THE ROUGH GUIDE TO
KENT, SUSSEX
& SURREY

WITHDRAWN

written and
Samanth

D1343589

Contents

Introduction to
Kent, Sussex & Surrey

Traditionally, the southeast corner of England was where London went on holiday. Throughout the nineteenth and early twentieth centuries, everyone from royalty to illicit couples enjoyed seaside fun at Brighton – a splash of saucy decadence in the bucolic county of Sussex – while trainloads of Eastenders were shuttled to the hop fields of Kent for a working break from the city, and boats ferried people down the Thames to the sands at Margate. Surrey has historically had a lower tourist profile, though its woodlands and hills have long attracted outdoors-lovers.

While many of its old seaside towns floundered in the late twentieth century – barring **Brighton**, which has always been in vogue – this stretch of England's coast is in the throes of an exciting renaissance. It's fashionable once more to enjoy the traditional resorts' cheeky charms, and the more laidback appeal of the quieter seaside towns. The cliff-fringed **coastline** itself provides excellent walking, swimming and watersports, along with heaps of bucket-and-spade fun. Inland, ancient **woodlands** and sleepy **villages** preserve their picturesque appeal – there are even pockets of comparative **wilderness**, perhaps surprising in a relatively populous area so close to London. Sandwiched between the lofty chalk escarpments of the North and South Downs, a vast sweep is taken up by the largely rural **Weald** – the name comes from the Saxon "wald", or forest, dating to the days when it was almost entirely covered by woodland.

This corner of the country is of huge **historical** significance, with the coast, just a hop away from the Continent, having served as a gateway for an array of invaders. **Roman remains** pepper the region – most spectacularly at **Bignor** and **Fishbourne** in Sussex and **Lullingstone** in Kent – and many roads, including the main A2 between London and Dover, follow the arrow-straight tracks laid by the legionaries. Christianity arrived in Britain on the **Isle of Thanet** (the northeast tip of Kent, long since rejoined to the mainland by silting and subsiding sea levels) and in 597 AD Augustine established a monastery at **Canterbury**, still the home of the Church of England. The last successful invasion of

KENT, SUSSEX AND SURREY

South Downs National Park

Area of Outstanding Natural Beauty

Feet
244
183
122
61
0

miles

N

NORTH SEA

ENGLISH CHANNEL

Strait of Dover

ESSEX
BERKSHIRE
HANTS

LONDON
SURREY
KENT
EAST SUSSEX
WEST SUSSEX

Margate
Broadstairs
Ramsgate
Sandwich
Worth
Deal
Dover
White Cliffs of Dover
Folkestone
Hythe
Channel Tunnel Terminal
Dymchurch
Dungeness
Romney, Hythe & Dymchurch Railway
Romney Marsh
Denge Marsh
Lydd
Camber
Winchelsea
Rye
Northiam
Tenterden
Kent & East Sussex Railway
Biddenden
Staplehurst
Hastings
Bexhill
Pevensey Bay
Eastbourne
Beachy Head
Seven Sisters
Battle
Burwash
Heathfield
Blackboys
Glyndebourne
Alfriston
Seaford
Newhaven
Rodmell
Lewes
Uckfield
Crowborough
Hartfield
Ashdown Forest
East Grinstead
Edenbridge
Bluebell Railway
Kingscote
Haywards Heath
Burgess Hill
Hassocks
Hurstpierpoint
Steyning
Brighton
Hove
Shoreham-by-Sea
Worthing
Littlehampton
Bognor Regis
Selsey
West Wittering
Chichester
West Dean
SOUTH DOWNS NATIONAL PARK
South Downs Way
Midhurst
Petersfield
Bordon
Haslemere
Petworth
Amberley
Pulborough
Arundel
Godalming
Guildford
SURREY HILLS AONB
North Downs Way
Farnham
Aldershot
Fleet
Farnborough
Camberley
Wokingham
Bracknell
Reading
Slough
Maidenhead
Windsor
Staines
Woking
Heathrow Airport
Leatherhead
Dorking
NORTH DOWNS
Reigate
Redhill
Horley
Gatwick Airport
Crawley
Horsham
Greensand Way
Sevenoaks
Royal Tunbridge Wells
Tudeley
Tonbridge
Paddock Wood
Maidstone
THE WEALD
THE NORTH DOWNS
Greensand Way
Borough Green
Eynsford
Gravesend
Tilbury
Grays
Rochester
Chatham
Gillingham
Sittingbourne
Faversham
Seasalter
Whitstable
Herne Bay
Isle of Sheppey
Sheerness
Medway Estuary
Saxon Shore Way
Canterbury
Ashford
THE DOWNS
Great Stour
Little Stour
Stour
Royal Military Canal
Rother
Ouse
Adur
Arun
Medway
Eden
Thames

North Downs Way

ART ALONG THE COAST

One of the defining features of the Kent and Sussex coastline is its crop of exciting art galleries, which with their cutting-edge architecture and top-notch collections have brought fresh energy and glamour to the faded seaside towns of the Southeast. Regenerating ailing coastal communities with high-profile buildings is no new thing, of course – the **De La Warr Pavilion** (1935), Bexhill's Modernist icon, was built partly for that very reason, although it was originally an entertainment hall and not a gallery. Within a couple of decades it had fallen into decline, but a gorgeous restoration in 2005 saw it brought back to life. Nearby, in Hastings, the Jerwood (relaunched as the **Hastings Contemporary** in 2019), whose shimmering black-tiled exterior echoes the look of the local fishing huts, opened in 2012 to display a modern British collection, and has played an important part in the upwards trajectory of that town. Even Eastbourne, more associated with OAPs than YBAs, has the **Towner**, open since the 1920s but moved in 2009 to a sleek new location. In Kent, the **Turner Contemporary** was instrumental in returning a smile to the face of once-merry Margate, and Folkestone's highly rated **Triennial** – a major public show that has featured artists from Tracey Emin to Cornelia Parker, first staged in 2008 – has become a major event.

England, in 1066, took place in Sussex, when the **Normans** overran King Harold's army at **Battle** near **Hastings** – and went on to leave their mark all over this corner of the kingdom, not least in a profusion of medieval **castles**. There are other important historic sights at every turn, from **Tudor** manor houses and sprawling Elizabethan and **Jacobean** estates to the old dockyards of **Chatham**, power base of the once invincible British navy.

You can also tackle some impressive long-distance **walks**, prime among them the glorious **South Downs Way** in Sussex and the gentler **North Downs Way** from Surrey to East Kent. Both Sussex and Kent – a county historically famed for its fruit and veg – are superb **foodie** destinations, with countless gastropubs, restaurants and farmers' markets providing delicious local produce, from asparagus and wild cherries to fresh seafood and Romney Marsh lamb, as well as award-winning **vineyards** and **breweries** producing excellent wines and ales.

Where to go

On Kent's north coast, the arty little fishing town of **Whitstable**, famed for its oysters, is a favourite getaway for weekending Londoners. **Margate,** gentrifying rapidly, and the charmingly retro **Broadstairs** make good bases on the **Isle of Thanet**, with its clean sandy bays, while the east coast has the low-key Georgian seaside town of **Deal**, the mighty **Dover Castle, Folkestone** – home to the art Triennial – and the strangely compelling shingle headland of **Dungeness**. Inland is the university city of **Canterbury**, where the venerable cathedral dominates a compact old centre crammed with medieval buildings, while Kent's Weald boasts a wealth of historic **houses**, among them the mighty **Knole** estate and **Hever Castle**, Anne Boleyn's childhood home, along with the glorious **gardens** at **Sissinghurst**, a stunning array planted by Vita Sackville-West. Exploring the many other historical attractions in the Weald – such as Winston Churchill's estate at **Chartwell** or Charles Darwin's family home at **Down House** – could fill a long and happy weekend; the Georgian town of **Royal Tunbridge Wells** makes an appealing base, as do countless peaceful villages.

The jewel of **Sussex** is the **South Downs National Park**, a glorious sweep of rolling downland that stretches from Hampshire into Sussex, meeting the sea at the iconic chalk cliffs of **Beachy Head** and **Seven Sisters**. There's wonderful walking along the Downs, not least along the South Downs Way, but equally rewarding are the less-tramped pockets of countryside, from the gorse-peppered heathland of **Ashdown Forest** on the edge of the sleepy High Weald to the sandstone cliffs of the **Hastings County Park** on the coast.

In East Sussex, buzzy **Brighton**, a university town with a blowsy good-time atmosphere, makes an irresistible weekend destination, as does handsome **Lewes**, in the heart of the South Downs; **Hastings**, east along the coast, is an up-and-coming seaside town with lots to recommend it, including a pretty Old Town and the scruffy but hip St Leonards neighbourhood to explore. On the edge of lonely **Romney Marsh**, picturesque **Rye**, with its cobbled streets and medieval buildings, lies within minutes of the family-friendly beach of **Camber Sands**. In West Sussex, the attractive hilltop town of **Arundel**, surrounded by unspoilt countryside, boasts a magnificent castle; **Midhurst** – headquarters of the South Downs National Park– is surrounded by gorgeous scenery and plenty of foodie pubs; while the lovely old cathedral town of **Chichester**, set between the sea and the South Downs, makes a perfect base for exploring the creeks and mudflats of **Chichester Harbour** and dune-backed **West Wittering** beach. Like Kent, Sussex abounds in great landscaped estates and gardens, among them seventeenth-century **Petworth House**, with its vast parkland roamed by deer, the Capability Brown-designed **Sheffield Park**, sprawling **Wakehurst Place** and the informal, imaginative garden at **Great Dixter**.

While **Surrey** boasts some attractive market towns, the chief appeal is in the **Surrey Hills**, in the North Downs, where ramblers and cyclists enjoy bluebell woods, mellow chalk grasslands and unspoiled hamlets such as **Shere** or Peaslake. The wild heathlands of the **Devil's Punchbowl** feel very different, but are equally good for walking. The county's main sights include the **Denbies** vineyard, where you can tour the winery and enjoy tastings; the stunning Arts and Crafts **Watts Gallery Artists' Village**; and the great gardens of **RHS Wisley**, dating back to Victorian times.

When to go

Kent, Sussex and Surrey often feel slightly warmer than the rest of the country, and the Sussex coast in particular sees a lot of sunshine – Eastbourne is regularly cited as the sunniest place on the UK mainland. Weather-wise, the **summer** is the best time to head for the coast, though it can get crowded – and more expensive – at this time, as well as at weekends and during the school holidays. Travel during the week, if you can, or book well in advance. **Spring** can be a lovely season, especially for ramblers and cyclists, with the wildflowers in bloom; given the profusion of woodlands, **autumn** is frequently glorious, with great banks of fiery foliage set off by bright skies and crisp air. **Winter** tends to be quiet, and is an ideal time to snuggle up with a pint of real ale in a country pub, or to enjoy the strange allure of an off-season English seaside town.

Author picks

Our authors have explored every corner of Kent, Sussex and Surrey, and here they share some of their favourite experiences.

Unique accommodation B&Bs are all very well, but for the utmost in unusual stays, try Margate's *Walpole Bay Hotel* (see page 93), the quirky experiences at Port Lympne (see page 128) and Knepp Castle estate (see page 295), the Belle Tout lighthouse at Beachy Head (see page 210) or the *Old Railway Station*, Petworth (see page 286).

Quirky churches There are some real gems in this region. Track down the Marc Chagall windows in Tudeley Church (see page 144), St Thomas à Becket, stranded in Romney Marsh (see page 129), and the beautiful Berwick Church with its Bloomsbury Group murals (see page 219).

Seaside fun Enjoy simple, old-fashioned pleasures at our favourite retro *gelaterias* – Morelli's in Broadstairs (see page 98) and Fusciardi's in Eastbourne (see page 208) – and while away a day crabbing at Whitstable (see page 80), East Head (see page 276) or Bosham (see page 274).

Vintage finds You can grab fabulous retro gladrags and funky vintage furnishings in Margate's Old Town (see page 89), along Harbour Street in Whitstable (see page 80) and in North Laine in Brighton (see page 238).

Festivals and events The Rochester Sweeps (see page 71), Jack-in-the-Green, Hastings (see page 181), Lewes Bonfire Night (see page 225) and the Bognor Birdman (see page 297): all fabulous fun and just a tiny bit bonkers.

Art off the beaten track The region has its fair share of big-hitting arty attractions (the Turner, Pallant Gallery and Charleston Farmhouse, to name but a few), but just as rewarding are the lesser-known gems of Ditching Museum of Art + Craft (see page 228), Farleys House and Gallery (see page 189), Derek Jarman's garden in Dungeness (see page 131) and the Watts Gallery Chapel in Surrey (see page 306).

> Our author recommendations don't end here. We've flagged up our favourite places – a perfectly sited hotel, an atmospheric café, a special restaurant – throughout the Guide, highlighted with the ★ symbol.

JACK IN THE GREEN FESTIVAL, HASTINGS
WATTS CHAPEL CEILING DETAIL

20

things not to miss

It's not possible to see everything that Kent, Sussex and Surrey have to offer in one trip – and we don't suggest you try. What follows, in no particular order, is a selective taste of the region's highlights, including gorgeous beaches, outstanding beauty spots, historic big-hitters and compelling cultural experiences. All highlights are colour-coded by chapter and have a page reference to take you straight into the Guide, where you can find out more.

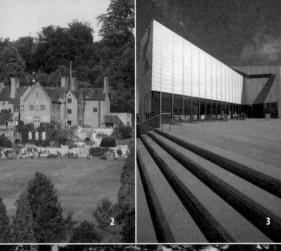

1 THE SEVEN SISTERS AND BEACHY HEAD
See page 210
The iconic, soaring Seven Sisters cliffs are the scenic highlight of the South Downs National Park.

2 CHARTWELL
See page 154
Winston Churchill's country estate offers fascinating insights into the man, along with lovely grounds and local woodlands to explore.

3 THE TURNER CONTEMPORARY
See page 90
The high-profile modern gallery that kick-started Margate's rebirth hosts excellent temporary exhibitions, and all for free.

4 THE DEVIL'S PUNCH BOWL
See page 305
Wild, raw and a little eerie – this Surrey heath is one of the county's more dramatic beauty spots.

5 RYE
See page 164
Beautifully preserved medieval town packed with good hotels, restaurants and independent shops, with Camber Sands' beachy fun just minutes away.

6 WEST WITTERING

See page 275

A splendidly uncommercialized dune-backed beach offering miles of sand and excellent watersports.

7 THE GOODS SHED

See page 56

In a region packed with fabulous farmers' markets, Canterbury's foodhall and restaurant tops them all.

8 PALLANT HOUSE GALLERY

See page 266

Chichester's modern art gallery offers a stupendous British collection in an elegant Georgian building with an airy, modern extension.

9 VINEYARDS

See page 146

English wine is going from strength to strength, and some of the very best is produced right here in the Southeast.

10 CHARLESTON FARMHOUSE

See page 217

The country base for the bohemian Bloomsbury Group, Charleston is a riot of ebullient decoration.

11 PROSPECT COTTAGE
See page 131
Derek Jarman's shingle beach garden typifies the strange, unsettling allure of Dungeness.

12 HASTINGS
See page 173
From its charming Old Town and still-working fishing quarter to its modern art gallery, independent shops and reimagined pier, there's a lot to love about this seaside town.

13 BROADSTAIRS FOLK WEEK
See page 97
A packed schedule of gigs brings a spirit of folksy anarchy to this pretty coastal resort.

14 CANTERBURY CATHEDRAL
See page 41
Mother Church of the Church of England, Canterbury Cathedral has an extraordinarily rich history.

15 BOTANY BAY
See page 92
With its towering chalk stacks, this is the most dramatic of Thanet's superb sandy beaches.

11

12

16 BRIGHTON

See page 234
The Southeast's favourite seaside city offers year-round fun beyond its famous beach, with great food and nightlife and an irresistible bohemian vibe.

17 SISSINGHURST

See page 148
Vita Sackville-West's ebullient, romantic garden is a blaze of colour, contrasts and surprising plantings.

18 PETWORTH HOUSE

See page 285
This magnificent stately home boasts an astonishing hoard of art treasures and a deer park designed by Capability Brown.

19 ALFRISTON

See page 213
With a beautiful setting, this is the picturesque village to end them all, with a village green, cosy smuggling inns and good local walks.

20 DOVER CASTLE

See page 114
You could spend a long, busy day in this vast fortress, exploring medieval tunnels, an Anglo-Saxon church, royal apartments and an underground World War II hospital.

17

18

19

20

Itineraries

Kent, Sussex and Surrey are wonderfully diverse, and these itineraries take in a variety of different pleasures – from lively seaside fun in Brighton to a wealth of amazing historical sights and some of England's finest gardens. Mixing the big names with secret gems, they should help you discover some of the richness and diversity of this lovely region.

A WEEKEND IN BRIGHTON

FRIDAY NIGHT

Dinner Start off the weekend in style with seafood and a sea view at the *Salt Room* restaurant. See page 250

Komedia Head to the hip Komedia theatre to catch some comedy or live music. See page 256

SATURDAY

Royal Pavilion Set aside a full morning to take in the splendours of George IV's pleasure palace by the sea. See page 236

The Lanes and North Laine Spend the afternoon exploring the independent shops of the Lanes and North Laine, and grab a roll from the *Flour Pot Bakery* for lunch. See pages 238 and 251

Dinner Book a seat at the counter at *64 Degrees* to enjoy some memorably inventive cooking. See page 250

Nightlife Head out on the town – Brighton is positively bursting at the seams with über-cool bars and clubs, as well as a great collection of traditional boozers. A top spot to start the night is *The Plotting Parlour* cocktail bar. See page 254

SUNDAY

Brunch Try the *Compass Point Eatery* or *Redroaster* for a lazy brunch. See pages 249 and 252

The seafront Amble to the end of the kitsch Brighton Pier, swoop up the i360 tower or burn off the breakfast calories with a game of beach volleyball. See page 240

Duke of York's cinema If it's raining, hunker down at Brighton's independent cinema, or take in the exhibits at the Brighton Museum. See pages 256 and 237

The South Downs If you fancy a complete change of scene, hop on a bus to Devil's Dyke or Ditchling Beacon (20min) for splendid walks and some of the finest views in the South Downs National Park. See pages 229 and 230

THE HISTORY TOUR

There are enough historical attractions in Kent, Sussex and Surrey to fill a trip of three weeks or more. Here we cover the biggest hitters on a tour that could easily last a fortnight.

❶ **Chatham Historic Dockyard** Explore historic ships, art and a working Victorian ropery

---

Create your own itinerary with Rough Guides. Whether you're after adventure or a family-friendly holiday, we have a trip for you, with all the activities you enjoy doing and the sights you want to see. All our trips are devised by local experts who get the most out of the destination. Visit **www.roughguides.com/trips** to chat with one of our travel agents.

in the colossal dockyard from England's Great Age of Sail. See page 72

❷ Canterbury With three sights – including the mighty cathedral and the ancient abbey – comprising a UNESCO World Heritage Site, this venerable city is full of historic splendour. You'll need a couple of days to do it justice. See page 38

❸ Dover Castle The mighty cliffside fortress packs in millennia of history, from its Roman lighthouse to its claustrophobic World War II bunkers. See page 114

❹ Battle Abbey Site of the most famous battle ever fought on English soil, the 1066 Battle of Hastings, which saw the end of Anglo-Saxon England. See page 185

❺ Royal Pavilion, Brighton Opulent, quirky and marvellously OTT, George IV's Regency pavilion is quite unlike any other palace in the country. See page 236

❻ Fishbourne Roman Palace Head west to Chichester to visit the largest and best-preserved Roman dwelling north of the Alps. See page 270

❼ Petworth House Seventeenth-century Baroque mansion, with sweeping parkland landscaped by Capability Brown – and immortalized by J.M.W. Turner. See page 285

❽ Polesden Lacey Elegant and utterly Edwardian, with wonderful grounds just perfect for picnicking. See page 309

❾ Knole The fifteenth-century childhood home of Vita Sackville-West, eulogized in literature and film, is an immense treasure-trove with an irresistible, faded beauty. See page 148

THE GARDEN OF ENGLAND

All three counties are heaven for garden fans, with a wide variety, from formal to natural, to inspire even the most tentative of gardeners. The following are the must-sees, visitable in a busy week; there are many more.

❶ Sissinghurst Abundant, romantic, nostalgic, witty – the bohemian cottage garden to top them all, designed by Vita Sackville-West and her husband. See page 148

❷ Prospect Cottage, Dungeness The late Derek Jarman's windswept shingle patch is a poignant, artistic memorial to an extraordinary filmmaker. See page 131

❸ Great Dixter The innovative, experimental garden of the late, great Christopher Lloyd features informal garden rooms set around a Wealden hall house. See page 187

❹ Sheffield Park Beautiful at any time of year but especially famed for its autumn colours, when banks of flaming foliage are reflected in the landscaped garden's lakes. See page 194

❺ Wakehurst Place A short hop from Sheffield Park, the country estate of Kew's Royal Botanic Gardens is a glorious 465-acre site taking in formal gardens, meadows, woodland, lakes and wetlands. See page 197

❻ Hannah Peschar Sculpture Garden An offbeat hideaway, with modern sculptures dotted around wild, lush woodland. See page 310

❼ RHS Wisley The Horticultural Society's flagship offers a huge amount, including a giant glasshouse and all manner of experimental gardens, plus an excellent shop. See page 311

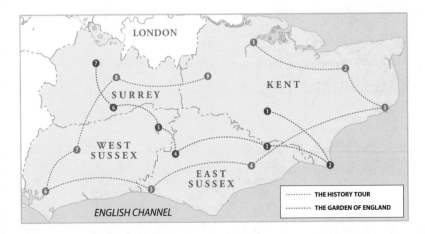

WALKERS ON THE SOUTH DOWNS WAY, SUSSEX

Basics

Getting there

With London on their doorstep, the Eurotunnel at their eastern end, and Gatwick – Britain's second-largest international airport – to the west, Kent, Sussex and Surrey are easily accessible by air, road or rail, with excellent transport connections that include the country's first high-speed rail line, in Kent.

By car

From the M25 London Orbital, several major **roads** strike off south: the A2/M2 to Canterbury and the North Kent coast; the M20 to Folkestone; and the M23/A23 to Brighton. The A27 runs west–east roughly parallel to the coast, giving access to coastal towns including Chichester, Brighton, Eastbourne and Hastings, though it can be slow going – the sixty-odd miles between Chichester and Hastings can take up to three hours to drive.

By train

Kent and the easternmost part of Sussex are served by **Southeastern** trains. By far the quickest way to travel into Kent is on Southeastern's regular **high-speed** services: one line zips from London St Pancras to Ashford International, taking under forty minutes; the other runs along the North Kent coast via Rochester, Faversham, Whitstable, Herne Bay, Margate, Broadstairs and Ramsgate, before heading inland to Canterbury and Ashford and across to Folkestone. There are also regular, slower services into Kent from London Bridge, Charing Cross, Waterloo and Victoria.

Sussex destinations served by Southeastern include Hastings (from Charing Cross or St Pancras via Ashford), Rye (St Pancras via Ashford) and Battle (Charing Cross). Hastings is also, along with the rest of Sussex, and parts of Surrey, served by **Southern Railways**. Southern's fast service to Brighton from London Victoria takes just fifty minutes; the company also runs trains from Southampton along the coast to Brighton, and from London Victoria to Eastbourne, Lewes, Arundel, Littlehampton and Chichester. You can also reach Brighton from London Victoria on the Gatwick Express, and from London Bridge and St Pancras International on Thameslink.

Southern also offers a service from London Victoria to Dorking in Surrey; elsewhere, the county is served by **South Western Railway**, with services from London Waterloo to Farnham, Guildford and Dorking.

By bus

National Express (⊕nationalexpress.com) runs coaches from London's Victoria Coach Station to **Kent** (including Ashford, Canterbury, Deal, Dover, Folkestone, Hythe, Maidstone, Margate, Ramsgate, Rochester and Tunbridge Wells), **Sussex** (Battle, Bexhill, Bognor Regis, Brighton, Chichester, Eastbourne, Hastings, Littlehampton, Shoreham and Worthing) and Guildford in **Surrey**.

By plane

Gatwick Airport, just north of Crawley in Sussex, is Britain's second-largest international airport, and has good rail connections on to Brighton and other destinations within Sussex.

By ferry, Eurotunnel and Eurostar

Ferries run from France to Dover (⊕doverport.co.uk) and Newhaven (just east of Brighton; ⊕newhavenferryport.co.uk). P&O Ferries (⊕poferries.com) and DFDS (⊕dfdsseaways.co.uk) operate the Calais-to-Dover route (hourly; 1hr 30min), and DFDS also runs services from Dunkirk to Dover (hourly; 2hr) and Dieppe to Newhaven (3–4 daily; 4hr). Consult ⊕directferries.com, ⊕ferrybooker.com or ⊕seaview.co.uk for up-to-date information, bookings and offers.

Often quicker and more convenient are the drive-on/drive-off shuttle trains operated by **Eurotunnel** (⊕eurotunnel.com) through the Channel Tunnel from Calais to Folkestone (35min). Book well ahead for the lowest prices, which start at less than €80 for a car with all passengers.

The **Eurostar** train service (⊕eurostar.co.uk) runs through the Channel Tunnel from Brussels, Amsterdam, Lille and Paris – plus, less frequently, from the south of France – to London St Pancras, with some trains stopping at Ashford International and Ebbsfleet International in Kent.

Getting around

Getting from A to B by public transport is generally pretty straightforward in Kent, Sussex and Surrey, at least when it comes to towns; the problem comes in getting to off-the-beaten-track attractions or villages deep in the countryside, which might only be served by one solitary bus, or involve a long hike from the nearest train station, making travel in anything but a car distinctly challenging.

Fortunately, some of the region's loveliest **country-side** – including Devil's Dyke, Beachy Head and the Seven Sisters in the South Downs National Park – has good public transport connections, and there is a huge range of wonderful long-distance walking and cycling routes too (see page 28).

Throughout the Guide we give public transport information for sights and attractions that are served by regular buses or trains.

By train

There are good connections around Kent, Sussex and Surrey with **Southeastern**, which covers Kent and the easternmost part of Sussex around Hastings, and runs the country's only high-speed rail services; **Southern Railways**, which serves the rest of Sussex and some of Surrey; and **South Western Railway**, which covers Surrey. The essential first call for information on routes, timetables, fares and special offers is **National Rail Enquiries**.

The key to getting the best **fares** is to book early and buy an "**advance**" ticket, which is only valid on the date and time specified; the most expensive tickets are "**anytime**" tickets bought on the day, which permit flexible travel on any train. You can buy tickets in person at train stations, or by phone or online from any train operator or simply by using a quick and easy online booking site like ⑩ thetrainline.com; the National Rail Enquiries website also offers direct links from its journey planner for purchasing specific fares. Bear in mind that some journeys (for example Hastings to London) are covered by more than one train operator, and an advance ticket bought from one operator will not be valid on the route run by the other. It's worth noting, too, that if you are travelling on one of the high-speed services operated by South-eastern you'll need a high-speed ticket, or else will be required to pay a supplement.

If you're spending time in Kent it may pay to buy the **Kent Rover** travel pass, which gives you three consecutive days of unlimited train travel on Southeastern for £45 per adult (with up to four kids at £5 each).

Finally, it's worth bearing in mind that the region's **heritage railways** can be a useful means of getting to attractions otherwise not easily accessible, as well as being fun trips in their own right; the Romney, Hythe & Dymchurch Railway (see page 129) is a good way of getting to and from Dungeness; the Kent & East Sussex Railway (see page 151) connects Tenterden in Kent to the picture-perfect Bodiam Castle just over the border; and the Bluebell Railway (see page 194) links East Grinstead mainline station in Sussex with Sheffield Park.

By bus

The bus network in **Kent** is split into two: Stagecoach covers the east and south of the county, including Ashford, the Canterbury, Herne Bay and Whitstable triangle, Dover, Deal, Faversham, Folkestone and Hythe; and Arriva covers the west and north, including Gravesend, the Isle of Sheppey, Maidstone, Sevenoaks, Tonbridge and the Medway towns.

In **Sussex** and **Surrey**, buses are run by a variety of operators including Arriva, Brighton & Hove Bus and Coach Company (which cover the surrounding area as well as the city itself), Compass Bus, Metrobus, Southdown Buses and Stagecoach, as well as smaller community operators. East Sussex County Council's website has links to bus timetables and a useful inter-active bus map (⑩ eastsussex.gov.uk; search for "bus timetables and maps"); West Sussex County Council (⑩ westsussex.gov.uk) lists local bus operators; and Surrey County Council's site (⑩ surreycc.org.uk) has an extensive section on local buses, including links to timetables.

In most cases, **timetables** and routes are well integrated. Buses between towns tend to be frequent and regular, but services can be sketchy once you get into the countryside, and on Sundays they sometimes dry up altogether.

Tickets are bought on board the bus, and it's generally cheaper to buy a return ticket than two single fares – check with the driver. Children under 5 travel free, and older children will generally pay half or two-thirds of the fare. For any but the shortest hops it's worth considering a **Discovery ticket**, which is accepted by all of the main bus operators in Kent, Sussex and Surrey; day tickets cost £9 per adult, £7.20 per child, or you can buy a family day ticket for £17.50.

The impartial official service **Traveline** has full details and timetable information for every bus route in Kent, Sussex and Surrey.

By car

Once you get away from the main towns and the coast, driving is, inevitably, the easiest way to get around the region – and in the case of many off-the-beaten-track attractions, it's the only practical means of transport.

If you are driving, keep plenty of change handy; some towns do still offer free parking but they're few and far between, and parking machines and meters never offer change (though increasingly, cards are also accepted). Pay-and-display car parks are generally cheaper than on-street meters. Both Brighton and Canterbury offer **park-and-ride** schemes, which can be a useful way to bypass the stress of parking, especially in Brighton where parking charges have risen through the roof in recent years.

The main **car rental** companies have branches all over the region; expect to pay around £60 for a weekend or from £120 per week. The price comparison website Ⓦ carrentals.co.uk is a good first port of call.

The AA (Ⓦtheaa.com), RAC (Ⓦrac.co.uk) and Green Flag (Ⓦgreenflag.co.uk) all operate 24-hour **emergency breakdown services** and offer useful online **route planners**. You can make use of these emergency services if you are not a member of the organization, but you will need to become a member at the roadside and will also incur a hefty surcharge.

PUBLIC TRANSPORT CONTACTS

Arriva ☎ 0344 800 4411, Ⓦ arrivabus.co.uk
Brighton & Hove Bus and Coach Company ☎ 01273 886200, Ⓦ buses.co.uk
Compass Travel ☎ 01903 690025, Ⓦ www.compass-travel.co.uk
Metrobus ☎ 01293 449191, Ⓦ metrobus.co.uk
National Express ☎ 0871 781 8181, Ⓦ nationalexpress.com
National Rail Enquiries ☎ 0845 748 4950, Ⓦ nationalrail.co.uk
Southdown Buses ☎ 01342 719619, Ⓦ southdown.net
Southeastern ☎ 0345 322 7021, Ⓦ southeasternrailway.co.uk
Southern Railway ☎ 0345 127 2920, Ⓦ southernrailway.co.uk
South Western Railway ☎ 0345 600 0650, Ⓦ southwesternrailway.com
Stagecoach ☎ 0345 600 2299, Ⓦ stagecoachbus.com
Traveline ☎ 0871 200 2233, Ⓦ travelinesoutheast.org.uk

Accommodation

Kent, Sussex and Surrey offer a good range of attractive accommodation, from simple guesthouses to cosy village pubs, luxurious country retreats and cool boutique hotels. Camping is a good option, with glampers particularly well catered for in Sussex.

It is usually best to **book in advance**, especially in summer, and at certain times it's essential. Accommodation in Brighton, and all the seaside towns, is at a premium on summer weekends while festivals such as the Whitstable Oyster Festival, Broadstairs Folk Week and the Goodwood events near Chichester fill up their towns very fast. Some places impose a **minimum stay** of two nights at the weekend and/or in high season – this is practically universal in Brighton and the bigger seaside destinations, but can also be true of some of the more remote guesthouses or glampsites, too – though these conditions can often be waived at the last minute if an establishment has not filled its rooms. Most accommodation options offer **free wi-fi** as standard; we've stated in the Guide where this is not the case.

Hotels, inns and B&Bs

Hotels run the gamut from opulent country piles to (quite) cheap and (mostly) cheerful seaside guest-houses. The absolute minimum you can expect to pay is around £70 for a reasonable double room in a simple B&B, rising up to at least £200 for something more luxurious, be it a country manor set in its own grounds or a sleek sea-view affair in Brighton. For a good level of comfort, service and atmosphere you're looking at paying about £80–100, though of course there are exceptions.

Though we have quoted **prices** in our reviews (see page 23), it is increasingly the case that rates are calculated according to demand, with online booking engines such as Ⓦ lastminute.com and Ⓦ booking.com often offering discounts on last-minute reservations, and establishments raising or lowering their prices according to how busy they predict they might be.

Staying in a **B&B** will generally, but by no means always, be cheaper than a hotel, and will certainly be more personal. While often little more than a couple of rooms in someone's house, many B&Bs aim to offer something special, and the houses themselves may well be part of the appeal – a converted oast house in Kent, for example, or a Sussex lighthouse. In Surrey, certainly, staying in a rural B&B is by far the best accommodation option, allowing you to

---

ACCOMMODATION PRICES

For all accommodation reviewed in this guide we provide **high season** (July–Sept) weekend prices, quoting the lowest price for one night's stay in a double or twin room in a **hotel or B&B**, the price of a dorm bed (and a double room, where available) in a **hostel**, and, unless otherwise stated, the cost of a pitch in a **campsite**. For **self-catering**, we quote the lowest rate you might pay per night in high season for the whole property – and we've made it clear where there is a minimum stay. Rates in hotels and B&Bs may well drop between Sunday and Thursday, or if you stay more than one night.

TOP FIVE CAMPSITES

Blackberry Wood Sussex. See page 230
Palace Farm Kent. See page 78
The Warren Kent. See page 126
Welsummer Kent. See page 160
WOWO Sussex. See page 198

see the best of the county. Tea- and coffee-making facilities, en-suite or private bathrooms and a hearty breakfast are generally standard – at least in the places featured in the Guide – and many will offer luxurious extras such as fluffy robes and posh bath products. Another good option, especially for foodies, is to stay in a **restaurant** (or gastropub) **with rooms**. Here the focus is mainly on the meal, which will invariably be good, with the added luxury of an extremely short and easy trip up to bed after dinner. Restaurants with rooms often offer meal-plus-bed deals, and a delicious breakfast to boot, which can prove good value.

Hostels

Even for those who can't face the idea of bunking up with snoring strangers, **hostel accommodation** is well worth considering. Most hostels nowadays, whether owned by the Youth Hostels Association (YHA) or independently run, have shaken off their institutional boy scouts/backpackers-only image, and offer a mix of dorms – with anything from four to twelve beds – as well as simple double, triple or family rooms.

There are nine **YHA** (⊛yha.org.uk) hostels in Kent, Sussex and Surrey: two in Kent – in Canterbury and out in the countryside near Gillingham; five in Sussex – Brighton, Eastbourne, Littlehampton, Southease (near Lewes) and Shoreham; and two in the Surrey Hills near Dorking. YHA hostels can offer very good value, especially for families. Many are in glorious rural locations, making great bases for walking or cycling holidays, and the costs (rates vary according to season and demand) are very competitive, with double rooms from as little as £30. Facilities, and atmosphere, vary; most have self-catering kitchens and some also have cafés, but all are reliable, clean and safe. Wi-fi provision, though free, also varies – where it does exist, it might only be available in communal areas. The YHA is a member organization, part of the global HI (Hostelling International) group, and members receive a 10 percent discount on bookings, which includes anyone travelling with you. Annual membership costs £20 for an individual.

There are also a handful of **independent hostels** and **camping barns** (⊛independenthostels.co.uk) in the region. Of these, the *Kipps* hostels, in Brighton and Canterbury, are both highly recommended.

Camping

Camping is an excellent option in Kent and Sussex, whether you want a simple, wild camping experience, pitching your own tent in a car-free field, or a more luxurious all-in glamping holiday, snuggling up in a tipi, a compact shepherd's hut or a vintage Airstream caravan. Smaller, quieter sites dominate the scene, with a number of beautifully situated camps in bucolic countryside – in the North and South Downs, say, or on the clifftops along the east coast – though there are larger caravan sites clustered around the more popular seaside destinations such as Camber and the Thanet resorts. Sussex in particular has taken up the **glamping** trend with relish, with some of the best-equipped and most enjoyable sites in the country.

Most campsites close in the winter, though exact dates vary according to the weather during any one year; we've included the closing months in our reviews. **Prices** for pitches start at as little as £7 per person for the most basic site, but you could pay as much as £280 for a couple of nights in your own two-yurt hideaway, warmed by a wood-burner with kitchen and shower.

Several small outfits offer **VW campers**, or "glampervans", which typically cost from £90 per night; check out ⊛beachwoodcamperhire.co.uk (Kent), ⊛activekampers.co.uk (East Sussex) or ⊛retrocampervan.com (Surrey). For an offbeat night, you could try "**champing**" in Kent or Surrey – setting up camp in an ancient church, with breakfast provided (April–Sept only; ⊛champing.co.uk).

Self-catering

Self-catering, whether in a rural cottage for two, a city-centre apartment or a family house by the sea, invariably proves cheaper than staying in a hotel and offers far more flexibility. Where once a week-long stay was standard, many places nowadays offer breaks of as little as one night, though there will usually be at least a two-night minimum stay at weekends and in the summer. Depending on the season, you can expect to pay around £375 a week for a small, out-of-the-way cottage or maybe three or four times that for a larger property in a popular spot. Note that properties owned by the National Trust and Landmark Trust, which are in historically significant and beautiful buildings, tend to be pricier than other options and are often booked up long in advance.

SELF-CATERING AGENCIES

Bramley & Teal Ⓦ bramleyandteal.co.uk. Stylish cottages in East Sussex and Kent, with good searches including "ecofriendly" and "dog-friendly".

Cottages.com Ⓦ cottages.com. Wide range of properties in the region, including some in Surrey.

Farm Stay UK Ⓦ farmstay.co.uk. Self-catering – plus B&B, bunkhouses and camping – on working farms throughout the region.

Kent & Sussex Holiday Cottages Ⓦ www. kentandsussexcottages.co.uk. More than three hundred pretty apartments, cottages and houses, on a user-friendly website with handy filters and searches for luxury, seaside and family-friendly properties.

Landmark Trust Ⓦ landmarktrust.org.uk. A preservation charity that has converted historically important properties into characterful accommodation – from tiny Tudor cottages to Arts and Crafts mansions.

Mulberry Cottages Ⓦ mulberrycottages.com. Upmarket self-catering focused on the south of England; there's a particularly good selection in Kent.

National Trust Ⓦ nationaltrustcottages.co.uk. The NT owns many cottages, houses and farmhouses, most of which are set in the gardens or grounds of their own properties – the eight or so in Kent, Sussex and Surrey include an Arts and Crafts style apartment in Standen House.

Stilwell's Cottages Direct Ⓦ cottagesdirect.co.uk. A good choice of properties in Kent and Sussex, with direct booking.

Food and drink

You're never far from somewhere really good to eat in Kent and Sussex, whether you want a simple Ploughman's lunch in a pub garden or exquisite Michelin-starred destination dining; Surrey, too, has its fair share of classy gastropubs and restaurants. Kent and Sussex, in particular, have embraced the local food movement with gusto, with countless gastropubs and restaurants sourcing food locally, naming their suppliers, and even growing their own.

Kent, which is traditionally famed for its fruit growing, still produces delicious veg, soft fruits and juices, along with fish and seafood – Whitstable's oysters are famed – tasty lamb fed on the nutrient-rich Romney Marsh and lots of good cheeses. **Sussex**, too, offers fresh juices, artisan cheeses and Romney lamb, with fresh fish from the Hastings fleet

and scallops from Rye Bay. **Surrey** has yet to attach itself to slow food principles with such vigour, but most of its best restaurants will list ingredients that have made the quick hop across the border from Kent and Sussex.

This part of the country is also excellent for **real ale** and **wine** – along with a couple of major historic breweries there are scores of local microbreweries and award-winning vineyards producing delicious tipples, and no shortage of traditional country pubs or good restaurants where you can enjoy them. For more on local food see Ⓦ producedinkent.co.uk, Ⓦ www.sussexfoodawards.biz and Ⓦ southdownsfood.org.

Restaurants and gastropubs

One of the great pleasures of a trip to this region is to head out to a country **gastropub**, filling up on delicious, locally sourced food before or after a bracing walk. The distinction between restaurant and gastropub is becoming fuzzier every day, with the gastropubs tending to lead the way when it comes to innovation and high cuisine principles: the Michelin-starred *Sportsman* (see page 85), in Seasalter near Whitstable, for example, which is one of the best places to eat in the country, belying its humble pub exterior.

Beware, though – most places have caught on to the "gastro" buzzword, and not everywhere that calls itself a gastropub is going to be good. We've reviewed the very best places in the Guide, but as a rule of thumb it's worth checking to see if an establishment names its suppliers, has a regularly changing menu, and doesn't try to cover too many bases on the menu.

As for **restaurants**, most towns of any size that are geared up for tourists will have some very good options, from veggie cafés to classy bistros and seafood joints. The most popular seaside towns, including Whitstable, Broadstairs, Margate, Hastings and Brighton, as well as the countryside surrounding Chichester and Midhurst, and the area around Faversham in North Kent, are foodie hotspots, with creative restaurants and gastropubs garnering national attention.

TOP FIVE GASTROPUBS

The Compasses Inn Crundale. See page 62
Fordwich Arms Fordwich, near Canterbury. See page 60
Griffin Inn Fletching. See page 199
Richmond Arms West Ashling, near Chichester. See page 268
The Sportsman Seasalter. See page 85

Markets and farm shops

Kent, Sussex and Surrey offer rich pickings when it comes to **farmers' markets**, with an array of delicious seasonal produce and artisan bread, cheese, chutneys, fruit juices, beers and wines from local producers. These are lively, well-attended affairs, and always worth a visit, even if just to browse. We've reviewed the best of them in the Guide; you can find a comprehensive list of farmers' markets in Kent on Ⓦkfma.org.uk; in West Sussex on Ⓦwestsussex.info/farmers-markets.shtml; and in Surrey on Ⓦvisitsurrey.com/whats-on/markets. Farm shops are also good places to pick up picnic supplies or deli treats to take home – many have diversified to sell posh food and produce from other farms as well as from their own. We've picked out a few to review in the Guide, but it's always worth stopping off to nose around any you may come across on your travels.

Drink

Kent, Sussex and Surrey excel in traditional **country pubs**, often picture-postcard places with wonky oak beams, head-bumpingly low ceilings and roaring open fires. The vast majority have local ales on offer, and the best will also list wines from the local vineyards, and fruit juices and ciders from local suppliers. Most serve food, and though many have been gussied up to within an inch of their lives, even the fanciest will have a room set aside for drinkers who simply want a quiet pint.

For cutting-edge **bars** and cool **cocktails** you'll do best in Brighton; even Kent's most popular tourist destinations, including Canterbury, Whitstable and the Thanet towns, have quite low-key drinking scenes, preferring quiet pubs over sleek see-and-be-seen joints. One trend that is making quite a stir in Kent is the arrival of the **micropub** – minuscule, independently run and very simple places, often set up in old shops and open for limited hours, where a small crowd of real-ale fans can hunker down to enjoy beer, conversation and – well, nothing much else, really; that's the whole point.

Real ale

Both Kent, the heartland of the old hopping industry, and Sussex, which was also scattered with hop farms, are known for their **real ales**. The biggest local names are **Shepherd Neame** (Ⓦshepherdneame.co.uk), the nation's oldest brewery, which operates from Faversham in Kent as it has for centuries, producing its characteristically earthy ales – Spitfire and Bishop's

---

LOCAL SPECIALITIES

Cobnuts This tasty Kentish hazelnut, harvested between mid-August and October, can be bought at local farmers' markets and found as an ingredient on menus throughout the county.

Fruit Kent's mild climate and rich soil provide excellent conditions for growing fruit. Wild cherries have been eaten here since prehistoric times, and cherry and apple trees were planted by the Romans and the Normans, but it was Henry VIII who really developed a taste for fruit and veg varieties as we recognize them today. In 1533 he employed the first royal fruiterer to plant orchards in Teynham, a few miles west of Faversham, and the county, "the fruitbowl of England", never looked back.

Hops Though the industry has declined drastically in the last sixty-odd years, Kent in particular still has a strong emotional attachment to the hop, which was such a crucial part of the economy in the nineteenth century (see page 139). Local breweries, including the venerable Shepherd Neame in Kent and Harvey's in Sussex, still use local hops in their beers, and you can also buy live plants to grow, or dried garlands of bines for decoration – as seen in countless pubs and hotels in the Weald. Some artisan food producers also add hops to crackers or biscuits to add a unique, slightly bitter flavour.

Huffkins An old-fashioned Kentish speciality – a soft, flat, small oval loaf with a deep dimple in the centre, occasionally filled like a bap, and often served warm.

Lamb Though many of the famed Romney Marsh lambs are now farmed elsewhere (see page 130), the appearance on menus of their prized, tender meat is the sure sign of a good restaurant; the sweet, succulent meat of Sussex's Southdown lamb is equally prized.

Oysters The old fishing town of Whitstable, on the north coast of Kent, is the place to eat these briny delicacies (see page 81); there's even an annual festival to give thanks for them.

Rye Bay scallops The season for Rye Bay's prized bivalves – some of the best in the country – lasts from November to the end of April, and reaches its peak in February, when more than fifteen thousand are consumed during Rye's week-long Scallop Festival.

BEST FARMERS' MARKETS AND FARM SHOPS

Aylesford Farmers' Market Kent. See page 158

Cliftonville Farmers' Market Kent. See page 92

Cowdray Farm Shop Sussex. See page 283

The Goods Shed Kent. See page 56

Lewes Farmers' Market Sussex. See page 226

Macknade Fine Foods Kent. See page 78

Middle Farm Shop Sussex. See page 218

Penshurst Farmers' Market Kent. See page 143

Quex Barn Farm Shop Kent. See page 94

Rochester Farmers' Market Kent. See page 66

Sharnfold Farm Shop Sussex. See page 209

Shipbourne Farmers' Market Kent. See page 155

Shoreham Farmers' Market Sussex. See page 298

Tonbridge Farmers' Market Kent. See page 143

Finger among them – and running a huge number of local pubs; **Harvey's** in Lewes, Sussex (Ⓦ harveys. org.uk), which dates back to 1792 and is known for its traditional cask ales, including the flagship Sussex Best bitter; and the **Dark Star Brewing Co** (Ⓦ dark-starbrewing.co.uk), which started out in 1994 in the basement of a Brighton pub and has grown to become Sussex's second largest brewery after Harvey's.

There is also an ever-growing number of **micro-breweries**, some of them very small indeed, producing interesting, top-quality ales and porters. These outfits often apply traditional methods and creative innovations, selling their seasonally changing selections in local pubs, restaurants and farm shops, and occasionally online. In **Kent** look out for beers from Ripple Steam Brewery (Ⓦ ripplesteambrewery. co.uk), which uses no mechanization in its brewing process; the Tonbridge Brewery (Ⓦ tonbridgebrewery. co.uk), whose spicy Rustic bitter is made with rare Kent-grown Epic hops; the Westerham Brewery (Ⓦ westerhambrewery.co.uk), which uses nine varieties of Kentish hops in its Spirit of Kent pale ale; and Larkins Brewery (Ⓦ larkinsbrewery.co.uk), whose peppery, chocolatey porter is particularly good. Great **Sussex** microbreweries include the Long Man Brewery in Litlington, which creates award-winning ales using barley grown on the farm (Ⓦ longman-brewery.com); Burning Sky in Firle, set up by ex-Dark Star brewer Mark Tranter and known for its pale ales (Ⓦ burningskybeer.com); FILO Brewery at the *First In, Last Out* pub in Hastings, which has been brewing since 1988 (Ⓦ thefilo.co.uk); the steam-powered Langham Brewery near Midhurst (Ⓦ langhambrewery. co.uk); and a clutch of microbreweries in Brighton, among them Brighton Bier (Ⓦ brightonbier.com) and the Hand Brew Co (Ⓦ handbrewpub.com). In **Surrey**, you can count on good ales from Hogs Back (Ⓦ hogsback.co.uk) and Frensham (Ⓦ craftbrews.uk) – both near Farnham – and the Surrey Hills Brewery (Ⓦ surreyhills.co.uk) on the Denbies wine estate.

Wine

Kent, Sussex and Surrey, where the soil conditions and geology are almost identical to those in France's Champagne region – and where the climate is increasingly similar, due to global warming – are home to some of the country's most highly regarded vineyards. These chiefly produce white and sparkling wines, for which nearly all of them can claim a raft of prestigious awards, but there are some fine rosés and interesting reds out there, too.

Most good restaurants – and some pubs – in Kent and Sussex will make a point of listing local wines, and you'll be able to buy them in farm shops and specialist stores such as the English Wine Centre near Lewes (see page 217). You can also find bottles from the major producers in supermarket aisles: Marks and Spencer and Waitrose are the main sources. The best place to buy, of course, is from the **vineyards** themselves – most offer free guided tours and generous tutored tastings. As a very broad rule of thumb, in Kent **Chapel Down** does superb fizz and excellent whites, **Biddenden** has some fine off-dry sparkling wines and a distinctive, very delicious Ortega, and **Hush Heath** produces a superb pink fizz. In Sussex, **Ridgeview**, **Rathfinny Estate** (on course to become England's largest vineyard), **Nyetimber** and **Wiston Estate** are all renowned for their bubbly, while **Sedlescombe** (Ⓦ englishorganicwine.co.uk) adopts innovative biodynamic principles for its wine making, with delicious results, and **Bolney**, unusually, is best known for its reds. Surrey's **Denbies** is another that specializes in excellent fizz.

While it's perfectly possible to visit the vineyards independently (see page 28), a number of **tours** are taking advantage of increased interest in English wine. In Kent and Sussex, English Wine Tasting Tours (Ⓦ englishwinetastingtours.co.uk) and Great British Wine Tours (Ⓦ greatbritishwinetours.co.uk) lead small-group tours of two or three vineyards a day, with tastings and lunch included.

ENGLISH WINE: A SPARKLING SUCCESS STORY

English wine is fast shucking off its image as somehow inferior to its longer-established European counterparts, and the industry is booming. Nearly five hundred vineyards across the country produce about fifteen million bottles a year (more than seventy percent of it sparkling), and the best of the harvest more than rivals the more famous names over the Channel; indeed, in recent years some of France's most prestigious Champagne brands have invested in English vineyards. **Sparkling wine** is the biggest success story, with several wines from the Southeast beating the best Champagnes in international blind-tasting competitions. New vineyards are springing up all the time: Rathfinny Estates, established in 2010 outside Alfriston, is on course to produce more than a million bottles of fizz a year, making it one of the biggest single vineyards in Europe. For more details of vineyards throughout Kent, Sussex and Surrey – including a downloadable wine routes map and an iPhone app giving full information on the region's growers and producers – check the website of the Southeastern Vineyard association, ⓦseva.uk.com. There's more information on English wine at ⓦwinegb. co.uk and on Sussex wineries at ⓦsussexwineries.co.uk.

Several vineyards offer tours and tastings. Among the best are:

Biddenden Kent. See page 150
Bolney Sussex. See page 195
Chapel Down Kent. See page 150
Denbies Surrey. See page 308

Hush Heath Kent. See page 146
Rathfinny Sussex. See page 215
Ridgeview Sussex. See page 229
Tinwood Estate Sussex. See page 273

Sports and outdoor activities

Kent, Sussex and Surrey offer a good range of outdoor activities, chiefly walking and cycling, along with excellent sailing, watersports and birdwatching. There are also good opportunities for adrenaline junkies, including rock climbing and paragliding. As for spectator sports, Surrey boasts the Epsom Downs racecourse, home to the Derby for nearly 250 years, and Sussex is home to Goodwood, site of the UK's major horse and motor races. For something gentler, cricket is king in this part of England, still played on quiet village greens as well as on the bucolic county ground at Canter-bury and at the lovely ground at Firle, near Lewes, home to one of the oldest cricket clubs in the world.

Walking

Perhaps unexpectedly, given how populated this corner of the country is, Kent, Sussex and Surrey are superb **walking** destinations, with plenty of trails, of all lengths and for all abilities, where you can get away from it all within minutes. From blustery seaside hikes atop towering chalk cliffs, to pretty rambles in ancient woodlands and undulating paths following ancient pilgrims' routes, the region offers a wide variety, whether you're after a country pub stroll or a long-distance trek.

The chalky hills of the **North Downs** and **Greensand Way** – both of which curve their way through Surrey to east Kent – along with the **High Weald** in Kent and Sussex, and the **South Downs** in Sussex, are all prime walking territory. **Long-distance paths** include the 150-mile-long **North Downs Way** (ⓦnationaltrail. co.uk/north-downs-way), which starts at Farnham in west Surrey and heads through the beautiful Surrey Hills, following old pilgrims' paths to Canterbury and Dover along the highest points of the Downs. Further south, and running roughly parallel, the 108-mile **Greensand Way** heads off from Haslemere in Surrey, traversing dramatic heathland, ancient woodlands and the pretty Kent Weald countryside before ending near the border with Romney Marsh.

In Sussex, the **Sussex Downs** – part of the **South Downs National Park** (ⓦsouthdowns.gov.uk), which spreads into Hampshire and is crisscrossed by nearly two thousand miles of footpaths – provide fantastic walking opportunities, whatever you're after; the website details some good options that start and finish at a bus stop or train station. The jewel of the South Downs is the one hundred-mile **South Downs Way** (ⓦnationaltrail.co.uk/south-downs-way), which follows ancient paths and droveways along the chalk escarpment from Winchester all the way to the glorious Beachy Head cliffs. Running north to south through the South Downs, the 38-mile-long **New Lipchis Way** (ⓦnewlipchisway.co.uk), from Liphook in Hampshire to West Wittering, affords you the special thrill of arriving in Chichester on foot. In the Weald, the largely rural and heavily wooded area that spreads through both Kent and Sussex, the 95-mile **High Weald Landscape Trail** (Ⓦhighweald.org), from Horsham to Rye via Groombridge and Cranbrook, takes you from bluebell woods to marshlands, via winding sunken lanes, past some of the area's prettiest villages. The North Downs Way and South Downs Way are linked by the eighty mile **Weald Way** (Ⓦexplorekent.org/activities/wealdway), a peaceful route that heads south from Gravesend to Eastbourne, spanning chalk downlands and valleys and taking you through Ashford Forest, and by the forty-odd-mile **Downs Link** (Ⓦwestsussex.gov.uk), which follows the traffic-free course of a disused railway line from near Guildford, winding through woods, heath and open country before linking up with the South Downs Way and following the River Adur down to Shoreham. The 150-mile **Sussex Border Path** (Ⓦsussexborderpath.co.uk), meanwhile, loosely follows that county's inland boundary with Hampshire, Surrey and Kent, starting in Thorney Island and ending in the lovely medieval town of Rye.

Long-distance **coastal paths** include the splendid 163-mile **Saxon Shore Way** (Ⓦexplorekent.org/activities/saxon-shore-way), which heads from Gravesend to Hastings, following the coastline as it would have looked 1500 years ago – which in some parts is now quite far inland – encompassing the bays of Thanet and the White Cliffs of Dover, and taking in the appealing small towns of Faversham, Deal and Rye. Curving a twenty-mile course along the Thanet shore, from Minnis Bay in the west to Pegwell Bay near

Sandwich, the **Thanet Coastal Path** (Ⓦthanetcoast.org.uk/projects-and-issues/thanet-coastal-path) is an excellent way to experience the lovely beaches in this part of Kent.

We've flagged up especially nice walks throughout the Guide, and recommend some of the best walking books in our Books section (see page 323). There are countless more walks in Kent, Sussex and Surrey; check Ⓦvisitkent.co.uk/see-and-do/active-and-outdoors/walking, Ⓦeastsussex.gov.uk, Ⓦwestsussex.gov.uk and Ⓦvisitsurrey.com/things-to-do/activities/walking-and-hiking, as well as the South Downs National Park website (Ⓦsouthdowns.gov.uk/enjoy/walking), which has over two dozen downloadable walking trails. The **National Trust** (Ⓦnationaltrust.org.uk/visit/activities/walking) is another good resource, with downloadable walks of varying lengths from most of their properties.

Cycling

Kent, Sussex and Surrey offer rich pickings for cyclists. From gentle traffic-free woodland trails suitable for family pottering to heart-thumping training routes, from invigorating coastal clifftop paths to sleepy country lanes, the routes are varied and well marked.

Of the **National Cycle Network** routes (Ⓦsustrans.org.uk), Route 1, which runs from Dover all the way up to Scotland, takes in the East Kent coast between Dover and Sandwich before heading inland via Canterbury to meet the North Kent coast at Whitstable and Faversham, while Route 2 – also known as the **South Coast Cycle Route** – follows most of the south coast

---

SEVEN SPLENDID WALKS

Ashdown Forest There are lots of good paths through the gorse-speckled heaths of Ashdown Forest, with the added fun for kids of tracking down Pooh Bear's favourite haunts. See page 192

The Crab and Winkle Way Follow the line of a disused steam railway from Canterbury to Whitstable, passing orchards and ancient woodland on your way. See page 59

The Cuckmere Valley and the Seven Sisters An eight-mile circular walk in one of the most beautiful parts of the South Downs National Park, offering magnificent views of soaring white cliffs and velvety green chalk grassland. See page 212

Herne Bay to Reculver A splendid stretch of the long-distance Saxon Shore Way, taking you from the old-fashioned seaside resort to the ruined clifftop church towers standing sentinel over wildlife-rich Reculver Country Park. See page 87

Kingley Vale Clamber up through dark, mysterious yew forest to rolling chalk grassland with panoramic views on this magical 3.5-mile circuit. See page 270

The Surrey Hills Using a country village like Shere or Peaslake as your base, the Surrey Hills offer countless rambles through Surrey's glorious old woodlands. See page 307

Whitstable to Seasalter Crunching along the shingle the two miles from the oyster-loving town of Whitstable to the superb *Sportsman* gastropub is a bracing way to experience this stretch of the North Kent coast. See page 82

ACTIVE FUN: A TOP FIVE

Paddle your own canoe along Kent's quiet waterways See page 60

Swoop above the South Downs on a paraglider See page 220

Outjump your opponents at Brighton beach volleyball See page 247

Pedal in the wake of Olympic champions at Box Hill See page 309

Catch some waves at the Joss Bay surf school See page 97

from Dover to Cornwall, dipping inland at various points, with an uninterrupted stretch between Dover and Worthing.

In Kent, the **Crab and Winkle Way**, also a walking path (see page 59), forms part of National Cycle Route 1 and provides a quick and scenic route between Canterbury and Whitstable on the coast. Just east of Whitstable, the seven-mile **Oyster Bay Trail** (W explorekent.org/activities/oyster-bay-trail) is a family-friendly seaside path that leads to Herne Bay and the beachfront Reculver Country Park; from there you can join the start of the 32-mile **Viking Coastal Trail** (W explorekent.org/activities/viking-coastal-trail), which follows the Thanet coast all the way round to Pegwell Bay, south of Ramsgate. You can also cycle from Hythe to Winchelsea in Sussex along the **Royal Military Canal** (W royalmilitarycanal.com), a gratifyingly flat thirty-mile ride through quiet marshes. Shorter rides include the six-mile **Tudor Trail** (W explorekent.org/activities/tudor-cycle-trail), a largely traffic-free route between Tonbridge Castle and Penshurst Place; the flat, marshy lands of the Hoo Peninsula and the Isle of Sheppey are also very good for cycling. If you're after something more active, head to **Bedgebury Forest** (W forestryengland.uk/bedgebury), which is crossed by National Cycle Route 18 and features off-road mountain bike trails.

In Sussex, the **South Downs Way** (see page 284) is as exhilarating for cyclists as it is for walkers, though bear in mind you'll be sharing the path with horses as well as pedestrians. The **South Downs National Park** website (W southdowns.gov.uk) has a number of downloadable cycle rides that start and finish at a bus stop or train station. Two popular off-road cycle trails along disused railways are the fourteen-mile **Cuckoo Trail** (see page 191) and the nine-mile **Forest Way** (see page 195), while another great place to cycle is the flat **Manhood Peninsula**, with a good network of canalside towpaths and a couple of routes from Chichester, including the eleven-mile **Salterns Way**

(W conservancy.co.uk/page/cycling), which leads to East Head via country lanes, roads and designated paths. You can combine cycling with a spot of culture on the eighteen-mile **Coastal Culture Trail** (W coastalculturetrail.com; see page 177), which links three art galleries along the Sussex coast; the section between Hastings and Bexhill is all off-road.

The pretty village of Peaslake in **Surrey** is a major centre for off-road cycling, with trails in the surrounding forest, while the steep zigzag road up **Box Hill**, long a popular route for training cyclists – and which formed part of the road race cycling event in the London 2012 Olympics – is particularly popular at weekends. A couple of National Cycle Network routes also run through Surrey – the quiet **Route 22** (W sustrans.org.uk), which follows tranquil paths and bridleways east–west through the county, and the stretch between Guildford and Cranleigh on the **Downs Link**, are particularly worthwhile.

Watersports

With its long, varied coastline, its marshlands and its rivers, the Kent and Sussex region offers excellent watersports. Sailing, windsurfing and kiteboarding are especially good around **Whitstable** (see page 83), with jet-skiing, sailing and kayaking in **Herne Bay** (see page 87), windsurfing and kiteboarding at **Margate** and superb surfing in Thanet's **Joss Bay** (see page 97), where there's a top-notch **surf school** (W kentsurfschool.co.uk). The seaside town of Hythe, on Kent's east coast, is also something of a windsurfing centre (see page 127), while the nearby **Action Watersports** (W actionwatersports.co.uk), inland in Lydd, offers waterskiing, wakeboarding, jet-skiing and other activities on a purpose-built lake. Further down the coast, just across the border in Sussex, blustery **Camber** is another major centre for wind- and kitesurfing and paddleboarding (see page 172); **Eastbourne** offers a host of watersports including sailing, diving, windsurfing, kayaking and stand-up paddleboarding (see page 298); the coast around **Worthing**, west of Brighton, is one of the best places in the country to learn how to kitesurf (see page 298); while at sandy **West Wittering beach** (see page 278) there's everything from surfing to kayaking to stand-up paddleboarding on offer.

Finally, if it's buff beach fun you're after, **Brighton** is the place, offering year-round beach volleyball and other sports at the excellent **Yellowave Beach Sports Venue** (see page 247); local operators also offer scuba diving, kayaking, wakeboarding and sailing, with windsurfing, stand-up paddleboarding and cable wakeboarding on a beachfront lagoon.

There are some particularly nice spots for open-air **swimming** in and around Brighton, too: at the Sea Lanes pool (see page 247) on the seafront near Yellowave; at the recently restored Grade II-listed Saltdean Lido (see page 243), accessible from the city along the Undercliff Walk; and in the nearby town of Lewes at Pells Pool (see page 224) – the country's oldest open-air freshwater pool. Arundel also has a fine lido (see page 289), which has the added bonus of a castle view.

Birdwatching

Birders are spoilt for choice in Kent and Sussex, with large swathes of lonely marshland, dense, ancient woods, and otherworldly shingle habitats all offering splendid twitching territory.

There are six major **RSPB reserves** (W rspb.org.uk) in **Kent**: the Blean Woods near Canterbury (see page 58); Cliffe Pools (see page 74) and Northward Hill (see page 74) on the Hoo Peninsula near Rochester; Capel Fleet on the Isle of Sheppey (see page 75); the headland of Dungeness down toward Sussex; and Tudeley Woods in the Weald near Tunbridge Wells (see page 136). There are also good sightings to be had in the **nature reserves** at Stodmarsh near Canterbury (see page 59), around the Swale Estuary (see page 77) and at Pegwell Bay near Ramsgate and Sandwich (see page 108). Other good locations include **Reculver Country Park** between Herne Bay and Thanet (see page 87); **Romney Marsh** (see page 129); and the **White Cliffs of Dover** (see page 116) – though sadly you categorically won't see bluebirds over those. For more on birdwatching in Kent, check the website of the **Kent Ornithological Society** (W kentos.org.uk).

In **Sussex**, the **WWT Arundel Wetland Centre**, one of just ten Wildfowl and Wetland Trust (WWT) sites in the UK, is home to endangered waterfowl from around the world as well as a host of native birds (see page 289). You'll also spot birds in the shingle-saltmarsh **Rye Harbour Nature Reserve** (see page 169); in the heathland habitat of **Ashdown Forest** (see page 192); in the **Loder Valley Nature Reserve** (see page 197) at Wakehurst Place in the High Weald; at the **RSPB Pulborough Brooks** nature reserve (see page 293); and on the Manhood Peninsula around the beautiful **Chichester Harbour** (see page 274) and at the **RSPB Pagham Harbour** (see page 278) and **RSPB Medmerry** (see page 279) nature reserves. You can find out more about birding in Sussex on W sos.org.uk, the website of the **Sussex Ornithological Society**.

In the **Surrey Hills**, there's an RSPB reserve at Farnham Heath, an area of restored heathland and bluebell woods abounding in crossbills, nightjars, tree pipits, woodcocks and woodlarks.

Paragliding and rock-climbing

Would-be **paragliders** should make a beeline for the **South Downs**, where local companies (see page 220) offer lessons that mean you can be up there on your own within just one day.

Meanwhile, there's superb **climbing** around Eridge Green and Groombridge, on the Sussex–Kent border near Tunbridge Wells: **Harrison's Rocks** (W thebmc. co.uk) offers challenging routes for experienced climbers, and outfitters nearby offer lessons (see page 193).

Golf

Kent, Sussex and particularly Surrey are home to some of the finest **golf** courses in the country, including two at the Goodwood Estate in Sussex, and three near Sandwich (see page 104). For details of courses in Surrey and Kent, see W surreygolfguide.com and W golfinkent.co.uk.

SPECIALIST OPERATORS

Canoe Wild W canoewild.co.uk. Guided and self-guided canoe trips along the backwaters of Kent. See page 60.

The Carter Company W the-carter-company.com. Cycling tours through Kent, with gourmet, arty, historic and family options.

Contours W contours.co.uk. Walking holidays in Kent, Sussex and along the North Downs Way in Surrey.

Electric Bike Tours W ukelectricbiketours.co.uk. Electric bike tours in Kent and East Sussex. Itineraries include vineyards, hop and fruit farms, gardens and castles.

Experience Sussex W experiencesussex.co.uk. Activity and pottery holidays in Sussex, including guided walks and cycle rides.

Footpath Holidays W footpath-holidays.com. Self-guided and guided walking holidays in the South Downs.

Footprints of Sussex W footprintsofsussex.co.uk. Self-guided walking holidays and short breaks in the South Downs National Park.

Hatt Adventures W thehatt.co.uk. Climbing, abseiling and kayaking in Sussex.

The Kayak Coach W thekayakcoach.com. Kayak trips along the Ouse, Cuckmere and Arun rivers in Sussex, and along the River Medway in Kent.

South Downs Discovery W southdownsdiscovery.com. Self-guided walking holidays in the South Downs National Park, plus baggage transfers along the South Downs Way.

Walk Awhile W walkawhile.co.uk. Self-led and guided walking holidays in the Kent Downs, through the Weald and along the White Cliffs, with luggage transfers.

Festivals and events

Kent, Sussex and Surrey have a packed festivals calendar, which includes plenty of arts and music events and foodie festivals showcasing and celebrating the region's fantastic local produce. There's no shortage, too, of wonderful, quirky festivals and events that you won't find anywhere else in the country, from Sussex Bonfire Night to the Bognor Birdman.

JANUARY TO MARCH

Fat Tuesday Hastings, Feb. See page 181

Rye Bay Scallop Week Late Feb. Nine days of foodie events dedicated to the noble scallop: tastings, cookery demonstrations, live music and special menus, culminating in a scallop barrow race through the streets of Rye. Ⓦ visitryebay.com

Sussex Beer Festival Brighton, mid-March. Around two hundred real ales, ciders and perries on offer – many local to the Southeast – at this rollicking annual fest. Ⓦ sussexbeerfestival.co.uk

APRIL & MAY

Wise Words Festival Canterbury, often in April, but date varies. See page 57

Jack-in-the-Green Festival Hastings Old Town, end April/early May. See page 181

Rochester Sweeps Festival Early May. See page 71

Brighton Festival May. See page 246

Brighton Fringe May. See page 246

Elderflower Fields Festival Ashdown Forest, May. Family-friendly festival in Sussex woodlands, with music, local food and drink, a woodland spa and loads of kids' activities. Ⓦ elderflowerfields.co.uk

Great Escape Brighton, mid-May. See page 246

Charleston Festival Late May. Ten days of author talks and events at Charleston Farmhouse, near Lewes, the former home of Sussex's Bloomsbury Set. Ⓦ charleston.org.uk

Glyndebourne Festival Late May to Aug. See page 220.

JUNE

Whitstable Biennale Date varies, June. See page 87

Dickens Festival Rochester, early June. See page 71

Broadstairs Dickens Festival Third week June. See page 97

Nature Valley International Eastbourne, late June. International ladies' and men's tennis in the fortnight preceding Wimbledon, in the leafy surrounds of Devonshire Park. Ⓦ lta.org.uk

Festival of Chichester Late June to late July. Month-long arts festival featuring music, theatre, film, spoken word, exhibitions, walks and tours. Ⓦ festivalofchichester.co.uk

Festival of Speed Goodwood Estate, late June. See page 273

Brighton Kite Festival Date varies, but generally June/July. Long-running kite festival, with arena displays, team flying and kite fighting. Ⓦ brightonkiteflyers.co.uk

JULY

Folkestone Triennial Date varies, but often starts in July. See page 124

Deal Music and the Arts Early July. See page 113

JAM on the Marsh Early July. Eleven days of art, theatre, performance, children's events and tours, centring on the atmospheric medieval Romney Marsh churches. Ⓦ jamconcert.org/jam-on-the-marsh

Paddle Round the Pier Hove Lawns, Brighton, early July. See page 246

Love Supreme Glynde, near Lewes, early July. Europe's biggest and best greenfield jazz festival, held over three days in the beautiful grounds of Glynde Place.

Beach Life Festival Eastbourne, mid-July. A free weekend of extreme sports action – from slalom to windsurfing, BMX to go-karting – with plenty of opportunities to get involved as well as watch. Ⓦ beachlifefestival.co.uk

Hastings Pirate Day Mid-July. See page 181

Petworth Festival Mid-July. Two weeks of music (mainly classical and jazz), theatre, comedy and art. Ⓦ petworthfestival.org.uk

Ramsgate Festival Third week in July. A multifaceted arts festival incorporating the Ramsgate Week sailing regatta, an old-style carnival with parades, floats and marching bands, and various exhibitions, concerts and events. Ⓦ ramsgatefestival.org

Kent Beer Festival Near Canterbury, late July. Lively three-day real ale fest, featuring more than two hundred brews; the venue changes, but recently it has been held at Canterbury Rugby Club. Ⓦ kentbeerfestival.com

Whitstable Oyster Festival End July. See page 87

Neverworld Hever, end July/early Aug. Increasingly popular three-day music festival, born in teenager Lee Denny's back garden in 2006, which now showcases everyone from heritage acts to the coolest big names. Performers have included Young Fathers and Grandmaster Flash. Ⓦ neverworld.co.uk

Margate Soul Festival End July/early Aug. Big-name gigs – from Soul II Soul to Janet Kay – by the harbour, plus DJ stages, street performances and club nights. Ⓦ margatesoulfestival.co.uk

Old Town Carnival Week Hastings, end July/early Aug. Nine days of festivities, which include concerts, walking tours, a procession and the ever-popular annual pram race. Ⓦ oldtowncarnivalweek.co.uk

AUGUST

Bognor Birdman Aug. See page 297

Chichester International Film Festival Aug. Excellent festival with around three weeks of new movies from around the world, including open-air screenings and a drive in. Ⓦ chichestercinema.org/festival

Herne Bay Festival Aug. Lively festival with lots of family events, fireworks, live music and workshops. Ⓦ hernebayfestival.com

Airbourne: Eastbourne International Airshow Eastbourne, early Aug. Eastbourne's pride and joy and the biggest free seafront air show in the world – four days of historic aircraft and military displays. Ⓦ eastbourneairshow.com

Brighton and Hove Pride Early Aug. See page 258

Chilli Fiesta Chichester, early Aug. A lively weekend devoted to the chilli, with cooking demos, talks and live music. Ⓦ westdean.org.uk

Glorious Goodwood Early Aug. See page 273

Broadstairs Folk Week Early to mid-Aug. See page 97

Arundel Festival Second half Aug. This creative ten-day arts festival features everything from dragon-boat racing to treasure hunts, jousting to community samba, plus theatre, walks, workshops and tours. Ⓦ arundelfestival.co.uk

Weyfest Near Farnham, third week Aug. Acclaimed grassroots music festival at the Rural Life Centre in Surrey – acts run the gamut from The Waterboys to The Wurzels, via The Orb, The Selecter and 10cc. Ⓦ weyfest.co.uk

Medieval Festival Herstmonceux Castle, Aug bank holiday. The largest medieval bash in the UK, with costumed knights, men-at-arms, jesters, minstrels and traders descending on the moated castle for three days of jousting, tournaments, falconry and more, the highlights being the reconstructed siege and battle. Ⓦ englandsmedievalfestival.com

Lewes Art Wave Late Aug to early Sept. The annual visual arts festival for Lewes and the surrounding area; a fortnight during which more than 140 artists and makers open up their houses and studios to the public. Ⓦ www.artwavefestival.org

Faversham Hop Festival Late Aug/early Sept. Ebullient weekend street festival celebrating the heyday of the hop with bands, food and lots of Shepherd Neame beer. Ⓦ favershamhopfestival.org

SEPTEMBER & OCTOBER

Coastal Currents Visual Arts Festival Hastings, St Leonards, Eastbourne and Rye, throughout Sept. One of the biggest arts festivals on the south coast, featuring open studios, events, exhibitions and performances by local, regional and national artists. Ⓦ coastalcurrents.org.uk

Rye Arts Festival Two weeks in Sept. Established festival taking in classical and contemporary music, opera and dance, exhibitions and literary sessions. Ⓦ ryefestival.co.uk

Goodwood Revival Mid-Sept. See page 273

Hastings Seafood and Wine Festival Mid-Sept. A weekend of live music, wine and local seafood down at The Stade. Ⓦ visit1066country.com

OctoberFeast Lewes, mid-Sept to early Oct. Annual food and drink festival featuring markets, workshops, pop-up suppers, wine tasting, foraging excursions, brewery tours and more. Ⓦ lewesoctoberfeast.com

Canterbury Food and Drink Festival Late Sept. This three-day weekend foodie fest sees local producers, suppliers, farms and restaurants set up stalls in Dane John Gardens, along with arts and crafts vendors. It ties in with Kent's Green Hop Beer Fortnight, which celebrates the distinctive ales made from fresh (rather than dried) green hops. Ⓦ facebook.com/CTFoodFest and Ⓦ kentgreenhopbeer.com

---

PUBLIC HOLIDAYS

New Year's Day (Jan 1)
Good Friday
Easter Monday
Early May Bank Holiday (1st Mon in May)
Spring Bank Holiday (Last Mon in May)
Summer Bank Holiday (Last Mon in Aug)
Christmas Day (Dec 25)
Boxing Day (Dec 26)
If Jan 1, Dec 25 or Dec 26 fall on a Saturday or Sunday, the next weekday becomes a public holiday.

Small Wonder Charleston Farmhouse, end Sept. Annual short-story festival held at Charleston Farmhouse near Lewes, featuring workshops, discussions and performances. Ⓦ charleston.org.uk/whats-on/festivals/small-wonder

Broadstairs Food Festival Early Oct. See page 97

Battle of Hastings re-enactment Mid-Oct. Annual re-enactment of the famous 1066 battle in Battle, featuring more than a thousand soldiers and living history encampments. Ⓦ english-heritage.org.uk/visit/places/1066-battle-of-hastings-abbey-and-battlefield

National Apple Festival Brogdale, near Faversham, mid-Oct. A two-day celebration of Kent's finest fruit at the National Fruit Collection. Hundreds of apple varieties on display (some available to buy), plus music, crafts, food stalls, kids' entertainment and cooking demos. Ⓦ brogdalecollections.org/national-apple-festival

Canterbury Festival Mid-Oct to early Nov. See page 57

NOVEMBER & DECEMBER

Petworth Literary Festival Early Nov. Five days of talks and readings. Ⓦ petworthfestival.org.uk

Folkestone Book Festival Nov. See page 127

London to Brighton Veteran Car Run First Sun in Nov. See page 246

Bonfire Night Lewes, Nov 5, or the day before if Nov 5 falls on a Sun. See page 225

Dickens Christmas Rochester, early Dec. See page 71

Burning the Clocks Brighton, late Dec. See page 246

Travel essentials

Costs

For the most part Kent, Sussex and Surrey, being generally well-heeled areas close to the capital, have prices on a par with London and the more **expensive** parts of England. There are some exceptions, but, especially when it comes to eating and drinking, you should be prepared to spend quite a bit. Your biggest expense will be **accommodation** (see page 23). If you camp, or stay in hostels, buy your own food from one of the region's excellent farm shops, and walk or cycle from place to place, you could get by on as little as £40 per person per day – more if you factor in sightseeing costs. Staying in a B&B and eating out once a day could easily double that, and above that the sky's the limit.

We have given full adult prices for **admission prices** in the Guide, and in the case of family attractions have quoted children's rates as well. Some places will have reduced prices for seniors, the unemployed and full-time students, but you will need to show ID.

Many of the region's major historic attractions are under the auspices of the private **National Trust** (@ nationaltrust.org.uk) or the state-run **English Heritage** (@ www.english-heritage.org.uk), both of which are membership organizations. Prices can be steep for non-members, especially at the major attractions, but some National Trust properties offer discounts for people arriving on foot or by bike, and the generally excellent experiences offered by both organizations makes the cost worthwhile. If you're going to visit more than a handful of places run by either, it is well worth looking into membership, which will allow you free entry to – and free parking at – all their properties for a year. We've quoted the admission prices for non-members in the Guide, adding "NT" or "EH" as appropriate to indicate that members will not have to pay.

Prices for other attractions vary widely. Local town museums may well be free, while some of the major private attractions can charge as much as £20 per adult. Some of these pricier options, like Leeds Castle or Chatham Historic Dockyard, do allow you to return as many times as you wish in a year, however, which can work out as good value.

LGBTQ travellers

Brighton, of course, is the biggest draw for LGBTQ travellers in this region, with the lively Kemp Town area offering hotels, restaurants and shops all geared toward the pink pound, and an exceptionally lively and laidback LGBTQ nightlife scene packed into a compact area; **Brighton Pride** (@ brighton-pride. org) is the big summer event. Countrywide listings, news and links can be found at @ gaytimes.co.uk, @ gaybritain.co.uk and @ gaytravel.co.uk.

Maps

For an **overview** of the region on one map, the AA's *South East England Road Map* (1:200,000) is probably your best bet, and includes some town plans. There are also several good **road atlases** available: A–Z publishes a *South East England Regional Road Atlas* (1:158,400); *Kent Visitors' Map* (1:158,400); and *Surrey, East and West Sussex Visitors' Map* (1:158,400), as well as **street atlases** to East Sussex, West Sussex and Surrey (all 1:19,000) and Kent (1:20,267). OS *Explorer* maps (1:25,000) are best for **walking**.

Opening hours

We've given full **opening hours** for attractions, restaurants, cafés, pubs and shops in the Guide, though these do sometimes change from year to year – or even, in the case of the seaside resorts, depending on the season or the weather – so it's always worth calling ahead or checking the website before you set off.

Opening hours for most businesses, shops and offices are Monday to Saturday 9am to 5.30/6pm, with many shops also open on Sundays, generally 10.30/11am until 4.30/5pm. Big supermarkets have longer hours (except on Sun), sometimes round the clock. Banks are usually open Monday to Friday 9am to 4pm, and Saturday 9am to 12.30pm or so. You can usually get fuel any time of the day or night in larger towns and cities. Businesses and most shops close on bank holidays (see page 33), though large supermarkets, small corner shops and many tourist attractions stay open.

Tourist information

The Southeast's regional tourist body, **Visit Southeast England** (@ visitsoutheastengland.com), has a comprehensive website, packed with useful tips and ideas. Within the region, **Visit Kent** (@ visitkent. co.uk) and **Visit Surrey** (@ visitsurrey.com) each have their own website; there's no official tourist body for **Sussex**. Further down the scale, individual cities, towns and groups of towns also have their own tourist information websites, which we list within the relevant destination in the Guide.

Local **tourist offices** are also listed in the Guide; at the best of these staff will nearly always be able to book accommodation, reserve space on guided tours and sell guidebooks, maps and walk leaflets. The **South Downs National Park** has its headquarters and information centre in Midhurst (see page 282).

Travellers with disabilities

Kent, Sussex and Surrey have good facilities for travellers with disabilities. All new public buildings, including museums and cinemas, must provide wheelchair access, train stations are usually accessible, many buses have boarding ramps, and kerbs and signalled crossings have been dropped in many places. The number of accessible hotels and restaurants is growing, and reserved parking bays are available almost everywhere.

The **tourist bodies** for Kent and Surrey, and for individual towns, have varying amounts of accessibility information on their websites; some allow you to search for accessible attractions and restaurants in the area. The **National Trust** gives general information about access at ⓦnationaltrust.org.uk/ accessforall, where you can also download a PDF listing access information for their properties in the Southeast; **English Heritage** (ⓦenglish-heritage.org. uk) lists access information for each property on their website. Details of "Miles without Stiles" – accessible walks in the **South Downs National Park** – can be found at ⓦsouthdowns.gov.uk/enjoy/explore/ walking/miles-without-stiles.

A useful point of reference is **Tourism for All** (ⓦtourismforall.org.uk), which has general advice and listings. Also worth checking out is **The Rough Guide to Accessible Britain** (ⓦaccessibleguide.co.uk), which has accounts of a few attractions in the region, reviewed by writers with disabilities.

Travelling with children

Kent, Sussex and Surrey have enough farm parks, castles, steam trains, off-road cycling trails, crabbing spots and beaches to keep even the most exacting of children happy. The best **beaches for families** are in Kent around the Isle of Thanet (see page 88), where there are fifteen sandy strands – seven of them have Blue Flag status, signifying a particularly good resort beach with safe water and lifeguard facilities – plus plenty of family-friendly entertainment; in Sussex, the beaches are mainly pebbly, though there are two glorious exceptions at sand-dune-backed Camber Sands (see page 172) and West Wittering (see page 275).

Excellent **farm parks and zoos** in the region include the wildlife parks of Port Lympne (see page 128) and Howletts (see page 61) in Kent, and Drusillas (see page 217) and Fishers Farm Park (see page 287) in Sussex; there are **steam trains** on the Romney, Hythe & Dymchurch Railway (see page 129), the Bluebell Railway (see page 194), and the Kent & East Sussex Railway (see page 151) – the last of these an excellent way to get to Bodiam Castle (see page 188), one of many fine **castles** in this history-rich corner of the country. In North Kent, there is a knot of excellent family attractions around Rochester, where the huge ships of the Chatham Historic Dockyard (see page 72) are just a hop away from Diggerland (see page 72) and the Chatham Snowsports Centre (see page 72). For older children, there are a host of outdoor activities to keep them happy, from cycling and walking to stand-up paddleboarding at Eastbourne and Brighton (see pages 208 and 247), canoeing in Kent (see page 60) or surfing at West Wittering beach or Joss Bay (see page 97). Finally, there are **treetop adventure courses** at Branching Out near Lewes in Sussex and at Bedgebury in Kent (see page 159) – the latter also has adventure playgrounds and a family bike trail, with bike hire available.

Child **admission prices** for all children's attractions are listed in the Guide. Attractions that are not geared specifically towards children generally admit under-5s for free, and have reduced prices for 5- to 16-year-olds. Under-5s travel free on **public transport**, and 5- to 16-year-olds generally at a fifty-percent discount.

Breastfeeding is legal in all public places, including restaurants, cafés and public transport, and **baby-changing** rooms are available widely in shopping centres and train stations, although less reliably in cafés and restaurants. Children aren't allowed in certain licensed (that is, alcohol-serving) premises – though this doesn't apply to restaurants, and many **pubs** have family rooms or beer gardens where children are welcome.

Canterbury and around

CANTERBURY CATHEDRAL

Canterbury and around

Canterbury offers a rich slice through two thousand years of English history, with Roman and early Christian remains, a ruined Norman castle and a splendid cathedral that looms over a medieval warren of time-skewed Tudor buildings. It's a rewarding place to spend a couple of days, with important historic sights, peaceful riverside walks and a good number of hotels and excellent restaurants, and its small size makes it easy to get to know. Almost everything you will want to see is concentrated in or just outside the compact old centre, which, partly ringed by ancient walls, is virtually car-free. It's a delight to explore – though if you visit in high summer you should expect to share it with milling crowds. For a university town, things are surprisingly quiet after dark, which makes for a relaxing and restorative city break.

Canterbury is pretty laidback, but should you want to slow the pace even further, you can do so within minutes. Beyond the city a number of picturesque villages make good stop-offs for lunch or an overnight stay; indeed, it would be perfectly possible to base yourself outside Canterbury and make day-trips in, combining a city break with walking along the North Downs Way or even a canoe tour along the Stour. **South** of town, the Downs offer a couple of appealing family attractions as they begin their inexorable roll south, while to the north and west spreads the ancient, dappled woodland of the Blean and its nature trails and walking paths. From here you're a hop away from North Kent's foodie heartland, with both Faversham (see page 76) and Whitstable (see page 80) within easy reach. To the east, on the way to Thanet (see page 88) or the east coast, Stodmarsh Nature Reserve is an important birding spot and a lovely place for a stroll.

Canterbury

Most of the things you want to see in **CANTERBURY**, including the **cathedral**, are minutes away from each other within the bounds of the walled city. Just a short walk outside the walls are a handful of key historical sights – **St Augustine's Abbey**, **St Martin's Church** and **St Dunstan's Church** – while you may also want to head over to the campus of the University of Kent to catch a performance at the Gulbenkian Theatre (see page 58).

Brief history
The city that began as a Belgic settlement, spreading out on either side of the River Stour, was known as **Durovernum Cantiacorum** to the Romans, who established a garrison and supply base here soon after arriving in Britain. Life changed almost immediately for the Cantii locals, who found themselves living in a thriving town with good roads, public buildings and a ring of protective city walls. After the Roman withdrawal from Britain the place fell into decline, before being settled again by the Anglo-Saxons, who renamed it Cantwaraburg. It was a Saxon king, **Ethelbert of Kent**, who in 597 AD welcomed the Italian monk Augustine, despatched by Pope Gregory the Great to reintroduce **Christianity** to the south of England. By the time of his death in 605, Augustine had founded an important monastery outside the city walls, and established Christ Church, raised on the site of the Roman basilica, which was to become the first cathedral in England.

Highlights

❶ Canterbury Cathedral Dominating this historic university town, the ancient cathedral – seat of the Primate of All England, the Archbishop of Canterbury – can't fail to inspire a sense of awe. See page 41

❷ Greyfriars Chapel This tiny Franciscan chapel, with its own pretty walled gardens, makes a tranquil hideaway just footsteps from the city centre. See page 48

❸ The River Stour Whether you stroll or cycle along its quiet banks, glide upon it in a punt, or leave the city behind on a kayaking adventure, the Stour provides charm in spades. See pages 52 and 60

❹ Crab and Winkle Way Cycling or walking along the old railway track between Canterbury and the seaside town of Whitstable, just seven miles away, is a lovely way to combine city, countryside and coast. See page 59

❺ Chilham An unfeasibly pretty village in the countryside surrounding Canterbury, this Tudor gem makes a great stop off, especially if you're walking or cycling the North Downs Way. See page 62

❻ Compasses Inn, Crundale This gorgeous country pub dishes up outstanding seasonal, rustic food, with lovely woodland and Downs walks all around. See page 62

HIGHLIGHTS ARE MARKED ON THE MAPS ON PAGES 40 AND 42

1

After the Norman invasion, a complex power struggle developed between the archbishops, the abbots from the monastery – now St Augustine's Abbey – and King Henry II. This culminated in the assassination of Archbishop **Thomas Becket** in the cathedral in 1170 (see page 41), a martyrdom that created one of Christendom's greatest shrines, made Canterbury one of the country's richest cities – and effectively established the autonomy of the archbishops. Believers from all over Europe flocked to the cathedral on long pilgrimages, hoping to be cured, forgiven or saved; Geoffrey Chaucer's **Canterbury Tales** (see page 48), written towards the end of the fourteenth century, portrays the festive, ribald – and not always very pious – nature of these highly sociable events.

Becket's tomb, along with much of the cathedral's treasure, was later destroyed on the orders of Henry VIII, who also ordered the dissolution of St Augustine's Abbey. With its pilgrimage days effectively over, the next couple of centuries saw a downturn in the city's fortunes. However, following a period of calm and prosperity in the wake of the Restoration, in 1830 a pioneering steam passenger railway service was built, linking Canterbury to the seaside at Whitstable, and resulting in another bout of growth. Canterbury suffered extensive damage from German bombing on June 1, 1942, in one of the "**Baedeker Raids**" – a Nazi campaign to wipe out Britain's most treasured

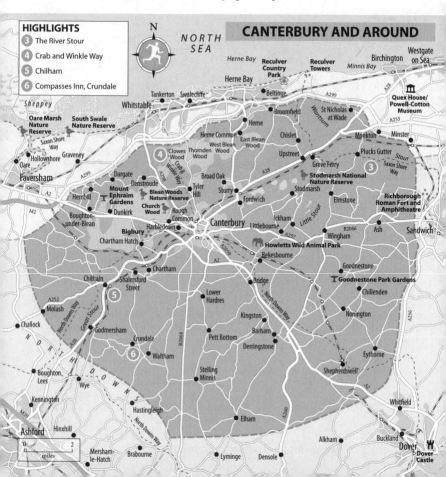

HIGHLIGHTS

CANTERBURY AND AROUND

1

THOMAS BECKET: THE TURBULENT PRIEST

The son of a wealthy merchant, Royal Chancellor **Thomas Becket** was appointed Archbishop of Canterbury in 1162 by his good friend and drinking partner Henry II. Becket had no particular experience in the Church, but Henry needed an ally against the bishops and monks who were, as the king saw it, getting far too above themselves and becoming a threat. The friends soon fell out, however, as Henry attempted to impose his jurisdiction over that of the Church and found that Becket seemed to have switched sides. After a six-year exile in France, Becket was reconciled with Henry and was allowed home in 1170 – only to find that his lands were being requisitioned by the king's officers. He incurred the king's wrath once more by refusing to absolve two bishops whom he had previously excommunicated, along with the family who had stripped him of his estates; Henry, in France, was told (untruthfully) that Becket was raising an army, provoking the king to utter the oft-quoted words, "Will no one rid me of this turbulent priest?" (Some sources claim he actually called him "low-born", or "meddlesome", but it is "turbulent" that has tended to stick.)

Hearing this, four knights took it upon themselves to seek out Becket and, on December 29, 1170, finding him in the cathedral, **murdered** him, hacking at him with their swords and slicing off the crown of his head. It was said he was praying when they found him, and was discovered to have been wearing a monk's habit under his robes, and a hair shirt underneath that – held to be proof of his great piety. The day after his murder, Becket's remains were taken to the crypt, for safety; within days miracles were said to be occurring at his simple stone tomb, and just three years later he was canonized. Hundreds of thousands of **pilgrims** from all over Europe, including kings and queens, flocked to the cathedral hoping to be healed or redeemed; one such pilgrim was Henry himself, who in 1174 walked barefoot and in sackcloth from St Dunstan's Church (see page 51) to the shrine, where he was theatrically beaten by eighty monks and a prior. Whether Henry was driven by a genuine sense of regret, or canny pragmatics – his pilgrimage was a statement to the world that he definitively did not order the murder of Becket, while also being an admission that his words may have inspired it – is open to debate.

historic sites as described in the eponymous German travel guides. Nine hundred buildings were destroyed, and the city smouldered for weeks; the cathedral survived, however, and today, along with St Augustine's Abbey and St Martin's Church, has been designated as a **UNESCO World Heritage Site**.

Canterbury Cathedral

Buttermarket, CT1 2EH · **Cathedral** April–Oct Mon–Sat 9am–5.30pm, Sun 9am–4.30pm; Nov–March Mon–Sat 9am–5pm, Sun 10am–4.30pm; last entry 30min before closing · **Crypt** April–Oct Mon–Sat 10am–5.30pm, Sun 10am–5pm; Nov–March daily 10am–5pm · £12.50, audio tours £4 · **Guided tours** Mon–Fri 10.30am, noon & 2pm (2.30pm in summer), Sat 10.30am (not in Jan), noon & 1pm; 1hr 20min; £5 ☏ 01227 762862, ⓦ canterbury-cathedral.org

The Mother Church of the Church of England, **Canterbury Cathedral** may not be the country's most impressive architecturally, but it lords over the city with a befitting sense of authority. A cathedral has stood here since around 600 AD, established by Augustine; it was enlarged by the Saxons, but the building you see today owes most to a Norman archbishop, Lanfranc, who in 1070 rebuilt the place after a huge fire. Already on the medieval pilgrim route to Rome, the cathedral became an enormously important pilgrimage centre in its own right after the murder of Archbishop **Thomas Becket** here in 1170 (see page 41). In 1174 it was rebuilt again, and modified over successive centuries; today, with the puritanical lines of the late-medieval Perpendicular style dominating, its exterior derives much of its distinctiveness from the upward thrust of its 235ft-high Bell Harry Tower, dating from 1498.

Inside, it is the reminders of earlier days that have the most emotional impact – from the amazing carved columns in the crypt to the steep flights of stone steps worn away by millions of pilgrims – along with a couple of modern sculptures that recall the

1

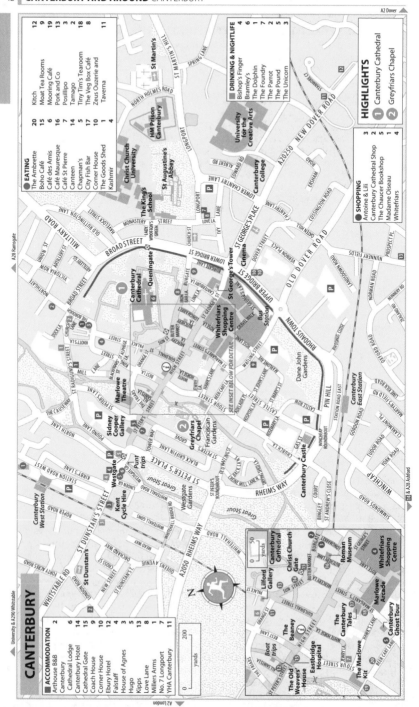

CANTERBURY

ACCOMMODATION

Arthouse B&B Canterbury	2
Cathedral Lodge	6
Canterbury Hotel	14
Cathedral Gate	15
Coach House	9
Corner House	10
Ebury Hotel	12
Falstaff	4
House of Agnes	3
Hugo	5
Kipps	13
Love Lane	8
Millers Arms	1
No. 7 Longport	7
YHA Canterbury	11

● EATING

The Ambrette	20
Boho Café	15
Café des Amis	6
Café Mauresque	16
Café St Pierre	7
Canteen	14
Chapman's	5
City Fish Bar	17
Corner House	10
The Goods Shed	1
Kashmir	4
Kitch	12
Moat Tea Rooms	9
Mooring Café	19
Pork and Co	13
Posillipo	3
Tamago	2
Tiny Tim's Tearoom	18
The Veg Box Café	8
Zeus Ouzerie and Taverna	11

■ DRINKING & NIGHTLIFE

Bishop's Finger	4
Bramley's	6
The Dolphin	1
The Foundry	7
The Parrot	2
The Pound	5
The Unicorn	3

● SHOPPING

Antoine & Lili	3
Canterbury Cathedral Shop	2
The Chaucer Bookshop	5
Madame Oiseau	1
Whitefriars	4

HIGHLIGHTS

1 Canterbury Cathedral
2 Greyfriars Chapel

enormity of the events of 1170. It's well worth taking a guided **tour** to peel away the many layers of the building's fascinating history. There's quite a lot of walking, and climbing of stairs, if you want to see everything; if you're short of time, concentrate on the **crypt** and **Trinity Chapel**.

The precincts

The cathedral **precincts** are entered through the ornate, early sixteenth-century **Christ Church Gate**, where Burgate and St Margaret's Street meet. This junction, the city's medieval core, was originally called "Bullstake" – cattle were baited in the street here in order to tenderize their meat – but was renamed **Buttermarket** in the eighteenth century. Having paid your entrance fee, you pass through the gatehouse to be confronted by one of the finest aspects of the cathedral, foreshortened and crowned with soaring towers and pinnacles.

Note that you can exit the precincts via the large gift shop (see page 58) on Burgate; just next to it, within the grounds, is a little **refreshments hut** with outdoor tables; the close-up view of the cathedral, and the peace and quiet, make this one of the city's best-kept secrets.

The nave

The fourteenth-century **nave**, the largest space in the cathedral, would have been a bustling arrival point for weary pilgrims. With its soaring Perpendicular pillars and vaulted arches, its sweeping views and lofty gilt bosses, it was designed to inspire awe, but was more sociable, and less formal than the areas beyond. At the eastern end, an elaborate **stone screen** marks the entrance to the Quire. In the distance beyond, though barely visible from the nave, are the high altar and the Trinity Chapel; in medieval times, obscuring the view of the double ascent up to the holy relics would have added to the sense of expectation as the pilgrimage drew to a close, and even today the screen provides a dramatic pausing point on your journey through the cathedral.

The Martyrdom

The actual spot where Thomas Becket was murdered, known as the **Martyrdom**, is just off the nave in the northwest transept, marked by a modern-day flagstone etched simply with the name "Thomas". Next to it, the **Altar of the Sword's Point** – where, in medieval times, the shattered tip of the sword that hacked into Becket's scalp was displayed as a relic – is today marked by a modern sculpture of the assassins' weapons, suspended on the wall. Taking the form of two jagged swords attached to a similarly jagged cross, and casting sinister shadows, it is a striking image, at once violent and spiritual.

The crypt

From the Martyrdom you can descend to the low, Romanesque **crypt**, one of the few surviving parts of the Norman cathedral and considered to be the finest of its type in the country. Beneath the Quire and the elevated Trinity Chapel – but not actually underground – it is an unusually large space, dimly illuminated with natural light and with a number of chapels branching off from the main area. Becket's original shrine stood down here, before being moved in 1220 to a more resplendent position in the Trinity Chapel.

Today, in the main body of the crypt, you can see amazingly well-preserved **carvings** on the capitals of the sturdy Romanesque columns, showing flowers, animals, scallops, sea monsters and winged beasts. There is a fine crop in **St Gabriel's Chapel**, which also boasts some intact, and colourful, twelfth-century wall paintings, uncovered in the 1860s. Among the usual stash of silver plate in the **treasury**, look out for the nineteenth-century brass high altar cross, studded with precious gems.

MURDER IN THE CATHEDRAL

A rain of blood has blinded my eyes. Where is England? Where is Kent? Where is Canterbury?
O far far far far in the past; and I wander in a land of barren boughs…
The Chorus, Part 2, Murder in the Cathedral

The American-born poet **T.S. Eliot** wrote his play **Murder in the Cathedral** for the 1935 Canterbury Festival, when it was performed in the cathedral itself. After converting to Anglicanism from Unitarianism in 1927 – the same year he took British citizenship – Eliot, a modernist, concerned himself increasingly with spiritual issues in his writing, and went on to become an important voice in the High Anglican Church, characterized by its emphasis on ritual and ceremonial. Written in a mixture of prose, blank verse and rhyme, and with its keening female chorus – who express their beautifully wrought, visceral anguish in lines like "O late late late, late is the time, late too late, and rotten the year" – *Murder in the Cathedral* recalls both Classical Greek drama and medieval morality plays. Though not quite as bleakly existential as Eliot's pre-conversion poems *The Waste Land* (1922) or *The Hollow Men* (1925), it is a profoundly personal work, written in his characteristically lean style. Even for non-believers, the genius he applies to both language and form in exploring vexed issues around faith, temptation, desolation and guilt render it a deeply moving piece of writing.

The Quire

In the main body of the cathedral, the **Quire** is one of the earliest examples of Gothic church architecture in Britain, built between 1175 and 1184 and replete with elegant pointed arches. As you enter from the nave, stop a while at the intricate **stone screen** and crane your neck upwards to gaze upon the interior of the **Bell Harry Tower**; a vertiginous pattern of arches, pillars and fan vaulting, this is a stunning sight, and all too easily missed. At the end of the Quire, at the top of the steps beyond the high altar, stands the thirteenth-century white marble **St Augustine's Chair**, on which all archbishops of Canterbury are enthroned.

Trinity Chapel

Beyond the Quire, climbing a flight of stone steps, polished and worn wonky by the knees of pilgrims, brings you to the **Trinity Chapel**, for centuries the cathedral's most venerated space. Becket's remains were moved up here from the crypt in 1220, with great pomp and ceremony; the new shrine, far more ornate than the earlier tomb, became a place of theatre and ritual. Each pilgrim would be shown the spot where Becket was murdered, taken to see the bust that contained the piece of skull dislodged by the fatal blow, and, as a grand finale, allowed to watch as a canopy was pulled up to reveal the ornate golden tomb, studded, according to the writer Erasmus in 1513, with jewels as big as goose eggs. The shrine shimmered in all its jewel-bedecked glory until being demolished during Henry VIII's Dissolution of the Monasteries in 1538, and all that remains today is a candle to mark where it once stood. You can get a sense of what it looked like, however, in the dazzling thirteenth-century stained-glass **Miracle Windows**, on the north side of the chapel, where along with Becket's life and miraculous works, you can see images both of the original tomb and the showier later version.

Also in the Trinity Chapel is the double tomb of **Henry IV** and his wife, **Joan of Navarre**, their heads resting on carved red cushions, and the (somewhat tarnished) gilt bronze effigy of Edward III's son, Edward Prince of Wales, or the **Black Prince**. The "achievements" hanging above him – his shield, gauntlets, sword and jerkin – are copies; the originals, which were carried in procession with his funeral in 1376, will return to the cathedral as part of a new display, currently scheduled for 2020.

1

The Corona
At the far eastern tip of the cathedral, the **Corona** is where, until Henry VIII destroyed it, a silver bust of Becket held the piece of Becket's skull hacked off by his assassin's sword. Today the chapel is dedicated to saints and martyrs of our own time, among them Dr Martin Luther King, Jr and an Anglican archbishop, Janani Luwum of Uganda, murdered by Idi Amin's forces in 1977.

The Great Cloister
On the cathedral's north flank are the fan-vaulted colonnades of the **Great Cloister**, an atmospherically weathered and beautifully peaceful space. Look above you to see expressive little faces, bulbous flowers and heraldic symbols carved into the vaulting, and check out the carved graffiti and ancient, crumbling columns. The **Chapter House**, off the cloister, is relatively plain, though it does boast an intricate web of fourteenth-century tracery supporting the roof and two huge stained-glass windows.

The High Street and around
As it cuts a northwest–southeast swathe through the city between Westgate and St George's Gate, Canterbury's predominantly pedestrianized **High Street** changes its name three times: the stretch from Westgate to the river is St Peter's Street, followed by the High Street proper down to Longmarket, where it turns into St George's Street for the remainder of its length.

Each section of the High Street has its own character; **St Peter's Street** is relatively quiet, with low-key restaurants and shops occupying its hotchpotch of half-timbered, gabled and more modern buildings, while chain stores predominate along the **High Street** proper. Here, though, the side streets offer photogenic medieval vistas – the view up **Mercery Lane** towards Christ Church Gate, for example, a narrow alley of crooked, overhanging shops at the end of which stand the elaborate gatehouse and the cathedral's handsome towers. Much of **St George's Street**, meanwhile, is consumed by the Whitefriars shopping centre (see page 58), before ending up at the edge of the old city walls.

Westgate
St Peters St, CT1 2BQ • Daily 11am–4pm (closed 30min for lunch) • £4 (£14.95 joint ticket with The Canterbury Tales, see page 47) • ☎ 01227 458629, ⓦ onepoundlane.co.uk

At the top of the High Street, the sturdy, 60ft-high **Westgate** is the largest and most important of Canterbury's seven city gates and the only one to have survived intact. With its massive crenellated towers, dating from 1380, it's a handsome structure, looming over the traffic below, and something of a city icon. A small museum inside includes intriguing historical snippets about the gate's days as a medieval and nineteenth-century gaol; best of all, you can climb up to the battlements for lovely **views** across to the cathedral and over the gardens below. The gate also houses an escape room, **Escape in the Towers** (1hr; from £19/person), with a choice of three different games involving an evil nineteenth-century doctor, World War II air attacks and a raid on the Magna Carta. Entry is in the lobby area of the neighbouring *The Pound* bar (see page 57).

Westgate Gardens
Westgate Grove, CT1 2BQ • Free • ⓦ westgateparks.co.uk

Across the road from the Westgate, and fringing the River Stour, the pretty, flower-filled **Westgate Gardens** make a splendid spot for a picnic or a riverside stroll. Like so many places in Canterbury, they're also historically significant, having been open to the public since medieval times. You'll hardly be able to miss the two-centuries-old, unfeasibly chubby Oriental plane tree, with a girth of a whopping 29ft, give or take; more difficult to spot, however, is the underwater sculpture by the Westgate Bridge. Here, two female statues, one cast in cement and the other in grass resin, float eerily beneath the surface of the reed-tangled, shallow water like latter-day Ophelias. This is **Alluvia**, the work of Jason de Caires Taylor, an ex-graffiti artist from Canterbury who now creates unsettling and sublimely beautiful underwater sculptures all over the world. It can be easiest to see the statues at night, when they are illuminated.

Sidney Cooper Gallery

22–23 St Peter's St, CT1 2BQ • Tues–Fri 10.30am–5pm, Sat 11.30am–5pm • Free • ☎ 01227 453267, ⓦ canterbury.ac.uk/sidney-cooper

An unobtrusive shopfront hides the **Sidney Cooper Gallery**, Canterbury Christ Church University's modern-art space. Hosting temporary shows from university staff, students and alumni, along with local and national artists of such calibre as Maggi Hambling, Louise Bourgeois and Anish Kapoor, it is always worth a look. Many, but not all, works have Kentish associations, and tend towards the cutting edge, featuring anything from sound installations to animation to sculpture.

The Old Weavers' House

1–3 St Peter's St, CT1 2AT

The wonky, half-timbered **Old Weavers' House**, standing at the King's Bridge over a branch of the Stour, is one of the most photographed buildings in Canterbury. Built around 1500, the structure appears to be quintessentially medieval, but is actually a hotchpotch, constructed on twelfth-century foundations and with alterations made between the sixteenth and twentieth centuries. A couple of restaurants now inhabit the place, making much of their picturesque riverside location.

Eastbridge Hospital

25 High St, CT1 2BD • April–Dec Mon–Sat 10.30am–5pm • £3 • ☎ 01227 471688, ⓦ eastbridgehospital.org.uk

Tiny **Eastbridge Hospital**, the ancient stone building standing just beyond the King's Bridge, was founded in the twelfth century to provide the poorest pilgrims with shelter (or "hospitality"). Following the Reformation, it continued as an almshouse, offering permanent accommodation for people in need; today it is home to a small community of elderly people.

Beyond the handsome pointed arch doorway, a couple of steps lead down into the Gothic **undercroft**, the original pilgrims' sleeping quarters; you can see the cubicles they slept in, along with a few exhibition panels recounting the history of the building, and of pilgrimage in Canterbury. Upstairs is the medieval **refectory**, where a striking thirteenth-century wall painting shows Jesus surrounded by the four Evangelists (though only two of them remain), and the light-filled **pilgrims' chapel**, with its beautifully crafted, thirteenth-century oak-beamed roof.

The Beaney

18 High St, CT1 2RA • Tues–Sat 10am–5pm, Sun 11am–4pm • Free • ☎ 01227 862162, ⓦ canterburymuseums.co.uk/beaney

A sturdy terracotta, brick and mock-Tudor ensemble, built in 1898, the **Beaney** – officially the **Beaney House of Art and Knowledge** – started its days with the aim of improving the masses and retains a populist, welcoming feel. Today, despite its modern library and lofty, airy rooms, some of the exhibits have the – not unlikeable – feel of a Victorian collection, with cases of stuffed animals, pinned butterflies and **antiquities and archeological finds** creating a cabinet-of-curiosities thrill. Look out for the little mummified cat, baring its tiny sharp fangs, the terrifying angled temple sword from eighteenth-century Malabar, and the nineteenth-century face-slapper, used to hit female prisoners in Kashgar. On a lighter note, the museum also pays homage to **Oliver Postgate**, with nostalgic TV footage and cabinets of real-deal Clangers, and to tartan-trousered philanthropist **Rupert Bear**, created by local-born Mary Tourtel, with all manner of bear memorabilia, including the very first Rupert book, dating from 1921.

There is a lot to see here, but perhaps most interesting of all are the **paintings**, from the seventeenth century onwards. Among the images of Kentish notables, landscapes and historical moments, many of them painted by local artists, perennial favourites include a Van Dyck portrait of Kent MP Sir Basil Dixwell (1638), displaying his long, aristocratic fingers and showing off his expensive black silk robes; the tall, thin and enigmatic *The Little Girl at the Door* (1910), by local artist Harriet Halhed; a Reculver scene by Walter Sickert (1936), painted during his four-year stay in Thanet; and the vigorous images of 1930s hop-pickers by English Impressionist Dame Laura Knight. In addition, high-profile **temporary exhibitions** have featured artists such as Grayson Perry, Gerald Scarfe and Martin Parr.

Roman Museum

Butchery Lane, CT1 2JR · Daily 10am–5pm · £9 (£19.95 joint ticket with The Canterbury Tales, see below · ☎ 01227 785575, ⓦ canterburymuseums.co.uk/romanmuseum

Following the devastating Canterbury bombings of 1942, excavations of the destroyed Longmarket area, between Burgate and the High Street, exposed the foundations of a Roman townhouse, complete with mosaic floors, now preserved in situ in the city's subterranean **Roman Museum**.

While historical panels give a good introduction to life in Durovernum Cantiacorum, it is the treasure-trove of **artefacts** excavated from the city and sites nearby that really brings it alive. This is a rich hoard: case after case filled with pottery, tiles and amulets (many of them phallus-shaped, a favourite among Roman soldiers), exquisite glass bottles, building tools, fashion accessories – the list goes on. Some are unexpectedly poignant – a commemorative stone for a 6-year-old girl, for example, marked with the words "May the earth lie lightly on thee"; the two crumbling military swords, found in a double grave; even the silver spoon marked with the words "I belong to a good man", which was buried for safety when the Romans withdrew in around 410, and which remained hidden underground for 1500 years.

The **remains** themselves come at the end of the display, protected behind glass in the dark. Here you can see the floor supports of an under-heated hypocaust, an undecorated stone corridor, and some stone floor mosaics decorated with geometric and floral patterns. If all this whets your appetite for Roman remains, plan a trip to Lullingstone Roman Villa, in the Weald (see page 153).

The Canterbury Tales

St Margaret's St, CT1 2TG · April–Aug daily 10am–5pm; Sept & Oct daily 10am–4pm; Nov–March Wed–Sun 10am–4pm · £10.95, under-16s £8.95 (£14.95/under-15s £10.95 joint ticket with Westgate, see page 45; £19.95/under-15s £8.95 joint ticket with Roman Museum, see above; £18.05/under-15s £13.15 joint ticket with St Augustine's Abbey, see page 49) · ☎ 01227 696002, ⓦ canterburytales.org.uk

Housed in an old church a few yards off the High Street, **The Canterbury Tales**, based on Geoffrey Chaucer's medieval stories (see page 48), is a quasi-educational, and fun, attraction. Equipped with audio guides, visitors set off on a 45-minute wander through atmospheric, odour-enhanced fourteenth-century tableaux, following the progress of a group of pilgrims (or rather, suitably scrofulous mannequins) from the *Tabard Inn* in London to Becket's atmospherically lit, and fabulously ornate, shrine. Each new space provides a setting for one of Chaucer's famous tales – edited-down versions of stories from the Knight, the Miller, the Wife of Bath, the Nun's Priest and the Pardoner. Each is told in a slightly different way, using animatronics, shadow play, video, or a combination of the three, with helpful interventions from costumed guides acting their hearts out in character – and it's all done rather well, with lively lighting, sound effects and tongue-in-cheek dialogue. The bare bum revealed in the scatological Miller's Tale is always a cheeky crowd-pleaser, and it's hard not to get caught up in the bawdy fun of it all.

The Marlowe Kit

Stour St, CT1 2NR · Sat 10am–5pm, Sun noon–5pm · Free · ☎ 01227 862268, ⓦ marlowetheatre.com

Run by the Marlowe Theatre and housed in a handsome twelfth-century Poor Priests' Hospital, the **Marlowe Kit** is chiefly a performance/arts workshop space. It does,

1

THE CANTERBURY TALES

Geoffrey Chaucer's (unfinished) **Canterbury Tales**, written between 1387 and the author's death in 1400, are a collection of stories within a story in which a motley bunch of thirty pilgrims exchange a series of yarns to while away the time as they journey from a tavern in London to the cathedral. The group is a colourful cross-section of medieval society, including a knight, a monk, a miller, a squire and the oft-widowed, rather raunchy, Wife of Bath. At a time when French was very much the official language of literature, Chaucer chose to write their earthy and often ribald tales in English. That, and the fact that each story has a different narrator, with his or her own voice and personality – and that each character is linked by their common journey – is a structure that feels entirely natural to modern readers but at the time was entirely new.

The tales themselves are reworked stories, popular at the time, from around the world, ranging from oral folk tales to classic myths – the *Prologue*, however, is entirely Chaucer's work, introducing each character and giving a wonderfully vivid, and humanistic, portrayal of early medieval England. All this, combined with the lively language and universal themes, keep the *Canterbury Tales* as fresh and engaging today as they ever were.

however, feature a low-key exhibit on local writers – playwright/poet and alleged spy **Christopher Marlowe**, novelist **Joseph Conrad**, who lived in Kent in his later years, and controversial author **Aphra Behn** – that outlines their relationship to Canterbury. There's also an escape room, "Marlowe's Ghost" (check website for days/hours; 1hr; from £19/person).

Greyfriars Chapel and Franciscan Gardens

Behind 6 Stour St, CT1 2NR • **Chapel** Easter–Sept Mon–Sat 2–4pm; Anglican Eucharist Wed 12.30pm • **Gardens** Easter–Sept Mon–Sat 10.30am–4pm • Free; donations welcome • ☎ 01227 471688, 🌐 eastbridgehospital.org.uk

A delightful surprise hidden off Stour Street, literally spanning the river and with pretty, peaceful gardens, the stone-built **Greyfriars Chapel** is the only surviving building from England's oldest Franciscan friary (1267). In the thirteenth century the friary was home to sixty or so friars; it was closed by Henry VIII in 1538 and sold on. This little building was, it is thought, the guesthouse of the friary, and home over the years to Huguenot and Belgian refugees; one room was also used as a prison in the nineteenth century, as its grim, studded iron door attests. In 2003 a group of Anglican Franciscan friars returned to Canterbury, and they now use Greyfriars as their chapel.

The interior, though unadorned, is fascinating, with its original beams and prisoners' graffiti carved into medieval wooden panelling. A small **exhibit** illuminates the history of Greyfriars and of the Franciscans; upstairs, the whitewashed, vaulted **chapel** still hosts a weekly Eucharist, open to all. Take time to stroll through the **Franciscan Gardens**, a haven of serenity with the river gurgling past a drift of scattered wildflowers.

Canterbury Castle

Castle St, CT1 2PR • Daily morning to dusk • Free • ☎ 01227 862162

Walking down Castle Street, which grows quieter and increasingly residential as it approaches the city wall, brings you to the ruins of **Canterbury Castle**. Replacing a simple wooden structure built by William the Conqueror around 1070, this motte-and-bailey affair sitting hard by the Roman town walls was started in around 1086 and considerably altered in subsequent years; by the late twelfth century its importance had dwindled to nothing in the light of Henry II's mighty castle at Dover. For many years it existed as a rather neglected prison, until it fell into ruin in the sixteenth century and was pretty much pulled apart in the eighteenth and early nineteenth centuries.

Today, you can explore the substantial roofless **keep**, built by Henry I and made of locally quarried flint, Kentish ragstone and Roman bricks. It's an evocative spot, with its sturdy walls silhouetted against the sky and sprouting luxuriant vegetation; most days it is silent but for the wheeling birds tending to their nests, stuffed in the many huge arches and empty windows.

Dane John Gardens

Watling St, CT1 2QX • Free • ☎ 01227 862162, ⓦ explorekent.org/activities/dane-john-gardens

Dane John Gardens, a well-used park near the castle, was laid out in the eighteenth century with lawns, flower beds and a stately avenue of lime trees, along with a bandstand that still hosts concerts in summer. Bordering the southern edge of the gardens are the city walls and the Dane John Mound, a Romano-British burial mound that was incorporated into the city's original castle and now affords good views across the city. There's a refreshment kiosk, and in late September a three-day **food and drink festival** (ⓦ canterbury.co.uk/fooddrinkfest), with more than one hundred food stalls, plus live music and children's entertainment. The park is best avoided at night.

The King's Mile

The **King's Mile** – the stretch from the cathedral up Sun Street and Palace Street, also including Guildhall and the Borough – is a quieter and more characterful place to shop than the High Street, its picturesque historic buildings housing a number of quirky independent shops, galleries and restaurants. Palace Street is the prettiest section; at the top, where it meets the Borough, a sturdy stone gate screens off the medieval buildings of the **King's School**. Commonly believed to be the oldest continually operating school in the world, King's has an impressive list of alumni, from Elizabethan dramatist Christopher Marlowe to author Patrick Leigh Fermor and movie director Michael Powell.

Outside the city walls

From Burgate, it's just a three-minute walk east of the city walls to the vestigial remains of the sixth-century **St Augustine's Abbey**, and then another five minutes on to **St Martin's Church**, possibly the oldest church still in use in the English-speaking world. The two, along with the cathedral, comprise UNESCO's **Canterbury World Heritage Site**; for any full account of the city's history, or indeed the history of Christianity in England, they are a must-see. Northwest of town, **St Dunstan's Church** – where Henry II paused on his 1174 pilgrimage to shed his shoes and don his hair shirt, and where the remains of another martyr, Sir Thomas More, are interred – is also worth a look.

St Augustine's Abbey

Longport, CT1 1PF • April–Sept daily 10am–6pm; Oct daily 10am–5pm; Nov–March Sat & Sun 10am–4pm • £7.20; EH (£18.05 joint ticket with The Canterbury Tales, see page 47) • ☎ 01227 767345, ⓦ www.english-heritage.org.uk/visit/places/st-augustines-abbey

Although Canterbury Cathedral gets most of the attention, the ruined **St Augustine's Abbey**, founded in 597, is just as historically important. Founded as a monastery by the Italian monk Augustine, tasked with re-introducing Christianity to the English, it was vastly altered by the Normans, who replaced it with a much larger abbey; in turn, most of this was later destroyed in the Dissolution before falling into ruin. Today, it is an atmospheric site, with more to see than its ruinous state might at first suggest. Its various ground plans, clearly delineated in stone on soft carpets of grass, along with scattered semi-intact chapels, altar slabs and tombstones, evoke the original buildings almost as powerfully as if they were still standing. Standouts include the ancient **tombs** of the early archbishops and the remains of the seventh-century **St Pancras Church**, which survived the Norman expansions, and where you can see the Roman brick used in its construction.

1

THE RISE AND FALL OF ST AUGUSTINE'S ABBEY

In 595 Pope Gregory the Great dispatched **Augustine**, a Benedictine monk from Rome, on an evangelical mission to restore Christianity to England after a couple of centuries of Anglo-Saxon paganism had all but wiped it out. The kingdom of Kent seemed like a good place to start: not only was it conveniently close to the continent, but its king – **Ethelbert**, the most powerful Anglo-Saxon ruler of the time – also had a Christian wife, Bertha, and was open to the idea of conversion.

Augustine, reluctantly, fearing he was not up to the task of converting the barbarian Angles, set off with between twenty and forty monks. At one point he turned back, begging the Pope to send someone else; his entreaties went unheard, however, and he finally arrived on the Kentish coast in late 596 or 597. He baptized Ethelbert in 601, an act that effectively rubber-stamped his mission, and immediately set about founding a church within the walled city (today's cathedral), and a **monastery** outside the walls to the east. Following a tradition that forbade burials within city walls, the monastery's first church, dedicated to saints Peter and Paul, became the final resting place of both Augustine (in 605) and Ethelbert (in 616), along with successive archbishops and kings of Kent right up until the middle of the eighth century.

Augustine's monastery continued to thrive after his death. Two more churches, St Mary and St Pancras, were added in the first half of the seventh century, with further extensions being made in the eighth and ninth centuries; by the 900s it was well established as a major seat of learning. The most dramatic changes came in the eleventh century, with the arrival of the **Normans**, who in 1072 established a Benedictine **abbey** here, replacing the relatively simple Anglo-Saxon structures – and moving the holy remains of St Augustine from their original tomb into a far more ornate, jewel-bedecked shrine – with a huge Romanesque church similar in size to today's cathedral. The abbey continued to grow, becoming an important centre of book production, until the **Dissolution**. After being disbanded in 1538, it was converted into a royal palace, with apartments for Anne of Cleves (who never actually stayed here); following Henry VIII's death it was rented by a string of noble families. In the eighteenth and nineteenth centuries the abbey precinct fell into relative ruin, though it was used variously as a brewery, hospital, jail and pleasure gardens; shocked at such sacrilege, local MP Alexander James Beresford Hope bought the site in 1844 and opened a missionary college four years later. These Victorian buildings are now part of the King's School (see page 49), while other buildings in the precinct are owned by Christ Church college, Canterbury prison and English Heritage.

Illustrated information panels admirably recount the changing fortunes of the abbey, but to get the most out of a visit, pick up an audio guide from the excellent interpretive centre. These describe not only the more dramatic incidents in the site's history, but also its domestic routines, and really bring the place to life. The centre also has a few virtual-reality headsets that allow you to visualize and "walk through" the abbey as it would once have appeared.

St Martin's Church

Corner of North Holmes Rd and St Martin's Lane, CT1 1PW • Tues, Thurs & Fri 11am–3pm, Sat (summer only) 11am–4pm, Sun 9.45–10.30am • Free • ☎ 01227 768072, ⓦ martinpaul.org

The lovely **St Martin's Church**, one of England's oldest churches, was built on the site of a Roman villa or temple and used by the earliest Christians. Although medieval additions obscure much of the Saxon structure, this is perhaps the earliest Christian site in Canterbury – it was here that the Frankish Queen Bertha worshipped with her priest Liudhard, welcoming Augustine and his monks after their arrival in England in 597. After King Ethelbert was baptized in St Martin's, Augustine's mission was deemed to be a resounding success, and he was able to go on to build the church and the abbey that dominated Canterbury for centuries.

Entering the church through an ancient shady graveyard, where nearly a thousand gravestones pepper the grassy hills, you'll find a few intriguing vestiges of the building's long history. Beyond the nave – a very early Anglo-Saxon structure of mortared brick and stone, with a fourteenth-century beamed roof – you can see a wall of long, flat Roman bricks in the chancel, dating back to the fourth century, and opposite it a flat-topped Roman doorway. Other highlights include an angled "squint", through which medieval lepers would have watched Mass from a safe distance outside the church.

St Dunstan's Church

80 London Rd, CT2 8LS • Mon–Sat 9am–5pm, Sun during services only; weekday hours dependent on volunteers, so call ahead to check • Free • ☎ 01227 786109

Though many people pass it without a second thought, the tenth-century **St Dunstan's Church** was an important stopping-point for medieval pilgrims on their journey to the city via Westgate – it was from here that King Henry II proceeded barefoot to the cathedral when doing penance in 1174 (see page 41). The church is also remarkable for holding the eternal remains of **Sir Thomas More**, executed upon the orders of Henry VIII in 1535 for refusing to accept the king's desire to split from the Catholic Church. More's head, removed from a spike outside the Tower of London by his daughter, Margaret Roper, is enclosed in a lead casket in the Roper family vault, beneath a stained-glass window portraying scenes from his life. A marble slab marks the spot.

ARRIVAL AND DEPARTURE CANTERBURY

BY TRAIN

Canterbury East Canterbury East station (in the south) is a 15min walk from the cathedral.

Destinations Bekesbourne (hourly; 5min); Chatham (every 20–40min; 45min); Dover (every 20min–1hr; 15–30min); Faversham (every 20–40min; 15min); London Victoria (every 40min–1hr; 1hr 35min); Rochester (every 20–40min; 40min–1hr).

Canterbury West Canterbury West (in the north), a 15min walk from the cathedral, is used by the high-speed train from London St Pancras.

Destinations Ashford (every 10–30min; 15–20min); Broadstairs (hourly; 25min); Chartham (hourly; 5min); Chilham (hourly; 10min); London Charing Cross (Mon–Sat hourly; 1hr 45min); London St Pancras (hourly; 55min); Margate (every 20min–1hr; 30min); Ramsgate (every 20min–1hr; 20min); Sevenoaks (hourly; 1hr 5min); Sturry (hourly; 5min); Tonbridge (hourly; 1hr); Wye (every 20min–1hr; 15min).

BY BUS

National Express services and local Stagecoach East Kent buses use the station just inside the city walls on St George's Lane beside the Whitefriars shopping centre.

Destinations Broadstairs (hourly; 1hr–1hr 30min); Chilham (Mon–Sat hourly; 30min); Deal (Mon–Sat every 30min–1hr; 45min–1hr 20min); Dover (every 15min–1hr; 45min); Faversham (every 10–20min; 30min); Folkestone (every 15min–1hr; 45min); Herne Bay (every 15min; 35min); Hythe (every 30min; 1hr); London Victoria (16 daily; 2hr); Margate (every 30min; 1hr); Ramsgate (hourly; 45min); Sandwich (every 20min; 40min); Whitstable (every 15min; 30min).

INFORMATION AND GETTING AROUND

Tourist office In the Beaney, 18 High St (Mon–Wed & Fri 9am–6pm, Thurs 9am–8pm, Sat 9am–5pm, Sun 10am–4pm; ☎ 01227 862162, ⓦ canterbury.co.uk). Also covers Herne Bay and Whitstable.

By car Parking in town can be problematic. There are off-street pay car parks throughout the centre, including on Watling Street, Castle Row, Rosemary Lane, Northgate and Pound Lane. Check ⓦ canterbury.gov.uk for a full list.

By bike Kent Cycle Hire, based at the *House of Agnes*, 71 St Dunstan's St (see page 51), rents bikes for £24/day or £90/week; kids' bikes, tandems and tagalongs are available (book in advance; ☎ 01227 388058, ⓦ kentcyclehire.com). You can drop off your bike at their sister outfit in Whitstable (see page 83) or in a restaurant in Herne Bay (see page 88).

ACCOMMODATION SEE MAP PAGE 42

A crop of fine old **hotels and B&Bs** in the city centre offer all the creaking, authentic antiquity you could ask for, and there are some good-value B&Bs just outside the city walls. Prices are reasonable for such a popular city, though many places ask for a two-night minimum stay at the weekend and it can be difficult to secure a room in July and August, when rates tend to increase; book well in advance if possible. If you're driving, check if your accommodation has on-site **parking** – many places in the centre don't, and this will add to the cost.

HOTELS AND GUESTHOUSES

Arthouse B&B 24 London Rd, CT2 8LN ☎ 07976 725457, ⓦ www.arthousebandb.com. Occupying an old fire station

1

CANTERBURY TOURS

Canterbury is small enough to find your own way around very easily, but various **tours** are available should you want a knowledgeable overview. A trip along the **River Stour**, in particular, either on a rowing boat or a chauffeured punt, is a relaxing and picturesque way to get to know the city.

RIVER TOURS

Canterbury Historic River Tours ☎ 07790 534744, Ⓦ canterburyrivertours.co.uk. Informative rowing-boat trips, with lively narration, along the River Stour (March–Oct daily 10am–5pm, weather permitting; every 15–20min; 40min; £11). No reservations necessary; simply turn up at the bridge by the Old Weaver's House (see page 46).

Canterbury Punting Company Next to Mooring Café (see page 54), Water Lane, CT1 1NQ ☎ 01227 464797, Ⓦ canterburypunting.co.uk. Chauffeured river tours (Feb–Dec; around 45min) on wooden punts, with historic commentary; cushions, blankets and rain canopies are provided if necessary. Choose from shared tours (10am–5pm; £12), private tours (10am–8pm; £15; six people minimum), candlelit "ghost" tours (6–8pm; £15) or a private "romantic" tour for couples (10am–8pm; £60 Mon–Fri/£80 Sat & Sun). Reservations can be made online, by phone or by email.

Westgate Punts Westgate Grove, CT2 8AA ☎ 07494 170640, Ⓦ canterburypunts.uk. Chauffeured punting trips (mid-March to Oct daily, weather permitting, 10am–5.30pm or later in summer) along the Stour through the city, with some jaunts into the countryside. These are private trips only, with a minimum of two adults/group (35min–1hr 5min; £13–24). They don't take bookings; find them at Westgate Bridge opposite *Café des Amis* restaurant (see page 56).

WALKING TOURS

The Canterbury Ghost Tour Ⓦ thecanterburytours. com. A tongue-in-cheek mix of supernatural spookery, history and local folklore, leaving from *Alberry's Wine Bar*, 38 St Margaret's St (Fri & Sat 9pm; around 1hr 30min; £10). Book online.

Canterbury Guided Tours ☎ 01227 459779, Ⓦ canterburyguidedtours.com. Informative walking tours of the city and the cathedral precincts, leaving from Christ Church Gate (daily 11am; April–Oct also 2pm; 1hr 30min; £10). Book online or buy tickets at the tourist office (see page 51) or the Roman Museum (see page 47).

---

a 10min walk from Westgate, the *Arthouse* offers a variety of options, and delicious seclusion. The main Victorian house has two doubles (each with private bathroom) sharing a lounge and kitchen – you could rent both and have the place to yourself. There's also a modern Scandinavian-style timber property, *Cedar House* (sleeps six) in the back garden, and more self-catering in a garden room next door (sleeps four). Two-night minimum stay. £125

Canterbury Cathedral Lodge The Precincts, CT1 2EH ☎ 01227 865350, Ⓦ canterburycathedrallodge. org. Modern hotel, owned by the cathedral and with an unbeatable location within the precinct grounds – you can eat breakfast outside in good weather. Rooms in the main building are unfussy and contemporary, with something of the feel of conference accommodation; cheaper annexe rooms lack the cathedral views. Rates vary depending on availability, but booking well in advance will bring costs down, as will special offers. Rates include one free admission/person to the cathedral. £100

Canterbury Hotel 140 Wincheap, CT1 3RY ☎ 01227 453227, Ⓦ thecanterburyhotel.co.uk. Solid hotel in a Georgian building, about a 10min walk from Canterbury East train station. The rooms are fine, but it's the suntrap garden and (small) heated indoor pool and spa that give this place the edge. £100

Cathedral Gate 36 Burgate, CT1 2HA ☎ 01227 464381, Ⓦ cathgate.co.uk. Built in 1438 and with a fantastic location next to the cathedral gate, this ancient pilgrims' hostelry is a warren of a place, all crooked, creaking floors, timber beams and narrow, steep staircases (no lift). It's not fancy, but it's comfortable and efficient, with cathedral views from many of the rooms. They also provide a simple continental breakfast, which you can eat in your room. The cheapest rooms share toilets and (tiny) showers but have basins, and all have tea- and coffee-making facilities. For singles (who pay around £50, with shared facilities), this is a particular bargain. £82

Coach House 34 Watling St, CT1 2UD ☎ 01227 784324, Ⓦ coachhouse-canterbury.co.uk. Six B&B rooms (including a good-value single and a family option) in a Georgian house, not luxurious but with creaky character. Some are en suite, others have private bathrooms; all are comfy, with original features, and there's a courtyard garden. On-site parking. Two-night minimum stay at weekends. £86

Corner House 1 Dover St, CT1 2NA ☎ 01227 780793, Ⓦ cornerhouserestaurants.co.uk. Set on a busy corner just outside the city wall, this superb Modern British restaurant (see page 56) offers four gorgeous B&B rooms that combine rustic charm and contemporary cool – the romantic attic features an in-room roll-top bathtub. £150

Ebury Hotel 65–67 New Dover Rd, CT1 3DX ☎ 01227 768433, ⓦ ebury-hotel.co.uk. Comfortable, reliable and rather – not unpleasantly – old-fashioned Victorian hotel, with fifteen en-suite rooms plus some apartments and cottages (ⓦ eburycottages.co.uk, from £140). There's plenty of on-site parking and a large leafy garden, which makes up for the slightly out-of-the-way location a 15min walk from the cathedral. Two-night minimum on summer weekends. **£130**

Falstaff 8–12 St Dunstan's St, CT2 8AF ☎ 01227 462138, ⓦ thefalstaffincanterbury.com. A handsome fifteenth-century coaching inn, with a little bar, by the Westgate. Rooms vary, so it's an idea to call to discuss your preferences: those in the old building have creaky historic atmosphere (some have four-poster beds), while the cheaper options in the annexes (£110) are less interesting. Some on-site parking. **£145**

★ **House of Agnes** 71 St Dunstan's St, CT2 8BN ☎ 01227 472185, ⓦ houseofagnes.co.uk. You can't fail to be charmed by the crooked exterior of this B&B near Westgate, and the experience inside is great, too. The main fifteenth-century house (mentioned in *David Copperfield*) has nine stylish rooms, each designed on a different theme, with eight more modern rooms in the old stable block in the large walled garden (£120). There can be street noise from the front, so if that bothers you, or if you want a more spacious room, let them know when you book. Some on-site parking. **£130**

Hugo 19 St Peter's St, CT1 2BQ ⓦ thehugo.co.uk. This small new hotel with a self-catering feel is administered by Airbnb, with entry via pin code and an off-site owner contactable via email (or an emergency number). The three rooms and one two-room apartment are contemporary, clean and very well maintained, though not huge, and prices are very competitive. A comfortable, central choice. **£80**

Love Lane 14 & 15 Love Lane, CT1 1TZ ☎ 01227 455367, ⓦ 7longport.co.uk. Two three-bedroom early Victorian cottages, each sleeping five, backing onto and owned by the same people as *No. 7 Longport* (see below). Each has a kitchen, sitting room and dining area, along with sweet courtyard gardens with barbecue; you can get a B&B room, or rent a whole cottage on a self-catering (minimum three nights in high season; £193/night) or, if available, B&B basis (minimum two nights; £270/night). Breakfasts are delicious. **£100**

Millers Arms 2 Mill Lane, CT1 2AW ☎ 01227 456057, ⓦ millerscanterbury.co.uk. The USP at this nineteenth-century Shepherd Neame pub, a 5min walk from the cathedral, is its location opposite a weir on the Stour – you can be lulled to sleep by the sound of rushing water from the rooms at the front. The en-suite B&B rooms come in a variety of sizes (including a single and a family room), with tasteful, contemporary decor – comfortable, friendly and good value. **£120**

★ **No. 7 Longport** 7 Longport, CT1 1PE ☎ 01227 455367, ⓦ 7longport.co.uk. This fabulous little hideaway – a tiny, luxuriously decorated fifteenth-century cottage with a double bedroom, wet room and lounge – is tucked away in the courtyard garden of the friendly owners' home, just opposite St Augustine's Abbey. The breakfasts are wonderful, with lots of locally sourced ingredients, and can be eaten in the main house or the courtyard. It gets booked up fast. The same owners run *Love Lane* (see above). **£100**

HOSTELS

★ **Kipps** 40 Nunnery Fields, CT1 3JT ☎ 01227 786121, ⓦ kipps-hostel.com. This early twentieth-century house, a 10min walk from Canterbury East station, is home to an excellent self-catering hostel. It's spruce and clean, with homely touches and a large cottage garden, but above all it's the friendly staff who make *Kipps* special. Along with mixed en-suite dorms (no under-18s), they have single, double and twin rooms with TV. Organized events mean you can be as sociable as you wish, but it's more a home from home than a party hostel, and quiet after 11pm. No curfew. Breakfast £3.50. Discounts for weekly stays. Dorms **£22.50**, doubles **£70**

YHA Canterbury 54 New Dover Rd, CT1 3DT ☎ 0345 371 9010, ⓦ yha.org.uk/hostel/canterbury. Half a mile out of town, and 15min on foot from Canterbury East station, this YHA hostel occupies a substantial Victorian villa. In addition to the four- and six-bed single-sex dorms (some of which are en suite), private rooms sleeping two (with shared facilities), three or five, they offer little wooden cabins, sleeping five, which are en suite with mini-kitchenette and allow pets. Breakfast costs £6.75, with evening meals also available, and there are self-catering facilities. Dorms **£23**, double **£89**, cabins **£119**

EATING

SEE MAP PAGE 42

With its lively student population and year-round tourist trade, Canterbury is not short on places to eat. The old core is **tearoom** territory, of course, but the city is establishing itself as a credible foodie destination, too, with a good number of places focusing on **Modern British** cuisine and Kentish produce – the **Goods Shed** farmers' market blazes the trail – and plenty of restaurants offering food from around the world. Meanwhile, if you have a car and fancy getting out of town, you can choose from some excellent gastropubs in the villages around Canterbury (see pages 60 and 62).

CAFÉS, COFFEE SHOPS AND TEAROOMS

Boho Café 27 High St, CT1 2AZ ☎ 01227 458931, ⓦ bohocanterbury.co.uk. This cheerful café-bar, with its quirky decor (paintbox colours, kitschy oilcloths, wonky lampshades, vintage clocks) is a popular spot with an informal neighbourhood feel. The menu (lunch dishes from

1

£6.50) offers something for most people, from full English fry-ups via tapas and overstuffed ciabatta sandwiches to homemade veggie burgers, gluten-free options and meaty Mediterranean-influenced mains. You could also simply pop in for coffee and cake. There's seating on the street, and a pretty suntrap garden at the back. Mon–Fri 9am–5.30pm, Sat 9am–9pm, Sun 9am–4pm.

Café St Pierre 41 St Peter's St, CT1 2BG ☎01227 456791. Bijou and very simple French patisserie and café with streetside tables and a small paved garden. The pastries are divine, from apricot *feuilleté* to buttery *palmier* biscuits, and you can make a light lunch of their *croques monsieur*, quiches, soups, salads or savoury croissants. The baguettes (£5.40; takeaway £4) include *du jour* specials (mushroom with melted raclette, say, or *andouillette* with Dijon mustard). Mon–Sat 8am–6pm, Sun 9am–5.30pm.

Canteen 17 Sun St, CT1 2HX ☎01227 470011, ⓦ canteen fresh.co.uk. With a super-convenient location near the cathedral, *Canteen* is a no-fuss spot for fresh juices and coffee, along with light lunch dishes (from £4.70) – flatbread wrap with roasted veg, perhaps, or a Mexican burrito. Take away or eat in one of their little rooms, ranged across three floors. Mon–Fri & Sun 10am–5pm, Sat 9am–6pm.

City Fish Bar 30 St Margaret's St, CT1 2TG ☎01227 760873. Sometimes only fish and chips will hit the spot, and this cheery, central family-owned chippie is a reliable place to get your fried fish fix. A fish supper costs around £8, but you can also get your chips with sausage, battered mushrooms or a pasty for less. There are a couple of tables squeezed into the shopfront, and a few more outside, but it's mostly takeaway. Mon–Sat 10am–7pm, Sun 10am–4pm.

Kitch 4 St Peters St, CT1 2AT ☎01227 504983, ⓦ www. kitchcafe.co.uk. This airily pretty, if slightly squeezed, café – in a heavily trafficked spot next to the Old Weaver's House – offers breakfasts, superfood salads and grazing plates using wholefoods and unprocessed and free-range ingredients. Try an all-day breakfast/brunch (£6–10), which range from acai berry smoothie bowls to kale pesto omelettes, or a lunch of vegan soup (£9) with a sandwich (£6–10). Mon–Fri 8.30am–5pm, Sat & Sun 9am–5pm (kitchen closes 4pm daily).

Moat Tea Rooms 67 Burgate, CT1 2HJ ☎01227 784514, ⓦ moattearooms.co.uk. Sweet, traditional little tearoom in a beamed and mullioned old building with cake stands piled high with scones, cupcakes and scrumptious homemade sponges. The loose-leaf teas include black, green and jasmine varieties – and although they serve decent breakfasts, light lunches and sandwiches, it's the good-value afternoon teas you should go for (cream teas from £7.50). Mon–Sat 9am–5pm, Sun 10am–5pm.

Mooring Café Water Lane, CT1 1NQ ☎01227 464797, ⓦ facebook.com/pg/themooringcanterbury. Laidback

riverside coffee house in a quiet corner, serving great coffee, with beers and ciders in the evening. Relax on a sofa in the light-bathed interior, then consider jumping on one of the punt trips that sets off from outside (see page 52). Regular community events include poetry, open-mic sessions, live music, film screenings and board-game nights. Daily 10am–5pm (later during events).

Pork and Co 27 Sun St, CT1 2HX ☎01227 764430, ⓦ porkandco.co.uk. Dude food comes to the pilgrim city at this carnivore haven, which specializes in slow-cooked pulled pork. Most people order it in a brioche bun (£10.50), but you can get those juicy scraps served in a variety of ways (£10.50–13) – with chips or nachos, or in toasties, for example. They also offer buttermilk-fried chicken, burgers, barbecue ribs and scotch eggs, with a few token veggie options. Takeaway available. Mon–Sat 11am–9pm, Sun 11am–8pm.

★**Tiny Tim's Tearoom** 34 St Margaret's St, CT1 2TG ☎01227 450793, ⓦ tinytimstearoom.com. There's actually nothing very Dickensian about this upmarket 1930s-style tearoom, which offers some thirty blends of loose-leaf tea, an indulgent choice of hot chocolates and filling afternoon teas (available all day, from £18.95) with finger sandwiches, scones, pastries and cakes all made in house. Smaller appetites might prefer the cream teas, all-day breakfasts or lunches – the Kentish huffkins (£6.95–8.95), large filled baps, are a tasty local choice, or you could simply choose a fat, fruit-packed "Plump Pilgrim" scone with butter and jam (£4.10). In good weather the cute back garden makes a good retreat from the tourist crowds. Mon–Sat 9.30am–5pm, Sun 10.30am–4pm.

★**The Veg Box Café** 17b Burgate, CT1 2HG ☎01227 456654, ⓦ thevegboxcafe.co.uk. This simple veggie café does delicious things with alfalfa and tofu, using organic, local ingredients, and with lots of vegan and gluten-free options. The daily changing menu always features soup, jacket potatoes, salad bowls, hotpots and bakes, plus fermented specials (mains £4.50–9.50), while breakfast (£4–5.50) features homemade granola, turmeric porridge and frittata. It's comforting, wholesome and nutritious, and the location, with tables under the arcades near the cathedral, is good. Takeaway available. Mon–Sat 8.30am–5pm, Sun 9am–4pm.

RESTAURANTS

★**The Ambrette** 14–15 Beer Cart Lane, CT1 2NY ☎01227 200777, ⓦ theambrette.co.uk. With a sister restaurant in Margate (see page 94), *Ambrette's* Canterbury branch brings Dev Biswal's nouvelle Indian cuisine to a smart, good-looking pub conversion on a quiet street. The focus on local produce is strong, with delicious flavours infusing everything from foreshank of goat with paprika and fenugreek potatoes to tilapia with local sea spinach and red lentils, and there are numerous vegan

1

THE GOODS SHED

The **Goods Shed farmers' market and foodhall** (Tues–Sat 9am–7pm, or 6pm in winter, Sun 10am–4pm, some food counters keep their own hours; ⓦthegoodsshed.co.uk), housed in an old brick goods shed next to Canterbury West train station, is a highlight of any foodie visit to Canterbury. With traders selling local cheeses, breads, charcuterie, fresh produce, wine, beer and deli items, along with a couple of places for coffee, breakfast, posh sandwiches, tapas and sharing plates, it's a fantastic place to pick up picnic food, to stock up (or fill up) before catching a train. Alternatively, treat yourself to a special meal at the mezzanine **restaurant** (see below).

options. Mains £13–20; sharing plates £16–18; lunch menus £13–22. Mon–Thurs 11.30am–2.30pm & 5.30–9.30pm, Fri 11.30am–2.30pm & 5.30–late, Sat & Sun 11.30am–late.

Café des Amis 2 Westgate Grove, CT2 8AA ☏01227 464390, ⓦcafedez.com. Don't be misled by the name (it's short for *Café des Amis du Mexique*) – this is not a French bistro, but a lively Mexican/Tex-Mex/South American place. Funky decor, carnival colours and papier mâché artwork set the scene for the vibrant food – from the hot goat's cheese *tostadas* (£6.95) to the paella (£26.95 for two) or the crispy duck confit fajitas (£28.95 for two), you can't go wrong. The weekday set menu (noon–6pm) gets you two courses plus nachos for £14.95. Mon–Thurs noon–10pm, Fri & Sat noon–10.30pm, Sun noon–9.30pm.

Café Mauresque 8 Butchery Lane, CT1 2JR ☏01227 464300, ⓦcafemauresque.co.uk. Moroccan-style restaurant with southern Spanish accents (all tiles, lanterns, scatter cushions and brass candlesticks) a few steps from the cathedral. You can go for tasty tapas (£3–7.25, mixed platters for two from £14.95) – anything from tabbouleh to squid and chorizo skewers – or plump for tagines, couscous or paella. The weekday lunch menu is more limited, but features soups, baguettes (from £7.20) and salads. Wash it all down with a jug of sangria or a pot of fresh mint tea, and save room for the sticky date cake. Mon, Tues & Thurs noon–3.30pm & 5pm–close, Fri noon–10pm, Sat & Sun noon–close.

Chapman's 89–90 St Dunstan's St, CT2 8AD ☏01227 780749, ⓦchapmanscanterbury.co.uk. An old-school seafood restaurant offering simple, well-executed food. The menu runs the gamut from sesame and chilli squid (£8.50) to an abundant *fruits de mer* platter (£38) via the likes of Dover sole, fish pie or fish and chips, plus daily specials. Regular themed evenings (all-you-can-eat mussels, perhaps) and a two-/three-course menu (Tues–Fri noon–2.30pm, Sat noon–3pm; £16/£19.50) bring the costs down. Mon 5.30pm–late, Tues–Thurs noon–2.30pm & 5.30pm–late, Fri noon–2.30pm & 5.30–10pm, Sat noon–late, Sun noon–3pm.

★ **Corner House** 1 Dover St, CT1 3HD ☏01227 780793, ⓦcornerhouserestaurants.co.uk. The location on the noisy main road isn't idyllic, but indoors all is calm in this

upmarket Modern British restaurant, with beams and bare-brick walls creating a rustic feel. Locally sourced ingredients are used in seemingly simple dishes such as confit pork belly or goat's cheese and pistachio fritters, with tempting desserts including homemade ice creams. Mains £16–24; hearty sharing plates (roasted rabbit saddle with polenta or Romney Marsh lamb with *Dauphinoise* potatoes; for two or four) £22/head; two-/three-course lunches £16–20. Mon–Sat noon–2.30pm & 5.30–9.30pm, Sun noon–3pm & 6–9.30pm.

★ **The Goods Shed** Station Rd West, CT2 8AN ☏01227 459153, ⓦthegoodsshed.co.uk. It doesn't get any more locally sourced than this – a buzzing, shabby-chic restaurant in the excellent Goods Shed farmers' market next to Canterbury West train station (see page 56), where most of the ingredients are provided by the stalls themselves. You can get anything from a build-your-own full breakfast to a formal supper: the regularly changing menu, modern British with flashes of Mediterranean flair, might feature dishes such as halibut gravadlax (£7.50), Jacob's ladder with roasted garlic and thyme mash or guineafowl with lentils, spinach and black pudding (both £17.50). Prices can mount, though at lunchtime they are happy for you to select a couple of starters. While the bustling ambience during the day is a delight, it can feel a little subdued at the end of the night, with the market stalls closed. Tues–Fri 8–10.30am, noon–2.30pm & 6–9.30pm, Sat 8–10.30am, noon–3pm & 6–9.30pm, Sun 9–10.30am & noon–3pm.

Kashmir 20 Palace St, CT1 2DZ ☏01227 462050, ⓦkashmirtandoori.co.uk. Though there's no reason to think it from the outside, this north Indian curry house is a winner: a large, friendly place with a long menu of tandooris, biryanis, baltis and the like (with some great Punjabi veg choices). House specials (chicken garlic masala, for example) from £8.50; *thalis* from £14; set meals from £13.95. Mon–Sat noon–2pm & 5–11.30pm, Sun noon–11.30pm.

Posillipo 16 The Borough, CT1 2DR ☏01227 761471, ⓦposillipo.co.uk. A long-established trattoria, a real local favourite, serving robust Neapolitan dishes, crispy wood-fired pizzas (£7.95–14.95), fresh pasta (from £10.95) and rustic fish and seafood specials, including a lip-smacking cod dish with olives, capers, anchovies and oregano (£14.95). The prices are reasonable, for such a classy place. Branches in Faversham and Broadstairs. Daily noon–late.

CANTERBURY **CANTERBURY AND AROUND** | 57
CANTERBURY **CANTERBURY AND AROUND** | 57

Tamago 64 Northgate, CT1 1BB ☏01227 634537, ⓦtamago.restaurant. This minimalist, casual Japanese café, just north of the King's Mile, brings an authentic slice of Tokyo to Canterbury, dishing up hearty *ramen*, *katsu* curries, *donburi* and *bento* boxes – along with beer and sake cocktails – to a brisk, youngish crowd. Mains £10.60–15.50; small plates from £3. Mon–Fri 5–9.30pm, Sat noon–3pm & 5–9.30pm, Sun noon–4pm.

Zeus Ouzerie and Taverna 2–3 Orange St, CT1 2JA ☏01227 788072, ⓦzeuscanterbury.com. Authentic Greek cuisine gets an update in this smart and stylish contemporary taverna, which does all the standards very well, from the meze (£3.50–9.50) to the moussaka, the *stifado* to the *souvlaki* (mains from £12.50). The delicious syrupy puds make a perfect finale. Tues–Thurs 5–10pm, Fri & Sat noon–11pm, Sun noon–10pm.

DRINKING AND NIGHTLIFE

SEE MAP PAGE 42
SEE MAP PAGE 42

Canterbury is a nice place for a drink, with more than its fair share of pubs serving **real ales** in cosy, historic buildings. The Shepherd Neame-owned places are in the majority, but look out, too, for beers from Canterbury's own Wantsum, Canterbury Brewers and Canterbury Ales breweries. Generally **nightlife** keeps a low profile – many people are happy to while away their evenings in the pubs.

Bishop's Finger 13 St Dunstan's St, CT2 8AF ☏01227 768915, ⓦbishopsfingercanterbury.co.uk. Unpretentious, popular old pub, just outside the Westgate, with Shepherd Neame ales, large-screen TVs showing major sports events and a patio at the back. Mon–Thurs noon–11pm, Fri noon–midnight, Sat 11am–midnight, Sun noon–10.30pm.

Bramley's 15 Orange St, CT1 2JA ☏01227 379933, ⓦbramleysbar.co.uk. One of the quirkier central venues, this cocktail bar offers bohemian-speakeasy ambience – all candles, sexy lighting and mismatched retro styling – and well-mixed drinks at not-bad prices (cocktails from £8; two for £10 6–8pm & all night Thurs). Live music Mon, Tues and occasional Weds. Mon–Thurs 6–11pm, Fri & Sat 6pm–12.30am.

★ **The Dolphin** 17 St Radigund's St, CT1 2AA ☏01227 455963, ⓦthedolphincanterbury.co.uk. A likeable old 1930s pub that's both quite cool, in a shabby way, and relaxed. With a good selection of local real ales, a real fire in winter and a big, grassy beer garden, the emphasis is on chatting, hanging out and playing board games, with no loud music or TVs to spoil the ambience. Tasty food, too, with few pretensions. Mon–Wed noon–11pm, Thurs–Sat noon–midnight, Sun noon–10pm.

The Foundry 77 Stour St, CT1 2NR ☏01227 455899, ⓦthefoundrycanterbury.co.uk. Tasty craft beers and lagers from the on-site Canterbury Brewers microbrewery in this big old foundry building; you can watch the whole brewing process as it happens, while you drink. They produce an excellent gin and offer guest ales, ciders and bottled beers, too, and the food (burgers, ribs, pies and the like), isn't bad. Mon–Sat noon–midnight, Sun noon–10pm.

The Parrot 1–9 Church Lane, CT1 2AG ☏01227 454170, ⓦtheparrotonline.com. Venerable hostelry – the oldest in Canterbury, in a fourteenth-century building groaning with dark-wood beams – in a quiet spot. The interior has loads of character, and they serve a choice of ales along with hefty portions of high-quality Modern British pub grub. Daily noon–11pm; kitchen Mon–Wed noon–3pm & 6–9pm, Thurs & Sun noon–9pm, Fri & Sat noon–10pm.

The Pound 1 Pound Lane, CT1 2BZ ☏01227 458629, ⓦonepoundlane.co.uk. Tucked away at the bottom of the medieval Westgate, this historic spot – which has housed both a Victorian jail and an Edwardian police station – has reinvented itself as a slick cocktail bar, its bare-brick vaults now filled with comfy armchairs, burnished bronze decor and vintage-style neon. There's some riverside seating, though it's on a busy road. Mon–Thurs 11am–2.30am, Fri & Sat 11am–3.30am, Sun 11am–1am.

The Unicorn 61 St Dunstan's St, CT2 8BS ☏01227 463187, ⓦunicorninn.com. There's a neighbourhood feel at this seventeenth-century, family-run tavern, popular with the CAMRA set; settle down by the wood-burning stove with a Kentish brew, or enjoy a game at the bar billiards table. Quiz night on Sun. Mon–Thurs & Sun 11.30am–11pm, Fri & Sat 11.30am–midnight.

CANTERBURY FESTIVALS

The year-long arts programme offered by Wise Words – chiefly focused on poetry, but with storytelling, arts workshops and music too – peaks during the **Wise Words literary festival** (ⓦwisewordsfestival.co.uk), held over ten days each spring. Centred on the beautiful Franciscan Gardens (see page 48), the quirky performances and events spill out all around town – from busy street corners to River Stour punts – creating a feel-good buzz.

The **Canterbury Festival** (mid-Oct to early Nov; ⓦcanterburyfestival.co.uk), meanwhile, is the *grande dame* of the city's arts events, a high-culture affair offering an international mix of music, theatre and performance, with poetry, lectures, classes, walks and live events thrown in. You'll catch anything from Americana to Gregorian chants, science lectures to magic shows, in a variety of venues including the cathedral, the Marlowe and the Gulbenkian.

ENTERTAINMENT

Gulbenkian University of Kent, CT2 7NB ☎ 01227 769075, ⓦ thegulbenkian.co.uk. The excellent arts centre on the university campus offers a consistently interesting programme of high-quality cultural events, including contemporary drama, dance, comedy, concerts and film.

Marlowe Theatre The Friars, CT1 2AS ☎ 01227 787787, ⓦ marlowetheatre.com. This modern theatre, cutting an audacious dash right in the centre of the city, is a popular venue for music, dance, stand-up, cabaret and plays. Shows range from the mainstream, with West End musicals and crowd-pleasing touring acts – Sarah Millican, The Proclaimers, Jimmy Carr and the like – to gigs from up-and-coming artists.

SHOPPING   SEE MAP PAGE 42

Antoine & Lili 46 Burgate, CT1 2HW ☎ 01227 785888. The oh-so-Parisian brand is brightening up Burgate with its playful, women's clothing, accessories and homewares in jewel colours and joyful bold prints. Mon–Thurs & Sat 9.30am–5.30pm, Fri 9.30am–6pm.

Canterbury Cathedral Shop 25 Burgate, CT1 2HA ☎ 01227 865300, ⓦ cathedral-enterprises.co.uk. You can enter the huge cathedral shop either from the precincts or from Burgate. It's worth a browse – though the wide range of products tends, naturally, towards the religious or spiritual (Thomas Becket tree decorations; stained-glass earrings; CDs of choral music), there is also a selection of books, foodie gifts, ceramics, magnets and the like. Mon–Sat 9.30am–5.30pm, Sun 10.30am–4.30pm; extended weekday hours in July & Aug.

★**The Chaucer Bookshop** 6–7 Beer Cart Lane, CT1 2NY ☎ 01227 453912, ⓦ chaucer-bookshop.co.uk. A bibliophiles' delight: a friendly, sixty-year-old secondhand bookshop in a crooked old building with two storeys packed to the rafters. It's strong on rare and antiquarian titles – hardbacks predominate, with lots of history and local interest,

plus vintage prints, maps and postcards – but you can hunt down anything from popular literary fiction to *Just William*, via art, travel, food and all sorts. Pretty cards and wrapping paper, too. Mon–Sat 10am–5pm, Sun 11am–4pm.

Madame Oiseau 8 The Borough, CT1 2DR ☎ 01227 452222, ⓦ madame-oiseau.com. A cupboard of a shop on the King's Mile, where they make and sell classy artisan chocolates. The emphasis is on the feminine – the heart-shaped bonbonière, for example – but there are big chunky slabs, too, crammed with fruits and nuts, along with chocolate gingers, chocolate-covered chillies and cute chocolate cats for the kids. Mon–Sat 10am–5.30pm.

Whitefriars Between St George's Lane and St George's, St Margaret's and Watling streets, CT1 2TF ☎ 01227 826760, ⓦ whitefriars-canterbury.co.uk. Gobbling up a substantial chunk of town between the bus station and the High Street, Canterbury's major mainstream shopping mall has the big high-street names – Fenwick to H&M, Specsavers to Boots – plus banks, supermarkets and places to eat (most of them fast-food, but there is a *Carluccio's* café in Fenwick). Daily; opening hours vary.

North of Canterbury

Covering around eleven square miles between Canterbury and Kent's north coast, the ancient broadleaf woodland of the **Blean** is a wonderful area for walking. Accessible from the North Downs Way – which passes the South Blean – the Saxon Shore Way in the north, the Pilgrims' Way from Winchester to Canterbury, and the Crab and Winkle Way between Canterbury and Whitstable (see page 59), these dappled and wildlife-rich **woodlands** feature around 120 miles of footpaths, taking in not only woods but villages, hop gardens, orchards and historical sites. Dominated by oak and sweet chestnut trees, but also featuring silver birch, hazel, beech and ash, among many others, it's an area rich in **birdlife**, with nightingales, nightjars, woodpeckers and tawny owls all making their homes here. The Blean is an easy place to head for a short day-hike from Canterbury, but there are also plenty of nice spots to stay and eat should you want to enjoy a more leisurely visit.

The area **northeast of Canterbury**, meanwhile, fanning out towards the coast, offers a number of water-based diversions. The **River Stour** courses through on its way to the sea at Pegwell Bay; bordering it to the east, the lonely **Stodmarsh Nature Reserve** is a fabulous birding spot.

Blean Woods Nature Reserve

Rough Common, CT2 9DD • Free • Access on foot at all times • ☎ 01227 464898, ⓦ rspb.org.uk/reserves/guide/b/bleanwoods • Buses #4/#4A from Canterbury

---

THE CRAB AND WINKLE WAY

A **cycling and walking route** that follows the line of the old steam railway from Canterbury to Whitstable (see page 80), and forms part of National Cycle Route 1, the **Crab and Winkle Way** is a delight. Some 7.5 miles long, and largely traffic-free, it starts at Canterbury West train station, heads up to the University of Kent campus (via two different routes), then passes through orchards, ancient woodland and gentle rolling pastures before ending in Whitstable; the midway point at Winding Pond is a nice spot to take a break, with a grassy area and picnic bench. Whitstable itself, a lovely little seaside town on the north coast, is well worth a stay of a night or two. For more, including a downloadable map, see ⓦ crabandwinkle.org.

Covering more than eleven square miles, **Blean Woods Nature Reserve**, near the hamlet of Rough Common a couple of miles northwest of Canterbury, offers some wonderful walking opportunities through the woods; five waymarked trails, the longest of which is eight miles, crisscross this peaceful site. In addition to the sparrowhawks, nightingales and woodpeckers, watch out for the flutter of the Heath Fritillary butterfly (June & July), seen in few other places in Britain. Note that dogs are only permitted on one of the trails (1.25 miles).

Mount Ephraim Gardens

Staplestreet Rd, Hernhill, ME13 9TX • April–Sept Wed–Sun 11am–5pm • £7 • ☎ 01227 751496, ⓦ mountephraimgardens.co.uk

The elegant Edwardian gardens at **Mount Ephraim**, a private estate a couple of miles west of Bossenden Wood in the Blean, provide an appealing contrast with the woodlands around them. Here you can wander through ten acres of landscaped, terraced gardens – among them a fragrant rose garden, a Japanese rock-and-water garden, and an unusual medieval-style "mizmaze", with soft raised turf paths fringed with wildflowers and swaying grasses. Many people bring picnics, but there is also a tearoom.

Stodmarsh National Nature Reserve

Stodmarsh, CT3 4BP • Dawn–dusk • Free • ☎ 07767 321053, ⓦ gov.uk/government/publications/kents-national-nature-reserves/kents-national-nature-reserves#stodmarsh • Buses along the A28 between Sturry (3 miles southwest) and Upstreet stop nearby

The lonely **Stodmarsh National Nature Reserve**, a square mile of reed beds, fens and pools in the Stour Valley, is accessible from the village of Stodmarsh, six miles northeast of Canterbury, and Upstreet/Grove Ferry, three miles further north. This marshy wetland is especially good for **birdwatchers**, with bitterns, kingfishers and marsh harriers, among many others, in residence – plus swallows and housemartins in summer, and starlings in winter – but it's a peaceful place for anyone to enjoy a bracing country walk. Footpaths (from 0.3 to 3 miles) include a couple of nature trails, with five designated hides.

ACCOMMODATION   NORTH OF CANTERBURY

The Grove Ferry Upstreet, CT3 4BP ☎ 01227 860302, ⓦ thegroveferry.co.uk. Location is everything at this friendly, relaxed pub, in a handsome ivy-festooned building with an unbeatable setting on the River Stour near Stodmarsh. The willow-fringed riverside terrace and big beer garden are lovely places to enjoy a local cask ale, and the six simple B&B rooms have lots of space. A couple have their own balconies overlooking the river at the back. Full meals are available in the pub. **£120**

★ **The Linen Shed** 104 The Street, Boughton-under-

Blean, ME13 9AP ☎ 01227 752271, ⓦ www.thelinen shed.com. Genteel shabby chic meets froufrou vintage glamour in this quirky weatherboard home, fronted by lavender gardens. The guest rooms, two of which have private bathrooms and one of which shares a bathroom with the friendly owners, are gorgeous, with more than a whiff of French provincial style, with French linen sheets, fresh flowers and fluffy robes. Gourmet breakfasts are served in the lovely garden in good weather. Minimum two-night stay at weekends. **£85**

1

MESSING ABOUT ON THE RIVER

Canoe Wild (☎07947 835688, ⓦcanoewild.co.uk), with bases in Fordwich (2.5 miles northeast of Canterbury) and Grove Ferry (some 5 miles further), offers canoe, kayak and paddleboard rental (March–Oct daily 9am–6pm, other times on request; SUP or single kayak: £18/hr, £33/half day, £55/full day; canoe or double kayak: £23/hr, £48/half day, £85/full day) and guided canoe/kayak paddles – from seal-watching at Pegwell Bay to sunset wildlife tours in Stodmarsh – for all abilities (March–Sept days and times vary; from £35/person for 3hr). Booking is advised, but may not be essential. For something less active, try a river cruise on the electric launch **Mary Ellen**, moored at the *Grove Ferry* inn (see page 59). Book to reserve (March, April & Oct Sat & Sun; May–July & Sept Wed–Sun; Aug daily; hourly from noon; 50min; £10; ☎07985 273070, ⓦgroveferryrivertrips.co.uk).

Nethergong Nurseries Upstreet, CT3 4DN ☎07901 368417, ⓦnethergongcamping.co.uk. A simple, peaceful and spacious riverside campsite, set in 26 acres 8 miles northeast of Canterbury, with camping space in woodland or open meadows, and glamping in shepherd's huts, Romany wagons and bell tents. There's also a shallow paddling pond and a fishing lake. Campfires are allowed (£5) and they sell their own fresh veg. Minimum two nights. Closed Nov–Easter. Tents **£32.50**, bell tents **£85**, shepherd's huts **£85**, wagons **£85**

EATING AND DRINKING

★ **Butcher's Arms** 29 Herne St, Herne, CT6 7HL ☎01227 371000, ⓦmicropub.co.uk. Fantastic micropub – open for more than a decade – in an old butcher's. Behind the unassuming shopfront is a fifteen-seater cubbyhole crammed with bric-a-brac, with a crowd of real-ale fans having a good old natter (no mobiles allowed). There are always at least four ales on the weekly changing selection. Tues–Sat noon–1.30pm & 6–9pm or later, Sun 1–3pm.

The Dairy 40 The Street, Boughton-under-Blean, ME13 9AS ☎01227 750304, ⓦthedairyrestaurant.co.uk. In an old 1930s dairy building, this family-friendly restaurant gives a nod to its original use with the vaguely retro decor. The informal menu – light bites (£4–12), meat-heavy bistro standards (steaks, burgers, pies; £13–25), coffee, shakes and puds – focuses on Kentish produce. Wed–Fri 6–11pm, Sat & Sun 11am–11pm.

The Dove Plumpudding Lane, Dargate, ME13 9HB ☎01227 751085, ⓦdovedargate.co.uk. A country gastropub that serves simple British food done well – smoked trout with horseradish mousse, rack of Kentish lamb, steamed golden syrup pud – in a smart-rustic space. Two/three courses £24.50/£28.50 at lunch, £35.50/£41.50 at dinner. The lovely garden has its own bar and traditional bat-and-trap game. Tues–Thurs noon–4pm & 6–10pm, Fri & Sat noon–11pm, Sun noon–6pm; kitchen Tues–Sat noon–3pm & 6.30–9pm, Sun noon–4pm.

★ **Fordwich Arms** King St, Fordwich, CT2 0DB ☎01227 710444, ⓦfordwicharms.co.uk. Behind the handsome ivy-strewn red-brick exterior, this cosy wood-panelled gastropub, helmed by *Clove Club* alumnus Dan Smith, is causing a considerable stir with its Michelin-starred modern British food that's as seasonal and local as it gets. Mains – roast blackface lamb with white asparagus, wild garlic and anchovy; Applewood-grilled Whitstable lobster; Jerusalem artichoke with morels, cracked wheat and coffee – start at £26, but the three-course weekday lunch menu (£35) and tasting menus (£65/£85/£95) offer good value. There's a gorgeous riverside garden and terrace, perfect on sunny days. Tues & Sun noon–6pm, Wed–Sat noon–11pm; kitchen Wed–Sat noon–2.30pm & 6–9pm, Sun noon–4pm.

Gate Inn Church Inn, Chislet, CT3 4EB ☎01227 860498, ⓦgateinnchislet.co.uk. Friendly Shepherd Neame pub, in a very pretty part of Kent, with a streamside garden shaded by willow. Inside it's cosy and unpretentious, with a big log fire, board games and an eclectic library. Good cask ales are offered, with a tempting menu of simple, homemade food including pies and black-pudding Scotch eggs (mains from £7). Mon–Fri 11am–3pm & 5.30pm–close, Sat & Sun 11am–close; kitchen Tues–Fri 11.30am–3pm & 6–9pm, Sat 11am–9pm, Sun noon–4pm.

Kathton House 6 High St, Sturry, CT2 0BD ☎01227 719999, ⓦkathtonhouse.com. Just a 7min drive from Canterbury, this quietly chic restaurant offers special-occasion fine dining in an intimate setting. The emphasis is on classic meat and sauces – duck breast in green peppercorn sauce, guinea fowl with watercress purée, supreme of halibut in lime and butter sauce – but there are good vegetarian and vegan menus, too. It's *prix fixe*: regularly changing two- and three-course menus cost £24/£28.50 at lunch (£25/£29 on Sun), £41/£48.50 at dinner. Reservations essential at weekends. Tues–Sat noon–2pm & 7–9pm, Sun noon–3pm.

Old Coach and Horses Church Hill, Harbledown, CT2 9AB ☎01227 766609, ⓦtheoldcoachandhorses.co.uk. This relaxed village pub, just a 20min walk from Canterbury, serves local ales and good, locally sourced food (starters from £7.50, mains from £13) from a regularly changing menu –

typical choices might be fish pie with creamed spinach or veggie stack with halloumi. The terraced courtyard garden is a nice spot in summer, with great woodland views. Mon–Sat noon–11pm, Sun noon–7pm; kitchen Mon–Fri noon–3pm & 6–9pm, Sat noon–9pm, Sun noon–4pm. **Red Lion** Crockham Lane, Hernhill, ME13 9JR ☎ 01227 751207, ⓦ theredlionhernhill.co.uk. On the village green, in a quaint fourteenth-century building, the *Red Lion* is a smartened-up but always welcoming old pub with a big grassy garden and a kids' play area. The seasonal menu focuses on gastropub staples including pastas, pies, steaks and burgers; starters from £6, mains from £13. Mon–Sat 11.30am–10pm, Sun 11.30am–7pm; kitchen Mon–Sat noon–2.30pm & 6–9pm, Sun noon–4pm.

South of Canterbury

The area **south of Canterbury**, though often overlooked in the dash from the city to the villages of the Weald or the iconic white cliffs of the coast, holds a couple of places of interest: the well-respected **Howletts Wild Animal Park** and gardens at **Goodnestone** are worthwhile paying attractions, while a number of sleepy little hamlets, including the village of **Chilham**, are appealing pit stops along the North Downs Way.

Howletts Wild Animal Park

Bekesbourne, CT4 5EL • Daily: April–Oct 9.30am–6pm (last admission 4pm); Nov–March 9.30am–5pm (last admission 3.30pm) • £22.95, under-16s £19.95 • **Treetop Challenge** Sat & Sun 10am–4pm • £7/person • **Animal Adventure Challenge** Sat & Sun 10am–4pm • £2.50/child • ☎ 01227 721268, ⓦ aspinallfoundation.org/howletts • Bekesbourne train station lies a mile to the southwest

Working alongside the Aspinall Foundation conservation charity, which also oversees Port Lympne near Folkestone (see page 128), **Howletts Wild Animal Park**, three miles south of Canterbury, is highly regarded for its conservation efforts, saving and breeding rare species from around the world, and, where possible, returning them to the wild. Spread across the hundred-acre site, the enclosures are, in the main, well designed and equipped, with scope for the creatures to retreat if necessary; this is not a zoo, as such, and you are not guaranteed to see all the animals if they are not in the mood to be seen. Though the park is home to black rhinos, snow leopards, Siberian tigers, giant anteaters and the largest **African elephant** herd in the UK, along with many other species – check out the extraordinary red river hogs – the stars here tend to be the primates, including **gorillas**, lemurs and a large number of lively langurs. Other diversions include the **Treetop Challenge**, an elevated adventure course with zip-lines, nets and rope-bridges, and the **Animal Adventure Challenge**, a less daunting adventure play area for smaller kids (aged 2–5). Reckon on a bare minimum of two hours for a visit.

Goodnestone Park Gardens

Goodnestone, off the A2 Canterbury to Dover, CT3 1PL • April–Sept Tues–Fri & Sun 11am–5pm • £7 • ☎ 01304 840107, ⓦ goodnestoneparkgardens.co.uk

Goodnestone Park Gardens, spread across eighteen acres around eight miles southeast of Canterbury, present a romantic ensemble. Part of an early eighteenth-century estate (which was home for a while to Jane Austen's brother and sister-in-law, and where the novelist was a frequent guest), the gardens were designed in the formal style so fashionable in the 1700s. The high point remains the seventeenth-century **walled garden**, its mellow, centuries-old walls tangled with clematis, wisteria and jasmine, and with deep borders spilling over in a profusion of English country flowers. There's also a **woodland** of old sweet chestnut and oak trees, carpeted with bluebells in spring and alive with vivid blue hydrangeas in autumn, and an **arboretum**, planted with ornamental trees that erupt into blossom in springtime. The *Old Dairy Café* (open garden hours; garden admission not necessary), with a courtyard, serves homemade scones, cream teas and light lunches.

1

Chilham

Country villages don't come much prettier than **CHILHAM**, a ten-minute drive southwest of Canterbury in the Stour Valley. This is chocolate-box stuff, a cluster of beamed and tiled fifteenth- and sixteenth-century dwellings, tangled with flowers and centring on a market square – no surprise, then, that it's been used in a number of movies, among them Michael Powell and Emeric Pressburger's delightfully odd *A Canterbury Tale*, and period TV adaptations from Jane Austen to Agatha Christie. It offers more in the way of dozy English charm than actual sights, though **St Mary's Church** (w friendsofstmaryschilham.org), with its looming tower, and **Chilham Castle**, a Jacobean country house whose gardens are occasionally open to the public (June–Sept Tues 10am–4pm; £5; ☎ 01227 733100, w chilham-castle.co.uk), give you something to look at on opposite ends of the square. There's also a tearoom and a pub on the square for food.

ACCOMMODATION

Duke William The Street, Ickham, CT3 1QP ☎ 01227 721308, w thedukewilliamickham.com. Owned by local celebrity chef Mark Sergeant, this smart village gastropub offers four contemporary B&B rooms, each named for a famous cook. Some have lovely countryside views and one has a balcony; all have Nespresso machines. Choose from a good full breakfast or a hamper in your room. The menu (mains from £14) is seasonal and creative, with tempting choices such as caponata tart with tempura courgette flowers and Kentish feta, or baked eggs with spicy nduja, wild mushrooms and pickled samphire. **£110**

The PIG at Bridge Place Bourne Park Rd, Bridge, CT4 5BH ☎ 0345 225 9494, w thepighotel.com/at-bridge-place. The casual-luxe PIG group of restaurants-with-rooms brings country-house chic and a dash of vintage rock and roll glam to this gorgeous Queen Anne mansion in the tiny village of Bridge, two miles from Bekesbourne. There are seven guestrooms in the main house, while scattered around the romantic ten-acre estate are a secluded barn for two, seven rustic huts and twelve rooms in the Coach House, which is also home to the *PIG* restaurant. Food, as at all the *PIGs*, focuses on homegrown or locally sourced ingredients. Spa treatments are available in the cute "potting sheds". Minimum two-night stay at weekends; breakfast costs extra. **£200**

Woolpack Inn The Street, Chilham, CT4 8DL ☎ 01227 730351, w woolpackinnchilham.co.uk. On the edge of Chilham, this Shepherd Neame pub, dating back to 1480, has fifteen en-suite guest rooms – including a single and three family rooms – spread through the main pub, a rear building and a converted stable block. A couple have four-poster beds and some have access to a little garden; all are decorated in a simple, rustic style. Dining in, on traditional British gastropub staples, is no hardship (mains from £14); breakfast is not included in rates. **£85**

EATING AND DRINKING

Artichoke Rattington St, Chartham Hatch, CT4 7JQ ☎ 01227 738316, w artichokechartham.co.uk. Quietly doing its thing, this fifteenth-century Shepherd Neame pub – with several good walks nearby – is pleasingly unreconstructed. The pub grub, from the simple (ham, egg and chips; pies) to slightly fancier (salt-and-pepper squid) is equally unpretentious, with starters from £5 and mains from £9. There's a cute beer garden, too. Mon 5–11pm, Tues–Thurs noon–11pm, Fri & Sat noon–midnight, Sun noon–10pm; kitchen Mon 5.30–8.30pm, Tues–Sat noon–2.30pm & 5.30–8.30pm, Sun noon–4.30pm.

★ **Compasses Inn** Sole St, Crundale, CT4 7ES ☎ 01227 700300, w thecompassescrundale.co.uk. Perhaps the perfect country inn, reached via winding hedgerow-lined lanes and with North Downs walks from the door – and offering outstanding eating in a quirky, hop-strewn space, all open fires, fresh flowers, vintage knick-knacks and horse brasses. The food, which is scooping accolades at a rate of knots, is a bit English, a bit French, quite meat-focused and very local; everything – from hunks of warm sourdough bread with home-churned butter to venison brioche bun with wild garlic pesto, from wild mushroom and spinach pudding to pan-fried cod with oxtail and parsnip purée – tastes amazing. Mains from £19, two-/three- course lunch menu £18.95/£22.95 (Wed–Sat). Book ahead. Wed–Sat noon–3pm & 6–11pm, Sun noon–6pm; kitchen Wed–Sat noon–2.30pm & 6–9.30pm, Sun noon–4pm.

The Duck Pett Bottom, CT4 5PB ☎ 01227 830354, w theduckpettbottom.com. The delightfully named hamlet of Pett Bottom is home to a great food pub – a favourite haunt for Ian Fleming, who supposedly wrote much of *You Only Live Twice* here. The modern British food is a cut above and full of flavour. Menus change daily, but you might start an evening meal with curried cauliflower soup with toasted coconut, following with bubble-and-squeak risotto with crispy hen's egg (mains from £17); there are two-/three-course lunch menus, too (£18.50/£21.50; £22.50/£26.50 on Sun). The nice garden is great for sunny days. Wed–Sat noon–11pm, Sun noon–8pm; kitchen Wed–Sat noon–2pm & 6.30–8.30pm, Sun noon–4pm.

★ **The George** The Street, Molash, CT4 8HE ☎01233 740323, ⓦthegeorgemolash.co.uk. The focus on local ingredients, including veg, fruit and salad from their own smallholding, has won this old North Downs coaching inn a firm following, with a daily changing menu listing traditional, well-executed dishes such as shoulder of lamb braised in ale or home-made suet steak-and-kidney pud. Mains start at £15, and there's a great-value two-/three-course set lunch menu (Mon–Sat) for £12/£14. The woodland walks on the doorstep, and the big beer garden, are bonuses. Booking advised, especially for Sunday lunch. Mon–Fri noon–2.30pm & 6–9pm, Sat noon–9.30pm, Sun noon–7pm.

Mama Feelgoods Chalkpit Farm, School Lane, Bekesbourne, CT4 5EU ☎01227 830830, ⓦmama feelgoods.com. This café, just a 10min drive southeast of the city, is a go-to spot for Canterbury locals. Food is simple, wholesome and inexpensive (from £7) – quiche, sandwiches and soups – with breakfast (until 11.45am), good coffee, fresh scones and – their speciality – sumptuous homemade cakes. Afternoon tea (from 2.30pm) £16.95. Mon–Sat 9.30am–5pm, Sun 10.30am–4pm.

North Kent

BOTANY BAY

North Kent

With a coastline that takes in creek-laced marshlands, shingle and sand beaches and dramatic, sea-lashed chalk cliffs, North Kent offers a splendid variety of attractions. It's perhaps best known for its bucket-and-spade resorts, but anyone with time to spend will uncover medieval castles and lonely bird reserves, ancient festivals and wacky museums, cutting-edge galleries and historic villages abounding in places to eat. This coast has traditionally been London's seaside playground, and today, easily accessible on the high-speed train from St Pancras, it still offers blasts of sunny fun within a hop of the capital.

Beyond the scruffy edges of London and Essex, the **Medway towns**, clustered around the estuary of the same name at the point where the North Downs fall down to the coast, have two big highlights in Rochester and Chatham, where a knot of important historic sights and family attractions – chief among them the mighty Chatham Historic Dockyard, founded by Henry VIII and for centuries the base of the Royal Navy – are less than an hour from London. From the estuary, the low-lying North Kent marshes creep along the coast to Whitstable, offering excellent birdwatching, particularly on the quiet Hoo Peninsula and Isle of Sheppey. Tucked just inland on the edge of the North Downs, alongside a winding creek, is medieval **Faversham**. Home to Shepherd Neame brewery and the National Fruit Collection, it's an underrated base for this part of Kent, with a good foodie scene. Most people are ploughing on to artsy **Whitstable**, a bolthole for weekending Londoners, famed for its oysters and its lively shops and restaurants. Neighbouring **Herne Bay** offers invigorating clifftop walks all the way to the **Isle of Thanet**, on Kent's northeastern tip – where you'll find an almost uninterrupted sequence of sandy beaches and bays fringed by tall chalk cliffs. The "isle", though not literally cut off from the mainland, has a distinct personality, its trio of appealing historic resorts – hip Margate, genteel Broadstairs and handsome Ramsgate – each offering something a little different. Focused on the Turner Contemporary in Margate, along with a number of independent galleries, Thanet's art scene is vibrant, linking it culturally both with Whitstable and Folkestone further down the east coast.

The Medway towns

The estuary towns of the **River Medway**, which stretches seventy miles from West Sussex to the sea, have historically been defined by their naval and shipbuilding industries – a heritage celebrated by the enormous **Chatham Historic Dockyard**, which records more than four hundred years of British maritime history. Of the towns themselves **Rochester** is by far the most appealing, with a clutch of interesting sights and good places to eat. The surrounding mudflats and saltmarsh are a big draw for **birdwatchers**, with the depopulated **Hoo Peninsula** and **Isle of Sheppey** boasting a number of important **nature reserves**.

Rochester

The handsome town of **ROCHESTER** was first settled by the Romans, who built a fortress on the site of the present **castle**; some kind of fortification has remained here ever since. With a Norman **cathedral** and an attractive high street, the town is probably best

WHITSTABLE

Highlights

❶ Rochester With its Dickens connections, cathedral and castle, plus Chatham Historic Dockyard on its doorstep, this good-looking Medway town makes a rewarding day-trip. See page 66

❷ Faversham Sweet little creekside town with a good food scene, a historic brewery and an orchard to explore, and lonely marshland walks all around. See page 76

❸ Whitstable It's hard not to fall for laidback, oyster-loving Whitstable, where weekenders rub shoulders with seasalts and artists. See page 80

❹ The Sportsman, Seasalter This "grotty pub by the sea", as it calls itself, is in fact a Michelin-

starred treat, one of the best restaurants in the UK. See page 85

❺ Margate's Old Town Pronounced "romantic, sexy and fucking weird" by local girl Tracey Emin, mad Margate is among south England's hippest destinations. See page 89

❻ Botany Bay Thanet has many superb beaches, but with its huge chalk pillars and its sweep of clean sand, Botany Bay is the most dramatic. See page 92

❼ Broadstairs Folk Week Quaint Broadstairs, the prettiest of the Thanet resorts, becomes a lively hotbed of music and street parades during this annual festival. See page 97

HIGHLIGHTS ARE MARKED ON THE MAP ON PAGE 68

known for its connections with **Charles Dickens**, who spent his youth and final years near here, and wrote about it often. Mischievously, perhaps, it appears as "Mudfog" in *The Mudfog Papers*, and "Dullborough" in *The Uncommercial Traveller*, as well as featuring in *The Pickwick Papers* and his last novel, the unfinished *The Mystery of Edwin Drood*. Many of the buildings he described can be seen today.

Everything you'll want to see is either on or just off the **High Street**, an unspoiled parade of wonky half-timbered, brick and weatherboard buildings that heads southeast from the River Medway. Lined with independent, old-fashioned shops and coffee houses, it's a nice place for a wander; there's an excellent **farmers' market** on the third Sunday of the month (9am–1pm), held in the Blue Boar Lane Car Park nearby.

Huguenot Museum

95 High St, ME1 1LX • Wed–Sat 10am–5pm; last admission 4.15pm • £4 • ☎ 01634 789347, ⓦ huguenotmuseum.org

The **Huguenot Museum** makes interesting connections between the fifty thousand French Protestants who fled France for Britain between 1685 and 1700 and modern-day refugees. The three-room display focuses on the dire religious persecution that drove them to flee their homes, the hostility they faced on arrival, and the huge contribution they made to British culture. Though many Huguenots settled in east London, there were significant populations in Kent – including an important silk-weaving community in Canterbury – and in 1960 the Huguenot Hospital (ⓦ frenchhospital.org.uk), established in 1718 in London, was moved to a new site on Rochester's high street. A couple of minutes' walk south of the museum, it still provides accommodation for Huguenot descendants fallen on hard times. The museum itself exhibits fine examples of Huguenot craftsmanship – in weaving, clockmaking, glassmaking, gold- and silversmithing – while temporary shows highlight specific strands of the Huguenot experience.

Guildhall Museum

17 High St, ME1 1PY • Tues–Sun 10am–5pm • Free • ☎ 01634 332900, ⓦ visitmedway.org

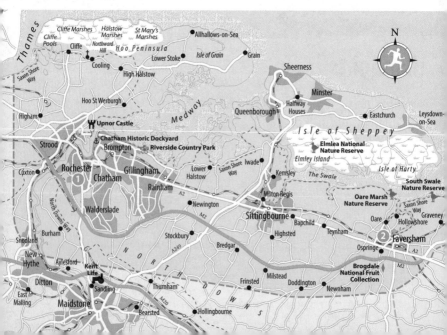

At the riverside end of the high street, the **Guildhall Museum** – the old magistrates' court, where Pip was bound over as apprentice to Joe in *Great Expectations* – holds a chilling interactive exhibition on the grim prison ships, or decommissioned **hulks**, used to house convicts and prisoners of war in the late eighteenth century.

Rochester Castle

Northwest end of the High St, ME1 1SW • Daily: April–Sept 10am–6pm; Oct–March 10am–4pm; last entry 45min before closing • £6.40; EH • ☎ 01634 335882, ⓦ www.english-heritage.org.uk/visit/places/rochester-castle

Built around 1127 by William of Corbeil, Archbishop of Canterbury, the dramatic **Rochester Castle**, though now ruined, remains one of the best-preserved examples of a Norman fortress in the country. The stark 113ft-high Kentish ragstone tower-keep – England's tallest – glowers over the town, while the interior is all the better for having lost its floors, allowing clear views up and down the dank shell. The outer walls and two of the towers retain their corridors and spiral stairwells, allowing you to scramble up rough and uneven damp stone staircases to the uppermost battlements.

Rochester cathedral

Boley Hill, ME1 1SX • Mon–Fri 7.30am–6pm, Sat 8.30am–5pm, Sun 7.30am–5pm • Free • ☎ 01634 843366, ⓦ rochestercathedral.org

Built on Anglo-Saxon foundations, Rochester's beautiful **cathedral**, at the northwest end of the high street, dates back to the eleventh century – though the building has been much modified since. Plenty of Norman features remain, however, particularly in the handsome west front, with its pencil-shaped towers, richly carved portal and tympanum, and in the nave, with its stout Romanesque columns, arches and jagged chevron carving. Look out, too, for the thirteenth-century wall painting (only half survives) in the quire – a remarkably vivid depiction of the Wheel of Fortune – and the zodiac image in the tiled floor in front of the high altar. The latter was the work of famed architect George Gilbert Scott, who remodelled the east end of the cathedral in the 1870s.

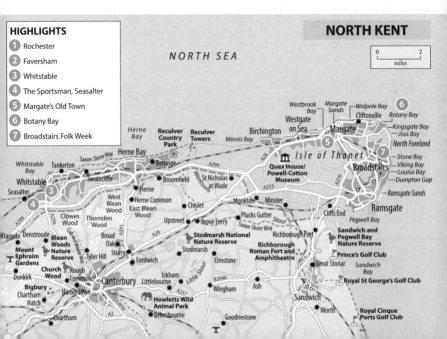

2

ON THE DICKENS TRAIL

Charles Dickens (1812–70) spent many of his formative years in Chatham, and returned to live near Rochester for the last thirteen years of his life with his long-time lover Ellen Ternan, a local actress. They met when she was 18 and he 45, and after his separation from his wife Catherine, lived together until her death.

In addition to the main **sights**, the town also hosts two Dickens **festivals** (see page 97); there's another, along with more Dickens-related sightseeing, in **Broadstairs**, along the coast in Thanet (see page 96).

ROCHESTER AND CHATHAM

Eastgate House High St. See below.
Royal Victoria and Bull Hotel 16 High St. This run-down hotel, opposite the Guildhall, stood in for the *Bull* in *Pickwick Papers* and the *Blue Boar* in *Great Expectations*.
Restoration House See below.
Six Poor Travellers House See below.
Chatham Historic Dockyard In 1817 Dickens' family moved to a small house in Chatham, where his father was a clerk in the dockyards, and lived there for six years. See page 72.

BEYOND ROCHESTER

Gad's Hill Place Higham, ME3 7PA. Now a private school, three miles west of town, this is the Georgian house that Dickens dreamed of owning as a child and bought at the height of his fame in 1856, and where he died in 1870. The Dickens Fellowship runs occasional tours, which must be prebooked (see ⓦ dickensfellowship.org for details).
St James's Church Cooling. See page 74.

Six Poor Travellers House

97 High St, ME1 1LX • Mid-April to Oct Wed–Sun 11am–1pm & 2–4pm • Free • ☎ 01634 823117, ⓦ richardwatts.org.uk/poor-travellers

The **Six Poor Travellers House**, an almshouse founded in 1579 to house impecunious travellers for the night – anyone, from scholars to blacksmiths, on the condition they were neither "rogues nor proctors" – was also used for a while in the eighteenth century as a prison for drunkards and runaway servants, and described by Dickens in his 1854 story *The Seven Poor Travellers*. "A clean white house", as the author put it, "of a staid and venerable air". Today you can wander through a set of small rooms, including three simple bedrooms with their truckle beds, and a fragrant courtyard herb garden.

Eastgate House

High St, ME1 1EW • Wed–Sun 10am–5pm (last admission 4.15pm) • £5.50 • ☎ 01634 332700, ⓦ visitmedway.org

A short distance from the Six Poor Travellers House, towards the bottom end of the High Street, sixteenth-century **Eastgate House** has been variously a private home, a museum and a boarding school. It also has a fair few Dickens connections, featuring as the Nuns' House in *Edwin Drood* and Westgate in *Pickwick Papers*. Inside you can explore the old rooms, where a few low-key exhibits illustrate the history of the building and those who lived there, while in the garden you can see Dickens' summer study, a Swiss chalet with gingerbread trimmings, which was moved here from his home at Gad's Hill in the 1960s.

Restoration House

17–19 Crow Lane, ME1 1RF • June–Sept Thurs & Fri 10am–5pm; check website for weekend openings • £8.50; gardens only £4.50 • ☎ 01634 848520, ⓦ restorationhouse.co.uk

Restoration House is not your usual house museum. An elegant Elizabethan mansion, given its current name after Charles II stayed here in May 1660 before his restoration, and the inspiration for Miss Havisham's Satis House in *Great Expectations*, it was, incongruously enough, owned for a while by Emu-toting entertainer Rod Hull. In fact, he saved it from being demolished – it was eventually taken from him by the taxmen, however, and left to dilapidation. The current owners have avoided the manicured restorations of so many old houses; its ragged, crumbling beauty reveals far more about the house's long life and many alterations than something more formal. This is a lived-in place, full of whimsical juxtapositions and evocative details: plaster is cracked and wood is buckled and chipped; mottled Georgian mirrors share space with Renaissance drawings and Gainsborough paintings, while Jacobean furniture sits upon undulating elm floorboards and fresh wildflowers tumble from vintage china. The large walled garden is charming, too, with fountains, fruit trees and fairytale topiary.

2

ARRIVAL AND INFORMATION
ROCHESTER

By train Trains arrive in the heart of town just east of the High St, opposite the back entrance of the tourist office.
Destinations Canterbury (every 20–45min; 40–50min); Chatham (every 5–25min; 3min); Faversham (every 10–20min; 30min); London Charing Cross (Mon–Fri every 30min; 1hr 20min); London St Pancras (every 30min; 35–40min); London Victoria (every 10–20min; 45min–1hr 20min); Ramsgate (every 5–40min; 1hr 10min).
By bus Arriva buses to and from Chatham stop on Corporation St (the A2), which runs parallel to the train line

and the High St (every 10–20min; 5min).
Tourist office 95 High St (April–Sept Mon–Sat 10am–5pm, Sun 11am–4pm; Oct–March Mon–Sat 10am–5pm; ☎01634 338141, ⓦvisitmedway.org). In a good central location, this is the hub for the Medway region, with lots of information, an art gallery and a café.
Tours The City of Rochester Society offers free guided walking tours, leaving from outside the tourist office (Sat, Sun & Wed 2.15pm; 1hr 30min; ⓦcity-of-rochester.org.uk/guided-tours).

ACCOMMODATION

Golden Lion 147–149 High St, ME1 1EL ☎01634 405542, ⓦjdwetherspoon.com. Rochester's most central option, with nine well-equipped, spick-and-span en-suite rooms above a Wetherspoons pub on the high street. Breakfast (available in the pub) is not included, but with a/c, double glazing and free tea and coffee this is very good value. **£75**
North Downs Barn Bush Rd, Cuxton, ME2 1HF ☎01634 296829, ⓦnorthdownsbarn.co.uk. Three luxurious en-suite B&B rooms, with garden or countryside views, in a gorgeous barn conversion on the North Downs Way four miles south of Rochester. **£95**

Ship & Trades Maritime Way, Chatham, ME4 3ER ☎01634 895200, ⓦshipandtradeschatham.co.uk. This waterside, Shepherd Neame-owned brasserie-bar near the dockyard offers smart, contemporary B&B rooms, many with Chatham marina views and some with capacious terraces. **£100**
YHA Medway 351 Capstone Rd, Gillingham, ME7 3JE ☎0345 371 9649, ⓦyha.org.uk/hostel/medway. Rochester's nearest hostel is four miles southeast, in an old oast house opposite the lovely Capstone Farm Country Park. There's a small kitchen. March–Oct Sat, Sun & school hols only; Nov–Feb groups only. Dorms **£19**, doubles **£49**

EATING

The Deaf Cat 83 High St, ME1 1LX ⓦthedeafcat.com. A hop away from the cathedral, this independent coffee shop, dedicated to the memory of Dickens' deaf cat, is a laidback place serving espresso drinks, cookies, cakes and sandwiches to a mixed crowd of tourists and locals. Try to bag a sofa seat. Mon–Sat 9am–5pm, Sun 10am–5pm.

The Seaplane Works 132 High St, ME1 1JT ⓦfacebook.com/TheSeaplaneWorks. Something a little different in these parts: a vegan coffee house/restaurant in a bare-bones, boho space (scrubbed wood, school chairs) that's as simple and appealing as the food. Dishes are creative and colourful – falafel with hummus, over-stuffed wraps, big

ROCHESTER FESTIVALS

Rochester hosts not one but two annual **festivals** devoted to **Charles Dickens** (ⓦrochesterdickensfestival.org.uk). Early June sees a weekend of parades, readings and street entertainment, while the Dickens Christmas in early December is a festive flurry of falling snow and candlelit parades, with much emphasis, of course, on *A Christmas Carol* and Scrooge. Just as much fun is the **Rochester Sweeps Festival** (ⓦmedway.gov.uk/sweepsfestival), a three-day May bank holiday celebration that re-creates the Victorian sweeps' May Day holiday; a rumbustious street affair featuring a Jack in the Green ceremony, folk music, parades and morris dancing.

2

FAMILY ATTRACTIONS AROUND ROCHESTER

Chatham Historic Dockyard (see below) makes a great family day out, and there are two more excellent family attractions, especially good for active types, nearby.

Chatham Snowsports Centre Capstone Rd, Gillingham, ME7 3JH ☎ 01634 827979, ⓦ jnlchatham. co.uk. Excellent skiing and snowboarding on the artificial ski slope, plus tobogganing and sno-tubing down the longest track in the UK. There are lessons for kids as young as 4. Prices vary. Mon–Fri 10am–10pm, Sat & Sun 10am–6pm.

Diggerland Roman Way, Medway Valley Leisure Park, Strood, ME2 2NU ☎ 0871 227 7007, ⓦ diggerland.com. Good mucky fun – especially on rainy days – on this small plot, crammed with diggers and dumpers of every shape and size, with plenty to drive, some to operate, and others mutated into fairground-type rides. Children can drive unaccompanied – but check the height restrictions before booking. £23.95; free for anyone under 90cm tall. Dates vary (July & Aug daily; closed Jan & Dec), see website.

---

salads and soups, raw cheesecake and the like, with top-notch Square Mile coffee to boot. Mains from £7. Mon–Fri 8am–5pm, Sat 9am–5pm, Sun 10am–4pm.

Smoke & Liquor 60 High St, ME1 1JY ☎ 01634 845270, ⓦ smokeliquor.co.uk. Very near the cathedral, in an atmospheric old building with wonky ceilings, this historic place offers relaxed dining, with cheese and charcuterie boards (£8.50), tapas (from £4) and open-fire charcoal BBQ dishes (from £10) served all day, or simple breakfasts in the morning (£1.50–6.50). Wed–Fri noon–9.30pm, Sat 9.30am–9.30pm, Sun 9.30am–4pm.

Sun Pier House Sun Pier, Medway St, Chatham, ME4 4HF ☎ 01634 401549, ⓦ sunpierhouse.co.uk. Friendly tearoom in a small gallery by the water. With its comfy sofas, board games and views across to Rochester, it's a relaxing spot for a coffee and cake, a light lunch or afternoon tea, all freshly made. Wed–Sat 11am–4pm.

SHOPPING

★ **Baggins Book Bazaar** 19 High St, ME1 1PY ☎ 01634 811651, ⓦ facebook.com/baggins.bazaar. England's largest secondhand bookstore is a never-ending warren of a place, filled with specialist, antique and rare titles on anything from fungi to UFOs. Daily 10am–5.45pm.

Chatham Historic Dockyard

About one mile north of Chatham along Dock Rd, main visitor entrance on Western Ave, ME4 4TZ • Daily: early to mid-Feb 10am–3pm; mid-Feb to end March & Nov 10am–4pm; end March to Oct 10am–6pm; Victorian Ropery and *Ocelot* tours by timed ticket only • £25; under-15s £15; family ticket from £66; discounts for online booking; tickets are valid for a year • ☎ 01634 823800, ⓦ thedockyard.co.uk • There are buses to the docks from Rochester; there are also trains to Chatham station from Rochester (see page 66), London Victoria and St Pancras International (every 30min; 40min) – from the station you can walk (30min), take a bus (10min) or hop in a taxi (£8)

Two miles east of Rochester, the colossal **Chatham Historic Dockyard**, founded by Henry VIII, was by the time of Charles II the major base of the Royal Navy. Britain led the world in ship design and shipbuilding for centuries, and many Royal Navy vessels were built, stationed and victualled here. The dockyards were closed in 1984, with the end of the shipbuilding era, but reopened soon afterwards as a tourist attraction.

With an array of fine historic ships, exhibitions and important buildings spread across the eighty-acre site it would take days to explore the whole place – if pushed for time, concentrate on the **Ocelot sub**, the **Victorian Ropery** and the **Command of the Oceans** displays. The main attractions are reviewed here, but there are more detailed accounts on the website and on the map boards dotted throughout the docks.

Command of the Oceans

The interactive **Command of the Oceans** exhibits offer some real highlights, vividly portraying the dockyard as a colossal, dynamic and ever-changing factory. The **Hearts of Oak** walkthrough experience uses digital graphics to follow a grandfather and grandson as they explore the docks in 1806 – just after Nelson's flagship *Victory*, devastated in the Battle of Trafalgar, returned here for repair – illuminating the processes of building timber-hulled sail-powered ships, and how Nelson's new "cutting the line" strategy changed the face of sea battle, and warship design, forever. **People, Tools and Trades**, meanwhile, focuses on 1803, with touchscreens zooming in on the individual workers – more than 2500 of them – and dockyard trades of that year.

Perhaps best of all, however, is the **Namur – the Ship Beneath the Floor** exhibit, which tells a fascinating tale. In 1995, archeologists discovered 168 frame timbers below the floorboards of Chatham's wheelwright's shop; these were identified as having come from *Namur*, a "second rate" ship launched in 1756. The ninety-gun *Namur* saw battle in the Seven Years War and the Battle of Lagos, among others; one member of its crew was slave boy Olaudah Equiano, who went on to become a famous abolitionist. The timbers were placed below the floor in 1834, but why there is quite so much of it is a mystery – saved as a mark of respect, perhaps, or, in a new age of iron and steam, as a memorial to a bygone era of timber and sails. Whatever the reason, they're a strangely moving sight in situ.

HMS Gannet

The Victorian sloop **HMS Gannet**, built at nearby Sheerness in 1878, is the most beautiful of Chatham's three historic ships, its elegant rigging and fine teak-planked hull evoking the glorious era of British naval supremacy. Unusually, *Gannet* also has a funnel – steam was not yet a tried and trusted form of naval power, so the ship was designed to be able to use both steam and sails. Nimble and fast, she was typical of the patrol ships deployed to impose the "gunboat diplomacy" that ensured Britannia ruled the waves.

HMS Cavalier

HMS Cavalier, built on the Isle of Wight in 1944, was known as the fastest destroyer in the fleet, equipped with all the latest technology and remaining active until 1972. You don't need to be a naval buff to get something from walking around this mighty "greyhound", the last of its kind in existence; the ship is kitted out as it would have been in the 1940s, and fascinating audio tours, which include testimony from men who served on destroyers, illuminate just how harsh conditions were on these mighty warships.

Ocelot submarine

Tours of the **Ocelot submarine** – the last Royal Navy warship to be built at Chatham, launched in 1962 – are not for the claustrophobic. You'll need to climb narrow, steep staircases, squeeze along low-ceilinged, one-person-wide passageways and shoot yourself from room to room through knee-high circular hatches. However, the opportunity to experience the astonishingly cramped quarters that housed a crew of 69 men for months at a time, and to peer through the periscope at the outside world, make it perennially popular; the fact that *Ocelot* was a Cold War spy ship, and that her movements are shrouded in a certain mystery, only lends it more intrigue.

The Victorian Ropery

The **Victorian Ropery** is one of the surprise hits of the dockyard; its lively tours, led by guides in Victorian costume, use the history of rope-making to illuminate the history of the docks themselves, and to reflect upon life at sea in the nineteenth century. Rope was made at Chatham from 1618 until the docks closed. During the "Age of Sail", warships would have needed some twenty miles of the stuff for the rigging alone; HMS *Victory* needed thirty miles at least, using it for everything from bucket handles to hammocks to cat-o'-nine-tails.

In 1790, the quarter mile-long **Ropewalk**, the longest brick building in Europe, was built at Chatham; it is now the only one of its kind left in the world, and rope is still made here for commercial use. Here you get the opportunity to make rope yourself, and during the week can watch ropemakers at work, "walking the rope out" in the lengthy hall upstairs, using traditional machinery dating from 1811.

2

No. 1 Smithery

Chatham's smithy – built in 1808, at the point when wooden ships were being replaced by iron and steam – now houses the **No. 1 Smithery**, which, along with temporary art exhibitions, features a splendid **Maritime Treasures** gallery. The highlights are undoubtedly the **ship models**, peaks of artistry and engineering made for a variety of reasons – as part of the design process, as prototypes, or simply as a way for sailors or naval POWs to pass the time. Look out for the fully rigged model of the wrecked HMS *Victory* (1806), carved by prisoners of war from bones saved from their meat rations, and a model of HMS *Ormonde* (1918), a World War I ship "dazzle painted" with jarring angular designs that, while looking for all the world like eye-catching Jazz Age modernism, provided highly effective camouflage at sea.

3 Slip: The Big Space

The Big Space is indeed very big, and full of very big things – including a Midget submarine, hulking mine-clearance equipment, massive steam hammers, a D-Day locomotive and a grim-looking tank. The building, a covered slip built in 1838, is impressive, a colossal wide-span timber structure with a cantilevered frame and an apsidal end that resembles the bow of a ship. From the mezzanine you can take a closer look at the roof, with its dramatic exposed timber skeleton.

The Hoo Peninsula

The marshy **Hoo Peninsula**, jutting out into the Medway and the Thames estuaries north of Rochester, is a lonely area rich in birdlife, attracting migrating and nesting waterfowl. The **Heron Trail** cycling route covers a loop of around seventeen miles, linking the **Cliffe Pools**, **Buckland Lake** and **Northward Hill** reserves, while the **Saxon Shore Way** walking path, which passes through Rochester, is also handy for Cliffe Pools and Northward Hill.

RSPB Cliffe Pools

Cliffe, ME3 7SX • Daily dawn–dusk • Free • ☏ 01634 222480, ⓦ rspb.org.uk/cliffepools • Bus #133 from Chatham (1hr) and Rochester stops in Cliffe; by car, park in Cliffe and walk down Pond Lane into the reserve

One of the most important wildlife reserves in the country, **Cliffe Pools**, a watery landscape of brackish pools, grasslands and salty lagoons right by the Thames, attracts large flocks of wading birds and waterfowl. Stars include avocets, little egrets, nightingales, cuckoos and lapwings, and, in summer, godwits, sandpipers and stints. A number of trails, including the Saxon Shore Way, cross the reserve, offering brilliant views.

Cooling

The village of **COOLING** is an isolated spot, stranded in the Hoo marshes around seven miles north of Rochester. On the main road, the thirteenth-century **St James's Church** (ⓦcoolingchurch.org.uk) is where Pip meets Magwitch by his brothers' gravestones in *Great Expectations*; you can still see the thirteen sad little lozenge-shaped stone tombs that inspired the scene. Nearby, within a private estate owned by musician Jools Holland, the ruined **Cooling Castle** was built in the fourteenth century to guard the River Thames; due to land reclamation it now sits around two miles inland.

RSPB Northward Hill

One mile from High Halstow, ME3 8DS • Daily dawn–dusk • Free, donations welcome • ⓦ rspb.org.uk/reserves/guide/n/northwardhill

Northward Hill is a working farm in a remote location on a ridge overlooking the marshes. With nearly 150 pairs of grey herons and around fifty pairs of little egrets, the marshes are also a rich breeding ground for lapwings, and the beautiful bluebell woods are filled with nightingale song in spring. Three trails, the longest at 2.3 miles, offer views of the marshes and the Thames Valley, and lead you to a heronry viewpoint.

Isle of Sheppey

The **ISLE OF SHEPPEY**, a flat clump of marshy land measuring just nine miles by four, separated from the mainland by the Medway and the Swale estuary, is often overlooked on a Kent itinerary. That's not to say it hasn't got a certain cut-off appeal: beyond its fifty-odd caravan parks, amusement arcades and industrial estates, beyond the ranks of enormous pylons and its trio of prisons, the island offers an odd, otherworldly sense of isolation and a few quiet attractions, from wide beaches crunching with London Clay **fossils** to empty, shimmering marshlands rich in **birdlife**. For an offbeat, nostalgic experience, the **Bluetown Heritage Centre** (see below) in **Sheerness**, Sheppey's main resort, can't be beat, but otherwise the south of the island is the most appealing – a serene, big-sky landscape where contented cows and fat sheep graze upon the salty marshlands of the isolated **Isle of Harty** and the wetland wilderness of **Elmley National Nature Reserve**.

2

Isle of Harty

The **Isle of Harty**, on Sheppey's southeastern tip, may not literally be an island, but separated from the rest of Sheppey by a number of channels it certainly feels cut off. With a few narrow country lanes winding through the watery landscape, this is good walking territory, and a favourite spot for birders; the **RSPB Capel Fleet viewpoint** is one of the best places in England to see birds of prey, including peregrines, while the coastal strip between **Shell Ness**, on the island's eastern tip, and Harty's *Ferry House Inn* (see page 76) is an excellent spot to see waders, waterfowl and birds of prey, along with rare plants and butterflies.

Elmley National Nature Reserve

Kingshill Farm, ME12 3RW • Mon & Wed–Sun 9am–5pm • £5/car • ☎ 07930 847520, ⊛ elmleynaturereserve.co.uk

The trip out to the **Elmley National Nature Reserve**, a 3300-acre wilderness area of open grassland, mudflats and saltmarsh on the southwest of the island, is half the fun. The sign from the A249 heralds a two-mile drive through lonely wetlands, with big skies stretching out to either side, before you even reach the farm car park – from there a couple of miles of footpaths provide fabulous views, with four bird hides. The privately owned reserve is famed among birders for its breeding waders and birds of prey; in spring and summer you'll see displaying waders, including redshanks and lapwings, along with rare breeding species including grey partridge and yellow wagtail, while in the cooler months you may spot short-eared owls and wigeon. Hares are also common. Uniquely for a national nature reserve, Elmley also offers **accommodation** (see below) – there could hardly be a more peaceful place to stay.

ARRIVAL AND INFORMATION   ISLE OF SHEPPEY

By car Sheppey is linked to the mainland by the A249 and the huge Sheppey Crossing bridge. You can also take the smaller road running alongside the A249, which has a small drawbridge and provides faster access to Elmley.

By train There are connections with Sittingbourne on the mainland from Sheerness (every 30min; 20min) and Queenborough (every 30min; 15min).

Tourist information The Bluetown Heritage Centre, 69 High St, Blue Town, Sheerness (Tues–Sat 10am–3pm, later for some movie/music hall shows; £2; ☎ 01795 662981, ⊛ thecriterionbluetown.co.uk), is a fascinating little volunteer-run information centre/museum – complete with a genuine old-time music hall and cinema (additional charge) – which concentrates on the history of Sheerness. The cosy tearoom serves homemade cakes and cream teas.

Website ⊛ visitsheppey.com.

ACCOMMODATION AND EATING

Elmley Kingshill Farm, ME12 3RW ☎ 07930 847520, ⊛ elmleynaturereserve.co.uk. A range of gorgeous accommodation dotted around a lovely wildlife-rich nature reserve (see above). Choose from romantic shepherds' huts sleeping two adults (some also have space for two kids), the charming Elmley Cottage (sleeping ten) or the glam eighteenth-century Kingshill Farmhouse (sleeping 14; available for group rental and occasionally on an individual B&B-room-basis). The beautiful, remote location makes this an extremely relaxing spot, and massages can be arranged.

2

Shepherds' huts (some with two-night minimum) **£115– 160**, cottage (two-night minimum) **£420**, farmhouse (two-night minimum) **£1150**

Ferry House Inn Harty Ferry Rd, Harty, ME12 4BQ ☏ 01795 510214, ⊛ theferryhouseinn.co.uk. A friendly sixteenth-century pub, in a remote spot on Sheppey's southern coast. With its sweeping Swale views, the large, flower-bedecked garden is a peaceful place to eat good, fresh, Kentish food; they have a kitchen garden, and all beef, lamb and game comes from their own farm (mains from £11; two-/three-course set lunch menu £14/£18). It's a popular venue for weekend weddings, so it's best to call

in advance if you want a meal. They also offer B&B rooms. Mon–Fri 11am–10.30pm, Sat 11am–11pm, Sun 11am– 5pm; kitchen Mon–Fri noon–2.30pm & 6–8.30pm, Sat 12.30–4pm & 6–8.30pm, Sun noon–4pm. **£80**

The Three Tuns The Street, Lower Halstow, ME9 7DY ☏ 01795 842840, ⊛ thethreetunsrestaurant.co.uk. On the way to Sheppey, this fifteenth-century country inn, with a huge streamside beer garden, serves great local ales and ciders and good, seasonal pub grub. Tuck into a "Kentish pub board" (Scotch egg, pork pie, toasted huffkin, Kentish cheeses; £14.95), farmhouse sausages, sea bream with fennel or a steak sandwich. Daily 11am–11pm; kitchen noon–9pm.

Faversham and around

Site of an important medieval abbey (long since gone), the good-looking creekside town of **FAVERSHAM** was famed from Elizabethan times for its thriving boatyards, fitting and repairing the wooden barges that worked their way along the estuary to London. Once surrounded by hop gardens, it is still home to the **Shepherd Neame Brewery**, while the importance of fruit-growing hereabouts is celebrated by the **Brogdale National Fruit Collection**. For many years, too, Faversham was at the centre of the nation's explosives industry, with **gunpowder** produced in the nearby marshes for three centuries before fizzling out in the 1930s. On the edge of the North Downs Area of Outstanding Natural Beauty, and separated from the Swale by a web of **marshes** and winding creek inlets, it's a neat, pretty place, its core boasting a well-preserved mix of buildings from medieval via Elizabethan to Victorian. **Market Place** (markets Tues, Fri & Sat 8.30/9am–3/4pm; ⊛ favershammarket.org) is the hub, fringed with cafés, the independent **Royal Cinema** (⊛ royalcinema.co.uk) and a handsome sixteenth-century Guildhall elevated on stout columns. From here, medieval **Abbey Street** runs down to the peaceful **creek**.

Fleur de Lis Heritage Centre Museum

10 Preston St, ME13 8NS • Mon–Sat 10am–4pm, Sun 10am–1pm • £5 • ☏ 01795 534542, ⊛ favershamsociety.org

The **Fleur de Lis Heritage Centre** should be your first stop; not only does it house the excellent information office and bookshop (see page 78) but also a fabulous local **museum** that punches way above its weight for a town of this size. Packed with lively exhibits on everything from brewing to boat building, agricultural riots to local pirates, the Tardis-like space also illuminates Faversham's social history with its reconstructed domestic interiors, while offbeat objects, from a mammoth's tooth to a magic lantern, greet you at every turn.

Faversham Creek

Faversham grew up alongside its **creek**, a tidal inlet of the Swale that was used from at least Roman times as a harbour. In the sixteenth century it was crowded with small merchant ships, many of them built locally, and it remained busy until Victorian times, swarming with deft Thames barges. **Standard Quay** (⊛ standardquay. co.uk), downstream of the swing bridge at the end of Abbey Street, was until 2012 one of just two remaining wooden boat repair yards in Britain; though you will still see old barges, fishing boats and historic ships moored by the quayside, the cluster of workshops, lopsided timber-framed buildings and weatherboard grain warehouses today hold antique, vintage and bric-a-brac stores, the excellent **Butcher**

of Brogdale (ⓦ thebutcherofbrogdale.co.uk), a wine bar and a garden centre (with coffee shop). You can walk along the creek to the nearby marshes and a couple of nature reserves.

Shepherd Neame Brewery

11 Court St, ME13 7AX • Daily, though closed occasional days; tour schedule varies, but there is usually a 2pm tour and often another in the morning, and occasionally more on Saturdays; allow 2hr; 18 years and above only • £18 • ☎ 01795 542016, ⓦ shepherdneame.co.uk/tours-functions/brewery-tours

It's rare to find a pub in these parts that isn't owned by the **Shepherd Neame Brewery**, the oldest in Britain, whose Spitfire, Bishops Finger and Master Brew ales are household names among beer fans. A brewery has stood on this site since at least 1573, drawing water from an artesian well; now this fifth-generation, family-owned business is best known for their quintessentially Kentish ales, made with hops from local fields. Lively **tours** take you through the process, from soaking the barley to conditioning the ales and adding special ingredients – oysters, rose petals – for their speciality brews. It's a working facility, thrumming, humid and pungent, and tours are enjoyably interactive: peer into the steaming, churning mash tuns, the oldest in England, and try all the key ingredients, from the burnt toast-tasting chocolate malt used in stout and porters, to wincingly bitter dried hop pellets and fresh spring water from the well. The grand finale is a tutored beer-tasting, after which you can choose a sample of your favourite to drink with free snacks. Be sure to wear covered shoes rather than sandals, flipflops or high heels.

Brogdale National Fruit Collection

Brogdale Rd, ME13 8XZ • Daily 10am–5pm; guided tours (1hr) April–Oct daily 11am, 1pm & 2.30pm; no booking required • £12, lasts a year • ☎ 01795 536250, ⓦ brogdalecollections.org

On the southern edge of town, **Brogdale Farm** is home to the largest collection of fruit trees in the world, with thousands of varieties of apple and hundreds of pears, plums, cherries and nuts. It's above all a research facility; you can wander around freely, but you'll get the most from your trip if you join a guided **tour** or come for one of their regular themed days or festivals. A little marketplace includes a nursery stocked with heritage fruit trees and a shop selling fruit, Brogdale honey and other local specialities.

The Swale

From the sixteenth to the twentieth century gunpowder was manufactured in the marshes northwest of Faversham on the south bank of the Swale; today these tranquil, sheltered mudflats and saltmarshes, cut through with fresh and brackish creeks, are prime habitat for migratory, overwintering and breeding birds, among them black-tailed godwit, dunlin, curlew, avocet, redshank and snipe. The **Oare Gunpowder Works Country Park** (April–Nov Mon–Fri 9am–5pm, Sat & Sun 10am–4pm; Dec–March Mon–Fri 9am–5pm; ⓦwww.gunpowderworks.co.uk), a mile west of town, just off the Western Link road to the village of Oare, is intriguing, its wildlife trails weaving through woodland, past abandoned works buildings and along ponds and canals. A couple of miles further north, the 80-acre **Oare Marsh Nature Reserve** (ⓦkentwildlifetrust.org.uk/nature-reserves/oare-marshes), at Harty Ferry, just north of Oare, has good birdwatching hides and views across the estuary to Sheppey. You can also walk along the creek east of Faversham, following the coast through the 420-acre **South Swale Nature Reserve** (ⓦkentwildlifetrust.org.uk/nature-reserves/south-swale) – rich in wading birds and wildfowl, and flecked with glorious wildflowers – the six or so miles to Seasalter and its famous gastropub, *The Sportsman* (see page 85).

ARRIVAL AND INFORMATION

By train The station is on Station Rd; it's a 10min walk up Preston St to Market Place.

Destinations Broadstairs (every 10–40min; 35min); Canterbury (every 15–40min; 15min); Dover (every 30min–1hr; 30–40min); Herne Bay (every 10–40min; 15min); London St Pancras (every 30min–1hr; 1hr 10min); London Victoria (every 30min; 1hr 10min–1hr 35min); Margate (every 10–40min; 30min); Ramsgate (every 10min–1hr; 40min); Rochester (every 10–20min; 30min); Whitstable (every 10–45min; 10min).

By bus Buses to Boughton (frequent; 20min) and Canterbury (every 15min–2hr; 40min) stop in the centre of town, on Court St near Market Place.

FAVERSHAM AND AROUND

By car Skirted by the A2, Faversham is just half a mile off the M2 and a 20min drive from the M20.

Fleur de Lis Heritage Centre 10 Preston St (Mon–Sat 10am–4pm, Sun 10am–1pm; ☏01795 534542, ⊛favershamsociety.org). Faversham's splendid visitor information centre has a fantastic local-history bookshop (there's a second branch, selling used books, around the corner on Gatefield Lane) and a museum (see page 76); it also organizes walking tours (April–June, Sept & Oct 1st Sat 2pm, other Sats 10.30am; July & Aug Sat 10.30am & 2pm; 1hr 30min–2hr; £5, including museum entry).

Website ⊛visitfaversham.org.

ACCOMMODATION

★**Palace Farm** Down Court Rd, Doddington, ME9 0AU ☏01795 886365, ⊛palacefarm.com. A peaceful family farm in a North Downs village six miles southwest of Faversham, with ten comfortable, hostel-style B&B rooms around a courtyard or in a converted granary. They're all en suite, with bunks and/or double beds, with a communal kitchen, lounge and dining room, plus outdoor eating areas. There's tent camping (Easter to mid-Sept) and a few bell tents (May–Sept; sleeping four), in a quiet field; you can rent firepits. Camping/person **£10**, bell tents **£70**, doubles **£60**

Railway Hotel Preston St, ME13 8PE ☏01795 533173, ⊛railwayhotelfaversham.co.uk. Opposite the station, this hotel has been hosting train travellers since Victorian times; today it's a Shepherd Neame inn, with en-suite rooms above the pub. It's not luxurious, but it's clean, comfortable

and friendly. The on-site *Carriage* restaurant is not bad, either, serving bistro favourites including Kentish lamb, fish pie or pork belly (mains from £11). Breakfast costs extra. **£80**

Sun Inn 10 West St, ME13 7JE ☏01795 535098, ⊛sun faversham.co.uk. Lovely old coaching inn, owned by Shepherd Neame, in a central location near Market Place. There are twelve rather luxurious B&B rooms, many of them crisscrossed with oak beams, and a good food menu in the pub. **£125**

Swan Quay Inn Conduit St, ME13 7DF ☏07538 106465, ⊛swanquayinn.com. A mere splash away from the creek, this eighteenth-century building offers comfortable, stylish accommodation in eight individually themed boutique rooms. **£120**

EATING AND DRINKING

As the home of Shepherd Neame, Faversham has more than its fair share of real ale **pubs**, most of them in lovely historic buildings – you can't go very wrong with any of them. Many also serve terrific **food**: this is one of Kent's foodiest towns.

Jittermugs 18A Preston St, ME13 8NZ ☏01795 533121, ⊛facebook.com/Jittermugs. Friendly little coffee shop, with distressed wooden floors, sofas and bookish bits and bobs scattered around the place. Come for an espresso with a slab of cake, a light meal (£5–7) of antipasti, salads, toasties and the like, or evening tapas (from £4). Mon & Tues 8am–5pm, Wed & Thurs 8am–5pm & 6–9.30pm, Fri & Sat 8am–5pm & 6–10pm, Sun 9am–5pm.

★**Macknade Fine Foods** Selling Rd, ME13 8XF ☏01795 534497, ⊛macknade.com. Just outside town, *Macknade*'s is more of a gourmet food hall than a farm shop. It's the foodies' go-to for the best local produce, from wines and fish to fruit and herbs, plus bread, cakes and posh deli stuff. The café serves excellent Italian espresso, cheese and artisan meat platters (£8–17), sandwiches, salads and all-day brunch (from £3 for a slice of sourdough with butter and

honey), all made with high-quality ingredients. Food hall Mon–Sat 9am–6pm, Sun 10am–4pm; café Mon–Sat 8.30am–5pm, Sun 9am–4pm.

Shipwrights Arms Hollowshore, ME13 7TU ☏01795 590088, ⊛theshipwrightsathollowshore.co.uk. Time seems to have stood still in this cluttered, seventeenth-century weatherboard pub – peacefully set in the marshes next to a boatyard – where the real ales are very local, as are the regulars. It's on the Saxon Shore Way, so you can walk here in around 40min through the marshes from Faversham, after which it's a treat to settle down to a quiet pint in the garden. Food is traditional pub grub (mains from £8). Hours vary seasonally, so it's worth calling ahead. Usually Tues–Fri 11am–3pm & 6–10pm, Sat 10am–10/11pm, Sun noon–10pm; kitchen Tues–Thurs & Sun noon–2.30pm, Fri & Sat noon–2.30pm & 6.30–8.30pm; shorter hours in winter.

★**Three Mariners** 2 Church Rd, Oare, ME13 0QA ☏01795 533633, ⊛thethreemarinersoare.co.uk. Appealing, smartish eighteenth-century pub, in a creekside village 1.5

miles north of Faversham, with a garden and terrace for alfresco dining. Serving good local ales, it excels with its food: perfectly executed dishes such as cauliflower panna cotta, pollock with fennel fondue, or Romney Marsh lamb with peas, pine nuts and goat's-cheese mash. Mains start at £14, with a three-course set dinner menu at £18.95 – you could cut costs with the three-course walkers' menu (Mon–Sat lunch; £16.95), or an early evening dish for £10 (Mon–Thurs 6–7pm). Book ahead. Mon–Thurs noon–10pm, Fri & Sat noon–11pm, Sun noon–8pm; kitchen Mon–Sat noon–2.30pm & 6–8.30pm, Sun noon–4.30pm.

★ **The Yard** 10 Jacob Yard, Preston St, ME13 8NY ☎01795 538265, ⓦfacebook.com/TheYardFaversham. This laidback community café, tucked away in a mews near the railway station, scores high for its fresh, creative, homemade food, on a daily changing menu – veggies will love the hot vegan sandwiches and "bliss bowls", but the sausage rolls are delicious, too. Good coffee and amazing cakes, and lots of community events, including yard sales and live music, make this a favourite local haunt; the little cobbled yard is a delight on sunny days. Dishes from £8.50. Mon–Sat 9am–5pm, Sun 9.30am–12.30pm.

Whitstable and around

The most charming spot along the North Kent coast, and a popular weekend destination for capital-dwellers, **WHITSTABLE** is a lively, laidback place. Fishermen, artists, yachties and foodies rub along here, and the sense of community, and tradition, is strong. By the Middle Ages this fishing village was celebrated for its seafood, and though it's nowadays more dependent on its commercial harbour and seaside tourism,

WHITSTABLE

■ DRINKING & NIGHTLIFE	
Black Dog	3
Duke of Cumberland	1
Old Neptune	2
Peter Cushing	6
The Rock Lodge	5
The Twelve Taps	4

● EATING	
Blueprint	16
Café and Kitchen	4
The Cheese Box	5
David Brown	9
Elliott's	3
The Forge	6
JoJo's	1
Pearson's Arms by Richard Phillips	10
Potato Tomato	17
Samphire	11
The Sportsman	14
Tower Hill Tea Gardens	2
V.C. Jones	7
Wheelers Oyster Bar	13
Whitstable Oyster Company	8
Whitstable Produce Store	12
Windy Corner Stores	15

■ ACCOMMODATION	
Duke of Cumberland	4
Fishermen's Huts	3
The Front Rooms	2
Hotel Continental	1

● SHOPPING	
Anchors Aweigh	3
Frank	2
Harbour Books	5
Harbour Market	1
Keam's Yard	6
Oxford Street Books	8
Valentines	7
The Whiting Post	4

Long Beach, Tankerton Beach, Tankerton Bay Sailing Club &

Kent Kitesurfing School

Whitstable Castle

Whitstable Harbour

Lifeboat Station

Whitstable Yacht Club/ Whitstable Watersports Centre

Kent Cycle Hire

Whitstable Bay

Horsebridge Arts & Community Centre

West Beach, Caravan Park, Seasalter &

Tennis Courts

Whitstable Playhouse Police Station

Whitstable Museum and Gallery

Whitstable Station

TOWER HILL

TANKERTON ROAD

NORTHWOOD ROAD

TOWER ROAD

TOWER PARADE

WESTGATE TERRACE

CROMWELL ROAD

CUCKOO DOWN LANE

DIAMOND ROAD

RAILWAY AVENUE

0   100
yards

N

2

WHITSTABLE NATIVES: THE WORLD'S YOUR OYSTER

Few molluscs have as much romantic allure as the **oyster**: unadorned, raw food redefined as a delicacy and attributed with aphrodisiac powers. For seafood fans, tucking into a half-dozen oysters is an essential part of any trip to Whitstable – ideally slurped down raw with a dash of Tabasco and a squeeze of lemon, accompanied by a crisp white wine or a hearty local stout – but their resurgence as a local icon is relatively recent. The shallow Swale estuary, fed by nutrient-rich brackish water from the marshy coast, has long been an ideal breeding ground for the bivalves, which are thought to have been eaten around here as far back as Neanderthal times. Certainly, the Romans were so taken by their delicate flavour that they towed them by sea back to Italy, and the industry as we know it began in earnest in the Middle Ages. By the mid-nineteenth century Whitstable had close to one hundred oyster dredgers, with the heavy, rocky-shelled "Whitstable Native" oysters being shucked in their millions and sent up the river to Billingsgate fish market in London. Though for centuries oysters were largely seen as poor people's food, in 1894 the Whitstable Oyster Company received the royal warrant to supply Native oysters to the queen. The twentieth century saw a run of bad luck – disease and overfishing, bad winters and big freezes – and by the 1970s oysters had fallen out of fashion, until the opening of the *Whitstable Oyster Company* restaurant (see page 86) in the 1990s saw the tide turn once more. Note that **Whitstable Natives** are strictly in season from September to March only; outside these months you may find yourself eating the perennial **Pacific oyster** – a larger, prolific breed, some of which are cultivated on the seabed and some of which are dredged wild. Occasionally, when the crop has been particularly bad, oysters have even been imported in order to meet demand.

the **oysters** for which it has been famed since classical times still loom large – you can tuck in at dozens of restaurants, or celebrate them with gusto at the lively annual **Oyster Festival** (see page 87).

Formal sights are few, which is part of the appeal. It's a great place simply to hang out, with a busy little **harbour** and an attractive **High Street** lined with independent restaurants, delis and shops. The **beach**, an uncommercialized shingle stretch backed by flower-filled gardens, weatherboard cottages and colourful beach huts, offers broad empty vistas and blustery walks for miles in each direction, and with its shallow bays and clean, flat waters Whitstable also offers good **watersports**.

Whitstable Harbour

Whitstable's **harbour**, a mix of pretty and gritty that defines the town to a tee, bustles with a fish market, whelk stalls and a couple of seafood restaurants, and offers plenty of places to sit outside and watch the activity. Built in 1832 to serve the **Canterbury & Whitstable Railway**, which carried day-trippers to the beach and back, today it's a mixed-use port, backed by a hulking asphalt plant; **Greta**, the handsome 1892 Thames sailing barge moored on the South Quay, offers boat trips around the estuary (see page 83).

The high street

Whitstable's high street runs through town from the railway up to the harbour. Adopting three different names as it goes, it links to parallel streets, and to the sea, via a number of narrow alleys. Starting as **Oxford Street** in the south, it segues into the **High Street** proper beyond **Whitstable Museum**, then transforms itself again at the **Horsebridge**, once home to the jetty where cargo was loaded and unloaded onto the Thames barges, and now a knot of activity where the town meets the beach. Here marks the start of **Harbour Street**, Whitstable's showpiece shopping stretch, lined with wonky and jauntily painted old buildings housing excellent restaurants and shops.

2

Whitstable Museum and Gallery

5 Oxford St, CT5 1DB • 10.30am–4.30pm: Jan–June & Sept–Dec Thurs–Sat; July, Aug & school hols Wed–Sat • £3 • ☏ 01227 276998,
🌐 whitstablemuseum.org

The friendly **Whitstable Museum** is full of curiosities. Here you can learn about ex-local **Peter Cushing** – the assertion that the actor best remembered as Baron Frankenstein or Dr Van Helsing was an accomplished model-maker, who also designed scarves for Marks and Spencer, may come as a surprise. Evocative photos recall the days of the **Canterbury & Whitstable Railway**, the world's first scheduled steam passenger service, while local maritime history is covered with figureheads, ships' models, old hulking tools, exhibits on helmet diving and oyster paraphernalia. The **fossils**, and an **Ice Age mammoth tooth** and tusk, both found nearby, are a hit with kids, while the local "pudding pan pots" are pretty extraordinary, too. Officially known as **Samian ware**, these pottery dishes date back to Roman times, conserved underwater in silt for thousands of years before being hauled up by fishermen and used in local homes.

The beaches

A swathe of shingle punctuated by weathered groynes, backed for most of its length by seaside houses and beach huts in varying states of repair, **Whitstable beach** is a glorious place for a stroll, a crabbing expedition or a lazy day's sunbathing, with a gentle slope that makes swimming possible in summer. Just steps away from the high street, it feels a world away, uninterrupted by commerce or cars and bathed in pearly light. Its elemental beauty, brightened by ragged clumps of tough beach plants, splashy wildflowers and peeling, upturned fishing boats, is picturesque without being twee; the skies are huge here, and the sunsets dramatic, with locals and tourists gathering most nights to watch the horizon bleed from orange to purple.

West to Seasalter

You mustn't leave Whitstable without taking a seaside walk **west from the Horsebridge**, where a beachside path takes you past abundant, unruly gardens, weather-beaten beach huts and covetable seaside houses on one side with the huge open horizon expanding on the other. The *Old Neptune* pub (see page 86), standing alone on the shingle, marks the start of the town's **West Beach**, a good spot for crabbing and fine for swimming at high tide. Busy with families in summer, the beach gets quieter the further west you go – beyond the caravan park you can either continue by crunching along the pebbles, or keep to the path behind the beach huts. Around two miles from town you arrive at lonely **Seasalter**, marooned between birdlife-rich marshes and a shell-strewn beach with muddy offshore oyster beds. It's an unlikely but lovely spot for the Michelin-starred *Sportsman* (see page 85), one of Britain's best restaurants.

Northeast to Tankerton

Walking **northeast from the Horsebridge**, passing the thicket of clattering masts next to the yacht club, then the lifeboat station and the harbour, and trudging along the shingle beyond, you'll join a broad seaside walkway. On the road above, accessible by a short path, sits **Whitstable Castle** – actually an eighteenth-century manor house and beautiful flower-filled public park, with great sea views, an excellent kids' **playground** and a couple of cafés. Well below and sheltered from the road, the path fringes Whitstable's broad, shingle **Long Beach** before emerging at the Blue Flag **Tankerton beach**, where there's good swimming and occasional **lifeguard service**. At low tide you can take a stroll along "**the Street**", a half-mile-long clay sandbank that juts out at a right angle to the beach and provides sandy bottomed, shallow swimming on either side. Ranks of brightly coloured beach huts sit staggered on the grassy **Tankerton Slopes** rising by the path – Tracey Emin's beach hut installation, *The Last Thing I Said To You Is Don't Leave Me Here*, which was bought by Charles Saatchi for £75,000 in 2000 and

WHITSTABLE WATERSPORTS

Whitstable is an excellent place for **watersports**, with a number of clubs based here and a laidback social scene. There are sailing races most summer weekends, and **windsurfing** and **kitesurfing**, concentrated around Long Beach and the Street, are popular.

Boardworx Watersports Store Beach Walk (☎ 01227 276566, ⊚ board-worx.com). Sells all the gear you need for kitesurfing, SUP, windsurfing, surfing, kayaking and the like. Mon–Sat 9.30am–5.30pm, Sun 10am–2pm (summer) or 10am–1pm (rest of year).

Tankerton Bay Sailing Club Tankerton Slopes (⊚ tbsc.co.uk). Small, friendly sailing club, below *JoJo's* restaurant (see page 85), offering a range of beginners' courses and "have a go" sessions (May–Sept).

2

later destroyed in a warehouse fire, hailed from here. Scattered with rare hog's fennel, the slopes are classified as a Site of Special Scientific Interest and provide a lovely barrier from the road above. Climbing the steps next to the sailing club brings you up to **Marine Parade**, the road to Herne Bay.

ARRIVAL AND DEPARTURE

By train From the station it's a 15min walk north to the harbour, or the same distance southwest along Cromwell Rd to West Beach; you can also walk to the high street via a short section of the Crab and Winkle Way (see page 59). Destinations Broadstairs (every 10–45min; 25min); Faversham (every 10–45min; 10min); Herne Bay (every 10–45min; 7min); London St Pancras (hourly; 1hr 15min); London Victoria (hourly; 1hr 30min); Margate (every 10–

WHITSTABLE AND AROUND

45min; 20min); Ramsgate (every 10–45min; 35min).
By bus Buses stop on the high street, running to Canterbury (every 15min; 30min).
By car Whitstable lies around five miles north of Canterbury on the A290, easily accessible from the M20. Parking is tight: if you can't find a space on the street, try the pay car park behind the harbour or at Keam's Yard near the Horsebridge.

INFORMATION AND ACTIVITIES

Tourist information The Whitstable Shop, 34 Harbour St (Jan–March Mon, Tues & Thurs–Sat 10am–4pm, Wed 10am–1pm, Sun 11am–4pm; April–Dec Mon, Tues & Thurs–Sat 10am–5pm, Wed 10am–1pm, Sun 11am–5pm; ☎ 01227 770060). You can also check ⊚ canterbury.co.uk/whitstable in advance.
Sailing trips The *Greta* (☎ 07711 657919, ⊚ greta1892.co.uk), a lovely old Thames barge moored in the harbour, offers regular trips around the Thames Estuary (April/May

to Sept/Oct; around 6hr; from £54).
Bike rental Kent Cycle Hire, by Goldfinch Galleries, Sea Wall, near the Whitstable Sailing Club (booking essential; ☎ 01227 388058, ⊚ kentcyclehire.com), rents bikes for £24/day or £90/week; kids' bikes, tandems and tagalongs are all available. Conveniently, you can drop off your bike in their sister branch in Canterbury (see page 51), or at a restaurant in Herne Bay (see page 88), if you wish.

ACCOMMODATION

Though there are some great places to stay in Whitstable, the choice of **hotels** and **B&Bs** is surprisingly limited, and prices aren't low, especially at the weekends (when there may be a two-night minimum). Many people choose **self-catering**: check ⊚ whitstableholidayhomes.co.uk, ⊚ whitstablecottagecompany.com and ⊚ placestostayin whitstable.co.uk.

★ **Duke of Cumberland** High St, CT5 1AP ☎ 01227 280617, ⊚ thedukeinwhitstable.co.uk. Eight comfortable and good-value en-suite B&B rooms above a friendly music pub (see below). It can be noisy on weekend nights, when they have live bands, but the music (which is generally excellent) tends to wind up around midnight. On sunny mornings breakfast in the flower-filled courtyard garden is a treat. **£80**

SEE MAP PAGE 80

★ **Fishermen's Huts** Near the harbour ☎ 01227 280280, ⊚ whitstablefishermanshuts.com. Run by the same people as the *Hotel Continental*, these two-storey weatherboard cockle-farmers' stores (sleeping two to eight) offer cute, characterful accommodation by the sea wall near the harbour. Most have sea views, and some have self-catering facilities. Rates include breakfast, served at the *Continental*; prices drop considerably out of season. Two-night minimum stay on Fri and Sat. Mon–Thurs & Sun **£150**, Fri & Sat **£225**
The Front Rooms 9 Tower Parade, CT5 2BJ ☎ 07738 013767, ⊚ thefrontrooms.co.uk. The three guest rooms in this B&B – a Victorian townhouse near Long Beach – are soothingly stylish, decorated in pale, heritage hues. Two en-suite rooms (one with balcony), and one with private shower. A continental breakfast is brought to your room.

2

CYCLING AROUND WHITSTABLE

The 7.5-mile **Crab and Winkle Way** (⊕crabandwinkle.org), following the old steam railway line to Canterbury (see page 59), is a popular cycling – and walking – route from Whitstable (though it's a little easier doing it in reverse), as is the enjoyable **Oyster Bay Trail**, a traffic-free seaside path that follows the coast round from Swalecliffe, just beyond Tankerton, to Herne Bay and Reculver Country Park (6.7 miles in total). From here you can hook up with Thanet's 32-mile-long **Viking Coastal Trail** (see page 30), which takes you along the shore to Birchington, Margate, Broadstairs and Ramsgate.

Two-night minimum stay on Fri and Sat. Mon–Thurs & Sun **£130**, Fri & Sat **£120**
Hotel Continental 29 Beach Walk, CT5 2BP ☎01227 280280, ⊕hotelcontinental.co.uk. The 1930s *Hotel Continental*, the only hotel in central Whitstable, has a

relaxed atmosphere and a peaceful location overlooking the sea at the start of the path to Tankerton. The rooms vary widely; the best have a seasidey vibe and balconies. Those with sea views are considerably more expensive than the cheapest quoted here. Rates include breakfast. **£125**

EATING
SEE MAP PAGE 80

Whitstable is one of the best places to eat in Kent, with a scene that extends beyond oysters and seafood into a relaxed and very good neighbourhood bistro scene. Many restaurants close surprisingly early – for all its pockets of sophistication, this is a sleepy place at heart – and opening hours may change during the off-season or at quiet times, when it's an idea to call ahead. There's a **farmers' market**, with lots of organic local produce, at St Mary's Hall, on Oxford Street, every second and fourth Saturday of the month (9.30am–2pm; ⊕whitstablefarmersmarket.co.uk).

CAFÉS AND DELIS
Blueprint 4 Oxford St, CT5 1DD ⊕blueprintcoffee. co.uk. Laidback little espresso bar serving expertly prepared, ethically sourced coffee and local baked goods in a relaxing, unfussy space – helped by the carefully curated selection of books and magazines that are available to buy. Mon, Wed & Fri 9am–4pm, Tues 9am–1pm, Fri 8.30am–4pm, Sat 9am–4.30pm, Sun 10am–4pm.
Café and Kitchen 61 Harbour St, CT5 1AG ☎01227 276941, ⊕cafeandkitchen.co.uk. Cute and informal café, with a very friendly vibe, serving tasty homemade breakfasts, brunches and lunches (rarebits, soups, sandwiches, salads and specials – also available to take away) with global food in the evenings. Wed–Sat 10am–3pm & 6–9pm, Sun 10am–4pm.
The Cheese Box 60 Harbour St, CT5 4LR ☎01227 273711, ⊕thecheesebox.co.uk. Heaven for turophiles, specializing in British farmhouse and artisan cheeses to take away. On Fri and Sat evenings you can eat in, dropping in for a cheese platter or a fondue with a glass of local wine, beer or cider. Summer Mon 10am–3pm, Wed & Thurs 10am–5pm, Fri 10am–9pm, Sat 10am–6pm or late bar, Sun 11am–3.30pm; shorter hours rest of the year.
David Brown 28a Harbour St, CT5 1AH ☎01227 274507, ⊕davidbrowndeli.co.uk. Excellent little deli with Mediterranean flair, selling posh store-cupboard staples

plus pastries, savoury tarts, sausage rolls, charcuterie, cheese and flavour-packed salads, along with superb coffee. You can eat in, in the tiny attached café – breakfast is popular, while lunch (from £9) might feature crab linguine or lamb cutlets with feta salad. On sunny days the two streetside tables are highly prized. Mon–Sat 8am–5pm, Sun 8am–4pm.
Elliott's 1 Harbour St, CT5 1AG ☎01227 276608, ⊕no1harbourstreet.co.uk. At a glance you'd have this pegged as a cheery neighbourhood café – which indeed it is – but the quality of the ingredients elevates the food to something special. Breakfasts range from porridge with brown sugar to shakshuka; at lunch you could try moules marinières, charred cauliflower steak, burgers or deliciously fresh crab sandwiches (£7; takeaway available). The evening menu changes regularly (mains from £10), but typical choices include lemon sole, rack of lamb or veggie stroganoff. Mon–Thurs & Sun 9am–4pm, Fri 9am–4pm & 7–9.30pm, Sat 8am–4pm & 7–9.30pm.
The Forge Chandlers Way, Sea Wall, CT5 1BX ☎01227 280280, ⊕whitstablefishermanshuts.com/the-forge. This rickety little shack, an oyster-shell's throw from the beach, is a real crowd-pleaser, with day-trippers enjoying Whitstable oysters (from £1.50 each), lobster and chips (£15.95) and glasses of chilled white wine, rubbing shoulders with families refuelling on mugs of tea and piping hot fresh doughnuts (five for £2.50). Local beers, too, plus ice cream. Sit at communal picnic tables, or bag a deckchair. Opening days and hours are weather dependent; if you're coming in winter, call ahead. Daily 9am–sundown, depending on weather.
Tower Hill Tea Gardens Tower Hill, CT5 2BW ☎01227 281726. A delightful spot towards Tankerton, across the road from but officially part of Whitstable Castle garden. The tearoom in the castle itself, the *Orangery*, may be smarter, but on a sunny day this simple hut has the edge, offering mugs of tea, ice creams, sarnies and snacks in a shady,

flower-filled garden with glorious sea views. April–Oct daily 10am–4pm, depending on weather.

Whitstable Produce Store 33 Harbour St, CT5 1AJ ⓦwhitstableproduce.co.uk. Friendly grocer-cum-deli specializing in Kent produce, with farm-fresh fruit and veg, juices and smoothies, homemade sausage rolls, quiches and tempting cakes. You can also eat in – simple breakfasts include granola and toasted teacakes, and soups are available at lunchtime. Mon 9am–4pm, Tues–Sat 9am–5pm, Sun 10am–5pm.

Windy Corner Stores 110 Nelson Rd, CT5 1DZ ☎01227 771707, ⓦfacebook.com/windycornerstoresandcafe. Homely neighbourhood grocery shop/café, where locals gather to enjoy coffee and homemade cakes, read the papers and chat; there are a couple of outdoor tables on the quiet residential street, and it's all very informal. The menu, freshly prepared with local ingredients, is short but tempting. Breakfasts (£3.50–7.50) include a great full veggie option or a bacon sarnie, while lunch (from £5) extends to creative salads and sandwiches. Mon–Wed 8am–4pm, Thurs–Sat 8am–5pm, Sun 8am–4.30pm.

RESTAURANTS

JoJo's 2 Herne Bay Rd, Tankerton, CT5 2LQ ☎01227 274591, ⓦjojosrestaurant.co.uk. With a breezy sea-view terrace atop Tankerton slopes, *JoJo's* is a great option, buzzing with happy diners feasting on Mediterranean-style tapas, small plates (from £6.50) and sharing plates (up to £45 for a mixed plate) while gazing out at the sea. Good choices might include grilled cod cheeks with white-wine butter, risotto balls with pea and mint, or chargrilled sardines with chorizo. Reservations recommended for dinner. Wed (school hols only) 6.30–11pm, Thurs–Sat 12.30–4pm & 6.30–11pm, Sun 12.30–4pm.

Pearson's Arms by Richard Phillips Horsebridge Rd, CT5 1BT ☎01227 773133, ⓦpearsonsarmsby richardphillips.co.uk. In a prime location at the edge of the shingle, this is a restaurant in a pub rather than a gastropub per se; local celeb chef Phillips produces gutsy Modern European food, served here in a warmly weather-beaten first-floor room with gorgeous sea views. The locally sourced, seasonal menu – Sussex goat's cheese parfait with roasted beets, maybe, or Dover sole with buttered greens – is wholesome and good (mains from £15; two-/three-course Mon–Sat lunch menu £15/£17). Mon noon–3pm, Tues–Sat noon–3pm & 5.30–9.30pm, Sun noon–6pm.

Potato Tomato 49 Oxford St, CT5 1DB ☎07708 821982, ⓦpotatotomato.co.uk. Cheery little vegan restaurant serving sizeable breakfasts and a range of tasty lunch dishes (from £7) – salads, dahls, mac and cheese, jackfruit burgers (from £10.50) and the like. There's a small suntrap terrace garden, and they host regular events including barbecues and comedy nights. All leftovers are used to feed rescued

pigs at a local sanctuary. Wed–Fri noon–4pm, Sat & Sun 10am–4pm.

Samphire 4 High St, CT5 1BQ ☎01227 770075, ⓦsamphirewhitstable.co.uk. This welcoming bistro – all timeworn wood, bright cushions, local art and fresh flowers – has been serving locally sourced modern British food for nearly a decade. Mains, from £14, might include sage polenta with butternut squash, feta and watercress pistou; bream with braised fennel; or mussels with Biddenden cider. One-/two-/three-course menus £15/£18/£21 (Mon–Fri noon–5pm, Sat noon–3.30pm). Mon, Tues, Thurs & Sun 9am–9.30pm, Wed 10am–9.30pm, Fri & Sat 9am–10pm.

★ The Sportsman Faversham Rd, Seasalter, CT5 4BP ☎01227 273370, ⓦthesportsmanseasalter.co.uk. The dull pub exterior belies the Michelin-starred experience within: *The Sportsman* gastropub, in a lonesome spot between marshes and beach four miles west of Whitstable, serves faultless, deceptively simple food. This is local sourcing to the extreme: fresh seafood, of course, plus lamb from the marshes, meat and veg from farms down the road, seaweed from the beach, bread and butter made right here – even the salt comes from the sea outside. Start, perhaps, with salt-baked celeriac, apple and fresh cheese (£10.95), and follow with thornback ray with brown butter, cockles and sherry vinegar dressing (mains from £22) – or splash out on the tasting menus (£55, no pre-order required/£70, book in advance). Tues–Sat noon–2pm & 7–9pm, Sun 12.30–2.45pm.

V.C. Jones 25 Harbour St, CT5 1AH ☎01227 272703, ⓦvcjones.co.uk. Friendly chippie, run by the same family since 1962, with a reassuringly unreconstructed old-timers' dining room at the back and takeaway at the front. From £8.95 for a huge portion, more if you add mushy peas and all the trimmings, and a little more than half that for takeaway. Cash only. Tues–Thurs 11.30am–8pm, Fri & Sat 11.30am–8.30pm, Sun noon–5pm.

★ Wheelers Oyster Bar 8 High St, CT5 1BH ☎01227 273311, ⓦwheelersoysterbar.com. A Whitstable institution, dating back to 1856 – and not related to Marco Pierre White's London oyster bar of the same name – this is a quiet contender for the best fish restaurant in Kent. It's an informal and friendly old place, with a cosy back parlour, a larger back room and a few stools at the (invariably sociable) fish counter at the front. The inventive, super-fresh seafood is stunning, whether you go for small dishes (John Dory ceviche with white crab salad; devilled herring roe on hot buttered toast; steamed prawn dumplings; £7–9), half a dozen oysters (£7–14) or more substantial mains such as pan-fried sea trout with charred lettuce, beets, fennel and goat curd. They offer takeaway, too, including delicious seafood tarts (£3/quarter). BYO (no corkage); cash only; reservations recommended. Mon & Tues 10.30am–9pm, Thurs 10.15am–9pm, Fri 10.15am–9.30pm, Sat 10am–10pm, Sun 11.30am–9pm.

Whitstable Oyster Company Horsebridge Rd, CT5 1BU ☎01227 276856, ⓦwhitstableoystercompany.com. With the best location in town, in the Victorian Oyster Stores building by the beach, the "oyster house" opened in 1989 and put Whitstable on the foodie map. Many former fans have moved on, put off by the high prices, but this remains a lovely spot for a treat, serving perfect, simply prepared fish – from roast gilthead bream with garlic and rosemary to whole cracked cock crab with mayonnaise – in a sun-warmed (or candlelit) room with bare brick walls and checked tablecloths. Mains from £17; half a dozen local oysters £16. Mon–Thurs noon–2.30pm & 6.30–9pm, Fri noon–2.30pm & 6.30–9.30pm, Sat noon–9.45pm, Sun noon–8.30pm.

DRINKING AND NIGHTLIFE

SEE MAP PAGE 80

Whitstable's nightlife revolves around its **pubs**, with a handful of places hosting excellent **live music**. Microbrews from the **Whitstable Brewery** (run by the people behind the *Oyster Company* restaurant, but based in a village some miles away; ⓦwhitstablebrewery.co.uk) are well worth trying – the oyster stout in particular is good, with a dark, chocolatey taste that goes down very well with briny oysters.

★ **Black Dog** 66 High St, CT5 1BB ⓦfacebook.com/TheBlackDog13. Don't be daunted by the vaguely Goth exterior – this quirky, cluttered little micropub, with something of the feel of an old gin palace, is all heart, with the focus on the (mainly) Kentish cask ales, natural ciders and wines, the inexpensive local snacks, and the friendly regular crowd. No cards, no vaping and no children. Tues, Wed & Sun noon–11.30pm, Thurs–Sat noon–midnight.

★ **Duke of Cumberland** High St, CT5 1AP ☎01227 272955, ⓦthedukeinwhitstable.co.uk. This roomy central pub, with cool music-themed decor and a pretty beer garden, has a name for its live weekend music – an impeccable programme from jazz, folk and blues to soul, big bands and retro pop. They have rooms, too (see above). Mon–Thurs 11am–11pm, Fri & Sat 11am–midnight, Sun noon–7pm.

Old Neptune Marine Terrace, CT5 1EJ ☎01227 272262, ⓦthepubonthebeach.co.uk. A white weatherboard landmark standing alone on the beach, the "Neppy" is the perfect spot to enjoy a sundowner at a picnic table on the shingle, gazing out across the Swale to the Isle of Sheppey, or to hunker down with a pint in the compact tongue-and-groove interior after a bracing beach walk. Some real ales, plus live acoustic music at the weekend. Mon–Wed 11.30am–10.30pm, Thurs–Sat 11.30am–11.30pm, Sun noon–10.30pm.

Peter Cushing 16–18 Oxford St, CT5 1DD ☎01227 284100, ⓦjdwetherspoon.com. Vast Wetherspoon's pub in a 1930s cinema, with a soaring, opulent Art Deco interior filled with retro movie memorabilia and Cushing paraphernalia. Join locals and old-timers for its inexpensive beer and grub and soak up the old-school glamour. Mon–Thurs & Sun 8am–11pm, Fri & Sat 8am–11.30pm.

The Rock Lodge 15–17 Oxford St, CT5 1DB ☎01227 770079, ⓦtherocklodge.co.uk Cosy, slightly kitsch and a little glam, this Alpine lodge-style cocktail bar/restaurant/music venue – check out the tartan curtains and log piles – has a kind of *Twin Peaks* vibe without the dark edge. Music (Thurs–Sat) runs the gamut from Motown, soul and funk to Mod classics, plus nostalgia nights devoted to anyone from Bob Dylan to Chuck Berry. Wed 11am–11pm, Thurs 11am–midnight, Fri & Sat 11am–1am, Sun 11am–6pm.

The Twelve Taps 102 High St, CT5 1AZ ☎01227 770777, ⓦthetwelvetaps.com. This welcoming, queer-run café-bar-style craft-beer place, with a little back garden, offers a rotating selection of twelve keykeg beers, plus speciality gins. They also do wine, cider and coffee, and sparkling wine on tap. No children after 6pm. Tues–Thurs 5–11pm, Fri & Sat 1pm–midnight, Sun 1–10pm.

ENTERTAINMENT

Horsebridge Arts Centre 11 Horsebridge Rd, CT5 1AF ☎01227 281174, ⓦthehorsebridge.org.uk. With a gallery and café, and lots of community events, this splendid arts centre also hosts acoustic gigs, theatre, comedy and movie screenings. Mon–Sat 9am–5pm, Sun 10am–4pm; performances from 7pm.

Whitstable Playhouse 104 High St, CT5 1AZ ☎01227 272042, ⓦplayhousewhitstable.co.uk. Variety, dance, movies, drama and music at this local theatre in a converted church.

SHOPPING

SEE MAP PAGE 80

Whitstable is a great place for shopping, with **Harbour Street** in particular known for its shabby-seaside-chic boutiques and vintage stores. The rest of the high street, while slightly less hip, has far more character than most, with barely a chain to be seen.

★ **Anchors Aweigh** 63 Harbour St, CT5 1AG ☎01227 263647, ⓦfacebook.com/anchorsaweighvintage. This little closet of a vintage store is always worth a browse for saucy seaside postcards, textiles, homewares, furniture, frocks and men's jackets, mainly from the mid-twentieth century, and all at good prices. Mon 10am–3pm, Thurs 10am–4pm, Fri & Sat 10am–5pm, Sun 11am–4pm.

Frank 65 Harbour St, CT5 1AG ☎01227 262500, ⓦfrankworks.eu. Creative and contemporary British graphic design and crafts, with handmade ceramics, prints, jewellery, cards and stationery, in a light, airy store. Mon–Fri 10.30am–

WHITSTABLE FESTIVALS

Based on a medieval thanksgiving ritual, the annual **Whitstable Oyster Festival** (ⓦwhitstableoysterfestival.co.uk), held for ten days or so at the end of July, is a high-spirited, very crowded, affair. There are food stalls, oyster-eating competitions, parades, live music, exhibitions and loads of kids' activities, with a symbolic "Landing of the Oysters" ceremony at Long Beach, featuring an oyster blessing. Quite different is the highly regarded **Whitstable Biennale**, a week or so of experimental art, film, theatre and performance, held in June in even years (ⓦwhitstablebiennale.com).

2

5pm, Sat 10.30am–5.30pm, Sun 11am–5pm; closed Tues in school term time.

Harbour Books 21 Harbour St, CT5 1AQ ☎01227 264011, ⓦharbourbooks.org. Two floors of novels, local titles and books on art, politics, travel and photography, many discounted, along with cards and gifts. Mon–Sat 9.30am–5.30pm, Sun 10.30am–4.30pm.

Harbour Market South Quay, Whitstable Harbour, CT5 1AB ⓦharbourmarketwhitstable.co.uk. A colony of fishermen's huts on the harbour, populated by around thirty local retailers – mostly food and drink stalls, but with crafts and gifts too. March–Oct Mon, Thurs & Fri 11am–5pm, Sat & Sun 10am–5pm, Tues & Wed some stalls open; Nov–Feb some stalls open on occasional days.

Keam's Yard On the shingle near the Horsebridge, CT5 1BU ☎07970 633112, ⓦfacebook.com/KeamsYard. Artist Bruce Williams' freestanding little workshop, facing the sea, exhibits quirky and interesting work in all media, much of it seaside-related, at good prices. Usually daily 11am–5pm.

★ **Oxford Street Books** 20a Oxford St, CT5 1DD ☎01227 281727, ⓦoxfordstreetbooks.com. Sprawling place selling a great selection of second-hand and antiquarian books, with out-of-print and rare titles, lots of novels and esoterica, and a cosy Art Deco-style reading room. Mon & Wed–Sat 10am–5pm, Sun 11am–4pm.

Valentines 21 Oxford St, CT5 1DB ☎01227 281224, ⓦvalentines-vintage.com. An excellent vintage furnishings store, selling good-looking, high-quality, handpicked homewares, ceramics and glass, from the 1950s to the 1970s, at competitive prices. Mon–Sat 10am–5.30pm, Sun 11am–4pm.

★ **The Whiting Post** 57 Harbour St, CT5 1HW ☎01227 772192, ⓦthewhitingpost.com. Colourful, feminine and whimsical womenswear store, with an irresistible selection of vintage-style frocks, accessories and shoes from brands including Saltwater, Seasalt, Emily & Fin and Noa Noa, plus homewares from the likes of Orla Kiely. A few men's clothes, too. Mon–Sat 9.30am–5.30pm, Sun 10.30am–5.30pm.

Herne Bay and around

The holiday destination of choice for Bertie Wooster's long-suffering butler Jeeves in the P.G. Wodehouse stories, **HERNE BAY** keeps a lower profile than the other seaside towns on Kent's north coast. Most of the appeal is on the seafront, where a two-mile prom fringes a typically British combination – caffs, ice-cream parlours, tourist shops and run-down amusements, alongside enormous bow-fronted houses, abundant flower gardens and a bandstand that recall the town's heyday as a Victorian resort. There's a stubby pier, with safe swimming nearby, and in summer the shingly beach is dotted with families. Look out to sea and you'll see the former end of the pier, marooned in the waves since a storm in 1978. Further out still are the menacing outlines of the **Maunsell Forts** – World War II anti-aircraft structures, long since abandoned to the elements. The waters around here are good for **jet-skiing**, and there are clubs in town devoted to dinghy sailing (ⓦhpyc.org.uk) and family-friendly sailing, canoeing and kayaking (ⓦhernebaysailingclub.co.uk). The main reason to come, however, is to take the invigorating walk to the **Reculver towers**.

Reculver Country Park

From Herne Bay you can take a glorious coastal walk along the Saxon Shore Way, or a cycle along the Oyster Bay Trail, to the twelfth-century **Reculver towers**, three miles east in **Reculver Country Park**. The park – an area of flat, fossil-flecked beaches and dramatically eroding soft sandstone cliffs topped with velvety meadows – is remarkably peaceful, with only the sound of waves crashing beneath you and wide-

2

open views across to Thanet stretching ahead. It attracts many migratory birds; you can check recent sightings at the visitor centre, which also fills you in on local history, in particular Reculver's fame as the testing ground for the bouncing bombs used by the World War II Dam Busters. From the towers it's another appealing walk or cycle of around four miles along the Viking Coastal Trail to **Minnis Bay**, where there's a sandy Blue Flag beach and good kitesurfing.

Reculver towers

Reculver, CT6 6SS · Daylight hours · Free; EH. Pay-and-display car park not owned by EH · ☎ 01227 740676, ⓦ www.english-heritage.org.uk/visit/places/reculver-towers-and-roman-fort

The flat-topped twin **Reculver towers** make a dramatic display on the clifftop, silhouetted against the sky. Built on the site of a Roman fort that protected the Wantsum Channel – which once separated Thanet from the mainland – the towers are pretty much all that remains of a twelfth-century remodelling of an earlier Anglo-Saxon monastery church. They were the only part of the structure to escape demolition in 1805 – by which time most of the local village had been abandoned due to drastic coastal erosion – and were kept here as navigational aids. Crouching low behind them are some rather more decrepit remains of the original church, bitten away by centuries of weather.

ARRIVAL AND DEPARTURE

By train The station is on Station Rd, on the south side of town; it's a 15min walk up Pier Ave or Station Rd to the sea. Destinations Broadstairs (every 10–30min; 22min); Faversham (every 10–40min; 15min); London St Pancras (hourly; 1hr 25min); London Victoria (hourly; 1hr 30min);

HERNE BAY AND AROUND

Margate (every 10–30min; 15min); Ramsgate (every 10–30min; 30min); Whitstable (every 10–45min; 7min).

By bus Buses from Canterbury (every 15min; 35min) and Margate (hourly; 50min) stop on the high street, a couple of blocks back from the seafront.

INFORMATION AND GETTING AROUND

Tourist information There is no tourist information office in Herne Bay; check out ⓦ canterbury.co.uk/hernebay.

Bike rental If you've rented a bike in Whitstable or

Canterbury with Kent Cycle Hire (ⓦ kentcyclehire.com) you can drop it off at *The Cookhouse*, Pier Approach, Central Parade.

EATING AND DRINKING

★ **A Casa Mia** 60 High St, CT6 5AJ ☎ 01227 372947, ⓦ acasamia.co.uk. This humble old-school pizzeria, the first in the UK to be approved by the rigorous Associazione Verace Pizza Napoletana, serves the best wood-fired pizza you'll get this side of Naples – authentically soft, charred and pliable, full of simple, good, Italian flavours, and a snip at £6.50–12. They also cook up a mean risotto and fresh pasta, but it's the pizza that steals the show. Takeaway available. Mon–Thurs 5–11pm, Fri & Sat noon–3.30pm & 5–11.30pm, Sun noon–10pm.

Green Door Deli 23 Williams St, CT6 5EG ☎ 07840 237642, ⓦ facebook.com/thegreendoordeli. A favourite for lunch, this cosy little deli, a couple of blocks back from the beach, makes a good pit stop, serving healthy salads – goat's cheese and walnut, say – homemade sausage rolls,

overstuffed sandwiches made with home-baked bread and tempting cakes. Mon–Fri 9.30am–3.30pm, Sat 9am–4pm.

Oyster and Chop House 8 High St, CT6 5LH ☎ 01227 749933, ⓦ oysterandchophouse.co.uk. Small, family-run and family-friendly surf 'n' turf restaurant specializing in lobster (£25), steaks (£11–18.50), burgers (£7.50–11.50) and BBQ platters (£10–15). Mon–Fri 5–10pm, Sat noon–10pm, Sun noon–9pm.

Wallflower The Mall, 116 High St, CT6 5JY ☎ 01227 740392. The homemade veggie/vegan food in this casual boho bistro is great. Most ingredients are sourced locally, and it's all delicious, from the generous breakfasts to the colourful, superfood-packed salads to the raw lemon cheesecake. Takeaway available. Mon–Sat 9am–5pm.

Isle of Thanet

Fringed by low chalk cliffs and sandy bays, the fist of land at Kent's northeastern corner, the **Isle of Thanet** (ⓦ visitthanet.co.uk), may now be attached to the mainland, but still has the feel of a place apart. That's not to say it's inaccessible – it's just ninety minutes from London by train, with regular transport connections to Canterbury and Dover – but taken together, the resorts of **Margate**, **Ramsgate** and **Broadstairs** have a distinct personality of their own. Having developed as seaside getaways in the eighteenth and nineteenth centuries, by the mid-twentieth century Thanet's sandy beaches had become the favoured bucket-and-spade destinations for Londoners seeking seaside fun. The arrival of cheap foreign holidays put paid to those glory days, but each town clings to its traditional attractions to varying degrees. There is a whiff of nostalgia about them all, from Broadstairs' quaint cobbled streets and old wooden pier to Margate's kiss-me-quick charms. J.M.W. Turner, who spent much of his time in Margate, said the Thanet skies were "the loveliest … in all Europe", and watching the sun set over the sea from one of its many glorious **beaches** – several of which have Blue Flag status – it's hard to disagree.

2

Margate and around

"There is something not exactly high class in the name of Margate. Sixpenny teas are suggested, and a vulgar flavour of shrimps floats unbidden in the air."
Marie Corelli, novelist, 1896

While the sixpenny teas and whiff of shrimps may have long gone, there is still something "not exactly high class" about **MARGATE**, a quirky resort that relishes eccentricity, nostalgia and brash seaside fun. As England's earliest seaside resort – in 1736 the country's first seawater baths were opened here, starting a craze for sea bathing and cures (among them a tasty concoction of seawater mixed with milk) – Margate grew in importance to score a number of firsts, including the first canopied bathing machines in 1750, seaside boarding house in 1770, donkey rides in 1790, and beach deck-chairs in 1898. At its peak, thousands of London workers were ferried down the Thames every summer to fill the beaches of "merry Margate", and on a fine weekend the place still throngs with day-trippers enjoying fish and chips, candyfloss

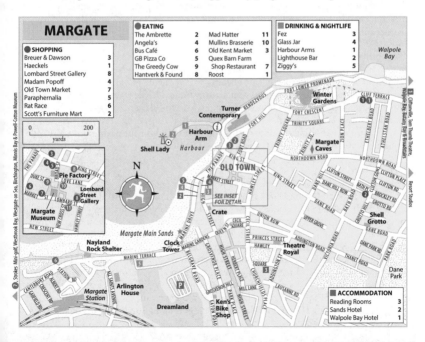

MARGATE

● **EATING**
The Ambrette	2
Angela's	4
Bus Café	6
GB Pizza Co	5
The Greedy Cow	9
Hantverk & Found	8
Mad Hatter	11
Mullins Brasserie	10
Old Kent Market	3
Quex Barn Farm	
Shop Restaurant	7
Roost	1

■ **DRINKING & NIGHTLIFE**
Fez	3
Glass Jar	4
Harbour Arms	1
Lighthouse Bar	2
Ziggy's	5

● **SHOPPING**
Breuer & Dawson	3
Haeckels	1
Lombard Street Gallery	
Madam Popoff	4
Old Town Market	7
Paraphernalia	5
Rat Race	6
Scott's Furniture Mart	2

■ **ACCOMMODATION**
Reading Rooms	3
Sands Hotel	2
Walpole Bay Hotel	1

2

THE THANET BEACHES

Thanet's chalk coastline, starting with Minnis Bay in the west and curving all the way round to Ramsgate Sands, features more than a dozen fine bays and clean, safe, sandy **beaches**. We've only covered the major beaches in this chapter, but each of them is worth visiting. All are accessible from the Thanet Coastal Path or by bike on the Viking Coastal Trail, and you could feasibly walk from Margate to Broadstairs, and then on to Ramsgate, at sea level – but you'd need to check the tides carefully. For more, see ⓦ thanetcoast.org.uk.

---

and sandcastle-building. As elsewhere along the British coast, the arrival of cheap overseas holidays in the 1970s ushered in long decades of decline; today, though the poverty of those years has left its mark, the tide in Margate is turning. Following the opening of the spectacular **Turner Contemporary** in 2011, a stream of artists and creatives was drawn to Margate by the faded seaside charm, the glorious skies so beloved of Turner and the low rents. Concentrated initially in the pretty **Old Town**, the artsy buzz – which fuels some cutting-edge indie galleries, scores of **vintage shops** and an increasingly good food scene – is slowly spreading. That energy – and not forgetting those huge, clean sandy **beaches** – has made Margate a hot spot once more.

Turner Contemporary

Rendezvous, CT9 1HG • Seasonal hours, but generally Tues–Sun 10am–5pm, daily in summer; check website • Free • ☎ 01843 233000, ⓦ turnercontemporary.org

Rearing up on the east side of the harbour, the angular, opalescent **Turner Contemporary** gallery is a landmark on the seafront. Named for J.M.W. Turner (who went to school in the Old Town in the 1780s, and who returned frequently as an adult to take advantage of the dazzling light), the modern gallery is built on the site of the lodging house where he painted some of his famous seascapes – and had a long love affair with his landlady, Mrs Sophia Booth. Inside, in addition to framing fantastic views of the seascape through its enormous windows, the gallery hosts regularly changing exhibitions of high-profile contemporary art, including shows devoted to Turner himself.

Harbour Arm

Margate's Georgian stone pier, or **Harbour Arm**, crooking out into the sea from next to the Turner gallery, is a funky little enclave, with a parade of old coal stores and fishermen's huts housing cafés, bars and artists' studios. It's de rigueur to walk over to the 85ft-high concrete **lighthouse** at the end, where the views across the little harbour and the broad sweep of Margate's beach are fantastic – especially at sunset. The oxidized bronze **"shell lady"** statue gazing out to sea is a homage both to kitsch seaside ornaments and to Mrs Booth, Turner's beloved landlady.

Marine Terrace

Fronting the beach, Margate's **Marine Terrace** has a rough-and-ready charm. You can sit in the Victorian **Nayland Rock shelter** where T.S. Eliot stared out to sea and drafted his poem *The Wasteland*. "On Margate Sands. /I can connect /Nothing with nothing", he wrote: who knows what existential angst he might have wrought from the seafront today, with its jangling amusement arcades – the flashy **Flamingo** sign has a dash of sub-Vegas pizazz – and the towering **Arlington House**, a brutish concrete 1960s housing block that's regarded as a hideous eyesore or a modernist treasure, depending upon your bent. To be fair, a growing number of good restaurants and bars, and the revitalized **Dreamland** amusement park, are bringing new life to this seafront stretch, and, surveyed from the sea or the Harbour Arm, the view of low-slung buildings fringing the long beach is undoubtedly appealing, evoking something of the resort's nineteenth-century heyday.

Dreamland

Marine Terrace/Belgrave Rd, CT9 1XJ • Days and hours vary, check website; generally Sat, Sun & school hols 10am–6pm; daily during summer school hols • Rides £1.50–5 – pay either with pay-as-you-go cards (from £5) or wristbands (over 1.25m £15–22.50, under 1.25m £12–19.50) • ⊕ dreamlandmargate.co.uk

Margate's **Dreamland**, which grew from Victorian pleasure gardens to become a wildly popular theme park in the 1920s, the very epitome of brash seaside fun, stood derelict on the seafront for nearly ten miserable years following its closure in 2003. Once a poignant symbol of the town's decline, in 2015 it became the flagbearer for the new, improved Margate, restored under the guiding eye of designers Wayne and Geraldine Hemingway. Targeted at first toward hipsters and hen dos, Dreamland today has settled down to become a family favourite. Certainly, many of the rides riff on beloved memories of the traditional British seaside – there's even a roller disco – but the place offers lots for today's kids, too. The park has a full calendar of cool **events**, including music festivals, DJ nights and free gigs; some very big names appear here, from Trojan Sound System to Mel C.

The beaches

It's not all about art and vintage shopping: even today most of Margate's visitors come to enjoy the sandy beaches. Though the mass community singsongs that were held here in the late nineteenth century are no more, the town beach, **Margate Main Sands**, a glorious golden swathe, is a family-friendly delight, with a tidal pool and kiddy rides. Quieter **Westbrook Bay**, to the west, offers shallow water that's great for paddling and watersports, especially windsurfing, and an eighteen-hole mini-golf course (⊕ strokesadventuregolf.com) nearby.

The Old Town

Margate's hipster reputation was largely spawned in the **Old Town**, a compact area roughly bounded by Hawley Street/Trinity Hill to the east, the waterfront to the west, and the blocks north of New Street up to Northdown Road. This is where Margate began, as a seventeenth-century fishing village, and in its narrow lanes is an energetic concentration of **vintage shops**, galleries and studio spaces, centring on lively little **Market Place**, lined with outdoor cafés.

Margate Museum

Market Place, CT9 1EN • 11am–5pm: May–Sept Sat, Sun & Wed; Oct–April Sat & Sun; last entry 4pm • £2 • ☎ 01843 231213, ⊕ margatemuseum.org

Secreted away in the old town hall/police station/magistrate's court (built in 1820), the volunteer-run **Margate Museum** is easy to miss but worth seeking out. Enjoyable exhibits illuminate the town's social history, covering a broad range of subjects from early sea bathing to Margate's role in the Dunkirk evacuations, with temporary shows adding even more local perspective.

Shell Grotto

Grotto Hill, CT9 2BU • Easter–Oct daily 10am–5pm; Nov–Easter Fri, Sat & Sun 11am–4pm • £4.50 • ☎ 01843 220008, ⊕ shellgrotto.co.uk

Discovered, or so the story goes, in 1835, by the children of the Newlove family who were renting the land above it, Margate's mysterious **Shell Grotto** opened as a paying attraction soon after and has been captivating visitors ever since. Resembling a slightly shabby gift shop from the outside, and reached via a short, winding and damp subterranean passageway, the grotto is an extraordinary and rather unsettling sight, its hallways and chambers entirely covered with intricate mosaics made from shells – more than 4.5 million of them, from clams to mussels to oysters, tinted silvery grey and black by the fumes of Victorian gas lamps. The origins and purpose of the grotto, decorated with all manner of symbols and imagery, remain a mystery. Some believe it to be an ancient pagan temple, others a more recent Regency folly, and others still are

2

ARTY MARGATE: THE INDIE GALLERIES

While Turner Contemporary rules the roost, Margate has a lot of indie art galleries for a town of its size, most of them artist-led and all of them exhibiting accessible contemporary works in most media. New venues pop up regularly, making use of Margate's interesting abandoned spaces, from one-time butchers' shops to old printworks, but the following are good bets. Opening days and hours will vary according to what's on.

Crate 1 Bilton Square, High St, CT9 1EE (ⓦ cratespace. co.uk).
Lombard Street Gallery See page 95.
Pie Factory 5 Broad St, Old Town, CT9 1EW (ⓦ pie

factorymargate.co.uk).
Resort Studios Pettman Building, 50 Athelstan Rd, Cliftonville, CT9 2BH (ⓣ 01843 449454, ⓦ resortstudios. co.uk).

---

convinced that the Newloves themselves built it, with a canny eye to the tourist trade. Whatever the truth, were it a hoax it was certainly an elaborate one – transporting and storing all the shells alone would have been a superhuman undertaking, not to mention the many years it would have taken to build such a place, and the impossibility of doing so in secret.

Cliftonville

A climb up from the main town, the clifftop neighbourhood of **Cliftonville** was, in Victorian times, Margate's snooty suburb, and until the 1930s its fashionable sea-facing hotels hosted such illustrious guests as T.S. Eliot, who recuperated from a nervous breakdown here in 1921. During Margate's dark years, Cliftonville declined and became one of the town's more impoverished neighbourhoods, its huge properties given over to bedsits and hostels. Today the creative types are moving in, and though gentrification would be too strong a word for it, it is definitely perking up. Other than the curious **Margate Caves** (ⓦ margatecaves.co.uk), excavated as a chalk mine in the eighteenth century and subsequently daubed with odd Georgian-era paintings – strange animals and battle scenes – there's not a huge amount to see. The sandy beach, **Walpole Bay**, has a Victorian tidal swimming pool, and you could also check out the striking, deserted 1920s Lido, clifftop adventure playground and historic **Walpole Bay Hotel** (see page 93). There are a couple of good places to eat, with an excellent **farmers' market** on the last Sunday of the month (Jan–Nov; 10am–1pm).

Botany Bay

Around 2.5 miles east of town, beyond Cliftonville, the Blue Flag **Botany Bay** is the flagship Thanet beach and quite different from others in the Southeast. Its towering chalk stacks, sheared off from the cliffs by narrow, winding sand corridors, create dramatic silhouettes, while the caves, shallow rockpools and stepping stones of creamy white boulders, capped with seaweed moptops, make a veritable seaside play- and fossicking ground.

Powell-Cotton Museum

Quex Park, Birchington, CT7 0BH • Tues–Sun: museum & gardens mid-Jan to mid-Dec 10am–5pm; house April–Oct 1–4pm • Museum, house & gardens £8.95, gardens only £4.95 • ⓣ 01843 842168, ⓦ quexmuseum.org/museum/

As if Margate itself wasn't offbeat enough, the **Powell-Cotton Museum**, in the village of Birchington, five miles west, offers another dose of magnificent eccentricity. Opened in 1896 to house the hunting trophies of Major Percy Powell-Cotton – whose expeditions, made between 1895 and 1939, included such far-flung corners as Abyssinia and Kashmir – this old-fashioned museum is most astonishing for its enormous **wildlife dioramas**. Crammed with staggering numbers of well-preserved and disarmingly expressive creatures, from aardvarks, bongos and dog-faced baboons to snarling tigers and mighty African elephants, these vivid scenes are even more astounding today than when they were made, giving a shocking sense of the abundance of wildlife that humans once took for granted. Highlights in the adjoining world-class **ethnographic collection** include bronze casts from Benin, an Angolan initiation costume woven from tree bark, and fabulous sacred and early Christian Abyssinian paintings.

Several rooms of the Powell-Cotton family home, a Regency mansion, are open to visitors, as are the lovely Victorian **gardens**, with pathways tumbling with abundant plantings and strutting peacocks. It's a great spot for picnics; stock up (or eat a meal) at the estate's excellent **Quex Barn Farm Shop** (see page 94).

Minnis Bay

Five miles west of Margate, near **Birchington**, the big, gently shelving sandy beach at **Minnis Bay** often has space when others get full, despite its many obvious charms. It's popular with kitesurfers, windsurfers and sea canoeists, and has good facilities, including showers and a paddling pool, along with a restaurant-bar on the cliff above.

ARRIVAL AND DEPARTURE

MARGATE AND AROUND

By train Margate's station is near the seafront on Station Rd. Destinations Broadstairs (every 5–30min; 5min); Canterbury (hourly; 30min); Faversham (every 10–30min; 30min); Herne Bay (every 10–30min; 15min); London St Pancras (every 25min–1hr; 1hr 30min); London Victoria (Mon–Sat hourly; 1hr 50min); Ramsgate (every 5–30min; 15min); Whitstable (every 10–45min; 20min).
By bus Buses pull in at the Clock Tower on Marine Terrace. Destinations Broadstairs (every 10–30min; 30min); Canterbury (every 30min; 1hr); Herne Bay (hourly; 50min); London (7 daily; 2hr–2hr 30min); Ramsgate (every 10–15min; 45min).

INFORMATION AND GETTING AROUND

Tourist office The visitor information centre for all Thanet is in the Droit House, Stone Pier, next to the Turner Contemporary (Wed–Sat 10am–5pm; hours may be reduced outside summer months; ☎01843 577577, ⓦvisitthanet.co.uk).

By bike Ken's Bike Shop, 26 Eaton Rd, opposite Dreamland's side entrance (shop Mon–Sat 10am–4pm, rental daily 9am–7pm; ☎01843 221422, ⓦkensbikes.co.uk) rents bikes from £15/day (£25 for two days, £30 for three) and offers a delivery and collection service.

ACCOMMODATION

SEE MAP PAGE 89

★ **Reading Rooms** 31 Hawley Square, CT9 1PH ☎01843 225166, ⓦthereadingroomsmargate.co.uk. Stunning boutique B&B set in a handsome, peaceful Georgian townhouse. The three big guest rooms have artfully distressed walls, gorgeous furnishings and huge, luxurious bathrooms; a classy breakfast is served in your room. Two-night minimum at weekends. No children. **£180**

Sands Hotel 16 Marine Drive, CT9 1DH ☎01843 228228, ⓦsandshotelmargate.co.uk. With an unbeatable location, this airy boutique refurb of an old seafront hotel is a popular choice. The twenty luxe rooms, some of which have balconies and sea views, are soothingly decorated, while the dining room has glorious sunset views – bag a table on the balcony if you can. **£140**

★ **Walpole Bay Hotel** Fifth Ave, Cliftonville, CT9 2JJ ☎01843 221703, ⓦwalpolebayhotel.co.uk. This family-run hotel has changed little since Edwardian times, and exudes an air of faded gentility from its pot-plant-cluttered dining room to its vintage trellis-gated lift. Offering a chunk of classic Margate eccentricity – the "living museum" and collection of napery art, for example – it's an old favourite of Tracey Emin, who threw parties here. Rooms vary, but most have sea views, many have small balconies, and all are comfy, clean and well equipped. The occasional wear and tear just adds to the character. **£95**

EATING

SEE MAP PAGE 89

OLD TOWN

The Greedy Cow 3 Market Place, CT9 1ER ☎01843 447557, ⓦthegreedycow.co.uk. Everything in this charming deli, from the simple, mismatched retro decor to the fresh, comfort-food menu, welcomes you in. The food ticks many boxes, whether you fancy a vegan peanut-butter maple toastie for breakfast or spiced pulled pork in a bun for lunch. Breakfast £5–8; lunch £6.50–8. Tues–Fri (plus Mon in summer) 10am–4pm, Sat & Sun 10am–5pm.

★ **Hantverk & Found** 16–18 King St, CT9 1DA ☎01843 280454, ⓦhantverk-found.co.uk. This tiny, pared-back café is a firm foodie favourite for its fabulous fresh fish menu,

2

poshed up with on-trend ingredients and the odd dash of Japanese/Korean and Mediterranean influence. From the deliciously simple (local haddock fish fingers with crème fraiche; dressed crab with charred sourdough) to the simply delicious (tagliatelle with sea urchin and bottarga; clams in spicy Korean broth with udon noodles), you can't go wrong – or just order half a dozen oysters (£12.50) with a glass of Kentish fizz. Starters from £7, mains £11–20; two-/three-course dinner menu £17.50/£21. Thurs noon–3pm & 6.30–9.30pm, Fri & Sat noon–3pm & 6.30–10pm, Sun noon–4pm.

Mad Hatter 9 Lombard St, CT9 1EJ ☎01843 232626, ⓦfacebook.com/TheMadHatterMargate. Friendly, quirky tearoom, in a crooked seventeenth-century building filled with Margate paraphernalia and Victoriana. The menu features old-school treats, but most people are here for the homemade cakes and scones. Mon & Thurs–Sat 9.30am–4pm, Sun 10am–4pm.

Mullins Brasserie 6 Market Place, CT9 1EN ☎01843 295603, ⓦmullinsbrasserie.co.uk. Lunch at this upscale, comfortable contemporary Caribbean/European restaurant sees jerk chicken, pastas and Creole mains from £11; more elaborate evening dishes (blackened halibut steak with truffle-potato-and-saltfish cake, say, or curried goat), start at £13. The two-/three-course menus are great value (lunch £12.95/£15.95; dinner £16.95/£19.95). Mon–Thurs noon–3pm & 6–9pm, Fri & Sat noon–3pm & 6–9.30pm.

OUTSIDE THE OLD TOWN

The Ambrette 10 Fort Hill, CT9 1HD ☎01843 231504, ⓦtheambrette.co.uk. Superlative modern Indian food served practically on the doorstep of the Turner Contemporary. Beautifully presented dishes are light and delicately spiced, featuring ingredients not often seen in Indian restaurants – pickled samphire, wood pigeon, wild salmon caviar – much of it locally sourced. Starters from £7, mains from £13; two-/three-course menus £18.95/£24.95 (pre-/post-theatre), £17.99/£21.99 (lunch). Mon–Thurs 11.30am–2.30pm & 6–9.30pm, Fri 11.30am–2.30pm & 5.30pm–late, Sat & Sun 11.30am–late.

★**Angela's** 21 The Parade, CT9 1EX ☎01843 319 978, ⓦangelasofmargate.com. They keep things elegantly simple at this unpretentious little fish restaurant, where farm-fresh veg is also given a starring role. The daily changing menu depends on the day's catch, but might include such dishes as scallops with kohlrabi or thornback ray with brown butter. Mains £12–20. Their sister place, a seafood bar/deli called *Dory's*, around the corner at 24 High St (Wed–Sun noon–7pm), follows the same philosophy but focuses on

small plates, with lots of raw, pickled and cured options. Wed–Sat noon–2.30pm & 6.30–9pm, Sun noon–3pm.

★**Bus Café** The Sun Deck, Royal Crescent Promenade, CT9 5AJ ☎07936 076737, ⓦthebuscafe.co.uk. The wraps and boxes dished up from this red double-decker bus, parked by the sea near the train station, are really tasty, fresh and locally sourced – filled with pulled chicken, falafel, halloumi, veg steaks or South African barbecue, and served with vibrant salads. Posh hash browns are also an option for weekend breakfasts, jumbling rösti with all manner of ingredients (including a vegan choice). Eat on board or, on sunny days, outside, in what has become a little street-food enclave. You'll be pushed to spend more than a tenner. Mon & Thurs–Sun 10am–3pm (Sun breakfast served only); check their Facebook page for seasonal variations.

★**GB Pizza Co** 14 Marine Drive, CT9 1DH ☎01843 297700, ⓦgreatbritishpizza.com. A Margate must – this buzzing contemporary pizza joint on the seafront, with smiley staff and a lively vibe, dishes up delicious gourmet crispy pizza (from £5.50) made with ingredients from small producers. Daily noon–9pm.

Old Kent Market 8 Fort Hill, CT9 1HD ☎01843 296808, ⓦfacebook.com/theoldkentmarket. A good stop if you're after food on the go, this indoor market, in an old cinema near the Turner Contemporary, has stalls selling anything from sushi to Afro-Caribbean curries and pies. Mon 9am–6pm, Tues–Sun 8am–6pm.

Roost 19 Cliff Terrace, Cliftonville, CT9 1RU ☎01843 229708, ⓦroostrestaurant.co.uk. Casual, very family-friendly dining with a creative twist in this funky restaurant, where the rotisserie chicken with which they made their name is joined by many delicious things – mac and cheese with jackfruit or crayfish, salt-and-pepper squid, Buddha bowls, burgers – all locally sourced. Dishes £9–32. Mon, Wed & Thurs noon–3pm & 5–8pm, Fri & Sat noon–3pm & 5–9pm, Sun noon–4pm.

AROUND MARGATE

Quex Barn Farm Shop Restaurant Quex Park, Birchington, CT7 0BB ☎01843 846103, ⓦquexbarn. com. A no-fuss, casual café with small garden, linked to the excellent Quex Park farm shop, one of the best in Kent, selling fabulous produce and deli specialities. Food, much of it organic and sourced from the Quex estate, is wholesome and good, whether it's the chunky sandwiches, homemade sausage rolls or the chickpea and coriander burger. Mains from £11. Mon–Thurs & Sun 9am–5pm, Fri 9am–5pm & 6–9pm, Sat 8.30am–5pm & 6–9pm.

DRINKING AND NIGHTLIFE
SEE MAP PAGE 89

★**Fez** 40 High St, CT9 1DS ☎07743 567006. Join an interesting mix of locals in this relaxed and eccentric micropub, stuffed to within an inch of its life with recycled vintage memorabilia, where young mods and old soulboys

alike perch on Waltzer ride carriages, barber chairs or cinema seats to enjoy a good chinwag and a pint of real ale or speciality cider. Occasional live music. Mon–Thurs 3–10.30pm, Fri & Sat noon–11.30pm, Sun noon–10pm.

Glass Jar 15 Marine Drive, CT9 1DH ☎ 01843 298825, ⓦ theglassjarmargate.co.uk. With its scrappy furniture, scuffed floorboards and skewiff piano on the wall, this little bar doesn't take itself too seriously, making it a popular local spot for artisanal cocktails (from £8.50) and mocktails (from £4). DJ sets Fri & Sat. Mon–Thurs noon–11pm, Fri & Sat noon–1am, Sun noon–10pm.

Harbour Arms Harbour Arm, CT9 1JD ☎ 07776 183273, ⓦ facebook.com/harbourarms.margate. Cosy, cluttered micropub, with a nautical, seasalty atmosphere, serving cask ales and ciders to a loyal local crowd. In warm weather the outside benches are at a premium – nursing a pint while watching the sun set over the sea is sheer delight. Occasional live music. Daily noon–11pm.

Lighthouse Bar Harbour Arm, CT9 1JD ☎ 01843 291153, ⓦ facebook.com/thelighthousebarmargate. This chilled-out bar has a prime spot at the end of the Harbour Arm, with windows overlooking the sea on two sides and more space than its neighbours. Sit outside to enjoy the fresh air, or on a comfy sofa inside; in winter the wood-burning stove keeps things toasty. Occasional live music and DJ nights. Mon–Thurs & Sun 11am–6pm, Fri 11am–9.30pm, Sat 11am–10pm.

Ziggy's 49 Marine Terrace, CT9 1XJ ☎ 01843 26943, ⓦ ziggysrooftop.co.uk. Casual rooftop bar up several flights of stairs near Dreamland, serving cocktails, Red Stripe and jerk BBQ. The relaxed, Caribbean vibe – Rasta colours, reggae playlist – amazing sunset views, and the feeling of being in on a local secret, set this place apart. Fri 5–10pm, Sat noon–10.30pm, Sun noon–8pm, though hours can be weather-dependent; call to check.

ENTERTAINMENT

Theatre Royal Addington St, CT9 1PW ☎ 01843 292795, ⓦ theatreroyalmargate.com. This grand old theatre, built in 1787 (but converted in Victorian times) is the second oldest in England. Crowd-pleasers and stand-up comedians share the schedules with contemporary theatre, dance and opera.

★ **Tom Thumb Theatre** 2 Eastern Esplanade, Cliftonville, CT9 2LB ☎ 01843 221791, ⓦ tomthumb theatre.co.uk. Nostalgic, witty and warm hearted, this is quintessential Margate: a tiny, family-owned rep theatre (just fifty or so seats) in a nineteenth-century coach house, offering cinema clubs, spoken word, live gigs (from bluegrass to electronica) and stand-up, along with straight theatre.

SHOPPING

SEE MAP PAGE 89

Margate's shopping scene yields rich pickings, with creative indie shops and pop-ups, once the preserve of the Old Town, spreading into the High Street and Cliftonville. The town is **vintage** heaven, with prices for clothes and furniture far lower than in the big cities.

Breuer & Dawson 7 King St, CT9 1DD ☎ 01843 225299, ⓦ breuerdawson.com. Though they do have the odd item for women, the focus here is on men's vintage gear, including Hawaiian shirts, 1940s jackets and 501s, in a handsome Old Town shop run by Portobello and Camden Market alumni. Pricey, but you can find some bargains. Usually Tues–Sun (plus sometimes Mon in summer) 11am–5pm.

Haeckels 18 Cliff Terrace CT9 1RU ☎ 01843 447234, ⓦ haeckels.co.uk. Margate reaches peak artisan in this exquisite lab/showroom where organic candles, fragrances, teas and beauty products are created by hand from natural ingredients – wild herbs, seaweed, chalk, saltwater – harvested from the local coast. Mon, Tues & Fri–Sun 10.30am–5pm, Wed & Thurs noon–8pm.

Lombard Street Gallery 2 Lombard St, CT9 1EJ ☎ 01843 292779, ⓦ lombardstreetgallery.co.uk. The shop at this sunny art gallery sells a very good, original range of postcards, posters, notebooks and crafts, much of it with a seasidey, Margate-specific bent. Tues–Sat (plus sometimes Mon in summer) 11am–5pm, Sun noon–4pm.

Madam Popoff 4 King St, CT9 1DA ☎ 01843 446072, ⓦ madampopoffvintage.patternbyetsy.com. Charming array of vintage clothes for women, some of them dating back to the 1930s, with an emphasis on glamour and feminine frocks. Fri & Sun 11am–5pm, Sat 11am–6pm.

Old Town Market Market Place, CT9 1ER ⓦ facebook. com/pg/MargateBazaarOldTownMarket. Small outdoor community market, with stalls selling funky crafts, antique jewellery, upcycled treasures and collectible junk. Easter–Oct Sat & Sun 10am–4pm, depending on the weather.

Paraphernalia 8 King St, CT9 1DA ☎ 07534 707105, ⓦ facebook.com/pg/paraphernaliaUK. Intriguing choice of stuff from around 1800 to 1980, including books, prints, furniture, stuffed stoats and saucy postcards – anything you might imagine – in this cut-above junk shop. Thurs–Sun 11am–5pm.

Rat Race 15 The Parade, CT9 1EY ☎ 01843 230397, ⓦ ratracemargate.co.uk. Mods, soulboys, rude boys and rockers kit themselves out here in classic British gear, new and vintage, including sharp suits, Harringtons and Brutus jeans for the men, and prom dresses, minis and pedal pushers for the women. Daily 10am–5pm.

★ **Scott's Furniture Mart** Bath Place, CT9 2BN ☎ 01843 220653, ⓦ scottsmargate.co.uk. Whether you're after a shell-encrusted poodle ornament or an old-school board game, you'll find it in this cheery, family-owned flea market, occupying an old ice factory. Also on the premises – which covers three floors and 16,000ft – is Junk Deluxe (Thurs–Sat only; ⓦ junkdeluxe.co.uk), specialists in Midcentury Modern furniture. Mon, Tues & Thurs–Sat 9.30am–1pm & 2–5pm.

Broadstairs and around

The smallest and quietest of the Thanet resort towns, unspoiled **BROADSTAIRS** stands on top of the cliff overlooking the golden arc of Viking Bay. At the northern end of the bay, a sixteenth-century timber **pier** curves out from the picturesque cluster of old flint and clapboard buildings that surround its venerable fishing **harbour**; the sandy **beach** alongside, which can only be reached by foot – or by elevator – feels deliciously sheltered from the town above. Up on the cliffs, the neat gardens, ice-cream parlours and seaview terraces of the large Victorian and Regency buildings give the place a refined flavour, while the large **bandstand** hosts concerts of all kinds, and the kitschy **Lillyputt crazy golf** course offers old-fashioned seaside fun and a nice tea garden (£5; ⓦlillyputt.co.uk). Linked to the prom by tiny alleys, sloping **Albion Street** behind is lined with higgledy-piggledy Georgian buildings housing restaurants, bars and shops.

A fishing village turned popular Victorian resort, Broadstairs still benefits from its location within walking distance of several excellent sandy **bays**. Renowned for its excellent **folk festival**, it also has strong connections with **Charles Dickens**: from 1837 until 1851 the author stayed in various hotels here, and eventually rented an "airy nest" overlooking the sea, where he finished writing *David Copperfield*. A festival and a small **museum** play up the associations.

The bays

Broadstairs' town beach, sandy **Viking Bay**, is a lovely golden crescent at the foot of the cliffs, and accessible, in summer, by lift. Fringed with beach huts, Viking Bay has a surf school (see page 97) and a few children's rides – and gets crowded on hot days. This is just one of seven sandy coves in the vicinity, however; on the northern

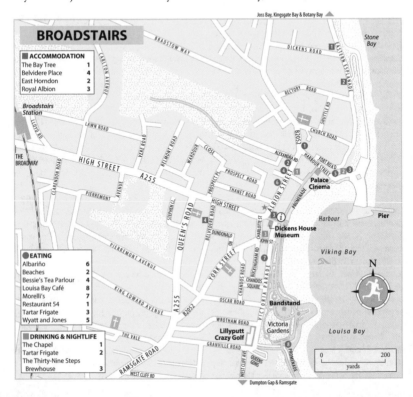

BROADSTAIRS FESTIVALS

The town bursts into life each August during **Broadstairs Folk Week** (Ⓦ broadstairsfolkweek. org.uk), one of England's longest-standing folk and roots music events, which features big names and up-and-coming singers, bands and dancing, with workshops, kids' events and a parade. Just slightly less crowded, the three-day **Dickens Festival** (Ⓦ broadstairsdickensfestival.co.uk), in the third week of June, sees enthusiastic Dickens fans, some of them dressed in Victorian garb, flock through the town enjoying Dickens dramatizations, tours, music, afternoon teas and film screenings. In early October, **Broadstairs Food Festival** (Ⓦ broadstairsfoodfestival.org.uk) is a three-day foodie event focused on locally sourced produce; there are more than one hundred exhibitors at the fair itself, with demos, tastings and events all around town.

2

edge of Broadstairs, walkable from Viking Bay, you'll find **Stone Bay**, where a staircase winds down the wildflower-tangled cliff-face to a curved Blue Flag beach, submerged at high tide. Quieter in summer than Viking Bay, it's great for rockpools and for sunny morning swims. Beyond is **Joss Bay**, which, with its long sands and shallow waters, offers the best surfing in the Southeast – it's home to the **Joss Bay Surf School** (see below) – and a refreshments kiosk. yFurther north are quiet **Kingsgate Bay**, with its sea caves, and best of all, the stunning **Botany Bay** (see page 92). In the other direction, **Louisa Bay**, easily reached on a sea-level prom from Viking Bay, is a quiet spot beneath cliffs shored up with concrete. Good for rockpooling, it does disappear entirely at high tide, but there's a superb beach caff.

Dickens House Museum

2 Victoria Parade, CT10 1QS • Mid-April to mid-June, Sept & Oct daily 1–4.30pm; mid-June to Aug daily 10am–4.30pm; Nov Sat & Sun 1–4.30pm • £3.75 • ☎ 01843 861232, Ⓦ dickensmuseumbroadstairs.co.uk

One block back from the clifftop prom, the broad balconied cottage that now houses the **Dickens House Museum** was once the home of Miss Mary Pearson Strong, on whom Dickens based the character of Betsey Trotwood in *David Copperfield*. (In the book, this "house on the cliff", outside which the donkey fights that so angered Miss Trotwood took place, was moved to Dover.) Its small rooms are crammed with memorabilia, including Dickens' letters, illustrations from the original novels, a reconstruction of Betsey Trotwood's parlour, and the author's desk, which he modified to include a rack for six bottles of wine. In addition, Victorian posters, maps, photography and costumes do a splendid job of evoking old Broadstairs.

ARRIVAL AND INFORMATION

BROADSTAIRS AND AROUND

By train Broadstairs station is at the west end of the High St, a 10min walk to the seafront.

Destinations Canterbury (hourly; 25min); Faversham (every 10–40min; 35min); Herne Bay (every 10–30min; 22min); London St Pancras (every 25min–hourly; 1hr 20min–1hr 45min); London Victoria (Mon–Sat hourly; 1hr 50min); Margate (every 5–30min; 5min); Ramsgate (every 5–30min; 6min); Whitstable (every 10–45min; 25min).

By bus Buses stop along the High St.

Destinations Canterbury (hourly; 1hr–1hr 30min); London (7 daily; 2hr 45min–3hr 20min); Margate (every 10–30min; 30min); Ramsgate (every 5–20min; 15min).

Tourist information The nearest tourist office is in Margate (see page 93); there's also a small, seasonal information kiosk on the Promenade by the *Royal Albion* hotel terrace (daily 10am–4pm in summer; Ⓦ visitthanet.co.uk).

ACTIVITIES

Watersports Joss Bay Surf School (lessons from £40; Ⓦ jossbay.co.uk), based at the area's prime surfing beach, offers lessons for all levels. Kent Surf School (Ⓦ kentsurfschool. co.uk), on Viking Bay, is great for beginners; it rents equipment and runs surfing, bodyboarding and stand-up paddleboarding lessons (from £35) and kayaking tours (£45).

ACCOMMODATION

SEE MAP PAGE 96

The Bay Tree 12 Eastern Esplanade, CT10 1DR ☎ 01843 862502, Ⓦ baytreebroadstairs.co.uk. In a good location near Stone Bay, just a 5min seaside stroll from the centre of Broadstairs, this solid red-brick Victorian house has been

2

restored into a friendly and very comfortable small hotel. Rooms, all different, are decorated in soothing heritage hues; some have sea views. The in-house restaurant (open to non-guests) offers simple dinners from £14 (prebooking required). **£190**

★ **Belvidere Place** 43 Belvedere Rd, CT10 1PF ☎ 07376 299296, ⊛ belvidereplace.co.uk. This stylish, quirky boutique B&B, in a gorgeous Regency townhouse, is at once warm-hearted and hip, its five rooms featuring sleek bathrooms, cool art and one-off vintage finds. The gourmet breakfasts are superb. No children. Minimum two-night stay at the weekend. **£160**

East Horndon 4 Eastern Esplanade, CT10 1DP ☎ 01843

868306, ⊛ easthorndonhotel.com. Friendly, comfortable, old-school B&B in a large Victorian house overlooking Stone Bay. Rooms are large, spruce and well equipped, some with sea views, and there's easy access to the sandy beach opposite. The hotel was taking a gap year at the time of research, so check on the website whether it has reopened. **£90**

Royal Albion 6–12 Albion St, CT10 1AN ☎ 01843 868071, ⊛ albionbroadstairs.co.uk. Grand eighteenth-century sea-facing hotel, now owned by Shepherd Neame, in a central location and with a sociable terrace bar (it's probably best to eat elsewhere, though). The 21 rooms are clean, contemporary and comfortable; the best have sea views and little balconies. **£135**

EATING   SEE MAP PAGE 96

★ **Albariño** 29 Albion St, CT10 1LX ☎ 01843 600991, ⊛ albarinorestaurant.co.uk. Authentic tapas served in a small, simple room that can get rather full. Cheese or meat platters start at £16, while the tasty tapas and sharing plates (£2.50–12.50) range from the familiar (tortilla; *gambas; padron* peppers) to the more unusual (crab on toast with pancetta; roasted cauliflower with pomegranate), all nicely washed down with a sherry or the eponymous Galician wine. Mon–Thurs 6–9.30pm, Fri 6–10pm, Sat noon–2.30pm & 5–10pm.

Beaches 49 Albion St, CT10 1NE ☎ 01843 600065, ⊛ facebook.com/beaches.broadstairs. With a surfy vibe and friendly crowd, *Beaches* is a colourful, laidback place with a casual menu of freshly made, veggie-focused food. Choose from fresh fruit smoothies, breakfasts (till noon), big salads, hefty sandwiches and more – all from £4.95. Occasional open mic poetry nights. Easter–Oct daily 9am–4pm.

Bessie's Tea Parlour 45 Albion St, CT10 1NE ☎ 01843 600189, ⊛ bessiesteaparlour.co.uk. This dinky café, all vintage crockery, fresh flowers and bunting, is the perfect spot for traditional home-baked cakes, scones, pastries and finger sandwiches accompanied by a pot of loose-leaf tea. They offer light lunches, but afternoon teas, of course, are the speciality (from £13.95), including a savoury option. Mon 10.30am–5.30pm, Tues–Sun 10am–5.30pm.

Louisa Bay Café Louisa Bay, CT10 1QE. It doesn't look much, but this beach cabin is a local hit for its fabulous bacon butties (from £4), made with the best back bacon and thick fresh bread, and eaten alfresco by the sand; the local sausages and breakfast baguettes are good too, with panini and Greek salads for a casual lunch (around £6). April–Oct daily 9.30am–4.30pm, weather permitting.

Morelli's 14 Victoria Parade, CT10 1QS ☎ 01843 862511, ⊛ morellisgelato.com/Stores/broadstairs. Deliciously retro, very pink, 1930s ice-cream parlour, whose formica,

leatherette and wicker decor, including an Italian water fountain, is a vintage lover's dream – as is the jukebox. Scoops of homemade gelato start from £2.70, with all sorts of fancy sundaes for a splurge; order a frothy cappuccino, too, for the full experience. Daily 8am–10pm.

Restaurant 54 54 Albion St, CT10 1NF ☎ 01843 867150, ⊛ restaurant54.co.uk. Fine modern British dining served in a soothing, candlelit room. Mains (£15.50–25) might include roast monkfish in a mustard-seed crust; honey-glazed duck with ruby and golden beets; or wild mushroom and pine nut strudel. Mon–Sat 6–9pm, Sun noon–3pm & 6–9pm; out of season sometimes closes Mon, Tues & Sun eve.

Tartar Frigate Harbour St, CT10 1EU ☎ 01843 862013, ⊛ tartarfrigate.co.uk. Reserve a window table if you can, and enjoy local seafood and sea views in this popular restaurant above a historic harbourside pub (see below). Classic fishy mains, including skate with capers and black butter or grilled sea bream, cost from £17.50, with meat options for non-pescatarians. Two-/three-course set menus £16.50/£19.50. Sun lunch sees things go off-piste, with a traditional four-course roast. Mon–Sat noon–1.45pm & 7–9.15pm, Sun seatings at 12.30pm & 3.30pm.

★ **Wyatt and Jones** 23–27 Harbour St, CT10 1EU ☎ 01843 865126, ⊛ wyattandjones.co.uk. This place looks great – fresh flowers, scrubbed-wood tables, soothing grey tongue-and-groove, Viking Bay views from the lower dining room – and the modern British food, all locally sourced, is fantastic. Options could include smoked mallard with pickled pear or a superb warm crab tart for starters; mains (from £14.50) might see cockle, mussel and smoked ham hock chowder or whole roasted poussin with charred sourdough sauce. Tasty breakfasts, too, whether you fancy granola with compote or crab Benedict. Wed & Thurs 9–11am, noon–3pm & 5–9pm, Fri & Sat 9–11am, noon–3pm & 5–10pm, Sun 9–11am & noon–4pm.

DRINKING AND NIGHTLIFE
SEE MAP PAGE 96

The Chapel 44 Albion St, CT10 1NE ☎ 07837 024259, ⓦ chapelbroadstairs.com. Offbeat, Brewdog-owned alehouse-cum-library in a dimly lit old chapel, with lots of nooks and crannies to curl up with an erudite or obscure used tome while you sip a local ale. Good local pub grub, too, and regular live folk/blues music. Mon–Wed & Sun noon–1am, Thurs–Sat noon–2am.

Tartar Frigate Harbour St, CT10 1EU ☎ 01843 862013, ⓦ tartarfrigate.co.uk. By the harbour, with a seafood restaurant (see above) upstairs, this eighteenth-century flint-and-weatherboard pub is a terrific place to spend an evening, especially during one of their folk jam sessions. Regular live music. Mon–Sat 11am–11pm, Sun 11am–10.30pm.

★ **The Thirty-Nine Steps Brewhouse** 11–13 Charlotte St, CT10 1LR. Friendly – and dog-friendly – pub with craft ales on tap and its own on-site brewery. The changing selection of cask ales, fruit ciders and unusual perries is always interesting, and the food is great – excellent cheese platters and homemade pork pies from just £3, much of it sourced from their deli down the road at no. 5. Occasional live acoustic music. Mon–Thurs & Sun noon–11pm, Fri & Sat noon–midnight.

ENTERTAINMENT

Palace Cinema Harbour St, CT10 1ET ☎ 01843 865726, ⓦ thepalacecinema.co.uk. Hidden away at the bottom of Harbour St, in a Grade II-listed 1911 flint building, Broadstairs' tiny indie cinema is a gem, with a programme that ranges from world cinema and silent classics to crowd-pleasers.

Ramsgate

RAMSGATE is the largest of the Thanet towns, its robust Victorian redbrick architecture and elegant Georgian squares set high on a cliff linked to the seafront by broad, sweeping ramps. Down by the bustling **harbour** (ⓦ portoframsgate.co.uk) – Britain's only royal harbour, designated after George IV visited in 1821 – a collection of cafés and bars overlooks the bobbing yachts, endowing the place, in summer at least, with a cosmopolitan buzz. The small, busy **Ramsgate Sands**, complete with children's rides and jet-ski area, lies just a short stroll away. Other sights include the **Maritime Museum**, in the old Clock House on the quayside, which chronicles local maritime history in great detail (usually Easter–Sept Tues–Sun 10am–5.30pm, but call to check; £2.50; ☎ 01843 570622, ⓦ ramsgatemaritimemuseum.org), and the excellent flea market **Petticoat Lane Emporium**, with hundreds of stalls selling arts and crafts, vintage and antiques, on Dumpton Park Drive (Mon–Sat 10am–5pm, Sun 10am–4pm; ☎ 01843 599005, ⓦ petticoatemporium.com).

Ramsgate Tunnels

Marina Esplanade, CT11 8FH • Tours Wed–Sun: April–Sept 10am, noon, 2pm & 4pm; Oct–March 10am, noon & 2pm; 1hr 30min • £7 • ☎ 01843 588123, ⓦ ramsgatetunnels.org

Many mocked when a team of engineers, championed by A.B.C. Kempe, Ramsgate's eccentric mayor, suggested in 1938 that a set of underground train tunnels could be refashioned into air-raid shelters. The scheme went ahead, however, and during a devastating air attack in August 1940 the **Ramsgate Tunnels** – equipped with bunk beds, electric lights and lavatories – saved thousands of lives. After World War II, the tunnels, which had provided safety, warmth and even a sense of makeshift, ragtag community to the many local families made homeless by the war, were closed. **Tours** today explore nearly a mile of largely empty, chilly tunnels, dotted with the odd piece of original memorabilia – though the atmosphere is palpable, it's the stories told by your guide that bring the place alive.

The Grange

St Augustine's Rd, CT11 9NY • Wed 2pm & 3pm, email or call the Landmark Trust to reserve; also occasional open days • £4 • ☎ 01628 825925, ⓦ landmarktrust.org.uk

The Grange is the former family home of **Augustus Pugin**, best known for designing the interiors of the Houses of Parliament, who lived his last ten years in Ramsgate. Designed by Pugin and built in 1843–44, the house is Gothic Revival in style and

2

filled with dark wood, rich wallpapers and decorative tiles – its emphasis on functional interior layouts over exterior symmetry marked a revolution in house design. Only some of the property is open to the tours, but you could stay here; it's rented out as self-catering accommodation (sleeping eight) by the Landmark Trust. Pugin and his family are buried at **St Augustine's church**, another of his works, and perhaps his favourite – "my own child", he called it – nearby (ⓦwww.augustine-pugin.org.uk).

ARRIVAL AND DEPARTURE   RAMSGATE

By train Ramsgate's station lies about 1.5 miles northwest of the centre, at the end of Wilfred Rd, at the top of the High St. Destinations Broadstairs (every 5–30min; 6min); Canterbury (every 20–40min; 20min); Faversham (every 10min–1hr; 40min); Herne Bay (every 10–30min; 30min); London St Pancras (every 10min–1hr; 1hr 15min–1hr 45min); London Charing Cross (hourly; 2hr 10min); London Victoria (Mon–Sat hourly; 2hr); Margate (every 5–30min; 15min); Whitstable (every 10–45min; 35min).

By bus Buses pull in at the harbour.

Destinations Broadstairs (every 5–20min; 15min); Canterbury (hourly; 45min); Margate (every 10–15min; 45min).

INFORMATION AND GETTING AROUND

Tourist information The nearest official tourist office is in Margate (see page 93) but there's an info point in Customs House, Harbour Parade (daily 10am–4pm; ☎01843 598750, ⓦvisitthanet.co.uk). Another useful resource is ⓦramsgatetown.org.

Bike rental Ken's Bike Shop in Margate (see page 93) also covers Ramsgate and Broadstairs.

ACCOMMODATION

★ **Albion House** Albion Place, CT11 8HQ ☎01843 606630, ⓦalbionhouseramsgate.co.uk. This elegant clifftop Regency house is now a boutique hotel, oozing luxurious, quirky charm. The fourteen rooms are all different, but most offer harbour views, some have balconies and each is decorated in soothing contemporary style. *Townleys*, the on-site brasserie/bar, is well worth a meal, serving anything from open crab sandwiches to sharing boards or locally reared pork chops. There's a good range of Kentish drinks, too. **£180**

The Corner House 42 Station Rd, Minster, CT12 4BZ ☎01843 823000, ⓦcornerhouserestaurants.co.uk. In the pretty old village of Minster, six miles west of Ramsgate, this corner restaurant has quietly been making a name for itself for its superb locally sourced food – Romney Marsh lamb; roasted cauliflower, tomato and Kentish blue cheese tart; Kentish gypsy tart (mains from £16). The two spacious, stylish en-suite rooms upstairs make it a very credible rural bolthole for a tour of the coast. **£90**

Royal Harbour Hotel 10–12 Nelson Crescent, CT11 9JF ☎01843 591514, ⓦroyalharbourhotel.co.uk. Welcoming hotel in two interconnecting Georgian townhouses above the harbour, with nautically themed decor and lots of personal touches. The 28 rooms range from singles and tiny "cabins" to larger options with balconies, and many have sea views; the walled herb garden, cosy lounges (with open fires) and complimentary evening cheese board are all plusses. **£100**

EATING

Flavours by Kumar 2 Effingham St, CT11 9AT ☎01843 852631, ⓦflavoursbykumar.co.uk. The food on offer at this cheery restaurant is a cut above your standard curry house, with tasty, traditional dishes executed with great flair by a chef who used to work at the famed *Ambrette* in Margate (see page 94). Mains from £10.25; the two-/three-course lunch menu, which offers lots of choice, is excellent value at £10.95/£12.95. Daily noon–2.30pm & 5.30–10pm.

Shakey Shakey 75 High St, CT11 9JF ☎01843 851248, ⓦfacebook.com/shakeyshakeyfishbar. Something slightly different – an excellent fish-and-chip shop serving a wide range of gluten-free and veggie/vegan options. Non-pescatarians can choose from such treats as tofish and chips or beefless onion pie, with perhaps a chip butty and a pickled gherkin on the side. Mon–Thurs 11am–9pm, Fri & Sat 11am–10pm, Sun noon–8pm.

Ship Shape Café 3 Military Rd, CT11 9LG ☎01843 597000. Cosy old-school caff tucked under the arches by the harbour, full of nautical bits and bobs and favoured by a seasalty crowd tucking into all-day fry-ups, mugs of strong tea and homemade puds. On a sunny day the outdoor tables make a fantastic vantage point. Daily 6.30am–5pm.

DRINKING AND NIGHTLIFE

Conqueror Ale House 4c Grange Rd, CT11 9LR ☎07890 203282, ⓦconqueror-alehouse.co.uk. Ramsgate's unassuming, award-winning micropub offers a quiet, friendly space to linger over excellent local ales and ciders. Tues–Sat 11.30am–2.30pm & 5.30–9.30pm, Sun noon–3pm.

Queen Charlotte 57 Addington St, CT11 9JJ ☎01843 570703. Cool and quirky little pub with an up-for-it, bohemian crowd, an eclectic playlist, exhibitions and events, tarot sessions, poetry and live music. It's a craft beer kind of place. Thurs 6–11pm, Fri & Sat 5pm–midnight, Sun 2–10pm.

Ramsgate Music Hall 13 Turner St, CT11 8NJ ☎01843 591815, ⓦramsgatemusichall.com. Outstanding live music venue – with room for just 125 people – with a fabulous roster of acts in all genres from the likes of Teleman to The Pop Group and Imaani.

2

East Kent

DUNGENESS

East Kent

As the closest part of Britain to the Continent, the east coast of Kent has long been a frontier. Historic evidence of its vulnerability to invasion is at every turn, from stout Tudor castles and Napoleonic fortifications to poignant memorials to World War II, when gunfire in France could be heard from across the sea and entire towns were evacuated. Proximity to the Channel has brought Kent good fortune, too – not least in medieval days, when its Cinque Ports were granted enormous privileges and wealth. In Victorian times tourism entered the fray, with Folkestone in particular attracting the great and the good to its grand seafront hotels. Things are far quieter today. Defined by its iconic White Cliffs and lacking the big tourist towns of Kent's north coast or the Sussex shore, the east coast abounds in quiet bays, rugged headlands and lonely marshes, its low-key seaside towns and villages offering plenty of laidback appeal.

Pretty, medieval **Sandwich**, once an important Cinque Port (see page 107) but now no longer even on the coast, makes a charming overnight spot, while further south the former smuggling haven of **Deal** has a certain raffish energy. Its two castles, built by Henry VIII, may be less famous than the mighty complex at Dover, but they're fascinating in their own right: Deal Castle reveals the most sophisticated military engineering of its day, while just a seafront walk away is Walmer Castle, once home to the Duke of Wellington, among other luminaries. **Dover** – Britain's principal cross-Channel port, a mere 21 miles from mainland Europe – is not immensely appealing in itself but it does provide a springboard for the magnificent **Dover Castle**, and for the stupendous chalk banks of the **White Cliffs**, which offer glorious walks. South of Dover lies **Folkestone**, a plucky resort valiantly re-energizing itself as an arts destination, and **Romney Marsh**, with the eerie, arty shingle headland of **Dungeness** at their southernmost tip.

The East Kent coast offers outstanding walking and cycling. The coastal stretch between Folkestone and Dover forms part of the North Downs Way, while the section of the Saxon Shore Way between Deal and Dover is one of the most picturesque on the entire path. **The Warren**, Folkestone's very own stretch of white cliff, offers dramatic vistas and a broad, fossil-studded beach, while **Samphire Hoe**, an incongruous knob of land created from spoil during construction of the Channel Tunnel, is an intriguing place for a stroll.

Sandwich and around

SANDWICH, on the River Stour six miles north of Deal, is one of the best-preserved medieval towns in England. It might seem hard to believe today, but this quaint little place was a major commercial port, chief among the Cinque Ports (see page 107), until the Stour started silting up in the 1500s; unlike at other former harbour inlets, however, the **river** hasn't vanished completely and still flows through town, its grassy, willow-lined banks adding to the sleepy charm.

Though the **Secret Gardens** are the biggest formal attraction, it's a pleasure simply to wander around Sandwich, with its crooked half-timbered buildings, narrow lanes, peaceful quayside and riverside path. Shops are few, and very low-key, while historical

Highlights

❶ **Sandwich** With its sleepy quayside and glorious Edwin Lutyens gardens, its nature reserves and its medieval streets, this little town is a delight. See page 104

❷ **Deal** The quiet seaside town of Deal boasts a proud maritime history, two Tudor castles, an atmospheric conservation area, great walking and some superb places to stay and eat. See page 109

❸ **Dover Castle** A visit to Dover's mighty castle, which dominates the skyline for miles around and spans Roman remains to World War II bunkers, could fill an entire day. See page 114

❹ **White Cliffs of Dover** An exhilarating

walk along these imposing white cliffs is an unmissable East Kent experience. See page 116

❺ **The Warren** Wildlife-rich and geologically fascinating, the cliffs and beach of the Warren have a rugged, handsome beauty. See page 126

❻ **Rocksalt, Folkestone** This glamorous harbourside restaurant, right on the water, is just one of the many good reasons to visit the up-and-coming town of Folkestone. See page 126

❼ **Prospect Cottage, Dungeness** Pay tribute to the artistic vision of late filmmaker Derek Jarman at his seaside garden, gazing out from the windswept shingle of Dungeness. See page 131

HIGHLIGHTS ARE MARKED ON THE MAP ON PAGE 106

markers relate intriguing snippets. Just outside town lie a handful of **nature reserves** and the remains of **Richborough Roman Fort**, which you can reach by boat. It's also a major destination for **golfers** – the **Royal St George's** course fringes the coast to the east, with the Prince's Golf Club to the north and the Royal Cinque Ports Club a mile or so south.

Secret Gardens of Sandwich

Knightrider St, CT13 9EW • Daily 10am–5pm • Jan & Dec free; Feb–Nov £8.50; free to RHS members on Mon • ☏ 01304 619919, ⓦ the-salutation.com/the-gardens

Designed in 1912 by Sir Edwin Lutyens and heavily influenced by his famous gardening partner Gertrude Jekyll, the 3.5-acre **Secret Gardens of Sandwich** were restored in 2007 after being abandoned to the wilderness for 25 years. While they largely retain the design of the original gardens, a few new features, including a tropical border, have been added; the lake, with its little island, dates back to the 1970s. It's a tranquil spot, with plenty of benches and secluded nooks, and a perfectly nice place simply to wander. The informal, country-garden style beautifully offsets the classical lines of the 1911 house (now a private residence and hotel, home to Steph and Dom of TV's *Gogglebox* fame), with bold, splashy plantings, unexpected combinations and discrete areas linked by winding brick paths.

HIGHLIGHTS

1. Sandwich
2. Deal
3. Dover Castle
4. White Cliffs of Dover
5. The Warren
6. Rocksalt, Folkestone
7. Prospect Cottage, Dungeness

EAST KENT

> **THE CINQUE PORTS**
>
> In 1278 Dover, Hythe, Sandwich, Romney and Hastings – already part of a long-established but unofficial confederation of defensive coastal settlements – were formalized under a charter by Edward I as the **Cinque Ports** (pronounced "sink", despite the name's French origin). In return for providing England with maritime support, chiefly in the transportation of troops and supplies during times of war, the five ports were granted trading privileges and other liberties – including self-government, exemption from taxes and tolls and "possession of goods thrown overboard" – that enabled them to prosper while neighbouring ports struggled. Some benefitted during peacetime, too, boosting their wealth by such nefarious activities as piracy and smuggling.
>
> Rye, Winchelsea and seven other **"limb" ports** on the southeast coast were later added to the confederation. The ports' privileges were eventually revoked in 1685; their maritime services had become increasingly unnecessary after Henry VIII had founded a professional navy and, due to a shifting coastline, several of their harbours had silted up anyway, stranding some of them miles inland. Today, of all the Cinque Ports only Dover is still a major working port.

3

The quayside

Sandwich's riverfront **quayside**, peaceful today, was once the heart of a great medieval port, when the wide river estuary known as Sandwich Haven lapped at its banks. While the Haven began silting up in the sixteenth century, and the sea is now miles away, the waterfront gives the place a breezily nautical atmosphere, with small boats moored by the toll bridge, open countryside stretching out across the river and the cry of seagulls raking the air. You may be lucky enough to find **boat trips** (see page 108) running from the toll bridge over the Stour – note the sixteenth-century **Barbican**, a stone gateway decorated with chequerwork, where tolls were once collected – down to the estuary to spot seals and birds. You can also **walk to Sandwich Bay** from the quayside, following the river and heading across the Royal St George's Golf Course to the sea – it's just a couple of miles, depending on the path you take.

The Guildhall

Cattle Market, CT13 9AH • Museum Wed–Sun 10am–4pm • Free • ☎ 01304 617197, ☮ sandwichtowncouncil.gov.uk/guildhall or ☮ sandwichguildhallmuseum.co.uk

At the centre of Sandwich, the handsome sixteenth-century **Guildhall** houses the tourist office (see page 108), various venerable council chambers, and an interesting **museum** recounting the history of the town. For centuries, the open square around it hosted a busy cattle market; today there's a small market every Thursday and Saturday morning.

Royal St George's Golf Course

1.5 miles east of Sandwich, CT13 9PB • Visitors will need to produce evidence of a handicap of 18 or below • ☎ 01304 613090, ☮ royalstgeorges.com

Sandwich is separated from the sandy beaches of Sandwich Bay by the **Royal St George's Golf Course**, perhaps the finest links course in England. Set in the undulating dunes, and boasting the deepest bunker in championship golf (on its fourth hole), St George's was established in 1887 and has been a venue for the British Open fifteen times since 1894 – including in 2020. Laid out in sympathy with its natural surroundings, it's a stunning spot, with wonderful views of the sea.

Richborough Roman Fort and Amphitheatre

Richborough Rd, Pegwell Bay, CT13 9JW • April–Sept daily 10am–6pm; Oct daily 10am–5pm; Nov–March Sat & Sun 10am–4pm • £6.80; EH • Parking free • ☎ 01304 612013, ☮ www.english-heritage.org.uk/visit/places/richborough-roman-fort-and-amphitheatre

> ## THE NOBLE SANDWICH
>
> Perhaps surprisingly, Sandwich makes little of what might seem an obvious claim to fame. The town's eponymous snack was created, so the story goes, in 1762, by John Montagu, the fourth Earl of Sandwich. Absorbed in a game of cards and on a winning streak, the peckish earl ate his beef between two bits of bread so as to be able to focus on the game, thus inadvertently inventing what went on to become the nation's favourite lunchtime staple. However, as this fabled event didn't happen in Sandwich, and as the earl's connections with the place were largely limited to his name, it seems fair enough that the town resolutely ignores any possible punning potential.

Marooned in the marshy lands that fringe Pegwell Bay, two miles northwest of Sandwich, stand the remains of **Richborough Roman Fort and Amphitheatre**, one of the earliest coastal strongholds built by the Romans. Originally a military garrison, the fort developed into first a civilian town and then a major port. Though its sheer size, and its lonely setting, is evocative – the coast that it guarded is now a couple of miles distant – Richborough's historical significance outshines its appearance. All that can be seen within the huge and well-preserved Roman walls are the remains of an early Saxon church and a little museum; nearby, a large hollow marks the site of the third-century amphitheatre.

Sandwich and Pegwell Bay Nature Reserve

Three miles north of Sandwich, off the A256, CT12 5JB · Daily 8.30am–7pm (or dusk if sooner) · Free · ☎ 01622 3577825, ⓦ kentwildlifetrust.org.uk/nature-reserves/sandwich-and-pegwell-bay

The broad expanse of the 615-hectare **Sandwich and Pegwell Bay Nature Reserve**, on the River Stour estuary between Sandwich and Ramsgate, is a superb spot for birdwatchers, boasting a wide variety of seashore habitats including tidal mudflats, shingle beach, dunes, saltmarsh, chalk cliffs and coastal scrubland. The best time to view the wading birds is in winter, or during the spring and autumn migrations, but even in summer you'll spot redshank, shelduck and oystercatchers, along with ringed plovers and little tern. The reserve is on the Viking Coastal cycling trail and the Saxon Shore Way (see page 29).

ARRIVAL AND DEPARTURE

SANDWICH AND AROUND

By train Sandwich station is off St George's Rd, from where it's a 10min walk north to the town centre and the quay.
Destinations Deal (every 30min–1hr; 6min); Dover (every 30min–1hr; 25min); Ramsgate (hourly; 15min).

By bus Buses pull in and depart from outside the Guildhall.
Destinations Canterbury (every 20min–1hr; 45min); Deal (every 20min–1hr; 25–35min); Dover (every 45min–1hr; 45min–1hr); Ramsgate (hourly; 45min–1hr).

INFORMATION AND TOURS

Tourist office The Guildhall (daily: Jan–March, Nov & Dec 10am–4pm; April, May, Sept & Oct 10am–5pm; June–Aug 10am–6pm; ☎ 01304 617197, ⓦ sandwichtowncouncil. gov.uk or ⓦ whitecliffscountry.org.uk).

River tours Sandwich Riverbus boats, by the toll bridge, have historically offered seal-spotting jaunts in the estuary

(30min–1hr) and longer wildlife-spotting trips (2hr), along with a ferry service to Richborough Roman Fort (1hr). There has been some disruption to the service in recent years, however, so you'll need to text, email or call to discuss options and reserve (☎ 07958 376183, ✉ sandriverbus@ gmail.com, ⓦ sandwichriverbus.co.uk).

ACCOMMODATION

Bell Hotel The Quay, CT13 9EF ☎ 01304 613388, ⓦ bellhotelsandwich.co.uk. Sandwich's largest hotel is a rambling hostelry that has stood on this site since Tudor times; the present building is largely Edwardian. Rooms are comfy, in an uncontroversial, upscale style; the best (£180–215) overlook the quayside and the Stour, and some even have balconies. There's a bar, and an in-house restaurant

serving modern European food (mains from £13). Minimum two nights at weekends June–Sept. __£130__

Kings Arms Strand St, CT13 9HN ☎ 01304 617330, ⓦ kingsarms-sandwich.co.uk. No surprises at this old pub, all carpets, dark wood and horse brasses, with a roaring fire in winter – it's geared up for eating (steaks, pies, curries, burgers), but there's a pretty garden in summer for when you just fancy a pint. Upstairs is a selection of plain, comfortable en-suite rooms; not fancy but good value, with a tasty full English breakfast included. **£85**

Molland Manor House Molland Lane, Ash, CT3 2JB ☎01304 814210, 🌐mollandhouse.co.uk. The history is palpable in this thirteenth-century manor, full of original features, 3 miles west of Sandwich. It's family friendly, with kind hosts and a big garden with swings and a slide; you'll be welcomed with a delicious cream tea and find lots of little luxuries. Six of the seven B&B rooms are en suite, and the other has a private bathroom. All are attractive, light and comfortable. Usually two nights minimum March–Oct, but it's worth checking if they have last-minute availability. **£125**

EATING

George and Dragon 24 Fisher St, CT13 9EJ ☎01304 614194, 🌐georgeanddragonsandwich.com. A fifteenth-century inn and popular, unpretentious gastropub, with great, good-value food, friendly staff, good ales, roaring real fires in winter and a courtyard garden for alfresco summer dining. The menu changes regularly, but dressed crab with new potato salad (£15) or steak and chips (£12) are typical. Booking advised in the evening. Mon–Sat 11am–11pm, Sun 11am–6pm.

Hop and Huffkin 10 New St, CT13 9AB ☎01304 448560, 🌐hopandhuffkin.co.uk. Locally sourced food, wines and ales served in a good-looking contemporary dining room or a courtyard. Many of the evening mains (£15–18) have a definite Mediterranean flavour – paella, sea bass with lentil cazuela, roast chicken with manchego – while lunch (£12–14) might include burger in a huffkin bap, lamb's liver, fisherman's pie or sausage and mash. Monthly live music. Mon–Sat 10am–10.30pm, Sun 10am–10pm.

Luigi's 3 The Quay, CT13 9EN ☎01304 615297, 🌐luigis restaurant.org. This convivial Italian restaurant serves good, old-school Italian food to an appreciative crowd. Mains (from £10) include all the classics done well, from oven-baked pasta to calzone and saltimbocca. Mon 6–10pm, Tues–Sat noon–2.30pm & 6–10pm, Sun noon–9pm.

No Name 1 No Name St, CT13 9AJ ☎01304 612626, 🌐nonameshop.co.uk. For picnic supplies, including baguettes, cheeses and artisan bread, look no further than this excellent French deli near the Guildhall. You can also eat in, choosing from a blackboard menu of light dishes – tartines, soups, quiches – with heartier mains such as baked mussels, duck confit and thyme-roasted chicken in the bistro upstairs. Dishes around £8–14. There's another branch in Deal (see page 113). Mon–Sat 8am–5pm, Sun 9am–4pm.

Deal

The low-key seaside town of **DEAL**, six miles southeast of Sandwich, is an appealing place, with a broad, steeply shelving shingle **beach** backed by a jumble of faded Georgian townhouses, a picturesque **old town** redolent with maritime history, and a striking concrete **pier** lined with hopeful anglers casting their lines. Henry VIII's two seafront **castles**, linked by a seaside path on the Saxon Shore Way, are the main attractions, along with walks and cycle rides along the coast, but above all Deal is a place to simply potter around. Its relaxed vibe and strong community spirit give it a likeable air of confidence; this, along with a very good selection of **restaurants** and B&Bs, makes it an increasingly popular weekend destination.

Brief history

It was on this stretch of coast that, in 55 BC, **Julius Caesar**, daunted by the vision

DEAL

■ **ACCOMMODATION**
Bear's Well	1
Garden Cottage/ Greenhouse Apartment	4
Number One B&B	3
Royal Hotel	2

0   200
yards

N

Deal Pier

● **EATING**
81 Beach St	5
Black Douglas Coffee House	4
Deal Pier Kitchen	6
Frog and Scot	3
No Name	2
Victuals & Co	1
Whits of Walmer	7

■ **DRINKING & NIGHTLIFE**
The Bohemian	3
The Just Reproach	2
The Lighthouse	5
Ship Inn	1
Zetland Arms	4

▼ 4, 5, 7, Paddling Pool, Bandstand & Walmer Castle

of Dover's colossal white cliffs further up the shore, first landed in Britain. **Henry VIII** built three castles in the area, compact coastal fortresses designed to scare off the Spanish and the French; having been named a **limb port** of the Cinque Ports in the thirteenth century (see page 107), by Elizabethan times Deal was one of the most important ports in the country. It was renowned for its skilled boatbuilders and courageous sailors – men able to navigate the perilous offshore Goodwin Sands, where countless ships had met their doom, to reach safe harbour in the "Downs" anchorage, the sheltered waters closer to land – and by the eighteenth century had become a notorious centre for smuggling. Privateering boosted the local economy until well into the Victorian era.

The seafront

At first glance, Deal's **seafront** promenade may not be the best advertisement for the town. Though handsome, many of its buildings have become a little shabby – on the outside at least – and lack the picture-postcard appeal of the sprucer old-town lanes just inland. That said, it has charm, with small, independent hotels and restaurants far outnumbering the few amusement arcades and tourist shops; **Beach Street**, the parade of pastel-painted Georgian and Victorian buildings north of the pier, is its prettiest stretch.

Deal beach

The **beach** itself is a long, uninterrupted shingle swathe, almost entirely uncommercialized and perfect for bracing walks. Steeply shelving, it's also a popular spot for sea fishing and even, for the very bold, a circulation-zapping swim. The wide coastal path alongside, suitable for walkers and cyclists, takes you past a picturesque ensemble of fishing boats, tatty lobster pots and chalky white fishing huts via **Walmer Castle**, the largest of Henry's local coastal defences, to the laidback little village of **Kingsdown**, at the edge of the White Cliffs.

Deal Pier

Built in 1957, **Deal Pier** is almost defiantly unprepossessing, a brutal concrete affair that replaced a more decorative Victorian iron pleasure pier destroyed by a run-in with a Dutch merchant ship in 1940. You can't leave town without walking its length – all 1026ft of it – however; lacking amusement arcades or end-of-the-pier entertainments, it has its own appeal, offering splendid views back over the town and a good café, *Deal Pier Kitchen*, at the end (see page 113). It's also a renowned spot for **fishing**, the water yielding bass, ray, smooth hound, dogfish and mackerel in summer, and codling, whiting and flatfish in winter.

Timeball Tower

Victoria Parade, CT14 7BP • 11.30am–4.30pm: May Sat & Sun; June–Sept Wed–Sun • £3 • ☎ 01304 362444, ⚲ dealtimeball.co.uk

Facing the sea, Deal's **Timeball Tower** was used, in the early nineteenth century, as a semaphore tower in an attempt to monitor local smuggling activity. Abandoned in 1842, the tower was transformed by the addition of a timeball in 1855; the ball dropped down a pole on the roof at exactly 1pm in summer, providing an accurate time check for ships at sea attempting to navigate the offshore Downs. Although the coming of radio put paid to that, the timeball still drops regularly in summer, and at midnight on New Year's Eve. Inside, you can see an array of exhibits relating to communications and signalling, including rare timepieces, telescopes and ingenious Victorian telegraph mechanisms.

The old town

Middle Street is the prettiest road in Deal's **old town**, its cute pastel cottages, elegant Georgian houses and narrow alleys making perfect photo opportunities. *Carry On* fans should stop by no. 117, a compact cottage with a blue plaque commemorating Charles Hawtrey, who by all accounts lived out his later years here in eccentric and alcoholic promiscuity. Middle Street's picturesque tranquillity belies the fact that this was the de facto high road for the town's smugglers and pirates – the northern end, marked by the small Alfred Square, was a particularly nefarious stretch, and it's said that a network of secret tunnels still lies beneath the street today.

Deal's lively **High Street** has more character than many of its kind; the best shops are to be found in its old town stretch, with a scattering of independent boutiques, delis, vintage stores and coffee shops north of Broad Street. Off the High Street, at 22 St George's Rd, the **Deal Maritime and Local History Museum** (April, May, Sept & Oct Tues–Fri 2–4.30pm, Sat 11am–4.30pm, Sun noon–4pm; June–Aug Tues–Sat 11am–4.30pm, Sun noon–4pm; £3 [no cards]; ⊚dealmuseum.co.uk) illustrates the town's social and seafaring history.

Deal Castle

Marine Rd, CT14 7BA • March Wed–Sun 10am–4pm; April–Sept daily 10am–6pm; Oct daily 10am–5pm; Nov–Feb Sat & Sun 10am–4pm • £7.60; EH • Parking free for members • ☎ 01304 372762, ⊚ www.english-heritage.org.uk/visit/places/deal-castle • Buses #12, #13, #13A, #14, #80A, #82, #82A and #93

Diminutive **Deal Castle**, at the south end of town, is one of the most striking of Henry VIII's forts. Hastily built in 1539–40, along with Sandown Castle (now destroyed) to the north and Walmer Castle to the south, as part of a chain of coastal defences against potential invaders – and in particular, Henry's French and Spanish Catholic enemies – this was a castle designed to face battle. Its distinctive **shape**, which viewed from the air looks like a Tudor rose, has less to do with aesthetics than sophisticated military engineering: squat rounded walls were effective at deflecting cannonballs and provided less surface area to be hit. Inside the six outer bastions, themselves mounted with heavy guns, a second set of six semicircular inner bastions protected the cylindrical central keep, its own 14ft-thick walls providing stout defence.

Perhaps disappointingly, after all this effort, the castle never did see serious fighting, though there was a brief skirmish during the Civil War. The castle was garrisoned one last time during the Napoleonic Wars, but again little fighting actually took place.

Self-guided **audio tours** outline every detail of the state-of-the-art military design. Bare rooms reveal how the castle changed over the years and give a good sense of how the soldiers lived; check out the claustrophobic privies with their deep, dark wells. Descending through gloomy cobbled passageways brings you to the basement and the Rounds, a subterranean warren equipped with yet more cannon, facing potential enemies across the dry moat.

Walmer Castle

Kingsdown Rd, 1 mile south of Deal, CT14 7LJ • Mid-Feb to March Wed–Sun 10am–4pm; April–Sept daily 10am–6pm; Oct daily 10am–5pm; Nov to mid-Feb Sat & Sun 10am–4pm • £12.20; EH • Parking free for members (weather dependent) • ☎ 01304 364288, ⊚ www.english-heritage.org.uk/visit/places/walmer-castle-and-gardens • Hourly buses (#82/#82A) from Deal; also accessible on foot along the seafront (30min) or from Walmer train station, a mile away; in addition to the on-site parking there's pay-and-display public parking opposite the entrance

The southernmost of Henry VIII's trio of "Castles in the Downs", **Walmer Castle** is another rotund Tudor-rose-shaped affair, built to protect the coast from its enemies across the Channel. Like Sandown Castle (which no longer stands) and its neighbour at Deal, Walmer saw little fighting; unlike those, however, it changed use when it became the official residence of the Lords Warden of the Cinque Ports in 1708 (which it still remains, though the title itself is now strictly ceremonial).

Adapted over the years by its various residents, today the castle resembles a heavily fortified **stately home** more than a military stronghold. The rooms – many of them fan-shaped, due to the unusual circular walls – are filled with the memorabilia of previous Lords Warden, including the late Queen Mother and Winston Churchill. Walmer is most associated, however, with the **Duke of Wellington**, who was given the post of Lord Warden in 1828. In his bedroom you can see his simple camp bed, with its original bedding, and the armchair in which he died in 1852. The Iron Duke lay in state in this room for two months before being buried at St Paul's Cathedral; in the two days before his body was taken to London, some nine thousand local mourners trooped past to pay their respects. Other Wellington memorabilia includes his sunken bronze death mask and a pair of original leather "Wellington" boots, designed by the Duke after the Battle of Waterloo to be cut lower than the usual boot and thus easier to wear.

The castle's eight acres of terraced **gardens** are as much a draw as the property itself. Begun by Lord Warden William Pitt in 1792, with help from his famous and eccentric adventuress niece, **Lady Hester Stanhope**, they offer all manner of walks – including some wonderful woodland trails – and picnic spots. Make a beeline for the Broadwalk, where colourful, cottage-garden-style borders are backed by a stunning yew "cloud" hedge, its surreal bulging undulations caused by a period of neglect during and after World War II.

ARRIVAL AND INFORMATION   DEAL

By train The station is on Queen St, a 10min walk from the sea.

Destinations Dover (every 15min–1hr; 15min); Ramsgate (every 30min–1hr; 20min); Sandwich (every 30min–1hr; 6min); Walmer (every 30min–1hr; 3min).

By bus Buses run from South St and Queen St near each other in the town centre.

Destinations Canterbury (hourly; 1hr 15min); Dover (every 30min–1hr; 45min); St Margaret's-at-Cliffe (hourly;

30min); Sandwich (every 20min–1hr; 25–35min); Walmer (every 15min–1hr; 15–30min).

By bike There are lots of good cycling paths around Deal. For rental – including kids' bikes and tagalongs – try Mike's Bikes, Hut 55 on the beach just off Marine Rd in Walmer (£18/day for an adult; ☎07484 727755, ✆mikesbikesdeal.com).

Tourist office Town Hall, High St (Mon–Thurs 10am–1pm, Fri 9.30am–12.30pm; ☎01304 369576, ✆deal.gov.uk or ✆whitecliffscountry.org.uk).

ACCOMMODATION   SEE MAP PAGE 109

Bear's Well 10 St George's Rd, CT14 6BA ☎01304 694144, ✆bearswell.co.uk. In a peaceful Old Town spot near the High St and the sea, this is an airy boutique B&B in a gorgeous Georgian home. The three en-suite rooms are comfortable and uncluttered, with views of the church or pretty back garden, and the breakfasts, made using local produce, are great. **£120**

Garden Cottage/Greenhouse Apartment Walmer Castle, Walmer, CT14 7LJ ☎0370 333 1187, ✆www.english-heritage.org.uk/visit/holiday-cottages/find-a-holiday-cottage/garden-cottage or ✆www.english-heritage.org.uk/visit/holiday-cottages/find-a-holiday-cottage/greenhouse-apartment. Breaks of three, four or seven nights in these self-catering options, both of which sleep four, in the castle grounds. In a gorgeous spot overlooking the eighteenth-century kitchen garden, both are decorated in an inoffensive contemporary style.

Minimum three-night stay; nightly rate lower for longer stays. Garden cottage **£280**; greenhouse apartment **£345**

Number One B&B 1 Ranelagh Rd, CT14 7BG ☎01304 364459, ✆numberonebandb.co.uk. Occupying a handsome Victorian townhouse, this high-quality B&B is near Deal Castle and just minutes from the beach. The four rooms each have a dash of design flair, with luxurious extras including bathrobes and coffee makers. Two-night minimum stay at weekends. **£110**

Royal Hotel Beach St, CT14 6JD ☎01304 375555, ✆theroyalhotel.com. Things have quietened down since Admiral Nelson scandalized society by entertaining Lady Hamilton in his bedchamber here, but there's still a thrill to staying a pebble's throw from the shingle beach – especially if you get one of the sea-facing rooms with large balconies. Rates include a breakfast buffet, and there's a bar and bistro on site. **£160**

EATING   SEE MAP PAGE 109

81 Beach St 81 Beach St, CT14 6JB ☎01304 368136, ✆81beachstreet.co.uk. Contemporary brasserie with sea views and a changing fusion menu. Dinner (small plates from £6, mains £12–28) might include homemade BBQ vegan burgers or whole baked catch of the day with tarragon-crushed potatoes. Daily noon–5pm & 5.45–10pm.

Black Douglas Coffee House 83 Beach St, CT14 6JB ☎01304 365486, ✆facebook.com/pg/blackdouglas coffeehouse. Boho seafront place, with a cosy, cluttered interior and a focus on locally sourced homemade food. While you can pop in for coffee and cake, they specialize in eggy breakfasts (eggs with chorizo, for example; £5–12).

There's lunch (maybe a feta, houmous and roast beetroot salad), too, and a short supper menu on Fri and Sat (mains £14–24). Mon 10am–3.30pm, Fri 10am–3.30pm & 7.30–11pm, Sat 9.30am–4pm & 7.30–11pm, Sun 10am–3pm.

Deal Pier Kitchen Deal Pier, CT14 6HX ☎01304 368228, ⓦfacebook.com/dealpierkitchen. With its picture windows and pared-down timber decor, perched over the water like a ship's lookout, *DPK* is a lively pier caff with panache. Dog- and family-friendly, it's particularly good for brunch (£5–9.50), when fishermen, laptop-toting freelancers and tourists alike tuck into eggs Benedict, pancakes, vegan Full Englishes and kedgeree. The crowd-pleasing lunch menu lists fish-finger sandwiches and mussels with chips. Various themed evenings and events. Daily 9am–5pm.

★ **Frog and Scot** 86 High St, CT14 6EG ☎01304 379444, ⓦfrogandscot.co.uk. The Scottish/French couple who own this bijou bistro have created a delightful neighbourhood haven where happy locals linger over genuinely delicious, authentic French dishes, from warm pork rillettes with honey mustard to lobster mayonnaise with frites or roast celeriac with beluga lentils, and a fabulous wine list. Dinner mains from £16; lunchtime sees a variety of two- and three-course lunch menus (£14.95/£17.95/£23.95/£26.95) and a dish of the day, with a glass of wine, for £10. Wed–Sat noon–2.30pm & 6–9.30pm, Sun noon–2.30pm.

No Name 110 High St, CT14 6EE ☎01304 375100, ⓦnonameshop.co.uk. This excellent French deli and coffee shop is a good place to stock up on baguettes, cheese, hams and olives for an upmarket beach picnic. There's another branch in Sandwich (see page 109). Mon–Thurs 8.30am–5pm, Fri & Sat 8.30am–4.30pm.

Victuals & Co 2 St George's Passage, CT14 6TA ☎01304 374389, ⓦvictualsandco.com. Tucked away in a lane off the High St, this relaxed, colourful restaurant is a reliable foodie choice for its unfussy fine dining. Short menus (two-/three-course lunch £22/£25; dinner mains from £17) might include such dishes as pan-fried cod with salsa verde, roasted sweet potato with crispy chickpeas and a variety of steaks. Wed & Thurs 6–8.30pm, Fri noon–2pm & 6–9.30pm, Sat 12.30–2.30pm & 6–8.45pm, Sun 12.30–2.30pm & 5.30–7.30pm.

Whits of Walmer 61 The Strand, Walmer, CT14 7DP ☎01304 368881, ⓦwhits.co.uk. Super-fresh fish and seafood, classically prepared – tuna millefeuille with local crab, mango and apple, perhaps, followed by crisp potato-crusted brill on braised baby leeks. There's a garden for alfresco dining. Mains from £19.50. Thurs–Sat 6–9pm (last seating), Sun 12.30–3.30pm (last seating).

DRINKING AND NIGHTLIFE SEE MAP PAGE 109

The Bohemian 47 Beach St, CT14 6HY ☎01304 361939, ⓦthebohemian.co.uk. The seafront "Boho" attracts a lively crowd with its mishmash decor – vintage mirrors, quirky art, retro bits and bobs – along with its suntrap garden and its long list of gins, real ales and bottled beers. Chunky sandwiches, gastropub pub grub and pizza are on offer, too (£5–167). Mon & Tues 11am–midnight, Wed 11am–1am, Thurs–Sat 11am–2am, Sun 10am–11.30pm; kitchen Mon–Fri 11am–3pm & 6–9pm, Sat noon–2pm & 6–9pm, Sun noon–4pm.

★ **The Just Reproach** 14 King St, CT14 6HX. With no phone or website, this dinky, dog-friendly micropub offers British microbrews, local cider and wines in a snug, bare-bones room livened up with retro memorabilia, and with no TV, music or digital devices to interrupt the conversation. Good, simple food – pickled onions, pork pies and cheese platters – too. Mon–Thurs noon–2pm & 5–9pm, Fri noon–2pm & 5–11pm, Sat noon–11pm, Sun noon–4pm.

The Lighthouse 50 The Strand, Walmer, CT14 7DX ☎01304 366031, ⓦthelighthousedeal.co.uk. Friendly, community-minded music pub with an eclectic range of live music (folk to Klezmer), DJ nights (Northern Soul to Disco), poetry and film screenings. Generally Thurs–Sun & occasionally other nights.

Ship Inn 141 Middle St, CT14 6JZ ☎01304 372222. Venerable little old-town pub, popular with a local and laidback crowd enjoying a quiet pint, with a gorgeous early nineteenth-century interior and a walled garden. Lots of cask ales on offer. No cards. Mon–Sat 11am–midnight, Sun noon–midnight.

Zetland Arms Wellington Parade, Kingsdown, CT14 8AF ☎01304 370114, ⓦzetlandarms.co.uk. Around a 45min walk from Deal along the beach, the *Zetland* is a favourite stop for walkers and cyclists, perched on shingle and with great views of the White Cliffs. Ales come from Shepherd Neame, and there's pub grub (from £9), too. Mon–Sat 10am–11.30pm, Sun 10am–10.30pm.

ENTERTAINMENT

The well-regarded **Deal Music and the Arts** festival (usually first fortnight of July; ⓦdealmusicandarts.com) is at the highbrow end of the scale. A variety of venues – as far afield as Sandwich, Dover and Margate – host chamber music, opera, classical music, modern dance and jazz from around the world, with big names, young performers, and a programme of talks and events.

Astor Community Theatre 20 Stanhope Rd, CT14 6AB ☎01304 370220, ⓦtheastor.org. A lively arts centre in a handsome old Edwardian theatre, hosting live music – local and low-key national bands – literary events, rep theatre, comedy, and the best world movies and classic films.

Dover and around

Given its importance as a travel hub – it's among the busiest ferry ports in Europe – **DOVER** is surprisingly small. Badly bombed during World War II, the town centre is unprepossessing, with just a few low-key attractions; the seafront is equally unassuming. The main attractions are **Dover Castle**, looming proudly above town and clearly visible from the sea, and just a walk along the legendary **White Cliffs**.

Dover Castle

Castle Hill, CT16 1HU • Mid-Feb to March Wed–Sun 10am–4pm; April–July & Sept daily 10am–6pm; Aug daily 9.30am–6pm; Oct daily 10am–5pm; Nov to mid-Feb Sat & Sun 10am–4pm; last entry 1hr before closing • £20.90, under-16s £12.50; EH • Parking free • ☏ 0370 333 1181, ⓦ www.english-heritage.org.uk/visit/places/dover-castle • Stagecoach buses from the centre of Dover #15, #15X, #80, #80A & #93 (hourly; 20min)

No historical stone is left unturned at **Dover Castle**, an astonishingly imposing defensive complex that has protected the English coast for more than two thousand years. A castle stood here as early as 1068, when **William the Conqueror**, following the Battle of Hastings, built over the earthworks of an Iron Age hillfort; a century later, the **Normans** constructed the handsome keep that now presides over the heart of the complex. The grounds also include a **Roman lighthouse**, a **Saxon church** and all manner of later additions, including tunnels built in the Napoleonic Wars and World War I signal stations. Indeed, the castle was in continuous use as some sort of military installation right up to the 1980s, and its network of **tunnels**, used during World War II, is a huge attraction in its own right. A more recent addition is the castle's **Bunker Escape Room**, set during the Cold War (hours vary; check website; from £44; ☏ 01304 211067).

Ideally you should allow a **full day** for a thorough visit, including time for a battlement walk (which takes around 1hr in total); if time is short, head first to Operation Dynamo, where long queues build up as the day proceeds, before making your way to the Great Tower.

Operation Dynamo: Rescue from Dunkirk

Tours leave every 15–20min; 50min

One of Dover Castle's most popular attractions is its network of **secret wartime tunnels**, dug during the Napoleonic Wars and extended during World War II. It was from these claustrophobic bunkers in 1940 that Vice Admiral Ramsay set out the plans for **Operation Dynamo**, the evacuation of Dunkirk, which successfully brought back some 330,000 stranded British and Allied troops from the Continent, helped by a small flotilla of local fishing and pleasure boats – the "little ships" – sailed by civilians. Defined by J.B. Priestley as "so absurd yet so grand and gallant that you hardly know whether to laugh or cry", Dunkirk marked a turning point in the war. Though "wars are not won by evacuations", as Churchill put it – and it was clear that the need to evacuate marked a serious defeat – a new determination to win, the so-called "Dunkirk Spirit", was born.

Operation Dynamo tunnel **tours** are lively and affecting affairs. Guides lead groups through the dark warrens while dramatic vox pops, sound effects and film footage flickering across crumbling tunnel walls shed light on the build-up to the war and how the evacuation came about. The detail is impeccable, from the graffiti on the walls, scrawled over a period of two hundred years, to the reconstructed chart rooms and repeater stations, eerily alive with the sounds of ringing phones and crackling messages.

The Underground Hospital

Tours leave roughly every 30min; 20min

In 1941–42, a new network of tunnels was hurriedly built beneath the castle to create a medical dressing station where patients, most of them from the castle garrison, could be bandaged and stabilized before being transferred to hospitals with better facilities. Billed as a walkthrough experience, tours of the **Underground Hospital** are impressionistic affairs, with rather less hard information than the Operation Dynamo tours next door. Loosely following the journey of a fictitious injured pilot brought to the hospital in 1943, you stride (at quite a pace) through corridors and wards, mess rooms and dorms, all filled with surgical instruments and the accoutrements of hospital life, as a somewhat surreal soundtrack booms around you. Dark, stuffy and claustrophobic, the tunnels can feel nightmarish as lights flicker and bombs rumble, spectral patients groan and shadowy nurses gossip; eerily, in the operating theatre, as you hear (invisible) doctors talking around their (invisible) patient, the smell of surgical spirit is overpowering.

The Great Tower

At the heart of Dover Castle is the inner bailey and the amazingly well-preserved **Great Tower**. Built by Henry II as a palace and a residence to welcome important visitors – including those on pilgrimage to Canterbury – this was the last and finest of the enormous rectangular royal towers that had begun with the Tower of London a century earlier. Despite subsequent modernization, notably under Edward IV and in the seventeenth century, it remains one of the best-preserved medieval royal towers in existence.

   Inside the tower itself, a series of rooms linked by steep and narrow stone staircases have been painstakingly re-created to look ready to receive Philip, Count of Flanders, in 1186. Everything from the pots and pans in the kitchen to the chess set and richly coloured furniture and wall hangings in the **King's Chamber** has been meticulously reproduced using, where possible, the materials and methods of the time. The chambers in particular reveal a surprising blaze of paint-box colours and jaunty designs – rich turquoises, reds and gloriously decorative golds designed to flaunt the king's colossal wealth and influence. Climbing to the **roof** of the tower, passing other visitors huffing and puffing as they descend, rewards you with fabulous views of the castle grounds, the sea and Dover itself.

The medieval tunnels

Following a nearly disastrous siege by the French Prince Louis and rebel barons in 1216–17, Dover Castle saw a number of improvements in its defence system – not least a complex set of subterranean **tunnels**, entered from a spot near the Great Tower. These were altered and expanded during the Napoleonic Wars and in the 1850s, but their original plan remains largely intact. There is little to actually see, although a set of lever-controlled doors that could be closed remotely to trap invaders is undeniably impressive, but the dramatically sloping declines, damp, drippy darkness, mysterious nooks and steep staircases are irresistibly atmospheric.

The Roman lighthouse

The Romans put Dover on the map when they chose the harbour – Portus Dubris – as the base for their northern fleet, and, probably in the second century AD, erected a clifftop **lighthouse** (*pharos*) to guide the ships into the river mouth. The remains of the chunky octagonal tower, made from local flint and bricks and refaced in medieval times, still stand – only the four lower stages survive, but you can walk inside the hollow shell.

St Mary-in-Castro

Standing beside the remains of the Roman lighthouse, the **St Mary-in-Castro** church dates back to around 1000 AD. Though subsequently remodelled, it remains a very fine, late-Saxon church, with original cruciform layout and soaring internal stone arches. Under Henry III, St Mary's became a church for soldiers – Richard the

Lionheart's knights took shelter here before setting out on a crusade, and you can see their graffiti scratched into the wall just above ground level in the original stone arches near the pulpit. Over the next few centuries the church fell into ruin, to be restored by famed Victorian architects Sir George Gilbert Scott and William Butterfield; the latter is responsible for the decorative mosaic tiling that covers the walls.

Roman Painted House

New St, CT17 9AJ • April & June–Sept Tues–Sat 10am–5pm, Sun 1–5pm; May Tues & Sat 10am–5pm; always call to check • £4 • ☎ 01304 203279, ⊕ theromanpaintedhouse.org.uk

Built around 200 AD, the **Roman Painted House**, once a rest house for official guests from across the Channel, was demolished around seventy years later. Today, in a purpose-built building near the Market Square, you can see the remains of five rooms, including evidence of the hypocaust (underground heating system) and various mosaics, along with – the chief attraction – vibrant Roman wall paintings relating to Bacchus, the god of wine. Roman objects found during the 1971 excavation are also on display.

Dover Museum

Market Square, CT16 1PH • April–Sept Mon–Sat 9.30am–5pm, Sun 10am–3pm; Oct–March Mon–Sat 9.30am–5pm • Free • ☎ 01304 201066, ⊕ dovermuseum.co.uk

Dover Museum is an appealing, slightly old-fashioned place, packed with enthusiastic displays on the town's past. The star attraction, protected behind glass in its own gallery, is a **Bronze Age boat** that was discovered in Dover in 1992, immaculately preserved by river silt for more than three thousand years. The vessel – the oldest-known seafaring boat in the world – is an astonishing sight, long, dark and sinewy like tough black seaweed; it took ten carpenters one month to build it, using holly, plum, oak, ash, apple, elm and yew, plus dense wodges of moss for waterproofing.

The White Cliffs of Dover

Shingly Dover beach may today lack the romance invested in it by Matthew Arnold (see page 118), but the iconic **cliffs** flanking the town on both sides retain their majesty. Stretching sixteen miles along the coast from Kingsdown to Folkestone, a towering 350ft high in places, these vast banks are composed of chalk – plus traces of quartz, shells and flint. Much of the cliffs lie within the Kent Downs Area of Outstanding Natural Beauty, and with their chalk grasslands home to an exceptional number of rare plants, butterflies and migrant birds, have been designated a Site of Special Scientific Interest.

The most dramatic **views** of the cliffs themselves, of course, come from miles out to sea, either from a ferry or on a short tourist cruise from Dover (see page 120). Best of all, though, is to take a **walk** along them, which affords you amazing views of the busy Straits of Dover. On a clear day it's even possible to catch a glimpse of France.

Shakespeare Cliff

A couple of miles west of Dover, **Shakespeare Cliff**, named for its mention in *King Lear* (see page 118), is almost ferociously daunting, a towering bastion of chalk leaning backwards as if straining to hold back the sea. The bracing clifftop walk here offers a sweeping panorama – and an excellent, unusual view of Dover and the surrounding cliffs – but anyone with vertigo will want to stay well clear of the edge.

THE WHITE CLIFFS OF DOVER

There is a cliff whose high and bending head
Looks fearfully in the confinèd deep
Bring me but to the very brim of it,
And I'll repair the misery thou dost bear
With something rich about me. From that place
I shall no leading need.

Earl of Gloucester, *King Lear*, Act 4 Scene 1

The sea is calm tonight,
The tide is full, the moon lies fair
Upon the straits; on the French coast the light
Gleams and is gone; the cliffs of England stand,
Glimmering and vast, out in the tranquil bay.
Come to the window, sweet is the night air!

Dover Beach, Matthew Arnold, 1867

Ah, God! One sniff of England
To greet our flesh and blood
To hear the traffic slurring
Once more through London mud!
Our towns of wasted honour
Our streets of lost delight!
How stands the old Lord Warden?
Are Dover's cliffs still white?

The Broken Men, Rudyard Kipling, 1902

There'll be bluebirds over
The White Cliffs of Dover
Tomorrow, just you wait and see.

(There'll Be Bluebirds Over) The White Cliffs of Dover, sung by Vera Lynn, 1942

As the first and last sight of England for travellers throughout the centuries, the **White Cliffs of Dover** play a complex role in the English psyche. A symbol of national fortitude, independence and pride, they have long represented a barrier for potential invaders; like mighty natural fortresses, they inspire awe and fear. **Julius Caesar** mentions them in his *Commentaries, Book IV*, recounting the Roman invasion of Britain in 55 BC – "steep cliffs came down close to the sea in such a way that it is possible to hurl weapons from them right down to the shore. It seemed to me that the place was altogether unsuitable for landing." Daunted, the invaders sailed further north to Deal and landed there instead.

In Shakespeare's **King Lear** the cliffs represent certain death to the abject and blinded Gloucester, who plans to commit suicide by jumping from them; in a later scene, his son Edgar, lying, convinces his father they are at the cliff edge with the words "the murmuring surge/That on the unnumber'd idle pebbles chafes/Cannot be heard so high. I'll look no more/Lest my brain turn, and the deficient sight/Topple down headlong". Poet Matthew Arnold, meanwhile, gives them a similarly melancholic resonance, invoking their massive grandeur in his famous elegy for lost belief, **Dover Beach**, while for Kipling's home-sick emigrants the cliffs, and the old Dover pub the *Lord Warden*, are among quintessential images of home.

Perhaps the most famous mention of the cliffs, however, comes in **Vera Lynn**'s wartime anthem, a rallying call for Britons to keep dreaming of a peaceful future in the wake of the Battle of Britain. It's ostensibly a hopeful song, but the plaintive tune, and the fact that no real bluebird ever flew over the cliffs, imbues the uplifting words with a poignant uncertainty.

Samphire Hoe

Below Shakespeare Cliff, off the A20 from Dover to Folkestone, CT17 9FL • Daily 7am–dusk • Free, but pay parking • ☎ 01304 225649, Ⓦ samphirehoe.co.uk

Created in 1997 from some 175 million cubic feet of chalk marl reclaimed during the building of the Channel Tunnel, **Samphire Hoe**, the nature reserve at the foot of Shakespeare Cliff, is an unsettling spot. Wild and exposed, its chalk meadows, dotted with rock samphire, orchids and wildflowers, have a raw beauty that evolves with each passing year. On the other hand, this is clearly a man-made landscape, blocked off from the sea by a sea wall and wire fence, and with brutish Channel Tunnel ventilation buildings welcoming you at the entrance. Walking around the Hoe (a total loop of around 45min) does, however, offer invigorating blasts of fresh air, along with splendid views of the sea and of the awe-inspiring Shakespeare Cliff looming above – this is a good **birdwatching** spot and you may see kestrels, guillemots and kittiwakes swirling overhead.

To reach Samphire Hoe, pedestrians, cyclists and cars alike enter through a dark single-lane **tunnel** that descends through the cliffs; this was built in the 1880s, an aborted early version of today's Channel Tunnel.

Langdon Cliffs

Langdon Cliffs, a couple of miles east of town, above the port of Dover, are home to the National Trust White Cliffs of Dover Visitor Centre (see page 120), and a popular starting point for clifftop **walks**. Following cliff-edge paths and ploughing through chalk downland meadows, you can walk in around fifty minutes to the Victorian **South Foreland Lighthouse** – via **Fan Bay**, with its World War II tunnel complex – but if time is short it's well worth taking a briefer stroll, enjoying unsurpassed views. Watch out for kittiwakes in the summer, along with pretty Adonis blue butterflies fluttering among the wildflowers, and perhaps even an Exmoor pony or two, grazing on the velvety grass.

Fan Bay Deep Shelter

Fan Bay • Tours April–Oct Mon & Thurs–Sun every 30min 11am–3pm; 45min; no under-8s • Admission on timed tours only; check availability at the National Trust White Cliffs Visitor Centre (see page 120) and then walk the 1.5 miles to the entrance • £10; no cards; NT • Parking (at the Visitor Centre) free for NT members, or £5 • ☎ 01304 207326, ⦿ nationaltrust.org.uk/white-cliffs-dover

In 1941, at the height of World War II, a **gun battery** was installed on the White Cliffs to monitor and attack enemy ships in the Channel. Below it, hidden behind the face of the cliffs and carved out in just one hundred days, lay an **underground labyrinth** that housed 185 troops. The battery and all visible traces on the surface were destroyed in the 1970s, but the tunnels themselves remained; they've since been cleared and restored by the National Trust as a historical attraction.

Visiting **Fan Bay Deep Shelter** is quite an undertaking. First you have to walk for around 1.5 miles (45min) along the clifftop trail from the White Cliffs Visitor Centre (see page 120); then you don a hard hat with head torch and set off on the tour, descending down into the cliff via 125 steep stairs. Guides lead you through the dark, damp warren that once held dorms, hospital beds and storage rooms. Though the tunnels are largely empty, the anecdotes, stray pieces of memorabilia and wartime graffiti etched into the chalk bring the place eerily alive. Some way down, you emerge onto an open-air ledge that holds two concrete "sound mirrors" – early-warning devices, designed to amplify the sound of approaching aircraft, built during the previous war in 1914.

South Foreland Lighthouse

The clifftop, St Margaret's Bay, CT15 6HP • Tours Mid-March to Oct Mon & Fri–Sun 11am–5.30pm • £6; NT • Parking (at the National Trust White Cliffs Visitor Centre, see page 120) free for members, otherwise £5 • ☎ 01304 853281, ⦿ nationaltrust.org.uk/south-foreland-lighthouse

South Foreland Lighthouse, a two-mile (50min) walk from the White Cliffs Visitor Centre, marks the end of the National Trust-owned clifftop path. Built in 1843 to guide ships past the perilous Goodwin Sands, three miles offshore, the chunky, icing-white tower offers (on clear days) amazing cross-Channel views. This was the site of Marconi's first international radio transmission, and the first lighthouse to be powered by electricity; guided **tours** detail the history, while touchscreens allow you to monitor the comings and goings on the busy Dover Strait. The **tearoom** downstairs (mid-March to Oct daily 11am–5pm) is a vintage-lover's dream, complete with vinyl playing on the record-deck and yellowing antique newspapers to flick through. You can **stay** in the lighthouse, too.

St Margaret's-at-Cliffe and around

Tucked away off the A258 Dover–Deal road, four miles northeast of Dover and around two miles inland, **ST MARGARET'S-AT-CLIFFE** was a major smuggling centre in the eighteenth century. There's very little evidence of that today, however; it's a sleepy spot, set on a glorious stretch of the **Saxon Shore Way** (see page 29) and on National Cycle Route 1. The local beach, **St Margaret's Bay**, is charming.

St Margaret's Bay

St Margaret's Bay, a twenty-minute walk down from the village, is the closest point on the British mainland to France, just twenty miles away. A secluded cove of shingle-sand beach, sheltered by white cliffs and with rockpools to explore and the odd fossil to be found, it's a nice spot for a seaside sojourn, with kayaking, canoeing and occasional surfing from the wave-cut platform off Ness Point. In the years following World War II, St Margaret's was quite the artistic colony, an exclusive summer getaway for wealthy Londoners; **Noël Coward** and friends bought up the four Art Deco houses at the end of the beach and hosted the great and the good for seaside sojourns. By 1951 Coward deemed the bay too "crowded with noisy hoi polloi", however, leased his house to his friend **Ian Fleming**, and returned to his home in Aldington, in Romney Marsh (see page 129).

If you fancy a break from the beach, pop into the organically managed six-acre **Pines Garden** (daily 10am–5pm; £4 donation suggested; ☎01304 851737), with its lake, mature trees, kitchen gardens and **tearoom** (April–Sept daily; Oct–March Wed–Sun; ☎01304 853173). If you're feeling more energetic, you could walk up to South Foreland Lighthouse (see page 119) – follow Lighthouse Road up for a mile or so, and note that the path is poor in places.

ARRIVAL AND DEPARTURE

DOVER AND AROUND

By train Dover Priory station is off Folkestone Rd, a 10min walk west of the centre.
Destinations Canterbury (every 30min–1hr; 15–30min); Deal (every 15min–1hr; 15min); Faversham (every 30min–1hr; 30–40min); Folkestone (every 10–50min; 20min); London Victoria (every 30min–1hr; 2hr); Sandwich (every 30min–1hr; 25min).
By bus The town-centre bus station is on Pencester Rd.

Destinations Alkham (5 daily; 20min); Canterbury (every 15min–1hr; 45min); Deal (every 30min–1hr; 45min); Folkestone (every 20–30min; 30min); Hythe (every 20–30min; 1hr); St Margaret's-at-Cliffe (hourly; 20min); Sandwich (every 45min–1hr; 45min–1hr).
By ferry P&O ferries run between Dover and Calais, while DFDS car ferries run to Calais and Dunkirk (☎doverport. co.uk/ferry).

INFORMATION AND TOURS

Tourist office Dover Museum, Market Square (April–Sept Mon–Sat 9.30am–5pm, Sun 10am–3pm; Oct–March Mon–Sat 9.30am–5pm; ☎01304 201066, ☎whitecliffs country.org.uk).
National Trust White Cliffs of Dover Visitor Centre Langdon Cliffs, Upper Rd (daily: March–June, Sept & Oct 10am–5pm; July & Aug 10am–5.30pm; Nov–Feb 10am–4pm; free, NT; parking free for members or otherwise £5; ☎01304 202756, ☎nationaltrust.org.uk/white-cliffs-dover). A few panels illuminate the ecology and history of the local coast and countryside, and there's a secondhand

bookshop, but most space is devoted to the coffee shop and its huge outdoor deck – the ideal vantage point from which to watch the port activity below.
Dover Sea Safari Based in the Dover Sea Sports Centre on the beach, Dover Sea Safari (☎01304 212880, ☎doverseasafari.co.uk) offers a selection of high-octane speedboat tours – including harbour and White Cliffs jaunts (1hr 30min; £35), seal-watching trips at Pegwell Bay (2hr; £45) and occasional low-tide trips out to Goodwin Sands, where you are left for 45min to roam free (3hr; £60).

ACCOMMODATION

DOVER

Maison Dieu Guest House 89 Maison Dieu Rd, CT16 1RU ☎01304 204033, ⓦmaisondieu.co.uk. Friendly guesthouse in a central location, with six comfy single, double, twin and family rooms, some en suite and others with private facilities. A couple have views over the walled garden to Dover Castle. An optional breakfast costs £8 extra. **£80**

Marquis of Granby Alkham Valley Rd, Alkham, 5 miles west of Dover, CT15 7DF ☎01304 873410, ⓦmarquis ofgranby.co.uk. Boutique-style accommodation within a 200-year-old inn. The ten rooms are each different, with opulent colour schemes and a chic mix of original features and contemporary furnishings – some have picture-perfect views across the Downs. Alkham itself, while pretty, is a sleepy place, perfect for a peaceful overnight stay. The cosy pub-restaurant (see below) means you don't have to travel to eat, though it's closed on Sunday evenings. **£105**

Peverell's Tower Dover Castle, CT16 1HU ☎0370 333 1187, ⓦwww.english-heritage.org.uk/visit/holiday-cottages/find-a-holiday-cottage/peverells-tower. Be king or queen of the castle at this lovely self-catering option (sleeps two), a thirteenth-century tower set within Dover Castle's walls. Well-equipped and contemporary – though keeping its twisty stairs and medieval quirks – it also has its own roof terrace with amazing views. A stay here includes access to the castle, and to all EH sites. Three-, four- or seven-night stays only; nightly rate lower for longer stays. **£270**

ST MARGARET'S-AT-CLIFFE AND AROUND

White Cliffs High St, CT15 6AT ☎01304 852229, ⓦthewhitecliffs.com. Chilled-out, friendly, family-run place – a great hit with walkers and cyclists – with a sociable restaurant/bar (see below) and a flexible range of accommodation. The rooms, tucked away in the warren of corridors in the main building – a sixteenth-century weatherboard house – come in all shapes, sizes and styles, from rustic and cosy to huge and glamorous, some with four posters; the smaller, less expensive options in outbuildings around the grassy beer garden are not quite so special, but all are super-comfortable. A tasty full breakfast is included. **£100**

EATING AND DRINKING

DOVER

Allotment 9 High St, CT16 1DP ☎01304 214467, ⓦthe allotmentrestaurant.com. A light-filled oasis on Dover's drab High St, this place serves tasty, unpretentious food in a soothing space with a pretty courtyard garden. They keep things simple at "brunch", which feels more like breakfast with its Full Englishes and bacon and eggs with toast, but the lunch menus branch out into such dishes as spring veg and fresh herb risotto, confit duck leg with cherries, Kentish venison or creamy crab and sweetcorn chowder. Burgers and baguettes, too, with afternoon tea from 2 to 5pm. Starters from £5.50; mains £9–17; afternoon tea (reserve 24hr in advance) £14.50. Tues–Fri noon–9.30pm, Sat 10am–9.30pm, Sun (July & Aug only) noon–6pm.

Blakes of Dover 52 Castle St, CT16 1PJ ☎01304 202194, ⓦblakesofdover.com. Cosy, wood-panelled basement bar offering real ales and local ciders, with a small beer garden at the back. Food – steaks and traditional pub grub – is served upstairs. Mon–Sat 11am–11pm, Sun noon–10pm.

Hythe Bay Seafood Restaurant at Dover The Esplanade, CT17 9FS ☎01304 207740, ⓦhythebay. co.uk. With a sister restaurant in Hythe (see page 129), this seafood place has a great location on Dover's seafront, and a traditional menu of simply prepared fish and seafood – from scallops to Dover sole, sardines to lobster – in a bright dining room with broad sea views. There's an outdoor deck for sunny days. Starters from £8, mains from £15. Daily noon–9.30pm; coffee served from 10am.

Marquis of Granby Alkham Valley Rd, Alkham, 5 miles west of Dover, CT15 7DF ☎01304 873410, ⓦmarquisofgranby.co.uk. This welcoming, contemporary country pub with rooms (see above) offers real ales and comforting pub grub, with locally sourced ingredients. Typical dishes might include chorizo Scotch egg, mushroom rarebit en croute or rump steak burger; mains from £12. There's also a sandwich menu (from £7), a good-value Sunday lunch (£15) and a kids' menu. It's particularly nice when they've got the real fires going. Mon–Fri 7.30–10am, noon–3pm & 6–9pm, Sat 8–11am, noon–9.30pm, Sun 8–10am & noon–5pm.

ST MARGARET'S-AT-CLIFFE AND AROUND

White Cliffs Kitchen and Bar White Cliffs, High St, CT15 6AT ☎01304 852229, ⓦthewhitecliffs.com. Informal local dining in a seasidey pub/restaurant/hotel (see above), lined with splashy art and with a big, walled beer garden. Kentish wine and keg ales are on offer, while seasonally changing menus list simple dishes such as ploughman's platters or grilled sea bass fillet with samphire (starters from £4, mains £13.50–22.50). Summer weekends (July–Sept Fri–Sun 5–9pm) see a short menu of sourdough pizzas from £11. Mon–Fri 7–10am, noon–5pm & 6–9pm, Sat 8–10am, noon–5pm & 6–9pm, Sun 8–10am & noon–5pm.

The Coastguard St Margaret's Bay, CT15 6DY ☎01304 853051, ⓦthecoastguard.co.uk. This nautically themed beachside pub/restaurant is a good spot for a summer drink;

enjoy a Kentish cask ale on their large terrace (separated from the beach by a car park) or the small beer garden that stretches practically down to the shingle. The menu lists fish and chips alongside fresh fish and local specials like Kentish hop sausages, plus steaks, burgers, risottos and ciabatta sandwiches. Lots of events, too, from BBQs to live music. Starters from £5.50; mains £13–23. Daily 10am–11pm; kitchen daily 10am–9pm.

Folkestone

In the early 2000s, depressed after the demise of its tourist industry and the loss of its ferry link to France, **FOLKESTONE** was a doleful place. Like all the settlements on the east coast, it had long been defined by its relationship to the sea: starting out as a fishing village, it thrived as a smuggling centre in the seventeenth century, then grew in Victorian times to become a busy cross-Channel ferry port and upmarket **resort**. The ravages of two world wars, followed by a rash of rebuilding, did the place no aesthetic favours, however, and the rise of cheap foreign travel hit hard. With the **Channel Tunnel**, west of town, whisking passengers direct from the M20 to the Continent, and the curtailment of the ferry service to Boulogne in 2000, reasons to stop in Folkestone were diminishing.

Thus began a concerted effort to start again, with many hopes pinned on the arts and the creative industries. Cue Folkestone's **Triennial**, which premiered in 2008. Spearheaded by the multimillionaire Roger de Haan (who once owned Saga holidays, which is based here) and his Creative Folkestone charity, the acclaimed art show brings considerable attention in festival years, and, spawning other cultural events in its wake, is gradually bringing Folkestone out of its extended limbo. Some parts of town remain bleak and shabby, but with the regenerating **Creative Quarter**, the salty little fishing **harbour** and the buzzy **harbour arm** (all three owned by de Haan), the glorious **Lower Leas Coastal Park**, a sandy town **beach**, and the wild **Warren** cliffs and beach nearby, Folkestone has plenty to offer. Less than an hour from the capital by train, and with some stylish places to eat and stay, it's making waves as a seaside weekender.

The Creative Quarter

Occupying a small corner of town down by the harbour, Folkestone's **Creative Quarter** (ⓦ creativefolkestone.org.uk/folkestone-creative-quarter) is a redeveloping slum area now owned by Creative Folkestone, which rents out the workspaces, commercial units and flats to artists. The steep and cobbled **Old High Street**, lined with brightly painted higgledy-piggledy seventeenth- and eighteenth-century buildings, holds most of the independent shops, cafés and galleries; it snakes its narrow way up to **Rendezvous Street**, another appealing little enclave. In Triennial years the Creative Quarter is Folkestone's beating heart; things are quieter at other times, with many shabby buildings boarded up or empty, but tantalizing pop-ups come and go and the community vibe is tangible, with flyers for local events and fundraisers plastered on windows everywhere.

Lower Leas Coastal Park and around

Folkestone exists on two levels – down by the sea and up on the cliffs, with steep hills and zigzag steps linking the two. Taking up a large, long swathe below the clifftop Leas promenade and above the beach, the **Lower Leas Coastal Park** is a glorious expanse of lush plantings, winding paths and pretty footbridges, all accompanied by sea views that on a sunny day have a distinctly Mediterranean flavour.

A man-made creation, made possible following a massive landslide in the eighteenth century, the park – which stretches west of the Leas Lift practically as far as the neighbouring village of Sandgate – was the talk of Victorian and Edwardian

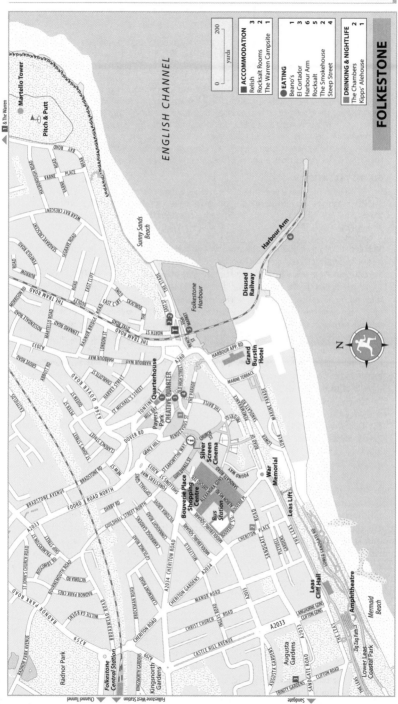

FOLKESTONE

■ ACCOMMODATION	
Relish	3
Rocksalt Rooms	2
The Warren Campsite	1

● EATING	
Beano's	1
El Cortador	3
Harbour Arm	6
Rocksalt	5
The Smokehouse	2
Steep Street	4

■ DRINKING & NIGHTLIFE	
The Chambers	3
Kipps' Alehouse	2

ENGLISH CHANNEL

3

3

THE FOLKESTONE TRIENNIAL

The **Folkestone Triennial** (dates change, generally two months in summer/autumn; ⓦ creativefolkestone.org.uk/folkestone-triennial), a public art project first held in 2008, has played a major part in changing the town's image. Attracting big British names from Tracey Emin to Cornelia Parker, Andy Goldsworthy to Martin Creed, as well as artists from around the world, the Triennial's importance to Folkestone as a confidence boost is inestimable. While many works are linked explicitly to the town, and most are location-specific, with soundscapes, performance art and mobile installations encouraging visitors to roam around and discover Folkestone itself, this is by no means a parochial event. Each year has a different theme, which, from dislocation and transience to the art of "looking", are universal. Talks, tours, workshops and live events keep energy levels high, with eminent critics and curators rubbing shoulders with curious locals – above all the Triennial aims for accessibility over elitism.

SIX INSTALLATIONS

Following each Triennial, a selection of the exhibits is made permanent, cumulatively transforming the town into a giant outdoor gallery. The following are particularly striking; there's a full list and detailed maps on ⓦ creativefolkestone.org.uk/folkestoneartworks/maps-and-routes.

18 Holes Richard Wilson (2008). Look twice and you'll see that the three concrete-and-green-felt beach huts on the coastal promenade, around 500m west of the old Leas Lift, are actually made from a crazy-golf course, the last remaining part of Folkestone's last remaining amusement park, finally demolished in 2007 after promises to redevelop and regenerate went by the wayside.

Baby Things Tracey Emin (2008). Blink and you'd miss them; these seven small bronzes from Kent-born YBA Emin – baby mittens, tiny cardies, teddies and lone bootees discarded on benches, railings and pavements – comment on the high teenage pregnancy rate in Folkestone and towns like it. Ostensibly ephemeral scraps of jetsam, they pack a surprisingly poignant punch.

The Folkestone Mermaid Cornelia Parker (2011). Parker's naturalistic version of Copenhagen's idealized Little Mermaid, a bronze life-cast sculpture modelled on a Folkestone woman, sits on a boulder by the harbour, overlooking Sunny Sands beach.

Out of Tune A. K. Dolven (2011). Norwegian-born artist Dolven has strung a discarded sixteenth-century church bell from a steel cable 65ft high, suspended between two posts on a lonely spot near the Leas Lift, where Folkestone's last amusement park once stood.

Lamp Post (As Remembered) David Shrigley (2017). Playing with notions of memory, nostalgia and heritage, this white lamppost on The Leas was created by one of Shrigley's artist friends, recalling from memory a lamppost she viewed for just 40 seconds.

The Luckiest Place on Earth Strange Cargo (2014). Folkestone Central's railway bridge is transformed into a site of great fortune – four 3D-printed sculptures, each representing a genuine Folkestone resident and clutching good luck talismans.

Folkestone, its landscaped promenades prime attractions of this genteel resort. Today it also features wildflower meadows and shady woodlands; behind the grassy outdoor amphitheatre, a dramatic zigzag path scales the rockface, complete with mysterious grottoes, up to the bandstand on the Leas. At the park's heart, thrillingly hidden in the woods, is an outstanding **children's playground** (free entry), with tube slides, zip-lines and all manner of adventure equipment for all ages. Beyond the point at which steps descend to the seafront *Mermaid Café* the park becomes wilder and less landscaped; it all culminates in a staircase leading up to the *Grand* and *Metropole* hotels on the Leas, relics of the resort's Edwardian heyday.

Leas Lift

Lower Sandgate Rd, CT20 1PR

The last of Folkestone's four Victorian lifts, and one of only three water-powered funicular lifts remaining in England, the 1885 **Leas Lift** used to chug up between the Leas seafront parade, with its lawns, formal flowerbeds and bandstand, down to the seafront at the end of Marine Parade. Closed since 2017 due to safety concerns, the lift is due to re-open in 2020.

Mermaid Beach

The shingle beaches below the coastal park are not bad for swimming, though you should watch out for rocks; the area around the *Mermaid Café*, unofficially called **Mermaid Beach**, is the best, a gently shelving slope with a rough sand bottom. The beach huts here – large concrete and hardboard boxes, painted in bright ice-cream colours – have a poignant, quintessentially Folkestone feel, being at once jaunty, pretty and a little rough.

The harbour and around

Split in two by a railway viaduct, Folkestone's **harbour** was crowded in Victorian days with ships and pleasure vessels, and with fishermen hauling in their huge catches. Today, it's an atmospheric spot, fishing boats bobbing in the tidal waters and wildflowers sprouting from its rocky walls, the cobbled **Stade** (or "landing place") studded with black weatherboard fishermen's huts. Small-scale fishing still goes on here, with a couple of seafood stalls (the whelks are delicious), plus a brace of excellent restaurants joining the chip shop, caff and pubs. On the other side of the harbour, beyond the 1980s *Grand Burstin* hotel – an outrageous eyesore looming over the water like a half-built cruise liner – the regenerated **Harbour Arm** (daily dawn to dusk; ⓦ folkestoneharbourarm.co.uk) is a lively spot. Terminus for Folkestone's old cross-channel boat trains, and fenced off for years, the arm now provides a good focus for seaside promenades, and its food carts, restaurants and bars, not to mention its live music and film screenings, provide a welcome blast of energy in this corner of town. While sitting on the arm, look out for **Another Time XVIII** (2013), one of Antony Gormley's characteristically haunting cast-iron human sculptures, which appears and disappears depending on the tide.

Sunny Sands beach

It may not always be sunny at **Sunny Sands**, the little beach by the fishing harbour, but it's undeniably sandy, which is a rarity along this shingly shore. The golden stuff is celebrated every summer with a popular annual sandcastle competition, a cheery affair watched over by the *Folkestone Mermaid* (see page 124), and on fine weekends it can get packed. From here you can climb a zigzag staircase and walk along the East Cliff to the very different beach at the Warren, enjoying glorious sea views as you go.

THE MARTELLO TOWERS

Built during the Napoleonic Wars, and based on a Corsican design that had thwarted British troops in 1794, Kent's clumpy **Martello towers** formed part of a chain of more than one hundred such defences that ran along the coastline from Sussex to Suffolk. Resembling giant – and malevolent – upturned flowerpots, around 30ft or 40ft high, with walls some 8ft thick on the landward side and 13ft thick seaward, the towers were designed to house more than twenty men in cramped quarters above the ground-floor arsenal and below the rooftop gun platform. The predicted French invasion never came, but the towers were handy for keeping an eye on local **smuggling**, and some served as observation decks during **World War II** before being left, as a rule, to rack and ruin.

Some forty or so towers survive in England, many of them listed, and they're becoming desirable as property conversions. Folkestone boasts four of them; walk along the clifftop to the Warren and you will first encounter the run-down **Martello No. 3**, now leased by Creative Folkestone, which acquired its ugly rooftop accretion in World War II. You can climb the rickety external staircase to the entrance (well above ground level, to confound attackers) for a bird's-eye view of the town and the Strait. There's another tower nearby, off Wear Bay Road, with more in Sandgate, Hythe and Dymchurch (in varying states of decay), and still more along the Sussex coast from Rye to Seaford.

The Warren

Accessible only on foot, fossil-bedecked **Warren Beach**, which fronts the **Warren**, a clifftop nature reserve and Site of Special Scientific Interest, feels wonderfully remote (though it's no secret in these parts, and when the tide is out you may well be joined by fossicking school groups and chilled-out families from the nearby campground). Getting there, a twenty-minute walk from Sunny Sands, is something of an adventure. Having ascended from Sunny Sands to the East Cliff clifftop, recent landslides mean you have to dip inland for a while, via a pitch-and-putt course, and passing a Martello tower on your way (see page 125), before rejoining the cliff-edge path. The gradual descent entails a bit of up and down along overgrown paths, and some minor scrambling over rocks – the official path takes the longer route round to the beach, but many people head down through the undergrowth to get to the sands sooner. Broad, flat and gleaming, punctuated by dilapidated groynes, seaweed-slick rocks, fossils and sea shells – and backed by a rather forbidding concrete sea defence – the Warren has a wild, raw magnificence, with huge, open views across to Samphire Hoe and the White Cliffs.

ARRIVAL AND INFORMATION
FOLKESTONE AND AROUND

By train Folkestone Central station is off Cheriton Rd, just under a mile northwest of the Cultural Quarter.
Destinations Dover (every 10–50min; 20min); London Charing Cross (every 30min–1hr; 1hr 40min); London St Pancras (every 30min–1hr; 55min); Sevenoaks (every 30min–1hr; 1hr 10min).

By bus The bus station is in the centre of town near Bouverie Place Shopping Centre.
Destinations Dover (every 20–30min; 30min).
Tourist office 20 Bouverie Place (Mon–Fri 9am–5pm; ☎01303 258954); also includes information on Hythe and Romney Marsh.

ACCOMMODATION
SEE MAP PAGE 123

Relish 4 Augusta Gardens, CT20 2RR ☎01303 850952, ⊛therelish.co.uk. An attractive Regency building next to the green Augusta Gardens and not far from the Leas, with ten quiet, comfortable boutique-style rooms, a comfy lounge and an outdoor terrace where you can eat your cooked breakfast. Little extras include complimentary homemade cake, coffee, juices and wine. No lift. **£98**

Rocksalt Rooms 1–3 Back St, CT19 6NN ☎01303 212070, ⊛rocksaltfolkestone.co.uk/rooms. Four "boutique bolt holes" (they're small) in an unbeatable harbourside location above the *Smokehouse* restaurant, and brought to you by the *Rocksalt* crew (see below). Those at the front are by far the best, with French windows and water

views – those at the back can get stuffy – but they're all chic and super-comfy, with scrubbed bare-brick walls, plump duvets, espresso-makers and tiny wet-rooms. A continental breakfast is delivered to your room in a hamper, or you can eat a full breakfast in the *Rocksalt* restaurant nearby. **£125**
The Warren Campsite The Warren, CT19 6NQ ☎01303 255093 (no calls after 8pm), ⊛campingandcaravanningclub.co.uk. Eighty pitches in a quiet cliffside location by the Warren nature reserve and beach, walkable (just about) from Folkestone. The views are glorious, but be prepared for the steep, narrow, pothole-scarred approach road. Minimum stay two nights in summer. Closed Nov–Easter. Non-members **£14.70**, members **£8.65**

EATING
SEE MAP PAGE 123

Beano's 43 Tontine St, CT20 1JT ☎01303 211817, ⊛beanosvegetarian.com. This simple little veggie/vegan restaurant is a reliable stalwart in the Creative Quarter. Come for creative breakfasts (till 11.15am), fancy cheese toasties and sandwiches, or fill up on falafel, seitan wraps or the dahl of the day. Mains £6–8. Tues–Fri 8.30am–5pm, Sat 9am–5pm.

El Cortador 41 Old High St, CT20 1RL ☎01303 243974, ⊛elcortadorfolkestone.com. Authentic, relaxed and roomy tapas bar serving all the classics – calamares, tortilla, chorizo, Manchego with membrillo – with a good selection of daily specials and Spanish wines. Most dishes around £3 to £6. Tues & Wed 11am–3pm & 6–10pm, Thurs–Sat 11am–10pm, Sun noon–4pm.

Harbour Arm Folkestone Harbour, CT20 1QH ⊛folkestoneharbourarm.co.uk. Long neglected and out of bounds, the restored Harbour Arm has become a real foodie focus in Folkestone, with a string of food carts serving global cuisine and restaurants and bars in the restored buildings behind. The waterside seating is a delight on sunny days. Note that individual businesses keep different hours. Hours vary; see website for individual outlets.

★ **Rocksalt** 4–5 Fishmarket, CT19 6AA ☎01303 212070, ⊛rocksaltfolkestone.co.uk. A beautiful cantilevered glass-and-wood restaurant with a deck on the harbour, a whelk's throw from the fishing boats, *Rocksalt* is a sophisticated setting for flawless Kentish food. The fresh

FOLKESTONE FESTIVALS

Other than the Folkestone Triennial (see page 124), the town's main event is the ten-day **Folkestone Book Festival** (Nov; ⓦ creativefolkestone.org.uk/folkestone-book-festival). Largely based at the Quarterhouse (see page 127), the book festival brings in a host of big-name crowd-pleasers, from Jonathan Coe to Rose Tremain, along with TV and radio folk and local historians. Events include screenings, plays and workshops; many are free. **Open Quarter**, meanwhile, an open studio event in mid-June, is a lively time to be in the Creative Quarter, with special exhibitions, performances, workshops and "meet the artist" events (ⓦ creativefolkestone.org.uk).

local fish is a winner, of course, from plump mussels via roast mackerel to whole local lobster with garlic butter, but the meat and veggie choices, made with produce from their own farm, are delicious too – whole grilled courgette with spiced freekeh and tempura courgette flower, say, or rump of Romney Marsh lamb with broad beans, spinach and pickled onion. Starters from £7, mains from £14; two-/three-course set lunch (Mon–Fri) £21.50/£25. Mon–Thurs noon–3pm & 6.30–10pm, Fri & Sat noon–3pm & 6.30–10.30pm, Sun noon–7pm.

The Smokehouse 1–3 Back St, CT19 6NN ☎ 01303 884718, ⓦ thesmokehousefolkestone.co.uk. *Rocksalt's* sister restaurant, a modern, brick-and-glass affair on the harbour, serves fantastic fish and chips (from £8.50) to eat in or take away. Though portions are unceremoniously heaped in cardboard boxes, this is no run-of-the-mill chippie – along with cod and haddock, and all the usual accompaniments, you could go for mackerel, sea bream or catch of the day, with starters including salt-and-pepper squid. The toughest choice is whether to have the fish healthily baked or in *Smokehouse's* fabulous, crackly crisp batter. Mon–Sat noon–8pm, Sun noon–6pm.

★ **Steep Street** 18–24 Old High St, CT10 1RL ☎ 01303 247819, ⓦ steepstreet.co.uk. This gorgeous coffee house, lined ceiling to floor with vintage books, buzzes with a Cultural Quarter crowd chatting, reading or tapping on laptops. The food, from sandwiches to salads, quiches to cakes, is simple but good, and inexpensive (cakes from £2). Arm yourself with a cappuccino, a homemade flapjack and a couple of books, head up to the mezzanine, settle down in a plump armchair and prepare to linger. Mon–Fri 8.30am–6pm, Sat 9am–6pm, Sun 9am–5pm.

DRINKING AND NIGHTLIFE   SEE MAP PAGE 123

The Chambers Radnor Chambers, Cheriton Place, CT20 2BB ☎ 01303 223333, ⓦ facebook.com/thechambers. The location, in the shopping streets some way from the seafront, isn't inspiring, but this friendly basement café-restaurant-bar is a popular spot for local ales and ciders, with good pub food, DJ nights and live music. Mon–Thurs noon–11pm, Fri & Sat noon–1am; kitchen closes a little earlier.

Kipps' Alehouse 11–15 Old High St, CT20 1RL ☎ 01303 246766, ⓦ facebook.com/Kippsalehouse. Informal pub/live music venue with a relaxed, cosy feel, serving real ales, craft beers, traditional ciders and inexpensive global food to a convivial crowd. Mon–Wed & Sun noon–10pm, Thurs noon–11pm, Fri & Sat noon–11.30pm; kitchen closes a little earlier.

ENTERTAINMENT

Quarterhouse Mill Bay, CT20 1BN ☎ 01303 760750, ⓦ quarterhouse.co.uk. The anchor of the Creative Quarter, the Quarterhouse hosts a variety of live music, comedy and theatre, along with festival events and film screenings, in a striking modern building.

Hythe and around

Just five miles south of Folkestone, at the northeastern edge of Romney Marsh, the ancient town of **HYTHE** was a Cinque Port (see page 107), and an important entry point for pilgrims crossing the Channel to visit Becket's tomb in Canterbury. Today it's an attractive little seaside town, the northern terminus of the **Romney, Hythe & Dymchurch Railway** (see page 129), with a broad pebbly beach. During Hythe's heyday and before the silting up of the harbour, the High Street was at the sea's edge; today it lies north of the A259 and the Royal Military Canal, which runs prettily through town on its thirty-mile journey to Sussex. The beach here is good for **watersports**, especially windsurfing; contact the Hythe and Saltwood Sailing Club (HSSC; ☎ 01303 265178, ⓦ hssc.net) on the waterfront.

Royal Military Canal

Ⓦ royalmilitarycanal.com

Fringed on both sides by tree-lined banks, the **Royal Military Canal** was built, like the Martello towers (see page 125) – of which Hythe has five – to defend the coast from potential attack by Napoleonic troops. Today it runs for nearly thirty miles from Seabrook, just east of town, through the marshes to a point south of Winchelsea in Sussex; you can walk or cycle its entire length. Cutting through town, the canal gives Hythe its distinctive character, its grassy banks dotted with sculptures and making a splendid place for a shady picnic. **Rowing boats** can be rented from next to Ladies' Walk Bridge (Easter–Sept; £12/hr; ☎ 07718 761236, Ⓦ electricboathythe.co.uk), and every year in August the canal hosts a **Venetian Fete** (Ⓦ hythe-venetianfete.com), with a floating costume parade. Further out of town, the canal becomes increasingly peaceful, with swans gliding on the water, herons and kingfishers in the trees, and bright-yellow water lilies and irises in the shallows.

St Leonard's Church

Oak Walk, CT21 5DN • Church daily 8am–5.15pm; ossuary Easter & May–Sept Mon–Sat 11am–1pm & 2–4pm, Sun 2–4pm • Church free; ossuary £1 • ☎ 01303 264470, Ⓦ slhk.org

The Norman church of **St Leonard's**, high on a hill on the north side of town, is a handsome building, with a soaring thirteenth-century chancel boasting some fine stone carving, but its main appeal is of a more eerie kind. Step into the ambulatory, where an **ossuary** confronts you with a startling pile of thousands of thigh bones and shelves of grinning jawbones and skulls, neatly packed as if on some ghoulish supermarket shelf. Dating back to medieval times and earlier, they're thought to be the remains of locals buried in the churchyard and moved when the church was expanded in the thirteenth century – some show signs of being descended from Roman settlers. Medieval church officials immediately saw the potential of such a gruesome tourist attraction, and charged pilgrims on their way to Becket's shrine in Canterbury for the privilege of a peep.

Port Lympne Reserve

Lympne, CT21 4PD • Reserve Daily: April–Oct 9.30am–6.30pm, last admission 3pm; Nov–March 9.30am–5pm, last admission 2.30pm • £26, under-16s £22 • ☎ 01303 264647, Ⓦ aspinallfoundation.org/port-lympne • **Dusk safaris** May–Aug Wed–Fri 5.45pm • £45 • ☎ 01303 234111

Set in around six hundred acres five miles west of Hythe, **Port Lympne Reserve**, along with Howletts near Canterbury (see page 61), works with the charitable Aspinall Foundation on a conservation and breeding programme for wild and endangered species. The park is home to more than seven hundred animals, many of them rare – along with a pair of adorable spectacled bears and some Western Lowland gorillas, it has the largest herd of endangered black rhino in the UK. Port Lympne isn't a zoo, so you're not guaranteed a view of all the animals – visits start off safari-style, with bone-rattling trucks taking you around the "South American Experience" (capybara, tapirs, spectacled bears), the "African Experience" (wildebeest, giraffes, zebras, black rhino), "Asian Experience" (bears, rhinos, cheetahs), "Carnivore Territory" (big and rare cats, including Barbary lions, now extinct in the wild), and the primate enclosure; some areas, including the Dinosaur Forest (populated with life-sized models of prehistoric crowd-pullers from T-Rex to pterodactyls) are also accessible on foot. The Serengeti it isn't, and the vision of exotic creatures, should you be lucky enough to see them, roaming through the gentle Kent countryside, with views over Romney Marsh to the Channel, is incongruous to say the least – but it's a commendable enterprise, and quite an adventure in this quiet corner of Kent if you manage to be here on a sunny day.

The best way to see the park can be outside opening hours: **dusk safaris** including drinks and dinner are available in summer, while a number of **accommodation** options

ROMNEY, HYTHE & DYMCHURCH RAILWAY

The **Romney, Hythe & Dymchurch Railway** (RH&DR), a fifteen-inch-gauge line running the 13.5 miles between Hythe and Dungeness (1hr), offers an enjoyable way to travel through this quirky corner of Kent – stops include Dymchurch, St Mary's Bay, New Romney and Romney Sands, named for the neighbouring holiday camp, near Greatstone Beach (April to Oct daily; Nov to April Sat & Sun, plus special events and tours; £18.60 for an all-day rover ticket including the railway exhibition at New Romney station; shorter journeys are cheaper; ☎01797 362353, ⓦrhdr.org.uk). Built in 1927 as a tourist attraction, its fleet of steam locomotives are mainly one-third-scale models made during the 1920s and 1930s, so taking a long ride can feel a little cramped, but if Laurel and Hardy – who reopened the line from New Romney to Dungeness after the war in 1947 – could do it, anyone can. Hythe station is a fifteen-minute walk west of the town centre, on the south bank of the canal by Station Bridge, while the end of the line, in Dungeness, is near the Old Lighthouse (see page 131). New Romney, the original station, is the railway headquarters, with play parks and a model railway exhibition (£2).

range from super-luxurious lodges in the lion enclosure (see below) to a formal hotel, a self-catering treehouse and woodland cabins.

ACCOMMODATION AND EATING — HYTHE AND AROUND

Coppers 26 Prospect Rd, CT21 5JW ☎01303 267707, ⓦcoppersinhythe.co.uk. Creative, intriguing Indian food served in a colourful dining room. Friendly staff will talk you through the menu, which offers a range of dishes from Kolkatta-style fish fry to Sindhi goat curry or bottle gourd dumplings, all prepared with good ingredients. They are happy to adjust the spicing according to taste. Starters £4.50–9, mains £10–17. Tues–Sun 5.30–11pm.

Hythe Bay Seafood Restaurant Marine Parade, CT21 6AW ☎01303 233844, ⓦhythebay.co.uk. With a nice setting on Hythe's seafront, this once-smart but now slightly tired dining room has a breezy front terrace. It's less upmarket than its sister branches in Dover (see page 121) and Deal, but the menu is mostly the same, and the simple, traditional fish dishes are largely good, especially if you choose the local catch. Starters from £8, mains from £15. Daily noon–9.30pm; coffee served from 10am.

Lion Lodge Port Lympne Reserve, Lympne, CT21 4LR ☎01303 234112, ⓦaspinallfoundation.org/port-lympne/short-breaks/lion-lodge. Two luxurious, timber-clad lodges (each sleeping four) with a balcony and huge picture windows overlooking Port Lympne's small pride of lions (see above). It's all very luxe, with Scandi-style wooden outdoor bathtubs, and rates include a reserve safari and after-hours access, plus a personal golf buggy for exploring. Port Lympne has a number of other accommodation options should your budget not stretch to these levels of luxury. **£1750**

Romney Marsh

In Roman times, what is now the southernmost chunk of Kent was submerged beneath the English Channel. The lowering of sea levels in the Middle Ages, however, along with later reclamation, eventually created a hundred-square-mile area of shingle and marshland now known as **ROMNEY MARSH**. Once home to important Cinque and limb ports (see page 107), along with villages made wealthy from the wool trade, this now rather forlorn expanse stretches inland for around ten miles from Hythe and skims the eastern edges of the Weald before curving around to meet Rye in Sussex. The "marsh" is in fact made up of three marshes – Romney proper extends as far south as the road from Appledore to New Romney, Walland lies to the south and west, and Denge spreads east of Lydd. Together they present a melancholy aspect, much given over to agriculture and with few sights as such, unless you count the **sheep**, the birdlife and several curious medieval **churches** (see page 130). While this flat, depopulated area makes grand walking and cycling country, its salt-speckled, big-skied beauty can also be appreciated on the **Romney, Hythe & Dymchurch Railway** (see above). The little train is an excellent way to reach lonely **Dungeness**, the shingle promontory presided over by two colossal nuclear power stations that is so beloved of artists.

3

ROMNEY SHEEP

The salty, mineral-packed Romney marshes are famed among foodies for their indigenous breed of **sheep**, a hardy, independent and low-maintenance creature with a stout body and stubby legs. In addition to producing excellent meat, Romney sheep have heavy, dense and long-woolled fleeces; the local woolmaking industry, which started in medieval times, was hugely profitable, spinning off a flourishing smuggling trade that lasted into the nineteenth century. In the 1800s nearly a quarter of a million Romneys roamed this waterlogged landscape, and in 1872 the first of them were exported to Australia. Itinerant shepherds, or "**lookers**", followed the flocks as they wandered, shacking up in small brick huts (just a few of these shed-like structures remain today, identifiable by their rusty iron roofs and squat chimneys). There are fewer genuine Romneys around the marsh nowadays – you'd see more in New Zealand – and, as improved drainage has seen much of the land turned over to agriculture, many are bred on farms elsewhere. You may spot a few as you explore, however, foraging in the lush grasses and samphire.

Much **Romney lamb**, which is juicy, tender and sweet (not, surprisingly enough, salty), is exported to France, but it's also a regular on the menus of good Kent and Sussex restaurants, and you can buy it at some of the better farm shops. Vegetarians can enjoy the bounty of the marshes at **Romney Marsh Wools**, a sheep farm near Ashford, which sells luxurious Romney wool products including throws, moccasins and wool-fat soaps (W romneymarshwools.co.uk).

Dymchurch and around

Five miles from Hythe, **Dymchurch** is torn between defining itself as a cheery family resort and playing up its smuggling associations, particularly its location as a base for the marvellously named Dr Syn, the smuggling, swashbuckling vicar featured in the early twentieth-century novels of Russell Thorndike. The wide, three-mile-long **beach** is a good one: clean, sandy and family-friendly. There's another nice beach at **St Mary's Bay**, the next stop down on the Romney, Hythe & Dymchurch Railway. Just a hop away is the hamlet of **St Mary in the Marsh**, a scrap of a place with a couple of literary associations – Noël Coward lived in a cottage next door to the *Star Inn* pub before moving to Aldington nearby, while his friend, Edith Nesbit, who also lived nearby, is buried in the twelfth-century churchyard. Once a busy Cinque Port at the mouth of the River Rother, **New Romney** lost its importance after a series of dramatic storms in the thirteenth century silted up its harbour and changed the course of the river, sending it out to the sea at Rye; today it's the hub of the RH&DR (see page 129), with an interesting Norman church whose western door is sunk beneath ground level.

Dungeness

An end-of-the-earth feel pervades **DUNGENESS**, the windlashed headland at the southern extremities of Romney Marsh. The largest expanse of shingle in Europe, presided over by two hulking nuclear power stations (one of them decommissioned), "the Ness" is not conventionally pretty, but there's a strange beauty to this lost-in-time spot with its landmark **lighthouses** and its clanking miniature **railway** (see page 129). Many of the little cottages standing higgledy-piggledy on the golden shingle date back to when this entire area was owned by Southern Railway, and train workers converted old carriages into simple homes; today they're joined by high-concept architectural conversions, fishing boats both dilapidated and jaunty, forbidding watchtowers, rusting winches, long-obsolete "listening ears" (pre-radar early warning devices built in the 1920s and 30s) and decrepit concrete bunkers. Stubborn wildflowers, grasses and lichens cling to the pebbles like spillages of bright paint, adding a palette of splashy colour. Many artists – most famously the late filmmaker Derek Jarman, whose **Prospect Cottage** continues to draw garden lovers and movie fans alike – have been inspired by the area's extraordinary light, its colossal skies and its quiet weirdness, setting up home in the ramshackle cottages and fashioning gardens from beachcombed treasures.

With its steep beach and fierce current, Dungeness Point is no place for a swim, although you can do so further north towards Lydd, if you take great care with the tides, and it's possible to fish from Dungeness beach. The headland has been designated a **National Nature Reserve**, with no new development allowed. Its unique and fragile ecology supports a huge variety of vegetation, from wild red poppies and deep-pink sea peas to inky-blue sea kale and animal life – including large populations of the endangered great crested newt – and it's renowned for superb **birdwatching**.

Old Lighthouse

Next to the RH&DR station, Dungeness, TN29 9NB • 10.30am–4.30pm: March–May, Sept & Oct Sat & Sun; June Tues–Thurs, Sat & Sun; July & Aug daily • £4.50 • ☎ 01797 321300, ⓦ dungenesslighthouse.com

Decommissioned since the erection in 1961 of its smaller successor nearby (the "New Lighthouse"), the 143ft-high **Old Lighthouse**, built in 1904 and painted the same velvety black as many of the beach cottages, displays navigational equipment and information panels on its four floors and affords sweeping views from the top. It's nearly two hundred steps up, with an extremely steep final stretch, and can be dramatically windy – vertigo sufferers should beware. The large, round structure next to the Old Lighthouse is the base of the oldest lighthouse of all, built in the eighteenth century and long since gone. It is now a private residence.

Prospect Cottage

Dungeness Rd, TN29 9NE • Roughly a 20min walk from the RH&DR station

The late **Derek Jarman** (1942–94), artist and avant-garde filmmaker, made his home at **Prospect Cottage**, a black weatherboard cottage with sunshine-yellow window frames, and the shingle garden he created in his final years from stones, rusty sea treasures and tough little plants remains a poignant memorial. The flowers may not always bloom quite as brightly today, without Jarman's guiding hand, but the poetry of his vision lingers, not least on the side of the house, where a long quote from John Donne's poem *The Sunne Rising* is carved black on black.

As everywhere in Dungeness, there is no fence – but do bear in mind that both the garden and the house are private.

FIVE ROMNEY MARSH CHURCHES

The dozen or so **medieval churches** of the Romney marshes are atmospheric and often isolated places, whose largely unrestored interiors provide evocative reminders of the days when the area thrived on the lucrative wool trade and wealth from its ports. The following are the pick of the bunch; for a full list, see ⓦ romneymarshchurches.org.uk.

St Augustine's Brookland. Decidedly odd thirteenth-century church, with its conical wooden belfry standing beside it rather than on top of it. Inside, note the wall painting on the south wall, showing the murder of Thomas Becket, and the unusual lead font marked with signs of the zodiac.

St Clement's Old Romney. Filmmaker Derek Jarman has his simple gravestone in the churchyard of this lovely Norman church. The restful whitewashed interior, with its Georgian minstrel gallery and rose-pink box pews, can be seen in the 1962 Disney movie *Dr Syn, Alias the Scarecrow*, which starred Patrick McGoohan of *The Prisoner* fame.

St Dunstan's Snargate. The terracotta wall painting of a ship (c.1500) in the north aisle of this thirteenth-century church is locally believed to have been a secret signal to smugglers that this was a safe haven.

St Mary the Virgin St Mary in the Marsh. This peaceful ancient church, parts of which date back to 1133, is notable for being the burial place of author E. Nesbit; her grave is marked by a simple wooden sign.

St Thomas à Becket Fairfield. The iconic Romney church, standing like a lonely sentinel upon the Walland Marsh, is all that survives of the lost village of Fairfield. Its largely Georgian interior, with herringbone floor and exposed beams, is beautifully tranquil.

3

ACTION WATERSPORTS

The coast around Camber in Sussex is renowned for its watersports (see page 172); just six miles away in Lydd, **Action Watersports** (📞 01797 321885, 🌐 actionwatersports.co.uk) is a top-notch facility offering sheltered waterskiing, wakeboarding, SUP-ing, flyboarding and jet-skiing, plus a floating inflatable aquapark, on a purpose-built, 22-acre freshwater lake. Lessons and equipment rental are available. Rates and packages vary – you might spend £29 for a fifteen-minute water-ski session or £99 for a flyboarding package. There's a huge pro shop and hot showers on site, along with relaxation areas.

RSPB Dungeness Reserve

Off the Lydd road, three miles from Dungeness, TN29 9PN • **Reserve** Daily 9am–9pm or sunset • £5 • **Visitor centre** Daily: March–Oct 10am–5pm; Nov–Feb 10am–4pm • Free • 📞 01797 320588, 🌐 rspb.org.uk/Dungeness

The marshy Dungeness promontory, poking out vigorously into the Channel, attracts huge colonies of gulls, as well as bitterns, little ringed plovers, Slavonian grebes, smews and wheatears. You can see them, and all manner of water birds, waders and wildfowl, from the huge picture windows at the excellent **RSPB visitor centre** and from half a dozen hides in the reserve itself, accessible on three easy trails.

ARRIVAL AND INFORMATION
ROMNEY MARSH

By train There's a mainline train station at Appledore, on the Ashford-to-Hastings line, while Dymchurch, St Mary's Bay, New Romney, Romney Sands and Dungeness are all on the miniature RH&DR (see page 129).

Romney Marsh Visitor Centre Dymchurch Rd, on the A259 between Dymchurch and New Romney (April–Oct daily 10am–5pm; Nov–March Wed–Sun 10am–4pm; 📞 01797 369487, 🌐 kentwildlifetrust.org.uk/nature-reserves/romney-marsh-visitor-centre-and-nature-reserve). This ecofriendly centre is packed with information on the wildlife of the marsh, with marked trails and organic gardens.

ACCOMMODATION

Beach Sun Retreat 21 Sycamore Gardens, Dymchurch, TN29 0LA 📞 07830 182380, 🌐 beachsunretreat. com. This self-catering house, sleeping thirteen in seven individually themed rooms, is perfect if you're sick of the British weather – its "sun room", complete with tropical mural and DJ decks, is bathed in replica natural sunlight. Though undeniably kitsch, it's more hip than tacky – occupying an old, timber-clad hotel, the property has a luxurious, airy feel with a film-screening room and extensive grounds with easy access to Dymchurch's sandy beach. Minimum three-night stay. **£750**

Romney Bay House Hotel Coast Rd, Littlestone, TN28 8QY 📞 01797 364747, 🌐 romneybayhousehotel. co.uk. Accessed down a potholed road near Dungeness and presiding alone over the lonesome shingle like a fading *grande dame*, this 1920s beauty was built by Sir Clough Williams-Ellis, who designed Portmeirion in Wales, for the Hollywood gossip columnist Hedda Hopper. Today it's a quirky hotel, with ten en-suite double/twins (some with sea views), a cosy drawing room and a light-filled lounge overlooking the sea, which is just footsteps away. The

restaurant (Tues, Wed, Fri & Sat) serves a four-course set dinner for £47.50. No children under 14. **£150**

Shingle House Dungeness Beach, TN29 9NE 🌐 living-architecture.co.uk. A breathtaking modern self-catering house, offered by Alain de Botton's Living Architecture programme, blending in beautifully with its surroundings. Behind the tarry black timber exterior, it's designed to the very last inch – all white tongue-and-groove, stained wood, warm concrete and vast glass walls opening out onto the shingle – and offers seriously luxurious accommodation for up to eight people. It books up very fast and very far in advance. Three-night or weekly stays only. **£800**

★ **The Watch Tower** Dungeness Rd, TN29 9NF 📞 01797 321773, 🌐 watchtowerdungeness.com. Originally a lookout post built in the Napoleonic Wars, this is a peaceful and very welcoming one-room B&B on the northern edge of the Ness. A private guest entrance leads through the arty back garden, via your own light, plant-filled conservatory – where a substantial breakfast is served – into the comfortable twin/double room with its cheery Dungeness-themed bathroom. **£100**

EATING AND DRINKING

Britannia Inn Dungeness Rd, TN29 9ND 📞 01797 321959, 🌐 britanniadungeness.co.uk. Squatting at Dungeness Point, very near the RH&DR station, this unfussy

place is a popular local destination for Shepherd Neame ales, pub grub and pizza. Mon–Sat 11am–9pm, Sun 11am–7pm; kitchen Mon–Fri & Sun noon–6pm, Sat noon–8pm.

★ **Dungeness Snack Shack** Fish Hut, Dungeness Rd, TN29 9NB ☎07549 377527, ⓦdungenesssnackshack. net or ⓦfacebook.com/snackshack.dungenessfish. It doesn't get much fresher, or more local, than this – the day's catch, brought ashore and sold straight off the boat, to take away from this little hut. Try a lobster or crab roll, a fisherman's roll (fresh grilled fish served in a bun), a Mexican roll (served in a flatbread with lime, chilli and sour cream) or fresh fish with fried potatoes. They're open in winter, too, dishing up a warming chowder – and all as cheap as chips (baps from £5). Some picnic tables outside. Usually Wed–Sun 11am–3.30pm, depending on weather; check Facebook page for updates.

Pilot Inn Battery Rd, TN29 9NJ ☎01797 320314, ⓦthepilotdungeness.co.uk. The vaguely nautical *Pilot* pub, just north of Dungeness lifeboat station, is a local favourite for fish and chips (from £11.95) – other options, from pies via burgers to a vegan stew with dumplings, are also on offer. Richardson's, opposite, sells superb smoked and fresh wet fish. Mon–Sat 11am–10pm, Sun 11am–9pm; kitchen Mon–Sat noon–9pm, Sun noon–8pm.

Red Lion Snargate, TN29 9UQ ☎01797 344648. Take a trip back in time at this gem of a pub, which has been in the same family for more than a century and changed little since the 1940s. World War II memorabilia fills the place, Kentish cask ales and ciders are served at a cluttered marble bar, and they've even got a selection of vintage pub games. Cash only. Daily; hours vary.

Woolpack Inn Beacon Lane, Brookland, TN29 9TJ ☎01797 344321, ⓦwoolpackinnbrookland.co.uk. Family-friendly country pub in a quiet village, retaining many of its fifteenth-century features, including a head-bangingly low ceiling and wattle-and-daub walls. You can drink in the large garden or the cosy, hop-strewn interior, and eat satisfying, homecooked pub grub – steaks, fresh local fish, veggie dishes and burgers. Mains £9–23. Mon–Fri 11am–3pm & 6–10pm, Sat 11am–11pm, Sun noon–10pm; kitchen Mon–Fri noon–2.30pm & 6–9pm, Sat & Sun noon–9pm.

3

The Kent Weald

SISSINGHURST

The Kent Weald

The Kentish Weald, wedged between the North Downs and the High Weald of Sussex, is defined by its gentle hills and country lanes, shallow valleys and tangled broadleaf woodlands. This landscape is at once quintessentially English, and, with its historic orchards and old brick oast houses – testament to the days when the Weald dominated England's hopping industry – has also come to symbolize Kent as a whole. The entire region, packed full of historic sites, royal estates, fairy-tale moated manor houses and some of England's loveliest gardens, makes splendid day-trip territory – the western Weald, in particular, is an easy journey from London.

It's perfectly feasible to plan a longer break, too, basing yourself in or around any one of numerous villages – Cranbrook, say – or in **Tunbridge Wells**, by far the nicest of the Weald's large towns. Both sit in the beautiful **High Weald**, scattered with gorgeous hamlets, with lots of country walking, peaceful places to stay and more gastropubs than you can shake a pint of real ale at. Some of England's finest **vineyards** are scattered around the east of the region, where the chalky soil yields dry whites and sparkling wines as good as any from France.

The commuter towns of **Sevenoaks** and **Maidstone**, on the fringes of the Weald, are surrounded by tourist attractions. Big hitters include Leeds Castle and **Hever Castle** – Anne Boleyn's family home – Winston Churchill's estate at **Chartwell**, and the jaw-dropping treasure house of **Knole**, the childhood home of Vita Sackville-West, who went on to create the sublime gardens at **Sissinghurst**. Less known, but with big appeal, are the Roman villa at **Lullingstone**; the fascinating **Down House**, where Charles Darwin lived and worked for forty years; and the delightful Elizabethan manor and gardens at **Penshurst**, along with a host of smaller historic houses and gardens. The Kentish Weald is renowned for its bluebells, which carpet the woodlands with a shimmer of mauve each spring – you'll find stunning woods around Chartwell and Sissinghurst, as well as near **Ightham Mote**, a charming Tudor manor house, and at the Edwardian **Emmetts Garden**.

Much of the Weald is commuter territory, so public transport to the main towns is good, but you'll need to drive – or even better, walk or cycle – to explore the countryside in depth. Long-distance walking routes include the Greensand Way from Surrey – which runs through the Weald before ending at Hamstreet, on the border with Romney Marsh – and many shorter loops and trails link the area's heritage sights. The North Downs offer excellent walking opportunities, with peaceful villages just a hop away from the busy Eurostar hub of **Ashford**.

Royal Tunbridge Wells

It seems unfair that **ROYAL TUNBRIDGE WELLS** is still associated, in many minds, with the fictional letter-writer known as "Disgusted of Tunbridge Wells", a whingeing Little Englander renowned for blustering and umbrage. Don't be misled – this handsome spa town, established after a bubbling spring was discovered here in 1606, and peaking during the Regency period, is an appealing destination. There are a couple of low-key sights, but above all it's a nice place simply to stroll around, with a pretty Victorian **high street** leading down to the pedestrianized **Pantiles**, and some excellent restaurants and pubs. Surrounded by gorgeous High Weald countryside, the town also has lots of lovely green space: the **Grove** and, to the north, **Calverley Grounds** offer formal gardens,

DEER AT KNOLE

Highlights

❶ Bedgebury This ancient broadleaf forest and world-renowned pinetum is a glorious spot to commune with nature, with countless options for all the family to get active. See page 145

❷ Vineyard tours Strolling through vineyards, learning about English viniculture and tasting excellent, award-winning wines is a wonderful way to spend a sunny Kent afternoon. See pages 146 and 150

❸ Sissinghurst Breathtaking gardens created by Vita Sackville-West – who defined her planting style as "cram, cram, cram, every chink and cranny" – and her husband. See page 148

❹ Smallhythe Place Picture-postcard Tudor cottage, once home to the glamorous Victorian

actor Ellen Terry. See page 150

❺ Knole This magnificent old estate, with its glorious medieval deer park, is a classic English beauty with a fascinating history. See page 152

❻ Chartwell Along with lovely gardens and countryside walks, Winston Churchill's family home reveals a touchingly personal side of this gruff statesman. See page 154

❼ Hever Castle Gardens Laid out between 1904 and 1908 by Waldorf Astor, these showpiece gardens include gorgeous Italianate statuary, rose gardens and trees planted in the time of Anne Boleyn, who spent her childhood here. See page 157

HIGHLIGHTS ARE MARKED ON THE MAP ON PAGE 138

THE KENT WEALD

HIGHLIGHTS

1 Bedgebury
2 Vineyard tours
3 Sissinghurst
4 Smallhythe Place
5 Knole
6 Chartwell
7 Hever Castle Gardens

HOPPING MAD

Unlike their neighbours on the Continent, medieval Brits preferred their ale syrupy sweet, made with malt and flavoured with spices. Tastes changed in the fifteenth century, however, after Flemish merchants introduced them to beer made with **hops** – which, quite apart from their distinctive flavour, have strong preservative qualities. In 1520 the first hop garden opened, near Canterbury – the Kentish soil provided perfect growing conditions, and the local woodlands supplied essential poles, for training the vines, and charcoal, for drying the hops. Just as significant, however, was the wealth of medieval Kentish farmers, which meant they could invest in new, labour-intensive and untried agricultural ventures. Almost immediately English beer was being exported to the Continent, much to the concern of the Dutch growers, and the industry boomed so dramatically that laws were passed preventing farmers rejecting all other forms of agriculture in favour of hop-growing. By the 1650s, hops were grown in fourteen English counties, with Kent producing one third of the total, and by the 1870s, around 72,000 acres – most of them in Kent – were devoted to the industry. The distinctive round **oast houses**, used for drying hops and topped with tiptilted white cowls, rapidly became as familiar a feature on the Wealden landscape as its woods and orchards.

The harvest required **casual labour** almost from the start. After the coming of the railway, thousands of "**hoppers**", generations of families and entire neighbourhoods, mainly from London's East End, were migrating to the fields of Kent for six weeks every autumn. Taking special "hopper trains", or piling into trucks and buses, joined by gypsy families in their caravans and itinerant workers chancing their luck, the hoppers originally lived in rough tents, but by the early twentieth century these had been upgraded to tiny "huts" – tin shacks, or stables. Some would bring bedding and curtains from home, covering unglazed windows and lining walls with newspapers; others would simply shack up in the straw, wrapping themselves in sacks. Everyone cooked and ate outside on faggot fires, sharing rudimentary washing and toilet facilities.

Days were strictly regulated, with hoppers working in teams (or "drifts"), tearing down the climbing vines ("bines"), stripping them of their cones, and filling their baskets as fast as they could. Pay was calculated per bushel, and often settled at the end of the season (by which time the rate had often plummeted); more skilled jobs, paid by the day, included that of the stiltmen, balanced on high stilts, who cared for the wires at the top of the wooden hop poles. **George Orwell**, who went hopping near Maidstone in 1931, stated that "as far as wages go, no worse employment exists" – and it was tiring, often painful, work, with hands ripped by prickly stems and covered in rashes from hop resin. But the chance to escape the cramped, polluted East End, the health benefits of fresh air and the opportunity to meet up with old friends seemed to override all that. Each farm effectively became its own community, with parties, dances and a Hop Queen crowned; temperance workers, the Salvation Army and the Red Cross would set up camp nearby to provide spiritual and medical care. In local villages, meanwhile, there was much mistrust of these rough Cockney incomers: shops battened down the hatches, and pubs, if they served them at all, consigned hoppers to special areas. Following mechanization in the 1950s the need for hoppers dwindled to almost nothing, and the majority of the oast houses that remain have been converted into private homes.

paths and splendid views, while the wilder, wooded **Common**, spreading out to the west behind the Pantiles, is laced with historic walking paths.

The Pantiles

Tucked off the southern end of the High Street, the colonnaded **Pantiles** – named for the clay tiles, shaped in wooden pans, that paved the street in the seventeenth century – is a pedestrianized parade of independent shops, delis and coffee houses that exudes a faded, almost raffish elegance. In Georgian times the fashionable set would gather here to promenade and take the waters, and it remains a lively stretch, especially in sunny weather, when the alfresco restaurant tables are buzzing with people-watching crowds. Hub of the Pantiles is the original **Chalybeate Spring**, in the 1804 Bath House. For £1, a costumed "dipper" will serve you a cup of the ferrous waters (Easter–Sept Thurs–Sun 10am–3pm), a tradition that dates back to the eighteenth century.

Tunbridge Wells Museum

Mount Pleasant Rd, TN1 1JN • ☎ 01892 554171, ⓦ tunbridgewellsmuseum.org

Tunbridge Wells Museum has a very good local-history collection, spanning everything from fossils to dandy Georgian glad rags, fading maps to scruffy stuffed animals, local cricket balls to spooky Victorian dolls. Particularly notable is its exquisite collection of **Tunbridge ware**, the finely crafted wooden marquetry, dating from the late eighteenth century and popular until the 1920s, that was applied to everything from boxes to book covers to furniture and created a wealth of Tunbridge Wells souvenirs. In November 2018 the museum closed for redevelopment. It promises to reopen bigger and better, under a new name, in 2021; watch the website to keep up to date on progress.

King Charles the Martyr

Chapel Place, TN1 1YX • Mon–Sat 11am–3pm, Sun 10am–noon & 6.30–7.30pm • Free • ☎ 01892 511745, ⓦ kcmtw.org

The first permanent building in Tunbridge Wells, the Restoration church of **King Charles the Martyr** (1676) was the brainchild of Thomas Neale, the entrepreneur

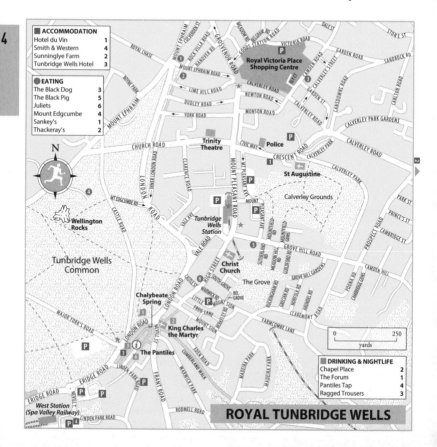

■ ACCOMMODATION	
Hotel du Vin	1
Smith & Western	4
Sunninglye Farm	2
Tunbridge Wells Hotel	3

● EATING	
The Black Dog	3
The Black Pig	5
Juliets	6
Mount Edgcumbe	4
Sankey's	1
Thackeray's	2

■ DRINKING & NIGHTLIFE	
Chapel Place	2
The Forum	1
Pantiles Tap	4
Ragged Trousers	3

ROYAL TUNBRIDGE WELLS

who, having built the Pantiles to exploit the tourist potential of the spring, went on to provide a place of worship and an assembly room for visitors. Behind the forbidding exterior lies a beautiful space. Its exquisite domed ceilings, their plasterwork emblazoned with flowers, grapes, cherubs and foliage, remain amazingly intact, while in the north gallery you can perch on the young Queen (then Princess) Victoria's very own pew. Other highlights include hand-written lists of early congregations, including Samuel Pepys, and, as you might expect from its name, a few pieces of memorabilia relating to Charles I.

ARRIVAL AND DEPARTURE ROYAL TUNBRIDGE WELLS

By train The train station stands where the High St becomes Mount Pleasant Rd.
Destinations Hastings (every 30min–1hr; 40–50min); London Charing Cross (every 15–30min; 55min); Sevenoaks (every 20min; 20–25min); Tonbridge (every 15–20min; 10–15min).
By bus Buses set down and pick up along London Rd and

Mount Pleasant Rd.
Destinations Brighton (every 30min–1hr; 1hr 50min); Cranbrook (every 30min–1hr; 1hr 10min); Hever (Mon–Sat 2 daily; 40–50min); Lewes (every 30min–1hr; 1hr 20min); Maidstone (every 30min; 1hr 20min); Sevenoaks (every 30min–2hr; 45min); Tonbridge (every 15–30min; 10min).

INFORMATION AND TOURS

Tourist office Corn Exchange, The Pantiles (April–Sept Mon & Wed–Sat 10am–3pm, Tues 10am–2pm; Oct–March Tues 10am–2pm, Wed–Sat 10am–3pm; ☎ 01892 515675, ⓦ visittunbridgewells.com). Occasional guided walking tours set off from here (1hr; £5).
Spa Valley Railway Based at West Station, a few minutes'

walk southwest of The Pantiles, this historic railroad, with steam and diesel locos, runs short trips via Groombridge to Eridge in Sussex, passing lovely Weald countryside (days vary, but generally Sat, Sun & hols Feb–Oct, with extra days in summer; £10 return; total 1hr–1hr 30min trip; ☎ 01892 537715, ⓦ spavalleyrailway.co.uk).

ACCOMMODATION SEE MAP PAGE 140

Hotel du Vin Crescent Rd, TN1 2LY ☎ 01892 320749, ⓦ hotelduvin.com. Elegantly set in a Georgian mansion overlooking Calverley Grounds, this member of the *Hotel du Vin* chain is quietly classy with a cosy bar and romantic French restaurant, and an atmospherically sloping old staircase leading up to the contemporary rooms. The best are at the back, with views of the lavender-filled grounds, the hotel vineyard and the park beyond. **£165**
Smith & Western Linden Park Rd, TN2 5QL ☎ 01892 550750, ⓦ smith-western.co.uk. The Tunbridge Wells branch of this Country and Western-themed mini-chain restaurant, atmospherically set in the old West train station, has nine comfortable, good-value rooms loosely themed around Native American imagery. **£110**
Sunninglye Farm Dundale Rd, TN3 9AG ☎ 01420 80804,

ⓦ featherdown.co.uk/location/sunninglye-farm. Four miles southeast of town, across the border on a hilltop copse in Sussex, this glampsite – one of the boutique Feather Down Farms chain – offers seven opulent tents (sleeping six), with beds, wood-burning stoves and flushing loos, on a family farm. The surroundings are bucolic, with a little nature-spotting area and a pond with rowing boats and materials for raft making, and campfires are permitted – you collect firewood yourself from the local woods. Two/three-night minimum. **£130**
Tunbridge Wells Hotel 58 The Pantiles, TN2 5TD ☎ 01892 530501, ⓦ thetunbridgewellshotel.com. Location is key in this period hotel, which offers quirky charm in cosy rooms above a smart modern British restaurant on the Pantiles – there's no lift, so ask if you don't fancy a room on the higher floors. **£150**

EATING SEE MAP PAGE 140

The Black Dog 20 Camden Rd, TN1 2PY ☎ 01892 549543, ⓦ blackdogcafetw.co.uk. This excellent little Aussie-run coffee house flies the flag for Camden Rd, the (slightly) boho face of Tunbridge Wells. It's not all flat whites and macchiatos; they're licensed, and offer tasty, on-trend food, from breakfast (new potato, ham and quinoa hash, say) via Sunday brunch (toasted banana bread with vanilla ricotta and honey) to lunch (sushi bowls, burgers). Dishes from £4. Mon–Fri 8am–4pm, Sat 8am–5pm, Sun 9am–2pm.

The Black Pig 18 Grove Hill Rd, TN1 1RZ ☎ 01892 523030, ⓦ theblackpig.net. Pig out at this gastropub, where dishes might include slow-roast pork belly, sirloin steak or pan-fried sea bream – or simply settle down with a charcuterie plate and a glass of wine in the sunny beer garden. Mains from £13.50. Mon–Sat noon–11pm, Sun noon–9pm; kitchen Mon–Sat noon–9.30pm, Sun noon–4pm.
Juliets 54 High St, TN1 1XF ☎ 01892 522931, ⓦ facebook.com/julietscafe. Don't be misled by the

4

twee window display; this is a lovely independent café whose warm, exposed-brick interior, filled with splashy paintings and mismatched furniture, invites you to linger. The homemade food is a winner, from the fab breakfasts (till 11.30am) – hop sausage sandwiches, pancakes with syrup, avocado on toast – to the daily-changing salads, soups, smoothies and cakes. Mains from £7. Takeaway available. Tues–Sun 8am–5pm.

Mount Edgcumbe The Common, TN4 8BX ☎01892 618854, ⊛themountedgcumbe.com. Hidden away on the Common, this friendly food pub makes a cosy, offbeat place for a meal – from halloumi and beetroot burgers to fish and chips – or a pint of local ale. With a lovely garden, it has a deliciously rural feel; in bad weather, check out the real cave in the bar area. Sharing boards and mains from £12. Mon–Wed 11am–11pm, Thurs–Sat 11am–11.30pm, Sun noon–10.30pm; kitchen Mon–Thurs noon–3pm & 6–9.30pm, Fri & Sat noon–9.30pm, Sun noon–8pm.

Sankey's 39 Mount Ephraim, TN4 8AA ☎01892 511422, ⊛sankeys.co.uk. Cosy seafood brasserie – with a sunny patio – serving great fish and shellfish (from crab spaghetti to fish cakes, oysters to paella) from £9. You can get the same menu, plus simple grub – grazing boards, burgers, Sunday roasts –in the buzzy pub upstairs, decked out with enamel signs and brewery mirrors, with comfy sofas around a wood-burning stove and a large selection of specialist beers. Brasserie Tues–Fri noon–3pm & 6–7pm, Sat noon–3pm. Pub Mon–Wed & Sun noon–11pm, Thurs–Sat noon–1am; kitchen Mon–Fri noon–3pm & 6–10pm, Sat noon–10pm, Sun noon–6pm.

★ **Thackeray's** 85 London Rd, TN1 1EA ☎01892 511921, ⊛thackerays-restaurant.co.uk. Named for the novelist William Makepeace Thackeray, who lived here for a time in 1860, this tile-hung seventeenth-century building offers top-notch modern European dining in a smart, relaxed room or alfresco courtyard. Dishes such as pan-fried gurnard with wilted kale and sea herbs or wild-garlic gnocchi with morchella mushrooms are conjured from fresh market produce, with fine wines to match. Mains from £24 (from £14 on the vegetarian menu); two-/three-course menus £20/£24 at lunch, £25/£30 at dinner. Tues–Sat noon–2.30pm & 6.30–10.30pm, Sun noon–2.30pm.

DRINKING AND NIGHTLIFE

SEE MAP PAGE 140

Chapel Place 18 Chapel Place, TN1 1YQ ☎01892 522304, ⊛chapelplacetw.co.uk. Bijou cocktail bar that pulls a cool but relaxed crowd for its on-trend rustic/ industrial decor and well-mixed drinks (from £6). They're big on the gin here, but also offer wine and Estrella. Tues–Sat noon–11pm, Sun noon–10pm.

★ **The Forum** Fonthill, The Common, TN4 8YU ☎08712 777101, ⊛twforum.co.uk. Highly regarded 250-capacity music venue that pulls an enthusiastic, in-the-know crowd for its lively programme of indie, up-and-coming and tribute bands, club nights, poetry slams and comedy.

Pantiles Tap 39–41 The Pantiles, TN2 5TE ☎01892 530397, ⊛thepantiles.com/shops/the-pantiles-tap. A brilliant destination for beer-lovers, this sweet spot is tucked away just behind the Pantiles with a tiny terrace and a frequently changing selection of keg and cask ales and ciders from microbreweries all around the UK. Local wines and an interesting range of bottled beers are on offer, too. Mon 4–11.30pm, Tues–Sat noon–11.30pm, Sun noon–10.30pm.

Ragged Trousers 44 The Pantiles, TN2 5TN ☎01892 542715, ⊛raggedtrousers.co.uk. This popular, relaxed bar, in the eighteenth-century Assembly Rooms, sees a high-spirited crowd enjoying real ales and lively chat, with decent pub grub during the day (£5–15). Daily noon–11pm; kitchen Mon–Fri noon–3pm, Sat & Sun noon–4pm.

ENTERTAINMENT

★ **Trinity Theatre** Church Rd, TN1 1JP ☎01892 678678, ⊛trinitytheatre.net. You'll catch art movies, world cinema and cult classics in the excellent Trinity, which also stages top-quality rep theatre, music and stand-up in an atmospherically converted church.

Around Royal Tunbridge Wells

Set in the High Weald, **Tunbridge Wells** is moments away from Sussex; the historic **Spa Valley Railway** (see page 141) chugs through lovely countryside from here to Eridge. This area is particularly good for **climbing**, with Nuts 4 Climbing in nearby Groombridge offering taster sessions and lessons (see page 193). To the north is the Elizabethan estate at **Penshurst**, with its glorious grounds, and **Tonbridge**, a quiet town long overshadowed by its neighbour, where you can tour the gatehouse of the once-mighty medieval castle. The tiny hamlet of **Tudeley** nearby offers a surprise in its local church – a set of ravishing windows designed by the artist **Marc Chagall**.

CYCLING THE TUDOR TRAIL AND BEYOND

The six-mile, mostly traffic-free **Tudor Trail** (download a map and guide at ⓦexplorekent.org), which runs along Regional Cycle Route 12, allows you to combine a cycle ride with some of the Weald's most popular sights. Starting from **Tonbridge**, which has a train station (see page 143), the route west to **Penshurst Place** takes you along the Medway, through broadleaf woodlands, and past wildflower meadows and lakes. From Penshurst you can extend your trip to **Hever Castle** (see page 157) along country lanes and peaceful bridleways, perhaps stopping off at the pretty village of **Chiddingstone** (see page 156). It's just a mile to Hever train station, or three miles to Edenbridge station, from Hever Castle.

Penshurst Place

Penshurst, TN11 8DG • April–Oct daily: house & toy museum noon–4pm; grounds & gardens 10.30am–6pm; parkland open all year • £12, grounds & gardens only £10; parkland free • ☎ 01892 870307, ⓦ penshurstplace.com • Bus #231 or #233 from Edenbridge train station (Mon–Sat)

Tudor timber-framed houses and shops line the pretty main street of **PENSHURST**, set in countryside five miles northwest of Tunbridge Wells. Presiding over it all is **Penshurst Place**, a magnificent fourteenth-century manor house that has been home to the Sidney family since 1552 and was birthplace of Sir Philip Sidney, the Elizabethan soldier, poet and all-round Renaissance Man. The jaw-dropping **Barons Hall**, dating from 1341, is the glory of the interior, with its 60ft-high chestnut-beamed roof still in place; it's all the more stunning for being largely unadorned, with amazingly well-preserved life-sized carved wooden figures – satirical representations of local peasants and manor workers – still supporting its vast arched braces. Elsewhere, the formal staterooms are packed with furniture and art, featuring important Elizabethan portraits, some fabulous tapestries and a fine room of armour with some savage-looking halberds; curiosities in the small **toy museum** include a painting on a cobweb and a Noah's Ark made from straw.

The 48 acres of grounds – and the surrounding 500 acres of parkland – offer good walks, while the eleven-acre walled **garden** is a beautiful example of Elizabethan garden design, with formal, yew-edged "rooms" ablaze with tulips, peonies, roses and lavender. There's also an adventure playground, and an excellent **farmers' market** on the first Saturday of the month (9.30am–noon; ⓦkfma.org.uk/penshurst).

Tonbridge and around

With its prime location and its good road and river connections, **TONBRIDGE** was for centuries far larger and more important than Tunbridge Wells. It's much quieter today – though Jane Austen's father was born here, and fans can pick up a self-guided walking-tour leaflet in the tourist office to follow in the family footsteps – and chiefly of interest for the mighty gatehouse of its medieval **castle**. If you're here on the second Sunday in the month, be sure to check out the big **farmers' market** (9.30am–1.30pm; ⓦtonbridgefarmersmarket.co.uk), which is one of the best in Kent.

Tonbridge Castle

Castle St, TN9 1BG • Mon–Thurs & Sat 9am–5pm, Fri 9am–4.30pm, Sun 10.30am–4.30pm; last tour 1hr before closing • Audio tours (1hr) £9, under-16s £5.85 • ☎ 01732 770929, ⓦ www.tonbridgecastle.org

A huge motte-and-bailey affair, later home to a large, self-sufficient feudal community, **Tonbridge Castle** was built in 1068 and heavily fortified over the following centuries. Controlling the bridge across the Medway, in a key position between London and the coastal ports, it remained effective as a fortress until the Civil War, using the most advanced design to repel attackers. Today, **audio tours** lead you around its impressively intact four-storey **gatehouse**, which in size and might is almost a castle in itself. Imparting lots of lively information on the castle's preparations for battle, it's all enjoyably interactive, with re-creations of thirteenth-century life including subterranean storerooms where disconcertingly life-like mannequins lurk in the half-light, and supper tables where rumbustious guards joke and banter. You might even come across the odd poor soldier taking a moment for himself in one of the gloomy privy chambers.

All Saints' Church

Tudeley Lane, Tudeley, TN11 0NZ • Summer daily 9.30am–6pm; rest of year daily 9.30am–4pm • £3 donation requested • ☎ 01892 836653, ⓦ tudeley.org/allsaintstudeley.htm

It would be easy to drive through **TUDELEY**, a scrap of a hamlet on the outskirts of Tonbridge, were it not for **All Saints' Church**. In this simple stone-and-brick structure, peacefully overlooking fields at the edge of the village, you'll find an unexpected surprise: twelve stained-glass windows designed between the 1960s and 1980s by the Russian artist **Marc Chagall** (1887–1985). Commissioned to create a memorial window by the parents of a local woman who died young, Chagall was so taken with the spot that he decided to design the rest of the windows too. They are an extraordinary sight, set low in the walls and easy to approach – the artist's marks are clear to see, while the dreamy golds, turquoises, rose pinks and inky violets wash over each other to create folkloric, almost abstract ensembles of birds, animals and deft floral motifs. It's undeniably moving to see the artist's humanistic and spiritual vision on such a grand, close-up scale, especially when the sunbeams stream through and flood the church with washes of jewel-like colour.

Tudeley Woods RSPB Reserve

Between Tunbridge Wells and Tonbridge on the A21, TN11 0PT • Daily 24hr • Free • ☎ 01892 752430, ⓦ rspb.org.uk

An invigorating mix of woods and heathland, **Tudeley Woods RSPB Reserve** is a haven not only for birds – lesser spotted woodpeckers, nightjars, woodlarks and marsh tits among them – but also butterflies and woodland flowers, including bluebells and rare orchids. It's especially interesting during the autumn migration season, and a profusion of **fungi** – more than a thousand species at last count, including the intriguingly named Puffballs, Deceivers and Chickens of the Woods – sprouts along the woodland floor. You can follow three nature trails, each between one and three miles in length.

ARRIVAL AND INFORMATION

By train Tonbridge train station is a 10min walk from the castle along the High St.

Destinations Ashford (every 30min; 35min); Canterbury West (every 30min–hourly; 55min); Edenbridge (hourly; 15min); Hastings (every 30min–1hr; 50min–1hr); London Bridge (every 30min; 45min); London Charing Cross (every 10–30min; 50min); London Victoria (hourly; 50min); Penshurst (hourly; 8min); Tunbridge Wells (every 15–30min; 10min).

Tourist office Castle grounds, Castle St, Tonbridge (Mon–Sat 8am–5pm, Sun 10am–4pm; ☎ 01732 770929).

EATING AND DRINKING

Bottlehouse Inn Coldharbour Rd, Penshurst, TN11 8ET ☎ 01892 870306, ⓦ thebottlehouseinnpenshurst.co.uk. A smart food pub in an updated fifteenth-century tavern, serving accomplished contemporary food, from ham hock, pea and mascarpone risotto to harissa halloumi (mains £11–25), on a seasonally changing menu. Eat outside on the flower-filled terrace or in the tasteful interior with its beams and plaster walls. Mon–Sat 11am–11pm, Sun 11am–10.30pm; kitchen Mon–Sat noon–10pm, Sun noon–9pm.

The Dovecote Alders Rd, Capel, TN12 6SU ☎ 01892 835966, ⓦ dovecote-capel.co.uk. Two miles southeast of Tudeley, this is an unreconstructed, friendly country pub with excellent real ales and reliable, unpretentious

pub grub (£6.50–13). It's usually buzzing with a cheery, laidback local crowd. Mon 5.30–10.30pm (7–11.30pm on music nights), Tues–Sat noon–3pm & 5.30–11.30pm, Sun noon–10.30pm; kitchen Tues–Sat noon–2pm & 6.45–8.45pm, Sun noon–3pm.

Fir House Tearooms Penshurst, TN11 8DB ☎ 01892 870382. Quaint Tudor tearoom, right outside Penshurst Place and once part of the estate, with a flower-filled cottage garden and a cosy open fire in winter, serving homemade cakes and scones, loose-leaf tea and soups and light snacks. April–Oct Wed–Sun 2.30–6pm.

George and Dragon Speldhurst Hill, Speldhurst, TN3 0NN ☎ 01892 863125, ⓦ speldhurst.com. Smart gastropub in a medieval inn three miles southeast of Penshurst. Mains such as slow-roast Old Spot pork belly start at £12.50. Make sure to pop into St Mary's Church across the road to see the Pre-Raphaelite Burne-Jones windows. Daily 11.30am–11.30pm; kitchen Mon–Sat noon–2.30pm & 6–9pm, Sun noon–4pm.

The Hare Langton Rd, Langton Green, TN3 0JA ☎01892 862419, ⓦbrunningandprice.co.uk/hare. Next to the village green, this family-, walker- and dog-friendly Greene King pub offers a nice beer garden, a lovely, spacious interior and great food, with global dishes – sesame-crusted teriyaki salmon, say, or Malaysian veggie curry – plus gastropub staples like bangers and pies. Mains from £12. Mon–Thurs 11am–11pm, Fri & Sat 11am–midnight, Sun 11am–10.30pm; kitchen Mon–Thurs noon–9.30pm, Fri & Sat noon–10pm, Sun noon–9pm.

Little Brown Jug Chiddingstone Causeway, Tonbridge, TN11 8JJ ☎01892 870318, ⓦthelittlebrownjug.co.uk. Good-looking pub with a huge beer garden and spacious interior – there's lots to look at here, from the walls lined with pictures and old news cuttings to the bookshelves packed with vintage titles. Food (takeaway available) runs the gamut from vegan burgers or butternut squash tagine to corned beef hash and award-winning fish and chips (mains from £11), and there's a good selection of beers. Mon–Thurs 10am–11pm, Fri 10am–midnight, Sat 9am–midnight, Sun 9am–11pm; kitchen Mon–Fri noon–9.30pm, Sat 9am–9.30pm, Sun 9am–9pm.

The Spotted Dog Smarts Hill, Penshurst, TN11 8EP ☎01892 870253, ⓦspotteddogpub.com. With its charming, old spotty dog sign, flower-bedecked weatherboard exterior and wonky tiled roof, this looks like the perfect country pub. Inside is just as attractive, a sixteenth-century burrow of sloping floors, low, beamed ceilings and inglenook fires, with a terraced garden at the back sheltered by tall trees. Reasonably priced local and guest ales are on offer, while the menu serves up traditional English favourites such as honey-glazed ham, fish pie and sausage with mash (mains from £11.50). Mon 11.30am–10pm, Tues–Sat 11.30am–11pm, Sun noon–9.30pm; kitchen Mon–Fri noon–2.30pm & 6–9pm, Sat noon–3pm & 6–9pm, Sun noon–4pm.

Kent's eastern High Weald

As you head further east into Kent's High Weald from Tunbridge Wells, things get sleepier. This is the domain of one-street villages and tidy market towns; the largest, like **Cranbrook** or **Tenterden** – their quaint, well-heeled high streets lined with antiques shops and upmarket restaurants – feel positively metropolitan compared with the rural hamlets hereabouts. Star attractions include the ravishing gardens at **Sissinghurst**, the award-winning vineyards at **Chapel Down** and **Hush Heath**, and **Bedgebury forest**, with its excellent cycling and walking opportunities, but you should seek out some quirkier destinations, too – Victorian actress Ellen Terry's Tudor cottage at **Smallhythe** and the idyllic **Scotney Castle** gardens among them.

Goudhurst and around

Surrounded by orchards, woods and hop fields, and offering uninterrupted views across the Weald, the hamlet of **GOUDHURST** has just one main street, its array of weatherboard, half-timbered and tile-hung buildings tumbling down from a sturdy ragstone church towards a duck pond. With some good places to eat and stay nearby, it's a handy base for a stay in this part of Kent.

Bedgebury National Pinetum and Forest

Lady Oak Lane, Goudhurst, TN17 2SJ • Daily: May–Aug 8am–8pm, Sept 8am–7pm, Oct 8am–6pm, Nov 8am–5pm; visitor centre 9.30am–3.30pm • Free; parking Mon–Fri £10, Sat & Sun £13 • ☎01580 879820, ⓦforestryengland.uk/bedgebury • Bus #254 from Tunbridge Wells to Flimwell Corner Farm

Brilliantly set up for outdoor activities, the Forestry Commission-owned **Bedgebury National Pinetum and Forest** comprises not only a glorious 2500-acre spread of broadleaf woodland, but also a world-renowned pinetum, established with Kew Gardens in the 1920s. The forest is a beauty, particularly stunning in spring when carpeted with drifts of bluebells, and a lovely place to spot wildlife, from goldcrests to wild boar; the pinetum, meanwhile, is home to more than twelve thousand **conifers** – 630 of the world's 810 species, from redwoods to Norway spruce, many of them rare and endangered.

Whether you fancy a gentle stroll and a lakeside picnic, a vigorous forest hike, a horseride or a high-adrenalin zip-line adventure at the **Go Ape** treetop park (ⓦgoape. co.uk), Bedgebury delivers. It's brilliant for kids, with tree-dappled adventure play areas, special orienteering trails and a junior Go Ape area. The forest is also very popular with **cyclists** (no bikes are allowed in the pinetum): National Cycle Route 18 runs through on its way between Goudhurst and Cranbrook, and there are off-road **mountain-bike trails** for all abilities, plus a freeride/dirt jump area, with **bike rental** (ⓦquenchuk.co.uk) and showers on site.

Scotney Castle

Lamberhurst, TN3 8JN • March–Oct daily: house 11am–5pm; garden and estate 10am–5pm; Nov–Feb: house 11am–3pm, garden 10am–4pm, estate 10am–3pm; last house admission 1hr before closing • £14.20; NT; parking £3 • ☎ 01892 893820, ⓦ nationaltrust.org. uk/scotney-castle • Bus #256 from Tunbridge Wells stops in Lamberhurst (Mon–Fri)

The ravishing ruin of **Scotney Castle**, a moated fourteenth-century manor house set in 770 gorgeous acres, presents a breathtakingly romantic vision, particularly in spring when tumbling white wisteria and tangles of old roses fight for space on the honey-coloured sandstone, and the **gardens** blaze with huge clouds of rhododendrons and azaleas. The gardens and castle – intentionally ruined by its owners in 1830, in order to create a picturesque folly in the grounds of their new home – are by far the main attractions, but you can also visit the mock-Elizabethan **"new house"**, a stolid Victorian pile. There's not a huge amount of interest inside, but the estate itself is a stunner, with three designated **trails** (30–45min) taking in bluebell woods, a working hop farm and wonderful views of rolling parkland.

Hush Heath vineyards

Five Oak Lane, Staplehurst, TN12 0HT • Daily: April–Oct 10am–6pm; Nov–March 10am–5pm • Self-guided tours (10am–5pm; 1hr 30min) free, no booking required; guided tours (2–3hr) from £20, pre-booking essential • ☎ 01622 832794, ⓦ hushheath.com

A family-owned estate of more than four hundred acres, centring on an early sixteenth-century manor house, **Hush Heath** devotes around twenty acres to Chardonnay, Pinot Noir and Pinot Meunier vineyards and thirty acres to apple orchards. While this is one of the newer Kentish wineries – its first wine was released in 2007 – Hush Heath soon became famed for its sparkling wines, made using traditional Champagne methods, and in particular the outstanding **Balfour Brut Rosé**, a delicate, very dry pink fizz that won the first gold medal for English wine at the prestigious International Wine Challenge. Other stars include a gorgeous ruby-red 1503 sparkling Pinot Noir, with its hint of cherry and berries, and a flinty Chardonnay reminiscent of a fine, crisp Chablis.

The self-guided **trail** through the estate is a stunner, a walk of an hour to ninety minutes, taking in not only ranks of vines, but also wildflower meadows, orchards and ancient woodlands, with generous Downs views sweeping off into the distance. Finishing up your walk with free **tastings** – on the terrace in good weather – is a delight.

ACCOMMODATION   GOUDHURST AND AROUND

Goudhurst Inn Cranbrook Rd, Goudhurst, TN17 1DX • ☎ 01580 211451, ⓦ thegoudhurstinn.com. Owned by the Hush Heath vineyard, a 10min drive away, this family-

friendly pub/restaurant (see below) has four contemporary B&B rooms, with super-comfy beds and quirky design features. **£100**

EATING AND DRINKING

★ **Frankie's** Staplehurst Nurseries, Clapper Lane, Staplehurst, TN12 0JT • ☎ 01580 890713, ⓦ frankies farmshop.co.uk. Let yourself in on a local secret and head for this superb farm shop café. Linked to an excellent plant nursery, the shop is stocked with local goodies, with a busy open kitchen baking bread and serving simple farm-fresh breakfasts

and lunches – Kentish rarebit, quiche of the day or tortilla with a herb salad, for example – plus amazing homemade cakes. It can get crowded at lunchtime, but on sunny days it's a pleasure to eat alfresco under the beady eye of the local alpacas. Mains from £8. Shop Mon–Sat 9am–5pm, Sun 10am–4pm; café Mon–Sat 9am–3.30pm, Sun 10am–2.30pm.

Goudhurst Inn Cranbrook Rd, Goudhurst, TN17 1DX ☎ 01580 211451, ⓦ thegoudhurstinn.com. You get good Downs views from the beer garden of this Hush Heath-owned hotel (see above) and restaurant, which also has a kids' play area. The menu (mains £12–16) focuses on tried-and-trusted pub grub staples, with a few contemporary veggie dishes featuring quinoa, kale and harissa; you can also get a gluten-free menu, clay-oven pizzas (Mon–Fri noon–9pm) and sandwiches in the bar. Kitchen Mon–Fri noon–3pm & 6–9pm, Sat 9–11am & noon–9.30pm, Sun 9–11am & noon–8pm.

Green Cross Inn Station Rd, Goudhurst, TN17 1HA ☎ 01580 211200, ⓦ greencrossinn.co.uk. This ordinary-looking little redbrick pub is actually more of a restaurant, specializing in fish and seafood – dressed Cornish crab,

Rye Bay skate, scallops, paella – prepared with love by the Italian chef-owner. Sunday sees a self-service carvery menu take over. Mains from £15. Kitchen Tues–Sat noon–3pm & 6–11pm, Sun noon–5pm.

★ **Halfway House** Horsmonden Rd, Brenchley, TN12 7AX ☎ 01892 722526, ⓦ halfwayhousebrenchley.co.uk. Unpretentious old country pub about five miles northwest of Goudhurst, popular with walkers, families (there's a big garden and separate play area) and beer lovers – there are at least seven real ales available at any time, with local cider, too. Crammed with old farm implements and dried hops, the interior is rustic, if a little hokey, and they serve simple, filling pub grub from around £9. Daily noon–11pm; kitchen Mon–Fri noon–2.30pm & 6–9pm, Sat noon–3pm & 6–9pm, Sun noon–5pm.

Cranbrook and around

Kent's smallest town, **CRANBROOK** (ⓦ cranbrook.org), was at the heart of the Weald's thriving medieval cloth industry, and home to a group of Victorian painters, the Cranbrook Colony, who enjoyed a brief spurt of popularity with wealthy London art collectors for their romanticized renditions of English country life. Today the place has the nostalgic and well-heeled air of a Sunday evening BBC TV drama: Stone Street, along with the busy little high street, offer a Wealden hotchpotch of medieval, Tudor and Georgian buildings, and lots of spruce, white weatherboard weavers' cottages, all watched over by the handsome 1814 **Union Windmill**, still grinding today (April–July & Sept Sun 2.30–5pm, plus occasional Weds & Sats; Aug Wed, Sat & Sun 2.30–5pm; free; ⓦ unionmill.org.uk). With excellent places to eat in town and nearby, it's an ideal base for the fabulous **Sissinghurst** gardens.

Sissinghurst

Biddenden Rd, off the A262, 2 miles northeast of Cranbrook, TN17 2AB • Gardens mid-March to Oct daily 11am–5.30pm; estate mid-March to Dec daily dawn–dusk; last admission 45min before closing • Mid-March to Oct £13.80; Nov & Dec £9.90; NT • Parking £3 (free for members) • ☎ 01580 710700, ⓦ nationaltrust.org.uk/sissinghurst

When she and her husband, Sir Harold Nicolson, took it over in 1932, **Vita Sackville-West** described **Sissinghurst** as "a garden crying out for rescue". Over the following thirty years they transformed the neglected five-acre plot into one of England's greatest and most popular country gardens, a romantic and breathtaking display that continues to inspire gardeners today. Spread over the site of an Elizabethan estate, which generations of neglect had left in a dismal condition (only parts of the old house remain), the gardens were designed to evoke the history not only of the ruined site itself, but also of Vita and Harold's beloved Kent – a heartfelt endeavour that was to absorb them for the rest of their days, and the anchor at the heart of their unconventional and open marriage.

The garden is in fact a set of gardens, each occupying different "rooms" within Tudor brick walls; the classic lines of the design are beautifully offset by the luxuriance of the planting, the flowers and foliage allowed to spill over onto the narrow pathways and the crumbling red brick. Perhaps most famous is the **rose garden**, stunning in late June and early July, when it's at its lush, overblown richest, and the fragrance, described by Vita as reminiscent of "those dusky mysterious hours in an Oriental storehouse", is heavy in the air. The exquisite abundance of tumbling old roses is set off by Japanese anemones, peonies, alliums and irises, among others, and vines, figs and clematis creep over the crumbling brick walls. The **cottage garden**, meanwhile, blazes in shades of orange, yellow and red – a fiery "sunset" scheme that is stunning year round. Sissinghurst has two areas that feel particularly unique: the **nuttery**, a glade of gnarled old Kentish cobnuts that is especially lovely in spring, when its carpet of woodland flowers is in full bloom, and the magical **White Garden**, with its froth of pale blooms and silvery grey-green foliage.

Focal point of the estate is the tall, brick Tudor **tower** that Vita restored and used as her quarters. You can climb 78 steep wooden stairs to the top, from where you get a bird's-eye view of the gardens, the estate and the ancient surrounding woodlands; halfway up, peep through the iron grille into Vita's **writing room**, which feels intensely personal still, with faded rugs on the floor and a photo of her lover, Virginia Woolf, on her desk. The **South Cottage** (timed tours only), meanwhile, hidden away in the cottage garden, reveals Vita and Harold's bedrooms and Harold's own writing room.

There are a number of **trails** in the woods around Sissinghurst – pick up a guide at reception or online – and, of course, a superb **plant shop** at the entrance. Meanwhile, regular talks, **workshops** and courses focus on all things garden related, from scything to garden writing.

ACCOMMODATION

★ Hallwood Farm Hawkhurst Rd, 1 mile south of Cranbrook, TN17 2SP ☎ 01580 712416, ⊚ hallwood farm.co.uk. Two spacious and pretty en-suite guest rooms – rustic beams and fragrant flowers, plus fresh milk and soft drinks in your own fridge – in an oast house conversion on a working fruit farm, surrounded by 200 acres of farmland, bluebell woods, blackcurrant fields and apple orchards. You can sample their produce at the huge farmhouse breakfasts (optional). No under-12s. Single night supplement £10. **£100**

The Queen's Inn Rye Rd, Hawkhurst, 4 miles southwest of Cranbrook, TN18 4EY ☎ 01580 754233, ⊚ thequeens innhawkhurst.co.uk. This sixteenth-century inn offers

CRANBROOK AND AROUND

smart boutique B&B rooms (including two family rooms; £150) and friendly service, plus good food in the gastropub downstairs (see below). **£110**

Sissinghurst Castle Farmhouse Sissinghurst, TN17 2AB ☎ 01580 720992, ⊚ sissinghurstcastlefarmhouse. com. Stunningly located on the estate, less than 100m from the gardens, Sissinghurst's Victorian farmhouse building – a huge, spacious affair, rich in old wood – offers seven luxurious, comfortable and tasteful B&B rooms. You can wander around the farmhouse's own pretty gardens, or just curl up in the comfy living room. Minimum two-night stay at the weekend. **£160**

EATING AND DRINKING

The Bull The Street, Benenden, 3.5 miles southeast of Cranbrook TN17 4DE ☎ 01580 240054, ⊚ thebullat benenden.co.uk. Though it can get crowded, especially during the Sunday carvery, this is a rustic-classy, very friendly pub in a charming hamlet. They serve excellent homemade pub grub – pies, fish and chips, suet puds and juicy burgers – from £11, plus a handful of modern European mains (from £13.50), good sandwiches and Ploughman's lunches, and local ales, ciders and perries. Try to sit in the pretty garden in good weather. There are three guest rooms, too. Daily noon–midnight; kitchen Mon–Sat noon–2.15pm & 6.30–9.15pm, Sun carvery 12.15pm, 12.45pm, 2.30pm & 3pm.

The Great House Gill's Green, Hawkhurst, 4 miles southwest of Cranbrook, TN18 5EJ ☎ 01580 753119, ⊚ elitepubs.com/the-great-house. Modern European kitchen in a smart but cosy sixteenth-century weatherboard pub. The regularly changing menu, focusing on seasonal, locally sourced ingredients, lists such treats as local asparagus with fried duck egg and salsa verde, Rye Bay stone bass or mint-and-chilli lamb burger, with mains from £12.50 and wood-fired sourdough pizza (takeaway available) from £10. The sunny terrace and pretty garden are great in summer. Mon–Sat 11.30am–11pm, Sun

11.30am–10.30pm; kitchen Mon–Thurs noon–3pm & 5.30–9pm, Fri noon–3pm & 5.30–9.30pm, Sat noon–9.30pm, Sun noon–8.30pm.

★ The Milk House The Street, Sissinghurst, TN17 2JG ☎ 01580 720200, ⊚ themilkhouse.co.uk. Lovely, light restoration of a sixteenth-century building, all whitewashed beams, pale wood, sisal flooring and plaster walls, with delicious, farm-fresh food – sourced from within twenty miles – and local ales and wines. The top-quality ingredients pack a massive punch in dishes that run the gamut from Old Spot ham, duck egg and chips to clam, cockle and corn chowder; from baba ganoush, white bean and spinach wraps to za'atar chicken schnitzel with romesco linguine. Mains (which are really quite big) range from £10 to £26. In good weather you can enjoy the outdoor bar and wood-fired pizza (not available in winter) served on the terrace. The four gorgeous B&B rooms (from £130) continue the soothing tone – this is a delightful place to spend the night. Mon–Thurs & Sun 9am–11pm, Fri & Sat 9am–midnight; kitchen Mon–Sat noon–9pm, Sun noon–4pm.

The Queen's Inn Rye Rd, Hawkhurst, 4 miles southwest of Cranbrook, TN18 4EY ☎ 01580 754233, ⊚ thequeens innhawkhurst.co.uk. Handsome tavern serving classy gastropub food (small plates from £2, mains from £12.50)

4

– superfood salads, roast chicken with nduja, roast rump of lamb with globe artichoke, steaks – made using fresh Kentish produce. Charcoal-grilled fish, meat and pizza are also on offer in *The Charcoal Kitchen* (mains and pizza from £9), and you can stay here, too (see page 149). Gastropub: Mon–Thurs noon–2.30pm & 6–9.30pm, Fri & Sat noon–2.30pm & 6–9.45pm, Sun noon–8pm; Charcoal Kitchen: Mon–Thurs 11am–11.30pm, Fri & Sat 11am–midnight, Sun 11am–11pm; kitchen Wed–Fri noon–2.30pm & 5–9pm, Sat noon–9pm, Sun noon–4pm.

Tenterden and around

Historically a major weaving centre and a limb port (see page 107) for Rye, **TENTERDEN** used to sit on the River Rother. Now lodged ten miles inland on the borders of the High Weald, it's a handsome, well-to-do little town, its broad, tree-shaded high street fringed with bow-windowed weatherboard and tile-hung buildings. From here you can hop on a **steam train** to Bodiam or take a trip out to lovely **Smallhythe Place**, once home to the great actor Ellen Terry, perhaps taking in one of the superb local **vineyards** on the way. The south-facing, chalky slopes nearby, very similar to those in the Champagne region of France, make perfect conditions for grape growing – you can stock up on award-winning wines at **Biddenden** and **Chapel Down**.

Biddenden vineyards

Gribble Bridge Lane, Biddenden, TN27 8DF · Jan & Feb Mon–Sat 10am–5pm; March–Dec Mon–Sat 10am–5pm, Sun 11am–5pm; guided tours (1hr) April–Sept Sat 10.15am · Self-guided tours free; guided tours £10 (booking essential) · ☎ 01580 291726, ⓦ biddendenvineyards.com

Spread across 23 acres on a gentle, sheltered south-facing slope, five miles northwest of Tenterden and just outside the half-timbered village of Biddenden, the family-owned **Biddenden vineyards** have been established here since 1969. With a long scroll of awards, they set the bar high for England's wine making, growing eleven varieties – mostly German, including Ortega, Schönburger, Huxelrebe and Bacchus – from which they produce single-variety white, red, rosé and sparkling wines, plus excellent ciders and juices. The medium-dry, fruity Ortega is particularly fine; it's worth trying the smoky, digestif-style, Special Reserve cider – aged in whisky casks – too, and the red apple juice made from red-fleshed and -skinned apples. The vineyards are free to visit, with a friendly, no-pressure atmosphere – either take a twenty-minute self-guided stroll, finishing with free **tastings** in the farm shop, or, to better understand what you're seeing, book a **guided tour**.

Chapel Down vineyards

Small Hythe, TN30 7NG · Daily 10am–5pm; check website for guided tours (1hr 45min) · Free; guided tours £17.50 · ☎ 01580 766111, ⓦ chapeldown.com

With 22 acres of vineyards, **Chapel Down**, established in 1977, is a multi-award-winning winemaker, growing eight varieties – chiefly Bacchus, Chardonnay, Pinot Blanc, Pinot Noir and the complex Rondo, as well as the Siegerrebe, which goes to make Chapel Down Nectar, their delicious and non-syrupy dessert wine. The country's biggest producer of English wine, using grapes grown here and in Sussex and Surrey, they supply Jamie Oliver and Gordon Ramsay, among others, and have branched out into brewing lager, too, using the same Champagne yeast as in their sparkling wines to create the zingy, refreshing and award-winning Curious Brew. The enjoyable **tours** are brisk and informative, following the wine-making process from vine to bottle and outlining the traditional methods used to create sparkling wines. A tutored **tasting** at the end gives you generous glugs of a number of the best wines – and with no compunction to spit them out. You can buy bottles (and taste more) at the **shop**, or order yourself a glass or two at the on-site **restaurant**, *The Swan*.

Smallhythe Place

Small Hythe, TN30 7NG · April–Oct Wed–Sun 11am–5pm · £8.80; NT; free car park nearby (not owned by NT) · 01580 762334, ⓦ nationaltrust.org.uk/smallhythe-place

THE KENT & EAST SUSSEX RAILWAY

From Tenterden you can take a nostalgic train excursion on the **Kent & East Sussex Railway** (most trains April–Sept, with intermittent and special services at other times, up to five services daily in Aug, fewer in other months; unlimited all-day travel £18, under-16s £12; ☎01580 762943, ⓦkesr.org.uk), a network of vintage steam and diesel trains that trundle their way 10.5 miles to the medieval Bodiam Castle in Sussex (see page 188). Following the contours of the land, the fifty-minute trip is a scenic, up-and-down affair, passing through the Rother Valley and the marshy, sheep-speckled Rother Levels; stops include Northiam (a mile from the village) near Great Dixter (see page 187).

An unfeasibly picturesque early sixteenth-century cottage, all beams, time-worn wood and warped mullioned windows, the rambling-rose-tangled **Smallhythe Place** is particularly interesting for having been home to the unconventional, charismatic actor **Ellen Terry** (1847–1928). The house was opened to the public after Terry's death by her daughter, Edith Craig, and thus it remains, packed with her belongings and all manner of theatrical memorabilia. (Edith was herself a fascinating character: theatre director, actor, costume designer and suffragette, she lived in a lesbian ménage à trois – the "three trouts", near-neighbour Vita Sackville-West called them – in a house on the grounds for thirty years until her death in 1947. But that's another story.)

Wandering through this crooked little dwelling, with its wonky floors and creaking staircases, is like following a treasure trail. Display cases are crammed with mementos, relics, letters and **costumes**, the walls cluttered with theatrical posters and illustrations. It's a dynamic and intimate exhibit, shedding light on the woman who, born into a family of travelling players, became a child actor and model, married three times, had two illegitimate children, lit up the stage with her naturalistic performances and became the toast of the theatrical, literary and artistic world.

Don't leave without a stroll around the lovely cottage **garden**: in summer, theatrical performances are staged in the rustic, thatched seventeenth-century **barn**, opened to the public by Edith in 1929, while the vintage-style **tearoom**, with tables beside the reed-fringed pond, is a treat at any time of year.

ACCOMMODATION

TENTERDEN AND AROUND

Bloomsburys Sissinghurst Rd, Biddenden, TN27 8DQ ☎01580 292992, ⓦbloomsburysbiddenden.com. Friendly, not over-manicured glamping in tipis, yurts and safari lodges. Good homemade food is served in the pretty flower-filled café/restaurant, and there's a wellness centre offering massage, yoga and various therapies. They even host occasional (low-key) acoustic live gigs. Prices based on minimum stay of two nights and four guests (couples pay the four-person rate). **£220**

Brook Farm Brook St, Woodchurch, TN26 3SR ☎01233 860444, ⓦbrookfarmbandb.co.uk. This seventeenth-century farmhouse, set in five acres three miles east of Tenterden, offers spacious and friendly B&B accommodation in a smartly converted barn. The en-suite rooms are

comfortable, un-chintzy and feature lots of warm oak – all have great views, and the largely organic breakfast, taken in the farmhouse, is something special. There's a heated outdoor swimming pool (summer only) and pond. No under-12s. **£95**

Little Dane Court 1 Ashford Rd, Tenterden, TN30 6AB ☎01580 763389, ⓦlittledanecourt.co.uk. Though this historic house near the centre of Tenterden offers a friendly welcome and comfortable, oak-beamed B&B rooms, it's the Japanese-themed cottage (sleeps four; £165) in the back garden, complete with futon and *shoji* window screens, that gives it the edge. The East-meets-medieval Kent combo can feel a little incongruous, but it's different, and nicely done – you could even order a Japanese-style breakfast, and eat it in the sunny courtyard garden. **£125**

EATING AND DRINKING

The Bakehouse 10 High St, Biddenden, TN27 8AH ☎01580 292270. Sweet and cosy hop-strewn coffeehouse/bistro, serving fresh homemade food – all-day breakfasts, hearty sandwiches, hot daily specials – in a cheery local atmosphere. The medieval building seeps history, with

gnarled beams and creaky floorboards. Mains from £5. Tues–Sat 9am–4pm.

The Lemon Tree 29–33 High St, Tenterden, TN30 6BJ ☎01580 763381, ⓦlemontreetenterden.co.uk. This traditional tearoom/restaurant, in a fourteenth-century timber-framed building, is great for afternoon tea (with homemade cakes, scones, crumpets and rarebit), but also offers cooked breakfasts, salads, sandwiches and old-school comfort food, including lamb's liver and bacon, fishcakes, and sausage and chips (mains £9–12), with lots of local ingredients. Mon–Sat 9am–5pm, Sun 10am–5pm.

Nutmeg Deli 3 Sayers Lane, Tenterden, TN30 6BW ☏ 01580 764125. You'll get the best espresso in town at this snug, buzzing little deli, tucked away on a pedestrianized lane off the north side of the High St. There are also cakes, healthy organic sandwiches, savoury tarts, salads and gluten-free options, along with local cheeses and deli goods. Dishes from £6. There are just a handful of tables, so you may have to wait. Mon–Sat 9am–5pm, Sun 10am–4pm.

Three Chimneys Hareplain Rd, Biddenden, TN27 8LW ☏ 01580 291472, ⊕ thethreechimneys.co.uk. Dating from 1420, this shabby-chic free house – blistered plaster and exposed bricks, dried hops tumbling over wonky beams – is a lovely place to stop for a pint of real ale. The locally sourced food is generally very good; mains on the seasonally changing menu can get pricey (£15–20), but the bar menu is good value (£7–9). Dishes might include duck and bacon hash, pan-roasted fish or three-cheese croquettes, all of which you can eat in the pub (candlelit in the evening), in the restaurant (in a light-bathed conservatory) or on the terrace. They also offer B&B rooms (£140). Pub Mon–Sat 11.30am–11.30pm, Sun noon–10.30pm; kitchen Mon–Thurs & Sun noon–2.30pm & 6.30–9pm, Fri & Sat noon–2.30pm & 6.30–9.30pm; snacks available Mon–Sat 2–6pm.

The West House 28 High St, Biddenden, TN27 8AH ☏ 01580 291341, ⊕ thewesthouserestaurant.co.uk. Michelin-starred Nouvelle British dining in a beamed sixteenth-century cottage. The ambience is laidback rather than stuffy, and – befitting the warm, rustic atmosphere – dishes, while small, are umami-packed and gutsy. Try fillet of John Dory with pickled gooseberry, caviar and elderflower butter sauce, perhaps, or lamb breast prosciutto with salsa verde and anchovy fritter. Two-/three-course dinner menus £38/£48; three-course weekday lunch menu £29; six-course tasting menus £55 (vegetarian)/£65 (non-veg). They also offer four upmarket contemporary guestrooms (from £340; rates include dinner and a breakfast hamper). Wed–Fri noon–1.45pm & 7–9.30pm, Sat 7–9.30pm, Sun noon–2.30pm.

Sevenoaks and around

Set among the greensand ridges of west Kent, 28 miles from London, **SEVENOAKS** is a thriving, well-heeled commuter town. Dating back to Saxon times, and with several historic buildings, mostly from the seventeenth and eighteenth centuries, it is not an unattractive place; its real appeal for visitors, though, is as a jumping-off point for the immense baronial estate of **Knole**, which is entered just off the High Street. Other day-trip attractions nearby include the mosaics at **Lullingstone Roman Villa**, Winston Churchill's home at **Chartwell** and the ravishing Elizabethan estate of **Ightham Mote**.

Knole

Entered from Sevenoaks High St, TN15 0RP (TN13 1HX for SatNav) • **House showrooms** March–Oct Tues–Sun 11am–5pm • £15.50; NT • **Gatehouse tower** Daily: March–Oct 11am–5pm; Nov–Feb 11am–4pm • Price included with showrooms, or £5 when showrooms are closed • **Attic tours** Wed, Fri & Sat 11.30am; reservations essential • £7.50 • ☏ 0344 249 1895 • **Conservation studio** Wed–Sat 11am–5pm • Free • **Courtyards, visitor centre and Orangery** Daily: March–Oct 10am–5pm; Nov–Feb 10am–4pm • Free • **Parkland** Daily dawn–dusk • Free • Parking £5; free for members • ☏ 01732 462100, ⊕ nationaltrust.org.uk/knole • The High St entrance to Knole estate is a mile south of Sevenoaks train station and half a mile south of the bus station; it's a 15min uphill walk from the entrance through the estate to the house

Covering a whopping four acres, **Knole** is an astonishingly handsome ensemble, with an endlessly fascinating history. Built in 1456 as a residence for the archbishops of Canterbury, it was appropriated in 1538 by Henry VIII, who lavished further expense on it and hunted in its thousand acres of **parkland**, still home to several hundred wild deer. Elizabeth I passed the estate on to her Lord Treasurer, Thomas Sackville, who remodelled the house in Renaissance style in 1605; it has remained in the family's hands ever since.

The house is given extra dash from being the childhood home of Bloomsbury Group writer and gardener **Vita Sackville-West**, whose bohemian tendencies, by all accounts, ran in the family; one of the great sadnesses of her life was the fact that as a girl, despite being an only child, she was not able to inherit the house she loved with an "atavistic passion". She wrote about it often, and in great detail in her loosely autobiographical novel, *The Edwardians* (see page 324); her one-time lover, Virginia Woolf, made it a fairy-tale castle in her novel *Orlando*, a flight-of-fancy love letter to West herself.

Following years of **major restoration work**, many of Knole's greatest treasures are once more open to the public. The **conservation studio** offers the chance to find out more about how the National Trust goes about its painstaking conservation work. While you could easily spend a whole day enjoying the **showrooms** in the house, make sure to schedule in some time to explore Knole's parkland, which offers splendid **walking**; pick up a map from the ticket office.

The house

Quite apart from the building itself, which, unusually for an English country estate, largely retains its Jacobean appearance, Knole is famed for its enormous collection of **Stuart furniture**. Much of this was acquired at the end of the seventeenth century, by Charles Sackville, Lord Chamberlain to William III, whose "perquisites" – or "perks" – of the job meant he could keep any unwanted royal furniture.

Beyond the **Great Hall**, it's in the showpiece **Great Staircase** that Knole's wow factor really kicks in: a Renaissance Revival delight with dashes of Rococo, it's alive with decoration and flamboyant murals. Upstairs, long galleries and apartments are packed with Jacobean portraits, eighteenth-century pictures of Tudor notables, Renaissance sculpture and fine old furniture. Highlights include the **Spangle Bedroom**, with its amazing bed, draped in a crimson silk canopy stitched with glittering sequins; the **King's Room**, gleaming with rare silver furniture and gold brocade; and, perhaps most evocative of all, the lustrous **Venetian Ambassador's Room**. This eighteenth-century beauty – described by Woolf in *Orlando* as shining "like a shell that has lain at the bottom of the sea for centuries" – boasts another staggering carved and gilded bed, once belonging to James II, with beautiful hangings of sea-green, blue and gold velvet. For a completely different look at Knole, you can book an anecdote-filled "behind-the-scenes" **attic tour** – an intriguing opportunity to glimpse the estate's secret spaces, some of which were inhabited over the years, and some of which were used for storage. The simplicity and emptiness here makes a striking contrast with the residence below; tours reveal areas of conservation work and the astonishing craftsmanship that went into creating this extraordinary building.

There's an altogether more domestic scene revealed in the **Gatehouse tower**, where two private rooms belonging to a more recent occupant, Eddy Sackville-West, a Bloomsbury Group stalwart who lived here from 1926 to 1940, are filled with his books, records and private possessions. Climbing the 77 steep steps to the top of the tower gives you amazing views over the estate.

Lullingstone Roman Villa

Lullingstone Lane, Eynsford, 8 miles north of Sevenoaks, DA4 0JA • Mid-Feb & March Wed–Sun 10am–4pm; April–Sept daily 10am–6pm; Oct daily 10am–5pm; Nov to mid-Feb Sat & Sun 10am–4pm • £8.10; EH • Parking £3; free for members • ☎ 01322 863467, ⓦ www. english-heritage.org.uk/visit/places/lullingstone-roman-villa • The villa is a 2-mile walk from Eynsford train station

The remains of **Lullingstone Roman Villa**, excavated in the 1950s and protected in a purpose-built building by a trickle of the River Darent, reveal much about how the Romans lived in Britain. Peacefully located in a rural spot, Lullingstone was typical of many houses in this area – indeed, the Darent Valley had the highest density of Roman villas in the country. Believed to have started as a farm around 100 AD, it grew to become a large estate, home to eminent Romans (including, it is thought, Pertinax, governor of Britain in 185–6 and, for just three months, emperor) and was occupied until the fifth century.

The site is known for its brilliantly preserved Roman **mosaics**, but excavations also unearthed rare evidence of early **Christian** practices – the so-called **Orantes paintings**, showing six large standing figures with their hands raised, and the Chi-Rho, an early Christian symbol. These unique finds are now held by the British Museum, but you can see reproductions here, along with replicas of fine marble **busts** found on the site.

The first-floor balcony is the best place from which to view the **mosaic floor**, which depicts Bellerophon riding Pegasus and slaying the Chimera, a fire-breathing she-beast. Displays throughout give lively glimpses into Roman domestic life – from decorated glass gaming counters to impossibly delicate bone needles and stunning bronze jewellery, with recipes for such dishes as mussels with lentils and peppered sweet cake, revealing the Romans to have eaten very well indeed. Clay slabs marked with the imprints of paws, hooves or the maker's fingerprints have a poignant immediacy, as do a couple of **human skeletons** – one of a young man in a lead coffin decorated with scallops, the other of a tiny baby, one of four found at the villa.

Ightham Mote

Mote Rd, Ivy Hatch, TN15 0NT • **House** Daily: March–Oct 11am–5pm; Dec 11am–3pm • **Gardens** Daily: March–Oct 10am–5pm; Nov–Feb 10am–4pm • **Estate** Daily dawn–dusk • March–Oct £14.40; Nov £4.75; Dec £9.50; NT • Parking £3; free for members • ☎ 01732 810378, ⊛ nationaltrust.org.uk/ightham-mote

Hidden in a pretty wooded valley around seven miles east of Sevenoaks, **Ightham Mote** – when you eventually find it – is a magical sight, a fourteenth-century, half-timbered beauty sitting on its own moated island, fringed with a soft stone wall spilling over with colourful wildflowers. There's plenty to see in its twenty-plus rooms, which, as they have been much adapted over the centuries by its various owners, from Tudor courtiers to a wealthy American businessman, are an intriguing mishmash. Every room is different, from the medieval **Great Hall** to the Victorian servants' quarters to the 1930s Oriel Room, where you can settle down on the sofa and listen to the old wireless; for anyone interested in architecture, or conservation, it's a treat. Highlights include the fifteenth-century **chapel**, with its stunning mid-sixteenth-century painted oak ceiling, and the **drawing room**, dominated by an elaborate Jacobean fireplace and lined with exquisite hand-painted eighteenth-century Chinese wallpaper. The 14-acre **gardens**, encompassing a historic orchard, woods and lakes, offer pretty walks, while the 550-acre estate, waymarked with trails, includes natural springs and bluebell woods to explore.

Emmetts Garden

Ide Hill, 4.5 miles west of Sevenoaks, TN14 6BA • Daily: March–Oct 10am–5pm (or dusk if sooner); Nov & Dec 10am–4pm (or dusk if sooner) • £9; NT; parking free • ☎ 01732 868381, ⊛ nationaltrust.org.uk/emmetts • Bus #404 from Sevenoaks (Mon–Fri) to Ide Hill, 1.5 miles south

Kent's ancient woodlands hold a good share of England's **bluebell woods**, and some of the very best are to be seen at the Edwardian **Emmetts Garden**. Sitting at the top of the Weald, one of the highest points in Kent – and with wonderful views over the grasslands of the North Downs – the six-acre garden is fringed with woodland whose slopes are carpeted with a violet haze in springtime. The woods, which include a wild play area for kids, make for gorgeous walks at any time of year, and in the formal garden itself you can see some surprisingly exotic plantings, many from East Asia, along with a rose garden and rock garden. There's plenty of space to stroll on hillside paths or picnic in the meadows.

Chartwell

Mapleton Rd, Westerham, 6 miles west of Sevenoaks, TN16 1PS • **House** Entry by timed ticket only, every 10min; last entry 1hr 10min before closing – tickets are allocated first-come, first-served on the day, with some afternoon slots bookable online 24hr in advance: March–Oct Mon–Fri 11.30am–5pm, Sat & Sun 11am–5pm; Dec Sat & Sun 11am–3pm • **Studio** Daily: March–Oct noon–4pm; Nov & Dec noon–3.30pm • **Garden** Daily: March–Oct 10am–5pm; Nov–Feb 10am–4pm • £15.50; garden & studio only £9; NT • Parking £4; non-members free • ☎ 01732 868381, ⊛ nationaltrust.org.uk/chartwell

Packed with the wartime Prime Minister's possessions – including his rather contemplative paintings – there is something touchingly intimate about **Chartwell**, the country residence of **Winston Churchill** from 1924 until his death in 1965.

SHIPBOURNE FARMERS' MARKET

A couple of miles south of Ightham, **Shipbourne Farmers' Market** (ⓦ shipbournefm.co.uk) is consistently rated as one of the best in England, with excellent local produce, a very friendly, sociable vibe, and a real focus on the community. Held every Thursday from 9am to 11am, in and around St Giles' Church, on Stumble Hill, it has some twenty stalls piled high with the freshest local fruit, veg, meat, cheese and bread; profits go to a variety of charities.

Churchill bought the house in 1922, bowled over by the expansive Weald views; his wife Clementine always had her doubts, however, fearing it would be too expensive to maintain. Indeed, Chartwell had to be put on the market in 1946, when it was bought by a consortium of the Churchills' supporters; the family then had the right to live there until they died, after which it was left to the nation.

Built on the site of a sixteenth-century dwelling, the house was extended greatly in the eighteenth and nineteenth centuries; the imposing 1920s exterior dates from Churchill's era. Filled with fresh flowers and personal effects, Chartwell is set up to look largely as it would have in the 1920s and 1930s, revealing the personal side of this gruff statesman – and Clementine's superb eye for design. A Monet hangs in the light-filled **drawing room**, with its colour scheme of soft primrose, lavender and rose, while the **dining room** features fashionable custom-designed Heals furniture. Cabinets of **memorabilia** include a medal given to Lady Churchill by Josef Stalin for her charitable work during World War II, Churchill's 1953 Nobel Prize for Literature and a Wanted poster offering £25 for his capture, dead or alive, following his escape in 1899 from a Boer POW camp. His flamboyant side is not forgotten, not least in his jaunty velvet **"siren suit"** – a self-designed boiler suit to be pulled on over pyjamas in the event of an Air Raid. An **exhibition** at the end includes a sweet series of notes between him and Clementine, and an illuminating letter from his father written when he was a young man, expressing his fears that he was to become "a social wastrel" and a "public school failure".

Chartwell's rolling **grounds**, bobbing with flowers, dotted with lakes and ponds and shaded by mature fruit trees, are perfect for a picnic. Take a stroll around the romantic English cottage garden, and look out for three small stones by a path – these are the **graves** of Churchill's beloved brown poodles, and his marmalade cat, Jock. The estate also makes a good starting point for a couple of appealing waymarked **walks**; pick up guide sheets from the visitor centre.

The studio

Churchill defined himself as a have-a-go artist, and openly acknowledged that he painted to combat the "black dog" – he coined the term – of his depression. His **studio**, lined ceiling to floor with more than one hundred canvases and including his easel, brushes and palette, reveals him to be an enthusiastic and not untalented painter; the works are of varying quality, however, and some of the best can be seen in the house itself. Of these, standouts include an effervescent black-and-white 1955 portrait of Clementine at the launch of HMS *Indomitable* in 1940, and a rather lovely, delicate *Magnolia* (1930).

Home of Charles Darwin – Down House

Luxted Rd, Downe, 10 miles northwest of Sevenoaks, BR6 7JT • Mid-Feb to March Wed–Sun 10am–4pm; April–Sept daily 10am–6pm; Oct daily 10am–5pm; Nov to mid-Feb Sat & Sun 10am–4pm • £12.70; EH; parking free • ☎ 01689 859119, ⓦ www.english-heritage.org.uk/visit/places/home-of-charles-darwin-down-house

Down House, where Charles Darwin lived and worked most of his life, is a treat, revealing a wealth of snippets about an extraordinary man and an extraordinary age. Darwin moved here from London in 1842 with his wife Emma and their first two children (they went on to have eight more), and remained until his death in 1882. This unremarkable family home – an "oldish, ugly" Georgian house, according to Darwin

– provided sanctuary from the social demands of the capital, and was itself a living laboratory. All the family were involved in his work – his children would collect and label specimens from the garden, help look after his pigeons and map the flight paths of local bees – as were his butler, the governess and even the local vicar.

Exhibition rooms offer an overview of Darwin's life and times, including a replica of his tiny cabin on the HMS **Beagle**, the ship that housed him on the five-year voyage that he called "by far the most important event in my life". The scrawled **list** of his father's objections to his *Beagle* trip – including it being a "wild scheme" and "disreputable to my character" – is just one of many lists on display. Darwin was an inveterate list-maker; they make fascinating reading, exposing a thoughtful, meticulous and somewhat anxious individual. Domestic rooms reveal a comfortable, well-worn upper-class Victorian family home, filled with pictures, mementos and memorabilia, but above all dominated by Darwin's work. In the **drawing room**, for example, look beyond the bourgeois trappings and you'll see a terracotta jar on Emma's beloved piano. This would have been filled with earthworms, as part of an experiment to see if they could hear or sense music. While you can see a reconstruction of Darwin's **bedroom**, the cluttered **study** perhaps reveals most. In the centre sits his battered old horsehair armchair and writing board; in the corner, a screened-off privy. Darwin suffered from regular vomiting, painful wind, dizzy spells and headaches, along with eczema and skin complaints. Some have attributed his symptoms to Chagas disease, caught after being bitten by a bloodsucking South American bug during his *Beagle* journey; others believe that his illness was aggravated by stress.

Don't miss the **garden** – Darwin's outdoor laboratory, where he could observe the natural world in situ, as well as cultivate plants for investigation. A gate opens onto the **Sandwalk**, the path through the meadows that he followed three times a day without fail on what he called his "thinking walks".

Chiddingstone

Some nine miles south of Sevenoaks, **CHIDDINGSTONE** (ⓌnationaItrust.org.uk/ chiddingstone-village), surrounded by soft rolling hills, ancient woodlands and hedge-tangled country lanes, is ridiculously picturesque. "Village" is too grand a name for this tiny place; the one street comprises just a handful of half-timbered Tudor gems and sixteenth- and seventeenth-century buildings. Things were not always so quiet; by the early sixteenth century this was a prosperous town, at the centre of the local wool and iron industries. Unsurprisingly, it has often been used as a movie location and stood in for the fictional village of Summer Street in Merchant Ivory's *A Room With a View*. Most of the buildings, and the **pub**, the *Castle Inn* (Ⓦcastleinnchiddingstone.co.uk), are owned by the National Trust. The **teashop** (Ⓦthetuliptree.biz), plus **Chiddingstone Castle**, **St Mary's Church** (Ⓦchiddingstonechurches.org.uk), the school and the general store – former residence of Thomas Boleyn, Anne Boleyn's father – are not NT owned.

Chiddingstone Castle

Hill Hoath Rd, TN8 7AD • April–Oct Mon–Wed & Sun 11am–5pm; last admission 4.15pm • £9.50 • ☎ 01892 870347, Ⓦ chiddingstonecastle.org.uk

Chiddingstone Castle is in fact a large country house, built in the sixteenth century and castellated in the early 1800s. It's an unusual place, half country manor and half museum, displaying the eclectic collection of the eccentric banker-cum-antiquarian **Denys Eyre Bower**, who bought it in 1955. The grounds include patches of woodland, a lake and a rose garden, and there's a pretty **tearoom** with a sunny cobbled courtyard.

The best of the collection is in the **Japanese** and **Ancient Egyptian** rooms, though Bower, who claimed to be the reincarnation of Bonnie Prince Charlie, also collected an excellent hoard of **Stuart and Jacobite** artefacts; note the snuff box with a hidden portrait of James III, the "Old Pretender", inside the lid, and the letter from James's son, the Bonnie Prince himself. Don't miss **Bower's study**, where an overwrought letter from a fiancée, chastising him for dreadful cruelty, sits beside news clippings about his conviction in 1957 for the attempted murder of a girlfriend. Bower always professed his innocence, and was released from prison after four years when his conviction was proved to be a miscarriage of justice.

Hever Castle

Hever, near Edenbridge, 9 miles southwest of Sevenoaks, TN8 7NG • **Castle** Feb & March daily noon–4.30pm; April–Oct & Dec daily noon–6pm; Nov Wed–Sun noon–4.30pm; last entry 1hr 30min before closing • **Grounds** Feb & March daily 10.30am–4.30pm; April–Oct & Dec daily 10.30am–6pm; Nov Wed–Sun 10.30am–4.30pm • Castle & grounds £17.75, gardens only £14.95; cheaper if booked online (no same-day online bookings) • ☎ 01732 865224, ⓦ www.hevercastle.co.uk • Hever train station is a mile west (no taxis)

A fortified manor house surrounded by a rectangular moat, **Hever Castle**, built in the thirteenth century, was the childhood home of Anne Boleyn, second wife of Henry VIII, and where Anne of Cleves, Henry's fourth wife, lived after their divorce. In 1903, having fallen into disrepair, it was bought by William Waldorf Astor, American millionaire-owner of *The Observer*, who had it assiduously restored, panelling the rooms with elaborate reproductions of Tudor woodcarvings. Surprisingly small, Hever has an intimate feel, and perhaps tells you more about the tastes and lifestyle of American plutocrats than Tudor nobles. Some original artworks and features are on display, however, along with pieces belonging to other owners, including a precious collection of Tudor portraits and a rare Jacobite sword, carved with verse claiming loyalty to Bonnie Prince Charlie.

Anne Boleyn's room is the most affecting, small and bare other than a huge wooden chest carved with the words "Anne Bullen" and a hulking piece of dark wood from her childhood bed. Next door you can see the book of prayers she carried with her to the executioner's block, inscribed in her own writing and with references to the Pope crossed out. Perhaps even more interesting than the house are the magnificent **grounds**, which cover 125 acres. Star of the show is Waldorf Astor's exquisite formal **Italian Garden** – decorated with statues, some of which are more than two thousand years old – but there's also a traditional yew maze, an adventure playground and a splashy water maze, along with ponds and weeping-willow-shaded lakes with rowing boats for rent; you can even try your hand at archery.

ARRIVAL AND INFORMATION

By train Sevenoaks train station is off London Rd, about a 20min walk to the main Knole entrance.

Destinations Ashford (every 30min; 45min); Eynsford (every 30min; 15min); Hastings (every 30min; 1hr–1hr 15min); London Charing Cross (every 30min; 45min); London Victoria (every 10–20min; 45min–1hr); Ramsgate (hourly; 1hr 30min); Shoreham (every 30min; 10min);

SEVENOAKS AND AROUND

Tunbridge Wells (every 30min–2hr; 25min).

By bus Buses to Sevenoaks stop on Buckhurst Lane, in the town centre, off the High St.

Destinations Eynsford (4 daily; 30min); Tunbridge Wells (every 30min–2hr; 45min); Westerham (every 1–2hr; 20min).

Website ⓦ visitsevenoaksdistrict.co.uk.

ACCOMMODATION

The Bakery Westmore Green, Tatsfield, TN16 2AG ☎ 01959 577605, ⓦ thebakeryrestaurant.com. Five clean, contemporary guestrooms above a lively modern European restaurant/bar – and in a ground-floor extension, with little decks – in a quiet village near Westerham. Friendly, comfortable and good value. **£115**

Becketts B&B Pylegate Farm, Hartfield Rd, Cowden, near Edenbridge, TN8 7HE ☎ 01342 850514, ⓦ beckettsbandb.co.uk. Characterful B&B in a beautifully appointed eighteenth-century barn three miles south of Hever, near the Sussex border. Each of the three en-suite bedrooms has a different character – one boasts an antique four-poster, another its own small garden area and there's another under the eaves – and there's a cosy drawing room, too.

You can eat summer breakfasts in the flower-filled garden, and country walks head off practically from the doorstep. Minimum two-night stay in summer. **£100**

Charcott Farmhouse Leigh, TN11 8LG ☎ 01892 870024, ⓦ charcottfarmhouse.com. This gorgeous red-tile-hung sixteenth-century farmhouse, around four miles east of Chiddingstone, is a relaxing B&B with a wild garden, a terrace and rolling fields outside the front door. There are also three cats and a gentle Labrador. The three twin rooms – two en suite, one with a private bathroom – are simple, and the homemade communal breakfasts are delicious. No cards. **£90**

Hever Castle B&B Hever, TN8 7NG ☎ 01732 861800, ⓦ hevercastle.co.uk/stay/bed-breakfast. If you want to live like a queen, or perhaps more accurately like an American

4

hotel magnate, this opulent B&B, in two Tudor-style wings that Astor added in 1903 next to the castle (see page 157), should fit the bill. The 28 luxurious en-suite rooms are each different, but all decorated in a classically tasteful style – some have four-posters. There's a swanky lounge and billiards room for guests' use and, best of all, staying here means you can wander the gardens at leisure after hours. **£180**

Ightham B&B Hope Farm, Sandy Lane, Ightham, TN15 9BA ☎07870 628760, ⓦwww.ighthambedand breakfast.co.uk. Tucked away in perfect tranquility – in the garden of your hosts' house but surrounded by greenery, flowers and trees – this contemporary barn conversion offers a splendid combination of B&B and self-catering. There's one twin and one double, with a shared bathroom, plus a huge guest lounge/kitchen and secluded terrace; the whole set-up is very family friendly, with toys and a play area. The tasty breakfast – of your choosing – is brought over to you to enjoy at your leisure. No cards. **£150**

EATING AND DRINKING

Food for Thought 19 The Green, Westerham, TN16 1AX ☎01959 569888, ⓦfacebook.com/fftwesterham. This unassuming tearoom, well placed for Chartwell on Westerham Green, is popular for its simple, homemade food. The light lunches (from £7) are tasty – salads, omelettes, soups, hearty veggie specials – as are the afternoon teas. You could also do far worse than simply stop for a cuppa and a slab of homemade cake or apple pie. Mon–Thurs, Sat & Sun 9am–5pm, Fri 9am–8pm.

George and Dragon 39 High St, Chipstead, TN13 2RW ☎01732 779019, ⓦgeorgeanddragonchipstead.com. This little village pub, effortlessly stylish with its whimsical feature wallpaper, fresh flowers, gnarled beams and bare floorboards, serves very decent food. Local sourcing is key on a menu that runs the gamut from courgette flowers stuffed with goat's cheese to steak sandwiches, pan-roasted duck breast to vegan Buddha bowls. Daily 11am–11pm; kitchen Mon–Fri noon–3pm & 6–9.30pm, Sat noon–4pm & 6–9.30pm, Sun noon–4pm & 6–8.30pm.

The Greyhound Charcott, Leigh, TN11 8LG ☎01892 870275, ⓦthegreyhoundcharcott.co.uk. Lovely, relaxed free house in a tiny village near Chiddingstone, serving real ales – many from local brewers including Larkins, Canterbury Ales and Whitstable Brewery – and really good, simple homemade pub food prepared with ingredients from their own farm. Try the lamb burger, halloumi salad or tempura prawns (mains £10–18). Tues–Sat noon–11pm, Sun noon–9pm; kitchen Tues–Sat noon–2.30pm & 6–9pm, Sun noon–3.30pm.

King Henry VIII Hever Rd, Hever, TN8 7NH ☎01732 862457, ⓦkinghenryviiihever.co.uk. Opposite the entrance to Hever Castle, this handsome tile-hung and half-timbered inn, now a Shepherd Neame pub, is an atmospheric place for a drink with its mullioned windows and wood-panelling, and its lovely beer garden. Hearty pub grub includes pies, sausages and steaks, with mains from £13. Mon–Sat noon–11.30pm, Sun noon–10pm; kitchen Mon–Thurs noon–3pm & 6.30–9pm, Fri & Sat noon–3pm & 6–9pm, Sun noon–6pm.

Maidstone and around

With a couple of Kent's most popular day-trip attractions within easy reach, plus good North Downs walking and a handful of lovely villages – **Aylesford** among them, which has an excellent **farmers' market** (third Sun of every month 9.30am–1.30pm; ⓦaylesfordfarmersmarket.co.uk) – there is little need to linger in the county town of **MAIDSTONE**. That said, its old centre, boasting attractive buildings dating from its seventeenth- and eighteenth-century heyday, repays a stroll. Along with the rather good **Maidstone Museum** on St Faith's Street (April–Oct Tues–Sat 10am–5pm, Sun noon–4pm; Nov–March Tues–Sat 10am–5pm; free; ☎01622 602838, ⓦmuseum. maidstone.gov.uk) with its impressive Anglo-Saxon hoard, ghoulish Egyptian mummy and important Japanese prints and decorative arts, there are attractive **riverside walks** along the Medway, which runs along the western edge of town.

Kent Life

Lock Lane, Sandling, 3 miles north of Maidstone, ME14 3AU • Jan Sat & Sun 10am–3pm; Feb, March & Nov daily 10am–4pm; April–Oct daily 10am–5pm; Dec Mon–Fri 10am–3pm, Sat & Sun 10am to various times (check website); last admission 1hr before closing • £9.95, under-16s £8.25 • ☎01622 763936, ⓦkentlife.org.uk

Though it offers more than a nod to Kent's agricultural history – leaning farm buildings, a working oast house, authentic hoppers' huts – the 28-acre **Kent Life**, which occupies an old farm estate on the banks of the Medway, is actually more of a giant outdoor playground than a museum of rural life, and very popular with small kids. Along with seasonal events from sheep racing to cider festivals, star attractions include the (indoor and outdoor) play areas, farmyard pens where you can cuddle a guinea pig or stroke a cockerel, bone-rattling tractor rides, and Big Top shows in the school holidays.

Leeds Castle

Near Leeds, 7 miles east of Maidstone, ME17 1PL · **Castle** Daily: April–Sept 10.30am–5.30pm (last entry 5pm); Oct–March 10.30am–4pm (last entry 3.30pm) · **Grounds & gardens** Daily: April–Sept 10am–6pm (last entry 4.30pm); Oct–March 10am–5pm (last entry 3pm) · **Playgrounds, maze & grotto** Daily: April–Sept 10am–5pm; Oct–March 10am–4pm · £26, under-16s £17.50; tickets valid for a year · 📞 01622 765400, 🌐 leeds-castle.com · Shuttle bus (£5; 🌐 spottravel.co.uk) from Bearsted train station, 3 miles northwest of the castle

Its reflection shimmering in a placid lake, the enormous **Leeds Castle** – it's named after the local village – resembles a fairy-tale palace. Beginning life around 1119, it has had a chequered history, and is now run as a commercial concern, hosting conferences, concerts and special events, with a branch of the zip-lining treetop adventure park **Go Ape** on site (🌐 goape.co.uk). The castle's interior, though interesting, fails to match the stunning exterior and the grounds, and twentieth-century renovations have tended to quash its historical charm; if you're happy to forego the paying attractions, you could simply cross the grounds for free on one of the **public footpaths**, while if you **stay the night** (see page 160), admission to the castle and attractions (though not Go Ape) is included.

The castle

Having started its days as a Saxon manor house, Leeds Castle was converted into a royal palace by Henry VIII. It is unusual in having been owned by six medieval queens, starting with Eleanor of Castile (wife of Edward I) and ending with Henry V's widow, Catherine de Valois; it was also home to Queen Joan of Navarre (c.1370–1437), wife of Henry IV, who was accused of being a witch. In 1926 it caught the eye of Anglo-American heiress Lady Baillie, who lived here for fifty years, entertaining guests from Charlie Chaplin to Noël Coward. Baillie upgraded many of the rooms in the 1920s and 30s, which makes it difficult to tell the originals from the reproductions – panels clarify what it is you are actually looking at. In the Gloriette, the keep, which housed the royal apartments, the **Queen's Room**, originally Eleanor's, is set up to look as it might have in 1422, while in the **Queen's Gallery** you can see a fireplace installed during Henry VIII's day, and a set of sixteenth-century busts portraying a morose Henry with his three children.

The remaining rooms look as they did in Baillie's day. Of most interest are her **dressing room and bathroom**, which were the last word in Deco chic, and the glorious **library**, flooded with golden light.

The grounds

With five hundred acres of beautifully landscaped grounds, crisscrossed with paths and streams, and with peacocks and black swans adding their elegant presence, Leeds Castle is a joy to walk around (note, though, that dogs are not allowed). There are plenty of diversions, including the excellent **falconry** displays near the **bird of prey centre**. A tricky **yew hedge maze** sits above a kitschy **grotto** – which, full of eerie, howling sound effects and glowing-eyed sea monsters, is a little baffling. There's even a **dog-collar museum** – should you yearn to see the collar worn by Sooty's squeaky sidekick Sweep, or a jagged medieval brass collar used for bear-baiting.

ARRIVAL AND INFORMATION	MAIDSTONE AND AROUND

By train Maidstone has two mainline stations, both of them central; Maidstone East, on the east side of the river, is a 15min walk from Maidstone West, which lies across the river to the southwest.

Destinations Ashford (every 30min–1hr; 30min); Aylesford (every 30min–1hr; 7min); Hollingbourne (every 30min–1hr; 9min); London Victoria (every 30min; 1hr); Tonbridge (hourly; 30min).

Website 🌐 visitmaidstone.com.

ACCOMMODATION

Black Horse Inn Pilgrims' Way, Thurnham, ME14 3LE ☎01622 737185, ⓦblackhorsekent.co.uk. B&B accommodation in garden chalets behind an eighteenth-century country pub/restaurant, four miles from Maidstone, on the southern slopes of the North Downs. The olde-worlde pub serves steaks, burgers, pies, *moules* and the like; mains from £13. **£95**

Leeds Castle Leeds Castle, Maidstone, ME17 1PL ☎01622 767823, ⓦleeds-castle.com/accommodation. The Leeds Castle estate offers various accommodation options: comfortable B&B at the *Stable Courtyard* and the sixteenth-century *Maiden's Tower*; seven self-catering properties, including a two-person hideaway and the former gamekeeper's house, which sleeps ten; and glamping in jaunty medieval-style pavilion tents for up to four people. Self-catering (four-night minimum) **£135**,

glamping **£180**, Stable Courtyard/Maiden's Tower **£260**

★ **Welsummer** Lenham Rd, Harrietsham, 8 miles southeast of Maidstone, ME17 1NQ ☎07747 304608, ⓦwelsummercamping.com. Well-run, almost-wild camping on the slopes of the North Downs, with walking trails all around. A tent-only site, with plenty of space for the kids to romp about, it offers pitches across two car-free meadows and a small woodland area, with bell tents, a Touareg tent and a Big Lodge tent (all sleeping six), a well-equipped little hut (for up to two adults plus two children; available year-round) and a B&B room in the owners' cottage. There are fire pits, and dogs are permitted (though not in the glamping options) on leads. Two-night minimum. Curfew 10.30pm. Closed Oct–March. Camping **£20**, bell tents **£70**, B&B **£75**, hut **£80**, Touareg **£90**, Big Lodge **£100**

EATING AND DRINKING

The Curious Eatery Albion Inn, 1 Church St, Boughton Monchelsea, ME17 4HW ☎01622 299359, ⓦthecuriouseatery.co.uk. Six miles southwest of Leeds Castle, this pretty restaurant, run by two sisters and located in a country pub, scores high for its friendly atmosphere and its short menu of fresh, contemporary food. Lunch mains (£9–15) might include lamb's liver with cassoulet, Moroccan vegetable ragu or lime-marinated prawns in a toasted tortilla, with a quiche and frittata of the day, while evenings mains (£13–22) include such dishes as ox tongue Madras or pan-fried hake in dashi broth. Tues–Thurs 9am–4.30pm, Fri 9am–11pm, Sat 9.30am–11pm, Sun noon–3pm.

The Dirty Habit Upper St, Hollingbourne, ME17 1UW ☎01622 880880, ⓦelitepubs.com/the-dirty-habit. In a building that dates from the eleventh century, this village pub at the foot of the North Downs – a couple of miles north of Leeds Castle – is at once cosy and rather smart with its rich oak panelling, gleaming flagstones and plump leather chairs. Alongside gastropub staples, the menu lists dishes such as vegan harissa and sesame falafel, garlic and pepper squid salad, and chicken, chorizo and padron pepper kebabs (mains from £13). There's good walking hereabouts. Mon–Sat 11.30am–11pm, Sun 11.30am–10.30pm; kitchen Mon–Thurs noon–3pm

& 5.30–9pm, Fri & Sat noon–9.30pm, Sun 12.30–8.30pm.

Frédéric Café Market Buildings, Maidstone, ME14 1HP ☎01622 297414, ⓦfredericbistro.com. If gastropubs get your goat, head to this buzzy brasserie, which brings a little slice of the Dordogne to Maidstone. Breakfast focuses on eggy specials; lunch (mains from £9) might tempt you with omelettes, *croques monsieur* and *tartines*, or more substantial dishes such as lamb cassoulet; dinner, meanwhile (mains from £13) could be *choucroute* or lemon sole. If you just fancy a glass of wine and a plate of cheese, head to their wine bar next door. Mon & Tues 9am–4pm, Wed–Sat 9am–midnight.

★ **Pepperbox Inn** Windmill Hill, Fairbourne Heath, Ulcombe, ME17 1LP ☎01622 842558, ⓦthepepperboxinn.co.uk. You get gorgeous country views from the garden of this lovely old Shepherd Neame pub – run by the same family since 1958 – on the edge of a tiny hamlet three miles south of Leeds Castle. If your appetite isn't up to the hearty a la carte dishes – pork tenderloin in smoked paprika, cumin and herb rub, say (mains from £13) – go for a fish special (£9–17.50) or a sandwich (from £6.50), and wash it all down with a pint of real ale. Mon–Sat 11am–3pm & 6–11pm, Sun noon–4.30pm; kitchen Mon–Sat noon–2.15pm & 6.45–9.45pm, Sun noon–3pm.

Ashford and around

The ever-expanding market town of **ASHFORD** is of most interest as a public transport hub and a jumping-off point for the Eurostar. Despite the tangle of historic narrow alleyways at its core, its handsome Norman church and scores of malls and designer outlets, there is little to keep you here – head out instead to the scattering of nearby villages in the North Downs and Low Weald, **Pluckley** and **Wye** among them, which make good bases for walking.

Pluckley

Owned from the seventeenth century until 1928 by the wealthy Dering family, who left their legacy in the village's many double-arched "Dering" windows, sleepy old **PLUCKLEY**, five miles west of Ashford, distinguishes itself from other local villages by being where the phenomenally successful 1990s TV series **The Darling Buds of May**, based on the novels by H.E. Bates, was filmed. Though the tourist buzz has shifted in recent years away from the rumbustious Larkins and towards spooky ghost tours (it is said to be "the most haunted village in England"), Pluckley still trades on the fame brought it by David Jason, Catherine Zeta-Jones et al; the Larkins' **Home Farm** itself, on Pluckley Road about 1.5 miles south of the railway station, has been transformed into Darling Buds Farm, offering self-catering accommodation (ⓦdarlingbudsfarm.co.uk).

Wye

WYE, some five miles northeast of Ashford, is a quiet village that makes a great base for hikes on the long-distance North Downs Way. The **Wye National Nature Reserve**, an area of chalky grassland, woods and hills a mile or so southeast of town, is a lovely spot for a short (occasionally steep) walk, with a 2.5-mile trail offering superb views out to Romney Marsh and the Weald; the **Devil's Kneading Trough**, one of a network of narrow, high-sided dry valleys cut into the Downs, is particularly dramatic. Look out, too, for the **white chalk crown** set into the grassy slopes to the east of Wye, created in 1902 to commemorate the coronation of Edward VII. The village hosts a good **farmers' market** (first and third Sat of the month; 9am–noon; ⓦwyefarmersmarket.co.uk).

4

ARRIVAL AND INFORMATION   ASHFORD AND AROUND

By train Eurostar services leave from Ashford International train station, while the domestic station, linked to it by a foot tunnel, sees regular services from London, the North Weald, East Sussex and the coast. Both are around a 10min drive from junction 10 of the M20.

Destinations Canterbury (every 10–30min; 15–20min); Dover Priory (every 15–45min; 30–35min); Folkestone (every 15–45min; 15–20min); Hastings (hourly; 40–50min);

London Charing Cross (every 30min; 1hr 20min); London St Pancras (every 30min; 40min); Maidstone (every 20–40min; 30min); Margate (every 30min–1hr; 50min–1hr); Pluckley (every 30min; 6min); Sevenoaks (every 30min; 45min); Tonbridge (every 30min; 35min); Wye (every 30min; 6min).

Tourist office Ashford Gateway Plus, Church Rd, Ashford (Mon–Fri 10am–1pm & 1.30–3.30pm; ☎01233 330316, ⓦvisitashfordandtenterden.co.uk).

ACCOMMODATION AND EATING

Dering Arms The Grove, Pluckley, TN27 0RR ☎01233 840371, ⓦderingarms.com. Fish is the speciality – fillet of black bream with marsh samphire, say – at this handsome creeper-covered hunting lodge by Pluckley station, but they also serve elegant meat dishes (starters from £5, mains from £15) along with a less formal tapas menu (tapas £5 each). There are three cosy B&B rooms, two of them en suite. Kitchen Tues–Fri noon–2.30pm & 6.30–9pm, Sat noon–3pm & 6.30–9pm, Sun noon–3pm. **£95**

Elvey Farm Elvey Lane, Pluckley, TN27 0SU ☎01233 840442, ⓦelveyfarm.co.uk. Set in 75 acres surrounded by undulating fields, this farmhouse hotel offers rustic rooms – in an oast house, a barn, a granary or stables – with stripped beams, exposed walls and modern bathrooms. Most are suites – the light-flooded Canterbury Suite comes with access to an outdoor hot tub, and there's a round room in the oast house, but there are standard doubles, too (some of which are beginning to look a little tired). The Italian restaurant features mains from £14. **£115**

★ **Five Bells** The Street, East Brabourne, TN25 5LP

☎01303 813334, ⓦfivebellsinnbrabourne.com. All log fires, dried hops and vintage paperbacks, this welcoming and stylish sixteenth-century inn, five miles southwest of Wye on the Pilgrims' Way, serves real ales, good wines, modern British/European mains (from £11), wood-fired pizza and BBQ. Upstairs are four fabulous, colourful B&B rooms – none has TV or tea-/coffee-making facilities (though they will bring drinks to your room), but two have real log fires, one has a copper bathtub, and all are deliciously eccentric, filled with retro and arty details. Daily 8am–11pm; kitchen Mon–Thurs 8am–9.30pm, Fri & Sat 8am–10pm, Sun 8am–9pm. **£135**

★ **King's Head** Church St, Wye, TN25 5BN ☎01233 812418, ⓦkingsheadwye.com. It's difficult to go wrong at this good-looking, friendly food pub on Wye's main road, where seasonal, local ingredients are deployed in simple but accomplished dishes such as crayfish croquettes, chard gratin or charcuterie boards. Mains from £14.50. The en-suite B&B rooms are attractive and comfortable, with dashes of contemporary style. Mon–Wed & Sun 8am–10pm, Thurs–Sat 8am–11pm. **£120**

The Sussex High Weald

ASHDOWN FOREST

5

The Sussex High Weald

Sandwiched between the lofty chalk escarpments of the North and South Downs, the Sussex High Weald is an unspoilt landscape of rolling sandstone hills, ancient woodland and wonky, hedgerow-lined fields, dotted with farmsteads and medieval villages. Most of this chapter – bar the towns of Rye and Hastings on the coast – lies within or on the fringes of the central High Weald AONB (Area of Outstanding Natural Beauty), which also stretches into Kent. There are no large towns to speak of in this tranquil pocket of Sussex countryside, and the landscape seems almost suspended in time. Steam trains puff through bluebell woods, crumbling castles guard against long-forgotten enemies, and venerable country estates gaze serenely over the glorious gardens that are one of the Sussex High Weald's defining features.

Best-known of the great gardens are Wakehurst Place, Sheffield Park, Nymans and **Great Dixter**, the last of these just a short hop from a romantic castle at **Bodiam** and Rudyard Kipling's country retreat at Bateman's. Kipling was one of many writers and artists who made their home in the area: you can also visit Henry James's townhouse at Rye, and Farleys House and Gallery, where Surrealist painter Roland Penrose and photographer Lee Miller entertained Picasso, Miró and Man Ray. A.A. Milne, creator of much-loved fictional bear Winnie-the-Pooh, had his weekend home at Hartfield in the heart of **Ashdown Forest**, at the northern edge of the **High Weald**. The landscape changes dramatically here, with hedgerow-fringed fields giving way to beautiful gorse-speckled heathland crisscrossed with trails – a great place to strike off and get lost.

Down on the coast, the High Weald meets the sea around Hastings. This is 1066 country: the most famous battle in British history was fought in nearby **Battle**, marking the end of Anglo-Saxon England. **Hastings** itself is a buzzy and vibrant (if rough-around-the-edges) seaside town with a picturesque old core and an atmospheric fishing quarter, while further east along the coast the perfectly preserved medieval town of **Rye** is one of the highlights of Sussex, even without the added draw of dune-backed Camber Sands beach on its doorstep. Both towns are crammed with stylish boutique hotels, and excellent restaurants making the most of fantastic local ingredients – fish from the Hastings fleet, scallops and shrimps from Rye, lamb from Romney Marsh and sparkling wine from local vineyards.

Rye and around

It's no mystery why **RYE** is one of the most popular destinations in Sussex: this ancient, pocket-sized, hilltop town – half-timbered, skew-roofed and quintessentially English – claims to have retained more of its original buildings than any other town in Britain, and has a street plan virtually unchanged since medieval times.

Rye lies perched on a hill overlooking the Romney Marsh, at the confluence of three rivers – the Rother, the Brede and the Tillingham, the first of which flows south to Rye Harbour and then out to sea. Though the town sees more than its fair share of tourists, especially in the summer months, it has managed – just – to avoid being too chocolate-boxy. There are plenty of good independent shops, a heartening absence of high-street chains, and you're positively spoilt for choice when it comes to great restaurants and places to stay. The main appeal of the town is simply to wander round and soak up the atmosphere: the jostling boats and screeching gulls down at **Strand Quay** (Rye's harbour

GREAT DIXTER

Highlights

❶ Rye A medieval gem, with cobbled streets and ancient inns, and dune-backed Camber Sands beach nearby. See page 164

❷ Hastings With a pretty Old Town, a still-working fishermen's quarter and miles of glorious coastline on its doorstep, Hastings makes the perfect seaside getaway. See page 173

❸ De La Warr Pavilion Bexhill-on-Sea's seaside pavilion is an unmissable Modernist masterpiece and a vibrant centre for contemporary arts. See page 182

❹ Battle Abbey Soak up the atmosphere at the site of the battle that changed the course of British history. See page 185

❺ Great Dixter One of the country's greatest gardens, with innovative, imaginative planting that can't fail to inspire. See page 187

❻ Bodiam Castle A classic picture-book castle, complete with moat and battlements, that's best reached by river boat or steam train. See page 188

❼ Farleys House and Gallery Don't miss the fascinating former home of Surrealist painter Roland Penrose and his wife, the model-turned-photographer Lee Miller. See page 189

❽ Ashdown Forest Hunt for heffalumps in the footsteps of Winnie-the-Pooh, the world's best-loved bear. See page 192

HIGHLIGHTS ARE MARKED ON THE MAP ON PAGE 166

5

in Tudor times); ancient **Landgate** – the town's only surviving medieval gate; and sloping, cobbled **Mermaid Street**, the town's main thoroughfare in the sixteenth century and today its most picturesque street.

Rye also makes a great base for the surrounding area. Within a couple of miles there's one of the finest beaches in Sussex, dune-backed **Camber Sands**, and in the other direction the once-mighty hilltop town of **Winchelsea**. Rye's acclaimed **arts festival** (Ⓦ ryefestival.co.uk) takes place over two weeks in September and features a wide range of musical and visual arts events, plus talks and walks. The other big annual event is **Rye Bay Scallop Week** (Ⓦ scallop.org.uk), held at the end of February.

Brief history

Rye was added as a "limb" to the original Cinque Ports (see page 107) in the thirteenth century, and under this royal protection it grew to become an important **port**. Over time, the retreat of the sea and the silting-up of the River Rother marooned Rye two miles inland, and the loss of its port inevitably led to its decline; **smuggling** as a source of income became widespread (see page 214), with the brutal Hawkhurst Gang making the town one of their haunts in the eighteenth century.

St Mary's Church

Church Square, TN31 7HF • April–Oct 9.15am–5.30pm; Nov–March 9.15am–4.30pm • Church free; bell tower £4 • ☏ 01797 224935, Ⓦ ryeparishchurch.org.uk

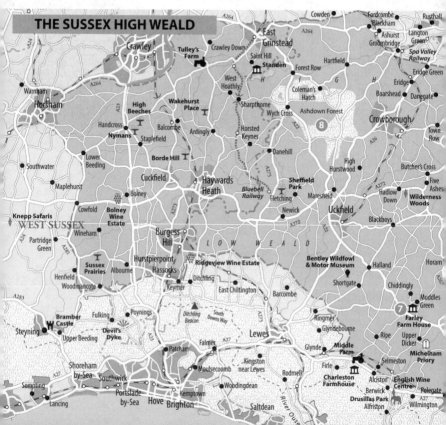

THE SUSSEX HIGH WEALD

The top end of town is crowned by the turret of the twelfth-century **St Mary's Church**, one of the oldest buildings in Rye, which dominates Church Square, a peaceful, shady oasis bordered by old tile-hung buildings. Inside the church, you can't fail to notice the massive 17ft-long pendulum beating time in front of you; St Mary's **clock** is the oldest working church-tower clock in the country, installed in 1561 – though the pendulum, the clock face and the quarterboys (so named because they strike the quarter hours) are all later additions. The ascent of the **bell tower** is a must, involving a fun squeeze through a 16in-wide passage and then a scramble up steep, narrow steps past the huge eighteenth-century bells to the rooftop, where there are fabulous views over the clay-tiled roofs and grid of narrow lanes below.

Rye Castle Museum

Ypres Tower Church Square, TN31 7HH • Daily: April–Oct 10.30am–5pm; Nov–March 10.30am–3.30pm • £4 • **East Street Museum** 3 East St, TN31 7JY • Normally April–Oct Sat, Sun & bank hols 10.30am–5pm, but call ahead to check • Free • ☎ 01797 226728, Ⓦ ryemuseum.co.uk

Rye Castle Museum is spread over two sites: the main museum is in the **Ypres Tower** (Rye's "castle") in the far corner of Church Square, and there's also a small, volunteer-run museum at 3 East Street, which contains an eclectic selection of relics from Rye's past. The Ypres (pronounced "Wipers") Tower was built, probably in the thirteenth century, to keep watch for cross-Channel invaders, though it didn't do a very good job of repelling the French raiding parties that struck in 1339 and 1377; the second

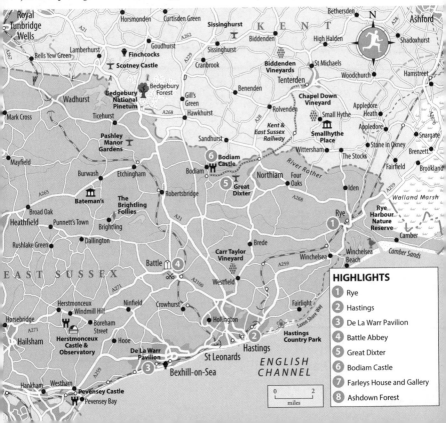

HIGHLIGHTS

1. Rye
2. Hastings
3. De La Warr Pavilion
4. Battle Abbey
5. Great Dixter
6. Bodiam Castle
7. Farleys House and Gallery
8. Ashdown Forest

5

attack virtually razed the town to the ground. The raids persuaded Edward III to open his purse and fund the construction of the town's walls and gates. In 1494 the tower became a prison, with the guardrooms in the turrets converted into cells, and it remained so for almost four hundred years, before setting up shop as a mortuary and finally becoming the town museum.

Inside the tower the modest range of exhibits includes a mocked-up cell, an interactive model showing Rye's changing coastline, medieval pottery, helmets and chainmail for kids to try on, and up the narrow stone staircase – with its "trick" steps, some deep and some shallow, to send intruders off-balance – a small exhibition on Rye's smuggling history. Another cell has been recreated in the neighbouring **Women's Tower**, which was built in 1837 to house female prisoners; thanks to reformers like Elizabeth Fry, the women's living conditions were a marked improvement on those of the unfortunate male prisoners next door. Out front, the **Gun Garden** (open access) looks out over Romney Marsh; it's hard to believe that everything you see in front of you would once have been sea.

Lamb House

West St, TN31 7ES · Mid-March to Oct Mon, Tues & Fri–Sun 11am–5pm · £7.50; NT · ☎ 01797 222909, ⓦ nationaltrust.org.uk/lamb-house

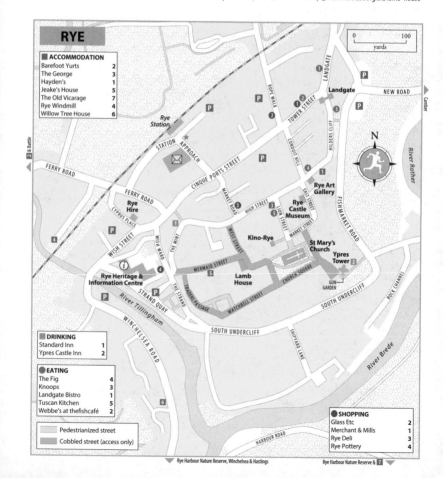

A stone's throw from Church Square, the elegant, redbrick Georgian **Lamb House** was the one-time home of author **Henry James** (1843–1916), who moved to Rye in 1897 after 22 years in London and fell in love with both the town and the house: "I have been to the South, the far end of Florida", he wrote in 1905, "but prefer the far end of Sussex! In the heart of golden orange groves I yearned for the shade of the old Lamb House mulberry tree." James wrote three of his best-known novels at Lamb House – *The Wings of the Dove*, *The Ambassadors* and *The Golden Bowl* – and entertained a wide circle of literary friends, including fellow Sussex writers H.G. Wells, Rudyard Kipling and Hilaire Belloc. Recent conservation work has opened up the first floor, where you can visit James's winter writing room (the garden room where he wrote in the summer was destroyed by a bomb in World War II) and the King's Room, where George I spent three nights in 1726 after he was driven ashore by a storm. James's manuscripts, letters and photos are on display around the house.

A few years after James's death, the writer **E.F. Benson** moved in, giving the house a starring role in his comic *Mapp and Lucia* novels (see page 323), in which Rye was thinly disguised as "Tilling", while Lamb House became "Mallards". **Tours** of Mapp and Lucia's Rye run by arrangement (1hr 45min; £12.50; ☎01797 223114, ⓦmappandluciarye.uk).

Rye Art Gallery

107 High St, TN31 7JE • Mon–Sat 10.30am–5pm, Sun & bank hols 11am–4pm • Free • ☎ 01797 222433, ⓦ ryeartgallery.co.uk

The bulk of the excellent **Rye Art Gallery** is given over to exhibitions of contemporary art, mainly pottery, prints and painting, while the top floor shows changing exhibitions drawn from the gallery's permanent collection of over 450 paintings, prints and photographs. The collection includes works by artists associated with Rye, including Edward Burra, Paul Nash and John Piper, who all lived in the town.

Rye Heritage and Information Centre

Strand Quay, TN31 7AY • Feb–June, Sept & Oct daily except Thurs 10am–4pm; July & Aug daily 10am–6pm; Nov & Dec Sat 10am–2pm; closed Jan; 20min sound-and-light show runs on demand • Free; sound-and-light show £3.50; audio guides £4; guided town walk or ghost walk £10 • ☎ 01797 226696, ⓦ ryeheritage.co.uk

Down by Strand Quay, it's well worth popping into the privately run **Rye Heritage and Information Centre** for its excellent **sound-and-light show**, which gives you a potted history of Rye using a model of the town as it would have looked in the early nineteenth century; it's fascinating to see how little its appearance has changed since then. The centre also hires out **walking tour** audio guides and offers **guided walks** including ghost walks. Upstairs there's a room of wonderfully clunky **penny arcade** machines, some dating back to the 1930s.

Rye Harbour Nature Reserve

Rye Harbour Rd, Rye Harbour, TN31 7TU • Nature Reserve open access; Information cabin open most days 10am–4pm • ☎ 01797 227784, ⓦ sussexwildlifetrust.org.uk • Free car park at Rye Harbour; bus #313 (roughly hourly) runs from Rye station to Rye Harbour

Until the late sixteenth century, most of the land that now makes up the **Rye Harbour Nature Reserve** – a triangle of land between Rye and the sea, bordered to the east by the River Rother and to the west by the River Brede – was a shallow harbour, but its slow silting up over the centuries has transformed it into a rare shingle habitat. By turns both bleak and beautiful, the reserve is at its most colourful in late spring, when the beach is speckled with spears of purple viper's bugloss, carpets of pink sea pea, and clumps of sea kale and yellow horned poppy. Miles of footpaths meander around the shingle ridges and saltmarsh, with five **birdwatching hides** set up overlooking lagoons and reed beds; you can download a map of the reserve from the website or pick one up from the temporary **information cabin** (soon to be replaced by a sleek new visitor centre) situated down the path opposite the car park.

5

Camber Castle

Tours normally Aug–Oct first Sat of month, 2pm (check ⓦ sussexwildlifetrust.org.uk) • £3

The reserve runs occasional guided tours of **Camber Castle**, which was built by Henry VIII as part of a chain of coastal fortifications that also included nearby Deal and Walmer (see page 109). The castle was completed in 1544, costing a princely £23,000, only to be abandoned less than a hundred years later after the build-up of shingle rendered its defensive position useless. Its crumbling walls now lie more than a mile inland, looking out over nothing more dangerous than munching sheep.

ARRIVAL AND GETTING AROUND
RYE AND AROUND

By train Rye's train station is at the bottom of Station Approach, off Cinque Ports St; it's a 5min walk up to High St. Regular trains run to Ashford (hourly; 20min), Hastings (hourly; 20min) and London St Pancras (hourly; 1hr 25min).

By bus Bus #100 runs into the centre of town from Hastings (Mon–Sat every 30min, Sun hourly; 40min).

By car The car park at the station costs £2.70/day (£3 on Sun).

By bike You can rent bicycles from Rye Hire, 1 Cyprus Place (Mon–Fri 8am–5pm, Sat 8am–noon, Sat afternoon & Sun by appointment only; £15/half-day, £20/day; ⓣ 01797 223033, ⓦ ryehire.co.uk).

INFORMATION

Rye Heritage and Information Centre Strand Quay (Feb–June, Sept & Oct daily except Thurs 10am–4pm; July & Aug daily 10am–6pm; Nov & Dec Sat 10am–2pm; closed Jan; ⓣ 01797 226696, ⓦ ryeheritage.co.uk). This privately run information centre (see above) sells town maps and rents out audio guides (£4).

ACCOMMODATION
SEE MAP PAGE 168

RYE

The George 98 High St, TN31 7JT ⓣ 01797 222144, ⓦ thegeorgeinrye.com. Rye's oldest coaching inn has almost everything you could want under one roof: 34 tasteful, individually styled bedrooms – from a Miami-themed suite with circular bed, to a cosy room lined with vintage Penguin paperbacks – plus a wood-beamed bar and a decent restaurant. It even has a shop next door selling bed linen, throws and other furnishings used in the hotel, so you can take a piece of hotel luxury home with you. **£135**

★ **Hayden's** 108 High St, TN31 7JE ⓣ 01797 224501, ⓦ haydensinrye.co.uk. Friendly, family-run and green-thinking, this popular B&B has eight impeccably elegant, contemporary rooms set above a restaurant in the heart of town. Rooms come with smart bathrooms, bathrobes and eco-friendly toiletries, and those at the back have lovely views out over Romney Marsh. **£140**

Jeake's House Mermaid St, TN31 7ET ⓣ 01797 222828, ⓦ jeakeshouse.com. This ivy-clad seventeenth-century guesthouse has a great location on Rye's most picturesque street, and inside oozes character, with sagging beams and creaky, sloping floors. Breakfast is served in an extraordinary high-ceilinged Baptist chapel, with such treats as devilled kidneys on the menu. The eleven rooms – most en suite – are traditional in style. **£99**

Rye Windmill Off Ferry Rd, TN31 7DW ⓣ 01797 224027, ⓦ ryewindmill.co.uk. Rye's 300-year-old white smock windmill is today a good-value B&B. There are eight smart en-suite rooms, plus two suites in the windmill itself: if you're splashing out, the one to go for is the Windmill Suite

(£200), set over the top two floors of the mill, with a balcony giving fabulous views over the river and rooftops. Minimum two-night stay at weekends. **£100**

Willow Tree House 113 Winchelsea Road, TN31 7EL ⓣ 01797 227820, ⓦ willow-tree-house.com. Immaculate, friendly B&B on the outskirts of Rye (a 5–10min stroll from the High St), with six luxurious rooms, great breakfasts and (rare for Rye) free parking. It's very popular, so book well ahead. Minimum two-night stay at weekends Easter–Oct. **£100**

RYE HARBOUR

★ **The Old Vicarage** Harbour Road, Rye Harbour, TN31 7TT ⓣ 01797 222088, ⓦ oldvicarageryeharbour.co.uk. One of the nicest places to stay in Rye isn't actually in Rye at all, but down the road in Rye Harbour. This super-friendly B&B has just three peaceful rooms and a fabulous location opposite the nature reserve; bikes are available to borrow if you want to explore. Rye Harbour village has a couple of good pubs and an excellent tearoom, so you don't need to venture into Rye for every meal. **£95**

AROUND RYE

★ **Barefoot Yurts** Stubb Lane, Brede, TN31 6BN ⓣ 01424 883057, ⓦ barefoot-yurts.co.uk. This magical spot, a 10min drive from Rye, comprises two beautiful yurts (hired together) nestled in their own tranquil clearing. One yurt is the bedroom, the other a sitting room (complete with sofa bed), and there's a separate hut containing a kitchen and shower room, with a covered veranda for sitting and watching the world go by. With wood-burning stoves in both yurts you could even brave a (cheaper) stay in winter. Two-night minimum stay April–Sept. **£140**

EATING

SEE MAP PAGE 168

There's no shortage of excellent places to eat in Rye; in addition to the places listed below, the restaurants at *The George* and *Hayden's* are recommended, as are the *Ship Inn* and the *Standard Inn* pubs. Rye Farmers' Market takes place every Wednesday on Strand Quay (10am–noon).

The Fig 2 High St, TN31 7JE ⓦthefigrye.com. Lovely contemporary café with a mostly veggie menu featuring imaginative salads, wraps and a good selection of tasty brunch options, from mushroom Benedict to Peruvian corn cakes. Produce is sourced locally, and the (locally roasted) coffee is great, too. Daily 10am–5pm.

★ **Knoops** Tower Forge, Hilders Cliff ☎01797 225838, ⓦfacebook.com/KnoopsChocolateBar. This little place, dedicated to hot chocolate, has a devoted following. First, choose your chocolate (from 28 percent to 99 percent cocoa solids; £3–4), add your extras (various spices, peppers, fruits, handmade marshmallow – all 50p, or a shot of something stronger for £1) and wait to be presented with your own bowl of made-to-order chocolately loveliness. Luxuriously rich chocolate milkshakes (£4.50) are also available. Mon & Fri–Sun 10am–6pm, plus Tues & Wed same hours in school hols.

★ **Landgate Bistro** 5–6 Landgate, TN31 7LH ☎01797 222829, ⓦlandgatebistro.co.uk. Perhaps the best restaurant in Rye, this small, intimate place – housed in two interconnected Georgian cottages – is known for its traditionally British food: there's plenty of fish from the local fishing fleet, Romney Marsh lamb and game in season. The three-course set menu is good value: £23.90 at lunch (Sat & Sun), £25.90 at dinner (Wed & Thurs). Wed–Fri 7–11pm, Sat noon–3.30pm & 6.30–11pm, Sun noon–3.30pm.

Tuscan Kitchen 8 Lion St, TN31 7LB ☎01797 223269, ⓦtuscankitchenrye.co.uk. Book ahead at this popular restaurant, which serves up fantastic, authentic Tuscan food – the likes of potato and thyme tortellini, or roast rabbit with rosemary – in unassuming rustic surrounds. Pasta dishes cost £8/9, meat and fish mains £10–19. Usually Thurs–Sat 6–11pm, Sun noon–4pm, but check website.

Webbe's at thefishcafé 17 Tower St, TN31 7AT ☎01797 222226, ⓦwebbesrestaurants.co.uk. Excellent fish restaurant (mains £13.50–18.50), with an on-site cookery school offering regular day courses (£105) throughout the year. Daily noon–2pm & 6–9.30pm.

DRINKING

SEE MAP PAGE 168

★ **Standard Inn** The Strand, TN31 7EN ☎01797 225231, ⓦthestandardinnrye.co.uk. There's been an inn on this spot since 1420, and the current incarnation – beautifully restored, with bare brick walls and beams – is a gem. There's a good selection of craft beer and local ale, including the pub's own *Standard Inn Farmer's Ale*, plus highly rated food (mains £13–18), which runs from pie of the day to Rye Bay fish. Daily noon–11pm/midnight; kitchen daily noon–3/4pm & 6–9/9.30pm

Ypres Castle Inn Gun Gardens, down the steps behind the Ypres Tower, TN31 7HH ☎01797 223248, ⓦyprescastleinn. co.uk. At the top end of town, the seventeenth-century "Wipers" pub offers real ales, a lovely beer garden with views over Romney Marsh and live music on Sunday from 5 to 7pm. There's decent food too, all locally sourced and cooked to order; at lunchtime there's the likes of fish and chips (£12) and ploughmans on the menu. Mon–Sat noon–11pm, Sun noon–9pm; kitchen Mon–Sat noon–3pm & 6–9pm, Sun noon–5pm.

ENTERTAINMENT

Kino Rye Lion St, TN31 7LB ☎01797 226293, ⓦkino digital.co.uk. Independent cinema, converted from an 1850s building that used to be the town's library, with a stylish café-bar and two screens showing blockbusters, foreign-language films and live streamings of performances from the National Theatre, Royal Opera House and others.

SHOPPING

SEE MAP PAGE 168

There are **antiques shops** dotted all around Rye. A good place to start browsing is the huddle of half a dozen shops just off Strand Quay (most open daily 10am–5pm), which sell everything from upcycled furniture to vintage kitchen equipment and crockery.

Glass Etc 18–22 Rope Walk, TN31 7NA ☎01797 226600, ⓦdecanterman.com. A treasure-trove of antique and twentieth-century glass, run by Andy McConnell, one of the country's leading authorities on glassware. Mon–Sat 10.30am–5pm, Sun 11am–5pm.

Merchant & Mills 14a Tower St, TN31 7AT ☎01797 227789, ⓦmerchantandmills.com. If this beautifully styled shop doesn't inspire you to get out your sewing machine, then nothing will: bolts of gorgeous fabrics sit alongside "sewing notions" (scissors, pins and the like) in utilitarian packaging, and Merchant & Mills' own patterns. There's also a small ready-to-wear section. Mon–Sat 10am–5pm.

Rye Deli 8–10 Market Rd and 28b High St, TN31 7JA ☎01797 227271, ⓦryedeli.co.uk. Pick up your picnic provisions or foodie souvenirs from this excellent deli. Goodies include homemade pies, smoked fish, a great selection of cheeses and ales from the Romney Marsh Brewery. Mon–Fri 9am–5pm, Sat 9am–5.30pm, Sun 11am–4pm.

5

Rye Pottery Wish Ward, TN31 7DH ☎01797 223038, ⓦ ryepottery.co.uk. Established in the late seventeenth century, this family-owned, design-led pottery still makes and decorates everything by hand. Its collection of homeware (some featuring its famous Cottage Stripe design), figures, animals and more isn't cheap, but you can occasionally pick up seconds and samples. Mon–Sat 10am–5pm, Sun 11am–4pm.

Winchelsea

Perched on top of Iham Hill two miles southwest of Rye, sleepy **WINCHELSEA** receives a fraction of the visitors of its neighbour, and is probably heartily thankful for it. The tiny town – a neat grid of quiet streets of white weatherboard and tile-hung buildings – is no bigger than a village really but, like Rye, it was once one of the most important ports in the country. Winchelsea was founded in the late thirteenth century by Edward I, after its predecessor, Old Winchelsea – an important member of the Cinque Ports confederation (see page 107) – was washed away by a series of violent storms. New Winchelsea was built on higher ground, and for a brief period it flourished until, ironically, the sea which had provided its wealth once again delivered its ruin, gradually retreating, silting up the harbour and leaving the town high and dry.

Church of St Thomas à Becket

High St, TN36 4EB · Daily 9am–6pm, closes 4pm in winter.

Perhaps the most obvious reminder of Winchelsea's illustrious past is the **Church of St Thomas à Becket**, the cathedral-like proportions of which seem strikingly out of place in pocket-sized Winchelsea. The magnificent Gothic church was erected by Edward I in 1288, with no expense spared, and would originally have covered most of the square in which it now sits – what you see today is only the chancel and side chapels, and remnants of the ruined transepts. Inside, the first things that strike you are the glorious, glowing **stained-glass windows**, the work of Douglas Strachan in the early 1930s. To your left, in the north aisle, are three beautiful **effigies** carved from West Sussex black marble that were brought from Old Winchelsea church before the sea submerged it.

Winchelsea Museum

High St, TN36 4EN · May–Oct Tues–Sat noon–4pm, Sun & bank hols 1.30–4.30pm · £2 · ☎01342 714559, ⓦ winchelsea.com/museum

Winchelsea Museum is housed in the old courthouse, one of the oldest buildings in town, and contains maps, models, local pottery and other local memorabilia, as well as a display on past residents of Winchelsea, which have included the actor Ellen Terry, artist John Everett Millais and comedy legend Spike Milligan, who is buried in the churchyard opposite under a gravestone inscribed (in Gaelic) with the immortal words "I told you I was ill".

Camber Sands

Three miles east of Rye, on the other side of the River Rother estuary, **CAMBER SANDS** is a two-mile stretch of sandy beach that's the stuff of childhood nostalgia: soft, fine sand backed by tufty dunes, with gently shelving shallows stretching for half a mile when the sea retreats at low tide. Along with West Wittering (see page 275), Camber is one of only two sandy beaches in Sussex, and accordingly popular: Camber Village is awash with holiday camps and caravan parks – and the odd chic beach house – and in summer you can find yourself bumper-to-bumper in traffic on the approach road from Rye. The quieter end of the beach is to the west: park at the Western Car Park (the first one you'll come to if arriving from Rye) and scramble up one of the footpaths weaving through the scrubby dunes for your first magnificent view of the beach.

ARRIVAL AND DEPARTURE   **CAMBER SANDS**

By bus Bus #101 (Mon–Sat hourly, Sun every 2hr; 15min) runs from Rye station.

By car There are three car parks: Western, Central and Old Lydd Rd, which are pay-on-entry in summer, pay-and-

WATERSPORTS AT CAMBER

Anyone who's ever struggled to put up a windbreak at Camber won't be surprised to learn that it's a renowned centre of wind-based **watersports**: you'll often see windsurfers or kitesurfers scudding along the waves. If you fancy having a go yourself you could try one of the two local outfits, or nearby Action Watersports in Romney Marsh ☎01797 321885.

The Kitesurf Centre Broomhill Sands car park ☎07563 763046, ⍟thekitesurfcentre.com. Lessons and courses in kitesurfing (£99/day), powerkiting (£49/2hr) and kitebuggying (£59/2hr 30min, £89/4hr) on Camber Sands, plus stand-up paddleboarding lessons

and trips on the rivers around Rye (£49/2hr).
Rye Watersports Northpoint Water, New Lydd Rd ☎01797 225238, ⍟ryewatersports.co.uk. Offers introductory windsurfing (£89/day) and paddleboarding (£48/2hr) lessons on its own coastal lake by Camber Sands.

display in winter. On sunny weekends in summer the car parks can be full by mid-morning, so get there early.

By bike A three-mile cycle path connects Rye and Camber; bike rental is available in Rye (see page 170).

ACCOMMODATION AND EATING

★**The Gallivant Hotel** New Lydd Road, TN31 7RB ☎01797 225057, ⍟thegallivant.co.uk. For the perfect grown-up getaway head to this "restaurant with rooms", set just back from the beach. The twenty serene rooms are decorated "with an eye to the Hamptons", there's a complimentary tea-and-cake happy hour at 4pm each day,

and the breakfast buffet includes unlimited Bloody Marys. Even if you're not staying, the restaurant is worth a visit: it sources 95 percent of its fresh ingredients from within a ten-mile radius (mains £18–24). Minimum two-night stay at weekends. Daily noon–2.30pm & 6–9.30pm. __£145__

Hastings and around

Move over Brighton – if you're planning a Sussex weekend away by the sea, you might want to consider heading to **HASTINGS** instead. It has all the ingredients for a perfect break: some fantastic places to stay; a picturesque Old Town crammed with great pubs, cafés and independent shops; a still-working fishing quarter down on the beach where you can tuck into fish hauled in that morning; a seafront that combines plenty of tacky seaside amusements with a sleek modern art gallery and an architecturally prize-winning pier; a packed festivals calendar; and miles of gorgeous countryside – the rugged Hastings Country Park – literally on your doorstep.

Sprawling along the seafront for over two miles, the town has several distinct neighbourhoods. At its eastern end, sandwiched between East and West Hills, lies the lovely **Old Town**, an enclave of handsome mossy-roofed houses, meandering twittens (passageways), antiques shops and upmarket boutiques and cafés, with the fishing quarter down on the beach. On the other side of West Hill is the **town centre**, very much the poor relation, where you'll find the station and the scruffy main shopping precinct, while further west still is fast-gentrifying, shabby-chic **St Leonards-on-Sea**, once a separate town but now more or less absorbed into Hastings.

Out of town, five miles west along the coast, the small seaside town of Bexhill-on-Sea is home to the **De La Warr Pavilion**, a peerless piece of Modernist architecture, and further along the coast you can visit **Pevensey Castle**, where William's troops encamped before marching on to Battle. Inland there's star-gazing and hands-on science at **Herstmonceux Castle and Observatory**, and wine tasting at **Carr Taylor Vineyard**.

Brief history

Hastings is perhaps best known for the eponymous **battle** of 1066 which in fact took place six miles away at Battle (see page 185); the victorious William I designated Hastings as one of the six Rapes (districts) of Sussex, and ordered that a castle be built to defend his newly conquered land. In the years that followed, the town became an

5

important **Cinque Port** (see page 107), but French raids and destructive storms in the thirteenth century saw the start of its decline as a port, though fishing remained the main industry. After a lucrative dalliance with **smuggling** in the eighteenth century, the town got a second lease of life as the fashion for **sea bathing** took off: in 1800 Hastings' population stood at around 3000, but by 1900 it was over 65,000, thanks in large part to the arrival of the railway. By the 1960s and '70s, seaside resorts had begun to go out of fashion, and Hastings was no exception; however, recent years have seen tourism bounce back, and it is becoming an increasingly popular destination for a weekend by the sea.

Old Town

By far the nicest part of Hastings is the pretty **Old Town**. **All Saints Street** is the most evocative thoroughfare, punctuated with the odd rickety, timber-framed dwelling from the fifteenth century. Running parallel to All Saints Street and separated from it by The Bourne – the town's busy main through-road – is the narrow **High Street**, lined with junk shops, galleries, hip retro shops, pubs and restaurants. Pedestrianized **George Street** – also chock-a-block with shops and restaurants – strikes off to the west; midway along, the West Hill Cliff Railway (see page 176) ascends West Hill.

Down at the southern end of the High Street, the view of the beach is obscured by gaudy fairground rides and arcades – the easternmost end of a long line of traditional **seaside amusements** that stretches west as far as Pelham Crescent, underneath West Hill.

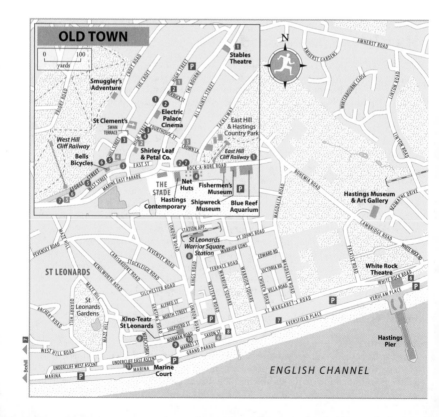

Shirley Leaf and Petal Company

58a High St • **Museum** Mon–Fri 10am–4pm, Sat 10.30am–4pm • £1 • **Shop** Mon–Fri 9.30am–5pm, Sat 10.30am–5pm • ⓦ martin-enterprises.eu/shirley.html

The tiny **Shirley Leaf and Petal Company** has been making artificial flowers and leaves for theatre, film and television sets around the world for over a hundred years; descend the stairs into the cluttered workshop-cum-museum to see the original Victorian tools and moulds (over 10,000 of them) that are still in use today. Cloth flowers are for sale in the shop above.

The Stade

At the eastern end of the seafront, tucked below East Hill, the area known as **The Stade** ("landing place") is home to Hastings' fishing fleet – the largest beach-launched fleet in Europe – and is characterized by its unique **net huts**, tall, black weatherboard sheds built in the mid-nineteenth century to store nets, and still in use today. The beach behind the net huts is a jumble of nets, winches and other fishing paraphernalia, with boats pulled up onto the shingle. Some of the day's catch doesn't travel far: seafront **Rock-a-Nore Road** is home to a clutch of fantastic fish **restaurants** as well as plenty of **fish shops** and stalls selling fresh-off-the-boat fish, pints of prawns and piping-hot, crispy fish rolls.

Just west of the net huts, on the far side of the Hastings Contemporary gallery, the wide expanse of the **Stade Open Space** is used for various festivals, concerts and other events throughout the year, including **Stade Saturdays** (ⓦ www.hastings.gov.uk/arts_culture/stadesat), a free programme of summertime performances.

5

HASTINGS' CLIFF RAILWAYS

You shouldn't leave Hastings without taking a ride on one of its stately Victorian **funiculars** (both March–Sept daily 10am–5.30pm; Oct–March Sat & Sun 11am–4pm; return ticket £3). The **West Hill Cliff Railway**, with its entrance tucked away in George Street, climbs up West Hill, depositing you a short walk from Hastings Castle, while the **East Hill Cliff Railway** – the steepest cliff railway in the country – trundles up the cliff face from Rock-a-Nore Road to Hastings Country Park (see page 182). The views from the upper stations of both funiculars are sensational.

Fishermen's Museum

Rock-a-Nore Rd, TN34 3DW • Daily: April–Oct 10am–5pm; Nov–March 11am–4pm • Free • ☎ 01424 461446, ⊛ ohps.org.uk/hastings-fishermans-museum

Just past the net huts on Rock-a-Nore Road, a converted seaman's chapel is now the **Fishermen's Museum**. The centrepiece is *The Enterprise*, one of Hastings' last clinker-built luggers (1912) – exceptionally stout trawlers able to withstand being winched up and down the shingle beach. Surrounding it is a wealth of photos, models, fishing nets, stuffed seabirds and other nautical paraphernalia.

Shipwreck Museum

Rock-a-Nore Rd, TN34 3DW • **Museum** April–Oct daily 10.30am–5pm; Nov–March Sat & Sun 11am–4pm • Free • **Wreck tours** Check website for details of times • £6; 1hr 45min • ☎ 01424 437452, ⊛ shipwreckmuseum.co.uk

The **Shipwreck Museum** details the dramas of unfortunate mariners, focusing on two wrecks: the Restoration seventy-gun warship *Anne*, which ran ashore in 1690 when it was damaged by the French in the Battle of Beachy Head; and the Dutch East Indiaman *Amsterdam*, beached in 1749. The latter was carrying textiles, wine and 27 chests of silver bullion when she ran aground, worth several million pounds in today's money; some of it was swiftly liberated by local smugglers before the rest was removed by the authorities. The wreck is now embedded in the sand three miles west of town, with low tide revealing the tops of its ribs; the museum runs occasional **tours** to the wreck site.

Blue Reef Aquarium

Rock-a-Nore Rd, TN34 3DW • Daily: March–Sept 10am–5pm; Oct–Feb 10am–4pm • £10.75, under-13s £8.25 (cheaper tickets available if bought in advance online); joint ticket with Smugglers Adventure & Hastings Castle £18.45/£14.33 • ☎ 01424 718776, ⊛ bluereefaquarium.co.uk

The **Blue Reef Aquarium** is a well-presented if pricey family attraction, with both tropical and native sea life on display, from giant crabs to rays and seahorses. A small walk-through underwater tunnel brings you face-to-fin with tropical fish, and hourly talks and feeding sessions take place throughout the day.

Hastings Contemporary

Rock-a-Nore Rd, TN34 3DW • Tues–Sun & bank hols 11am–5pm • £8, free entry first Tues of month 4–8pm • ☎ 01424 728377, ⊛ hastingscontemporary.org

Adjacent to the fishing quarter, the **Hastings Contemporary** – previously the Jerwood Gallery – hosts changing exhibitions of modern and contemporary art. The building's striking exterior, of shimmering black ceramic tiles, is a nod to the vernacular architecture of the nearby fishing huts. Up on the first floor there's an airy café with floor-to-ceiling windows and a small terrace looking out over the fishing boats on the beach below.

West Hill

West Hill, which separates the Old Town from the less interesting modern town centre, can be ascended by the wonderful old West Hill Cliff Railway from George Street (see box above), or on foot by climbing up through the steep twittens from the junction of Croft Road and Swan Terrace, by St Clement's Church. From the top you'll be rewarded with wonderful views back over the Old Town.

Hastings Castle

West Hill • Generally Feb–Oct daily 10am–4pm but check website • £4.95, under-13s £3.95 (cash only); joint ticket with Smugglers Adventure & Blue Reef Aquarium £18.45/£14.33 • ☎ 01424 422964, ⓦ smugglersadventure.co.uk

William the Conqueror erected his first castle on West Hill in 1066, a prefabricated wooden structure brought over from Normandy in sections and then built on the site of an existing fort, probably of Saxon origins. It was soon replaced by a more permanent stone structure, but in the thirteenth century storms caused the cliffs to subside, tipping most of the castle into the sea. Today **Hastings Castle** is little more than a shell, but the ruins that do survive offer a great view over the town. An **audiovisual show** inside a mocked-up siege tent describes the events of the last successful invasion of the British mainland, though for the real deal you're better off visiting Battle Abbey (see page 185).

Smugglers Adventure

West Hill, TN34 3HY • Generally Feb–Oct daily 10am–5pm but check website • £8.45, under-13s £6.25; joint ticket with Hastings Castle & Blue Reef Aquarium £18.45/£14.33 • ☎ 01424 422964, ⓦ smugglersadventure.co.uk

Re-creating the eighteenth-century heyday of smuggling (see page 214), **Smugglers Adventure** is set in the winding subterranean passageways and caverns of St Clement's Caves, which burrow their way into West Hill. The interactive displays, eerie sound effects and narration by "Hairy Jack the Smuggler" offer a fun introduction to the town's long history of duty-dodging, though some of the exhibits are looking a little tired. As well as being used by smugglers to store their contraband, the caves have also served variously as a military hospital, a Victorian tourist attraction and a World War II air-raid shelter.

Town centre

For the most part, Hastings' down-at-heel **town centre** lacks the charm of the Old Town or the buzz of St Leonards to the west and is eminently missable. That said, the triangle of land known as the **America Ground** – an eclectic enclave with a fascinating history (see page 178), dotted with coffee shops, bars, tattooists and independent shops selling everything from vinyl to health foods – is worth a wander, and no trip to the town would be complete without a stroll along **Hastings Pier** (ⓦ hastingspier.org. uk), beautifully restored and reopened in 2016 after decades of neglect. Just east along the seafront from the pier is the popular **Source Park** (see website for details of sessions; ☎ 01424 460943, ⓦ sourcebmx.com), a huge underground skatepark converted from a long-abandoned Victorian Turkish baths and swimming pool.

Hastings Museum and Art Gallery

John's Place, Bohemia Rd, TN34 1ET • April–Oct Tues–Sat 10am–5pm, Sun noon–5pm; Nov–March Tues–Sat 10am–4pm, Sun noon–4pm • Free • ☎ 01424 451052, ⓦ www.hmag.org.uk

As well as hosting temporary exhibitions, the eclectic **Hastings Museum and Art Gallery** contains permanent displays on the local area and further afield, with exhibits on everything from Hastings smugglers and Native Americans to iguanodons and **John**

THE COASTAL CULTURE TRAIL

The **Coastal Culture Trail** (ⓦ coastalculturetrail.com) was set up to draw attention to the 25-mile-long coastal path that links the Hastings Contemporary gallery (see page 176), the De La Warr Pavilion in Bexhill (see page 182) and the Towner Gallery in Eastbourne (see page 205). The Coastal Culture Trail website and accompanying map and guide (downloadable from the website, or available to buy from the art galleries themselves, tourist offices and cycle outlets) have lots of useful information about walking or **cycling** the route. The stretch of cycle path between Hastings and Bexhill is especially recommended as it's off-road all the way – perfect for families. There are bike hire shops in all three towns, and bikes are allowed on the Hastings–Bexhill–Eastbourne train, making it easy to cycle one way and return by train.

5

THE AMERICA GROUND

There is a small corner of Hastings that shall remain forever star-spangled, in name at least. The **America Ground**, the area of town bordered by Robertson, Claremont and Trinity streets, gained its name almost two hundred years ago. When huge storms in the thirteenth century altered the coastline, over a long period of time creating land where once there was sea, canny locals saw an opportunity to claim the newly created no-man's-land for themselves and escape tax and rent. A ramshackle but thriving settlement gradually developed, of warehouses, farm holdings, lodging houses, even a school, and by the 1820s around a thousand people lived there. When the Corporation of Hastings attempted to seize control of the area, the inhabitants rioted, and raised the American flag, declaring themselves the 24th state of America, and independent from Hastings. Unsurprisingly the powers-that-be weren't having any of it, and in 1828 the site was claimed for the Crown; it was cleared seven years later, and stood empty until Patrick Robinson started the construction of the Crown Estate in 1850, the buildings of which still stand today.

A huge mural on Robertson Passage, on the corner of Trinity and Robinson streets, commemorates the original America Ground, while the annual **America Ground Independence Day** in early July celebrates the area's attempted American citizenship with live music and market stalls.

Logie Baird, whose experiments in the town led him to transmit the first television image in 1925. Don't miss the ornately carved **Durbar Hall**, created for the Colonial and Indian Exhibition held in South Kensington in 1886.

St Leonards-on-Sea

Shabby, arty, quirky and a bit rough around the edges, **St Leonards** presents a very different side to Hastings. Some years back the national press dubbed the area "Portobello Road-on-Sea", and while the accolade is a bit far-fetched, St Leonards is definitely a part of Hastings that's on the up. It's well worth spending a morning or afternoon here admiring the impressive Regency architecture (see page 179) or checking out some of the cool art galleries, shops, cafés and restaurants along **Norman Road** and **Kings Road**.

ARRIVAL AND DEPARTURE
HASTINGS AND AROUND

By train Hastings station is a 10min walk from the seafront along Havelock Rd. There's another station, St Leonards Warrior Square, at the north end of Kings Rd. Southern services along the coast and Southeastern services to London call at both Hastings and St Leonards.
Destinations Ashford (hourly; 40min); Battle (every 30min; 15min); Brighton (every 30min; 1hr 5min); Eastbourne (every 20min; 25min); Lewes (every 20min; 55min); London Victoria (hourly; 2hr–2hr 15min); Rye (hourly; 20min);

Tunbridge Wells (every 30min; 35–50min).
By bus Bus services operate from outside the train station. Destinations Battle (Mon–Sat hourly; 15min); Eastbourne (Mon–Sat every 20–30min, Sun hourly; 1hr 15min); London Victoria (1 daily; 2hr 35min); Rye (Mon–Sat hourly, Sun every 2hr; 40min).
By car The most convenient place to park for the Old Town is the 450-space Rock-a-Nore car park, accessed via Rock-a-Nore Rd.

GETTING AROUND AND INFORMATION

By bike A 7km traffic-free route stretches along the seafront from Hastings Old Town to Bexhill, making bikes a great way to get around. Bike hire is available at Bells Bicycles, 4 George St (Tues–Sat 10am–5pm, Sun 11am–5pm; ☎01424 716541, ⓦbellsbicycles.co.uk; £15/half day, £20/day, advance booking recommended), and Seaside

Cycles, on the beach side of the adventure golf complex (school summers holidays and selected weekends only; ☎07432 181966, ⓦwww.hastings.gov.uk/cycle; £14/day).
Tourist office On the seafront at Aquila House, Breeds Place, TN34 3UY (Mon–Fri 9am–5pm, Sat & Sun 10am–3pm; ☎01424 451111, ⓦvisit1066country.com).

ACCOMMODATION
SEE MAP PAGE 174

OLD TOWN
★ **The Laindons** 23 High St, TN34 3EY ☎01424

437710, ⓦthelaindons.com. There's lots to love about this friendly boutique B&B, set in a Georgian townhouse with bags of character. The six rooms have a crisp Scandi vibe and are flooded with light; the Yellow Room (£164) is the pick of them, with a great view over the rooftops to East Hill. Breakfast includes home-baked bread and coffee made with beans roasted in-house. **£130**

Old Rectory Harold Rd, TN35 5ND ☎01424 422410, ⓦtheoldrectoryhastings.co.uk. Elegant, double-fronted Georgian pad next to All Saints Church, with nine luxurious, quirkily styled rooms; those at the front are grander, while the smaller rooms at the back look out over the tranquil walled garden. The breakfast menu is a treat, featuring own-cured bacon, homemade sausages, kippers and locally smoked haddock from the Hastings fleet. Minimum two-night stay at weekends during busy periods. **£140**

Swan House 1 Hill St, TN34 3HU ☎01424 430014, ⓦswanhousehastings.co.uk. This boutique B&B was one of Hastings' first, and still ticks all the boxes. It couldn't have a more perfect setting, in a lovely half-timbered fifteenth-century building on a quiet Old Town street. Rooms are luxurious and tasteful, with muted paintwork and wooden floors, and there's a pretty decked patio garden for sunny breakfasts. Minimum two-night stay at weekends. **£140**

TOWN CENTRE

The Printworks 14 Claremont, America Ground, TN34 1HA ☎01424 425532, ⓦ14claremont.com. This hip B&B in the old *Observer* building offers loft-style living in the America Ground, with vaulted ceilings, wooden floors and bare plaster-and-brick walls, jazzed up with eclectic vintage furnishings.

The two bedrooms have plenty of character, with original features from the building's days as a newspaper office. **£120**

Senlac Guesthouse 46–47 Cambridge Gardens, TN34 1EN ☎01424 435767, ⓦsenlacguesthouse.co.uk. Stylish yet affordable, this friendly B&B near the station is fantastic value for money – rooms are bright and contemporary, and bathrooms gleaming. The cheapest rooms share bathrooms. Breakfast is an additional £8.50. Next door, *Number 46 Rooms & Apartments* is similar in price and quality. **£65**

White Rock Hotel White Rock, TN34 1JU ☎01424 422240, ⓦthewhiterockhotel.com. Clean, comfortable rooms and a fab location on the seafront overlooking Hastings Pier. The cheapest rooms are at the back of the hotel; sea views will cost you £20 more. **£76**

ST LEONARDS-ON-SEA

Hastings House 9 Warrior Square, TN37 6BA ☎01424 422709, ⓦhastingshouse.co.uk. Friendly boutique B&B in a Victorian house overlooking a garden square, close to the beach. Each of the modern, luxurious rooms sports a different look; those at the front boast lovely views over Warrior Square gardens to the sea. **£105**

Zanzibar 9 Everfield Place, TN37 6BY ☎01424 460109, ⓦzanzibarhotel.co.uk. Boutique hotel with rooms themed around the owner's travels, set in a beautifully styled townhouse overlooking St Leonards' seafront – the rooms with the real wow factor face the sea. On the ground floor, the *Pier Nine* restaurant serves up excellent (though not cheap) food. **£145**

EATING
SEE MAP PAGE 174

Hastings has some fantastic places to eat, especially when it comes to fish: some of the best seafood places are along **Rock-a-Nore Road**, where the day's catch appears on menus and in fish shops a pebble's throw from where it was landed that morning. As well as the restaurants and cafés listed below, check out the recommended pubs and wine bars, many of which also serve excellent food.

OLD TOWN

Di Polas 14 Marine Parade, TN34 3AH ☎01424 203666. The best gelato in Hastings, made on site by the Italian owner. Daily in summer 11am–6pm; winter hours vary.

Petit Fi 16 George St, TN34 3EG ☎01424 272030,

ⓦfacebook.com/petitfihastings. This lovely little café, with big windows looking out onto pedestrianized George St and a few tables outside, is a great spot for lunch, with a menu that ranges from sandwiches to Sussex Smokies, plus cream teas and cakes. Mon–Sat 9–5.30pm, Sun 10am–5pm.

Thai Café and Boulevard Books 32 George St, TN34 3EA ☎01424 436521, ⓦthaicafeandbookshop.com. The town's most unique eating experience, this tiny secondhand bookshop serves up fantastic home-cooked Thai food in the evenings, with half a dozen tables nestled among the bookshelves. Two courses £17; BYO (corkage £2/person). Bookings essential. Tues–Sun 6–10pm, Mon by arrangement.

Two Bulls Steakhouse 61c High St, TN34 3EJ ☎01424

ST LEONARDS ARCHITECTURE

St Leonards was planned and built by the late-Georgian developer **James Burton** (1761–1837) and his son, **Decimus Burton** (1800–81), and was the first ever planned Regency seaside town. The resort was centred on a private park, now St Leonards Gardens, and the streets around it today contain some of the best examples of the Burtons' elegant architecture. A booklet (£2.50) available at the tourist office describes a **walking tour** around some of the highlights. For more information on the history of the area see ⓦburtonsstleonardssociety.co.uk.

5

436443, ⓦtwobulls.co.uk. Tuck into a 45-day-aged steak, grilled over charcoal and served with home-cut chips and a choice of sauces and butters, at this relaxed, informal steakhouse. Set lunches are great value, starting at £10. Orders taken Wed 6.30–8.30pm, Thurs noon–2pm & 7–8.30pm, Fri noon–2pm & 6.30–9pm, Sat 12.30–3pm & 6.30–9pm, Sun 12.30–3pm & 6.30–8.30pm.

THE STADE

Maggie's Rock-a-Nore Rd, TN34 3DW ☎01424 430205. For great fish and chips look no further than this unpretentious first-floor café, right on the beach overlooking the fishing boats. Tues–Sun noon–3pm.

Rock-a-Nore Kitchen 23a Rock-a-Nore Rd, TN34 3DW ☎01424 433764, ⓦrockanorekitchen.com. Excellent informal restaurant serving "boat-to-plate" fish and other dishes in an old tannery building facing the net huts. Mains such as steak and oyster pudding, scallop risotto or roasted plaice cost £14–20, and on sunny days in summer the kitchen hatch is opened up to serve scoops of freshly cooked calamari to passers-by. There are a dozen or so tables and just one sitting a night, so book ahead. Thurs, Fri & Sat 12.30–3.30pm & 7–9pm, Sun 12.30–3.30pm.

Webbe's 1 Rock-a-Nore Rd, TN34 3DW ☎01424 721650, ⓦwebbesrestaurants.co.uk. Top-notch seafood restaurant opposite the Hastings Contemporary gallery. Mains such as steamed panache of fish cost around £15, or you can pick and choose from tasting dishes at £3.95 each. There's plenty of outside seating in summer. Fish cookery-school mornings with lunch included take place throughout the year – check the website. Wed & Thurs noon–2.30pm & 6–9pm, Fri noon–2.30pm & 6–9.30pm, Sat noon–9.30pm, Sun noon–8.30pm.

ST LEONARDS-ON-SEA

FIKA 44 Kings Rd, TN37 6DY ☎01424 552142, ⓦfacebook.com/fikacoffee44. Popular coffee shop with a Scandi-cool interior and a pretty sun-trap courtyard, serving excellent coffee, homemade cakes (espresso banana cake and the like) and delicious veggie food including a weekly changing spread of imaginative salads – check out the photos on their Facebook page if you want to get a flavour of what might be on offer. Wed–Fri 9am–5pm, Sat & Sun 10am–5pm.

Half Man, Half Burger 7 Marine Court, TN38 0DX ☎01424 552332, ⓦhalfmanhalfburger.com. Great burgers (£7–9), "trashy desserts", craft beers and cocktails are a winning combination at this funky, cheerful place on the seafront. Burgers range from the Gonzo (with Memphis Screamin'Whiskey BBQ sauce) to the Halloumi Be Thy Name. Mon–Sat noon–10pm, Sun noon–8pm.

St Clement's 3 Mercatoria, TN38 0EB ☎01424 200355, ⓦstclementsrestaurant.co.uk. Fish is the main focus at this well-regarded, intimate restaurant: ninety percent of it comes from the Hastings fleet's daily catch, and dishes on the constantly changing menu might include grilled Hastings plaice or seafood linguine (mains £16–20). A good-value lunch and early evening set menu is also available on selected days. Wed–Fri noon–3pm & 6–9pm, Sat noon–3pm & 6–9.30pm, Sun noon–3pm.

Tommy's Pizzeria 28 Norman Rd, TN37 6AE ⓦtommypizzeria.co.uk. Laid-back pizzeria serving up delicious sourdough wood-fired pizzas (£7.50–12) and small plates such as fritto misto and wood-roasted Romano peppers (£3–7), with Hastings fish and other local produce playing a starring role. There's courtyard seating outside, plus sociable communal seating in the pared-back, black-walled interior. Mon & Wed–Sat noon–10pm, Sun noon–5pm.

DRINKING AND NIGHTLIFE

SEE MAP PAGE 174

OLD TOWN

The Albion 33 George St TN34 3EA ☎01424 439156, ⓦalbionhastings.com. Managed by the team behind the Hastings Fat Tuesday (see page 181), this hip Old Town pub has a great live music programme, covering everything from jazz to country. Good food, too, especially if you're a pie fan; there's a whopping nine different varieties on the menu, including a weekly guest pie, all homemade and delicious. Mon–Thurs & Sun 11am–11pm, Fri & Sat noon–midnight; kitchen Mon–Fri noon–9pm, Sat noon–7pm, Sun noon–5pm.

★ **The Crown** 64–66 All Saints St, TN34 3BN ☎01424 465100, ⓦthecrownhastings.co.uk. Great pub with a lovely ambience and a trendy crowd. There's plenty of local produce on the menu (Hastings fish, Rye Bay coffee, and so on) and behind the bar (Sussex ales, gins and ciders), and the classy dark-painted interior features changing exhibitions of local artists' work. Mon–Sat 11am–11pm,

Sun 11am–10.30pm; kitchen Mon–Fri noon–5pm & 6–9.30pm, Sat & Sun 11am–5pm & 6–9.30pm.

Dragon 71 George St, TN34 3EE ☎01424 423688, ⓦdragon-bar.uk. Part bar, part bistro, this cool, buzzy little hangout has good music, scuffed wooden floors and dark-painted walls hung with art. Interesting beers and a good wine list, plus top-notch food, with a menu that changes almost daily. Mon–Sat noon–11pm, Sun noon–10.30pm; kitchen Mon–Thurs noon–10pm, Fri–Sun noon–9pm.

★ **First In, Last Out (FILO)** 15 High St, TN34 3EY ☎01424 425079, ⓦthefilo.co.uk. Tiny, ever-popular traditional pub with snug booths, no jukeboxes or fruit machines, a huge roaring fire in winter, and its own microbrewery. Excellent (and good-value) food is an added bonus, and there's regular live music, too – check the website for details. Mon–Sat noon–11.30pm, Sun noon–11pm; kitchen Mon 6–8.30/9pm, Tues–Sat noon–2.30pm & 6–8.30/9pm, Sun noon–4pm.

Porter's Wine Bar 56 High St, TN34 3EN ☎01424 427000, ⓦporterswinebar.com. Wine bar with jazz and acoustic music on Wed and Thurs nights and Sun afternoons, including a regular spot by acclaimed jazz pianist and local resident Liane Carroll. Good, home-cooked, bistro-style food is on offer too. Mon, Tues & Sun noon–11pm, Wed–Sat noon–midnight; kitchen Mon–Sat noon–10pm, Sun noon–5pm.

ST LEONARDS-ON-SEA

Graze on Grand 16 Grand Parade, TN37 6DN ☎01424 439736, ⓦgrazeongrand.com. Wine bar, bottleshop, café-restaurant and gallery rolled into one, this light-flooded place on the seafront has a great choice of wine (over seventy bottles – also available to take away) and a menu that ranges from brunches to lunch platters to sophisticated à la carte options. The art on the wall is all for sale, and there are regular wine-tasting events. Tues–Thurs 10am–9pm, Fri & Sat 10am–10pm, Sun 10am–4pm; kitchen Tues–Thurs 10am–3pm & 6–9pm, Fri & Sat 10am–3pm & 6pm–late, Sun 10am–4pm.

ENTERTAINMENT

The Electric Palace 39 High St, TN34 3ER ☎01424 720393, ⓦelectricpalacecinema.com. Tiny independent cinema showing arthouse and world cinema, with a licensed bar. Screenings Thurs–Sun; £8.

★ **Kino-Teatr St Leonards** 43–49 Norman Rd, St Leonards, TN34 3EA ☎01424 237373, ⓦkino-teatr. co.uk. Arthouse films, new releases and live arts cinema, plus regular live music (including afternoon jazz) at this cool little cinema-theatre with a bar at the back of the auditorium and armchairs at the front. It's attached to the Baker-Mamonova Gallery, which shows changing exhibitions alongside its permanent collection of twentieth-century Russian art, and there's a lovely café-restaurant, *Liban@Kino*, perfect if you want to eat before or after a performance.

Stables Theatre and Arts Centre The Bourne, TN34 3BD ☎01424 423221, ⓦstablestheatre.co.uk. Small theatre hosting amateur and touring productions.

White Rock Theatre White Rock, TN34 1JX ☎01424 462280, ⓦwhiterocktheatre.org.uk. The town's main venue, putting on comedy, bands, theatre, ballet, shows and the annual panto.

SHOPPING   SEE MAP PAGE 174

Hastings has a great array of independent shops. We've picked out some favourites below, but new shops pop up all the time. In the Old Town the main shopping streets are **High Street** and **George Street**, lined with antiques shops, galleries, upmarket florists and quirky homeware stores; in St Leonards the main drag is **Norman Road**, with a scattering of galleries and hip vintage shops. It's also worth exploring the independent shops in the up-and-coming **America Ground** (see page 178), just inland from the Hastings Pier. Be aware that many independent shops close for a day at the start of the week.

OLD TOWN

★ **Alastair Hendy's Home Store** 36 High St, TN34 3ER ☎01424 447171, ⓦaghendy.com. Artfully styled utilitarian essentials – including brooms, vintage linen, woollen bedsocks, enamelware, hand-forged scissors and reclaimed furniture – arranged over three floors of a

---

PARADES, PIRATES AND CRAZY GOLF: HASTINGS FESTIVALS

Hastings has some brilliant (and sometimes quite bonkers) festivals. Biggest and best of the lot is the **Jack-in-the-Green Festival** (ⓦhastingsjack.co.uk) held over May Day weekend, which culminates in a riotous parade of leaf-bedecked dancers and drummers through the streets of the Old Town up to Hastings' hilltop castle, where "the Jack" – a garlanded leaf-covered figure whose origins date back to the eighteenth century – is ritually slain and the spirit of summer released.

In July, thousands of buccaneers descend on the town for **Hastings Pirate Day**, a phenomenally popular day of shanties, sword-fighting and other swashbuckling fun that currently holds the Guinness World Record for the largest gathering of pirates in one place – a title occasionally snatched by the scurvy pirates in Penzance.

The UK's largest Mardi Gras festival, **Fat Tuesday** (ⓦhastingsfattuesday.co.uk), is held over five days in February, and sees hundreds of gigs, many free, taking place around town. On Fat Tuesday itself, bands move from venue to venue in the Old Town, playing a twenty-minute set in each, so you can put your feet up and let the music come to you.

Other events include the **Coastal Currents arts festival** in September; two separate **foodie festivals** celebrating Hastings' unique fishing industry; **Hastings Week** in October; and, last but not least, the nail-biting **World Crazy Golf Championship** in June. For full details of all festivals, see page 32.

stunning Georgian town house that's been pared back to its original framework, all bare plaster and stripped wood. Even if you're not going to buy anything, it's a fascinating building to poke around. Out the back a small seafood kitchen opens up for weekend lunches in the summer. Tues–Sun & bank hols 11am–5.30pm.

★ **Butler's Emporium** 70 George St, TN34 3EE ☎ 01424 430678, ⊚ butlersemporium.com. A cornucopia of gorgeous odds and ends – from cashmere scarfs and candles to Moroccan slippers and bolts of Merchant & Mills linen – displayed in a fabulous 1830s hardware store complete with original shop fittings. Mon–Fri 10am–5pm, Sat & Sun 11am–5pm.

Judges Bakery 51 High St, TN34 3EN ☎ 01424 722588, ⊚ judgesbakery.com. Pick up organic artisan breads, tarts, quiches, cookies and meringues the size of melons at this bakery that's been making its own bread since 1826. If you're visiting in summer, look out for the famous Mack-a-Rolls (puff pastry filled with local smoked mackerel). Mon–Fri 7.45am–5.30pm, Sat 7.45am–6pm, Sun & bank hols 8.45am–5pm.

Made in Hastings 82 High St, TN34 3EL ☎ 01424 719110, ⊚ facebook.com/Made-In-Hastings. As the name suggests, everything in this little shop is made locally, from prints to pottery, notebooks to tea towels. It's a great spot to pick up a souvenir or gift. Daily 10.30am–5pm.

Penbuckles 50 High St, TN34 3EN ☎ 01424 465050, ⊚ penbuckles.co.uk. Great deli with goodies including artisan cheeses, charcuterie, Portuguese custard tarts, wines and Monmouth coffee. Mon–Sat 10am–6pm, Sun 11am–5pm.

Warp & Weft 68a George St, TN34 4EE ☎ 01424 437180, ⊚ warpandweftstyling.com. Beautiful handmade clothes, shoes and accessories in muted tones and natural fabrics, mixed with one-off vintage pieces, plus jewellery and other accessories from local craftspeople. A made-to-measure service is also available. Mon–Fri & Sun 11am–5pm, Sat 10.30am–5.30pm.

THE STADE

Rockanore Fisheries 3 & 4 Rock-a-Nore Rd, TN34 3DW ☎ 01424 445425, ⊚ rockanore.co.uk. One of several great fish shops along Rock-a-Nore Rd, this long-established family business is particularly well known for its smoked-on-the-premises salmon, but is also a great place to pick up wet fish. Tues–Sat 9am–5pm, Sun 10am–2pm.

TOWN CENTRE

Dyke & Dean The Printworks, 14 Claremont, TN34 1HA ☎ 01424 429202, ⊚ dykeanddean.com. Hip interiors and homewares store on the ground floor of The Printworks – a former newspaper building – in the America Ground, selling everything from lighting and utilitarian kitchenware to Welsh throws and soap from Oregon. Thurs & Fri 11am–5pm, Sat 11am–5.30pm.

ST LEONARDS-ON-SEA

SHOP 32–34 Norman Rd, TN38 0EJ ☎ 07763 579908. Fab little shop crammed with kitchenware, cards, furniture, home furnishings, fashion and accessories, with a small café at the back. Mon–Sat 10am–5pm, Sun 11am–4pm.

Hastings Country Park

Visitor centre Coastguard Lane, off Fairlight Rd, TN35 4AD • Fri–Sun 10am–3.30pm, though hours can vary as the centre is volunteer-run • ☎ 01424 812140, ⊚ hastingscountrypark.org.uk • To reach the East Hill end of the park, take the funicular (see page 176) or climb up the steep steps from Tackleway, parallel to All Saints St; for access to the eastern end of the park, take bus #101 from the Old Town to the visitor centre; there are also car parks at various locations throughout the park

Hastings Country Park extends three miles east from East Hill to Fairlight, a gorgeous and uniquely diverse stretch of coastline with more than 650 acres of gorse-speckled heathland, dramatic sandstone cliffs, rolling grassland and ancient woodland ravines cut by gushing streams and waterfalls. Most of the park is designated a Special Area of Conservation and a Site of Special Scientific Interest: its ancient gill woodlands – **Fairlight Glen**, **Ecclesbourne Glen** and **Warren Glen** – are home to rare liverworts and mosses, and are especially beautiful in the spring, when they're carpeted with bluebells and wood anemone. The **visitor centre** and main car park is at the eastern end of the park in the Firehills heathland.

The De La Warr Pavilion

Marina, Bexhill-on-Sea, TN40 1DP • Daily 10am–6pm • Free • ☎ 01424 229111, ⊚ dlwp.com • Bus #99 from Hastings (Mon–Sat every 20min, Sun hourly; 30min); train from Hastings (every 15min; 10min); or seafront cycle path from Hastings to Bexhill (see page 177)

Five miles west of Hastings is the seaside town of Bexhill-on-Sea, home to the iconic **De La Warr Pavilion**, a sleek Modernist masterpiece overlooking the sea. It was built in 1935 by architects Erich Mendelsohn and Serge Chermayeff – the first Modernist

5

public building in the country, and the first to use a welded steel frame – and was the brainchild of the progressive ninth Earl de la Warr, local landowner and socialist, who had a vision of a free-to-all seaside pavilion for the education, entertainment and health of the masses. In its brief heyday the Pavilion flourished, but it slid gradually into disrepair in the years following World War II. After decades of hosting everything from bingo to wrestling while the building crumbled and corroded, today the Pavilion has been lovingly restored to its original glory – all crisp white lines and gleaming glass – and hosts changing **exhibitions** of contemporary art, and an eclectic mix of **live performances**, from big-name bands to comedy and film nights. Up on the first floor a **café** and restaurant offer glorious views from the floor-to-ceiling windows and balcony.

Pevensey Castle

Castle Rd, Pevensey, 12 miles west of Hastings, BN24 5LE • End March to Sept daily 10am–6pm; Oct daily 10am–5pm; Nov–March Sat & Sun 10am–4pm • £6.80 (includes audio tour); EH • ☏ 01323 762604, ⓦ www.english-heritage.org.uk/visit/places/pevensey-castle

If truth be told, there isn't an awful lot left of **Pevensey Castle**, and you'll need to use your imagination – or take advantage of the excellent audio tour – to really bring the rich history of the place to life. When William the Conqueror landed here in 1066, he set up camp within the crumbling walls of an old Roman fort – one of the largest of the Saxon shore forts built on the south coast in the third century. After his victory at Battle (see page 186), he gave the Rape of Pevensey to his half-brother, **Robert Count of Mortain**, who built a wooden castle within the southeast corner of the Roman fort, and repaired its walls for use as an outer bailey; over two-thirds of the **Roman walls** still remain today. Mortain's wooden castle was replaced by a sturdier stone castle in the twelfth and thirteenth centuries.

The castle survived several dramatic sieges through the centuries, but was eventually overcome – not by invading troops but by the changing coastline, which left it without access to the sea and so without a strategic purpose. By 1500 the castle was no longer in use, though it was pressed back into action again at various times when foreign invasion threatened – the Spanish Armada in 1580, Napoleon in 1805 and Hitler in 1940. The **gun emplacements** added in World War II can still be seen today.

Entry into the Roman walls is free; you only pay to cross the moat and enter the Norman castle walls. Inside, much of what you see lies in ruins, but you can clamber down into the dungeons, and up a wooden staircase to the North Tower.

Herstmonceux Castle and Observatory Science Centre

Wartling Rd, Herstmonceux, BN27 1RN • **Castle gardens & grounds** Daily: March, Oct & Nov 10am–5pm; April–Sept 10am–6pm; last entry 1hr before closing • £6, joint ticket with observatory £13.50; children aged 4–16 £3/£9 • **Castle tours** 1 or 2 tours run most days between 11.30am & 2pm but check website ahead of visit • £3 • ☏ 01323 833816, ⓦ herstmonceux-castle.com • **Observatory** Feb, March, Oct & Nov daily 10am–5pm; April–Sept daily 10am–6pm; Jan & Dec open occasional weekends only; last admission 2hr before closing • £8.75, joint ticket with gardens £13.50; children aged 4–16 £7.45/£9 • ☏ 01323 832731, ⓦ the-observatory.org

Moated **Herstmonceux Castle**, thirteen miles from Hastings, was built in the fifteenth century, one of the first buildings in the south to be constructed from brick – at the time a new and fashionable building material. In 1946 the castle was sold to the Admiralty, who moved the **Royal Greenwich Observatory** to the castle grounds, away from London's lights and pollution. When the Observatory's prized Isaac Newton telescope was moved to the clearer skies of La Palma in the Canaries in 1979 it signalled the beginning of the end for the Observatory, and it was closed down in 1990.

The castle was subsequently bought by the **Queen's University of Canada** and is now closed to the public except on **guided tours**. You can still stroll round the lovely Elizabethan **walled garden** and surrounding **parklands**, but undoubtedly the best time to visit is during the **Medieval Festival** (see page 32) – the largest in the country – when the castle grounds are taken over by knights-at-arms, jesters and minstrels for three fun days of battle re-enactments, jousting, archery displays, workshops, theatre, music and story-telling.

Next door to the castle, the old observatory buildings now house the **Observatory Science Centre**, which is really two attractions in one: a fantastically well-run science centre, with over a hundred interactive exhibits, all enticingly hands-on for kids; and an observatory that's home to historic telescopes, now fully restored to working order – telescope tours (free; 45min) normally run daily. **Star-gazing open evenings** offer you the chance to use the telescopes on selected dates.

Carr Taylor Vineyard

Wheel Lane, outside Westfield village, 4 miles north of Hastings, TN35 4SG • Daily 10am–3/4pm • Self-guided tours £2.50 • ☎ 01424 752501, ⓦ carr-taylor.co.uk

Family-run **Carr Taylor Vineyard** was not only one of the very first commercial vineyards in the country, but it was also the first to produce traditional-method sparkling wine (Champagne in all but name), the real success story of English wine. This remains one of its mainstays today, together with still white wine and fruit wines. You can visit the beautiful 37-acre vineyard on a **self-guided tour**, which takes you through the vineyards, winery and bottling room and finishes at the shop.

Battle

The town of **BATTLE**, six miles inland of Hastings, occupies the site of the most famous land battle in British history. Here, on October 14, 1066, the invading Normans swarmed up the hillside from Senlac Moor and overcame the Anglo-Saxon army of King Harold, in what would be the last ever successful invasion of Britain (see page 186). Battle Abbey, built by the victorious William the Conqueror in penance for the blood spilled, still dominates the town today, its impressive gatehouse looming over the southern end of the narrow, appealingly venerable **High Street**, lined with a mix of medieval timber-framed, tile-hung and Victorian buildings.

Battle Abbey and 1066 battlefield

At the south end of High St, TN33 0AD • Feb half term daily 10am–4pm; mid-Feb to March Wed–Sun 10am–4pm; April–Sept daily 10am–6pm; Oct daily 10am–5pm; Nov to mid-Feb Sat & Sun 10am–4pm; manor house tours (included in entry fee) run most days in Aug; 30min • £12.30; EH • ☎ 01424 775705, ⓦ www.english-heritage.org.uk/visit/places/1066-battle-of-hastings-abbey-and-battlefield

The magnificent structure of **Battle Abbey**, founded by William in the aftermath of his victory, was ostensibly built to atone for the thousands of lives lost in the battle, but it was also a powerful symbol of Norman victory – not for nothing did William decree that the high altar in the abbey church should be built on the exact spot where Harold met his death. The completed abbey was occupied by a fraternity of Benedictines, and over the next four hundred years grew to become one of the richest monasteries in the country, being rebuilt and extended along the way. When the Dissolution came, the land was given to King Henry VIII's friend, Sir Anthony Browne, who promptly knocked down the church and converted the abbot's lodging into a fine manor house.

The **manor house** still stands today, though it's out of bounds to visitors for most of the year, having been occupied by Battle Abbey School since 1912; tours run in the August school holidays. All that remains of the Norman **abbey church** is its outline – with the site of the high altar marked by a memorial stone – but some buildings survive from the thirteenth century, including the monks' rib-vaulted **dormitory range**. The impressive 1330s **gatehouse** holds an exhibition on the history of the site, and allows you to clamber up to a rooftop viewing platform, but the best place to start your visit is in the modern **visitor centre**, where a short film takes you through the background to the events of the day itself.

Audio guides (40min) take you round the site of the **battlefield**, vividly re-creating the battle and its aftermath, which local chroniclers recorded as a hellish scene –

5

THE BATTLE OF HASTINGS

The most famous date in English history – October 14, 1066 – and the most famous battle ever fought on English soil, the **Battle of Hastings** saw the defeat of King Harold and the end of Anglo-Saxon England.

LEAD-UP TO THE BATTLE

The roots of the battle lay in the death of Edward the Confessor in January 1066. With no children of his own, the succession was far from clear: Edward's cousin, **William, Duke of Normandy**, had reportedly been promised the Crown by Edward during a previous visit to England, fifteen years before, but it was **Harold**, Edward the Confessor's brother-in-law, whom Edward named as his successor on his deathbed. William was enraged, his sense of injustice not helped by the fact that Harold had previously sworn an oath, on holy relics no less, that he would support William's claim to the Crown.

William quickly gathered together an army and sailed for England, landing at Pevensey on September 28. Harold heard the news in Yorkshire, where he'd just been celebrating victory over another claimant to the throne – **Harald Hardrada**, King of Norway – at the Battle of Stamford Bridge on September 22. He quickly raced his troops south to meet William, but instead of giving his footsore and battle-worn army time to recuperate, he rushed to engage William in battle.

THE BATTLE

The forces met at **Senlac Hill**. Harold's army of 5000–7000 troops occupied the superior position on the brow of the hill, his soldiers forming a protective shield wall. William's Norman army – a similar size – congregated below. Statistically, the odds were in Harold's favour, but the Saxon troops made an error: when Norman soldiers made an unsuccessful charge and retreated down the hill, some of Harold's troops, instead of staying put in their unassailable hilltop position, pursued them. Separated from the rest of their army, they were surrounded by Norman soldiers and killed. William pressed his advantage, his men feigning several more retreats, each time drawing the Saxon army down the hill, only for them to be surrounded and hacked to death. It wasn't enough to defeat the English entirely, but William had two other advantages: his mounted knights, who had greater mobility in the battlefield than the Saxon foot soldiers, and his archers, who were able to breach the English line. The advantage steadily moved in William's favour, and by nightfall the battle was his, and Harold lay dead on the battlefield. The total casualties lay at around 7000, which, at a time when the population of a large town was around 2500, would have been a shockingly large number.

THE BAYEUX TAPESTRY AND THE DEATH OF HAROLD

That we know so much about the battle and its lead-up is in part due to the existence of the **Bayeux Tapestry** – a 70m-long piece of embroidery created within twenty years of the battle. The most famous scene in the tapestry – the **death of Harold** – is, however, famously ambiguous. Harold's death by means of an arrow through the eye was first reported in 1080 (although it was not noted in any of the accounts written immediately after the battle), and by the following century had become an accepted fact. The scene in the tapestry seems to bear out the arrow story, but over the years scholars have variously argued that the figure with an arrow through his eye and "Harold" written above his head was not actually the king; that Harold was felled by an arrow through the eye and then hacked to death; and that the "arrow" through Harold's eye is just a spear he is holding, and that the fletching on it was added later in over-zealous restoration. The truth of the matter will probably never be known.

"covered in corpses, and all around the only colour to meet the gaze was blood-red". The best time to visit the abbey is during the annual **re-enactment** of the battle, held on the weekend nearest to October 14, and performed by a cast of over a thousand chain-mailed soldiers, entering into their Norman and Saxon roles with gusto.

Battle Museum of Local History

The Almonry, High St, TN33 0EA • April–Oct Mon–Sat 10am–4.30pm • Free • ☎ 01424 775955, ⊛ battlelocalhistory.com/battle-museum

At the top end of the High Street in the medieval Almonry, the small, volunteer-run **Battle Museum of Local History** contains what is possibly the only battle-axe discovered at Battle, as well as a rare hand-coloured print of the Bayeux Tapestry, made in 1819 after a watercolour painting by Charles Stothard. The museum is also home to the oldest **Guy Fawkes** in the country, with a pearwood head dating back to the eighteenth century. Every year, on the Saturday nearest to November 5, the effigy is paraded along High Street at the head of a torch-lit procession culminating at a huge bonfire on the Abbey Green, in front of the gatehouse.

ARRIVAL AND DEPARTURE
BATTLE

By train The train station is a well-signposted 10min walk from the High St.

Destinations Hastings (every 30min; 15min); London Charing Cross (every 30min; 1hr 30min); Tunbridge Wells (every 30min; 30min).

By bus Buses #304 and #305 run from Hastings to Battle High St (Mon–Sat hourly; 15min).

By car The car park next to Battle Abbey is the best value for stays of more than 2hr (£4.50/day; discount for EH members).

EATING

Battle Deli & Coffee Shop 57 High St, TN33 0EN ☎ 01424 777810. Lovely little deli-cum-café crammed with delicious stuff for a picnic or an eat-in lunch. Mon–Sat 8.30am–5pm, Sun & bank hols 10am–4pm.

★ **Bluebells Café Tearoom** 87 High St, TN33 0AQ ⓦ bluebellstearoom.co.uk. Just across the road from Battle Abbey, this fab tearoom is very popular for its delicious homemade cakes, breakfasts, sandwiches and light lunches. The (very generous) afternoon teas are especially recommended. Tues–Sat 9am–4.30pm.

Cut and Grill 17 High St, TN33 0AE ☎ 01424 774422, ⓦ cutandgrill.co.uk. All the produce at this exemplary burger and steak place is sourced from within a 20-mile radius of the restaurant — meat, fish, cheeses, ice cream and more. Burgers and hot dogs start at £8, grills at £10 and steaks at £14. There's a great kids' menu, too. Daily noon–9pm.

The eastern High Weald

A feeling of remoteness characterizes the **EASTERN HIGH WEALD**, which spills over the border into neighbouring Kent (see chapter 4). There are no really big towns – the small market town of Heathfield is the only place of any size – and most of the landscape is given over to rolling farmland and wooded hills, peppered with quiet, sleepy villages. The two big sights in the area are **Great Dixter** – one of the country's most famous gardens – and picture-perfect **Bodiam Castle**. Less known is the fascinating **Farleys House and Gallery**, the former home of the Surrealist artist Roland Penrose and photographer Lee Miller, which became a vibrant meeting place for leading figures in twentieth-century art. Other attractions include Rudyard Kipling's sleepy countryside retreat at **Bateman's**, gorgeous **Pashley Manor Gardens** and the moated Augustinian **Michelham Priory**.

Great Dixter

Half a mile north of Northiam, signposted from the village, TN31 6PH • End March–Oct Tues–Sun & bank hols: gardens 11am–5pm; house 1–4pm • House & gardens £12, gardens only £10 • ☎ 01797 252878, ⓦ greatdixter.co.uk • Stagecoach bus #2 passes through Northiam on its way from Hastings to Tenterden (Mon–Sat hourly; 45min from Hastings)

One of the best-loved gardens in the country, **Great Dixter** has come to be known above all else for bringing innovative and experimental planting to the English country garden. Exuberant and informal, it spreads around a medieval half-timbered house, which was home to the gardener and writer **Christopher Lloyd** until his death in 2005. Lloyd's parents bought the house in 1912 and, with the help of a dazzling young architect, **Edwin Lutyens**, stripped it back to its medieval splendour, ripping out partitions and restoring the magnificent Great Hall – the largest surviving timber-framed hall in the country – to its original double-height. A new wing (to the left

5

of the lopsided porch) was built, and another medieval house was moved piece-by-painstaking-piece from nearby Bendenden and tacked on to the back of the building.

Lutyens also helped design the **garden**, planting the hedges and topiary, incorporating old farm buildings where possible and laying the paving (recycled London pavement). As you wander round it today, through a series of intimate garden "rooms", the first thing you're struck by is its informality; all around are sweeps of wildflower-speckled meadow, and flowers spilling out of crammed, luxuriant borders. Christopher Lloyd loved change and colour, and with his head gardener **Fergus Garrett** (who continues to manage the garden today) he experimented with unusual juxtapositions and imaginative plantings, most famously ripping out his parents' rose garden to plant dahlias, bananas and other exotics. Look out, too, for occasional reminders that this was a personal garden; Lloyd's beloved dachshunds, which had a tendency to nip unwelcome visitors, are remembered in a pebble mosaic by the entrance.

Bodiam Castle

Bodiam, 9 miles north of Hastings, TN32 5UA • Daily 11am–5pm (or dusk if sooner) • £9.80; NT • ☎ 01580 830196, Ⓦ nationaltrust.org. uk/bodiam-castle • Parking £3 non-members; bus #349 from Hastings (daily; every 2hr; 40min); steam train from Tenterden (see page 151); or boat from Newenden (April–Sept; up to 3 boats daily – check timetable for details; 45min one way; £12 return; ☎ 01797 253838, Ⓦ bodiamboatingstation.co.uk)

Ask a child to draw a castle and the outline of the fairytale **Bodiam Castle** would be the result: a classically stout, square block with rounded corner turrets, battlements and a wide moat. When it was built in 1385 to guard what were the lower reaches of the River Rother against the French, Bodiam was state-of-the-art military architecture, but during the Civil War, a company of Roundheads breached the fortress and removed its roof to reduce its effectiveness as a possible stronghold for the king. Over the next 250 years Bodiam fell into neglect until restoration in 1826 by "Mad Jack" Fuller (see page 189) and later Lord Curzon.

Inside the castle walls it's a roofless ruin, but a wonderfully atmospheric one nonetheless, with plenty of nooks and crannies to explore and steep spiral staircases leading up to the crenellated battlements. It also boasts its original portcullis – claimed to be the oldest in the country – and murder holes in the ceiling of the gatehouse, through which defenders would fire arrows or drop rocks, boiling oil, tar or scalding water on to their enemies.

The nicest way to arrive at Bodiam is on a **steam train** from Tenterden, operated by the Kent & East Sussex Railway (see page 151), or on a **boat trip** from Newenden, four miles down the River Rother.

Bateman's

Bateman's Lane, Burwash, off the A265, TN19 7DS • Garden daily 10am–5pm (or dusk if sooner); house April–Oct daily 11am–5pm, Nov–March daily 11.30am–4pm • £11.50; NT • ☎ 01435 882302, Ⓦ nationaltrust.org.uk/batemans

Bateman's, the idyllic home of the writer and journalist **Rudyard Kipling** from 1902 until his death in 1936, lies half a mile south of **Burwich**, a pretty Sussex village of redbrick and weatherboard cottages with a Norman church tower. For Kipling, the seventeenth-century manor house was a haven from the outside world. By the turn of the century he was one of the most popular writers in the country, and he had grown heartily sick of the fame that came with his success. Bateman's gave him the seclusion that his previous home in Rottingdean (see page 243) had not.

In his book-lined **study** – which is today laid out much as he left it, with letters, early editions of his work and mementoes from his travels on display – he wrote *Pook's Hill* and *Rewards and Fairies*, the latter containing his most famous poem, *If*. Outside in the garage you can see Kipling's beloved 1928 Rolls Royce Phantom I, which despite his childlike enthusiasm for motor cars he never drove himself, preferring to be

"MAD JACK" FULLER AND THE BRIGHTLING FOLLIES

John Fuller of Brightling (1757–1834), or **"Mad Jack" Fuller** as he's affectionately known, was a true eccentric, one of the great characters of Sussex. A wealthy landowner, Fuller was a corpulent 22 stone, wore his hair in a pigtail (despite the style falling out of fashion long before), had a bellowing voice, and drove around the countryside in a heavily armed barouche. His turbulent parliamentary career ended with him hurling abuse at his fellow MPs and being expelled from the House. And yet Fuller was also a man of remarkable philanthropy, and his name crops up again and again all over Sussex: it was he who provided Eastbourne with its first lifeboat (see page 204), bought Bodiam Castle (see page 188) in 1828 to save it from demolition and built the Belle Tout lighthouse (see page 211), saving countless lives. He was also a champion of science, founding a reference library and two professorships at the Royal Institute.

His fame endures today in the main because of the **follies** he erected around his country estate at **Brightling**, a small village five miles northeast of Battle. In true Fuller fashion each one has an outlandish tale attached to it: the **Rotunda Temple** in Brightling Park was supposedly used for gambling sessions and carousing with ladies of the night; the 35ft-high circular **Tower**, just off the Brightling–Darwell road, was perhaps erected so that Fuller could keep an eye on the restoration work going on at nearby Bodiam Castle; and the **Sugar Loaf** (visible from the Battle–Heathfield road), was built after Fuller made a wager he could see the spire of nearby Dallington church from his estate – when it turned out he couldn't he had the tower, a replica of Dallington's church spire, built overnight so that he could win his bet. All three follies are accessible by footpath, but the easiest of Fuller's follies to visit is the incongruous blackened stone **pyramid** in the churchyard of squat-towered **Brightling church**: this is Fuller's burial place, though the story that he was interred bolt upright, dressed for dinner and with a bottle of claret on the table in front of him, has sadly been proved apocryphal.

chauffeured around the countryside. At the far end of the garden, across the stream, is a still-working **watermill** which was converted by Kipling to generate electricity. Special **events** run throughout the year, including occasional talks on the author and *Jungle Book* days and *Just So* story days for kids.

Pashley Manor Gardens

Off the B2099 south of Ticehurst, TN5 7HE • April–Sept Tues–Sat & bank hols 10am–5pm • £11 • ☎ 01580 200888, ⌨ pashleymanorgardens.co.uk

Romantic and quintessentially English, **Pashley Manor Gardens** are a gorgeous confection of lakes, follies and fountains, ancient oak trees, walled gardens and luxuriant borders, all set against the backdrop of Pashley Manor itself (closed to the public); the manor house dates from Tudor times, though the handsome Georgian facade added to the back of the house gives it an entirely different character. **Sculpture** (changing every year) is displayed dotted around the lawns and lakes, and special **events** include the late spring Tulip Festival, when over thirty thousand bulbs erupt into bloom.

Farleys House and Gallery

Muddles Green, Chiddingly, BN8 6HW • **Garden** April–Oct Sun 10am–3.30pm • £3.50 • **House tours** April–Oct Sun 10.30am, 11.30am, 12.30pm, 1.30pm, 2.30pm & 3.30pm; 50min • £13.50 (includes garden access) • **Private tours** Several times a year, led by members of the Penrose family; 3.5hr • £40 • ☎ 01825 872691, ⌨ farleyhouseandgallery.co.uk

Though nowhere near as well known as nearby Charleston Farmhouse (see page 217), **Farleys House and Gallery** is just as fascinating. After World War II this redbrick house became the home of painter and biographer **Roland Penrose**, American photographer **Lee Miller** and their son, Antony (who still lives at the farmhouse today), and over the years that followed it became a meeting place for some of the leading lights of the modern art world – Picasso, Man Ray and Max Ernst among them. Penrose was a key figure in the English Surrealist movement, curating the first International Surrealist Exhibition in 1936, and writing biographies of Picasso, Miró, Man Ray and

5

RUDYARD KIPLING

God gave all men all earth to love,
But, since our hearts are small
Ordained for each one spot should prove
Beloved over all…
Each to his choice, and I rejoice
The lot has fallen to me
In a fair ground – In a fair ground
Yea, Sussex by the Sea!   *Sussex*, by Rudyard Kipling (1902)

The reputation of **Rudyard Kipling** (1865–1936), author of *Kim*, *The Jungle Book* and the *Just So Stories*, has taken a bit of a battering over the years. In 1907, when he won the Nobel Prize for Literature, he was at the peak of his popularity, but just 35 years later George Orwell was famously writing of him: "Kipling is a jingo imperialist, he is morally insensitive and aesthetically disgusting."

Kipling was very much an author of his time. He was born in India in 1865, and after a childhood spent in England he returned aged 16 to take up a position on a small local newspaper in Lahore, where he started publishing his poems and short stories, and soaking up the sights, smells and experiences that would inform so much of his later writing. Kipling left India in 1889, travelling, writing, marrying and finally settling in Vermont, and by the time he returned to England in 1896, he had published *The Jungle Book* and its follow-up, and was famous.

In the successful years that followed he captured the mood of the nation with his poem *The White Man's Burden* (1899), a celebration of noble-spirited British empire-building that was regarded by just a small minority as imperialist propaganda. *Kim* (1901) and the *Just So Stories* (1902) followed, and Kipling's fame grew so great that he decamped to **Bateman's**, in the heart of the Sussex countryside, to escape his fans. Behind the scenes, however, all was not rosy. Kipling's beloved daughter, Josephine, died of pneumonia in 1898, and his son, John, was killed in 1915 at the Battle of Loos, having been encouraged to enlist by Kipling himself. Bateman's was indeed a haven, but it was also the place Kipling retreated to lick his wounds, and – if Orwell is to be believed – to "sulk" at the collapse of British colonialism, and perhaps his tarnished reputation too.

Despite it all, though, even Orwell admitted that Kipling could write a good line, a sentiment seemingly echoed by modern readers, who in recent years have crowned Kipling's *If* the nation's favourite poem.

Tàpies. Miller, too, was known for her Surrealist images, though she also found fame as a portraitist and a World War II photographer; she was one of the few female war reporters to witness battle first-hand.

Informative **tours** of the house take you through the ground-floor rooms, in the main left as they were in Penrose and Miller's day, decorated with Penrose's Surrealist paintings, sketches by artist friends and an eclectic array of *objet trouvé* and tribal art. The homely **kitchen** was the heart of the house: Miller was a gourmet cook, and dinner parties would feature copious amounts of whisky alongside eclectic creations ranging from blue spaghetti to pink cauliflower breasts. A couple of Picasso lithographs (one produced at the farmhouse during a visit) hang on the far wall, facing a well-worn tile by the artist above the Aga – the Surrealists believed art was there to be lived with and for all to enjoy. The **dining room** showcases Penrose's paintings and his journey to Surrealism, while the photographs and objects in Lee Miller's **office** tell the story of this most extraordinary women, whose life included spells as a supermodel in New York, as student, lover and muse to Man Ray in Paris, and as a war photographer who witnessed the liberation of Paris and of Dachau concentration camp. Outside, the beautiful **garden** contains sculptures by Roland Penrose and his friends, as well as rotating works by contemporary guest sculptors.

Check the website for dates of the engrossing **extended tours** led by Antony Penrose (who grew up at the farmhouse and was a favourite with the visiting Picasso) or his daughter, Ami.

Michelham Priory

Upper Dicker, BN27 3QS, signposted from the A27 and A22 • Daily: mid-Feb to end Feb & Nov to mid-Dec 11am–4pm; March–Oct 10.30am–5pm • £10.50 • ☎ 01323 844224, ⓦ sussexpast.co.uk

Venerable **Michelham Priory** has a lovely setting amid immaculate gardens and is encircled by the longest water-filled moat in the country. The Augustinian priory was founded in 1229, with the medieval gatehouse and moat added at the end of the fourteenth century, but in 1537 it was dissolved and partly demolished under Henry VIII, and transformed into a private country house. Only the refectory, the undercroft (now the main entrance) and the prior's room above it remain from the original structure; the Tudor wing of the house was added in the late sixteenth century.

Inside, you'll find Tudor rooms and furnishings, including a re-created kitchen complete with working spit, and a goggin – an early baby-walker. It's the **grounds**, though, that are the real treat, with a beautiful little kitchen garden, a medieval orchard, a working watermill and a moat walk giving lovely views back towards the house. Most weekends there's have-a-go **archery** on the sweeping South Lawn.

Branching Out Adventures

Bentley, Harvey's Lane, Halland, BN8 5AF, 7 miles northeast of Lewes • Feb–May Sat & Sun 10am–5pm; June–Oct Wed 10am–2pm, Thurs–Sun 10am–5pm (daily during school holidays); Nov–early Dec Fri–Sun 11am–5pm • Adults/under-16s: high ropes £19/17; low ropes £17/15; giant swing, zip wires & climbing wall £6/5 each, Bounce About cargo nets £7 (children) • ☎ 01825 280250, ⓦ branchingoutadventures.co.uk

Zip through the trees, wobble your way round a high ropes course or brave the adrenaline-pumping Giant Swing at **Branching Out Adventures**, nestled in woodland a few miles northeast of Lewes. If you're bringing kids, note that they need to be age 6 (and 1.2m) for the low ropes course and climbing wall, and age 8 (and 1.3m) for the high ropes, giant swing and zip wires; there's a woodland play area for littler ones.

ACCOMMODATION   THE EASTERN HIGH WEALD

The Bell High St, Ticehurst, TN5 7AS ☎ 01580 200234, ⓦ thebellinticehurst.com. The seven rooms at *The Bell* are as quirky as the rest of this eccentric pub (see below); for starters, each comes with its own silver birch tree growing up out of the floor. Outside are three similarly funky, eclectically styled lodges (sleep 2–4 people) – one featuring a turntable and selection of vinyl – and a "Love Nest" with roof terrace and fire pit. Doubles £117, lodges (2 people) £230

Dernwood Farm Little Dernwood Farm, Dern Lane, Waldron, near Heathfield, TN21 0PN ☎ 01435 812726, ⓦ dernwoodfarm.co.uk. Lovely car-free campsite, with pitches in a large meadow or nestled in woodland. The farm sells its own field-to-fork bacon, sausages, beef and lamb for cooking on the fire pit, and has an all-day café serving breakfast baps, milkshakes and more. More expensive glamping options, including a cabin with wood-fuelled hot tub, are also available. April–Oct. Two nights' minimum stay at weekends. Per adult £12

THE CUCKOO TRAIL

One of the most popular traffic-free cycle rides in Sussex is the **Cuckoo Trail**, which runs for fourteen miles – almost entirely off-road – past broadleaf woods and farmland along the path of a disused railway from Heathfield down to Hampden Park in Eastbourne. The Cuckoo Trail **leaflet** can be downloaded from ⓦ eastsussex.gov.uk. There's **parking** at Heathfield, Horam, Hellingly, Hailsham, Polegate and Hampden Park, and **train** stations at Polegate and Hampden Park. The trail slopes very gently downhill as it runs south, so there's much to be said for starting at the southern end to make your return trip slightly easier.

5

George Inn High St, Robertsbridge, TN32 5AW ☎ 01580 880315, ⊛ thegeorgerobertsbridge.co.uk. The four comfortable, well-priced rooms in this eighteenth-century former coaching inn make a great base for the area. There's excellent food, too, sourced where possible from within a thirty-mile radius of the pub. Tues–Sat noon–11pm, Sun noon–8pm. **£120**

Original Hut Company Quarry Farm, Bodiam, TN32 5RA ☎ 01580 830932, ⊛ original-huts.co.uk. Ten quirky "shepherd's huts", with wood-burners and their own fire pit, plus "tin tabernacles" (tin-roofed wooden camping pods) and camping pitches, all dotted about the tranquil woodland of a working farm. It's a great location – just a fifteen-minute stroll to Bodiam Castle, the battlements of which you can see peeking up over the trees. Loads of activities can be arranged, from paddleboarding to bushcraft; electric bike hire is available, and there's also an on-site spa, café and shop selling local food and crafts. There's an additional per-person charge of £3.30 for camping and tabernacles. Three nights' minimum stay (two nights for camping) at weekends and school holidays. Huts **£115**, tabernacles **£80**, camping **£23**

★ **Railway Retreats** Station Rd, Northiam, TN31 6QT ☎ 01797 253850, ⊛ railwaycarriageholiday.co.uk. For a unique and memorable stay, look no further than one of the four beautifully converted railway carriages overlooking the platform at Northiam station on the Kent & East Sussex Railway line (see page 151), mere metres away from the puffing steam trains. Pick of the bunch is the MK1 carriage (sleeps 6), which comes with three bedrooms, two bathrooms, an open-plan living space and an elevated glass balcony, but smaller carriages sleeping two are also available. Two nights' minimum stay. **£100**

EATING AND DRINKING

★ **The Bell** High St, Ticehurst, TN5 7AS ☎ 01580 200234, ⊛ thebellinticehurst.com. There's a bit of an Alice in Wonderland feel to this great village local: on the surface it's all old beams, wooden floors and battered sofas, but look a little closer and you'll see bowler hat light fittings dangling from the ceiling, coat hooks fashioned from old cutlery and, in the gent's, a row of upturned tubas for urinals. Food (mains £13–17) is excellent, seasonal and local, and there are plenty of Sussex ales on tap. Mon–Sat noon–11.30pm, Sun noon–10.30pm; kitchen Mon–Sat noon–3pm & 6.30–9.30pm, Sun noon–4pm & 6.30–9pm.

Blackboys Inn Lewes Rd, Blackboys, TN22 5LG ☎ 01825 890283, ⊛ theblackboys.co.uk. This lovely old 1300s coaching inn comes into its own on a summer's day, when drinkers spill out onto the terrace and front lawn under the chestnut trees. Decent food (mains £13 and up) includes burgers, pies and steaks, and they have Harveys and guest beers on tap. Daily noon–11pm; kitchen Mon–Fri noon–2.30pm & 6–9pm, Sat noon–3pm & 6–9.30pm, Sun noon–6pm.

Six Bells The Street, Chiddingly, BN8 6HE ☎ 01825 872227, ⊛ the-six-bells-chiddingly.business.site. A proper pub, old-fashioned and unpretentious, with plenty of cosy nooks and crannies, log fires, Harveys on tap, excellent-value pub grub (lots around the £8/9 mark) and a great atmosphere. Try to catch one of the regular folk and blues nights if you can (alternate Tues nights; ⊛ 6bellsfolk.co.uk). Mon–Thurs & Sun noon–11pm, Fri & Sat noon–midnight; kitchen Mon–Thurs noon–2pm & 6–9pm, Fri–Sun noon–9pm.

Ashdown Forest

The first thing that surprises visitors to **ASHDOWN FOREST** is how little of it is actually forest. Almost two thirds of the Forest's ten square miles is made up of high, open **heathland** – particularly lovely in late summer, when the gorse and heather flower and the heath becomes a riot of purple and yellow. It's a peculiarly un-Sussex scene, a complete departure from the rolling green hills and patchwork fields that surround it, and all the more beautiful for it.

Walking in the Forest couldn't be easier, with footpaths and bridleways striking off in every direction. Orientation can be difficult, so it's well worth getting hold of the official map (£2.50), which marks all the trails; it's available at the Ashdown Forest Centre Information Barn (see page 193) or you can download it from ⊛ ashdownforest.org. The Barn also has plenty of free leaflets (also downloadable from the website) describing individual walks. With one notable exception – Pooh Bridge (see page 194) – the Forest never really gets too busy, and you'll generally find yourself able to enjoy the expansive views in solitude, with only the odd free-wandering sheep for company. Ashdown Forest Riding Centre (☎ 07818 093880, ⊛ ashdownforestriding.co.uk) offers one- to three-hour **horseriding** sessions (£35–75), while the Llama Park at Wych Cross (☎ 01825 712040, ⊛ llamapark.co.uk) leads daily **llama walks** (1hr 30min; £40). Note that off-road **mountain biking** in the Forest isn't allowed.

ROCK-CLIMBING NEAR ERIDGE GREEN

Some of the best **climbing** to be had in the Southeast is around Eridge Green, straddling the Sussex–Kent border. Two of the sites – Eridge Rocks (owned by the Sussex Wildlife Trust; ⓦ sussexwildlifetrust.org.uk) and Harrison's Rocks (owned by the British Mountaineering Council; ⓦ thebmc.co.uk) – are open access, while a third, Bowles Rocks, is owned by the Bowles Outdoor Centre (ⓦ bowles.ac; £5/adult; climbing courses and lessons also available). The sites are all open to experienced climbers with their own equipment, while novices can get roped up with **Nuts 4 Climbing** (☎ 01892 860670, ⓦ nuts4climbing.com), which offers a one-day intensive course (£225) – a perfect introduction to the sport.

ARRIVAL AND INFORMATION

By bus Compass Travel bus #261 (Mon–Fri every 2hr) runs between East Grinstead and Uckfield via the Llama Park, Coleman's Hatch and the visitor centre. Metrobus #291 runs between East Grinstead and Tunbridge Wells, stopping at Coleman's Hatch and Hartfield (Mon–Sat hourly, Sun every 2hr), and #270 runs from Brighton to East Grinstead via Wych Cross (Mon–Sat hourly).

ASHDOWN FOREST

Tourist information Ashdown Forest Centre Information Barn, Wych Cross (March–Oct Mon–Sun 11am–5pm; Nov–March Sat & Sun 11am–dusk; ☎ 01342 823583, ⓦ ashdownforest.org).
By car There are dozens of free parking sites dotting the main roads through the forest; the Information Barn sells a map (£2.50) with parking spots marked.

ACCOMMODATION AND EATING

Hatch Inn Colemans Hatch, TN7 4EJ ☎ 01342 822363, ⓦ hatchinn.co.uk. The nicest pub in the Forest itself is this ancient weatherboard inn, dating from 1430, which ticks all the boxes for a perfect pub lunch: a cosy, beamed interior, a gorgeous garden for the summer, well-kept Harveys on tap and good, home-cooked food. At lunchtimes you can opt for a sandwich or ploughman's (£7.50–11.50), or more expensive mains such as haddock kedgeree or belly of pork (£11–16.50). Mon–Fri 11.30am–3pm & 5.30–11pm, Sat 11am–11pm, Sun noon–11pm; kitchen Mon–Fri noon–2.15pm & 7–9.15pm, Sat noon–2.30pm & 7–9.30pm, Sun noon–3.30pm.
Piglet's Tearoom High St, Hartfield, TN7 4AE ☎ 01892 770456, ⓦ poohcorner.co.uk. If it's time for a little something, make a beeline for the tearoom in the Pooh Corner shop (see page 194), with plenty of seating outside and a menu that runs from cream teas to tasty "Smackerels" (snacks). Mon–Sat 10am–5pm, Sun & bank hols 11am–4pm.
St Ives Farm Butcherfield Lane, Hartfield, TN7 4JX ☎ 01892 770213, ⓦ stivesfarm.co.uk. This lovely low-key campsite has three shady camping fields set around a fishing lake, three miles from the nearest main road. Evening brings the crackle of campfires; barbecue supplies can be bought from Perryhill Orchards farm shop, a 20min walk away. April–Oct. Two nights' minimum stay at weekends. Per person **£10**

The western High Weald

The **WESTERN HIGH WEALD** feels surprisingly sleepy and remote, given that it's sandwiched between sprawling Crawley and East Grinstead to the north, Horsham to the west, and Haywards Heath and Burgess Hill to the south, with the busy A23 roaring through the centre. Scattered villages and stately manor houses pepper the landscape: when the railway arrived in the mid-nineteenth century, making the area easily accessible from London, this was a popular spot for wealthy Londoners to buy or build a mansion and a slice of rural living.

The main draw of the area is its **gardens**: the big hitters are **Sheffield Park**, **Nymans** and **Wakehurst Place**, but **Borde Hill** and **High Beeches** come a close second, and the modern **Sussex Prairies** garden provides a wonderful modern counterpoint. There's another beautiful garden surrounding the Arts and Crafts house of **Standen**, though it's the house itself which is the real star, crammed full of decorative treasures by William Morris and his contemporaries. To the south lies the **Bluebell Railway**, a vintage steam railway that puffs its way north from Sheffield Park through the bluebell-speckled woodlands that gave it its name.

5

A BEAR OF VERY LITTLE BRAIN

Probably the most famous bear in the world, Pooh Bear, also known as **Winnie-the-Pooh**, is the much-loved creation of **A.A. Milne**, who wrote the classic children's books – *Winnie the Pooh* (1926) and *House at Pooh Corner* (1928) – from his weekend home at Cotchford Farmhouse near the small village of **Hartfield**, on Ashdown Forest's northeastern edge. The stories were inspired by Milne's only son, Christopher Robin, who appears in the books along with his real-life stuffed toys: Edward Bear, Piglet, Kanga, Roo, Eeyore and Tigger (Owl and Rabbit were invented for the books).

The places described in the stories were modelled closely on Ashdown Forest: the fictional **100 Aker Wood**, where the animals live with Christopher Robin, is named after the real-life Five Hundred Acre Wood; **Galleon's Leap** was inspired by the hilltop of Gills Lap; while a clump of pine trees near Gills Lap became the **Enchanted Place**, where Christopher Robin never managed to work out whether there were 63 trees or 64. The original illustrations by **E.H. Shepherd** took direct inspiration from the Forest, and perfectly capture the heathland landscape, with its distinctive hilltop clusters of pine trees.

POOH WALKS

The *Pooh Walks from Gills Lap* **leaflet**, available from the Ashdown Forest Centre Information Barn (see page 193), details two short walks that take you past some of the spots featured in the book, including the Enchanted Place, the Heffalump Trap, the Sandy Pit where Roo played and the North Pole, but by far the most popular Pooh destination is **Pooh Bridge**, where the bear-of-very-little-brain invented the game of **Poohsticks** one lazy sunny afternoon with his good friend Piglet. The bridge is an easy one-mile walk from the Pooh Bridge car park, at the Forest's northern edge, just off the B2026.

POOH CORNER

The shop where real-life Christopher Robin went with his nanny to buy bulls' eyes is now **Pooh Corner**, High St, Hartfield, TN7 4AE (Mon–Sat 10am–5pm, Sun & bank hols 11am–4pm; ☎01892 770456, ⊛poohcorner.co.uk), a small **shop** – with attached tearoom (see page 193) – selling a wide array of Pooh memorabilia, from soft toys, books and T-shirts to Sussex honey, as well as maps and guidebooks of the Forest, and a rule-book for playing Poohsticks.

Sheffield Park and Garden

On the A275 East Grinstead–Lewes main road, about 2.5 miles north of the junction with the A272, TN22 3QX • Garden daily 10am–5pm (or dusk if sooner); parkland dawn–dusk • £13.10; NT • ☎01825 790231, ⊛nationaltrust.org.uk/sheffield-park-and-garden • Free parking; bus #121 from Lewes (Sat every 2hr; 30min); Bluebell Railway (see page 194) Sheffield Park station is a 10min walk away through the parkland

The beautiful landscaped garden at **Sheffield Park and Garden**, first laid out by Capability Brown in the eighteenth century, is at its very best in autumn, when it puts on the most spectacularly colourful show in the Southeast. Pick a cloudless sunny day and you'll have peerless views of the brilliantly hued foliage reflected in the mirror-like waters of the garden's five deep lakes, linked by cascades and waterfalls – though if you want to enjoy the views in relative solitude you're best off avoiding weekends and the busier, middle part of the day, when it can seem as though the whole of Sussex has turned up to see the spectacle. The 120-acre garden is equally lovely – and much quieter – in the springtime, when daffodils and bluebells start to emerge, and in May and June when the azaleas and rhododendrons are out.

On the other side of the access road lies the estate's 265-acre **parkland**, dotted by grazing sheep. A ten-minute walk from the car park brings you to a small copse where you'll find a natural play trail and a "sky glade" for cloud watching.

The Bluebell Railway

Sheffield Park station, on the A275 East Grinstead–Lewes main road, about 2 miles north of the junction with the A272, TN22 3QL • Timetable varies, but trains run most days April–Oct, plus Feb half term & weekends in March & Dec – see website for details • Day-ticket with unlimited travel £19 • ☎01825 720800, ⊛bluebell-railway.co.uk • The railway is connected to the mainline station at East Grinstead; bus #121 from Lewes (Sat every 2hr; 30min) runs to Sheffield Park station

Probably the best-known vintage steam railway in the country, the **Bluebell Railway** was started by a small group of enthusiasts in 1959, just four years after the old London–Lewes line was closed, and today has blossomed into a huge operation, with more than thirty steam locos, over one hundred pieces of rolling stock and more than eight hundred volunteers keeping the wheels rolling. The locos take around forty minutes to puff the nine miles north from Sheffield Park station – the southern terminus of the railway – via Kingscote and Horsted Keynes stations to East Grinstead, where they chug into a platform alongside the mainline station.

The three original stations have all been beautifully restored to different periods: **Horsted Keynes** in 1920s splendour, with old posters and newspaper headlines on the walls and luggage on the platforms; **Kingscote** with 1950s trimmings; and **Sheffield Park** in the style of the 1880s, decorated with wonderful reclaimed enamel signs proclaiming the benefits of Gold Flake cigarettes and Virol ("anaemic girls need it"). Sheffield Park is also home to the **railway sheds**, where you can wander amongst some splendid old locomotives, and a small **museum** which charts the development of railways from horse-drawn to electric, and also tells the story of the Bluebell Railway.

Special services run throughout the year, everything from afternoon tea services to Santa specials. Especially popular is the **Golden Arrow** Pullman dining train, re-creating the luxurious *Golden Arrow* which once linked London and Paris (£85 including dinner).

Sussex Prairies Garden

Morlands Farm, Wheatsheaf Rd, near Henfield on the B2166, BN5 9AT • June to mid-Oct Mon & Wed–Sun 1–5pm • £8 • ☎ 01273 495902, ⓦ sussexprairies.co.uk

In comparison to the grand old gardens of the Sussex Weald the **Sussex Prairies Garden** is a mere whippersnapper – it was only established in 2009 – but it's already made a bit of a name for itself. The naturalistic planting of the eight-acre site features extraordinary, vibrant drifts of summer-flowering perennials and tall ornamental grasses – some sixty thousand plants in total – with pathways snaking between them. It's quite an experience weaving your way between the borders in late summer when you're dwarfed by grasses 8ft high. Every year the work of a different group of sculptors is featured, and there's also a lovely tearoom, with tables outside overlooking the riot of colour.

Bolney Wine Estate

Bookers Vineyard, Foxhole Lane, Bolney, RH17 5NB • **Vineyard trail** June to mid-Sept Tues–Sat 10am–3pm • Trail map £3 • **Tours** Drop-on tour £10, taster tour £20, afternoon tea tour £35, lunch tour £45 • **Shop** Mon–Fri 9am–5pm, Sun 10am–5pm • **Café** Daily 9am–5pm • ☎ 01444 881894, ⓦ bolneywineestate.co.uk

Grapes have been grown on the land that is now the **Bolney Wine Estate** since the Middle Ages, but the tradition was only reinstated in 1972, when Rodney and Janet Pratt planted their first three acres of vines. The vineyard is perhaps best known for

---

CYCLING THE FOREST WAY

Running for just over nine miles from East Grinstead in the west to Groombridge in the east, the **Forest Way** follows the path of a disused railway line that skirts the northern fringes of Ashdown Forest. The route is flat and peaceful, shadowing the River Medway as it wriggles its way east past patchwork fields, farms, small villages and wooded hills. With dragonflies darting over the water and swallows flitting above you, it's an idyllic ride – perfect for families – and gives you a real taste of the beautiful High Weald. There are picnic benches along the track, or you can detour off to pubs along the way or the excellent tearoom at Hartfield (see page 193). A map of the route can be downloaded from ⓦ eastsussex.gov.uk.

There's **bike rental** at Forest Row Cycle Hire in Forest Row (☎ 07539 927467, ⓦ forestrow. gov.uk/Cycle-Hire; £2.50/hr), towards the western end of the route.

5

its red wines – unusual in the UK – but it's also won awards for its sparkling wines. A variety of pre-bookable **tours** are available, some including lunch or afternoon tea in the on-site café with its open-air balcony overlooking the vines, and there's also a **vineyard trail** and a handy **drop-on tour**, which lasts 45 minutes, includes a couple of tastings and allows kids to tag along.

Borde Hill Garden

Borde Hill Lane, near Haywards Heath, RH16 1XP • April–June & Sept–Oct Mon–Fri 10am–5pm, Sat & Sun 10am–6pm (or dusk if sooner); July & Aug daily 10am–6pm • £9.15 • ☎ 01444 450326, ⦿ bordehill.co.uk

Beautiful **Borde Hill Garden** ranges around a handsome honey-coloured Elizabethan manor house (not open to the public) on a narrow ridge of the Sussex Weald, with fantastic sweeping views all around. The gardens were planted by **Colonel Stephenson R. Clarke**, an enthusiastic naturalist, in the 1890s, from exotic trees and shrubs collected by famous plant-hunters (see page 197).

The **formal gardens** closest to the house form a series of "garden rooms", ranging from a formal English rose garden and terraced Italian garden (originally the house's tennis court), to a fabulous secret, subtropical sunken dell. Further afield the estate's **woodland** is blanketed by drifts of bluebells and anemones in spring, and later ablaze with rhododendrons – a favourite of the Colonel's. By the entrance there's a small adventure playground, as well as a café and the excellent *Jeremy's Restaurant* (see page 199).

Nymans

Handcross, just off the A23, RH17 6EB • Garden daily: March–Oct 10am–5pm; Nov–Feb 10am–4pm; house March–Oct daily 11–4pm • £14; NT • ☎ 01444 405250, ⦿ nationaltrust.org.uk/nymans • Free parking; Metrobus #271/273 (Mon–Fri hourly, Sat & Sun every 2hr; 1hr) from Brighton to Crawley stops nearby

The thirty-acre gardens at **Nymans** were the work of the Messel family, who took on the estate in 1890 and set about creating one of Sussex's great gardens. The main draw of the garden is its plant collection – the Messels sponsored many plant-hunting expeditions that brought back rare, exotic trees and shrubs from the remotest corners of the world. It's also a garden that prides itself on its year-round interest: daffodils, bluebells, rhododendrons and rare Himalayan magnolias in spring; stunning borders and the rose garden in full bloom in summer; autumn colour at the back of the garden; and witch hazel, winter-flowering bulbs and camellias in winter.

The gardens are arranged around the ruins of a mock-Gothic **manor house**, which burnt down one winter shortly after World War II: the night of the fire was so cold that although fire engines arrived in plenty of time, the water was frozen solid and they were forced to stand by and watch the house burn. Only a change of wind direction spared the portion of the house that remains open to the public today: the last of the Messels, Anne, lived in these few, modest rooms until her death in 1992, and they are preserved as they were when she died, decorated with flowers from the garden.

High Beeches

High Beeches Lane, near Handcross on the B2110, just off the A23, RH17 6HQ • April–Oct Mon, Tues & Thurs–Sun 1–5pm • £8.50 • ☎ 01444 400589, ⦿ highbeeches.com

The landscaped woodland garden of **High Beeches** has a wilder feel to it than the other great Sussex gardens, with steep, meandering paths cut through long grass, tumbling streams, woodland glades and a gorgeous wildflower meadow speckled with golden buttercups and ox-eye daisies in early summer. The 27-acre garden has beautiful displays of autumn colour, but it really comes into its own in spring, when the woodland is cloaked in bluebells, magnolias are in bloom and early rhododendrons, followed by azaleas, set the garden aflame with splashes of red and pink.

PLANT HUNTERS AND GATHERERS: GREAT GARDENS OF THE WEALD   **5**

Some of the greatest gardens in the Southeast – **Wakehurst Place**, **Nymans**, **Borde Hill** and **High Beeches** – can be found in a pocket of sleepy Sussex countryside, all within a few miles of each other. Their proximity is no coincidence: they were established at roughly the same time, in the 1890s and the decade that followed, by men who knew and influenced each other, and who would often visit one another's gardens and exchange ideas, advice and plants.

In contrast to the prevailing Victorian fashion for orderly formal planting, the Sussex gardens share a love of **naturalism**, partly due to the influence, encouragement and advice of the great gardener **William Robinson**, whose own garden at *Gravetye Manor* – now a hotel (see page 198) – was only a stone's throw away. The other defining feature of the Sussex gardens is their **exotic planting**, which often includes rare and important trees and shrubs. The fertile acid soil and high rainfall of the Weald provided perfect conditions for experimentation with non-native species, and Messel, Stephenson R. Clarke and the Loders all helped finance the perilous **plant-hunting expeditions** around the globe, which brought back some of the rare and exotic rhododendrons, azaleas, magnolias and camellias which are today such a central feature of the gardens.

The estate's grand house was destroyed when a stray Canadian bomber crashed into it in World War II, but the garden – much of which was created by **Colonel Giles Loder**, who ran the estate for sixty years until his death in 1966 – survived the neglect of the war. On the Colonel's death the garden was bought by another noted plant-loving family, the Boscawens, who had heard it described as the most beautiful in Sussex.

Wakehurst Place

On the B2028 between Ardingly and Turners Hill, RH17 6TN • Daily 10am–6pm; Millennium Seedbank closes 1hr earlier • £13.95 including parking; NT members and other groups with reciprocal arrangements get free entry but are required to pay for parking (£3/1hr 30min, £5.50/2hr 30min, £10/day) • ☎ 01444 894066, ⓦ kew.org/visit-wakehurst • Metrobus #272 from Haywards Heath (Mon–Sat every 2hr; 15min)

The country cousin of Kew's Royal Botanic Gardens, **Wakehurst Place** sprawls over 465 acres and you'll need a whole day if you want to explore it properly. The main appeal of Wakehurst is its diversity, from the formal gardens surrounding the Elizabethan mansion (of which a few rooms are open) near the entrance, to the wilder meadows, wetlands, steep-sided valleys and ancient woodland further afield. At the far end of the site is the **Loder Valley Nature Reserve**, a mix of meadow, woodland and wetland, with several bird hides, which allows access to a maximum of fifty people a day (no booking).

The garden was originally planted by **Sir Gerald Loder**, a member of the illustrious local family also responsible for High Beeches. Many of the exotic and rare trees Loder planted in the early twentieth century were torn down in the great storm of 1987, but Kew – which has managed the site since 1965, when it took on a long-term lease from the National Trust – responded with its trademark emphasis on conservation, by replanting Wakehurst with different types of woodland from around the world, re-creating endangered habitats.

The Millennium Seedbank

Wakehurst is also home to the **Millennium Seedbank**, which opened in 2010 with the aim of conserving the most endangered and important seeds from around the world. It has already collected and stored around ten percent of the world's plant species, including all of the UK's native species (the first country in the world to do so). The vast storage vaults are hidden underground beneath the laboratories, which you can look into from the **exhibition room**.

5

Standen

West Hoathly Rd, 2 miles south of East Grinstead, RH19 4NE · Jan garden daily 10am–4pm, house Sat & Sun 11am–3.30pm; Feb–Oct garden daily 10am–5pm, house daily 11am–4.30pm; Nov & Dec garden daily 10am–4pm, house daily 11am–3.30pm · £12.60; NT · ☎ 01342 323029, ⊛ nationaltrust.org.uk/standen-house-and-garden · Free parking

Set in lovely countryside at the end of a long winding lane, **Standen** is a beautiful Arts and Crafts house, creaking at the seams with treasures from many of the key figures in the **Arts and Crafts movement** (see page 199).

The building was the creation of the architect **Philip Webb**, friend of William Morris, and a central player in the foundation of the Arts and Crafts movement. Webb was at pains to make the house functional as well as beautiful, and it was at the cutting edge of modern technology for its time, with both electricity and central heating fitted. The beautiful original light fittings – by **W.A.S. Benson**, one of Morris's protégés – can still be seen today. Webb was famed for his attention to detail, and this is evident all over the house, from the intricate fingerplates on the doors to the meticulously designed fireplaces.

The highlight, however, is Morris's exuberant **wallpapers and textiles**, deliberately offset by plain, wood-panelled walls. Look out for Morris's trellis wallpaper, his first marketed wallpaper design, in the conservatory corridor – the birds were drawn by Webb because Morris wasn't happy with his own efforts. Other gems include red lustreware and Islamic-inspired ceramic tiles by **William De Morgan** in the billiard room, and paintings and drawings by Edward Burne-Jones, Dante Gabriel Rossetti and Ford Madox Brown.

Surrounding the house are twelve acres of terraced hillside **gardens**, encompassing formal gardens and wilder areas, as well as a traditional Victorian kitchen garden.

ACCOMMODATION   THE WESTERN HIGH WEALD

Gravetye Manor Vowels Lane, West Hoathly, RH19 4LJ ☎ 01342 810567, ⊛ gravetyemanor.co.uk. Unashamedly old-fashioned, in a thoroughly good way, this sixteenth-century manor house hotel nestles amid beautiful gardens planted a hundred years ago by former owner William Robinson, the pioneer of the natural-style English garden. The seventeen bedrooms – named, fittingly, after trees found on the estate – are elegantly luxurious, there's a Michelin-starred restaurant, and afternoon tea can be taken in the flower-filled garden. **£395**

★ **Ockenden Manor** Cuckfield, RH17 5LD ☎ 01444 416111, ⊛ hshotels.co.uk. This stately Elizabethan manor house has not one but two trump cards up its sleeve: an award-winning restaurant, and a sleek spa housed in a separate modern building. The rooms vary from traditionally styled doubles to glamorous open-plan spa suites. Look out for dinner, bed and breakfast packages, which are often excellent value. **£194**

★ **WOWO Wapsbourne Farm** Sheffield Park, TN22 3QS ☎ 01825 723414, ⊛ wowo.co.uk. This lovely streamside campsite is a local favourite. Campfires are encouraged, there's bags of open space for kids (with rope swings aplenty), plus regular bushcraft workshops, a "wellbeing space" offering yoga, massage and the like, and a "village" area offering live acoustic music on Saturday evenings. Yurts, shepherd's huts and bell tents (sleeping 3–7 people) are also available. Camping available March–Oct, yurts and shepherd's huts available all year; two-night minimum stay at weekends. Camping/person **£12.50**, yurts & huts from **£105**

SPOOKS AND SCARES: SHOCKTOBER FEST

The month of October sees zombies, ghouls and other blood-splattered creatures of the undead take over **Tulley's Farm** near Crawley for one of the largest Halloween events in the country (⊛ halloweenattractions.co.uk). There's family-friendly spooky fun in the daytime at the **Spook Fest**, followed by properly terrifying immersive scare experiences for grown-ups in the evenings at the **Shocktober Fest**, including a horror hayride through the woods and several different interactive haunted houses, plus street theatre and live music.

Both events run on selected dates in October/early November. **Tickets** for the Shocktober Fest cost from £33 (including access to the interactive attractions); for the Spook Fest they are £11–13, or £15–18 for children aged 5–13.

THE ARTS AND CRAFTS MOVEMENT

5

The **Arts and Crafts movement** started out in Britain in the nineteenth century as a reaction against the evils of mass production. There was a strong vein of socialism underpinning it – the movement believed that mechanization threatened to dehumanize the lives of the ordinary working classes – and both John Ruskin and Alexander Pugin were influences.

The central ideas were a rejection of shoddy, mass-produced goods in favour of handcrafted objects; an emphasis on simple, honest design – in contrast to the over-elaborate showiness and artificiality of much Victorian design; and the use of nature as a source of inspiration.

The father of the Arts and Crafts movement was **William Morris**, one of the most influential designers of the nineteenth century, who in 1861 set up Morris, Marshall, Faulkner & Co (later Morris & Co), with other figures including Edward Burne-Jones, Dante Gabriel Rossetti and Philip Webb, to make and sell beautiful handcrafted objects for the home. "Have nothing in your home that you do not know to be useful or believe to be beautiful" was Morris's motto. Many of the designs that came out of Morris & Co were inspired by nature, and Morris named many of his own hand block-printed wallpapers after trees and flowers.

The Arts and Crafts movement flourished in the 1880s and 1890s but by the early twentieth century it became clear that its grand ideals were flawed; only the very wealthy could afford to buy Morris & Co's handcrafted designs, which were much more expensive to manufacture than the mass-produced items they were intended to replace.

EATING AND DRINKING

The Ginger Fox Muddleswood Rd, on the A281 at the junction with the B2117, near Albourne, BN6 9EA ☎ 01273 857888, ⓦ thegingerfox.com. This relaxed foodie pub is the country outpost of the Brighton-based "Ginger" empire, and it's equally popular, with a lovely big garden, great food (mains £15–18) and a play area for kids. Daily 11.30am–midnight; kitchen Mon noon–2.30pm & 6–9pm, Tues–Thurs noon–2.30pm, Fri noon–2.30pm & 6–10pm, Sat noon–3pm & 6.30–10pm, Sun noon–4pm & 6–9pm.

★ **The Griffin Inn** Fletching, TN22 3SS ☎ 01825 722890, ⓦ thegriffininn.co.uk. On a summer's day none further than this fabulous country pub, which boasts what is surely the most perfect beer garden in Sussex, with views across the Weald from the huge sloping lawn. Weekend lunchtimes in summer see the barbecue lit, with lobster, tuna, steak and local bangers all sizzling on the coals. Year-round there's local ale on the pump, twenty wines by the glass and excellent food (mains £15–19). Daily 11am–late; kitchen Mon–Fri noon–2.30pm & 7–9.30pm, Sat noon–3pm & 7–9.30pm, Sun noon–3.30pm & 6.30–9pm (bar food only).

Jeremy's Restaurant Borde Hill Garden, Balcombe Rd, near Haywards Heath, RH16 1XP ☎ 01444 441102, ⓦ jeremysrestaurant.com. This award-winning restaurant in Borde Hill Garden (see page 196) is especially lovely on a summer's day, when tables are set up on the terrace overlooking a Victorian walled garden. The a la carte menu (mains £16–28) might feature suckling pig or South Coast John Dory, or there's a cheaper set menu (two/three courses £24/29; available Tues–Sat lunch & Tues–Thurs dinner). Tues–Sat 12.30–2.30pm & 7–9.30pm, Sun noon–3pm.

The Royal Oak Wineham Lane, Wineham, BN5 9AY ☎ 01444 881252, ⓦ theroyaloakwineham.wordpress. com. Everything a traditional English country pub should be, this ancient, unspoilt boozer sits on a quiet country lane, with plenty of tables on the lawn out front. Inside the thirteenth-century building it's all low beamed ceilings and uneven brick floors. Don't be thrown by the lack of hand pumps at the bar – the beer (Harveys, Dark Star and guests) is served straight from the cask. There's good, seasonal food on offer, too, including chunky ploughman's boards (starting at £8.95). Mon–Fri 11am–3pm & 5.30–11pm, Sat 11am–3pm & 6–11pm, Sun noon–4pm & 7–10.30pm; kitchen Mon–Sat noon–2.30pm & 7–9pm, Sun noon–3pm.

East Sussex Downs

THE SEVEN SISTERS

East Sussex Downs

6

The South Downs, a range of gently undulating chalk hills protected within the South Downs National Park, stretch across much of Sussex, but nowhere are they more beautiful – or more dramatic – than in the pristine pocket of countryside just west of Eastbourne. Here, the Downs meet the sea at the Seven Sisters, a series of spectacular chalk cliffs culminating in the dizzying 530ft-high Beachy Head, the tallest chalk sea cliff in the country. The gorgeous countryside continues as the South Downs sweep westwards towards Ditchling Beacon – the highest point in Sussex – with splendid views all around, over sleepy villages and spired churches, rolling grassland dotted with munching sheep, poppy fields, vineyards and patchwork fields that change colour with the seasons. Little wonder that this bucolic corner of Sussex is so popular.

The nicest way to soak up the views is on foot: the long-distance **South Downs Way** footpath follows the ridge of the Downs, crisscrossed by any number of other footpaths – the South Downs have one of the densest networks of public rights of way in the country. But the area's charms aren't all scenic: there's also a renowned opera house at **Glyndebourne**, an ever-growing number of vineyards producing award-winning sparkling wine, plenty of fine country pubs and dozens of pretty little villages, the pick of the bunch being the old smugglers' haunt of **Alfriston**. One of the biggest draws of the area is its associations with the **Bloomsbury Group**: Virginia Woolf settled at Monk's House near Lewes, while her sister Vanessa Bell and other members of the set made Charleston their bohemian home. More of Sussex's art trail can be explored in the village of **Ditchling**, where the beautifully designed Ditchling Museum of Art + Craft displays the work of a group of artists and craftspeople – Eric Gill among them – who set up a community here in the early years of the twentieth century.

All of the sights in this chapter are an easy drive from buzzy Brighton (see chapter 7), but two other towns make great (and quieter) alternative bases. The seaside town of **Eastbourne** has an elegant promenade, a fine modern art museum and the chalk cliff of **Beachy Head** on its doorstep. Or just northeast of Brighton, straddling the River Ouse, there's the county town of **Lewes**; with a handsome centre, a Norman castle, its own brewery and a lively, arty vibe, it's full of character and charm.

Eastbourne

The archetypal English seaside resort, elegant **EASTBOURNE** has a certain timeless appeal. A stroll along the three-mile-long prom will take you past old-fashioned ice-cream parlours, brass bands playing in the bandstand, floral displays and grand hotels offering afternoon tea. Over the years it's gained a reputation as a retirement town by the sea, derided as "God's waiting room", and "a graveyard above the ground". But Eastbourne is slowly changing, with families and creative types, priced out of Brighton, moving into the area; it even has that hallmark of seaside-town regeneration – a state-of-the-art contemporary art gallery, the Towner. Eastbourne may still lack the hipness of neighbouring Brighton, but some would say it's all the better for it.

CHARLESTON FARMHOUSE

Highlights

❶ Beachy Head and the Seven Sisters The unmissable scenic highlight of the South Downs National Park: soaring white cliffs backed by wildflower-rich chalk grassland. See page 210

❷ Alfriston A contender for the title of prettiest village in Sussex, with a picturesque main street, an idyllic village green and a clutch of historic smuggling inns. See page 213

❸ Charleston Farmhouse The Bloomsbury Group's uniquely decorated country home gives a fascinating glimpse into the lives of Sussex's most famous bohemians. See page 217

❹ Paragliding on the Downs You can be flying solo in a day, in one of the country's finest paragliding destinations. See page 220

❺ Lewes One of Sussex's loveliest towns, with a medieval castle, a brewery, the Downs on its doorstep and even its own currency. See page 222

❻ Sussex Bonfire Night Bonfire Night as it should be: spectacular costumed processions, flaming torches and plenty of proud tradition. See page 225

❼ Ditchling Museum of Art + Craft Admire the work of Eric Gill and his contemporaries in the beautiful village where it was made. See page 228

❽ Devil's Dyke Any view described by painter John Constable as "the grandest in the world" has got to be worth seeing for yourself. See page 230

HIGHLIGHTS ARE MARKED ON THE MAP ON PAGE 204

6

The seafront

Eastbourne's well-conserved seafront is an elegant ribbon of Victorian terraces and villas, entirely unblemished by shops – thanks to an edict of **William Cavendish**, one of the two landowners who developed the upmarket seaside resort ("planned by gentlemen for gentlemen") in the nineteenth century. With its palm trees and fairy lights there's a distinct holiday vibe to it on balmy summer evenings. The seafront strip stretches for three miles from one of Europe's largest marinas, **Sovereign Harbour** (ⓦeastbourneharbour.com), in the east to the cliffs of **Holywell** in the west. From Holywell, paths zigzag back up to the main seafront road and the start of the footpath up to Beachy Head (see page 210). The beach is resolutely pebbly, but stretches of sand emerge at low tide. In August huge crowds on the beach and the roar of jet engines overhead announce the arrival of the **Airbourne** International Air Show (see page 32).

Eastbourne Pier and Bandstand

Grand Parade, BN21 3EL • Daily 9am–6pm • Free • ⓦ eastbournepier.com

The focal point of the seafront is the elegant **pier**, designed by master pier-builder Eugenius Birch and opened in 1872. The much-loved landmark lost its ballroom pavilion in 2014 when a devastating fire ripped through the shore end (a bare expanse of decking now stands in its place), but a stroll along the pier remains an essential part of any Eastbourne visit.

The seafront's other pride and joy is the much-loved **bandstand** (ⓦeastbournebandstand.co.uk), just west of the pier, with its jaunty azure-blue domed roof. In summer, traditional brass bands take to the stage on Sundays (May–Sept Sun 3pm; 1hr 30min; £3.50), and big bands and tribute shows play on occasional evenings; check online for details.

Eastbourne Lifeboat Museum

King Edward's Parade, BN21 4BY • Daily: Jan & Feb 10am–3pm; March, Nov & Dec 10am–4pm; April–Oct 10am–5pm • Free • ⓦ eastbournernli.org/museum

A five-minute walk west of the pier, the tiny **Eastbourne Lifeboat Museum** recounts some of the more daring rescues the town's lifeboatmen have made since 1822, when

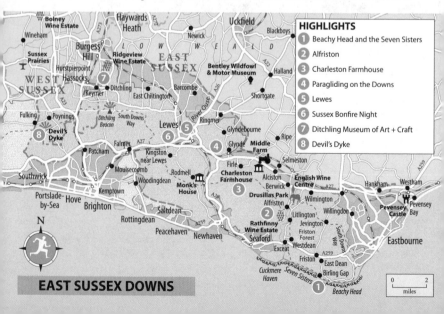

HIGHLIGHTS

1. Beachy Head and the Seven Sisters
2. Alfriston
3. Charleston Farmhouse
4. Paragliding on the Downs
5. Lewes
6. Sussex Bonfire Night
7. Ditchling Museum of Art + Craft
8. Devil's Dyke

EAST SUSSEX DOWNS

local eccentric John "Mad Jack" Fuller (see page 189) donated Eastbourne's first lifeboat. Cork lifejackets weren't introduced until 1854, making the bravery of those first volunteers, who generally couldn't swim, all the more astonishing. The museum is overlooked by a grassy mound topped by the **Wish Tower**, one of a series of Martello towers (see page 125) built along the south coast at the end of the eighteenth century.

Redoubt Fortress

Royal Parade, BN22 7AQ • Check website for opening hours • ☎ 01323 410300, ⓦ eastbourneredoubt.co.uk

The splendid **Redoubt Fortress**, at the eastern end of the seafront, was one of three fortresses built at the same time as the Martello towers to counter the threat of Napoleonic invasion, and was garrisoned on and off until World War II. The 24 vaulted casemates (rooms) built around the circular parade ground housed up to two hundred men (up to 350 in emergencies), as well as supplies and ammunition. Above the parade ground is the gun platform, where ten 24-pounder cannons (with a range of around a mile) kept a beady watch across the Channel. The Redoubt building was closed for restoration at the time of writing, although the outside spaces continue to be used for film screenings and other events – check the website for the latest information.

The Devonshire Quarter

Eastbourne's **Devonshire Quarter** is centred on **Devonshire Park**, best-known for its world-class **lawn tennis courts** which play host to big-name players during the Aegon International Eastbourne in June. Two elegant Victorian **theatres** – the Devonshire Park Theatre and the Winter Garden – lie on the park's southern edge, alongside the post-war Congress Theatre and the modern **Towner Art Gallery**. A £54-million regeneration of the area, due for completion by the end of 2020, has included the refurbishment of the iconic theatre buildings.

Towner Art Gallery

Devonshire Park, BN21 4JJ • Tues–Sun & bank hols 10am–5pm • Free • **Art store tours** alternate Sundays; 1hr • £6 • ☎ 01323 434670, ⓦ townereastbourne.org.uk

First opened in 1923 in a former manor house in Manor Gardens, the venerable **Towner Art Gallery** was relocated to a glamorous new home in Devonshire Park in 2009 – a sleek modern edifice of glass and smooth white curves. The award-winning gallery is the largest in the Southeast, and shows four or five major exhibitions of contemporary art a year, alongside rotating displays from its own permanent collection; it's especially well-known for its modern British art, in particular the work of **Eric Ravilious** (see page 206). Fascinating **tours** of the collection store (showing some of the four thousand-odd works not on display at any one time) run a couple of times a month, and there's a busy programme of events for children and families. Up on the second floor there's a lovely **café-bar** with a small terrace looking over the Eastbourne rooftops to the Downs beyond. The Towner is one of three contemporary art galleries along the **Coastal Culture Trail** (see page 177), a joint initiative between the Towner, Hastings Contemporary and the De La Warr Pavilion in Bexhill.

Eastbourne Heritage Centre

2 Carlisle Rd, BN21 4BT • Mid-March to Oct Mon, Thurs, Fri & Sun 2–5pm; Sat 10am–4pm; Nov to mid-March Sat 10am–4pm • £3 • ☎ 01323 411189, ⓦ eastbourneheritagecentre.co.uk

The compact **Eastbourne Heritage Centre** houses a modest collection of exhibits about the town, including old maps showing its growth from a few small villages into a grand Victorian resort. Changing exhibitions run a couple of times a year, and a small cinema in the basement shows films about the town, including a couple of fun promotional

6

ERIC RAVILIOUS

Of all Sussex artists, **Eric Ravilious** (1903–42) – painter, wood engraver and designer – is perhaps the one who captured the local landscape the best. Ravilious was a local lad: he grew up in Eastbourne, the son of a shopkeeper, and in 1919 won a scholarship to the Eastbourne College of Art. In 1922 he started at the Royal College of Art in London, where he studied under Paul Nash, became close friends with Edward Bawden and spent much of his time chatting up women. He accepted a part-time teaching job at his old Eastbourne college in 1925, during which time he took his students sketching in Alfriston, Jevington and Wilmington, but it was only in the mid-1930s that Ravilious really rediscovered Sussex, travelling back to stay at **Furlongs**, a shepherd's cottage near Beddingham belonging to his friend and fellow artist Peggy Angus – a radical with a fondness for folk songs, home-made elderflower champagne and wild Midsummer's Eve parties. It was during these visits that Ravilious painted some of his best-known watercolours – quintessentially English evocations of prewar Sussex, where people are almost completely absent, and the landscape takes centre stage.

By this point Ravilious was one of the best-known artists of the time, not only for his watercolours but also for his ceramic designs for Wedgwood and his wood engravings – one of which, of two top-hatted cricketers, graced the front cover of *Wisden Cricketer's Almanack* from 1938 to 2002. When war broke out, Ravilious served in the Observer Corps before becoming an **Official War Artist**. In 1942 he was out on a search-and-rescue mission in Iceland when his plane came down, and his life was cut tragically short, aged just 39.

films from the 1960s and 1970s which enthusiastically extol the delights of the "suntrap of the South". The small shop is a good place for Eastbourne-themed souvenirs.

ARRIVAL AND DEPARTURE EASTBOURNE

By train Eastbourne's splendid Italianate station is a 10min walk from the seafront up Terminus Road.

Destinations Brighton (every 20min; 35min); Hastings (every 20min; 25min); Lewes (every 20min; 30min); London

Victoria (Mon–Sat 4 hourly, Sun 2 hourly; 1hr 20min–1hr 50min).

By bus The National Express coach station is on Junction Rd, right by the train station. Most local bus services are run

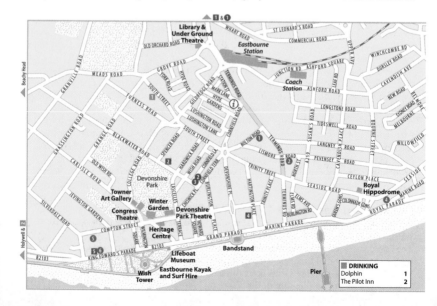

DRINKING
Dolphin 1
The Pilot Inn 2

by Stagecoach.

Destinations Brighton (every 10–15min; 1hr 15min); Hastings (Mon–Sat every 20–30min, Sun hourly; 1hr 15min); London Victoria (Sat & Sun 1 daily; 3hr 40min).

By car There's pay-and-display parking all along the seafront.

GETTING AROUND AND INFORMATION

Dotto Train This land train (ⓦ stagecoachbus.com/dotto) runs along the seafront in summer, from Sovereign Harbour in the east to Holywell in the west, stopping en route at the Redoubt Fortress, the pier and the Wish Tower. June Sat & Sun, July & Aug daily 10am–5pm; hourly; £2.30, day-ticket unlimited travel £5.

Eastbourne Sightseeing bus Hop-on, hop-off open-top buses (ⓦ eastbournesightseeing.com) run along the seafront and in a loop to Beachy Head, Birling Gap and East Dean. April–Oct daily 10am–5pm; up to every 30min in peak season; 1hr for circuit; £10, valid 24hr.

Taxis Eastbourne and Country Taxis ☎ 01323 720720.

Tourist office 3 Cornfield Rd, just off Terminus Rd (March–April & Oct Mon–Fri 9am–5.30pm, Sat 9am–4pm; May–Sept Mon–Fri 9am–5.30pm, Sat 9am–5pm, Sun 10am–1pm, bank hols 10am–4pm; Nov–Feb Mon–Fri 9am–4.30pm, Sat 9am–1pm; ☎ 01323 415415, ⓦ visit eastbourne.com).

ACCOMMODATION

SEE MAP PAGE 206

The Grand Hotel King Edwards Parade, BN21 4EQ ☎ 01323 412345, ⓦ grandeastbourne.com. The best address in town is the "White Palace", a grand Victorian edifice at the western end of the seafront, which over the years has welcomed Winston Churchill, Charlie Chaplin and – most famously – Charles Debussy, who worked on La Mer during a stay in 1905. Standard rooms are traditional in style, and there are two excellent restaurants and an in-house spa. **£215**

The Guesthouse East 13 Hartington Place, BN21 3BS ☎ 01323 722774, ⓦ theguesthouseeast.co.uk. Six of the seven en-suite suites in this award-winning guesthouse come with their own small, well-equipped kitchenettes – perfect for families. If you're feeling too lazy to cook your own eggs in the morning you can pay extra for a delicious breakfast delivered to your door, or eat at the communal table. **£109**

Pebble Beach 53 Royal Parade, BN22 7AQ ☎ 01323 431240, ⓦ pebblebeacheastbourne.com. Popular B&B with six stylish, good-value rooms set across three floors of a Victorian seafront townhouse, at the eastern end of town by the Redoubt. The nicest room (£110) is up on the first floor, with floor-to-ceiling windows and a private balcony looking out to sea. Two-night minimum stay year-round. **£85**

Ravilious 16 Blackwater Rd, BN21 4AJ ☎ 01323 733142, ⓦ ravilioushotel.com. Stunning rooms – wooden floors, high ceilings and contemporary furniture – and a great location by Devonshire Park make this townhouse B&B a winner. The attic rooms (up three flights of stairs) are a

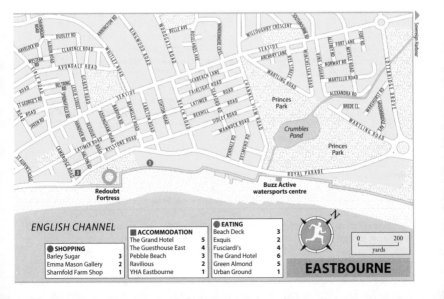

ENGLISH CHANNEL

Redoubt Fortress

Buzz Active watersports centre

Sovereign Harbour

Princes Park

Crumbles Pond

Princes Park

ROYAL PARADE

● SHOPPING	
Barley Sugar	3
Emma Mason Gallery	2
Sharnfold Farm Shop	1

■ ACCOMMODATION	
The Grand Hotel	5
The Guesthouse East	4
Pebble Beach	3
Ravilious	2
YHA Eastbourne	1

● EATING	
Beach Deck	3
Exquis	2
Fusciardi's	4
The Grand Hotel	6
Green Almond	5
Urban Ground	1

0   200
yards

EASTBOURNE

6

WATERSPORTS IN EASTBOURNE

If you thought tea dances were as animated as things got in Eastbourne, think again. Several outfits offer you the chance to get out and active on the water, whether exploring underwater wrecks or paddling a sea kayak.

Buzz Active Spray Watersports Centre, Royal Parade, BN22 7LD ☎ 01323 417023, ⓦ buzzactive. org.uk. Taster windsurfing, sailing, kayaking and stand-up paddleboarding lessons (from £22, depending on size of group), plus longer courses. The last two activities are also available at their base at Cuckmere Haven (see page 212). Jan–April & Dec Mon–Fri; May–Nov daily.

Diving charters The Sussex coast has some of the best

wreck dives in the country, and a handful of charter companies offer trips from Sovereign Harbour – check out ⓦ channeldiving.com, ⓦ sussexshipwrecks.co.uk and ⓦ dive125.co.uk.

Eastbourne Kayak and Surf Hire By the Wish Tower ☎ 07917 863791. Sea-kayak and paddleboard hire on the beach (May–Sept daily in good weather; from £10/1hr).

bargain, but even the standard rooms (£105) are good value for the quality. Licensed bar. **£95**

YHA Eastbourne 1 East Dean Rd, BN20 8ES ☎ 0845 371 9316, ⓦ yha.org.uk/eastbourne. Modern hostel in a

quiet, leafy location on the western outskirts of town, just a mile from the centre. It's 400m from the start of the South Downs Way footpath (see page 210), so a good location for walkers. Dorms **£19**, doubles **£69**

EATING

SEE MAP PAGE 206

Beach Deck Royal Parade, BN22 7AE ☎ 01323 720320, ⓦ thebeachdeck.co.uk. There's no better place in town for an alfresco lunch than this lovely spot, with a big suntrap deck overlooking the beach and crowd-pleasing food (including gluten-free options), ranging from burgers to pizza. Daily 8.30am–10pm.

Exquis 1 Pevensey Rd, BN21 3HJ ☎ 01323 430885. What this unprepossessing French bistro lacks in kerb appeal it more than makes up for with its fabulous food – and it's good value, too. Two courses of traditional homemade food (Toulouse sausages, confit duck, tartiflette and the like) cost £14.95 (£3 more at weekends), with free pre-dinner nibbles thrown in. A little gem. Tues & Thurs–Sat 6–11pm.

★ **Fusciardi's** 30 Marine Parade, BN22 7AY ☎ 01323 722128, ⓦ fusciardiicecreams.co.uk. Established in 1967, this ice-cream parlour is an Eastbourne institution, with queues out the door on summer weekends. More than sixteen flavours of homemade ice cream are on offer, as well as light meals and piled-high sundaes that are a work of art. Daily 9am–9pm.

The Grand Hotel King Edwards Parade, BN21 4EQ ☎ 01323 412345, ⓦ grandeastbourne.com. Of the

two restaurants at *The Grand Hotel*, the award-winning *Mirabelle* is the one to go to for if you want to treat yourself, with a dining room that's all timeless elegance and crisp white linen. Three courses at dinner cost £46 (£28 at lunch), or there's a tasting menu for £67. Elsewhere in the hotel, afternoon teas are served in the grand surrounds of the Great Hall (daily 2.45–6pm; £26). Tues–Sat 12.30–2pm & 7–10pm.

Green Almond 12 Grand Hotel Buildings, Compton St, BN21 4EJ ☎ 01323 734470, ⓦ thegreenalmond. com. Tucked away round the back of *The Grand Hotel*, this lunchtime-only vegetarian bistro is abidingly popular. Fill up your plate from the buffet with whatever you fancy – delicious salads, hot dishes and bread and butter – for £7.50 (£1 more for a large plate). Tues–Sat noon–3pm.

★ **Urban Ground** 2A Bolton Rd, BN21 3JX ☎ 01323 410751, ⓦ urbanground.co.uk. Fab little independent coffee shop – with a second branch on South Street – serving up Square Mile coffee alongside sandwiches, soups, flatbreads and cakes. Mon–Sat 7.30am–5.30pm, Sun 9am–5pm.

DRINKING

SEE MAP PAGE 206

Dolphin 14 South St, BN21 4XF ☎ 01323 746622, ⓦ thedolphineastbourne.co.uk. Victorian pub in the centre of town, with a beautifully restored interior featuring open fires and comfy leather chesterfields. There's Brakspear and local ales on tap, and good home-cooked food (burgers, pies, fish and the like). Mon–Thurs 11am–11pm, Fri & Sat 11am–midnight, Sun noon–10.30pm; kitchen Mon–Thurs noon–2.30pm & 6–9.30pm, Fri & Sat noon–9.30pm, Sun noon–8pm.

The Pilot Inn 89 Meads St, BN20 7RW ☎ 01323 723440, ⓦ pilot-inn.co.uk. Lovely, laidback pub in leafy Meads that's handy for lunch or a drink after a walk up Beachy Head (see page 210). It's dog- and walker-friendly, and (a big plus) the excellent seasonal pub food is available throughout the day (most mains £12–14). Mon–Sat 11am–11pm, Sun noon–8pm; kitchen Mon–Sat noon–9pm, Sun noon–6pm.

ENTERTAINMENT

Eastbourne is well-known for its plethora of **theatres**, three of which are clustered side-by-side in Eastbourne's Devonshire Quarter, backing onto Devonshire Park. Recent multi-million-pound refurbishment has seen the interior of the Grade II-listed Congress Theatre returned to its 1960s heyday and a new Welcome Centre built. Restoration works on the Victorian Winter Garden are due to be completed by the end of 2020.

Congress Theatre Carlisle Rd, BN21 4BP ☎ 01323 412000, ⓦ eastbournetheatres.co.uk. Modern, large theatre with an eclectic programme of live bands, comedy, musicals, theatre, ballet, classical music and more.

Devonshire Park Theatre Compton St, BN21 4BP ☎ 01323 412000, ⓦ eastbournetheatres.co.uk. Drama, musicals and children's theatre are the mainstays of this Victorian theatre, as well as the annual panto.

Royal Hippodrome 108–112 Seaside Rd, BN21 3PF ☎ 01323 802020, ⓦ royalhippodrome.com. For many years the home of music hall in Eastbourne, the Hippodrome shows a year-round programme of comedies, musicals and variety shows.

Under Ground Theatre Below Central Library, Grove Rd, BN21 4TL ☎ 0843 289 1980, ⓦ undergroundtheatre. co.uk. Small, independently run performance space, hosting everything from jazz and folk bands to drama and film. Tickets available on the door, from the tourist information office or from the box office (☎ 0845 680 1926).

Winter Garden Compton St, BN21 4BP ☎ 01323 412000, ⓦ eastbournetheatres.co.uk. Once a skating rink, the Winter Garden now hosts comedy, children's theatre, music, tea dances and big bands.

SHOPPING

SEE MAP PAGE 206

★ **Barley Sugar** 1 Cornfield Terrace, BN21 4NN ☎ 01323 734442, ⓦ barley-sugar.co.uk. This "artisan deli and lifestyle store" has a great deli counter and lots of goodies from Sussex and further afield, plus a small selection of homeware and antique finds. There's also a lovely little café-restaurant attached. Tues & Wed 9am–4pm, Thurs–Sat 9am–8pm.

Emma Mason Gallery 3 Cornfield Terrace, BN21 4NN ☎ 01323 727545, ⓦ emmamason.co.uk. This little gallery sells original prints by British printmakers, from the postwar period to the modern day, as well as books and cards. Regular exhibitions held throughout the year. Thurs–Sat 10am–5pm.

Sharnfold Farm Shop Stone Cross, BN24 5BU ☎ 01323 768490, ⓦ sharnfoldfarm.co.uk. A 10min drive from Eastbourne, this excellent farm shop sells the farm's produce, homemade bread, cheeses and chutneys; it's also one of the best pick-your-own spots in this corner of Sussex. Tues–Sat 9.30am–5pm, Sun 9.30am–4pm.

Sussex Heritage Coast

The glorious stretch of coast between Eastbourne and Seaford, known as the **Sussex Heritage Coast**, is one of the longest expanses of undeveloped coastline on the south coast, a stunning, nine-mile-long pocket of pristine shoreline, dizzying white cliffs and sweeping chalk grassland, with beautiful views at every stride. It's one of the undoubted highlights of the South Downs National Park (see page 202), and there's always a steady stream of walkers tramping along the blowy clifftops, enjoying what is arguably the finest coastal walk in the Southeast.

Beachy Head is the tallest of the cliffs and the closest to Eastbourne; to the west of it is the tiny hamlet and pebbly beach of **Birling Gap**, and then come the gently undulating cliffs of the **Seven Sisters**, which end at beautiful **Cuckmere Haven**. Inland lie the pretty villages of **East Dean** and **West Dean**, the latter nestled among the beech trees of **Friston Forest**.

Note that cliff falls are a regular occurrence along this coast, so stay well away from the cliff edge and the base of the cliffs.

ARRIVAL AND GETTING AROUND

SUSSEX HERITAGE COAST

By bus Bus #12 runs daily every 20min between Eastbourne and Brighton, via East Dean and Exceat. Bus #13X takes a detour along the clifftops and runs between Eastbourne and Brighton via Beachy Head, Birling Gap, East Dean and Exceat (May to mid-June Sun & bank hols 3 daily; mid-June to end Aug Mon–Sat 3 daily, Sun & bank hols 2 hourly). The Cuckmere Valley Ramblerbus runs between Berwick Station, Alfriston, Seaford, Exceat, Friston Forest (West Dean) and Wilmington (May–Oct Sat, Sun & bank hols; hourly; ☎ 01323 870920, ⓦ cuckmerebuses.org.uk).

6

THE SOUTH DOWNS WAY

The glorious, long-distance **South Downs Way** rises and dips for over a hundred miles along the chalk uplands between the city of Winchester and the spectacular cliffs at Beachy Head. If undertaken in its entirety, the bridle path is best walked from west to east, taking advantage of the prevailing wind, Eastbourne's better transport and accommodation, and the psychological appeal of ending at the sea: the heart-pumping hike along the Seven Sisters and Beachy Head makes a spectacular conclusion to the trail. Steyning, the halfway point, marks a transition from predominantly wooded sections to more exposed chalk uplands.

The OS *Explorer* **maps** OL11 and OL25 cover the eastern end of the route; you'll need OL10, OL8, OL3 and OL32 as well to cover the lot. A **guidebook** is advised, and several are available, including the official *South Downs Way National Trail Guide* (east–west; 1:25,000 OS mapping; Aurum Press); *The South Downs Way* (either direction; 1:25,000 OS mapping; Cicerone Press); and the *South Downs Way Trailblazer Guide* (west–east; 1:20,000 maps and downloadable GPS waypoints; Trailblazer). Cicerone also publish *Mountain Biking on the South Downs*, which includes the South Downs Way. For more **information**, including details on **accommodation**, see ⓦnationaltrail.co.uk/south-downs-way.

By sightseeing bus Hop-on, hop-off Eastbourne Sightseeing buses run from Eastbourne (see page 207).
By car Pay-and-display car parks at Beachy Head, Birling Gap (NT), Crowlink (NT), Exceat and Friston Forest (on the western side of the forest on the Litlington road; and on the eastern side at Butchershole on the Jevington road). There's also a free car park at East Dean.

INFORMATION

Seven Sisters Country Park Visitor Centre Exceat, on the A259 between Seaford and Eastbourne (March & Nov Sat & Sun 11am–4pm; April–Sept daily 10.30am–4.30pm; Oct daily 11am–4pm; volunteer run, so opening times can vary, especially in winter; ☎0345 608 0194, ⓦsevensisters. org.uk). Information on walks and activities in the park, plus displays and exhibitions on its history, geology and wildlife.
Beachy Head Visitor Centre Beachy Head Rd (April–Oct Mon 1–4pm, Tues–Sun & bank hols 10am–4pm; volunteer run, so opening times can vary; ☎01323 737273, ⓦbeachyhead.org). Mainly a souvenir shop (which also sells maps and walking guides), but has a small exhibition on the area's plant and animal life, too.
Birling Gap National Trust Visitor Centre Birling Gap (daily: Jan–June & Sept–Dec 10am–5pm, or 4pm in winter; July & Aug 9am–5.30pm; ☎01323 423197, ⓦnationaltrust.org.uk/birling-gap-and-the-seven-sisters). Lots of information on walks and the local area, with displays on wildlife, fossils and the changing coastline, including a dramatic video of a previous cliff fall. Free tracker packs for kids are available.

Beachy Head

At 530ft, majestic **Beachy Head** is the tallest chalk sea-cliff in the country, and probably the most famous, too, having been the backdrop for music videos, television dramas and films from *Quadrophenia* to *Atonement*. Every year the cliff recedes a little further, eroded by the battering waves below – up to 1.5ft a year, though in 1999 a record 20ft were lost in one spectacular early morning cliff fall, a warning to anyone tempted to stray too close to the edge. The views from the top on a clear day stretch as far as Dungeness in one direction and the Isle of Wight in the other, while down below at the foot of the cliffs is **Beachy Head lighthouse**, with its cheery red and white stripes, looking exactly as a lighthouse should. The construction of the lighthouse, completed in 1902 to replace the Belle Tout lighthouse further west (see page 211), was no mean feat; 3600 tonnes of granite had to be winched down from the top of the cliff.

Beachy Head can be accessed by car or bus, but the nicest way is of course on foot. A steep two-mile-long path climbs up from the western end of Eastbourne to the blowy clifftop, where you'll find the Beachy Head Visitor Centre (see above) on Beachy Head Road.

ACCOMMODATION **BEACHY HEAD**

★ **Belle Tout** Beachy Head ☎ 01323 423185, ⓦ belle tout.co.uk. For a real treat book into this old lighthouse (see page 210), perched high up on the dramatic cliffs just west of Beachy Head. The cosy rooms boast stupendous views, there's a snug residents' lounge and – best of all – there's unrestricted access to the lamproom at the top of the lighthouse, where you can sit and watch the sun go down. **£200**

Birling Gap

Heading 2.5 miles west along the windswept clifftops from Beachy Head will bring you to **Birling Gap** – as its name implies, a natural dip in the cliffs. The cliff here is just 40ft high, and the pebbly **beach** below can be accessed via a metal staircase. It's a magical spot – totally unspoilt and never really overrun, with endless rockpools and even a stretch of sand at low tide, and all with the stunning backdrop of the Seven Sisters.

Up on the clifftop, the tiny hamlet of Birling Gap consists of little more than a few cottages and a National Trust-owned **visitor centre** (see page 210) and café, and is set to shrink even further; the cliff is retreating by more than 2ft a year – with a whopping 9ft collapsing during winter storms in 2014 – and the National Trust is implementing a policy of "managed retreat", which in essence means abandoning the hamlet to its inevitable fate. Of the row of eight **coastguard's cottages** built in 1878, only four remain, and in a century the whole hamlet will have vanished and Birling Gap will have reverted to grassland. The National Trust runs special **events** throughout the year, everything from rockpool rambles to guided archeology walks – see ⓦ nationaltrust.org.uk/birling-gap-and-the-seven-sisters for details.

East Dean

A mile inland from Birling Gap, **EAST DEAN** village is a popular starting point – or lunch stop – for walks along the Seven Sisters and Beachy Head. The old part of the village lies on and around the idyllic green, encircled by flint-walled cottages and a scattering of places to eat and drink.

ACCOMMODATION AND EATING **EAST DEAN**

Beehive on the Green The Green, BN20 0BY ☎ 01323 423631, ⓦ thebeehiveonthegreen.co.uk. This great little deli-café can provide everything you need for a picnic, from freshly baked pastries and artisan bread to local chutneys, cured hams, cheeses, local beer and homemade cakes. There are a few tables available. Tues–Sat 9.30am–4pm, Sun 10am–4pm.

Tiger Inn The Green, BN20 0DA ☎ 01323 423209, ⓦ beachyhead.org.uk. With an idyllic location on the green in East Dean, this quintessentially English pub is the perfect spot for a summertime drink; ales include the award-winning Legless Rambler from the village's own Beachy Head Brewery. Five understated yet luxurious rooms make a good base for the area. Mon–Thurs 11am–10.30pm, Fri & Sat 11am–11.30pm, Sun 11am–10pm; kitchen Mon–Sat noon–3pm & 6–9pm, Sun noon–7pm. **£120**

> ### BACK FROM THE BRINK: THE BELLE TOUT LIGHTHOUSE
>
> Perched in glorious isolation on the clifftop between Beachy Head and Birling Gap, just 70ft from the crumbling edge, dumpy **Belle Tout lighthouse** was erected in 1832 and remained operational until 1902, when a more effective replacement was built at the foot of nearby Beachy Head. It hit the headlines in 1999 when its then owners, faced with the prospect of their home tumbling into the sea, had the 850-tonne building lifted up onto runners and slid back onto safer ground – an astonishing feat of engineering by any stretch of the imagination. The lighthouse has since been converted into a smart and stylish B&B (see above).

6

The Seven Sisters

From Birling Gap, the majestic, undulating curves of the **Seven Sisters** cliffs swoop off to the west, ending at Cuckmere Haven, where the River Cuckmere meets the sea. The three-mile walk along the springy turf of the clifftops, counting off the cliff summits (the Sisters) as you go, is exhilarating, though out-of-puff walkers beware – the "Seven" Sisters are actually eight, the result of the coastline retreating since they were named. The peaceful **Crowlink Valley** runs inland between two of the Sisters, Flagstaff and Brass Point, leading to a handy car park; the four-mile **circular walk** from Crowlink along the Seven Sisters to Birling Gap, then north to East Dean village and back to Crowlink (marked on OS *Explorer* map OL25), gives a perfect taster of the scenery.

At the western end of the Seven Sisters, Haven Brow rewards you with a wonderful view over Cuckmere Haven, before the trail heads down to the grassy valley floor. On the far side of the estuary you can see Seaford Head and the old **coastguard's cottages** that feature in the iconic view of the Seven Sisters you'll see on all the postcards; you can't cross the river mouth here, so to climb Seaford Head and see the view for yourself you'll need to head inland for 1.5 miles and then back to the coast along the river's western bank.

Cuckmere Haven

Beautiful **Cuckmere Haven**, the only undeveloped estuary in Sussex, is a famed beauty spot, and always busy with walkers, families and tourists ambling along the 1.5-mile-long main path that runs between the beach and the Exceat car park and visitor centre (see page 210) on the A259. Despite the steady flow of visitors it's still a gorgeous spot, with chalk downland, saltmarsh and shingle habitats all encountered in a half-hour stroll. The river's much-photographed **meanders** are actually nothing more than picturesque relics – the river itself flows through an artificial arrow-straight channel to the west, and has done since the channel was built in the 1840s.

As you follow the paved path you'll notice several **pillboxes** – squat concrete forts – set into the hillsides, and the remains of a tank trap between the beach

---

ACTIVITIES AT CUCKMERE HAVEN AND THE SEVEN SISTERS

While most visitors to Cuckmere Haven do little more than stroll the three-mile round-trip down to the sea and back, there's plenty to entertain more energetic types. **Walking trails** strike off in every direction and it's easy to lose the crowds; a couple of classic walks from Exceat are suggested below (both routes marked on OS *Explorer* map OL25). For cyclists there are excellent **mountain-bike trails** through Friston Forest, with climbs, drops and singletrack. There's even the opportunity to get out on a **canoe** or **paddleboard** on the River Cuckmere's famous meanders.

WALKING

Exceat – Seven Sisters – East Dean – Friston Forest – Exceat 8 miles. This full-day walk takes in many of the area's scenic highlights, heading down along the beautiful Cuckmere Valley before climbing up and along the Seven Sisters, turning inland just before Birling Gap. The village of East Dean makes a perfect lunch stop, before you continue north to Friston Forest, where shady trails lead back to Exceat.

Exceat – Chyngton Farm – South Hill – Hope Gap – Cuckmere River – Exceat 4.5 miles. This walk takes you up onto the other side of the Cuckmere estuary, for superlative views of the Seven Sisters. From Exceat Bridge, you follow the west bank of the Cuckmere River for 200m before heading up a gentle incline to Chyngton Farm, and then south up to South Hill. From here a trail leads down to Hope Gap – where there's beach access at low tide for rockpooling – and then along the clifftop to the classic viewpoint of the Seven Sisters with the coastguard's cottages in the foreground. Once down at the beach, you can follow the west bank of the river upstream back to Exceat.

CANOEING AND STAND-UP PADDLEBOARDING

Buzz Cuckmere ☎ 01323 491289, ⊚ buzzactive. org.uk. Taster kayaking and stand-up paddleboarding lessons (from £22/person, depending on size of group), plus longer courses.

LIE OF THE LAND

Chalk downland is one of Britain's richest **wildlife habitats**, thanks in large part to the sheep which have been grazing the Sussex downland since the Middle Ages, keeping the turf cropped short and allowing a unique – and rare – ecosystem of slow-growing plants to develop. More than forty different types of plants can grow in a single square yard, supporting an equally rich diversity of insects and small animals, including skylarks, six species of grasshopper and the rare Adonis blue butterfly.

Chalk downland is in fact made up of a few different habitats, of which **grassland** – with its short, springy turf – is just one. Others include **scrub**, characterized by low-growing shrubs or bushes such as yellow-flowered gorse, hawthorn and blackthorn, which you'll see bent double by the wind up on Beachy Head; and **dew ponds**, man-made, clay-lined ponds built to retain rainwater for watering livestock.

Along the length of the Downs you'll see plenty of evidence, if you look closely enough, of **ancient settlements** and people, including flint mines dug by Neolithic man at Cissbury Ring; and Iron Age hillforts at Cissbury, Devil's Dyke, Chanctonbury Ring and Mount Caburn above Lewes, to name but a few. Even the footpaths that cut across the hills tell a story: many are old **drovers' routes** that have been worn away through centuries of use.

6

and the saltmarsh – reminders of the role the valley played in **World War II**, when defences were put into place against a possible invasion. At night the valley was lit up to look like a town, in the hope that German planes would mistake the lights for Newhaven and so set their coordinates wrongly and miss their targets further north.

ACCOMMODATION AND EATING   CUCKMERE HAVEN

Saltmarsh Jevington, BN26 5QB ☎ 01323 484442, saltmarshfarmhouse.co.uk. The big draw of this café, housed in a sixteenth-century farmhouse just behind the Visitor Centre at Exceat, is its lovely courtyard garden, but it's equally nice inside, with a big fireplace and a counter piled high with goodies (delicious salads, quiches, freshly baked pastries and more). It's a bit on the pricey side, but the location and ambiance are unbeatable. Elsewhere in the farmhouse there are six beautiful guestrooms. Daily 10am–5pm. **£120**

Friston Forest

The hilly slopes of tranquil **Friston Forest** (🖥 forestry.gov.uk/fristonforest), which covers two thousand acres north of the A259 coast road, are popular with **walkers** and **mountain-bikers** alike; a free leaflet on the main trails is available from the car park. Buried away among the trees at the forest's western edge is the tiny village of **West Dean**, with a duck pond and squat-towered Norman church, while to the east, just outside the forest boundaries, is the old flint-walled smuggler's village of **Jevington**.

EATING AND DRINKING   FRISTON FOREST

Eight Bells Jevington, BN26 5QB ☎ 01323 484442, 🖥 theeightbellsjevington.co.uk. A proper country pub with loads of character and plenty of history too: the colourful Jevington Jig, leader of the Jevington smugglers' gang (see page 214), was once innkeeper here. Good home-cooked food features the likes of steak and ale pie (£11.50) and the Eight Bells burger (£11.50), and there's a lovely garden. Mon–Sat 11am–11pm, Sun noon–10.30pm; kitchen Mon–Sat noon–3pm & 6–9pm, Sun noon–9pm.

Alfriston

As the River Cuckmere draws close to the sea, the final part of its journey takes it through the lower reaches of the beautiful Cuckmere Valley, where it loops lazily

6

SMUGGLING ON THE SOUTH COAST

In the heyday of **smuggling**, in the late eighteenth to the early nineteenth centuries, there was scarcely a community along the Sussex and Kent coast that remained untouched by it, from Chichester in the west right up to Deal in the east. The counties were perfectly situated for the smuggling trade, just a short hop across the Channel from France – source of much of the contraband – and within easy distance of the rich consumers of London. Smuggling actually started with illegal exporting, when "owlers" smuggled wool to the continent to avoid paying wool tax. Later tobacco, brandy, tea and other luxuries were brought in from France in huge quantities; illegally imported gin was supposedly so plentiful in Kent at one point that villagers used it for cleaning their windows.

Smuggling was very much a community-wide affair, with whole villages involved in the trade, from wealthy landowners providing the capital and members of the clergy receiving the illegal goods to farm workers carrying and hiding the contraband. In Rottingdean near Brighton, the local vicar himself reportedly acted as a lookout.

Despite the air of romance, smuggling was often a brutal and unpleasant business, carried out by well-organized **gangs** with a reputation for violence. The gang leaders were often hardened criminals, and the locals who helped them generally did so due to a combination of fear and extreme poverty: a farm labourer could earn a week's salary in one night as a "tubman", carrying cargo from the beach to its hiding place.

Almost every village in the Alfriston area has its own infamous smuggler. At East Dean it was **James Dippery**, who managed to retain his enormous fortune by informing on his fellow smugglers. In Jevington, colourful petty criminal and innkeeper James Petit, known as **Jevington Jig**, ran a local gang that reputedly stored its ill-gotten booty in the tombs of the churchyard and the cellars of the local rectory. The Alfriston gang was led by the notorious **Stanton Collins**, and had its headquarters at *Ye Olde Smugglers Inn* – a perfect smugglers' hideaway, with 21 rooms, 6 staircases, 48 doors (some of them false) and secret tunnels thought to lead as far away as Wilmington.

The smuggling trade met little resistance from the authorities. The power of the Customs men was limited, and they could often be bribed to turn a blind eye. Although the arrival of the **coastguards** and blockade men had some success in curtailing the smugglers' activities, it wasn't until **free trade** – and reduced import duties – was introduced in the 1840s that smuggling finally came to an end.

---

through the water meadows around **ALFRISTON**, one of the prettiest villages in Sussex. Its main street is a handsome huddle of wonky-roofed flint cottages, narrow pavements and low-slung timber-framed and tile-hung cottages, punctuated with not one but three creaky old hostelries, each awash with history and tales of smuggling derring-do. The weathered stump of the medieval **Market Cross** marks the High Street's northern end, while a hundred metres south a twitten cuts down to the idyllic village green, **The Tye**, and a view that's remained virtually unchanged for centuries, with the spire of fourteenth-century St Andrew's Church rising above a ring of trees.

Clergy House

The Tye, BN26 5TL • March–June, Sept & Oct Mon–Wed, Sat & Sun 10.30am–5pm; July & Aug Mon–Wed & Fri–Sun 10.30am–5pm; Nov to mid-Dec Sat & Sun 11am–4pm • £5.60; NT • ☎ 01323 871961, ⊛ nationaltrust.org.uk/alfriston-clergy-house

The small but perfectly formed **Clergy House**, a fourteenth-century Wealden hall house, was the very first building to be saved by the newly formed National Trust, who bought it in 1896 for the princely sum of £10 and rescued it from demolition. The thatched, timber-framed dwelling has been faithfully restored, with a large central hall and a floor made in the Sussex tradition from pounded chalk sealed with sour milk. The brick chimney was a later addition – fires would originally have been lit in the open hall in the middle of the house, with smoke rising up to escape from the eaves.

Rathfinny Wine Estate

Alfriston, BN26 5TU · **Cellar door** Wed, Thurs & Sun 10am–5pm, Fri & Sat 10am–9pm · **Tours** May–Sept · £20, or £55 with lunch · 1hr 45min · ☎ 01323 871 031, ⊛ rathfinnyestate.com

The **Rathfinny Wine Estate**, on the southern outskirts of Alfriston, was founded in 2010 with the aim of producing some of the world's best sparkling wine, and is on track to become one of the largest single vineyards in Europe. You can sample its first sparkling wines, launched in 2018, as well as its still wines (bottled under the Cradle Valley label), gin and vermouth at the cellar door, or on a tasting tour of the vineyard and state-of-the-art winery. There's an excellent restaurant too, as well as accommodation.

6

ARRIVAL AND DEPARTURE

ALFRISTON

By train and bus The nearest train station, in Berwick, has hourly connections to Brighton, Lewes and Eastbourne. The Cuckmere Valley Ramblerbus operates an hourly circular service (50min) from Berwick Station via Alfriston, Seaford, the Seven Sisters Country Park and Wilmington (May–Oct

Sat, Sun & bank hols; ☎ 01323 870920, ⊛ cuckmerebuses. org.uk).

By car The village's two car parks – one pay-and-display, the other free (max 2hr) – are on either side of the road at the northern edge of the village.

ACCOMMODATION AND EATING

★ **Badgers** North St, BN26 5UG ☎ 01323 871336, ⊛ badgersteahouse.com. Once the village bakery, this sixteenth-century cottage is now a classy tearoom with a courtyard garden and a cosy, flagstone interior. Tea is served the way it should be – in silver teapots and with bone china crockery – and cakes are freshly baked on the premises. Especially recommended are the cheese and pecan scones, and the signature cake – a gloriously artery-clogging fresh cream, gooseberry and elderflower sponge. Breakfasts, sandwiches, soups and salads are also available. Mon–Fri 9.30am–4pm, Sat & Sun 10am–4.30pm.

Flint Barns Rathfinny Estate, BN26 5TU ☎ 01323 874030, ⊛ rathfinnyestate.com. Set amidst the vines at Rathfinny Estate, this beautifully converted barn has a mix of doubles

and family rooms (ten in all) – all equally tasteful, with oak floors, crisp white duvets and woollen throws – plus a cosy lounge and snug. Dinner is available to residents on Fridays and Saturdays (order in advance – two courses £22.95). Closed Mon– Thurs during harvest and pruning (generally mid-Sept to mid-Oct). Doubles **£100**, family rooms **£210**

George Inn High St, BN26 5SY ☎ 01323 870319, ⊛ thegeorge-alfriston.com. Venerable timber-framed inn with sloping floors, low beams and a huge inglenook fireplace, plus a peaceful walled garden out the back. The food ranges from sharing boards (£13.50–16.50) to mains (£10–17) such as rack of South Downs lamb or lamb and mint burger. Mon–Sat 11am–11pm, Sun noon–11pm; kitchen noon–9pm.

GUARDIAN OF THE DOWNS: THE LONG MAN OF WILMINGTON

Ancient fertility symbol or eighteenth-century folly? No one really has a clue what the **Long Man of Wilmington** is, how long he's been there or why he was carved into a Sussex hillside in the first place. This huge figure – 231ft tall, and designed to look in proportion when seen from below – is sited on the steep flank of Windover Hill, two miles northeast of Alfriston by the tiny village of Wilmington. He's one of only two human hill figures in the country (the other is the Cerne Abbas Giant in Dorset).

Various **theories** have been put forward for his origin: some believe that the figure is Roman or Anglo-Saxon; others that it is the work of a medieval monk from the nearby Wilmington priory; while recent studies have suggested that the figure may well date from the sixteenth century, perhaps the work of a landowner "marking" his land.

The Long Man was originally an indentation in the grass rather than a solid line – the pin-sharp outline you can see today was only created in 1874 when the lines were marked out in yellow bricks, replaced by concrete in 1969 (and briefly painted green during World War II, to prevent enemy planes using the landmark for navigation). The earliest known drawing of the figure, made in 1710, suggests that it once had facial features, and a helmet-shaped head. Sadly, local folklore claiming that the Long Man once sported a penis, later removed by prudish Victorians, is probably apocryphal.

A **car park** lies at the southern end of Wilmington village, from where footpaths lead up to the figure.

6

The Tasting Room Rathfinny Estate, BN26 5TU ☎ 01323 874030, ⓦ rathfinnyestate.com. The Rathfinny Estate's elegant restaurant offers high-class, impeccably presented food (two-course lunchtime set menu £30, six-course set dinner menu £60 or £90 with wine flight) and stunning views over the vines to the rolling hills beyond through floor-to-ceiling windows. A cheaper "light bites" menu is also available for those who just want a nibble while enjoying a glass of Sussex fizz. Wed, Thurs & Sun noon–3pm, Fri & Sat noon–3pm & 6–10.30pm.

★ **Wingrove House** High St, BN26 5TD ☎ 01323 870276, ⓦ wingrovehousealfriston.com. A stay at this stylish, colonial-style "restaurant and rooms", with a cosy lounge and a leafy outside terrace, is a treat from start to finish. There are just seven rooms, and it's popular, so book ahead. The excellent restaurant serves dinner in the evenings (mains £16–20) as well as lighter meals throughout the day and a splendid afternoon tea, all using local, free-range, seasonal ingredients. Mon–Sat noon–9pm, Sun noon–8.30pm. **£165**

SHOPPING

Alfriston Village Store By the Market Cross, BN26 5UE ☎ 01323 870201. This great little village store, with a well-preserved 1891 interior, has all you could possibly need for a picnic on the riverbank, including freshly baked bread and a well-stocked deli. Mon–Sat 8am–7pm, Sun 10am–5pm.
★ **Much Ado Books** 8 West St, BN26 5UX ☎ 01323

871222, ⓦ muchadobooks.com. Award-winning bookshop with a great selection of both new and secondhand books (including lots on the Bloomsbury Group and the local area). Craft workshops and other events are held in the neighbouring barn. Mon–Sat 10am–5.30pm, Sun 11am–5pm.

From Alfriston to Lewes

A mile north of Alfriston, the Alfriston Road meets the A27, which zips west towards Lewes, shadowing the hulking South Downs ridge. Detours off the busy main road include **Charleston**, the fascinating country home of the Bloomsbury Group, as well as lovely village pubs at **Berwick**, **Firle** and **Glynde** – each of them perfectly sited for post-pub rambles into the hills. Foodies should make a point of stopping off at **Middle Farm**'s excellent farm shop and at the **English Wine Centre**, where you can pick up a few bottles of Sussex's world-class bubbly – essential if you're planning on an interval picnic on the lawns of the famous **Glyndebourne** opera house.

GETTING AROUND   FROM ALFRISTON TO LEWES

By train Hourly trains run from Lewes to Eastbourne via Glynde and Berwick stations.
By bus Bus #125 runs from Lewes along the A27 via Glynde, Firle, Berwick and Alfriston to Eastbourne (Mon–Sat 4 daily).

On foot A 14-mile section of the South Downs Way long-distance footpath runs between Alfriston and Lewes, along the top of the Downs escarpment. A low-level alternative, the Old Coach Road, threads along the foot of the Downs between Alfriston and Firle.

Berwick

The village of **Berwick** is split in two by the A27: the village proper – where you'll find a beautiful **church** decorated by the Bloomsbury Group – lies just south of the road, while Berwick train station sits two miles north. The big-hitter tourist attraction in the parish is **Drusillas Park**, a few hundred metres east of the village, which calls itself (with some justification) the best small zoo in the country.

Berwick Church
Berwick village, off the A27, BN26 5QS • Daily 9am–dusk • Free • ⓦ berwickchurch.org.uk
From the outside, the little flint-walled **Berwick Church** looks distinctly ordinary, but step inside and you'll see why there's a steady trickle of tourists to this quiet spot. During World War II, **Duncan Grant** and his lover **Vanessa Bell** – residents of nearby Charleston Farmhouse (see page 217) – were commissioned by Bishop George Bell of Chichester to decorate the church with murals, a rather enlightened move given that the couple were unmarried, not practising Christians and pacifists to boot. Bell was

keen to promote the relationship between Art and the Church, and also to continue the tradition of mural painting in Sussex churches, which had come to an end after the Reformation. What resulted was a series of murals painted by the couple and Vanessa's son, **Quentin Bell**, depicting biblical events set against a backdrop of rural wartime Sussex. Sir Charles Reilly, who had recommended Grant to Bishop Bell, commented that entering the church was "like stepping out of a foggy England into Italy".

The artists used themselves, locals and friends as models. In **The Nativity** (north side of the nave), Vanessa's daughter, Angelica, was the model for Mary, with farm workers posing as the shepherds, and the spruced-up children of Vanessa's housekeeper and gardener forming the onlookers – all set against the local Sussex landscape. The largest painting in the church, on top of the chancel arch, is **Christ in Majesty**; here Christ is flanked on the right by the then Rector of Berwick and Bishop Bell, and on the left by three local men representing the three armed forces; the soldier, Douglas Hemming, son of the stationmaster, was later killed in action. Perhaps the most beautiful of the murals, however, are also the simplest: four roundels on the rood screen depicting the **Four Seasons**, scenes of ordinary rural life, interspersed with two panels depicting the pond at Charleston at dawn and dusk.

Drusillas Park

Alfriston Rd, just off the A27, BN26 5QS • Daily: March–Oct 10am–6pm; Nov–Feb 10am–5pm • £17.95–21.50 depending on season; cheaper tickets available if booked online in advance • ☎ 01323 874100, ⓦ drusillas.co.uk

Multi-award winning **Drusillas Park** is a massive hit with kids, though it does get full to bursting in the summer holidays. There's been a zoo here since the 1930s and today it houses more than a hundred different small species, everything from penguins to porcupines. There are plenty of other attractions alongside the animals, including a brilliant adventure playground, rides and a water play area.

English Wine Centre

Alfriston Rd, by the A27, BN26 5QS • Tues–Sun 10am–4pm • Free • ☎ 01323 407807, ⓦ english-wine-centre.co.uk

If you've not yet caught on to the success story of English wine (see page 28), make sure you stop off at the **English Wine Centre**, showcasing 150 varieties, including many from the local area. The shop generally has a few wines out for tasting, and also runs tutored **wine-tasting** events. There's also a lovely tearoom where you can tuck into afternoon tea accompanied by a glass of Sussex bubbly.

EATING   **BERWICK**

Cricketers' Arms Berwick village, just off the A27 (south side), BN26 6SP ☎ 01323 870469, ⓦ cricketersberwick. co.uk. Get here early in summer to bag one of the picnic tables in the flower-filled cottage garden of this pretty flint village pub – one of the nicest spots in the area for an alfresco pint. Food ranges from ploughmans (£14) to Harvey's beer-battered haddock (£13), and there's well-kept Harvey's on tap. Mon–Sat noon–11pm, Sun 11am–8pm; kitchen Mon–Fri noon–2.30pm & 6–8.30pm, Sat noon–8.30pm, Sun noon–5pm.

Charleston Farmhouse

Six miles east of Lewes, signposted off the A27, BN8 9LL • **House** March–Oct Wed–Sat 11.30am–5pm, Sun & bank hols noon–5pm (note that Wed–Sat entry is by 1hr guided tour only, while on Sun & bank hols rooms are stewarded and you can move about freely); Nov–Feb Wed–Sun 11.30am–2.30pm (entry is by 40min guided tour only – only ground-floor rooms are visited); last entry 1hr before closing **Garden and galleries** Wed–Sun 10am–5pm • House and garden £14.50 (March–Oct), £10 (Nov–Feb), garden only £5, exhibitions £7 • ☎ 01323 811626, ⓦ charleston.org.uk

Hidden away at the end of a meandering lane under the hulking Downs, **Charleston Farmhouse** was the country home of the **Bloomsbury Group**, an informal circle of writers, artists and intellectuals who came together in the early decades of the twentieth century. The farmhouse was rented by **Vanessa Bell** and the love of her life **Duncan Grant**, who moved here in 1916, in order that Grant and his lover **David Garnett** –

6

pacifists and conscientious objectors – could work on local farms (farm labourers were exempt from military service). It was a rather unconventional household to say the least, housing not only the amicable love triangle of Vanessa, Grant and Garnett, but also Vanessa's two young sons from her marriage-in-name-only to **Clive Bell**, who himself was an intermittent visitor, until he settled permanently there in 1939. The farmhouse became a gathering point for other members of the Bloomsbury Group, including the biographer and historian **Lytton Strachey**, the novelist **E.M. Forster**, economist **John Maynard Keynes** and Vanessa's sister **Virginia Woolf**.

Vanessa's children enjoyed a childhood of almost complete liberty, and perhaps not surprisingly all grew up embracing the artistic life, her eldest son Julian becoming a poet, second son Quentin an art historian and potter, and Angelica, her daughter with Duncan Grant, a painter. Vanessa died in 1961, and Duncan Grant in 1978. The dilapidated house was bought by the Charleston Trust, restored and opened to the public, retaining the warm, lived-in feeling of a family home.

The house

Bell and Grant saw the house as a blank canvas: almost every surface is **decorated** – fireplaces, door panels, bookcases, lamp bases, screens. Many of the fabrics, lampshades and other artefacts bear the unmistakeable mark of the **Omega workshops** (see page 219), the Bloomsbury equivalent of William Morris's artistic movement. In the **dining room**, the dark distempered walls with a stencilled pattern might seem commonplace to modern eyes but at the time would have been daringly modern; so too the painted circular table, signifying equality between the sexes, where women were not required to leave the table after dinner and could enter into discussions with men on an equal footing.

Around the house, the walls are hung with **paintings** by Picasso, Renoir and Augustus John, alongside the work of the residents. Portraits of friends and family abound, nowhere more so than in **Vanessa's bedroom**; above her bed is a large portrait of her beloved son Julian, who was killed in 1937 while working as an ambulance driver in the Spanish Civil War. Vanessa never really recovered, and a further blow came in 1941, when her sister committed suicide.

The garden, gallery and other buildings

Charleston's **walled garden** was created by Vanessa and Duncan Grant, working to the designs of their friend, the art critic Roger Fry. The garden was very much a painters' garden, crammed with plants chosen for their colours and shapes, and dotted with idiosyncratic sculptures by Duncan Grant and Quentin Bell; Quentin wrote that it was "as though the exuberant decoration of the interior had spilled through the doors". The garden was neglected after Vanessa's death, but over the last thirty years it has been beautifully brought back to life.

Elsewhere on the Charleston site, the purpose-built **art gallery** hosts changing exhibitions exploring the Bloomsbury Group's artistic and literary heritage. Other buildings are used for the Trust's programme of creative **workshops, talks and events**, including the **Charleston Festival** at the end of May and the **Small Wonder** short-story festival in September.

Middle Farm

Firle, 4 miles east of Lewes on the A27, BN8 6LJ • **Farm shop, restaurant & cider centre** Daily 9.30am–5.30pm (4pm in winter) • Free •
Open farm Generally daily 9.30am–4pm • £6 (April–Oct), £5 (Nov–March), under-3s free • ☏ 01323 811411, ⓦ middlefarm.com

Opened in the 1960s, **Middle Farm** is one of the oldest farm shops in the country, and is a great place to stock up on local produce. The main draw for many, however, is the **National Collection of Cider and Perry**, a small barn crammed floor-to-ceiling with barrels housing more than one hundred varieties of draught cider and perry, alongside meads, country wines, ales and more; tasting glasses are provided so you can compare

THE BLOOMSBURY GROUP

The group of artists, writers and thinkers that came to be known as the **Bloomsbury Group** had its beginnings in Cambridge, where the brother of **Virginia Woolf** and **Vanessa Bell**, Thoby, studied alongside Leonard Woolf (Virginia's future husband), Clive Bell (Vanessa's future husband), E.M. Forster, John Maynard Keynes, Roger Fry and Lytton Strachey (whose cousin, **Duncan Grant**, would later set up home with Vanessa at Charleston Farmhouse). The men graduated in 1904, the same year that Virginia and Vanessa's father died. Vanessa promptly rented a property in Gordon Square in **Bloomsbury**, painted the door a defiant red, and set up home with her siblings. Thoby's Cambridge friends began to meet at the house, sharing ideas and discussing their work with each other and the sisters, and in time, the "Bloomsbury Group" was born.

Artistically, the art critic **Roger Fry** was a huge influence on the group. It was he who brought over the first post-Impressionist exhibitions from France in 1910 and 1912, which were greeted with horror by the general public whose idea of proper art was the photorealist representation of the Victorian age. In the wake of the exhibitions, Fry, Grant and Vanessa set up the **Omega workshops** in 1913, to bring post-Impressionism to the decorative arts – furniture, ceramics, textiles and more. The idea that art did not have to be confined to a picture frame was a guiding principle behind the exuberant decorations at **Charleston Farmhouse**, where Vanessa and Grant moved in 1916.

The **values** of the Bloomsbury Group were, primarily, a loathing and rejection of Victorian conventions – its worthiness, hypocrisy, prudishness, militarism, sexism and homophobia. Instead there was a focus on individual pleasure, friendship, pacifism and truth to oneself and one's sexuality – the last of these resulting in a bewildering amount of bed-hopping and all sorts of complicated **love triangles**: Keynes was a lover of both Strachey and Grant before he settled down with a Russian ballerina; while Vanessa, though married to Clive Bell, lived with Grant and had a child with him, **Angelica** (who was recognized by Bell to avoid scandal). Grant slept with any number of men during his years with Vanessa, among them Keynes, Strachey and writer **David Garnett**, who eventually ended up – in a move that horrified Vanessa and Grant – marrying the young Angelica.

6

ciders before filling a bottle with the tipple of your choice. Elsewhere on the site there's an open farm for children and a café-restaurant.

Firle

Four miles from Lewes, tiny **West Firle** – known generally as **Firle** – is a perfect Sussex village, with brick- and flint-walled cottages lining the main street, a handsome old pub, the *Ram Inn*, and an idyllically sited cricket ground fringed by swaying oaks – home to **Firle Cricket Club** (w firlecc.com), one of the oldest in the world, formed in 1758.

Several members of the Bloomsbury set, Vanessa Bell among them, are buried in the churchyard of **St Peter's**, at the far end of The Street. Inside the church, there's a beautiful piece of modern stained glass in the organ vestry – a depiction of Blake's *Tree of Life*, designed in 1985 by English artist John Piper; look out for the local Southdown sheep at the bottom of the window.

Firle Place

The Street, Firle, BN8 6NS • Generally July–Sept Mon–Thurs & Sun 2–4.30pm • £9 • ☎ 01273 858567, w firle.com

Beyond St Peter's church lies handsome **Firle Place**, originally Tudor but remodelled in the eighteenth century with Caen stone, probably taken from the Priory ruins in nearby Lewes (see page 222). Firle Place has been the home of the Gage family for over five hundred years – Sir John, who built the manor house, served as Lord Chamberlain under Henry VIII, while his son, Edward, has a rather more ignominious place in history, having supervised the arrest and burning of the Lewes martyrs (see

6

UP, UP AND AWAY: PARAGLIDING IN SUSSEX

On balmy summer's days, you can't fail to notice the colourful canopies of **paragliders** floating in the thermals above the Downs near Lewes. Two local companies offer lessons; you can be up in the air flying solo in just one day.

Airworks Paragliding Centre Old Station, Glynde ☎ 01273 434002, ⓦ www.airworks.co.uk. Small-group tuition in paragliding and paramotoring (powered paragliding). One-day introductory paragliding or paramotoring courses £150; five-day Elementary Pilot course £740; 20min tandem rides £99.

FlySussex Paragliding On the A27, 2 miles east of Lewes, between Glynde and Firle ☎ 01273 858170, ⓦ flysussex.com. The largest flying centre in the UK, with their own private flying sites and year-round lessons. One-day introductory paragliding courses £165 (£185 weekends), five-day Elementary Pilot course £760; 30min tandem rides £165 (£185 weekends).

---

page 225). The family still lives in the house today, giving it an appealingly homely air, with family knick-knacks sitting alongside Gainsborough family portraits, Chippendale cabinets and Sèvres porcelain. It's best to visit on a weekday if you can, when visits are by informative guided **tour**.

ACCOMMODATION AND EATING   FIRLE

Beanstalk Tea Garden Old Coach Road, Firle Estate, BN8 6PA ☎ 01273 858906, ⓦ facebook.com/BeanstalkTeaGarden. Idyllic summer-only tea garden – complete with resident peacock – hidden away at the foot of the Downs, a 20min walk (or bumpy drive) from Firle along the Old Coach Road. Cakes, afternoon teas and light lunches are served all day. Generally April to early Sept Wed–Sun & bank hols 11.30am–5.30pm.

Firle Camp Heighton St, Firle Estate, BN8 6NZ ☎ 07733 103309, ⓦ firlecamp.co.uk. Lovely back-to-basics campsite in a gorgeous meadow location, overlooked by the Downs, and with the Middle Farm shop (see page 218)

and a handful of good pubs within walking distance. Fires allowed. Per adult £11.50

Ram Inn Firle village, BN8 6NS ☎ 01273 858222, ⓦ raminn.co.uk. This sprawling brick-and-flint pub is a corker, with a lovely walled garden and, inside, wooden floors, slate-grey walls and roaring fires in winter. Food is good, and local – bread is baked in nearby Glynde, and game comes from the Firle Estate; mains are £12–22, though there is a cheaper bar menu available during the day. There are five gorgeous rooms above the pub. Daily 9am–11pm; kitchen daily 9–11am, noon–3pm & 6.30–9.30pm. £150

Glynde

Three miles east of Lewes, just north of the A27, the tiny estate village of **Glynde** is a bit of a backwater, best known for its world-famous opera house, **Glyndebourne**, which lies just up the road.

Glynde Place

Glynde, BN8 6SX • Generally May, June & Aug bank hol Wed, Thurs & Sun; entry by tour only at 2pm & 3.30pm • £5 • ☎ 01273 858224, ⓦ glynde.co.uk

Glynde village was built – and is still owned – by the Glynde Estate; the estate's manor house, **Glynde Place**, a handsome Elizabethan affair built in Sussex flint, lies at the northern fringe of the village. The house opens up for a few months in the summer for guided tours, allowing a glimpse into the magnificent interior of one of Sussex's finest manor houses. In early July, the idyllic parkland surrounding the house hosts the Love Supreme festival (see page 32), regarded as one of the best jazz festivals in Europe.

Glyndebourne

1 mile north of Glynde, BN8 5UU • ☎ 01273 812321, ⓦ glyndebourne.com

Founded in 1934, **Glyndebourne** is one of the world's best opera houses, and Britain's only unsubsidized one. It's best known for the **Glyndebourne Festival** (May to Aug), an indispensable part of the high-society calendar, when opera-goers in evening dress

throng to the country house with hampers, blankets and candlesticks to picnic on the lawns; the operas themselves are performed in an award-winning theatre, seating 1200. **Tickets** for the season's six productions sell out quickly, and are eye-wateringly expensive, but there are some standing-room-only ones available at reduced prices (from £15), as well as discounts for under-30s (register beforehand to be eligible).

6   Lewes and around

East Sussex's county town, **LEWES**, couldn't be in a lovelier spot, straddling the River Ouse and with some of England's most appealing chalk downlands right on its doorstep. With a remarkably good-looking centre, a lively cultural and artistic scene, plenty of history and a proud sense of its own identity (it even has its own currency), Lewes is one of Sussex's finest towns.

Lewes Castle

169 High St • Mon & Sun 11am–5.30pm (dusk in winter), Tues–Sat 10am–5.30pm (dusk in winter); closed Mon in Jan • £8.20, joint ticket with Anne of Cleves House £13 • ☏ 01273 486290, ⓦ sussexpast.co.uk

The town's splendid Norman fortress, **Lewes Castle**, was the work of William de Warenne, who was given the land by William I after the Conquest. Originally a simple motte-and-bailey construction, the castle was enlarged in 1100 and a second motte (or mound) was added, together with a gateway and curtain walls. Castles built on two mottes were very unusual: Lewes is one of only two examples in England (Lincoln is the other). Just a single wall remains of the Norman gateway today; the majestic arrow-slitted gateway you see in front of it – the **Barbican** – was built in the early fourteenth

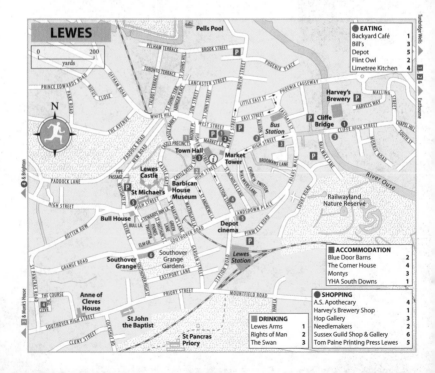

LEWES

● EATING	
Backyard Café	1
Bill's	3
Depot	5
Flint Owl	2
Limetree Kitchen	4

■ ACCOMMODATION	
Blue Door Barns	2
The Corner House	4
Montys	3
YHA South Downs	1

● SHOPPING	
A.S. Apothecary	4
Harvey's Brewery Shop	1
Hop Gallery	3
Needlemakers	2
Sussex Guild Shop & Gallery	6
Tom Paine Printing Press Lewes	5

■ DRINKING	
Lewes Arms	1
Rights of Man	2
The Swan	3

THE LEWES POUND

Created to encourage the local economy, the **Lewes pound** was launched to much fanfare and national press attention in 2008. The currency's still in circulation – though it's rare to be handed one in your change – and is available in £1, £5, £10 and £21 denominations, with the same value as sterling. It's accepted by more than a hundred businesses around town, including stallholders at the farmers' markets, and is issued at various locations, among them the Town Hall, the Harvey's Brewery Shop (see page 227) and the Depot cinema (see page 227). Lewes pound collector packs are available to buy from the website. Visit ⓦ thelewespound.org to find out more.

6

century for added fortification. The last of the De Warennes died without heir in 1347 and the castle began its slow slide into decay, until the romantic ruins were reinvented as a tourist attraction in the eighteenth century.

Inside the complex, narrow stone steps climb up inside the Barbican to the roof, with its excellent views over the town. The best views, however, can be had from the eleventh-century **Shell Keep**, which tops one of the castle's two mottes. From here you can see the other motte, **Brack Mount**, now just a grassy hillock and closed to the public, as well as the hills to the north of town where the **Battle of Lewes** took place in 1264. The battle was the bloody culmination of a clash between Henry III and a rebel army of barons under Simon de Montfort; the king was defeated and the resulting treaty, the **Mise of Lewes**, restricted his authority and forced him to assemble a governing council – often described as the first House of Commons.

Barbican House Museum

The castle ticket office is also the entrance to the **Barbican House Museum**, which has exhibits on Sussex life from the Stone Age through to medieval times. A twelve-minute film tells the history of Lewes with the help of a model of the town as it would have looked in the 1880s. You can also see a tapestry created in 2014, using thirteenth-century embroidery techniques, to mark the 750th anniversary of the Battle of Lewes.

The High Street

Georgian and crooked older dwellings line Lewes's handsome **High Street**. A few minutes' walk west from the castle you'll pass **St Michael's Church**, one of the oldest in Lewes, with unusual twin towers, one wooden shingle and the other flint. On the opposite side of the road is the fifteenth-century **Bull House**, where revolutionary and pamphleteer **Thomas Paine** lived from 1768 to 1774 before emigrating to America, where he wrote *Common Sense*, the pamphlet that made his name and earned him the title "Father of the American Revolution".

On either side of the High Street, enticing narrow lanes – "twittens" – strike off into the backstreets; most photogenic is steep, cobbled **Keere Street**, down which the reckless Prince Regent (see page 238) is alleged to have driven his carriage for a bet.

Southover

The part of Lewes known as **Southover**, to the south of the High Street, grew up around St Pancras Priory (see page 224) and was separated from Lewes by the Winterbourne stream. The stream still trickles, sporadically, through beautiful **Southover Grange Gardens** (daily dawn–dusk), a favourite picnic spot with locals. A hole-in-the-wall kiosk (Easter–Oct) sells ice creams, sandwiches and snacks. The gardens surround **Southover Grange**, built in 1572 from St Pancras Priory's remains, and once the childhood home of the diarist John Evelyn. A section of the Grange is given over to the Sussex Guild Shop & Gallery (see page 227).

Anne of Cleves House

52 Southover High St, BN7 1JA • Feb & Nov Mon & Sun 11am–4pm, Tues–Sat 10am–4pm; March–Oct Mon & Sun 11am–5pm, Tues–Sat 10am–5pm; sometimes closed for private functions – call to check • £6.30, joint ticket with Lewes Castle £13 • ☎ 01273 474610, ⓦ sussexpast.co.uk

Despite the name, Anne of Cleves never actually lived in the timber-framed **Anne of Cleves House**: it was one of nine Sussex properties given to her in 1540 after Henry ignominiously cast her aside after less than a year of marriage, making her one of the richest women in the country – not a bad deal considering the fate of some of Henry's other wives. The building, a Wealden hall house, was constructed in the late fifteenth century by a wealthy yeoman farmer and would originally have been open to the rafters like the Clergy House in Alfriston (see page 214). The house today is for the most part presented as it would have been in Tudor times – the highlight being a magnificent oak-beamed bedroom complete with a 400-year-old Flemish four-poster – but two rooms are given over to exhibits on the Sussex Wealden **iron industry** and the **history of Lewes**.

St Pancras Priory

Access via Cockshut Lane or Mountfield Rd • Always open • Free • ⓦ lewespriory.org.uk

South of Southover High Street sprawl the evocative ruins of **St Pancras Priory**, founded around 1078 by William de Warenne, who also built Lewes Castle. Little remains of the priory today, but interpretive boards do an excellent job of conjuring up what the crumbling stones would have looked like in its heyday, when it was one of the largest and most powerful monasteries in England, with a church the size of Westminster Abbey and land holdings as far north as Yorkshire. Most of the priory was destroyed during the Reformation, and the site became a quarry for building materials – stones from here ended up being used all over Lewes.

Cliffe

At the east end of the High Street, School Hill descends towards **Cliffe Bridge** – the entrance to **Cliffe**, commercial centre of the medieval settlement. On the far side of the bridge you can't miss the Victorian Gothic tower of **Harvey's Brewery**, while semi-pedestrianized **Cliffe High Street** strikes off ahead, with antiques shops and cafés spilling out onto the pavements. At the end of the street, steep, narrow **Chapel Hill** leads straight up on to the Downs – the start of a lovely three-mile walk to the village of Glynde (see page 220) – while South Street runs south to the *Snowdrop Inn*, named after the deadliest avalanche in British history when, in 1836, a ledge of snow fell from the cliff onto the houses below, killing eight people.

Harvey's Brewery

The Bridge Wharf Brewery, BN7 2AH • ☎ 01273 480209, ⓦ harveys.org.uk

Affectionately known locally as Lewes Cathedral, **Harvey's Brewery** is the oldest brewery in Sussex. Sussex Best bitter – one of a handful of cask ales – is the most popular brew, but the brewery also produces a dozen or so seasonal ales, including Bonfire Boy (timed for the November 5th celebrations) and the popular Old Ale, available in the autumn and winter months. The brewery **shop** (see page 227) on Cliffe High Street is a great place to stock up on the award-winning cask ales and bottled beers.

Pells Pool

Brook St, BN7 2PW • May Mon–Fri 7–9am & noon–7pm, Sat & Sun noon–7pm; June–Aug Mon–Fri 7–9am & 10am–7pm, Sat & Sun 10am–7pm; Sept & Oct Mon–Fri 7–10am & 3–6.30pm, Sat & Sun noon–6.30pm; sometimes stays open later in fine weather • £4.50 • ☎ 01273 472334, ⓦ pellspool.org.uk

A five-minute walk from the High Street brings you to the Pells area, where you'll find **Pells Pool**; built in 1861, it proudly holds the claim of being the oldest freshwater

LEST WE FORGET: LEWES BONFIRE NIGHT

Each November 5, while the rest of the country lights small domestic bonfires or attends municipal fireworks displays to commemorate the 1605 foiled Catholic plot to blow up the Houses of Parliament, Lewes puts on a more dramatic show – not for nothing has it been called the "**Bonfire Capital of the World**". The town closes to traffic, shops are boarded up and, come nightfall, the narrow streets are thronged by dozens of processions of elaborately costumed locals wielding flaming torches, burning crosses and flares, accompanied by marching bands and drummers. Each of Lewes's six tightknit **bonfire societies** – Borough, Cliffe, Commercial Square, Southover, South Street and Waterloo – has their own colours and themed costumes (Mongol warriors, monks, Vikings and more), and every year each produces a massive (often controversial) tableaux of a contemporary public figure, which is paraded through town and later burnt; the 2016 event saw no fewer than four tableaux of Donald Trump wheeled through the streets. After the main procession of the night (normally around 7.30pm), each society heads off to its own bonfire site and fireworks display on the outskirts of town.

The origins of Lewes's celebrations lie in the deaths of the town's seventeen Protestant martyrs during the Marian Persecutions of 1555–57, when Mary Tudor sentenced 288 Protestants around the country to be burned alive for their heretical views. By the end of the eighteenth century, Lewes' **Bonfire Boys** had become notorious for the boisterousness of their anti-Catholic demonstrations, in which they set off fireworks indiscriminately and dragged flaming tar barrels through the streets. Lewes's first bonfire societies were established in the 1850s to try to introduce a little more discipline into the proceedings, and in the early part of the last century they were persuaded to move their street fires to the town's perimeters.

The Lewes Bonfire experience is undeniably brilliant, but it does get packed, especially on years when November 5 falls on a weekend, and the official line is that it's an event for the people of Lewes only. If you decide to come, be aware that roads close early, parking is restricted and there can be horrendously long queues for trains at the end of the night; it's best to stay over if you can (book early). With loud bangs, flying sparks and lots of open flames, the event is definitely not suitable for small children. If the 5th falls on a Sunday, the celebrations take place on the 4th. For more, see ⓦ lewesbonfirecouncil.org.uk.

OTHER SUSSEX BONFIRE CELEBRATIONS

Although Lewes is the best known of Sussex's bonfire celebrations, dozens of other villages and towns have their own societies which celebrate with torchlit processions and fireworks between September and the end of November, attending each other's processions, as well as the big one in Lewes. Though on a smaller scale, these events are a great way to experience the unique Sussex bonfire tradition; you can check dates on the societies' websites below. In Lewes itself, a seventh bonfire society, **Nevill Juvenile** (ⓦ www.njbs.co.uk), is specifically for children and holds its celebrations in October.

September Burgess Hill (ⓦ burgesshillbonfire society.co.uk), Crowborough (ⓦ crowboroughbonfire andcarnival.com), Mayfield (ⓦ mayfieldbonfire.co.uk), Uckfield (ⓦ uckfieldcarnival.co.uk).

October Eastbourne (ⓦ eastbournebonfiresociety. co.uk), Ewhurst & Staplecross (ⓦ esbs.org.uk), Firle (ⓦ firlebonfire.com), Fletching, Hailsham (ⓦ hailsham bonfire.org.uk), Hastings (ⓦ hbbs.info), Littlehampton (ⓦ littlehamptonbonfiresociety.co.uk), Newick (ⓦ newick

bonfire.com), Ninfield (ⓦ ninfieldbonfire.co.uk), Northiam (ⓦ northiambonfiresociety.co.uk), Rotherfield (ⓦ rmcbs. co.uk), Seaford (ⓦ seafordbonfire.co.uk).

November Barcombe (ⓦ barcombebonfire.co.uk), Battle (ⓦ battlebonfire.co.uk), Chailey (ⓦ chaileybonfire.co.uk), Hawkhurst (ⓦ hawkhurst-gang-bonfire-society.org.uk), Lindfield (ⓦ lindfieldbonfiresociety.co.uk), Robertsbridge (ⓦ robertsbridgebonfiresociety.com), Rye (ⓦ ryebonfire. co.uk), South Heighton (ⓦ southheighton.org/bonfire).

open-air swimming pool in the country. Fed by an icy freshwater stream, a dip here is certainly not for the fainthearted, but that doesn't seem to put off the locals, who throng here at summer weekends to sprawl on the tree-lined lawn surrounding the pool. There's also a paddling pool, and a kiosk selling ice creams and home-baked goodies. It gets very busy on hot days at weekends and in the summer holidays, when you'll need to arrive early and queue to get in.

6

ARRIVAL AND INFORMATION

LEWES

By train The station lies south of High St down Station Rd; there are good connections with London and along the coast.

Destinations Brighton (every 10–20min; 15min); Eastbourne (every 20min; 30min); London Victoria (Mon–Sat every 30min, Sun hourly; 1hr 10min).

By bus The bus station is on Eastgate St, near the foot of School Hill.

Destinations Brighton (Mon–Sat every 10min, Sun every 30min; 30min); Tunbridge Wells (Mon–Sat every 30min,

Sun hourly; 1hr 10min).

By car There's no free parking in the centre of Lewes, and wardens are vigilant. There are plenty of car parks around town.

Tourist office At the junction of High St and Fisher St (April–Sept Mon–Fri 9.30am–4.30pm, Sat 9.30am–4pm, Sun & bank hols 10am–2pm; Oct–March Mon–Fri 9.30am–4.30pm, Sat 10am–2pm; ☎ 01273 483448, ⓦ www.lewes-eastbourne.gov.uk). They hold copies of the excellent free monthly magazine *Viva Lewes* (ⓦ vivalewes.com).

ACCOMMODATION

SEE MAP PAGE 222

The website ⓦ lewesbandb.co.uk is a good directory of B&B **accommodation** in Lewes and the surrounding area. If you're hoping to get a room on Bonfire Night, book as far in advance as possible.

Blue Door Barns Beddingham, just outside Lewes, BN8 6JY ☎ 01273 858893, ⓦ bluedoorbarns.com. Stylish B&B and holiday lets in four luxurious barns, complete with on-site treatment room. Horseriding packages are available. Two-night minimum stay at weekends. **£135**

The Corner House 14 Cleve Terrace, BN7 1JJ ☎ 01273 567138, ⓦ lewescornerhouse.co.uk. There's a real home-from-home feeling about this friendly B&B, set back from Southover High Street on a quiet Edwardian terrace. The two rooms have cheery patchwork quilts on the beds, wooden floors, plenty of books and small, immaculate bathrooms. **£85**

Montys Broughton House, 16 High St, BN7 2LN ☎ 01273

476750, ⓦ montysaccommodation.co.uk. Boutique B&B in a nineteenth-century townhouse, with two rooms in the basement and a third stunning loft-style room (£125 – cheaper outside summer season) occupying the entire top floor. All three rooms come with kitchenettes, and a breakfast of warm croissants and homemade granola is delivered to your door. **£80**

YHA South Downs Itford Farm, Beddingham, 5 miles south of Lewes ☎ 0870 371 9574, ⓦ yha.org.uk/hostel/south-downs. The nearest hostel to Lewes is a gem, renovated from a characterful old farm, and in a great location right on the South Downs Way footpath, with good transport connections (Southease station – with regular connections to Lewes – is just 200m away). Camping pods (sleeping 2 or 4) and bell tents (sleeping 4) are available, and there's a café and licensed bar too. Camping pods **£79**, bell tents **£99**, dorms **£25**, doubles **£69**

EATING

SEE MAP PAGE 222

Lewes's weekly **food market** (ⓦ lewesfoodmarket. co.uk) takes place in the Market Tower on Market Street every Friday (9.30am–1.30pm). There's a larger **farmers' market** in the shopping precinct at the bottom of the High Street on the first and third Saturday of the month (9am–1pm). As well as the cafés and restaurants listed below, check out the town's pubs, many of which do excellent food.

Backyard Café Needlemakers, 14 West St, BN7 2NZ ☎ 01273 480219, ⓦ backyardcafelewes.co.uk. Located in a characterful old needle manufacturing (and later candle) factory, this cosy café with bare-brick walls has a delicious selection of cakes, quiches, salad plates (£5–8), sandwiches and toasties, as well as loose-leaf tea and locally roasted coffee. It's a good choice for brunch too, with an all-day breakfast menu featuring homemade banana bread with berry compote and baba ganoush on olive bread. Mon–Thurs 10am–5pm, Fri & Sat 10am–4pm, Sun 11am–4pm.

Bill's 56 Cliffe High St ☎ 01273 476918, ⓦ billsproduce store.co.uk. Now a countrywide restaurant chain, *Bill's* started life as a greengrocer's right here in Lewes and it remains as popular as ever, helped in part by its great

location on pretty Cliffe High Street, with tables outside. Breakfasts are a particular treat, served till 4pm and ranging from buttermilk pancakes to a legendarily good vegetarian breakfast. Daily 8am–10.30pm.

Depot Pinwell Rd, BN7 2JS ☎ 01273 525354, ⓦ lewesdepot.org. In the stylish Depot cinema building (see below), this café-bar and restaurant is one of the town's nicest places to stop for a bite to eat or drink, especially in the summer when you can take advantage of its outdoor seating (rare in Lewes). There's a simple brunch/lunch menu, and a larger evening menu featuring the likes of sea trout or mushroom risotto (mains £11–14). Food served daily 10am–3pm & 4–9pm.

★ **Flint Owl** 209 High St, BN7 2DL ☎ 01273 472769, ⓦ flintowlbakery.com. The café of the Glynde-based Flint Owl Bakery – which supplies its pastries and artisan bread (made using stoneground organic flour and little or no yeast) around Sussex – is a stylish space with a small courtyard garden out the back, and counters piled high with freshly baked pastries, savouries and cakes. Sandwiches, quiches and salads are also served, and there's a great selection of bread for sale, too, if you just want to pop in to buy a loaf. Mon–Sat 9am–5pm.

Limetree Kitchen 14 Station St, BN7 2DA ☎01273 478636, ⓦlimetreekitchen.co.uk. Tapas-style "small plates" and an extensive range of gins are the signatures of this intimate little restaurant. There are a dozen or so main dishes to choose from, most in the £7–8 range – expect the likes of soft-shelled crab with samphire, crispy pig's head with kimchi or smoked Sardinian ricotta – plus a range of sides at £3.50 each. Wed–Sat noon–3pm & 8–10.30pm, Sun noon–3pm.

DRINKING

SEE MAP PAGE 222

★ **Lewes Arms** Mount Place, BN7 1YH ☎01273 473252, ⓦlewesarms.co.uk. One of Lewes's best-loved locals, this friendly pub has bags of character, with several cosy bare-boarded rooms and a tiny bar serving a good selection of real ales, including Harvey's. Annual events range from spaniel-racing and dwyle-flunking (tossing a beer-soaked dishcloth) to the World Pea Throwing Championships (the record currently stands at over 44m). The home-cooked pub food is great value, too. Mon–Thurs 11am–11pm, Fri & Sat 11am–midnight, Sun noon–11pm; kitchen Mon–Fri noon–4pm & 5–9pm, Fri & Sat noon–9pm, Sun noon–6pm.

Rights of Man 179 High St, BN7 1YE ☎01273 486894. This traditional pub on the High Street has a good range of Harvey's beer, a lovely roof terrace with views of the castle and a good-value menu of home-cooked, locally sourced food, ranging from sandwiches (£7) to burgers to fish and meat mains (£12–15), with a separate (excellent) tapas menu. Mon–Sat noon–11pm, Sun noon–10.30pm; kitchen Mon–Sat noon–3pm & 6–9.30pm, Sun noon–6pm.

The Swan 30 Southover High St, BN7 1HU ☎01273 480211, ⓦfacebook.com/theswanlewes. Friendly, always-busy pub at the end of Southover High St, a 5–10min walk from the station, with four or five different Harvey's on tap, a vinyl-only music policy and a small, sunny beer garden out the back. Great home-cooked food, too, including lots of good veggie options and enormous and very tasty roasts. Daily noon–late; kitchen Mon–Sat noon–9pm, Sun noon–5pm.

ENTERTAINMENT

Depot Pinwell Rd, BN7 2JS ☎01273 525354, ⓦlewes depot.org. Award-winning independent cinema with a stylish café-bar/restaurant (see above) and three screens showing a mix of mainstream, arthouse and independent films, plus live streamings of arts events. Special events and workshops often run.

SHOPPING

SEE MAP PAGE 222

A.S. Apothecary 31 Western Rd, BN7 1RL ☎01273 253186, ⓦasapoth.com. Flagship store of this luxury natural skincare brand, which produces natural scents, creams and essential oils in small batches from flowers and other plants foraged locally and further afield. The beautiful little shop, arranged around a copper still, smells heavenly and is packed with products you can test and buy (including some not available online). There's a treatment room downstairs. Fri & Sat 10am–5pm or by appointment.

Harvey's Brewery Shop 7 Cliffe High St, BN7 2AH ☎01273 480217, ⓦharveys.org.uk. The brewery shop is crammed floor-to-ceiling with award-winning cask ales and seasonal bottled beers. Mon–Sat 9.30am–5.30pm, Sun 11am–3pm.

Hop Gallery Castle Ditch Lane, off Fisher St, BN7 1YJ ☎01273 487744, ⓦfacebook.com/hopgallery. Well-regarded art gallery within the eighteenth-century Star Brewery building, with regularly changing exhibitions of contemporary art for sale. Check their Facebook page for exhibition times.

Needlemakers West Street, BN7 2NZ. A collection of independent shops set over two floors of an old factory, selling everything from jewellery, homeware and ceramics to vintage gear and fairtrade goods. Most shops Mon–Sat 10am–5pm.

Sussex Guild Shop & Gallery Southover Grange, Southover Rd, BN7 1TP ☎01273 479565, ⓦthesussex guild.co.uk. A wonderful selection of textiles, prints, ceramics and jewellery produced by Sussex craftspeople. Daily 10am–5pm.

Tom Paine Printing Press Lewes 151 High St, BN7 1XU ⓦtompaineprintingpress.com. This tiny shop-cum-gallery is home to a working eighteenth-century-style printing press, of the type that would have been used to produce Thomas Paine's pamphlets (see page 223). Prints and cards printed on the press are on sale, alongside the work of contemporary printmakers. Tues–Sat 10am–5pm.

Monk's House

Rodmell, BN7 3HF • Easter–Oct Wed–Sun & bank hols: house 1–5pm; garden 12.30–5.30pm • £6.30; NT • Free parking • ☎01273 474760, ⓦnationaltrust.org.uk/monks-house

Three miles south of Lewes on the Lewes–Newhaven road, the pretty, weatherboard **Monk's House** was the home of novelist **Virginia Woolf** and her husband, Leonard,

6

> ## BOATING AT BARCOMBE
>
> At **Barcombe**, four miles upstream of Lewes, you can take to the water for a gentle paddle along the **River Ouse**, one of the South's most beautiful and unspoilt waterways. The eighteenth-century *Anchor Inn* (☏ 01273 400414, ⓦ anchorinnandboating.co.uk) – actually half a mile northeast of Barcombe, but signposted from the village – hires out two-, four- and six-seater **canoes** (1hr £6/person) for the two-mile trip upstream past grassy banks and meadows to Fish Ladder Falls. The only building visible en route is the spire of Isfield Church, and if you're lucky you'll spot kingfisher, heron and cormorant – though on summer weekends your most likely sightings will be boatloads of other paddlers.

first as a summer and weekend retreat, until their London house was bombed in 1940 and it became their permanent residence. Like Charleston Farmhouse, where Virginia's much-loved sister Vanessa Bell lived, Monk's House hosted gatherings of the Bloomsbury Group (see page 219), and over the years E.M. Forster, Maynard Keynes, Vita Sackville-West, Lytton Strachey and Roger Fry all visited; informal snapshots of these guests, accompanied by Virginia's occasionally acerbic comments, are on show in the writing room in the orchard.

The **house** – of which you can see just four rooms – is presented as though the Woolfs had just popped out, and is unmistakeably "Bloomsbury" in style, with painted furniture, decorated ceramics and paintings by Vanessa and her partner Duncan Grant in every room, though on a much smaller, calmer scale than at Charleston. The real highlight of the property is the **garden**, with its beautiful views over the Ouse Valley, and paths weaving between overflowing borders.

When World War II broke out Virginia sank into one of the deep depressions that had afflicted her throughout her life. On March 28, 1941, she wrote a letter to Leonard – "We can't go through another of those terrible times" – and walked to the River Ouse, where she filled the pockets of her coat with stones and drowned herself.

Ditchling and around

The pretty, affluent village of **DITCHLING** lies eight miles west of Lewes at the foot of the Downs, overlooked by famed beauty spot **Ditchling Beacon** – one of the highest spots on the escarpment. Handsome half-timbered and tile-hung buildings cluster around the traffic-clogged crossroads at the centre of the village, with two great lunch spots, *The Bull* and *The Green Welly*, facing each other across the street. A few steps away, the village green is overlooked by the striking **Ditchling Museum of Art + Craft** and the chunky flint **church of St Margaret's**, where many of the artists featured in the museum are buried, amongst them Edward Johnston and Hilary Pepler.

Ditchling Museum of Art + Craft

Lodge Hill Lane, BN6 8SP • Tues–Sat 10.30am–5pm, Sun & bank hols 11am–5pm • £6.50 • ☏ 01273 844744, ⓦ ditchlingmuseumartcraft.org.uk

The small but beautiful **Ditching Museum of Art + Craft** houses a fascinating assortment of prints, paintings, weavings, sculptures and other artefacts created by the artists and craftspeople who lived in Ditchling in the last century, amongst them typographer and sculptor **Eric Gill**. Gill moved to Ditchling in 1907, and was later followed by like-minded artists and craftspeople, amongst them **Edward Johnston** (who designed the iconic London Underground font and roundel while living in the village), printer and writer Hilary Pepler, poet and painter David Jones, weaver Ethel Mairet and artist Frank Brangwyn. In 1920 Gill, Pepler and two others co-founded the **Guild of St Joseph and St Dominic**, an experimental Catholic community of artists and makers inspired by the Arts and Crafts movement – "a religious fraternity for those who make things with their hands" – with its own workshops, chapel and printing press on Ditchling Common just outside the village. Gill left Ditchling for Wales in 1924, but the Guild continued to flourish, only disbanding in 1989.

The museum's **permanent collection** includes small carvings and pencil drawings by Gill, paintings by David Jones – including a beautiful *Madonna and Child* set against a lowering Sussex landscape – and weavings by Ethel Mairet, her apprentice Valentine KilBride, and Hilary Bourne and Barbara Allen (who designed the textiles for the Royal Albert Hall in 1951). One room centres on Hilary Pepler's printing press which, as well as being a creative outlet, also functioned as the village's press, printing everything from beer labels to posters advertising productions by the Ditchling Dramatic Circle. Temporary **exhibitions**, changing every six months, feature contemporary commissions alongside objects loaned from other collections, plus there's a busy programme of **talks, events** and **workshops**.

Ridgeview Wine Estate

Fragbarrow Lane, Ditchling Common, off the B2112, BN6 8TP • **Cellar door** Daily 11am–4pm • **Tours** Run at weekends and occasional weekdays (check dates on website; pre-booking essential); 1hr 30min • £20 • ☎ 01444 241441, ⓦ ridgeview.co.uk

Just north of Ditchling, the **Ridgeview Wine Estate** has picked up a staggering array of trophies over the last ten years, including best sparkling wine in the world. Its sparkling whites and rosés – produced using traditional Champagne grape varieties and methods – are available nationwide, but it's much more fun to pitch up at the cellar door and taste before you buy. The vineyard also runs **tours** most weekends.

Ditchling Beacon

Towering above Ditchling village, 820ft-high **Ditchling Beacon** is one of the highest points in the South Downs, and from its breezy summit there are glorious views out over the patchwork of fields, copses and tiny villages of the Weald, to the hazy outline of the North Downs beyond. The summit gained its name from its warning beacon, one of a chain of bonfire sites across the Downs lit to warn of the Spanish Armada and other invasions.

ERIC GILL IN DITCHLING

One of the country's great twentieth-century artists, **Eric Gill** (1882–1940) is probably best known for his sans-serif **Gill Sans typeface**, which was famously used on the covers of the early Penguin books with their two coloured stripes. He was also a lauded sculptor, who revived the technique of direct carving in Britain and was a major influence on British sculptors such as Moore and Hepworth. His commissions included the *Stations of the Cross* at Westminster Cathedral, and *Prospero and Ariel* on the front of the BBC's Broadcasting House.

Gill was a complicated character. He was deeply **religious**, and had a horror of the twentieth century's mechanistic culture, despising everything that went with it, including typewriters, contraception, Bird's custard powder and the fashion for tight trousers that constricted "man's most precious ornament". Having moved with his wife to Ditchling in 1907 he relocated in 1913 to a run-down cottage outside the village, where he and his family lived in ascetic squalor, eschewing all modern conveniences and to all outward appearances living a life of pious simplicity.

Beneath the surface, however, Gill's family set-up was anything but wholesome. When his **biography** was published in 1989, he was revealed to be an incestuous polygamist, who regularly had sex not only with two of his sisters, but also with two of his daughters, not to mention the family dog. For Gill, sex was inseparable from his deeply held religious beliefs – he believed that "sexual intercourse is the very symbol for Christ's love for his church" – but whatever bizarre morality underpinned his actions, his reputation has never completely recovered.

6

A 1.5-mile lung-busting path leads up the hill from Ditchling village, or there's a car park at the summit, from where **trails** strike off in all directions; an easy 1.5-mile stroll westwards along the South Downs Way footpath brings you to the two **Clayton Windmills**, also known as Jack and Jill; the latter, a white wooden post mill built in 1821, is open to the public most Sunday afternoons in summer (normally May–Sept Sun 2–5pm, but check website; ⓦjillwindmill.org.uk). Continue along the South Downs Way for another 3.5 miles – past Saddlescombe Farm (see page 231) – to reach Devil's Dyke, just over the county border in West Sussex.

Devil's Dyke

One of the most-visited beauty spots in the South Downs, **Devil's Dyke** has been luring tourists for more than one hundred years. In its Victorian heyday it was a positive playground of new-fangled delights, featuring swingboats, a funicular, a single-track railway running from Hove, and most thrillingly of all, a cable car – the country's first – that took tourists across the 275m-wide Devil's Dyke valley. Thankfully, only the concrete footings of the cable car's pylons remain today.

The **views** from the grassy slopes of the summit, described by John Constable in 1824 as "the grandest view in the world", are really something special: the hill drops off steeply in front of you giving a stupendous panorama over the Weald and westwards along the grand sweep of the Downs.

The **Dyke** itself, a steep chasm on the north side of the escarpment, is often overlooked; it lies around the other side of the *Devil's Dyke* pub and a hundred yards back along the access road. The longest, widest and deepest chalk valley in the country, it was formed by melting water in the last Ice Age – or, if you're to believe local legend, dug by the Devil to allow the sea to flood in and drown the infuriatingly pious parishioners of the Weald. The Devil was only thwarted when an old lady, hearing a noise, lit a candle to investigate and the Devil fled, fearing the light was the rising sun.

ARRIVAL AND INFORMATION   DITCHLING AND AROUND

By train The nearest station is Hassocks (on the Brighton–London line), two miles away.

By bus From Brighton, Breeze up to the Downs buses run throughout the year: bus #77 to Ditchling Beacon (Sat, Sun and bank hols only; every 1hr–1hr 15min; 30min; £5 return) and bus #79 to Devil's Dyke (mid-June to Aug daily; rest of the year Sat, Sun and bank hols only; every 45min–1hr; 35min; £5 return).

On foot or by bike Both Ditchling Beacon and Devil's Dyke

are on the South Downs Way footpath, eight miles apart; if you're staying in Brighton you can use the Breeze up to the Downs buses (see page 210) to walk or cycle between the two. From Lewes it's a beautiful six-mile walk or cycle to Ditchling Beacon across the Downs.

By car There's free parking (2hr max stay) in Ditchling's village hall car park, and there are National Trust car parks at the summits of Ditchling Beacon and Devil's Dyke.

Website ⓦvisitditchling.co.uk.

ACCOMMODATION AND EATING

DITCHLING

The Bull 2 High St, BN6 8TA ☎01273 843147, ⓦthebullditchling.com. Splendid (and award-winning) sixteenth-century village inn, with beamed ceilings, huge fireplaces and the smell of wood smoke in the air. The menu changes daily, but mains (around £13–16) might include ale-battered cod or pork belly. Upstairs are eight stylish rooms with sleek en-suite bathrooms. Mon–Sat 8am–11pm, Sun 8am–10.30pm; kitchen Mon–Fri 8–11am, noon–2.30pm & 6–9.30pm, Sat & Sun 8–10.30am & noon–9/9.30pm. **£135**

★ **Green Welly** 1 High St, BN6 8SY ☎01273 841010, ⓦthegreenwellycafe.co.uk. Lovely little café with lashings of charm. All the food – soup, quiche, cakes, sandwiches and the like – is made on site in the open kitchen, and there's a pretty walled garden out the back. It's walker- and dog-friendly, too. Tues–Sun & bank hols 8.30am–4pm.

AROUND DITCHLING

★ **Blackberry Wood** Streat Lane, near Ditchling, BN6 8RS ☎01273 890035, ⓦblackberrywood.com. Book early if you want to get your hands on one of the twenty tent pitches at this fab campsite, each in its own secluded woodland glade, complete with fire pit. Elsewhere on the site, there's an eclectic range of accommodation including a fire engine, a double-decker bus, treehouses and a 1960s search-and-rescue helicopter. Camping/person $\overline{£17}$, fire engine $\overline{£115}$, bus $\overline{£109}$, helicopter $\overline{£99}$, treehouses $\overline{£245}$

Saddlescombe Farm Saddlescombe Rd, near Poynings, BN45 7DE ☏01273 857712 (camping), ☏01273 857062 (B&B), ⓦnationaltrust.org.uk/saddlescombe-farm-and-newtimber-hill. Right on the South Downs Way, National Trust-owned Saddlescombe Farm offers camping (backpackers only) April–Sept. Alternatively, the tenant farmers run a comfy B&B in the farmhouse, and stays can be combined with lambing open days and shepherd-for-the-day events. There's also a simple café on site. While you're at the farm check out the seventeenth-century donkey wheel – one of only four left in the Southeast. Camping/person $\overline{£5}$, B&B doubles $\overline{£85}$

6

Brighton

FAIRGROUND RIDES ON BRIGHTON PIER

Brighton

Sandwiched between the sea and the South Downs, Brighton (or Brighton & Hove, to give it its official name) is the jewel of the south coast – colourful and creative, quirky and cool. On a summer's day, with the tang of the sea in the air, the screech of seagulls overhead and the crowds of day-trippers streaming down to the beach, there's a real holiday feel to the city. Vibrant, friendly and tolerant, this is a city that knows how to have fun. The essence of Brighton's appeal is its bohemian vitality – a buzz that comes from its artists, writers, musicians and other creatives, its thriving LGBTQ community and an energetic local student population from the art college and two universities. Despite the middle-class gentrification that's transformed the city over the last decade or so, it still retains the appealingly seedy edge that led Keith Waterhouse to famously describe it as a town that always looks as if it's helping police with their enquiries.

A visit to Brighton inevitably begins with a visit to its most famous landmarks – the exuberant **Royal Pavilion** and the wonderfully tacky **Brighton Pier**, a few minutes away – followed by a stroll along the pebbly beach, lined with beachfront bars and shops, to the futuristic **i360**, the city's observation tower. Just as fun, though, is an unhurried meander around some of Brighton's distinct neighbourhoods: the car-free **Lanes**, a maze of narrow alleys marking the old town, crammed with restaurants, jewellery shops and boutiques; the more bohemian **North Laine**, where you'll find the city's greatest concentration of independent shops, and some fabulous cafés and coffee shops; **Kemp Town** village, the heart of Brighton's LGBTQ community, with antiques shops and some cool little cafés; and **Hove**, with its elegant beachfront.

Brighton's other great joy is its fantastically vibrant and eclectic **cultural life**. On any given night of the week there'll be live music, comedy, plays, concerts, talks and films, so whether you want to catch a big-name band in an intimate venue, a free acoustic gig in a pub, a string quartet in a concert hall, a subversive theatre production or a family-friendly mainstream show, you'll find something to entertain you. The city's packed **festival calendar** partly accounts for this, with festivals devoted to film, literature, music and comedy taking place throughout the year, as well as the Brighton Festival – the country's largest arts festival after Edinburgh – which runs for three weeks in May.

Brief history

Recorded as the tiny village of Brithelmeston in the Domesday Book, Brighton remained an undistinguished fishing town until the mid-eighteenth century, when the new trend for **sea bathing** established it as a resort. The fad received royal approval in the 1780s, after the decadent **Prince Regent** (the future George IV) began patronizing the town in the company of his mistress, thus setting a precedent for the "dirty weekend", Brighton's major contribution to the English collective consciousness. By the end of the 1700s the town was the most fashionable resort in the country, visited by the great and good of high society – though the arrival of the train in 1841 soon put paid to that, kickstarting mass tourism and a level of popularity with day-trippers from the capital that's continued unabated to this day.

KEMP TOWN

Highlights

❶ Royal Pavilion This extraordinary Oriental-style palace is the city's must-see sight, with jaw-dropping, no-expense-spared opulence. See page 236

❷ North Laine Brighton at its bohemian, buzzy best, heaving with hip coffee stops and quirky independent shops. See page 238

❸ British Airways i360 Get a bird's-eye view of the city from the futuristic viewing pod of the world's tallest moving observation tower. See page 241

❹ Brighton Festival and Fringe The biggest arts festival in England is an all-singing, all-dancing three-week culture-fest of art, dance, music, comedy and theatre. See page 246

❺ Beach sports Feel the sand between your toes at the beach volleyball courts, or brave the bracing English sea on a stand-up paddleboard or kayak. See page 247

❻ Eating out From Indian and Mexican street food to cutting-edge cooking showcasing the best of Sussex produce, Brighton's eating scene covers all budgets and tastes. See page 249

❼ Komedia You're spoilt for choice when it comes to nights out in the city, but make sure at least one of them is spent here, at this great arts venue that puts on comedy, cabaret, film, live music and club nights. See page 256

HIGHLIGHTS ARE MARKED ON THE MAP ON PAGE 236

Royal Pavilion and around

4/5 Pavilion Buildings • Daily: April–Sept 9.30am–5.45pm; Oct–March 10am–5.15pm; last entry 45min before closing • £15 (cheaper if bought online in advance), audio guides £2 or free if you use your mobile phone; Brighton Explorer Pass with British Airways i360 & Sea Life Brighton £36.50 (cheaper if bought online in advance); 3-day History Pass with Brighton Museum & Preston Manor £20 • ☏ 0300 029 0900, ⓦ brightonmuseums.org.uk/royalpavilion

In any survey to find Britain's most loved building, there's always a bucketful of votes for Brighton's exotic extravaganza, the **Royal Pavilion**, which flaunts itself in the middle of the Old Steine, the main thoroughfare along which most of the seafront-bound road traffic gets funnelled. Commissioned by the fun-loving **Prince Regent** (see page 238) in 1815, the Pavilion was the design of **John Nash**, architect of London's Regent Street. What Nash came up with was an extraordinary confection of slender minarets, twirling domes, pagodas, balconies and miscellaneous motifs imported from India and China, all supported on an innovative cast-iron frame, creating an exterior profile that defines a genre of its own – Oriental-Gothic.

Inside, one highlight – approached via the restrained Long Gallery – is the **Banqueting Room**, which erupts with ornate splendour and is dominated by a one-

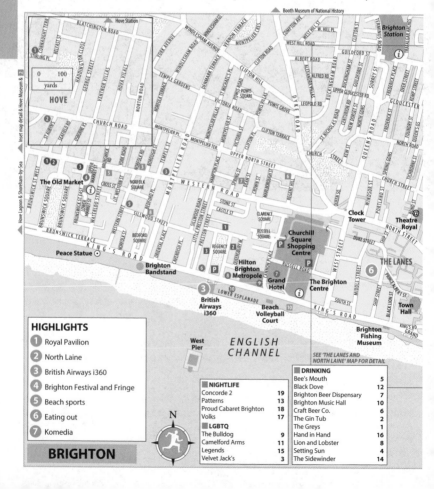

HIGHLIGHTS

1. Royal Pavilion
2. North Laine
3. British Airways i360
4. Brighton Festival and Fringe
5. Beach sports
6. Eating out
7. Komedia

BRIGHTON

NIGHTLIFE	
Concorde 2	19
Patterns	13
Proud Cabaret Brighton	4
Volks	17

LGBTQ	
The Bulldog	9
Camelford Arms	11
Legends	15
Velvet Jack's	3

DRINKING	
Bee's Mouth	5
Black Dove	12
Brighton Beer Dispensary	7
Brighton Music Hall	10
Craft Beer Co.	6
The Gin Tub	2
The Greys	1
Hand in Hand	16
Lion and Lobster	8
Setting Sun	4
The Sidewinder	14

SEE 'THE LANES AND NORTH LAINE' MAP FOR DETAIL

tonne chandelier hung from the jaws of a massive dragon cowering in a plantain tree. Next door, the huge, high-ceilinged **kitchen**, fitted with the most modern appliances of its time, has iron columns disguised as palm trees. The stunning **Music Room**, the first sight of which reduced George to tears of joy, has a huge dome lined with more than twenty-six thousand individually gilded scales and hung with exquisite umbrella-like glass lamps. After climbing the famous cast-iron staircase with its bamboo-look banisters, you can go into Victoria's sober and seldom-used bedroom and the **North-West Gallery** where the king's portrait hangs, along with a selection of satirical cartoons. More notable, though, is the **South Gallery**, decorated in sky-blue with trompe l'oeil bamboo trellises and a carpet that appears to be strewn with flowers.

Brighton Museum

Royal Pavilion Gardens, BN1 1EE • Tues–Sun & bank hols 10am–5pm • £6 (cheaper if bought online in advance), free to Brighton & Hove residents; 3-day History Pass with Royal Pavilion & Preston Manor £20 • ☎ 0300 029 0900, ⓦ brightonmuseums.org.uk/brighton

7

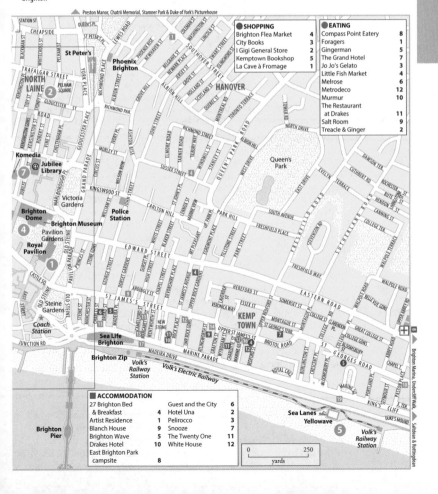

SHOPPING

Brighton Flea Market	4
City Books	3
I Gigi General Store	2
Kemptown Bookshop	5
La Cave à Fromage	1

EATING

Compass Point Eatery	8
Foragers	1
Gingerman	5
The Grand Hotel	7
Jo Jo's Gelato	3
Little Fish Market	4
Melrose	6
Metrodeco	12
Murmur	10
The Restaurant at Drakes	11
Salt Room	9
Treacle & Ginger	2

ACCOMMODATION

27 Brighton Bed & Breakfast	4	Guest and the City	6
Artist Residence	1	Hotel Una	2
Blanch House	9	Pelirocco	3
Brighton Wave	5	Snooze	7
Drakes Hotel	10	The Twenty One	11
East Brighton Park campsite	8	White House	12

0   250
yards

7

THE FIRST GENTLEMAN OF ENGLAND: GEORGE IV

Born on August 12, 1762, **George, Prince of Wales**, was the eldest son of George III and Queen Charlotte, and a constant source of disappointment to his straight-laced father. He was vain, indolent and profligate, with a life devoted almost entirely to pleasure – gambling, heavy drinking, dining, mistresses, racing and fine clothes.

George's love affair with Brighton started in 1783, when on the advice of his physicians he visited the small seaside town – by that stage already a popular health resort. He liked it so much that he rented a farmhouse, which he later transformed into a lavishly furnished villa. His presence over the next forty or so years was instrumental in the town's meteoric transformation into a fashionable and slightly racy "London by the sea". George had the time of his life there, building up unspeakably large debts (running to tens of millions of pounds in today's money), and spending his days in the pursuit of pleasure – promenading, horseriding, partying, and frolicking with his mistress, **Mrs Maria Fitzherbert**, whom he secretly – and illegally – married in 1785, and installed in a house on the west side of the Old Steine. A twice-widowed commoner, and Roman Catholic to boot, Fitzherbert couldn't have been a more unsuitable partner.

In 1795 George's disapproving father forced a marriage with **Princess Caroline of Brunswick**. It was not a success. Caroline had as much contempt for her portly husband as his father did, and George continued his dissolute lifestyle unrepentant, with the couple separating soon after the birth of their only child the following year.

In 1811, George became **Prince Regent** after his father was declared insane, and within a few years he hired John Nash to transform his villa into the extravagant palace that stands today. When his father died in 1820, he was crowned **King George IV** – by this time morbidly obese, suffering from gout and digestive problems, and frequently caricatured in the national press as being completely out of touch with a nation reeling from famine and unemployment in the aftermath of the Napoleonic Wars. When George died in 1830, aged 68, his passing was neatly summed up by *The Times*: "There never was an individual less regretted by his fellow-creatures than this deceased king."

Across the gardens from the Pavilion stands the wonderful **Brighton Museum**, which houses an eclectic mix of modern fashion and design, archeology, art and local history in a grand building that used to form part of the royal stable block.

Downstairs, the central hall houses the museum's collection of **twentieth-century art and design**, a procession of classic Art Deco, Art Nouveau and modern furniture that includes Dalí's famous sofa (1938) based on Mae West's lips. Across the hall the **Ancient Egypt** galleries contain some mummified animals and wonderful painted coffins from 945–715 BC, courtesy of famous Egyptologist – and Brightonian – Francis Llewellyn Griffith. Two other rooms on the ground floor take you through the **history of Brighton**, covering everything from the rise of the dirty weekend to the famous 1964 clash of the Mods and Rockers on Brighton seafront that inspired the film *Quadrophenia*. Upstairs are three **Fine Art** galleries, as well as a **Costume gallery** containing garments belonging to George IV, whose love of fashion (and his own appearance) led his wife to comment rather sniffily "I ought to have been the man and he the woman to wear petticoats."

Adjacent to the museum, and part of the same complex of buildings, is the town's main concert hall, **Brighton Dome** (see page 256).

North Laine

If you're looking for the Brighton that's bohemian, hip and slightly alternative, you'll find it in **North Laine**, which sprawls west and north of the Royal Pavilion as far as Trafalgar Street, bordered by Queens Road to the west and the A23 to the east. What used to be the city's slum area is now its most vibrant neighbourhood, packed with coffee shops and pavement cafés, cool boutiques and quirky independent shops

THE LANES AND NORTH LAINE

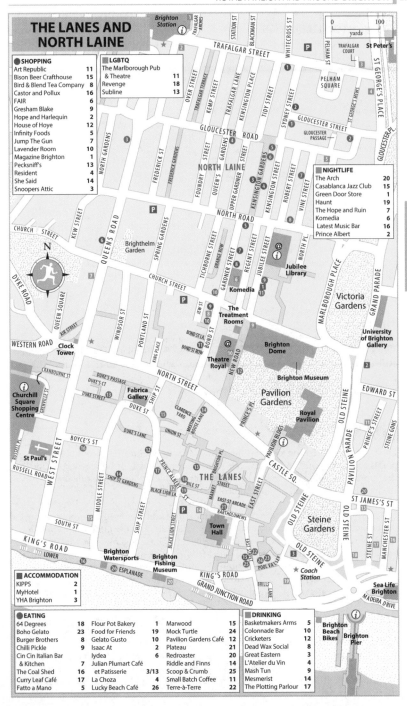

● SHOPPING

Art Republic	11
Bison Beer Crafthouse	15
Bird & Blend Tea Company	8
Castor and Pollux	16
FAIR	6
Gresham Blake	9
Hope and Harlequin	2
House of Hove	12
Infinity Foods	5
Jump The Gun	7
Lavender Room	10
Magazine Brighton	1
Pecksniff's	13
Resident	4
She Said	14
Snoopers Attic	3

■ LGBTQ

The Marlborough Pub & Theatre	11
Revenge	18
Subline	13

■ NIGHTLIFE

The Arch	20
Casablanca Jazz Club	15
Green Door Store	1
Haunt	19
The Hope and Ruin	7
Komedia	6
Latest Music Bar	16
Prince Albert	2

7

■ ACCOMMODATION

KIPPS	2
MyHotel	1
YHA Brighton	3

■ EATING

64 Degrees	18	Flour Pot Bakery	1	Marwood	15
Boho Gelato	23	Food for Friends	19	Mock Turtle	24
Burger Brothers	8	Gelato Gusto	10	Pavilion Gardens Café	12
Chilli Pickle	9	Isaac At	2	Plateau	21
Cin Cin Italian Bar		Iydea	6	Redroaster	20
& Kitchen	7	Julian Plumart Café		Riddle and Finns	14
The Coal Shed	16	et Patisserie	3/13	Scoop & Crumb	25
Curry Leaf Café	17	La Choza	4	Small Batch Coffee	11
Fatto a Mano	5	Lucky Beach Café	26	Terre-à-Terre	22

■ DRINKING

Basketmakers Arms	5
Colonnade Bar	10
Cricketers	12
Dead Wax Social	8
Great Eastern	3
L'Atelier du Vin	4
Mash Tun	9
Mesmerist	14
The Plotting Parlour	17

7

selling everything from vintage homeware and vinyl to mod clothing and manga comics. Several streets are pedestrianized, while others become temporarily car-free at the weekend, when the crowds descend en masse and café tables and stalls spill out onto the streets. The city's striking, state-of-the-art central **library** is also down this way, on Jubilee Square. The North Laine **website** (ⓦ northlaine.co.uk) features a downloadable map, as well as reasonably comprehensive listings for the many shops and eating places.

The Lanes

Tucked between the Pavilion and the seafront is a warren of narrow, pedestrianized alleyways known as **the Lanes** – the core of the old fishing village from which Brighton evolved. It's a great place to wander, with some excellent cafés and restaurants, and plenty of interesting independent shops and boutiques, including the long-established jeweller's shops for which the area's known.

The seafront

Every visitor to Brighton will find their way down to Brighton's **seafront** at some point, and in summer it certainly feels that way, with crowds of holidaymakers and Brightonians soaking up the sun in the beachfront cafés, or crunching their way over the pebbly beach to find an unoccupied spot.

The section of seafront between the two piers is where most of the action takes place. Here, down beneath the street-level prom with its distinctive turquoise-blue railings, the **Lower Esplanade** runs west from Brighton Pier along to the **i360** tower, lined for much of the way by bars, clubs, cafés, galleries and gift shops, many snuggled into the old redbrick **fishermen's arches**, and with stalls or tables out by the pebbles. The beach is quieter farther west, around Brighton's beautiful Victorian **bandstand** – the only one to survive of eight that once graced the seafront; during summer it puts on free Sunday afternoon concerts. Keep heading west and you'll soon reach **Hove Lawns** (see page 244).

East of Brighton Pier the beach is much quieter. The venerable **Volk's Railway** trundles along for a mile or so past the **Sea Lanes pool** to the **naturist beach** – the first public naturist beach in the country, and usually the preserve of just a few thick-skinned souls – and then on to Brighton Marina. Running parallel is Madeira Drive, end point for some of the city's biggest events, including the London to Brighton Bike Ride, the Veteran Car Run, the Brighton Marathon and the Burning the Clocks parade.

Brighton Pier

Madeira Drive, BN2 1TW • Daily 10am–10/11pm; opening hours can vary depending on weather • Free; various fees apply to rides • ☎ 01273 609361, Ⓦ brightonpier.co.uk

Every inch of kitsch, brash **Brighton Pier**, opened in 1899, is devoted to fun, from the side stalls and cacophonous amusement arcades to the kiosks selling bubblegum-pink candyfloss and striped Brighton Rock. The **fairground rides** at the end of the pier range from the traditional (helter-skelter, carousel and dodgems) to the downright terrifying (the Booster, which lifts you 40ft in the air, leaving you dangling over the sea).

Brighton Fishing Museum

201 King's Rd Arches, Lower Esplanade (at beach level), BN1 1NB • Normally daily 9.30am–5pm; opening hours can vary depending on weather • Free • Ⓦ brightonfishingmuseum.org.uk

The golden days of Brighton's local fishing industry are revisited at the **Brighton Fishing Museum**, which displays old photos, video footage and memorabilia, and houses a large Sussex clinker, a boat once common on Brighton beach. Before Brighton's rise as a fashionable resort it was the most important fishing town in Sussex, with four out of every five men working as fishermen. The rise of tourism led to the decline of the fishing fleet, with unsightly boats being removed from the fashionable Steine, leading some resourceful fishermen to turn to tourism instead, offering pleasure cruises or becoming dippers or bathers for Brighton's bathing machines.

British Airways i360

Lower King's Road, BN1 2LN • Open daily; hours vary so check website • £16.50 (cheaper if bought online in advance); Brighton Explorer Pass with Royal Pavilion & Sea Life Brighton £36.50 (cheaper if bought online in advance) • ☎ 0333 772 0360, Ⓦ britishairwaysi360.com

There's no missing Brighton's newest attraction, the **British Airways i360**: at 162m high, it's the world's tallest moving observation tower, and it dominates the skyline from its seafront site by the ruined West Pier (much to the disapproval of some locals). Designed by the architects of the London Eye, the i360 is essentially a pod on a pole: visitors board the gleaming, saucer-shaped pod – complete with champagne bar serving local fizz – and are whisked up for 360-degree views over the city and beyond. On a clear day the views, extending up to 26 miles, are great: inland to the South Downs, west as far as Chichester and east to the Seven Sisters cliffs and beyond. The whole experience is a bit pricey, given you're only aloft for fifteen minutes or so, but it's a fun one-off; just be sure to plan your visit around the weather.

At the bottom of the tower there's a restaurant, the *West Beach Bar & Kitchen*, and a tearoom housed in one of the restored nineteenth-century tollbooths that previously marked the entrance to the West Pier.

BEST OF BRIGHTON FOR KIDS

Brighton Pier Arcade games, stalls, scary rollercoasters and gentler rides – a sure-fire hit with most ages. See above

Yellowave This beach sports venue is a great spot for kids, and you can take an old electric train along the seafront to get to it. See page 247

Biking along the prom Rent bikes at the seafront and you can cycle for miles along the promenade; the quieter end around Hove Lawns is best for smaller cyclists. See page 246

Gelaterias Ice cream is bound to feature in your stay – just make sure it's from one of the city's top-notch *gelaterias*. See page 252

Komedia This brilliant, family-friendly venue has a regular programme of shows for kids. See page 256

West Pier

All that remains of the once-grand **West Pier** is a blackened skeleton, no longer connected to the mainland. Built in 1866 by Eugenius Birch, the pier was one of the finest in the country – and the first to be Grade I-listed – but after decades of neglect it was all but destroyed by storms and two separate fires in 2002 and 2003. Today the rusting carcass has become an iconic sight, especially in winter, when the skies above the pier are filled at dusk with swirling clouds of **starlings**.

Sea Life Brighton

Marine Parade, BN2 1TB • Daily 10am–4/5/6pm; last entry 1hr before closing • £15–19 depending on ticket type (cheaper if bought online in advance); Brighton Explorer Pass combined entry with Royal Pavilion & British Airways i360 £36.50 (cheaper if bought online in advance) • ☎ 01273 604234, ⓦ visitsealife.com/Brighton

Sea Life Brighton is the world's oldest operating aquarium, opened in 1872. The atmospheric main aquarium hall still looks largely as it would have done in Victorian times, lined with tanks and with a wonderful vaulted ceiling, and is the real star of the show. Elsewhere there's a short tunnel leading you through a tank populated by sharks and stately giant turtles, and a small, dark room of jellyfish floating mesmerically in glowing, colour-changing tubes. Talks and feeding sessions take place throughout the day.

Volk's Electric Railway

Madeira Drive, BN2 1EN • Easter–Oct Mon & Fri 11.30am–5.15pm, Tues–Thurs 10.30am–5.15pm, Sat & Sun 10.30am–6.15pm • £3.80, £4.90 return • ⓦ volksrailway.org.uk

Just east of Brighton Pier, the antiquated locomotives of **Volk's Electric Railway** – the first electric train in the country, dating back to 1883 – trundle from Aquarium Station eastward for just over a mile to Black Rock Station, by the Marina, stopping off halfway near the Yellowave beach sports venue and Sea Lanes open-air pool (see page 247). A visitor centre at Aquarium Station tells the history of the railway, which was built by **Magnus Volk**, a nineteenth-century inventor and engineer, who was also responsible for setting up the first telephone line in the city and installing its first electric lighting.

Brighton Marina

One mile east of Brighton Pier, BN2 5UF • ⓦ brightonmarina.co.uk • Bus #7; free parking

The antithesis of boho central Brighton, **Brighton Marina** – the largest in Europe – is a somewhat soulless sprawl of factory outlet shops and chain restaurants, with a cinema, bowling alley, indoor mini golf (ⓦ globalls.co.uk), casino and superstore. On a summer's day, however, it's pleasant to wander around, trying out the free ping pong and chess tables in Marina Square and finishing off with an alfresco lunch overlooking the bobbing, clanking boats. Various boat trip operators and **watersports** outfits operate out of the Marina (see page 247).

Kemp Town

East of the city centre, **Kemp Town** is the heart of the city's LGBTQ community and one of Brighton's liveliest, most colourful neighbourhoods. From the city centre, head along busy, bustling **St James's Street** (Brighton's "Gay Village"), which strikes off east from the Old Steine. St James's Street runs east to its quieter continuation, **St George's Road**, where you'll find a clutch of antique and vintage shops, delis, cosy pubs and laidback coffee shops. Here, you can't miss the elaborate copper dome of *Proud Cabaret*

THE UNDERCLIFF WALK

Built between 1928 and 1935 to provide sea defences for the crumbling cliffs, the **Undercliff Walk** stretches 3.5 miles from Brighton Marina east to Saltdean. It's one of Brighton's lesser-known treasures, and makes a wonderful day-trip from the city if combined with a wander around the pretty village of Rottingdean or a swim in Saltdean's Art Deco lido. The walk is lovely on a summer's day at low tide, when you can drop down to the beach to poke around the rockpools, but it's definitely best – and most exhilarating – in stormy weather, when at high tide the wind carries the spray right over the sea wall onto the promenade.

If you're walking the route in one direction, you can catch **buses** #12, #14 or #27 back to Brighton (every 10–15min) from bus stops on the coast road at Rottingdean or Saltdean.

ROTTINGDEAN

Two and a half miles along the Undercliff Walk you'll come to the Gap – a natural break in the cliffs, which allows access to the little village of **Rottingdean**. Cross over the busy coast road and head up the High Street to reach The Green, the picturesque, leafy hub of the village. It was here that Pre-Raphaelite painter **Edward Burne-Jones** and his nephew **Rudyard Kipling** both moved in the late nineteenth century: the Burne-Jones' former holiday house, North End House, sits on the western side, just a stone's throw from Kipling's house, The Elms, on the village green itself. Neither building is open to the public today, but you can wander through the peaceful flint-walled **Kipling's Gardens** (daily until dusk; free) beside his old home.

Kipling wrote many of his best-known works while in Rottingdean, including some of his *Just So* stories, but eventually he lost patience with tourists coming to gawp at him and removed himself to a more secluded haven at Bateman's near Burwash (see page 188). Burne-Jones remained in Rottingdean until his death in 1898 and is buried at the flint-walled thirteenth-century **church of St Margaret's** on the northeastern corner of The Green, which contains some wonderful **stained-glass windows** created by him in collaboration with William Morris. Just south past the duck pond the **Grange Museum and Gallery** (Tues–Sat 10.30am–4pm, Sun 2–4pm; ☎01273 301004, ⊕ rottingdeanpreservationsociety.org.uk), originally the vicarage, has plenty of material dedicated to its two famous residents.

SALTDEAN LIDO

A mile further on from Rottingdean, you'll come to **Saltdean** with its wonderful **Art Deco lido** (⊕ saltdeanlido.co.uk), open during the summer months. Designed by architect Richard Jones and opened in 1938, it's the only Grade-II listed lido in the country; the design – two curved wings swooping away from a main block topped by sun terraces – is intended to emulate the bridge of an ocean liner.

Brighton (see page 254), originally built as a **mausoleum** by Sir Albert Sassoon in 1892, in the same Oriental-Gothic style as the Pavilion. One can't help but wonder what the old baronet would make of the exotic burlesque supper clubs held under the dome today.

Farther east is **Sussex Square**, part of the grand **Kemp Town Estate** erected by the neighbourhood's namesake, Thomas Kemp, in the early nineteenth century. The author **Lewis Carroll** was a regular visitor to no.11, and it's said that the tunnel that runs down to the beach from the Estate's private gardens was the inspiration for the rabbit hole in *Alice in Wonderland*. If you're heading down to the beach yourself you can take the restored Victorian **Madeira Lift**, which will whisk you down from Marine Parade to the *Concorde 2* club, close to the Yellowave beach sports venue.

Hove

Although it forms a continuous conurbation with Brighton – and to most visitors' eyes is just another neighbourhood – **Hove** was, until quite recently, a completely separate town. It grew up as the resort of Brunswick Town in the 1820s, separated from Brighton by open fields, and it was only in 1997 that it was merged with its flashier neighbour to form the borough of Brighton and Hove, which achieved city status three years later.

Hove has always been rather protective of its separate identity: its tongue-in-cheek slogan, "Hove, actually", originates in the sniffy response of local residents to outsiders asking if they live in Brighton. It definitely has a calmer, less raffish air to it, with handsome Regency architecture around **Brunswick Square** and an elegant lawn-backed **seafront** – where the division between Brighton and Hove is marked by the **Peace Statue**. The wide grassy expanses of **Hove Lawns** start just beyond here, backed at their western end by a row of brightly coloured beach huts. Further west still is **Hove Lagoon**, one of the best places in the city to try out a new watersport (see page 247).

Hove Museum

19 New Church Rd, BN3 4AB • Mon, Tues & Thurs–Sat 10am–5pm, Sun & bank hols 2–5pm • Free • ☎ 0300 029 0900, ⓦ brightonmuseums.org.uk/hove • Buses #1, #1A, #6, #49 or #49A from North St or Churchill Square (20min)

Like its sister museum in Brighton, **Hove Museum** is a bit of an eclectic treasure-trove. Its single most prized possession is the 3500-year-old **Hove amber cup** – discovered nearby in 1856 and considered to be one of Britain's most important Bronze Age finds – but it's equally known for its wonderful **contemporary crafts collection**, one of the finest in the country, comprising over two hundred pieces of ceramics, textiles, metalwork and other crafts by local and international makers. You also shouldn't miss the **Film Galleries**, which record Hove's important role in the early silent film industry, and show some of the wonderful films made in a tiny six-seat cinema.

Elsewhere there's an interesting display on the **history and architecture** of Hove, with some great pictures of the earliest stages of development, with a ribbon of grand seafront crescents and squares backed by open fields. For kids, the **Wizard's Attic**, an imaginatively interactive room stuffed full of antique toys, is a sure-fire hit.

Out of the centre

Most of Brighton's sights are very central, but there are a few a little further afield that are well worth seeking out. Remember also that Brighton sits on the edge of some stunning countryside, and in a surprisingly short time you can be out of the city and soaking up glorious views at some of the loveliest spots in the South Downs National Park (see page 202).

Booth Museum of Natural History

194 Dyke Rd, BN1 5AA, 1 mile from the centre of town • Mon–Wed, Fri & Sat 10am–noon & 1.15–5pm, Sun 2–5pm • Free • ☎ 0300 029 0900, ⓦ brightonmuseums.org.uk/booth • Buses #14, #27

A half-hour walk from the city centre, the **Booth Museum of Natural History** is a wonderfully fusty old Victorian museum with beetles, birds, butterflies and animal skeletons galore. The museum was purpose-built by nineteenth-century natural historian and eccentric Edward Thomas Booth to house his prodigious collection of stuffed birds – one of the largest in the country. Rumour had it that Booth kept a locomotive under steam at Brighton station so that he could be ready to set off in pursuit of a rare species at a moment's notice. Booth's technique of mounting birds in a diorama of their natural habitat, rather than on a simple wooden perch, was completely new, and copied around the world.

BREEZE UP TO THE DOWNS

The year-round **Breeze up the Downs** bus service (ⓦ brighton-hove.gov.uk/breezebuses) connects the city to three nearby beauty spots in the South Downs National Park: Devil's Dyke (see page 230), Ditchling Beacon (see page 229) and Stanmer Park (see below) – all just a twenty-minute ride away from the centre of Brighton. Buses run at weekends and bank holidays throughout the year, with daily departures to Devil's Dyke in high summer. The Breeze Return ticket (£5) allows you to travel to one destination and return from another; the six-mile walk from Devil's Dyke to Ditchling Beacon is a splendid way to soak up some of the national park's finest scenery.

Preston Manor

Preston Drove, just off the A23, BN1 6SD • April–Sept Tues–Sat 10am–5pm, Sun 2–5pm • £7.40; 3-day History Pass with Royal Pavilion & Brighton Museum £20 • ☎ 0300 029 0900, ⓦ brightonmuseums.org.uk/prestonmanor • A 5min walk from Preston Park train station, or buses #5, #5A, #17, #40, #40X or #273

Two miles north of Brighton, pretty **Preston Manor** dates from 1738, though it was extensively remodelled in 1905 by the Stanford family, who lived there for 138 years before gifting it to the city of Brighton in 1932. Its series of period interiors engagingly evokes the life of the Edwardian gentry, from the servants' quarters downstairs to the luxury nursery upstairs; the Stanfords were ferocious entertainers, counting Queen Victoria's daughters and Rudyard Kipling among their regular visitors.

7

Chattri memorial

ⓦ chattri.org • Bus #5A runs to Old London Rd in Patcham (where there is also free parking), from where it's a 1-mile walk

On the outskirts of the city, up on the Downs and only accessible by footpath, the **Chattri memorial** commemorates the Indian soldiers who died during World War I. Around 12,000 wounded Indian soldiers were brought to Brighton for treatment – some ending up at the Royal Pavilion Hospital – and the 53 Hindus and Sikhs who died were cremated at this peaceful site. The simple marble memorial was erected in 1921.

Stanmer Park

Two miles from Brighton, off the A270 • Bus #78 (Sat, Sun & bank hols only) or buses #23 or #25

Covering around twenty square miles of woods and downland, sweeping **Stanmer Park** lies just within the South Downs National Park, and is a lovely place to escape the city, especially in spring when bluebells speckle the woods. One of the nicest walks – with buses back to Brighton at each end – is the three-mile stroll across to Ditchling Beacon (see page 229).

ARRIVAL AND DEPARTURE   **BRIGHTON**

BY TRAIN

Brighton station At the top of Queen's Rd, which descends to the Clocktower and then becomes West St, eventually leading to the seafront, a 10min walk away. Destinations Arundel (hourly; 1hr 10min); Bognor (every 30min; 45min); Chichester (2 hourly; 45–55min); Eastbourne (every 20min; 35min); Hastings (every 30min; 1hr 5min); Lewes (every 10–20min; 15min); Littlehampton (every 30min; 45min); London Bridge (Mon–Sat 2 hourly; 1hr); London Victoria (1–2 hourly; 55min); Shoreham-by-Sea (every 30min; 15min); Worthing (every 30min; 25min). **Hove station** At the top of Goldstone Villas; it's a 10min walk south along Goldstone Villas and then George St to reach Church Rd, the main drag. Destinations Chichester (1–2 hourly; 45min); Littlehampton (every 20min; 35–45min); London Victoria (1–2 hourly; 1hr 10min); Shoreham-by-Sea (every 10–15min; 10min); Worthing (every 10min; 15–20min).

7

BRIGHTON'S BEST FESTIVALS AND EVENTS

Scarcely a week passes in Brighton without a festival or event taking place. We've picked out some of the best below, but there are many more; check out ⓦvisitbrighton.com.

Brighton Festival ⓦbrightonfestival.org. One of Europe's leading arts festivals, taking place over three weeks in May, with a different Guest Artistic Director each year.

Brighton and Hove Fringe Festival ⓦbrightonfringe.org. Running at the same time as the Brighton Festival, this is one of the largest fringe festivals in the world, with over a thousand acts, from cabaret to club nights to comedy.

Artists Open Houses ⓦaoh.org.uk. Hundreds of artists around the city open up their houses and studios to the public in this biannual event (May & Nov/Dec).

Great Escape ⓦgreatescapefestival.com. Three-day music festival in May, showcasing the best new and up-and-coming local, national and international bands.

Paddle Round the Pier ⓦpaddleroundthepier.com. Weekend beach festival held in July, featuring watersports, live music and a pier-to-pier race.

London to Brighton Veteran Car Run ⓦveterancarrun.com. Taking place in early November on a Sunday, this long-established event (which first took place in 1896) sees hundreds of vintage vehicles – all built before 1905 – attempt the 60-mile run from the capital.

Burning the Clocks ⓦsamesky.co.uk/events/burning-the-clocks. To mark the winter solstice on December 21, hundreds of beautiful paper and willow lanterns are carried through the streets before being burnt on the beach.

BY BUS

The bus station is just in from the seafront on the south side of the Old Steine.

Destinations Arundel via Littlehampton (Mon–Sat every 30min, Sun hourly; 2hr); Chichester via Bognor, Littlehampton, Worthing & Shoreham-by-Sea (every 10min; 1hr 45min); Eastbourne (every 10–15min; 1hr 15min); Lewes (Mon–Sat every 10min, Sun every 30min; 30min); London Victoria (hourly; 2hr 20min).

BY CAR

The main A23 road into Brighton often suffers from traffic jams at weekends in summer, and once you're in the centre free on-street parking is non-existent, so it's best to avoid driving if you're just coming for the day. If you're staying overnight, most accommodation options can supply you with parking vouchers.

Park-and-ride Free at Withdean Sports Complex, north of the city centre (Tongdean Lane, BN1 5JD, signposted from the A23); bus #27 runs into town every 15min Mon–Sat, every 20min Sun. A City Saver bus ticket costs £5 (see below).

Parking Pay-and-display parking in central Brighton costs £3.60/hr, £6.20/2hr and £10.40/4hr (max stay). Seafront parking charges drop outside the central zone (east of Yellowave, and west of Hove Street), and allow longer stays (up to 11hr). The cheapest central long-stay multistorey car parks are Regency Square and Trafalgar St (both £18/24hr). Brighton and Hove Council's website ⓦbrighton-hove.gov.uk/content/parking-and-travel/journeyon has a useful car parking map.

GETTING AROUND

BY BUS

Most of the city is walkable, but buses can be useful for west Hove and some further-flung sights. The City Saver ticket gives you one day's unlimited travel in the city for £5. Short-hop journeys cost £2.

BY TAXI

The main taxi ranks are at Brighton and Hove stations, East St, Queens Square near the Clock Tower, outside St Peter's church and outside Hove Town Hall.

Brighton and Hove Streamline Taxis ☎01273 202020.
Brighton and Hove Radio cabs ☎01273 204060.

BY BIKE

There's a downloadable cycling map of the city at ⓦbrightonandhovecyclemap.com; a cycle path runs the length of Brighton seafront, meeting up just east of the Marina with the Undercliff Walk (see page 243) – note that cyclists must give way to pedestrians here. Bike tours are also available (see page 247). The two most central bike hire outlets are:

Brighton Cycle Hire Unit 8, under the station, off Trafalgar St (Mon–Fri 9am–5pm, Sat, Sun & bank hols 10am–4pm; ☎01273 571555, ⓦbrightoncyclehire.com). Bikes cost £7/3hr, £10/24hr.

Brighton Beach Bikes 250 King's Rd Arches, west side of Brighton Pier (daily 10.30am–6pm; ☎07917 753794, ⓦbrightonbeachbikes.co.uk). Californian beach-cruiser-type bikes cost £12/3hr, £16/4hr or longer.

INFORMATION

Tourist office There are fourteen staffed visitor information points throughout the city (☎ 01273 290337, ⓦ visitbrighton.com), including at the train station, the Royal Pavilion Shop, Brighton Pier, Jubilee Library and Churchill Square. Opening times vary; see the website for a full list.

Listings magazines and websites The best listings magazine is *Source Magazine* (ⓦ brightonsource.co.uk), but *XYZ* (ⓦ xyzmagazine.co.uk) and *BN1* (ⓦ bn1magazine.co.uk) are also worth a look. Viva Brighton (ⓦ vivabrighton.com) is a monthly magazine of articles and reviews, with covers designed by local artists, distributed free around the city and also available online.

ACTIVITIES

BEACH SPORTS

★ Yellowave Beach Sports Venue 299 Madeira Drive, BN2 1EN ☎ 01273 672222, ⓦ yellowave.co.uk. The country's only year-round beach sports venue is a brilliant spot, with six sand courts offering volleyball (courts and ball £24/hr; beginners' classes £6.50) and other beach sports. Even if you don't want to play it's a great place to hang out, with a sandpit to keep youngsters happy, and a great café with plenty of tables outside. March–Oct Mon & Fri–Sun 10am–8pm, Tues–Thurs 10am–10pm; Nov–Feb Tues–Thurs 10am–9pm, Fri–Sun 10am–5pm.

Lower Esplanade beach volleyball ☎ 01273 292716. There's a council-run beach volleyball court on the Lower Esplanade between the piers. Pre-booking is required April–Sept (£26/hr, or £18/hr before noon Mon–Fri); the rest of year it is free for anyone to use. April–Sept daily 10am–6pm; Oct–March daily open access.

WATERSPORTS

Brighton Watersports 185 King's Rd Arches, on the Lower Esplanade, BN1 1NB ☎ 01273 323160, ⓦ thebrightonwatersports.co.uk. Right down by the pebbles, this well-established outfit offers stand-up paddleboarding (board rental £15/hr; 2hr 30min introductory lesson £45), wakeboarding (30min; £45) and kayak rental (£15/person/hr).

Lagoon Watersports Hove Lagoon, BN3 4LX ☎ 01273 424842, ⓦ lagoon.co.uk/hove-lagoon. This sheltered beachfront lagoon offers windsurfing (3hr taster £75); stand-up paddleboarding (2hr taster £55); and wakeboarding (1hr taster £45). Their sailing school based at Brighton Marina offers longer dinghy sailing courses and high-speed powerboat rides (30min; £37.50).

OPEN-AIR POOLS AND LIDOS

Saltdean Lido The Oval Park, Saltdean Park Rd, Saltdean, BN2 8SP ☎ 01273 069984, ⓦ saltdeanlido.org. Wonderful Art Deco lido in Saltdean, 3 miles east of Brighton Marina (buses #12, #14 and #47; 25min). Tickets cost £7.90, or £12 all day, and can be pre-booked online. June Mon & Fri–Sun 7am–7pm; July to mid-Sept Mon, Wed & Fri–Sun 7am–7pm, Tues & Thurs 9am–9pm.

Sea Lanes Madeira Drive, BN2 1EN ⓦ sealanesbrighton.co.uk. This open-air, heated 25m swimming pool, at the

---

CITY TOURS

In addition to the recommended tours below, you can take advantage of the **Brighton Greeters** scheme, which pairs up visitors with a volunteer Brighton resident tour guide for a free two-hour tour; see ⓦ visitbrighton.com/greeters for more information.

The Grand Brighton Bike Tour ☎ 07914 786843, ⓦ brightonbiketour.com. A fun 2hr 30min tour of the city by bike (£22.50); morning and afternoon tours available.

Brighton City Walks ☎ 07941 256148, ⓦ brightoncitywalks.com. This 1hr 30min traditional tour of the city runs most days; the price depends on the number of people on the tour.

Ghost Walk of the Lanes ☎ 01273 328297, ⓦ ghostwalkbrighton.co.uk. Fun (and family-friendly) ghost walks around Brighton's atmospheric Lanes, visiting eight apparently haunted sites (Wed–Sat; 1hr 10min; £8).

Only in Brighton ☎ 07954 482112, ⓦ onlyinbrighton.co.uk. Equally popular with locals and visitors, this quirky tour (April–Oct Fri & Sat; 1hr 30min; £10) answers all the important questions about Brighton life: how did a song performed at the Brighton Dome help trigger the Portuguese Revolution? Why did the Prince Regent need a stiff brandy when he met his future wife? And just what connects Mount Everest and the Hove branch of Tesco? The same guide runs "Piers and Queers" tours, exploring the city's LGBTQ history, and a tour of the Lanes (check website for dates; prices vary).

Sightseeing bus Hop-on, hop-off buses run around the city's main sights (April–Oct daily 10am–5pm, every 1hr; 1hr for whole circuit; £14, valid 24hr; ⓦ city-sightseeing.com).

eastern end of the seafront next to the Yellowave Beach Sports Venue, is scheduled to open in 2020.

ZIP WIRE

Brighton Zip Madeira Drive, BN2 1EN, just east of the pier ☎01273 671405, ⊕brightonzip.com. One of Brighton's newest attractions, with a 300m-long twin zipline along the seafront (£16) plus the Drop Zone, a 17m freefall drop (£9.50). Daily 10am–late in summer, weather-dependent; reduced hours in winter.

BOAT TRIPS

Ross Boat Watertours Pontoon 5, West Jetty, Brighton Marina, BN2 5WA ☎07958 246414 & ☎07836 262717, ⊕rossboats.co.uk. Mackerel fishing trips (March–Nov; 1hr 30min; £22), powerboat rides (25min; £20) and sea cruises (45min; £9.50).

SIGHTSEEING FLIGHTS

Brighton Scenic Shoreham Airport, Shoreham-by-Sea, BN43 5FF ☎07918 902721, ⊕brightonscenic.co.uk.

Scenic flights in a four-seater aircraft. Lots of options, from a short city flight (30min; £82), to a longer tour that takes you over the Downs and along the coast (1hr 30min; £169).

WINE-TASTING

Great British Wine Tours ☎01273 278474, ⊕greatbritishwinetours.co.uk. Minibus tours (£89) of two or three Sussex vineyards, leaving from Brighton, including tutored wine-tastings, lunch and a vineyard tour.

SPA TREATMENTS

Brighton HARSpa Kings Road, BN1 1NA ☎01273 323221, ⊕harbourhotels.co.uk/brighton. Atmospheric subterranean spa housed in old smugglers' tunnels beneath the seafront *Brighton Harbour Hotel*, featuring a heated indoor pool, sauna, steam room, hot tubs, hydrotherapy pool and gym. Half-day and day passes are available.

The Treatment Rooms 21 New Road, BN1 1UF ☎01273 818444, ⊕thetreatmentrooms.co.uk. Aromatherapy, facials, wraps and other treatments, for both men and women.

ACCOMMODATION

SEE MAPS PAGES 236 AND 239

Accommodation is pricey in Brighton. The prices we give are weekend, high-season rates, but if you're visiting out of summer – especially during the week – these rates can fall dramatically, so it pays to check out a few options online. Year-round, you'll be required to stay a minimum of two nights at the weekend. Some of the nicest, most characterful B&Bs are in **Kemp Town**, on the eastern side of the city; with some excellent cafés, restaurants and antique shops up at the "village" end of Kemp Town, this can be a great place to base yourself.

CENTRAL BRIGHTON

★ **Artist Residence** 33 Regency Square, BN1 2GG ☎01273 324302, ⊕artistresidencebrighton.co.uk. Characterful, cool and quirky, this uber-stylish 23-room townhouse hotel sits at the top end of a seafront square overlooking the i360. Rooms are individually decorated – some of them by local and international artists – plus there's a buzzy cocktail bar, *The Fix*, and a very good restaurant. **£165**

Hotel Una 55/56 Regency Square, BN1 2FF ☎01273 820464, ⊕hotel-una.co.uk. One of the city's best hotels, with a splendid location on one of Brighton's prettiest seafront squares, and seventeen beautiful, luxurious high-ceilinged rooms, all named after rivers and featuring bespoke furniture and contemporary artwork. The most expensive rooms come with their own sauna or whirlpool bath. **£160**

KIPPS 76 Grand Parade, BN2 9JA ☎01273 604182, ⊕kipps-brighton.com. This hostel – an antidote to the party hostels of Brighton – feels more like a small

hotel, and has an unbeatable location opposite the Royal Pavilion. Rooms and dorms are plain but comfy, plus there's a licensed bar and excellent-value breakfasts (£2.50 for dorms, included for rooms). Dorms **£22.50**, doubles **£72**

MyHotel 17 Jubilee St, BN1 1GE ☎01273 900300, ⊕myhotels.com/my-hotel-brighton. This hip, fun contemporary hotel has a great location, right in the heart of North Laine, and incorporates not only one of the city's best restaurants, *Chilli Pickle*, but also one of its best coffee shops, *The Small Batch Coffee Co*. The rooms have been designed along feng shui lines, so you'll find curved walls inset with crystals, vibrant colour and spiritual artwork. Rates vary according to demand, and can drop as low as £75 out of peak times, so check online for bargains. **£130**

★ **Pelirocco** 10 Regency Square, BN1 2FG ☎01273 327055, ⊕hotelpelirocco.co.uk. "England's most rock'n'roll hotel" is a real one-off, featuring extravagantly themed rooms inspired by pop culture and pin-ups. There's a Pop Art "Modrophenia" room featuring bedside tables made from scooters, a cosy "Do Knit Disturb" room created by a Brighton knitwear/crochet artist, and the decadent "Lover's Lair" suite that comes with a circular bed with a mirrored canopy and a pole-dancing pole in the corner of the room. **£135**

★ **YHA Brighton** Old Steine, BN1 1NH ☎01273 738674, ⊕yha.org.uk/hostel/brighton. The cheapest sea views in Brighton can be found at the stylish YHA hostel, less than a minute's walk from the pier. All of the 51 rooms (including twenty doubles – the smartest of them with roll-top baths) are en suite, and there's a lovely café-bar. Prices drop dramatically mid-week and out of season; book well ahead for weekend stays. Breakfast not included. Dorm **£35**, double **£109**

KEMP TOWN

★ **27 Brighton Bed & Breakfast** 27 Upper Rock Gardens, BN2 1QE ☎01273 694951, ⓦbrighton-bed-and-breakfast.co.uk. The five rooms at this Georgian townhouse B&B – each of them named after someone or something associated with the Prince Regent – are beautifully elegant, featuring old-fashioned brass beds, antiques and Chinese-inspired furnishings, and the hosts couldn't be more welcoming. Decanters of sherry in the rooms are one of many lovely touches. **£120**

Blanch House 17 Atlingworth St, BN2 1PL ☎01273 603504, ⓦblanchhouse.co.uk. Brighton's original boutique hotel is still going strong, with a mix of styles and prices across its twelve chic rooms. The high-ceilinged champagne and cocktail bar down on the ground floor makes a perfect start to a night on the town. **£150**

Brighton Wave 10 Madeira Place, BN2 1TN ☎01273 676794, ⓦbrightonwave.com. This friendly B&B has a lovely relaxed feel, with a bright and cheery breakfast room that features art for sale on the walls and fairy lights in the fireplaces. Rooms are smart and contemporary, with en-suite showers, and welcome extra touches include a large DVD library and breakfast served late at weekends. **£130**

Drakes Hotel 33–34 Marine Parade, BN2 1PE ☎01273 696934, ⓦdrakesofbrighton.com. The seafront location is the big draw at this chic, minimalist boutique hotel, which boasts the best sea views in town: the most expensive rooms come with freestanding baths by floor-to-ceiling windows looking out over the twinkling lights of the pier. The excellent in-house restaurant (see above) is one of Brighton's best. **£160**

East Brighton Park campsite Wilson Ave, BN2 5TS ☎01273 626546, ⓦexperiencefreedom.co.uk. Brighton's leafy campsite lies a mile or so inland from Brighton Marina (take bus #1 or #1A from the centre to Wilson Ave), on the far side of Kemp Town, a 40min walk from the city centre. The site is mainly for caravans, but there are eighty tent pitches and camping pods. Camping **£30**, pods **£60**

★ **Guest and the City** 2 Broad St, BN2 1TJ ☎01273 698289, ⓦguestandthecity.co.uk. A great central location, super-friendly hosts and stylish rooms. If you want to treat yourself, spend a bit more to bag one of the two rooms (£160) with stained-glass windows of classic Brighton scenes and a covered balconette. **£90**

★ **Snooze** 25 St George's Terrace, BN2 1JJ ☎01273 605797, ⓦsnoozebrighton.com. This cool B&B in the heart of Kemp Town is crammed with fun touches, including a graffiti-style re-creation of the Sistine Chapel in the breakfast room. The six en-suite rooms are styled with a hotchpotch of retro furnishings, plus there are two uber-cool 1970s-style suites. **£125**

★ **The Twenty One** 21 Charlotte St, BN2 1AG ☎01273 686450, ⓦthetwentyone.co.uk. This Regency townhouse is a super-friendly home from home, with stylish rooms – chandeliers, fluffy cushions and cream linens – immaculate bathrooms, a DVD library, iPads, bathrobes and a well-stocked hospitality tray. The lovely owners and their attention to detail make it very popular. **£155**

White House 6 Bedford St, BN2 1AN ☎01273 626266, ⓦwhitehousebrighton.com. Set back from the road slightly, and facing south, this lovely townhouse B&B seems flooded with light. The eight serene rooms are impeccably tasteful, and those at the front even boast that elusive thing in Brighton – a proper sea view. **£140**

EATING

SEE MAPS PAGES 236 AND 239

As you'd expect from cool, cosmopolitan "London-by-the-sea", there's a thriving café culture in Brighton, with hip little cafés and **coffee shops** sprouting up all over the city, but especially concentrated around the lively North Laine area; Brighton consumes more coffee than anywhere else in the UK (the city even has its own coffee festival – ⓦbrightoncoffeefest.com), and sitting over a coffee and watching Brighton life go by is an essential box to tick on any trip to the city. Brighton also boasts the greatest concentration of **restaurants** in the Southeast after London, among them some highly rated fine-dining options and some long-established gems including, appropriately enough for a town that embraced lentils and tofu long before they became mainstream, two of the country's best vegetarian restaurants. If you're visiting on a Friday, be sure to check out **Street Diner** (ⓦstreetdiner.co.uk), a weekly open-air street food market held in Brighthelm Garden, a couple of minutes' walk from the station (11am–3pm).

THE SEAFRONT

CAFÉS, SNACKS AND AFTERNOON TEA

Compass Point Eatery 127A King's Rd, BN1 2FA ☎01273 672672, ⓦcpeatery.com. Welcoming, laidback café decked out with American memorabilia and with an American-inspired menu featuring burgers (£14), old-fashioned milkshakes, cocktails and a fine selection of buttermilk pancakes. Mon–Sat 9am–late, Sun 9.30am–5pm.

The Grand Hotel 97–99 King's Rd, BN1 2FW ☎01273 224300, ⓦgrandbrighton.co.uk. With its elegant lounge and peerless sea views, you really can't beat afternoon tea (£29.95) at *The Grand*, Brighton's iconic seafront hotel. Two sittings daily at 2.30pm & 4.30pm, plus 12.30pm on Sat & Sun.

Lucky Beach Café 171 King's Rd Arches, BN1 1NB ☎01273 728280, ⓦluckybeach.co.uk. Popular beach café, with lots of outdoor seating and a great menu of

7

7

BEST PLACES FOR...

Afternoon tea *The Grand Hotel* (see page 249), *Metrodeco* (see page 252), *Terre-à-Terre* (see page 251).

Treating yourself *64 Degrees* (see page 250), *Gingerman* (see page 250), *Isaac At* (see page 251), *Little Fish Market* (see page 252), *The Restaurant at Drakes* (see below), *Salt Room* (see below).

Veggies and vegans *Food for Friends* (see page 251), *Iydea* (see page 252), *Terre-à-Terre* (see page 251).

burgers made from organic beef (£9), fish landed in Brighton, sandwiches and local beers. Excellent coffee too, as you'd expect from the sister café to the *Redroaster* roastery. Mon–Fri from 8.45am, Sat & Sun from 8am; closing times vary depending on season and weather.

RESTAURANTS

Melrose 132 King's Rd, BN1 2HH ☎01273 326520, ⓦmelroserestaurant.co.uk. Along with the *Regency* next door, this traditional seafront establishment is a bit of a Brighton institution – it's been dishing up tasty, excellent-value fish and chips (£8.75), seafood platters, roasts and custard-covered puddings for more than forty years. Daily 11.30am–10.30pm.

Murmur 91–96 King's Rd Arches, BN1 2FN ☎01273 711900, ⓦmurmur-restaurant.co.uk. Sister restaurant to the award-winning *64 Degrees*, this casual seafront restaurant is set right on the beach, overlooking the ruined West Pier – its name comes from the spectacular starling murmurations that can be seen here in the winter. The menu features the likes of Harissa lamb and roast cod (mains £14–18), and there's plenty of seating outside on the terrace. Mon–Thurs noon–4pm & 5.30–9pm, Fri & Sat noon–4pm & 5.30–9.30pm, Sun noon–4pm.

The Restaurant at Drakes 33–34 Marine Parade, BN2 1PE ☎01273 696934, ⓦdrakesofbrighton.com/restaurant. The stylish restaurant in the basement of one of the city's best hotels is an absolute winner (two courses £37). Arrive early if you can, for a pre-dinner drink in the cocktail bar with its lovely sea views. Daily noon–2pm & 6–9pm.

Salt Room 106 King's Rd, BN1 2FU ☎01273 929488, ⓦsaltroom-restaurant.co.uk. One of the city's best fish and seafood restaurants, with a stylish exposed-brick interior, peerless sea views and fantastic charcoal-grilled fish and seafood (mains £20 and up). Make sure you leave room for the "Taste of the Pier" dessert, a fun confection of candyfloss, ice-cream cones, doughnuts and chocolate pebbles. Mon–Thurs & sun noon–4pm & 6–10pm, Fri & Sat noon–4pm & 6–10.30pm.

CITY CENTRE

Gingerman 21a Norfolk Square, BN1 2PD ☎01273 326688, ⓦgingermanrestaurant.com. You can't spend long in Brighton without stumbling on one of the foodie outposts of the Ginger empire – there's a *Ginger Pig* in Hove, a *Ginger Dog* in Kemp Town and a *Ginger Fox* in nearby Albourne – but this one-room restaurant was where it all started. Chic and minimalist, it still serves up some of the best food in Brighton: a three-course dinner will set you back £45, just over half that at lunchtime. Tues–Sun 12.30–2pm & 7–10pm.

THE LANES

CAFÉS AND COFFEESHOPS

Marwood 52 Ship St, BN1 1AF ☎01273 382063, ⓦthemarwood.com. A real one-off, this quirky coffee shop's eclectic, cluttered decor includes Action Men abseiling from the ceiling and a stuffed cat mounted on the wall. Stop by for a coffee or a cocktail and soak up the quintessentially Brighton vibe. Mon 8am–7pm, Tues–Sat 8am–11pm, Sat 9am–11pm, Sun 10am–7pm.

Mock Turtle 4 Pool Valley ☎01273 327380. If you're after an antidote to Brighton's hip coffee shops, look no further than this old-fashioned teashop, which has been here for donkey's years and is always packed. The traditional menu offers loose-leaf teas, inexpensive homemade cakes, giant doughnuts filled with homemade jam and cream teas featuring amply proportioned scones, served warm with lashings of cream. Daily 9am–6pm.

RESTAURANTS

★ **64 Degrees** 53 Meeting House Lane, BN1 1HB ☎01273 770115, ⓦ64degrees.co.uk. This pocket-sized restaurant in the Lanes is one of the best places to eat in the city. The seats to go for are up at the counter of the open kitchen: choose several small plates of food (£8–19) to share from the short menu, which features four options each of fish, veg and meat dishes (example dish: "pig head, corn, mustard"). The food's inventive and delicious, and the whole experience is brilliant fun. Mon–Thurs & Sun noon–2.45pm & 6–9.15pm, Fri & Sat noon–2.45pm & 6–9.45pm.

The Coal Shed 8 Boyces St, BN1 1AN ☎01273 322998, ⓦcoalshed-restaurant.co.uk. Seriously good steak, aged for 35 days and cooked on a charcoal grill, is the main draw here, though the fish is equally good (mains £13–28). Worth a special mention are the Sunday sharing roasts (£40 for 2 people): a 500g sirloin presented on a platter with all the trimmings. Mon–Thurs & Sun noon–4pm & 6–10pm, Fri & Sat noon–4pm & 6–10.30pm.

★ **Curry Leaf Café** 60 Ship St, BN1 1AE ☎01273 207070, ⓦcurryleafcafe.com. Delicious South Indian street food in the heart of the Lanes; tuck into masala dosas, thalis and street food platters at lunch, or more formal mains (£14/15) in the evening. Craft beers and delicious cocktails are added bonuses. Mon–Thurs noon–3pm & 6–10pm, Fri & Sat noon–3pm & 6–10.30pm, Sun 1–9pm.

Food for Friends 18 Prince Albert St, BN1 1HF ☎01273 202310, ⊛foodforfriends.com. Brighton's original veggie restaurant has been going strong since 1981, and its sophisticated cooking is imaginative enough to please die-hard meat-eaters too. Mains around £15. Mon–Thurs & Sun 9am–10pm, Fri & Sat 9am–10.30pm.

Plateau 1 Bartholomews, BN1 1HG ☎01273 733085, ⊛plateaubrighton.co.uk. "Wine, beats and bites" is the tagline of this buzzy little restaurant-cum-wine bar. Sharing platters and small bites (£7/8) run alongside a good range of cocktails, organic beers and organic and biodynamic wines (some from Sussex producers). Daily noon–late; kitchen noon–3.30pm & 6–10pm.

Riddle and Finns 12b Meeting House Lane, BN1 1HB ☎01273 328008; ⊛riddleandfinns.co.uk. This bustling champagne and oyster bar is justifiably popular. There's a huge range of fish and shellfish on offer, served on communal marble-topped tables in a white-tiled candelit dining room. No bookings. Mon–Fri & Sun noon–10pm, Sat 11.30am–11pm.

★ **Terre-à-Terre** 71 East St, BN1 1HQ ☎01273 729051, ⊛terreaterre.co.uk. One of the country's best vegetarian restaurants, this multi-award-winning place is famed for its inventive cuisine (mains around £17). The taster tapas plate for two (£35) is a good way to sample some of the weird and wonderful creations on offer, everything from Sneaky Peeking Steamers to Better Batter and Lemony Yemeni Relish. Daily noon–10pm.

NORTH LAINE

CAFÉS AND COFFEESHOPS

Flour Pot Bakery 40 Sydney St, BN1 4EP ☎01273 621942, ⊛flour-pot.co.uk. Tuck into crumbly pastries, cakes and sandwiches made with artisan bread at this hip bakery/café, with bench seating in the bare-brick interior and more tables outside. Further branches of the Brighton-based chain are scattered around the city. Mon–Sat 8am–6pm, Sun 9am–5pm.

Julian Plumart Café et Patisserie 48 Queens Rd, BN1 3XB ☎01273 777412, ⊛julienplumart.com. This little French patisserie showcases the glorious creations of chef Julien Plumart – trained by Raymond Blanc. Choose from exquisite tarts, classic pastries or jewel-like macarons, which come in over a dozen flavours (£1.65 each). There's a separate shop and *salon de thé* on Duke St. Mon–Fri 7.30am–7pm, Sat & Sun 8.30am–7pm.

Pavilion Gardens Café Royal Pavilion Gardens, BN1 1UG ☎01273 730712, ⊛paviliongardenscafe.co.uk.

Run by the Sewell family ever since it opened back in 1941, this no-frills café serves up sandwiches, jacket potatoes and legendary rock cakes from its idyllic location in Pavilion Gardens. All seating is outside. Hours weather dependent; closed in winter.

Small Batch Coffee 17 Jubilee St, BN1 1GE ☎01273 697597, ⊛smallbatchcoffee.co.uk. This Brighton-based coffee chain, with its own roastery in Hove, has seven branches around the city but the sleek flagship shop is here, in the ground floor of *MyHotel*. Coffee lovers can choose from espresso, cold-brew (brewed for five hours to create a delicate flavour), pour-over (filter), or a brewed coffee at the syphon bar. Beans change seasonally. Mon–Sat 7am–7pm, Sun 8am–6pm.

RESTAURANTS

Burger Brothers 97 North Rd, BN1 1YE ☎01273 706980, ⊛facebook.com/burgerbrothersbrighton. "Strictly burgers, no chips!" reads the sign at this independent no-frills burger joint, whose offerings – from the Simple Jack (£5) to the Benetton burger with stilton, wasabi mayo, Portobello mushrooms and a choice of charcuterie (£9.50) – have won a string of awards. There are a few seats but it's mainly takeaway. Tues–Sat noon–9pm.

★ **Chilli Pickle** 17 Jubilee St, BN1 1GE ☎01273 900383, ⊛thechillipickle.com. You really can't go wrong with a meal at this fantastic, award-winning restaurant. From thalis (£16) to tandoori platters to street food, everything on the menu is innovative and delicious. Mon & Tues noon–3pm & 6–10pm, Wed–Fri noon–3pm & 6–10.30pm, Sat 12.30–10.30pm, Sun 12.30–9.30pm.

Cin Cin Italian Bar and Kitchen 13–16 Vine St, BN1 4AG ☎01273 698813, ⊛cincin.co.uk. This tiny Italian restaurant, housed in a former garage, has just twenty seats set around a counter surrounding the bar and open kitchen. The menu is equally tiny, but everything on it is delicious: authentic homemade pasta (£12–14) and small plates of *arancino*, *burrata* and Italian *salumi*. Tues–Sat noon–3.30pm & 6–11pm.

Fatto a Mano 25 Gloucester Rd, BN1 4AQ ☎01273 693221, ⊛fattoamanopizza.com. The pillowy-soft Neapolitan-style pizza (£7–10) that comes out of the wood-fired oven at this family-run pizzeria is arguably the best in the city. There are other branches in Hove and on London Rd. Mon–Thurs noon–10pm, Fri & Sat noon–10.30pm, Sun noon–9.30pm.

Isaac At 2 Gloucester St, BN1 4EW ☎07765 934740, ⊛isaac-at.com. A unique fine-dining experience: choose the seven-course (£60) or the four-course (£40) menu, with optional alcohol or Sussex juice pairings (£30/25 respectively). The food – inspired by Sussex and all sourced locally – is prepared in front of you in the open kitchen, and

7

GLORIOUS GELATO

Happily for ice-cream lovers, Brighton has a handful of top-class *gelaterias*.

Boho Gelato 6 Pool Valley, BN1 1NJ ☎01273 727205, ⓦbohogelato.co.uk. Weird and wonderful flavours abound (Gorgonzola and rosemary, anyone?) at this tiny hole-in-the-wall place. There's another branch nearby on Ship St. Daily 11am–6pm.

Gelato Gusto 2 Gardner St, BN1 1UP ☎01273 673402, ⓦgelatogusto.com. *Sorbettos* and ice creams to eat in or take away, plus fabulous sundaes, waffles and crepes. Mon–Fri 11.30am–6pm, Sat & Sun 11am–6pm.

Jo Jo's Gelato 123–124 Western Rd, ☎01273 771532, ⓦjojosgelato.co.uk. Big, bright and beautiful, with a massive selection of gelato (over fifty flavours), and long opening hours. Daily 8am–11pm.

Scoop & Crumb 5–6 East St, BN1 1HP ☎01273 202563, ⓦscoopcrumb.com. Sundaes (more than fifty of them) are the big draw here, but you can also tuck into waffles, hot dogs and toasties. Mon–Fri 11am–6pm, Sat & Sun 10am–6.30pm.

---

served to guests by the chefs. Tues–Fri 6.30–10.30pm, Sat 12.30–2.30pm & 6.30–10.30pm.

★ **Iydea** 17 Kensington Gardens, BN1 4AL ☎01273 667992, ⓦiydea.co.uk. Good value, wholesome and delicious veggie and vegan food served up cafeteria-style. What's on offer changes every day, but there tends to be a quiche, a lasagne, a curry and enchiladas, alongside half a dozen other dishes; pick one main, add two vegetable dishes or salads and two toppings, and you're away (from £4.70). Daily 9.30am–5.30pm; lunch served Mon–Thurs & Sun noon–4pm, Fri & Sat 11.30am–5pm.

La Choza 36 Gloucester Rd, BN1 4AQ ☎01273 945926, ⓦlachoza.co.uk. Fun and flamboyant Mexican street-food restaurant, with great-value food: snacks such as deep-fried jalapeños or calamari with chipotle mayo cost £5–6; more filling burritos, quesadillas and tostadas are around £9. Mon 11.30am–4pm, Tues–Sun 11.30am–10pm.

HOVE

Foragers 3 Stirling Place, BN3 3YU ☎01273 733134, ⓦtheforagershove.co.uk. Relaxed and unpretentious, this gastropub serves up seasonal, sustainable food, with meat and fish sourced from Sussex and Kent suppliers. Mains are around £12–15. The Sunday roasts (including vegetarian/vegan options) are particularly recommended. Daily noon–late.

★ **Little Fish Market** 10 Upper Market St, BN3 1AS ☎01273 722213, ⓦthelittlefishmarket.co.uk. This exceptionally good fish restaurant, set in a converted fishmonger's, isn't cheap (all that's on offer is a multi-course

set menu for £69) but it gets rave reviews and is well worth it for a special occasion. It only serves twenty diners a night, so book ahead, especially at weekends. Tues–Sat 7–9pm.

Treacle & Ginger 164 Church Rd, BN3 2DL ☎01273 933695, ⓦtreacleandginger.com. Lovely little café with a simple menu (Welsh rarebit, pies, sandwiches and the like, in the £7–8 range) and good homemade cakes and tarts. Mon–Fri 9am–5pm, Sat & Sun 9.30am–5pm.

KEMP TOWN

CAFÉS AND COFFEESHOPS

Metrodeco 38 Upper St James's St, BN2 1JN ⓦmetrodeco.com. Choose from over twenty blends of tea at this 1930s Parisian-style tearoom, which also has a good selection of boutique gins and tea cocktails – served in teapots, of course. The afternoon teas (£23.50), served on vintage crockery, are a real treat. Mon–Thurs & Sun 11am–6pm, Fri & Sat 9.30am–8pm.

Redroaster 1d St James's St, BN2 1RE ☎01273 686668, ⓦredroaster.co.uk. This beautifully revamped place serves great coffee (as you'd expect of one of Brighton's first independent coffee houses, with its own roastery) alongside upmarket brunches and lunches. In the evenings, it switches coffee for cocktails and transforms into *Lucky Khao* restaurant, dishing up northern Thai BBQ food. Coffeeshop Mon–Sat 7am–5pm, Sun 8am–5pm; Lucky Khao restaurant Tues–Thurs 5–11pm, Fri & Sat 4pm–midnight.

DRINKING

Brighton has an illustrious history of catering to drinkers and partygoers: in 1860 the town boasted 479 **pubs** and **beer shops** – more than the combined number of all the other local shops. Though drinking establishments no longer make up the majority of the town's businesses, the perfect venue and tipple can still be found for all comers, from traditional boozers to indie hangouts, and sleek and chic **cocktail bars**.

SEE MAPS PAGES 236 AND 239

THE SEAFRONT

Brighton Music Hall 127 King's Rd Arches, BN1 2FN ☎01273 747287, ⓦbrightonmusichall.co.uk. The main draw of this bar is the fantastic location, right on the beach with a huge open-air heated terrace, and free live music when the sun shines. Hours vary but generally summer daily 9/10am–late; winter most days from noon – call ahead to check.

CITY CENTRE

Brighton Beer Dispensary 38 Dean St, BN1 3EG ☎01273 710624, ⓦfacebook.com/BRTNDispensary. This appealingly down-to-earth pub has a regularly changing selection of nine keg beers, six cask beers and three ciders, including offerings from the city's own Brighton Bier. Daily noon–late.

★ **Craft Beer Co.** 22–23 Upper North St, BN1 3FG ⓦthecraftbeerco.com. A must for beer aficionados, this pub boasts an incredible range of nine cask ales changing daily, eighteen keg taps dispensing beer from around the world, and two hundred bottled varieties on offer at any one time. Staff are super friendly and keen to talk about the beers, and they offer free tasters. Mon 4–11pm, Tues–Thurs noon–11pm, Fri & Sat noon–1am, Sun noon–10.30pm.

★ **Lion and Lobster** 24 Sillwood St, BN1 2PS ☎01273 327299, ⓦthelionandlobster.co.uk. One of the best pubs in Brighton, the *Lion and Lobster* has a traditional feel – patterned carpet, velvet seats and framed prints and pictures – but a young and fun atmosphere. Though usually busy, various booths offer privacy. Pub quiz on Mon nights, and regular live music. Good food is served until late. Mon–Thurs 11am–1am, Fri & Sat 11am–2am, Sun noon–midnight.

Mesmerist 1–3 Prince Albert St, BN1 1HE ☎ 01273 328542, ⓦmesmerist.pub. Describing itself as "a twenty-first-century gin palace", this large, welcoming and perennially popular bar attracts a diverse clientele, and has a good range of cocktails plus live music events (from jazz to burlesque) during the week. Daily noon–late.

★ **The Plotting Parlour** 6 Steine St, BN2 1TE ☎01273 621238, ⓦtheplottingparlour-brighton.co.uk. This dimly lit, snug cocktail bar is a real treat, with inventive cocktails (£9 and up), table service and stylish decor that includes flip-up cinema seats and copper-clad walls. Mon–Thurs & Sun 3pm–midnight, Fri & Sat 3pm–1am.

THE LANES

Colonnade Bar 10 New Rd, BN1 1UF ☎01273 328728, ⓦthecolonnadebrighton.co.uk. Right next to the Theatre Royal, the *Colonnade Bar* has an appropriately traditional feel, with plenty of tasselled velvet, and black-and-white headshots of actors who have graced the boards next door. Mon–Thurs noon–11pm, Fri & Sat noon–1am, Sun noon–10.30pm.

Cricketers 15 Black Lion St, BN1 1ND ☎01273 329472, ⓦcricketersbrighton.co.uk. Brighton's oldest pub – all red velvet and gilt – was immortalized in Graham Greene's *Brighton Rock*, and remains an old favourite. Mon & Tues 11am–11pm, Wed & Thurs 11am–midnight, Fri & Sat 11am–2am, Sun noon–10.30pm.

Mash Tun 1 Church St, BN1 1UE ☎01273 684951, ⓦmashtun.pub. This very popular studenty pub is often

heaving, particularly at the weekend. The inside is fairly basic, but cool tunes, trendy bar staff and a "celebrity wall of death" sweepstake contribute to the young and lively atmosphere. It serves great burgers, too. Mon–Wed & Sun noon–2am, Thurs–Sat noon–3am.

NORTH LAINE

★ **Basketmakers Arms** 12 Gloucester Rd, BN1 4AD ☎01273 689006, ⓦbasket-makers-brighton.co.uk. A cosy, traditional boozer, serving a wide selection of real ales, craft lagers and whisky. The only downside is that the pub is more popular than it is spacious; at the weekend it can be difficult to find a seat. Mon–Thurs 11am–11pm, Fri & Sat 11am–midnight, Sun noon–11pm.

Dead Wax Social 18a Bond St, BN1 1RD ☎01273 683844, ⓦdeadwaxsocial.pub. Vinyl, craft beer and crispy sourdough pizzas are the USPs of this cavernous bar. Every evening DJs play some of the bar's five thousand-strong vinyl collection – or you can bring your own along. Mon–Wed & Sun noon–2am, Thurs–Sat noon–3am.

Great Eastern 103 Trafalgar St, BN1 4ER ☎01273 685681. This cosy, candlelit pub at the bottom of Trafalgar St eschews TV screens and fruit machines in favour of bookshelves stocked with well-thumbed books and board games. The craft ales and impressive array of whiskies on offer make it a local fave. Daily noon–midnight.

L'Atelier du Vin ☎01273 622519. Low lighting and jazz set the mood at this cosy, prohibition era-themed wine and cocktail bar. The "bootlegger bar" offers drinkers the city's biggest selection of wines (some 800) and champagnes (200) alongside a classically inspired cocktail list. Daily noon–late.

HOVE

Bee's Mouth 10 Western Rd, BN3 1AE ☎01273 770083, ⓦfacebook.com/beesmouth123. Stepping into this dimly lit, surreal pub is a little like falling down the rabbit hole. The pub descends three floors and the subterranean levels host life-drawing classes and a diverse schedule of live music (particularly jazz) and DJs. A fantastic range of bottled beers, too. Mon–Thurs 4.30pm–12.30am, Fri 4.30pm–1.30am, Sat 2pm–1.30am, Sun 3.30pm–12.30am.

The Gin Tub 16 Church Rd, BN3 2FL ☎01273 772194, ⓦthegintub.co.uk. Gin is the main event at this Hove cocktail bar (it stocks more than a hundred), and the fun Gin Slider boards (a selection of four different gins in taster-sized glasses) is the best way to sample them. A Faraday cage installed around the bar prohibits the use of mobiles (a move intended to "bring back the art of conversation") and orders are placed using the old-style phones set on each table, which can also be used by braver souls to call other tables. Mon–Thurs & Sun 4pm–late, Fri & Sat 1pm–late.

7

KEMP TOWN AND HANOVER

Black Dove 74 St James's St, BN2 1PA ☎ 01273 671119, ⓦ blackdovebrighton.com. This trendy, justifiably popular bar at the top of St James's St has a cool, speakeasy vibe, with lots of dark wood and antiques, plus a decent cocktail list and a wide selection of bottled beers and ciders. Live acoustic music throughout the week. Daily 4pm–late.

The Greys 105 Southover St, BN2 9US ☎ 01273 232615, ⓦ thegreysfreehouse.co.uk. There seems to be a pub on every street in this part of Hanover, but *The Greys* is particularly nice, with a chilled-out atmosphere, cosy decor and a good selection of beer and bottled cider, plus regular live music. The Sunday roasts are pretty good, too. Mon–Fri 4pm–midnight, Sat noon–1am, Sun noon–11pm.

Hand in Hand 33 Upper St James's St, BN2 1JN ☎ 01273 699595, ⓦ handbrewpub.com. This tiny, eccentric brewpub is the downstairs room of a yellow-and-red building which also houses the Hand Brew Co brewery (established in 1989). The ale made upstairs is sold downstairs, along with a wide selection of other interesting beers. Mon–Sat noon–midnight, Sun noon–11pm.

Setting Sun 1 Windmill St, BN2 0GN ☎ 01273 230778, ⓦ thesettingsunpub.co.uk. The name of this hilltop pub sums up what makes it such a popular destination, in spite of the hike required to reach it. It has fantastic views over Brighton – particularly impressive at sunset – which can be enjoyed from the decking in warm weather or from the conservatory in winter. There's also good-value food. Daily noon–late.

The Sidewinder 65 St James's St, BN2 1JN ☎ 01273 679927, ⓦ sidewinder.pub. This large, comfortable pub has a lot going for it, not least the two enormous beer gardens. During the day the atmosphere is relaxed, while at weekends the pub hosts DJs. Mon–Thurs & Sun noon–midnight, Fri & Sat noon–2am.

NIGHTLIFE

SEE MAPS PAGES 236 AND 239

Brighton is renowned for its vibrant nightlife, which, reflecting the city's personality, comes in various flavours. From the kiss-me-quick, stag and hen, messy hedonism of West St, right through to a flourishing alternative and live music scene, the party never stops. Although there's plenty of dependable, mainstream clubbing to be had, some of the more interesting nights are in smaller, quirkier venues. Note that, while the following listings have been split into "Clubs" and "Live music", there's a lot of crossover between the two.

CLUBS

The Arch 187–193 King's Rd Arches, BN1 1NB ☎ 01273 208133, ⓦ thearch.club. The first-rate sound and lighting system at this mid-sized seafront club no doubt helps its pulling power, frequently attracting big-name DJs, particularly at weekends. The programming is balanced between emerging talent and big-name DJs and live performers. Drinks prices are moderate.

Casablanca Jazz Club 3 Middle St, BN1 1AL ☎ 01273 321817, ⓦ casablancajazzclub.com. Established in 1980, this Brighton stalwart has ensured its longevity with a dependable mix of jazz, funk, Latin and disco, washed down with cheap drinks. Head downstairs for live bands and to salsa 'til you sweat.

★ **Green Door Store** Trafalgar Arches, Lower Goods Yard, BN1 4FQ ⓦ thegreendoorstore.co.uk. Hip young things dance the night away in this uber-cool club and live music venue in the arches under the train station. Bare brickwork and an alternative array of music that covers anything from psych, blues, punk and rock 'n' roll to powerdisco make it eye-wateringly trendy but still good fun. Best of all, the bar is always free entry.

Haunt 10 Pool Valley, BN1 1NJ ⓦ thehauntbrighton. co.uk. Set in a converted cinema, this club and music venue is a great space, with a dancefloor and raised stage overlooked by a balcony. Club nights are on-trend electro and indie, and retro 80s and 90s. Also regularly hosts up-and-coming live acts.

★ **Komedia** 44–47 Gardner St, BN1 1UN ☎ 0845 293 8480, ⓦ komedia.co.uk/brighton. This top-notch arts venue (see page 256) also hosts live music and fun, unpretentious and frequently retro-themed club nights, playing rock 'n' roll, 60s and alternative 80s. Devoted punters of all ages turn up in era-appropriate attire.

Patterns 10 Marine Parade, BN2 1TL ☎ 01273 894777, ⓦ patternsbrighton.com. Trendy seafront venue set on two floors. Watch the sunset from the laidback terrace and soak up the LA vibes, then move downstairs to the basement club. The range of club nights is broad but specializes in electronic music and attracts internationally renowned DJs, including a residency from Horsemeat Disco.

★ **Proud Cabaret Brighton** 83 St Georges Rd, BN2 1EF ☎ 01273 605789, ⓦ proudcabaretbrighton.com. Evenings at this decadent burlesque and cabaret venue kick off with dinner and a show, before the tables are cleared away for dancing. Dinner, show and club £45 (Fri), £60 (Fri).

Volks 3 The Colonnade, Madeira Drive, BN2 1PS ☎ 01273 682828, ⓦ volksclub.co.uk. This small, long-running club peddles all things bass, with a schedule chock-full of dubstep, drum 'n' bass, reggae, jungle and breaks. The venue is appropriately dark and sweaty, and has some of the latest opening hours of any Brighton club, often keeping the party going until 7am.

7

LIVE MUSIC

★ **Concorde 2** Madeira Shelter Hall, Madeira Drive, BN2 1EN ☎ 01273 673311, ⓦ concorde2.co.uk. It's worth the walk along the seafront to get to this slightly out-of-the-way live venue and club. Housed in a high-ceilinged Victorian building, it feels intimate but not cramped, and has a much better atmosphere than the city's larger live venues. The line-up ranges from big-name acts (The White Stripes, Kaiser Chiefs and Florence + the Machine have all played here) to up-and-coming musicians and varied club nights.

The Hope and Ruin 11 Queens Rd, BN1 3WA ☎ 01273 325793, ⓦ hope.pub. This cool indie music pub is modelled on Budapest's famous ruin bars, making it the only pub in Brighton with a caravan and a (purposefully) broken piano inside. Upstairs, the 150-capacity venue showcases mainly rock and indie bands, with weekend club nights. There's a great range of craft beers.

Latest Music Bar 14–17 Manchester Street, BN2 1TF ☎ 01273 687171, ⓦ latestmusicbar.co.uk. Housed over two floors of a beautiful listed building, this little venue has played host to everyone from Amy Winehouse to the Kooks over the years. Gigs and other events (comedy, spoken word and more) take place in the intimate setting of the downstairs cabaret bar, decorated with fairy lights and 3D rooftop scenes from an old West End stage set.

Prince Albert 48 Trafalgar St, BN1 4ED ☎ 01273 730499, ⓦ facebook.com/ThePrinceAlbert. A Brighton institution, this pub-cum-music venue is immediately recognizable from the Banksy kissing policemen (a replica, after the original was sold) and graffiti portrait commemorating John Peel emblazoned on the building's side wall. The ground floor is a spacious pub, while upstairs a small venue hosts alternative live acts of various stripes.

ENTERTAINMENT

CINEMA

★ **Duke of York's Picturehouse** Preston Circus, BN1 4NA ☎ 0871 704 2056, ⓦ picturehouses.com/cinema/Duke_Of_Yorks. Grade II-listed cinema – one of the oldest still-functioning cinemas in the country, opened in 1910 – with buckets of character, velvet seats and a licensed bar. The programme is a great mix of arthouse, independent and classic films, alongside live-streamed opera and ballet, all-nighters and themed evenings. If you don't want to trek out to Preston Circus, there's always Dukes at Komedia, its sister cinema in North Laine (see below).

THEATRE, COMEDY AND CABERET

B·O·A·T Dyke Road Park, Hove BN3 6EH ⓦ brighton openairtheatre.co.uk. The Brighton Open Air Theatre operates from May to Sept and hosts national touring productions, local theatre and some music, comedy, screenings and spoken-word events.

Brighton Dome 29 New Rd, BN1 1UG ☎ 01273 709709, ⓦ brightondome.org. The Royal Pavilion's former stables is home to three venues – Pavilion Theatre, Concert Hall and Corn Exchange – offering theatre, concerts, dance and performance.

The Dance Space Circus St ☎ 01273 696844, ⓦ south eastdance.org.uk. Part of the Circus Street regeneration project, just off Grand Parade, The Dance Space is due to open in 2020 and will provide a permanent home for South East Dance. The building will incorporate performance space, too – check the South East Dance website for the latest.

★ **Komedia** 44–47 Gardner St, BN1 1UN ☎ 0845 293 8480, ⓦ komedia.co.uk/brighton. A Brighton institution set across three floors, this fantastic arts venue hosts comedy and cabaret, as well as live music and club nights. The Duke of York's cinema (see above) has three screens upstairs.

The Marlborough Pub & Theatre 4 Princes St, BN2 1RD ☎ 01273 273870, ⓦ marlboroughtheatre.org.uk. This sixty-seat venue specializes in provocative and unusual LGBTQ theatre, music, comedy and spoken word events.

The Old Market (TOM) 11a Upper Market St, BN3 1AS ☎ 01273 201801, ⓦ theoldmarket.com. Theatre, comedy and live music all feature on the programme of this stylish performing arts venue on the border of Hove.

Rialto Theatre 11 Dyke Road, BN1 3FE ☎ 01273 725230, ⓦ rialtotheatre.co.uk. Theatre, comedy and cabaret in a Grade II-listed building; the main space is upstairs, plus there's a less formal studio bar downstairs.

Theatre Royal New Rd, BN1 1SD ☎ 01273 764400, ⓦ atgtickets.com/venues/theatre-royal-brighton. One of the oldest working theatres in the country, offering predominantly mainstream plays, opera and musicals.

SHOPPING

SEE MAPS PAGES 236 AND 239

Brighton's a great shopping destination, with plenty of interesting independent shops. The places to head for are the **Lanes** and (especially) **North Laine** (ⓦ northlaine. co.uk), though for antiques shops you'll need to head out to **Kemp Town**, where a wander along the main street – which changes name from Upper St James's St to Bristol Rd to St Georges Rd – will uncover lots of gems. For work by some of Brighton's thriving population of artists and makers, there are galleries scattered throughout town but the best – and most fun – time to buy is during the biannual **Artists Open Houses** events (May & Dec; ⓦ aoh.org.uk), when you can visit the artists in their homes. Brighton's high-street chains are around **Churchill Square**, with higher-end chains concentrated on and around **East St** at the bottom end of the Lanes.

THE SEAFRONT

Castor and Pollux 165 King's Rd Arches, Lower Promenade, BN1 1NB ☎01273 773776, ⓦfacebook. com/castorandpolluxart. This great beachfront gallery sells limited edition prints (by Rob Ryan and others), alongside posters, art and design books, jewellery, pottery, stationery and more. Daily 10am–5pm.

THE LANES AND AROUND

Bison Beer Crafthouse 7 East St, BN1 1HP ☎01273 809027; 57 Church Rd, Hove, BN3 2BD ☎01273 774266; ⓦbisonbeer.co.uk. Independent bottle shop stocking over 350 craft beers from around the world, including their own small batch beers. There's a second branch (with attached bar) in Hove. East St Mon–Thurs 11am–7pm, Fri & Sat 11am–8pm, Sun 11am–6pm; Church Rd Mon & Tues 4–11pm, Wed & Thurs noon–11pm, Fri & Sat noon–midnight, Sun noon–10pm.

House of Hoye 22a Ship St, BN1 1AD ☎0845 094 3175, ⓦjeremy-hoye.co.uk. A favourite of the fashion press, contemporary jeweller Jeremy Hoye's creations include silver charms featuring Brighton landmarks (£65). Mon–Fri 10am–6pm.

Pecksniff's 45–46 Meeting House Lane, BN1 1HB ☎01273 723292, ⓦpecksniffs.com. Brighton's very own independent fragrance house, which has been creating its own upmarket perfumes and bespoke blends for over 25 years. Its perfumes and body products (made in the upstairs laboratory) make great gifts. Mon–Sat 10am–5pm, Sun 10.30am–4pm.

She Said 12 Ship St Gardens, BN1 1AJ ☎01273 777811, ⓦshesaidboutique.com. As you'd expect from the home of the dirty weekend, Brighton has its fair share of erotic emporiums, but this one is a touch above the rest: it's even been featured in *Vogue*. The ground floor is largely devoted to undies and corsets, with the saucier stuff kept downstairs. Mon–Wed 10am–6pm, Thurs–Sat 10.30am–6.30pm, Sun 11.30am–5.30pm.

NORTH LAINE AND AROUND

Art Republic 13 Bond St, BN1 1RD ☎01273 724829, ⓦartrepublic.com. Limited-edition prints from both local and big-name artists, plus open-edition museum prints and poster art. Mon–Fri 9.30am–6pm, Sat 9am–6pm, Sun 11am–6pm.

Bird & Blend Tea Company 41 Gardner St, BN1 1UN ☎01273 325523, ⓦbirdandblendtea.com. Award-winning tea mixology company, selling a huge variety of fine leaf teas (over 70) from Gingerbread Chai

and Rooibos Earl Grey to Enchanted Narnia (with Turkish Delight) and Brighton Rock (with mint). Mon–Thurs 10.30am–6.30pm, Fri 10.30am–6pm, Sat 10am–7pm, Sun 11am–5.30pm.

FAIR 21 Queen's Rd, BN1 3XA ☎01273 723215, ⓦthe fairshop.co.uk. A pioneer in ethical fashion, this boutique stocks the big-name ethical fashion brands, plus fairtrade homeware, jewellery and more. Mon & Tues 10am–5pm, Wed–Sat 10am–6pm, Sun noon–5pm.

Gresham Blake 20 Bond St, BN1 1RD ☎01273 609587, ⓦgreshamblake.com. Bespoke tailoring, made-to-measure and ready-to-wear suits, plus a range of eye-catching ties and bright shirts, at this hip contemporary designer-tailor. Mon–Thurs & Sat 10am–6pm, Fri 10.30am–6pm, Sun 11am–5pm.

Hope and Harlequin 31 Sydney St, BN1 4EP ☎01273 675222, ⓦhopeandharlequin.com. Beautifully presented vintage shop stocking clothing and modern collectables from the late 1800s to the 1970s, though it's especially strong on the 1930s and 1940s. Mon & Wed–Sat 10.30am–6pm, Tues & Sun 11am–5pm.

Infinity Foods 25 North Rd, BN1 1YA ☎01273 603563, ⓦinfinityfoodsretail.coop. This organic vegetarian and vegan store – run as a workers' cooperative – has been going for over forty years, and sells seasonal fruit and veg, fresh bread, natural bodycare products and more. Mon–Sat 9.30am–6pm, Sun 11am–5pm.

Jump The Gun 36 Gardner St, BN1 1UN ☎01273 626333, ⓦjumpthegun.co.uk. This much-loved gentleman's outfitters – often with a moped parked outside – has been selling mod and early Sixties clothing (parkas, shirts, suits, T-shirts and button badges) for over twenty years. Mon–Sat 10am–6pm, Sun 11am–5pm.

Lavender Room 16 Bond St, BN1 1RD ☎01273 220380, ⓦlavender-room.co.uk. There's a bit of a boudoir vibe at this pretty boutique; inside you'll find fragrances, bath oils, lingerie, silk robes, jewellery and vintage-inspired home accessories. Mon–Sat 10am–6pm, Sun 11am–5pm.

Magazine Brighton 22 Trafalgar St, BN1 4EQ ☎01273 687968, ⓦmagazinebrighton.com. Cool, Scandi-styled North Laine shop selling an eclectic selection of more than 200 indie magazines, on everything from travel, crafts and sport to food, fashion and feminism. Mon–Fri 11am–5pm, Sat 10am–6pm, Sun noon–4pm.

Resident 28 Kensington Gardens, BN1 4AL ☎01273 606312, ⓦresident-music.com. This award-winning independent record shop often has limited editions and indie exclusives, and also sells tickets for local venues. Mon–Sat 9am–6.30pm, Sun 10am–6pm.

★**Snoopers Attic** 1st floor of Snooper's Paradise, 7–8 Kensington Gardens, BN1 4AL ☎01273 945898, ⓦsnoopersattic.co.uk. Run by a cooperative of over a dozen designers, makers and vintage collectors, this attic space is crammed full of vintage and handmade treasures

7

7

– clothes, jewellery, hats, homewares and textiles. Downstairs, the stalls of Snooper's Paradise are a treasure trove of eclectic bric-a-brac. Mon–Sat 10am–6pm, Sun 11am–4pm.

HOVE

★ **City Books** 23 Western Rd, BN3 1AF ☎ 01273 725306, Ⓦ city-books.co.uk. Brighton's largest independent bookshop is a thriving and much-loved fixture in the city, organizing big-name literary talks and readings. Mon–Sat 9.30am–6pm, Sun 11am–4.30pm.

I Gigi General Store 31a Western Rd, BN3 1AF ☎ 01273 775257, Ⓦ igigigeneralstore.com. Beautifully styled little shop stocking homeware and gifts: pottery, hand-blown glassware, antique linen tablecloths, scented candles, bangles and more. Upstairs there's an equally chic café, while the stylish I Gigi Women's Boutique is a few doors along at no. 37. Mon–Sat 10am–6pm, Sun 11am–4.30pm.

La Cave à Fromage 34–35 Western Rd, BN3 1AF ☎ 01273 725500, Ⓦ la-cave.co.uk. There are over two hundred cheeses – plus thirty types of cured meats and fifty wines – at this cheese emporium, which also has a tasting café and runs regular cheese-and-wine-tasting events on Thursday evenings. Mon–Wed 10am–5.30pm, Thurs 10am–10pm, Fri & Sat 11am–10pm, Sun 11am–6pm.

KEMP TOWN

Brighton Flea Market 31a Upper St James's St, BN2 1JN ☎ 01273 624006, Ⓦ brightonfleamarket.com. The unmissable pink facade of this long-established flea market houses over a hundred stalls and cabinets on two levels, selling furniture, bric-a-brac, jewellery and more. Mon–Sat 10am–5.30pm, Sun 10.30am–5pm.

Kemptown Bookshop 91 St Georges Rd, BN2 1EE ☎ 01273 682110, Ⓦ kemptownbookshop.co.uk. Award-winning independent bookshop, with a good selection of cards, prints and book-related gifts. Mon–Sat 9am–5.30pm.

LGBTQ BRIGHTON

SEE MAPS PAGES 236 AND 239

As you would expect from a city as synonymous with gay life as Brighton, the nightlife here doesn't disappoint. Radiating outwards from St James's St in **Kemp Town**, the scene is surprisingly compact but varied. **Brighton Pride** (date varies each summer; Ⓦ brighton-pride.org) is one of the best Pride events in the world: alongside a parade and ticketed party in Preston Park, the weekend celebrations include a range of cultural events covering film, theatre and performance art.

INFORMATION AND TOURS

GScene Magazine Ⓦ gscene.com. LGBTQ lifestyle, listings and community magazine for the local area.

Piers and Queers tour ☎ 07954 482112, Ⓦ onlyin brighton.co.uk. Fun, illuminating walking tour looking at the city's LGBTQ history, personalities and stories.

Switchboard ☎ 01273 204050, Ⓦ switchboard.org.uk. Running since 1975, the Switchboard provides information about the Brighton LGBTQ scene, support and advice and a counselling service.

BARS AND CLUBS

The Bulldog 31 St James's St, BN2 1RF. Brighton's longest-running gay bar is packed at weekends, and is popular both as a post-club spot and for the karaoke and cabaret upstairs. Daily noon–late.

Camelford Arms 30–31 Camelford St, BN2 1TQ Ⓦ camelfordarmsbrighton.co.uk. This cosy community pub, with a welcoming atmosphere and excellent food, is a popular first stop at the weekend for a crowd that includes plenty of bears, otters and their admirers. The Sunday roasts are legendary. Mon–Wed & Sun noon–11.30pm, Thurs noon–midnight, Fri & Sat noon–1am.

Legends 31–34 Marine Parade, BN2 1TR Ⓦ legends brighton.com. Comprised of the ground-floor *Legends Bar* with terrace overlooking the sea, and the free-entry *Basement Club*, this venue has a friendly, mixed crowd. Downstairs the music runs from chart pop to dance; upstairs the bar hosts cabaret nights with local drag stars. Opening times vary; check website.

The Marlborough Pub & Theatre 4 Princes St, BN2 1RD Ⓦ marlboroughtheatre.org.uk. Attracting a truly diverse crowd and welcoming to all, *The Marlborough* is unarguably Brighton's queerest pub; it's particularly popular with Brighton's lesbian and trans communities. There are regular DJs, open-mic nights and quizzes, and upstairs in the sixty-seat theatre, provocative and entertaining queer theatre and performance art is programmed. Mon–Thurs noon–midnight, Fri & Sat noon–2am, Sun noon–11.30pm.

Revenge 32–34 Old Steine, BN1 1EL ☎ 01273 606064, Ⓦ revenge.co.uk. A leading presence on the city's gay scene and a key player in Brighton Pride, with a young studenty crowd regularly packing out the two floors and roof terrace. Nights include foam parties and themed events. Opening times vary; check website.

Subline 129 St James's St, BN2 1TH Ⓦ sublinebrighton. co.uk. *Subline* is Brighton's only men-only cruise bar. Dark and subterranean, with industrial decor, the bar runs theme nights including leather, underwear-only and foam parties. Members only; join via the website prior to visiting. Opening times vary; check website.

Traumfrau Various venues, check website for details Ⓦ traumfrau.co.uk. Monthly queer club night that moves location every month, with a varied roster of DJs playing everything from electro, disco and pop to punk and rockabilly. With provocative live performances and a DIY aesthetic that encourages the crowd to get truly involved, *Traumfrau* is lively, joyous, unpredictable and always truly inclusive.

Velvet Jack's 50 Norfolk Square, BN1 2PA ☎01273 661290, ⓦfacebook.com/velvetjacksbrighton. Cosy and friendly lesbian café-bar – a great spot for coffee during the day, and in the evening the bar has a welcoming community feel. Tues & Sun 11am–11pm, Wed–Sat 11am–midnight.

7

West Sussex

WEST WITTERING BEACH

West Sussex

One of the surprising but wonderful things about West Sussex is that over half of it is protected countryside. A large swathe of the county lies within the South Downs National Park, which sweeps west to east across the whole of the region, encompassing not only the steep scarp slopes of the South Downs themselves but also, to the north, the beautiful woodland and heathland of the Western Weald around Midhurst. Down on the coast, the estuarine landscapes of Chichester Harbour are protected as one of the county's two Areas of Outstanding Natural Beauty (AONBs); the other lies northeast in the High Weald (and is covered in Chapter 5, The Sussex High Weald). The only city in West Sussex is Chichester, and the only other settlements of any size are concentrated in the east around the busy A23 or along the built-up coastal strip, leaving the rest of the county in splendid rural tranquillity.

The county town of West Sussex is **Chichester**, a pocket-sized, culture-rich city with an unbeatable location sandwiched between the South Downs National Park to the north and the sea, sand and sails of Chichester Harbour and the **Manhood Peninsula** to the south; with the city as your base it's perfectly possible to be tramping the Downs in the morning and basking on the beach by the afternoon. Chichester Harbour aside, the jewel in the crown of the Manhood Peninsula is pristine, dune-backed **West Wittering Beach** – one of only two sandy beaches in Sussex, and consequently besieged by windbreak-toting holidaymakers in summer. There are plenty of opportunities on the peninsula for watersports, walks and cycling, or you can simply relax and take in the shifting tidal landscapes of Chichester Harbour on a leisurely boat trip.

The South Downs National Park begins just a few miles north of Chichester and, unsurprisingly, there's plenty of wonderful walking to be had, including along the South Downs ridge at Harting Down, and at Kingley Vale, one of the country's finest yew forests. The cluster of sights up this way includes the Weald & Downland Open Air Museum, where you can get a fascinating snapshot of Sussex rural life in days gone by, the Cass Sculpture Foundation with its outdoor displays of modern British sculpture nestled amongst the trees, and the Goodwood Estate, host to three of the county's biggest events (see page 273) which book up hotels in the area months in advance. Further north is the attractive market town of **Midhurst**, home to the national park visitor centre, and nearby **Petworth**, a handsome town crammed with independent shops that has grown up around magnificent Petworth House. Nearby, you can get one of the best views in the national park at **Black Down**.

Moving east, the picturesque town of **Arundel** makes a lovely alternative base for a visit, with a splendid castle, some great places to eat, and a clutch of sights nearby that includes the industrial heritage museum at Amberley, Elizabethan Parham House and Bignor Roman Villa – a fascinating counterpart to the larger **Fishbourne Roman Palace** near Chichester. Further east again is **Steyning**, with two ancient hillforts nearby and a ruined Norman castle. From Arundel, the River Arun meanders gracefully downstream through water meadows to the coast at **Littlehampton**, one of a handful of low-key seaside towns along the **West Sussex coast**.

STATUE OF SAINT RICHARD AND CHICHESTER CATHEDRAL

Highlights

❶ **Chichester Cathedral** Chichester's great medieval cathedral is as well known for its modern devotional art as for its more ancient treasures. See page 265

❷ **Pallant House Gallery** This modern art gallery is Chichester's pride and joy: a roll call of the great and the good in twentieth-century British art. See page 266

❸ **Fishbourne Roman Palace** One of the country's most important collections of Roman remains, and the biggest Roman dwelling ever discovered north of the Alps. See page 270

❹ **Chichester Harbour** The stunning watery landscapes of Chichester Harbour are best enjoyed on a boat trip. See page 274

❺ **West Wittering Beach** Even the summertime crowds that flock to this undeveloped sandy beach can't quite dispel its magic. See page 275

❻ **Black Down** Climb to the highest point of the South Downs National Park to see the sweeping view that inspired Tennyson. See page 284

❼ **Petworth House** One of the finest stately homes in the Southeast, with a magnificent haul of art, and a deer park immortalized by Turner. See page 285

❽ **Arundel Castle** This splendid castle, with a Norman keep and richly furnished state rooms, dominates the skyline of sleepy Arundel. See page 288

HIGHLIGHTS ARE MARKED ON THE MAP ON PAGE 264

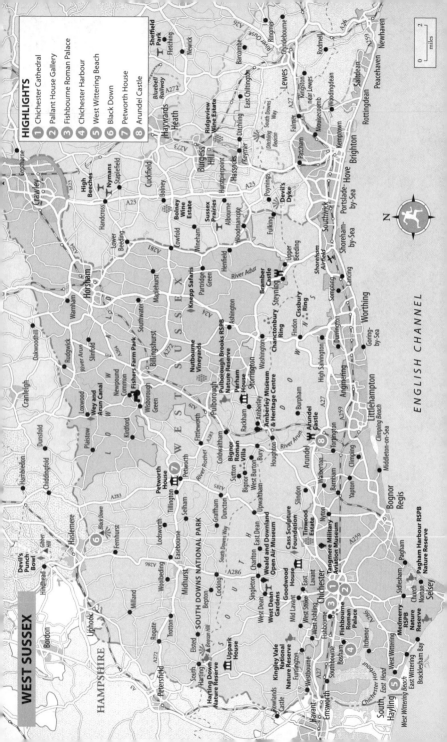

WEST SUSSEX

HIGHLIGHTS

1. Chichester Cathedral
2. Pallant House Gallery
3. Fishbourne Roman Palace
4. Chichester Harbour
5. West Wittering Beach
6. Black Down
7. Petworth House
8. Arundel Castle

ENGLISH CHANNEL

N

0   1   2
miles

SOUTH DOWNS NATIONAL PARK

HAMPSHIRE

WEST SUSSEX

Chichester and around

The handsome market town of **CHICHESTER** has plenty to recommend it: a splendid twelfth-century cathedral, a thriving cultural scene centred on its highly regarded Festival Theatre (see page 270), and one of the finest collections of modern British art anywhere in the country at the Pallant House Gallery. There are some excellent attractions within just a few miles of the city, too: the Roman ruins at **Fishbourne**; ancient woodland in **Kingley Vale** nature reserve; beautiful **West Dean Gardens**; the **Weald & Downland Open Air Museum**, which contains more than fifty reconstructed historic buildings; the **Cass Sculpture Foundation**, home of contemporary British sculpture; and finally, the dashing **Goodwood Estate**, host to three big annual events. Only very slightly further afield are the Witterings and Chichester Harbour (see page 274), and the scenic splendour of the South Downs National Park.

Market Cross and around

The centre of Chichester is marked by its splendid Gothic **Market Cross**, an octagonal rotunda topped by ornate finials and a crown lantern spire, built in 1501 to provide shelter for the market traders. The buzz of commerce still dominates the surrounding area today, with the four main thoroughfares leading off from the Cross – North, East, South and West streets – each lined with shops, and a **farmers' market** setting up its stalls on the first and third Friday of the month (9am–2pm; ⓦchichester.gov.uk/farmersmarket). There are several fine buildings up North Street, including the dinky little **Market House** (also known as the Butter Market), built by Nash in 1807 and fronted by a Doric colonnade; a tiny flint **Saxon church** with a diminutive wooden shingled spire; and the redbrick **Council House**, built in 1731, with Ionic columns on its facade.

The city walls

The centre's cruciform street plan, and the **city walls** that encircle it, are a legacy of Chichester's Roman beginnings. The city started life as the settlement of Noviomagus Reginorum, connected to London by the arrow-straight Stane Street. The **Roman city walls** were built in the third century, and large sections (much restored over the years) still stand today, though the ancient gateways are long gone. Pavement markers, signposts and interpretive boards guide you round the 1.5-mile circuit; for much of the route there's a footpath on top of the walls, and it's a fun way to see the city, hopping on and off at various points to visit Chichester's other sights.

Chichester Cathedral

West St, PO19 1RP • Mon–Sat 7.15am–6.30pm, Sun 7.15am–5pm; tours (45min) Mon–Sat 11.15am & 2.30pm • Free • Café Mon–Sat 9am–6pm, Sun 10am–4pm • ⓣ 01243 782595, ⓦ chichestercathedral.org.uk

Chichester's splendid **cathedral** has stood at the heart of the city for over nine hundred years. Building began in 1076, after the Norman conquerors moved the bishopric from Selsey, ten miles away. The cathedral was consecrated by Bishop Luffa in 1108, and since about 1300 has only been minimally modified, with the exception of the unique freestanding fifteenth-century bell tower and the slender spire; the latter had to be rebuilt after it came spectacularly crashing down in 1861 when the choir screen was dismantled.

The interior is renowned for its prestigious **modern devotional art**, which includes a font of smooth Bodmin stone and beaten copper by **John Skelton** just inside the entrance; an enormous altar-screen tapestry by **John Piper**; and a stained-glass window – an exuberant blaze of ruby-red – by **Marc Chagall** nearby. Perhaps the cathedral's greatest artistic treasures, however, are its oldest: in the south aisle, close to the tapestry, you'll see a pair of exquisite Romanesque carvings – the **Chichester Reliefs** – created

8

around 1125, and showing the raising of Lazarus. Notable for the wonderfully expressive faces of the figures, the reliefs would once have been brightly painted, with semiprecious stones set in the eyes.

Elsewhere you can see a couple of enormous **Renaissance wooden panel paintings** by Lambert Barnard – depicting the past bishops of Chichester (north transept), and Henry VIII confirming the Chichester bishopric (south transept) – as well as the fourteenth-century **Fitzalan tomb** of Richard Fitzalan, thirteenth earl of Arundel. The earl's stone effigy, lying sweetly hand-in-hand with his countess, inspired Philip Larkin's poem *An Arundel Tomb*, which famously concludes "What will survive of us is love."

Behind the cathedral, Canon Lane leads to the fourteenth-century gateway to the Bishop's Palace; the Palace itself is not open to the public, but the beautiful **Bishop's Palace Gardens** (daily 8am–dusk; free) are one of the city's hidden gems and a perfect picnic spot, with expansive lawns, great views of the cathedral, a Tudor walled garden and sections of Roman wall.

Pallant House Gallery

9 North Pallant, PO19 1TJ · Tues, Wed, Fri & Sat 10am–5pm, Thurs 10am–8pm, Sun & bank hols 11am–5pm · £11, Tues £5.50, Thurs 5–8pm permanent collection free (£5.50 for temporary exhibitions) · ☎ 01243 774557, ⓦ pallant.org.uk

Hidden away off South Street, in the well-preserved Georgian quadrant of the city known as the Pallants, is the wonderful **Pallant House Gallery**, Chichester's answer to

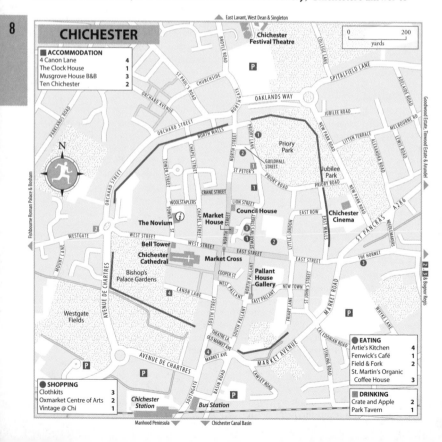

CHICHESTER'S FALCONS

If you're visiting the cathedral in spring (April–June), you'll get a chance to spot the cathedral's pair of **peregrine falcons**, which have been returning here to nest every year since 2000. There's a webcam of the nest in the café garden, and telescopes in front of the cathedral – the southwest lawn is a good place to catch them in flight, especially in the early evening. Check out ⓦ chichesterperegrinesblog.co.uk for more on the birds.

---

the Tate Modern. Housed in a creaky-floored Queen Anne townhouse and an award-winning contemporary extension, the gallery contains one of the most important collections of modern British art in the country, with works by almost every notable British artist of the last hundred years, including Moore, Freud, Sickert, Hepworth, Blake, Piper, Hodgkin, Sutherland and Caulfield. The collection started with the bequest of **Walter Hussey**, the dean of Chichester Cathedral – who commissioned much of the modern art in the cathedral, including the Piper tapestry and the Chagall window – and has grown with subsequent bequests to become an eclectic "collection of collections", encompassing paintings, ceramics, furniture, sculpture and more. Alongside the rotating permanent collection, the gallery also shows several excellent **temporary exhibitions** each year, and has a designated room for **prints and drawings**.

The Novium

Tower St, PO19 1QH • April–Sept Mon–Sat 10am–5pm, Sun 10am–4pm; Oct–March Mon–Sat 10am–5pm • Free • ☎ 01243 775888, ⓦ www.thenovium.org

The city's museum of local history – the **Novium** – is housed in a state-of-the-art building a stone's throw from the cathedral. The first sight that greets you as you walk in is the recently excavated **Roman bath house**, which stood on this site nearly two thousand years ago; after its discovery in the 1970s it was buried under a car park for safekeeping until the Novium build allowed it to see the light of day once again. If you've seen the remains at Bignor (see page 292) or Fishbourne (see page 270) you might be a bit underwhelmed, but a film projected onto the wall behind does a good job of bringing the excavation to life. Also here are the incomplete but beautiful fourth-century **Chilgrove mosaic**, discovered in the Chilgrove valley nearby, and the second-century **Jupiter Stone** statue base, unearthed during excavations in West Street.

The other two floors display artefacts from the museum's huge, eclectic collection – over 500,000 items in all. The first floor tells the story of Chichester using artefacts that range from prehistoric stone tools to Roman hipposandals (protective horseshoes), Saxon grave goods and the old toll board and weighing scales once used at the Butter Market. The second floor concentrates on thematic displays; from the foyer up here there are views of the cathedral. The whole museum is very child-friendly, with dressing-up, games and child-height drawers labelled "open me".

Chichester Ship Canal

Canal Basin, Canal Wharf, PO19 8DT • **Boat trips** Mid-Feb to early Nov 2–4 trips daily; 1hr 15min return • £8 • **Rowing boats** £7 for first 30min, £5/30min thereafter • ☎ 01243 771363, ⓦ chichestercanal.org.uk

Just outside the southern city walls, Chichester Canal Basin is the start of the **Chichester Ship Canal**, which skirts the fringes of the city before flowing lazily through flat countryside to Chichester Marina at Birdham, four miles away. The canal opened in 1822 to carry cargo between the sea and the city, but it was never a commercial success and was abandoned in 1928. Today the Chichester Canal Trust hires out **rowing boats** and runs **boat trips** as far as the Crosbie Bridge at Donnington two miles away; the more energetic might fancy a go at **stand-up paddleboarding** (see page 298) – the non-tidal water makes it a perfect place to learn. A **towpath**, part of the long-distance Lipchis Way (see page 278), runs the length of the canal down to the marina. Whether on foot or on the river the canal makes a lovely, peaceful outing from the city, with wildflowers speckling the riverbanks in summer, dragonflies flashing above the water, and swans and mallards gliding along; from Hunston Bridge you also get a great view back across the meadows to the cathedral, a vista immortalized by J.M.W. Turner in 1829.

ARRIVAL AND DEPARTURE — CHICHESTER AND AROUND

By train The station, on Stockbridge Rd, is a 10min walk south of the Market Cross.

Destinations Arundel (Mon–Sat 2 hourly, Sun hourly; 25–50min); Brighton (2 hourly; 45–55min); London Victoria (Mon–Sat 2 hourly, Sun hourly; 1hr 35min).

By bus The bus station lies across the road from the train station on Southgate.

Destinations Brighton via Bognor, Littlehampton, Worthing & Shoreham-by-Sea (every 10min; 1hr 45min); Midhurst (Mon–Sat every 30min, Sun hourly; 40min).

By car Chichester has plenty of long-stay (3hr-plus) car parks – at Cattle Market, Westgate, Northgate, Basin Rd and Ave de Chartres – all signposted from the city's approach roads.

GETTING AROUND

By bike There's bike rental at Barreg Cycles, two miles from the centre in Fishbourne (£18/day; ☎ 01243 786104, ⓦ barreg.co.uk).

By taxi Chichester Taxis (☎ 01243 330015).

INFORMATION AND ACTIVITIES

Tourist office At the Novium, Tower St (April–Sept Mon–Sat 10am–5pm & Sun 10am–4pm; Oct–March Mon–Sat 10am–5pm; ☎ 01243 775888, ⓦ visitchichester.org).

City walks Guided city walks run throughout the year, bookable through the tourist office (April–Sept Tues & Wed 11am, Sat 2pm; Oct–March Tues 11am, Sat 2pm; 1hr 30min; £5).

Stand-up paddleboarding TJ Board Hire (☎ 07548 619578, ⓦ tjboardhire.co.uk) offers fun SUP lessons on the flat waters of Chichester Ship Canal – perfect for beginners and families (£45; 2hr).

ACCOMMODATION

There's generally no problem finding a place to stay in or around Chichester other than during **Goodwood**'s three big annual events (see page 273), when the most popular accommodation can fill up more than a year in advance. Note that the prices below exclude the Goodwood periods, when rates rise across the board.

IN TOWN **SEE MAP PAGE 266**

4 Canon Lane 4 Canon Lane, PO19 1PX ☎ 01243 813586, ⓦ chichestercathedral.org.uk. What makes a stay here special is the location: this eight-bedroom Victorian house, once home to the Archdeacon of Chichester, is owned by the cathedral and located in the grounds, just by the Bishop's Palace gateway. The rooms are big, comfortable and tranquil, if a little bland; two come with baths, the others showers. An added bonus is the top-notch art on the walls, lent by the Pallant House Gallery. Breakfast costs extra. **£110**

The Clock House St Martin's Square, PO19 1NT ⓦ clock housechichester.com. This bijou converted coach house is a stylish self-catering option for two people, with a cosy lounge complete with wood-burner (logs included), a small kitchen out the back and a courtyard garden. Lovely extra touches include Molton Brown toiletries and fluffy robes; hampers and meals are available on request. It's in a fab location, too, set on a quiet back road between North St and Priory Park. Minimum two-night stay. **£160**

Musgrove House B&B 63 Oving Rd, PO19 7EN ☎ 01243 790179, ⓦ musgrovehouse.co.uk. This friendly, stylish boutique B&B, just a short walk from the centre, is a real bargain. The three lovely rooms are all impeccably tasteful, decked out in cocooning shades of grey, with shutters on the windows and super-comfy beds with silk duvets. **£95**

Ten Chichester 10 Whyke Rd, PO19 7AL ☎ 01243 532068, ⓦ tenchichester.co.uk. Friendly and reasonably central B&B with three pretty en-suite rooms (one with a sofa bed, ideal for families), a courtyard garden and a guest sitting room with a woodburner and lots of local maps and books. Private off-street parking is another bonus. Minimum two-night stay at weekends April–Nov. **£110**

OUT OF TOWN

As well as the options listed below, check out the Goodwood Hotel (see page 273) and the Tinwood Estate Lodges (see page 273).

Richmond Arms Mill Rd, West Ashling, 5 miles from Chichester, PO18 8EA ☎ 01243 572046, ⓦ therichmond arms.co.uk. There are just two B&B rooms above this excellent village pub, a 10min drive from Chichester. Rooms are smart and luxurious, with bathrooms featuring polished wooden floors, roll-top baths and walk-in showers; the larger room (£135) comes with a sofa bed, so is a good option for families. The real selling point, however, is the great food on offer downstairs, though bear in mind the restaurant's not open every day. **£125**

Royal Oak Pook Lane, East Lavant, 3 miles from Chichester, PO18 0AX ☎01243 527434, ⓦroyaloak eastlavant.co.uk. This lovely dining pub, set on a quiet lane just north of Chichester, offers a range of gorgeous, stylish rooms – five rooms and three cottages (sleep 3), all kitted out with DVD players, plump down duvets and local aromatherapy toiletries. **£175**, cottages **£210**

EATING

IN TOWN
SEE MAP PAGE 266

Artie's Kitchen 33 Southgate, PO19 1DP ☎01243 790365, ⓦartieskitchen.com. Tuck into authentic, beautifully cooked tapas (£6–9 each) at this stylish bare-brick and beams tapas bar. Tues–Sat 11.45am–3pm & 6–11pm.

Fenwick's Café Priory Park, PO19 1NL ☎01243 839762, ⓦfenwickscafe.com. In a lovely spot in tranquil Priory Park, this friendly café is a top pick for a simple summer lunch – sandwiches, salads, platters and a small selection of hot food, including stone-baked pizzas. Mon & Sun 9.30am–5pm, Tues–Sat 9.30am–8pm.

Field & Fork 4 Guildhall St, PO19 1NJ ☎01243 789915, ⓦfieldandfork.co.uk. One of the best places to eat in the city, serving up imaginative, locally sourced food in a tranquil restaurant with a sun-flooded conservatory at the back. Mains such as wild sea trout with local broad beans or maple-glazed short rib of beef will set you back £15–22, or there's a cheaper set menu (2 courses £19.50). Tues–Sat noon–2.45pm & 5pm–late.

St. Martin's Organic Coffee House 3 St Martin's St, PO19 1NP ☎01243 786715, ⓦorganiccoffeehouse.co.uk. Housed in a higgledy-piggledy eighteenth-century town house, this relaxed café has been going since 1979. It serves organic (mostly veggie) food and drink, all prepared on the premises, and has Scrabble and other games, plus a piano that anyone is welcome to play. Tues–Sat 10am–6pm.

OUT OF TOWN

Some of the best food in the Chichester area is found in the country pubs around the city.

Earl of March Lavant Rd, 3 miles from Chichester, PO18 0BQ ☎01243 533993, ⓦtheearlofmarch.com. Renowned foodie pub a few miles north of the city, with a lovely terrace garden which backs right onto the surrounding fields and has fabulous views across to the Downs. Mains cost £18–25, though lighter lunches (including sandwiches and salads; from £7) are also available, and there's a good-value set menu (2/3 courses £24.50/27.50). Daily 11am–11pm; kitchen Mon–Sat noon–2.30pm & 5.30–9.30pm, Sun noon–3pm & 5.30–9pm.

Fox Goes Free Charlton, 6 miles from Chichester, PO18 0HU ☎01243 811461, ⓦthefoxgoesfree.com. This seventeenth-century flint country pub oozes character – well-worn brick floors, sagging beams and inglenook fireplaces – and history: back in the 1600s William III used to drop in to refresh his hunting party here. The large garden is the crowning glory, with picnic tables under the apple trees and beautiful views of the Downs. Food is traditional and homemade, and runs from sandwiches to the pie of the day (£7–16). Mon–Sat 11am–11pm, Sun noon–10.30pm; kitchen Mon–Fri noon–5pm & 6.15–9.30pm, Sat noon–10pm, Sun noon–5pm & 6.15–9.30pm.

★ **Richmond Arms** Mill Rd, West Ashling, 5 miles from Chichester, PO18 8EA ☎01243 572046, ⓦtherichmond arms.co.uk. West Ashling's village pub is a real find, with heaps of style and great food: a meal here might start with hot and runny chorizo Scotch egg with pickled fennel and saffron aioli, followed by hot molten Selsey crab Kiev, and finish with a hot white chocolate, cherry and pistachio spring roll served with cherry ripple ice cream. Most mains £15–18. On Fri and Sat evenings woodfired small plates and artisan-style pizzas are available. Wed–Sat noon–2pm & 6–9pm, Sun noon–3pm.

Royal Oak Pook Lane, East Lavant, 3 miles from Chichester, PO18 0AX ☎01243 427434, ⓦroyaloak eastlavant.co.uk. Two-hundred-year-old, vine-covered coaching inn in a pretty village just outside Chichester, with bags of character and tables out the front overlooking the quiet village lane. The food is great, sourced from local suppliers where possible: mains (£15–22) might include wild local sea bass or local pheasant. Cheaper sandwiches (£7–9) are also available at lunch. Daily 9am–11pm; kitchen Mon–Fri 7.30–9.30am, noon–2.30pm & 6–9pm, Sat 8–10am, noon–2.30pm & 6–9.30pm, Sun 8–10am, noon–3pm & 6–8pm.

DRINKING
SEE MAP PAGE 266

Crate and Apple 14 Westgate, PO19 3EU ☎01243 539336, ⓦcrateandapple.co.uk. This smart, family-friendly pub is justifiably popular. Craft ales, local gins and cocktails sit alongside really good locally sourced food (mains £13–17), and there's a small beer garden out the back. Mon–Fri 10am–11pm, Sat & Sun 10am–late; kitchen daily 10–11.30am, noon–3pm & 6–9pm.

Park Tavern 11 Priory Rd, PO19 1NS ☎01243 785057, ⓦparktavernchichester.co.uk. A proper pub with a great atmosphere, overlooking Priory Park. Great-value food such as sandwiches and ploughman's (£5–7), plus mains around the £10 mark and superior homemade bar snacks

8

and pickles (£4–5). Fuller's ales on tap, plus a seasonal guest beer. Mon–Sat 11am–11pm, Sun noon–10.30pm; kitchen Mon noon–3pm, Tues–Fri noon–3pm & 6–9pm, Sat 11am–9pm, Sun noon–4pm.

ENTERTAINMENT

Chichester Cinema New Park Rd, PO19 7XY ☎ 01243 786650, ⓦ chichestercinema.org. Chichester's excellent arthouse cinema screens up to four films a day.

Chichester Festival Theatre Oaklands Park, PO19 6AP ☎ 01243 781312, ⓦ cft.org.uk. One of the best regional theatres in the country, the refurbished Chichester Festival Theatre opened in 1962 when it was the very first thrust-stage theatre, with Laurence Olivier as artistic director. Today, many productions from the theatre's annual season (roughly Easter–Oct) move on to the West End and abroad; in winter it hosts touring shows.

SHOPPING   SEE MAP PAGE 266

★ **Clothkits** 16 The Hornet, PO19 7JG ☎ 01243 533180, ⓦ clothkits.co.uk. Chichester-based Kay Mawer has breathed fresh life into the much-loved Clothkits brand of ready-to-sew mail-order clothes, which dressed a generation of 1970s children. The shop here in Chichester sells clothing kits for women and children (featuring unique prints by contemporary artists and textile designers) alongside a vast array of fabrics and haberdashery, and there's a busy programme of workshops running upstairs. Next door is Draper's Yard, an alley of pop-up market stalls and studios selling everything from jewellery to prints to furniture. Mon–Sat 9.30am–5.30pm.

Oxmarket Centre of Arts St Andrews Court, off East St, PO19 1YH ☎ 01243 779103, ⓦ oxmarket.com. Housed in a twelfth-century church, this gallery houses the work of local artists, with exhibitions changing monthly. Tues–Sun 10am–4.30pm.

Vintage @ Chi 2 Jays Walk, St Martin's St, PO19 1NP ☎ 01243 773644, ⓦ facebook.com/VintageAtChi. For good-quality vintage clothing look no further than this tiny shop, crammed with great pieces. Tues–Sat 10am–4.30pm.

Fishbourne Roman Palace

Salthill Rd, Fishbourne, PO19 3QR • Feb & Nov to mid-Dec daily 10am–4pm; March–Oct daily 10am–5pm; mid-Dec to end Jan Sat & Sun 10am–4pm • £9.80 • ☎ 01243 789829, ⓦ sussexpast.co.uk • Train from Chichester to Fishbourne (hourly; 3min), then 10min walk

Fishbourne Roman Palace, two miles west of Chichester, is the largest and best-preserved Roman dwelling in the country, and the largest north of the Alps. Roman relics have long been turning up in Fishbourne, and in 1960 a workman unearthed their source – the site of a depot constructed by the invading Romans in 43 AD, which is thought later to have become the vast palace of the Romanized king of a local tribe, Cogidubnus. The palace was built around 75–80 AD, on a huge scale, with around a hundred rooms, 160 columns, 43,000 roof tiles and up to two miles of masonry walls. The one surviving wing – the **north wing** – represents just a quarter of the site; a large part of the complex lies buried beneath Fishbourne village.

Fishbourne has the largest collection of in-situ **mosaics** in the country, and some of the earliest too. When the palace was built, craftsmen laid the black-and-white geometric mosaics that were popular in Rome at the time, but as tastes changed from the early second century onwards, these were supplanted by polychrome mosaics, which featured a central panel surrounded by a large border – the dolphin-riding cupid being Fishbourne's most famous example. Nearby Bignor Roman Villa (see page 292) also has some stunning polychrome mosaics, and makes a fascinating follow-on visit.

An **audiovisual programme** gives a fuller picture of the palace as it would have been in Roman times, and the extensive **gardens** attempt to re-create the palace grounds – which might well have been the earliest formal gardens in the country – with new planting in the original bedding trenches. There is at least one **guided tour** a day (free), as well as occasional handling sessions, and special events take place throughout the year.

Kingley Vale National Nature Reserve

5km northwest of Chichester, near West Stoke village • Download Natural England's leaflet (including a map of the reserve) at ⓦ publications. naturalengland.org.uk/publication/32044 • Car park near West Stoke village (signposted); the reserve is a 15min walk from here

The magical **Kingley Vale National Nature Reserve**, a few miles northwest of Chichester in the South Downs National Park, is perhaps best known for its ancient **yew trees**, which are thought to be amongst the oldest living things in Britain. The massive, twisting trees here are at least 500 years old and probably much, much older – one story goes that they were planted back in 859 to commemorate a victory against Viking invaders. The 3.5-mile circular Nature Trail (accessed from the West Stoke car park) climbs up through the dark, atmospheric yew forest to rolling chalk grassland with wonderful panoramic views over Chichester Harbour; look out for the Devil's Humps nearby, Bronze Age burial mounds.

West Dean Gardens

West Dean, PO18 0RX • Feb & Nov to mid-Dec Mon–Fri 10.30am–4pm, Sat, Sun & bank hols 9am–4pm; March–Oct Mon–Fri 10.30am–5pm, Sat, Sun & bank hols 9am–5pm • March–Oct £9.50, Feb, Nov & Dec £6.25 • ☎ 01243 818210, ⊛ westdean.org.uk/gardens • Stagecoach Coastline bus #60 from Chichester or Midhurst (Mon–Sat 2 hourly, Sun hourly)

With wildflower meadows, sweeping lawns, flower gardens and fruit orchards, all set against a backdrop of the South Downs, **West Dean Gardens**, five miles north of Chichester, are among the loveliest in Sussex. You could happily spend half a day or more exploring: highlights include the walled **Kitchen Garden** – one of the most perfect examples you'll see anywhere, with neat, white-painted Victorian glasshouses, fruit trees trained into sculptural shapes, and supernaturally neat rows of flawless vegetables – and the pretty **Spring Garden**, where you'll find dinky flint bridges spanning the crystal-clear River Lavant, and two Surrealist fibreglass **tree sculptures**. The sculptures were created by poet and writer **Edward James**, who once owned the West Dean Estate and is best known for his early support and patronage of Surrealist art; Salvador Dalí's iconic *Mae West Lips Sofa* and *Lobster Telephone* were both created in collaboration with James. James is buried up in the fifty-acre **arboretum**, half a mile or so uphill across sloping parkland dotted with grazing sheep; it's at its most beautiful in spring, when rhododendrons and azaleas daub the pathways with splashes of red and pink.

Edward James's mansion, at the centre of the gardens, operates as **West Dean College**, an internationally renowned residential college dedicated to creative arts and conservation. To get a taster, you can enrol on one of the dozens of **day courses**, which span everything from stained-glass making and woodcarving to blacksmithing and botanical painting.

Weald & Downland Open Air Museum

Singleton, PO18 0EU • Daily: April–Oct 10.30am–6pm; Nov–March 10.30am–4pm; Downland Gridshell tour daily 1.30pm • £14 • ☎ 01243 811363, ⊛ wealddown.co.uk • Stagecoach Coastline bus #60 from Chichester or Midhurst (Mon–Sat 2 hourly, Sun hourly)

Five miles north of Chichester, the **Weald & Downland Open Air Museum** is a brilliantly engaging rural museum. More than fifty buildings from the last seven hundred years – everything from a medieval farmstead to a Tudor market hall and a pair of Victorian labourers' cottages – have been dismantled from sites around the Southeast and reconstructed on this fifty-acre site. None would have survived without the museum's intervention: some were virtually tumbledown, while others were due to be demolished to make way for development.

Many of the buildings have been decked out as they would have been originally, using replica furniture and artefacts. In the working Tudor kitchen in sixteenth-century **Winkhurst Farm** you can even taste some of the food of the period – handmade butter and cheese, griddle bread and pottage. Stewards inside the buildings are on hand to talk about what life would have been like for those who lived there, and there are regular **demonstrations** – different every day – of rural crafts and trades, from spinning and dairying to thatching and scything. Spend some time at the **information galleries** at the entrance to get the most out of your visit; the daily **tour** of the modern, innovative

8

Downland Gridshell building, the museum's vast workshop and store containing 15,500 artefacts, is also recommended. Numerous events and activities run throughout the year.

Cass Sculpture Foundation

Goodwood, 5 miles north of Chichester, PO18 0QP • April–Oct daily 10am–4.30pm • £12.50 • ☎ 01243 538449, ⓦ sculpture.org.uk

The magical **Cass Sculpture Foundation** is an absolute must for anyone interested in contemporary art, with more than fifty large-scale works nestled among the trees in a beautiful 26-acre woodland setting. Uniquely, all of the sculptures are for sale – ranging in price from a few thousand pounds to well over a million – meaning that the pieces on display change from year to year as they are sold. The dynamo behind the operation is retired businessman **Wilfred Cass**, whose own Modernist house lies hidden among the trees. Plenty of big names have been on show over the years – Tony Cragg, Antony Gormley, Thomas Heatherwick, Eduardo Paolozzi, Andy Goldsworthy, Rachel Whiteread and more – but the Foundation also commissions sculpture from lesser-known British talent, meeting the cost of the materials and then taking a share of the profits when the piece is sold, before ploughing the money back into the Foundation.

The Goodwood Estate

Goodwood, 4 miles north of Chichester, PO18 0PX • **Motor Circuit** Track Days from £160/half-day • **Aerodrome** A range of flights are available, from a 20min sightseeing flight (£135) to the "Top Gun Air Combat" (£499) • **Golf** Day membership £125 • ☎ 01243 755055, ⓦ goodwood.com

Goodwood's name is synonymous with glamorous sporting pursuits, and its three big annual events – **Glorious Goodwood**, the **Festival of Speed** and the **Goodwood Revival** (see page 273) – draw spectators from around the world. At the centre of the estate is the magnificent **Goodwood House**. Surrounding it are a famous **racecourse** high up on the Downs, which has hosted horse racing since 1802; a celebrated **motor-racing circuit**; an **aerodrome**; two **golf courses** (one ranked in the top 100 in the country); a hotel (see page 273); and a members-only **sporting club**, The Kennels, built in 1787 to house the third Duke of Richmond's hounds and huntsman – the prized dogs apparently had central heating in their quarters a hundred years before it was installed in the main house.

If you've got deep pockets, all of the above is yours to enjoy. You can drive your car round the historic Goodwood Motor Circuit on a **Track Day**, take the controls of an aircraft on a short flight from the aerodrome or play a round of golf on the prestigious Downs Course. A day at the horse races is a positive bargain by comparison, with the cheapest tickets under £15; see ⓦ goodwood.com for fixtures.

Goodwood House

March–July & Sept–Oct most Mon & Sun 1–4.30pm; most of Aug Mon–Thurs & Sun 1–4.30pm; check website for exact dates • Entry by obligatory guided tours (6 daily; 1hr 15min) • Tour £9.50, tour & afternoon tea £25 • ☎ 01243 755055, ⓦ goodwood.com

Seat of the Dukes of Richmond, Lennox, Gordon and Aubigny, **Goodwood House** is every bit as splendid as the rest of the estate. When the first Duke of Richmond – the illegitimate son of Charles II and his French mistress – bought the house in 1697 it was little more than a hunting lodge, but over the years successive generations improved and enlarged it into what you see today. The Earl and Countess of March live in the house, so only the **state apartments** are open to the public, and those only on certain days of the week for parts of the year. The rooms are furnished in opulent Regency style, a fitting home for the family's stellar art collection which includes Sèvres porcelain and paintings by Stubbs, Reynolds, Van Dyck and Canaletto. Tours can be combined with **afternoon tea** served in the opulent ballroom.

GLORIOUS, GLORIOUS GOODWOOD

Goodwood's three big **events** are all incredibly popular. Book your accommodation as far in advance as you can – many hotels and B&Bs are booked up more than a year in advance – and be prepared for **accommodation** prices to soar. For exact dates, prices and further details, see ⓦ www.goodwood.com.

Festival of Speed 4 days in late June/early July. This long weekend of vintage and special cars – featuring everything from Formula One racers and supercars to motorbikes, rally cars and classics – bills itself as "the largest motoring garden party in the world", and is held in the grounds of Goodwood House, attracting around 150,000 petrolheads. The 1.16-mile hill climb is the main event of the weekend (Sat & Sun), but there's plenty of other stuff going on, and the public can wander around the paddocks and get up close to the cars and the stars. Tickets cost £39–70, depending on the day.

Glorious Goodwood 5 days in late July/Aug. One of *the* events of the social and racing year, as much about celeb-spotting, champagne and fashion as it is about

horse racing – Edward VII famously described it as "a garden party with racing tacked on". Ticket prices depend on which enclosure you're in: cheapest is the Lennox Enclosure (£25); then comes the Gordon Enclosure (£49); the Richmond Enclosure is members-only.

Goodwood Revival 3 days in mid-Sept. This nostalgic motor-race meeting relives the glory days of the Goodwood Motor Circuit, welcoming the cars and motorbikes that would have competed during the 1940s, 1950s and 1960s. Many cars are driven by famous names from the past and present, and the entire event is staged in an authentic period setting, with staff – and most of the 100,000 spectators – dressing up in period garb. Tickets cost £59–79, depending on the day.

ACCOMMODATION
THE GOODWOOD ESTATE

Goodwood Hotel Goodwood Estate, 4 miles from Chichester, PO18 0QB ☏ 01243 775537, ⓦ goodwood. com. The Goodwood Estate's country-house hotel isn't cheap, but you're not just paying for the rooms – which are suitably deluxe – but for the whole Goodwood experience. A night here gives you access to the health club and spa, two golf courses and a couple of excellent restaurants supplied in part from the estate's own farm. Rates vary according to demand. **£170**

Tinwood Estate

Tinwood Lane, Halnaker, PO18 0NE • Daily 9am–6pm • Free; wine-tasting £5 • **Tours** Daily at 3pm, plus extra tour at noon on Sat (book ahead); 1hr 30min • £18 • ☏ 01243 537372, ⓦ tinwoodestate.com

The **Tinwood Estate** planted its first vines in 2007, and today the smart 65-acre estate produces three sparkling wines, all made from classic Champagne-variety grapes. You can pitch up to taste the wines in the stylish, modern tasting room, or buy a bottle and enjoy it on one of the picnic benches outside, looking out over the vines; book in advance to join one of the **tours**, which take you around the vineyard and include tastings of the three different fizzes. Tinwood also runs special events throughout the year, including a pop-up restaurant and grape picking.

ACCOMMODATION
TINWOOD ESTATE

Tinwood Estate Lodges Tinwood Lane, PO18 0NE ☏ 01243 537372, ⓦ tinwoodestate.com. Three ultra-smart wooden lodges, named after the vines grown on the estate – Chardonnay, Pinot Noir and Pinot Meunier. Each lodge has big windows looking out onto the vines, an enormous bathroom with two-person jacuzzi and walk-in shower, a fridge well-stocked with wine and a lovely decked terrace on which to drink it. The lodges share a wine barrel-shaped sauna, and free mountain bikes are available for exploring the area. It's not cheap, but it's all done impeccably. **£245**

Tangmere Military Aviation Museum

Tangmere, PO20 2ES • Daily: Feb & Nov 10am–4.30pm; March–Oct 10am–5pm • £10 • ☏ 01243 790090, ⓦ tangmere-museum.org.uk

An operational airfield from 1916 through to 1970, RAF Tangmere, just east of Chichester, is perhaps most famous for the pivotal role it played during the Battle of

Britain in World War II, when it defended an area of the south coast from Portland Bill to Brighton, including the crucially important Portsmouth dockyard. Today a corner of the historic airfield houses the **Tangmere Military Aviation Museum**, an Aladdin's cave of aviation memorabilia covering both World Wars and the Cold War, with a couple of flight simulators and a clutch of historic aircraft thrown in for good measure, amongst them the red Hawker Hunter in which Neville Duke set the world airspeed record in 1953, and the poignant remains of a Hurricane shot down during the Battle of Britain. Displays range from stories of individual heroism by RAF pilots to a recreated ops room; particularly fascinating is an exhibit about Tangmere's role in delivering SOEs (special operations executives) into Europe under the cover of darkness, armed with maps concealed in the false interiors of thermos flasks, and fountain pens loaded with capsules of deadly gas.

The Manhood Peninsula

Just south of Chichester lies the flat **MANHOOD PENSINULA**, with Selsey Bill – the southernmost point of Sussex – at its tip, Bognor Regis (see page 296) to the east, and the beautiful creeks of **Chichester Harbour** on its far western edge. Its rather wonderful name probably comes from the Old English *maene-wudu*, meaning "men's wood" or common land, though there's no remaining woodland to speak of today, with the peninsula mainly given over to agriculture. Inland the landscape is flat and featureless, but the main appeal of the area is around the coast, where you'll find some of the last remaining stretches of undeveloped coastline in Sussex. The best way to enjoy the peninsula, known locally as "God's pocket" for its benevolent microclimate, is to make the most of the great outdoors, whether by taking a boat trip, enrolling in a watersports taster course or simply striking off on a coastal footpath.

ARRIVAL AND GETTING AROUND   THE MANHOOD PENINSULA

By bike Bike routes crisscross the peninsula (see page 278), most of which is no more than 6m above sea level, making it easy cycling territory.

By bus Stagecoach bus #52 runs from Chichester to West Wittering, East Wittering and Bracklesham (Mon–Sat every 15–30min, Sun every 30min–1hr), and #56 to Old Bosham (Mon–Sat every 1hr 30min).

By car Be aware there can be daily traffic jams on the road to and from West Wittering beach on summer weekends; get there early, or consider hiring a bike (see page 278). There's plentiful pay-and-display parking around the peninsula.

Chichester Harbour

Chichester Harbour is the Southeast's smallest Area of Outstanding Natural Beauty, a glorious estuarine landscape of inlets and tidal mudflats, pretty creekside villages and hamlets, big skies and sparkling water dotted with sails. One of Sussex's few remaining tracts of undeveloped coastline, the harbour shelters a rich diversity of habitats (shingle banks, saltmarsh, mudflats, sand dunes and ancient woodland) and wildlife – over 50,000 birds use the harbour every year, making it a top site for birdwatching, especially in winter. Exploring is easy: boat trips (see page 276) run all year, and 28 miles of footpaths wiggle around the coastline. **Chichester Harbour Conservancy** (ⓦconservancy.co.uk), which manages and conserves the harbour, also runs an excellent programme of **activities**, everything from canoe safaris to birdwatching and bat and butterfly walks.

Bosham

One of the prettiest villages on the harbour, and certainly the most popular, is historic, creekside **Bosham** (pronounced "Bozzum"). The village's appearance changes dramatically throughout the day as the tidal creek fills and empties: at low tide it's surrounded by green- and dun-coloured mudflats and marooned boats, while at high tide the water comes slapping right up against the back walls of the buildings along waterfront Shore Road. Despite warning signs, and tell-tale seaweed on the road, you still get the odd hapless parked car caught out by the tide; pop into the village pub, the *Anchor Bleu* (see below), and you'll see photos up on the walls of cars in various sorry states of submersion.

Fittingly, Bosham is one of the places put forward as the possible location of **King Cnut**'s (994–1035) failed attempt to turn back the tide – a deliberate display to show the limits of his power to his fawning courtiers. Cnut's young daughter is said to be buried in pretty, shingle-spired **Bosham Church**, parts of which date back to Saxon times. Look out for the reproduction of a scene from the **Bayeux Tapestry** in the north aisle, which depicts Harold, the Earl of Wessex and soon-to-be last Saxon King of England, praying in the church in 1064 before sailing off to Normandy to settle the matter of the English throne's succession with his rival, William of Normandy.

Beyond the church, over the millpond stream, lies National Trust-managed **Quay Meadow**, with **Bosham Quay** at its southern end; in summer it's a popular picnic spot, with good crabbing from the quay wall at high tide.

EATING AND DRINKING   BOSHAM

Anchor Bleu Bosham High St, PO18 8LS ☎01243 573956, ⓦanchorbleu.co.uk. The back terrace of this whitewashed eighteenth-century inn is the perfect spot to sit and watch the tide turn; at high water the sea laps right up against the terrace wall. Inside there are low, beamed ceilings and flagstone floors; the food is classic, well-done pub grub – baguettes and ploughman's (£6–10), fish and chips (£12), fresh dressed crab (£9) and the like at lunch, plus proper, satisfying puds like spotted dick and treacle sponge. Mon–Sat 11am–11pm; kitchen Mon–Fri noon–2pm & 6–9pm, Sat noon–3pm & 6–9pm, Sun noon–4pm & 5–8pm.

Itchenor

The long, winding country lane leading to the quiet sailing village of **Itchenor** ends at the slipway, with lovely views across to Bosham Hoe on the far side of the creek across a sea of masts and sails. There's a viewing platform next to the slipway, a lovely place to sit and watch the bobbing, clinking boats, but most people come to Itchenor to get out on the water themselves: **boat trips** run throughout the year, and from spring to autumn a small **passenger ferry** shuttles across the creek to Bosham Hoe, a thirty-minute walk south of picturesque Bosham (see page 274). Just by the slipway, the office of the **Chichester Harbour Conservancy** (Mon–Fri 9am–5pm, plus Easter–Sept Sat 9am–1pm; ☎01243 513275, ⓦconservancy.co.uk) has plenty of information on the harbour, boat trips, walks and other activities.

EATING AND DRINKING   ITCHENOR

Ship Inn The Street, PO20 7AH ☎01243 512284, ⓦtheshipinnitchenor.co.uk. Just up the lane from Itchenor's slipway, this redbrick pub is always busy in summer with boaties and tourists, and the picnic tables out front are a fine spot to settle down with a pint. Food is decent pub grub (sausages, burgers, fresh fish, steaks), with most mains in the £12.50–15 range, and there are Sussex-brewed beers and guest ales on tap. Daily 10am–11pm; kitchen Mon–Fri noon–2.30pm & 6.30–9pm, Sat noon–5pm & 6.30–9pm, Sun noon–5pm.

West Wittering Beach and around

Beach daily: mid-March to mid-Oct 6.30am–8.30pm; mid-Oct to mid-March 7am–6pm • Café mid-March to mid-Oct daily 9am–6pm; mid-Oct to mid-March Fri, Sat & Sun 10am–4pm • Parking £2–8.50 depending on season, day & time • ☎01243 514143 (Estate Office), ⓦwestwitteringbeach.co.uk

The wonderful thing about unspoilt **West Wittering Beach** is what *isn't* there: no amusement arcades, caravan parks or lines of shops selling garish seaside tat. Instead you'll find acres of soft white sand dimpled by shallow pools at low tide, a line of candy-coloured beach huts, grassy dunes and a beautiful new **café** with a wildlife-

CHICHESTER HARBOUR BOAT TRIPS

The best way to appreciate gloriously scenic Chichester Harbour is on the water. The harbour is one of the most popular boating waters in the country, with over 12,500 craft using it annually, and there are several ways you can join in.

HARBOUR TOURS

Chichester Harbour Conservancy ☏ 01243 513275, ⓦ conservancy.co.uk. The Conservancy runs boat trips on the *Solar Heritage*, a solar-powered catamaran with virtually silent engines that allow it to glide peacefully along the inlets and creeks, getting up close to wildlife; various cruises are available, including the standard "harbour discovery" tour, evening cruises, nature tours and winter-only birdwatching cruises. Departures are from Itchenor (1hr 30min; £10) throughout the year, apart from June to early September, when most trips depart from Emsworth (1hr; £10), just over the border in Hampshire; advance booking is essential.

Chichester Harbour Water Tours ☏ 01243 670504, ⓦ chichesterharbourwatertours.co.uk. Boat trips around the harbour leave from Itchenor up to four times a day during high summer, daily during spring and autumn, and weekends only during April and Oct (1hr 30min; £9).

BOAT HIRE

Itchenor Boat Hire ☏ 01243 513345, ⓦ itchenor boathire.co.uk. Offers self-drive, small-boat hire to those with prior experience, by the day or half-day (mid-June to mid-Sept only). A six-person dory costs £85–95/half-day, £125–145/day.

ITCHENOR–BOSHAM FERRY

Itchenor Ferry ⓦ itchenorferry.co.uk. Runs from the end of the jetty at Itchenor across the channel to Smugglers Lane at Bosham Hoe (April & Oct Sat & Sun 9am–6pm; May to Sept daily 9am–6pm; Nov–March Sat & Sun 10am–4pm; £2.50, bikes 50p).

friendly vegetated shingle roof – and that's about it. It could all have been so different, had a band of foresighted locals not scraped together £20,546 in the 1950s to buy the land and prevent it being turned into a Butlin's holiday camp; the West Wittering Estate is now managed as a conservation company, with parking fees paying for the maintenance of the beach and surrounding area.

The big grass field behind the beach serves as the car park; at its eastern end by the entrance you'll find a small cabin housing 2XS, which offers **watersports** tuition and equipment hire (see page 278), and at its western end is National Trust-owned East Head (see below). **West Wittering village** – which counts among its residents Rolling Stones guitarist Keith Richards – lies less than a mile inland.

The beach gets incredibly busy on summer weekends, when as many as 15,000 holidaymakers can descend in a day. Queues on the access road can snake back for miles; if you're staying in Chichester and don't want to spend an hour or two in traffic, your best bet is to hire a bike and cruise past the jams on the Salterns Way cycle route (see page 278).

East Head

Coast Guard Lane, Chichester, PO20 8AJ • Open access • Park at West Wittering beach car park (see page 275) • ☏ 01243 814730, ⓦ nationaltrust.org.uk/east-head

At the mouth of Chichester Harbour, National Trust-managed **East Head** is a pristine salt-and-shingle spit that's prized for its rare sand dune and saltmarsh habitats. It's connected to the western end of West Wittering Beach by a narrow strip of land known as "The Hinge", and covers around ten hectares – you can walk its length in just fifteen minutes, but despite its proximity to West Wittering's hordes it never really gets too busy. Boardwalks snake across the spit, protecting the fragile dune system. On the western (seaward) side there's a **beach** of fine sand backed by constantly shifting dunes knitted together with clumps of shaggy marram grass; on the eastern side there's a large area of saltmarsh which fills and empties with each tide – a popular **birdwatching** site, especially in winter. At the far northern end of the spit you'll often see boats anchored in the summer and, in winter, the occasional seal basking on the beach.

From The Hinge, a **footpath** runs north for a quarter of a mile to a specially constructed **crabbing pool**, and on to the village of Itchenor, a further 3.5 miles away. The path skirts the shoreline all the way, with flat farmland on one side and beautiful views across the water on the other.

ACCOMMODATION AND EATING · WEST WITTERING

Beach House B&B Rookwood Rd, PO20 8LT ☎ 01243 514800, ⊛ beachhse.co.uk. The best option if you want to stay close to West Wittering Beach is this friendly, family-run B&B with just seven lovely rooms (including some family rooms sleeping five); it's just a 15min walk from the beach, in the heart of West Wittering village. Minimum two-night stay April–Sept. **£130**

The Lamb Inn Chichester Rd, PO20 8QA ☎ 01243 511105, ⊛ thelambwittering.co.uk. Midway between West Wittering and Itchenor, this tile-hung country pub has a lovely ambience and locally sourced food (seafood linguine, rabbit pie, fish of the day, and the likes) in the £13–16 range. There's a nice garden out the back for summertime eating or drinking. Mon–Sat 11.30am–11pm, Sun 11.30am–10pm; kitchen Mon–Thurs noon–2.30pm & 6–9pm, Fri & Sat noon–3pm & 5.30–9pm, Sun noon–8pm.

The Landing Pound House, Pound Rd, PO20 8AJ ☎ 01243 513757, ⊛ facebook.com/thelandingcoffeeshop. This tiny coffee shop brings a dash of style to West Wittering, with its bare boards, Eames chairs and art on the walls. On the menu you'll find great coffee, cakes, fresh crab sandwiches and artisan ice cream. Mon–Fri 8am–5pm, Sat & Sun 9am–5pm.

East Wittering and Bracklesham Bay

Along the southwest coast of the Manhood Peninsula, the seaside villages of **East Wittering** and **Bracklesham Bay** merge together in an unremarkable modern sprawl of bungalows and shops. The beach along this stretch lacks the wow-factor of famous West Wittering; it's pebbly for a start (though there's plenty of sand at low tide), and is backed by modern residential blocks in place of West Wittering's grass-flecked dunes. It does, however, have some of the best places to eat on the peninsula, and is also one of the best stretches of coast for **fossil-hunting**, in particular around Bracklesham Bay, where every day at low tide hundreds of fossils including bivalve shells, shark's teeth and corals are washed up on the sand – the easiest fossil-hunting going, and perfect for families. The best hunting ground is around Bracklesham Bay car park and the few hundred yards east towards Selsey.

East Wittering is a popular location for **surfing**; you can hire boards and wetsuits from the Wittering Surf Shop (see page 278).

ACCOMMODATION AND EATING · EAST WITTERING AND BRACKLESHAM BAY

Billy's on the Beach Bracklesham Lane, Bracklesham Bay, PO20 8JH ☎ 01243 670373, ⊛ billysonthebeach.co.uk. Blue-and-white-striped Billy's has a great location right on the beach, cheerful beach-themed decor and a menu of pancakes, toasties (from £5.25), fish and chips, seafood platters (£13.50), ice cream sundaes and more. June to early Sept daily 9am–9pm; mid-Sept to May Mon–Wed & Sun 9am–5pm, Thurs–Sat 9am–9pm.

Drift-In Surf Café Wittering Surf Shop, 11–13 Shore Rd, East Wittering, PO20 8DY ☎ 01243 672292, ⊛ witteringsurfshop.com/pages/drift-in-cafe. As you might expect from a café that's connected to a surf shop, this place has a cool, laidback vibe, and a menu full of perfect energy fodder after a morning catching waves – smoothies, shakes, hot chocolate, doorstop sandwiches, wraps and salads, and an enormous selection of pancakes. Mon–Sat 9am–5pm, Sun 10am–4pm.

Drifters Kitchen & Bar 61 Shore Rd, East Wittering, PO20 8DY ☎ 01243 673584, ⊛ drifters-ew.co.uk. On a sunny day make a beeline for the big outside deck at this relaxed restaurant a pebble's throw from the beach. The crowd-pleasing menu runs from burgers (from £11.50) wraps through to chilli, mezze and tapas-style "small plates" (around £7 each), and there's a good kids' menu too. Craft beers, cocktails and wine are all available. Mon, Wed & Thurs 9am–7.30pm, Fri & Sat 9am–late, Sun 9am–4pm.

Stubcroft Farm Stubcroft Lane, East Wittering, PO20 8PJ ☎ 01243 671469, ⊛ stubcroft.com. This no-frills, eco- and wildlife-friendly campsite is the nicest place to camp on the Manhood Peninsula, and very popular, so book ahead in summer. The slightly cramped pitches are spread over three paddocks on a working sheep farm; BBQs and campfires are allowed, there's a small shop, and as an added bonus you can help bottle-feed the lambs in springtime. The nearest beaches (East Wittering and Bracklesham Bay) are a 20min walk away. **£20**

WALKS, WATERSPORTS AND TWO WHEELS ON THE MANHOOD PENINSULA

The great outdoors is what the Manhood Peninsula does best. The area is very well set up for walkers and cyclists, with miles of footpaths and cycle paths crisscrossing the peninsula – bikes can be rented in Fishbourne near Chichester (see page 270). If you want to get out on the water, sample the huge variety of watersports on offer around the coast.

WATERSPORTS

2XS West Wittering Beach (daily 9am–5.30pm; ☎ 01243 513077, ⓦ 2xs.co.uk). This well-established outfit is the only one on the sands of West Wittering. Taster sessions run for most watersports, with longer sessions/courses available: windsurfing (2hr/£55); surfing (2hr/£40); stand-up paddleboarding (2hr/£48); kitesurfing (5hr/£115). Equipment rental (wetsuits, body- and surfboards, SUPs, kayaks etc) is also available.

Fluid Adventures Unit 1A Keynor Farm, Chalk Lane, Sidlesham (Mon, Tues & Thurs 8am–6pm, Wed & Fri–Sun 8am–9pm; ☎ 01243 942777, ⓦ fluidadventures.co.uk). This excellent paddlesport company runs a variety of kayaking trips around Chichester harbour (£55) and can also arrange kayak and canoe hire from Itchenor (book in advance).

Wittering Surf Shop 11–13 Shore Rd, East Wittering (Mon–Sat 9am–5pm, Sun 10am–4pm; ☎ 01243 672292, ⓦ witteringsurfshop.co.uk). Surfboard hire costs £10/half-day, £15/full day.

CYCLING

Maps for the cycle routes below are available at ⓦ conservancy.co.uk/page/cycling.

Bill Way Signposted route from Chichester Canal Basin to Pagham Harbour nature reserve along a canalside path and minor roads.

Chichester–Itchenor–Bosham circular This summer-only route follows the Salterns Way as far as Chichester Marina, then continues to Itchenor, where you can pick up the ferry (see page 275) across to Bosham Hoe. You then cycle back up through Bosham and Fishbourne before returning to Chichester. This route is easily accessible if you're hiring bikes from Barreg Cycles in Fishbourne (see page 270).

Salterns Way This signposted route runs for 11.5 miles from the Market Cross in Chichester to the dunes of East Head, partly on cycle paths, partly on country lanes and roads.

WALKING

Chichester Harbour Walks There are lots of downloadable walks on the Chichester Harbour Conservancy website, including a lovely four-mile low-tide circular walk around West Wittering and East Head – see ⓦ conservancy.co.uk/page/walking.

Lipchis Way This long-distance north-to-south footpath (ⓦ newlipchisway.co.uk) runs from Liphook in Hampshire to West Wittering. The latter part of the walk runs from Chichester along Chichester Ship Canal, past Itchenor and along the coast to West Wittering (10 miles), where you can pick up bus #52 back to Chichester (Mon–Sat every 15–30min, Sun every 30min–1hr).

★ **Three Veg @ Samphire** 57 Shore Rd, East Wittering, PO20 8DY ☎ 01243 672754, ⓦ threeveg.co.uk. Vegetables are the star at this brilliant and imaginative flexitarian restaurant, which creates memorably delicious food from simple, fresh ingredients: mains (£11/12) are all vegetarian or vegan – expect the likes of charred peach and goat's cheese salad, or springtime risotto – but you can add fish or meat as an "add-on" if you choose (£5–7). Tues–Sat noon–2pm & 5–10pm.

Pagham Harbour RSPB nature reserve

Nature reserve Near Sidlesham, PO20 7NE • Open access • Free • **Visitor centre** Selsey Rd, 1 mile south of Sidlesham, PO20 7NE • Daily 10am–4pm • ☎ 01243 641508, ⓦ rspb.org.uk/paghamharbour • Car parks at visitor centre (donation suggested) & Church Norton; bus #51 from Chichester (20min); cycle route #88 (Bill Way) from Chichester Canal Basin

On the east side of the Manhood Peninsula, **Pagham Harbour nature reserve** feels blissfully remote – you wouldn't think that brash Bognor lies just five miles away along the coast. The bay at the heart of the reserve is intertidal, and the landscape transforms dramatically throughout the day: at high water it's filled by the sea, while low tide sees the water ebb away to reveal expanses of mudflats and saltmarsh, picked over by wading birds. Surrounding the bay is a patchwork of meadows, farmland, copses, lagoons, reed beds and, on either side of the harbour mouth, two long shingle spits that are speckled with sea kale and yellow horned poppies in early summer.

The reserve is an important wetland site for wildlife, with the tidal mudflats attracting scores of **bird** species throughout the year, including thousands of Brent geese in winter; there's a hide at Church Norton and a second near the **visitor centre** just south of Sidlesham. The visitor centre is also the starting point for the circular 1.75-mile **Discovery Trail**, which takes you along the edge of Pagham Harbour as far as Sidlesham, home to the excellent *Crab and Lobster* pub. The RSPB, which manages the reserve, runs **guided walks** and activities.

ACCOMMODATION AND EATING	PAGHAM HARBOUR

Crab & Lobster Mill Lane, Sidlesham, PO20 7NB ☎01243 641233, ⓦ crab-lobster.co.uk. If you want to treat yourself, this classy sixteenth-century inn on the edge of Pagham Harbour is the place: the rooms are effortlessly stylish, and the restaurant has an upmarket menu (mains £17–26) focused on local produce. At the back of the pub there's a peaceful terrace and beer garden with lovely views over the countryside. Mon–Fri noon–2.30pm & 6–9.30pm, Sat & Sun noon–9.30pm. **£200**

Medmerry RSPB nature reserve

PO20 7NE • Open access • Free • ⓦ rspb.org.uk/medmerry • Car parks at Earnley & Pagham Harbour visitor centre (see above)

A few miles southwest of Pagham Harbour, a new intertidal nature reserve has been created at **Medmerry**. The scheme, completed in 2013 and designed to reduce flood risk, involved constructing over four miles of new clay banks inland and then breaching the shingle beach, allowing the sea to flood in; the new wildlife habitats created are still developing, but already you can see plenty of birdlife. Access to the reserve's footpaths, cycle paths and viewing mounds is from either Earnley, on the western side of the reserve, or the Pagham Harbour visitor centre (see above).

Midhurst and around

Lying smack-bang in the middle of the South Downs National Park, and home to the park's headquarters, the small market town of **MIDHURST** proudly trumpets itself as "the heart of the national park". The sleepy town has plenty of charm and a lovely location, bordered to the north and east by the wiggling, willow-fringed River Rother, but the main draw is the surrounding countryside – a gorgeous patchwork of ancient woodland, heathland and sweeping, humpbacked hills. A few miles to the north lies wild and beautiful **Black Down**, the highest point in the national park, while just south is the South Downs Way, which threads east along the rolling chalk downlands to **Harting Down** nature reserve. Just south of here is the fascinating **Uppark House**, destroyed by fire in 1989 and since painstakingly restored by the National Trust.

Market Square and around

Midhurst grew up around the medieval market in **Market Square**, still the most picturesque corner of town. In the centre of the square, the **Church of St Mary Magdalene and St Denys** (ⓦ midhurstparishchurch.net) has Norman foundations but has been much rebuilt over the years. By the church stands the **Old Town Hall**, now *Garton's Coffee House*, which was built in 1551 as the town's market house, originally open-sided for traders to display their goods. In 1760 the building became the town hall, with law courts on the first floor and cells below (which you can still see in the coffee shop today). The town **stocks**, last used in 1859, sit in an alcove underneath the steps at the side of the building.

THE SOUTH DOWNS NATIONAL PARK

The **South Downs National Park** came into being in April 2010. Covering over six hundred square miles, it stretches for seventy miles from eastern Hampshire through to the chalk cliffs of East Sussex, encompassing rolling hills, heathland, woodland and coastline – and plenty of towns and villages, too. More than 112,000 people live and work in the national park – more than in any other – and it is crisscrossed by a dense network of over 1800 miles of footpaths and bridleways.

The South Downs themselves, a range of gently undulating chalk hills famously described by Rudyard Kipling as the "blunt, bow-headed, whale-backed downs", form the backbone of the park; the southern slopes slant gently down to the sea, while the steep escarpment on the northern side drops abruptly to give spectacular views over the low-lying Weald. West of Arundel, the South Downs become more wooded on their journey into Hampshire, and the boundaries of the national park extend northward to cover the Western Weald, an area of woodland and heathland that, after much debate, was included in the park in recognition of its outstanding natural beauty.

In 2016, the South Downs National Park was designated an **International Dark Sky Reserve** (IDSR), only the second IDSR in England and one of only thirteen in the world. Check out ⓦsouthdowns.gov.uk/communicating-south-downs/dark-night-skies for more information about the International Dark Sky Association, as well as tips on stargazing, details of events and a list of the darkest skies in the national park.

PARK PRACTICALITIES

Information The park's headquarters, the South Downs Centre (see page 282), is in Midhurst. ⓦsouthdowns. gov.uk has comprehensive information on public transport, food and drink, walks, cycling, horse-riding and other activities, plus an events calendar.

Getting around If travelling by public transport, the Discovery Ticket (£9, family ticket £17.50) is a good option, allowing a day's unlimited bus travel across the National Park; see ⓦsouthdowns.gov.uk/enjoy/plan-a-visit/getting-around/discovery-ticket for details.

Walking and cycling ⓦsouthdowns.gov.uk has over two dozen downloadable walks and cycle rides, and the National Trust – which manages some of the finest tracts of land within the Park – also has a series of downloadable walks on its website (ⓦnationaltrust. org.uk/visit/activities/walking). There's a list of bike hire outlets at ⓦsouthdowns.gov.uk/enjoy/cycling/hire-a-bike.

Food and drink The ⓦsouthdownsfood.org portal has lots of information on local produce, everything from Southdown lamb to award-winning Sussex fizz. The site's interactive food-finder map lists over two hundred businesses that champion locally produced food and drink – from farmers' markets and farm shops to vineyards, microbreweries, pubs and restaurants. The website also lists foodie events in the South Downs, from wine and beer tastings to food festivals and foraging events.

Behind the Old Town Hall on **Edinburgh Square** you'll see a row of redbrick houses with distinctive saffron-yellow paintwork, a sign they belong to the local **Cowdray Estate**, which covers 16,500 acres northeast of Midhurst; the colour, now known as "**Cowdray Yellow**", was chosen by the second Viscount Cowdray in the 1920s as a statement of his Liberal politics and has remained ever since.

Opposite Market Square is the gloriously higgledy-piggledy *Spread Eagle* (see page 282), one of Midhurst's two splendid **coaching inns**, dating back in part to 1430. Its rival, the Georgian-fronted *Angel Inn* on North Street, was the favoured drinking hole of a certain Guy Fawkes, who masterminded his infamous plot while butler at Cowdray House (see page 281).

North Street and the Cowdray ruins

Midhurst's main thoroughfare is **North Street**, which cuts through town to the west of Market Square. At the north end of the street is turreted **Capron House**, headquarters of the South Downs National Park Authority and home to its visitor centre (see page 282). A plaque on the wall recalls the building's past life as Midhurst Grammar

School, which was attended in the 1880s by novelist **H.G. Wells** while his mother worked as housekeeper at nearby Uppark House (see page 283).

On the opposite side of the street, across the water meadows, you can make out the castle-like gatehouse and crenellated walls of the **Cowdray House ruins**, assessible via a 300m-long causeway. From afar the building appears relatively intact, but as you draw closer, jagged walls come into view, glimpses of sky can be seen through the window frames and the gutted, roofless shell of a once-grand Tudor house is finally revealed. When Cowdray House was built in the sixteenth century, it was one of the grandest homes in the country (see below), but in 1793 a disastrous fire broke out which destroyed almost all of it. It was left to rot, and by the nineteenth century had become a romantic ruin, painted by Turner and Constable. You're not able to visit the ruins except during special events – see ⓦcowdray.co.uk for details.

Woolbeding Gardens

Poundcommon, Woolbeding, 2 miles north of Midhurst, GU29 9RR • Mid-April to Sept Thurs & Fri 10.30am–4.30pm, plus Weds in July & Aug; pre-booking required • £9.60; NT • ☎ 0344 249 1895, ⓦ nationaltrust.org.uk/woolbeding-gardens • No parking at site; a minibus shuttle service operates from Midhurst

You'll need to pre-book to visit hidden-away **Woolbeding Gardens**, which are only open to the public a few days a week in the summer. The magical gardens, which occupy a lovely spot by the River Rother just north of Midhurst, were created over a period of forty years by the late Sir Simon Sainsbury and his partner, Stewart Grimshaw, and vary hugely in style, from formal "garden rooms" divided by neat clipped hedges to a wilder water garden, complete with grotto, ruined chapel and Chinese bridge.

ARRIVAL AND INFORMATION

MIDHURST AND AROUND

By train and bus The closest stations are at Haslemere (connected by bus #70 to Midhurst: Mon–Sat hourly; 25min); Petersfield (bus #92: Mon–Sat hourly; 25min); and Chichester (bus #60: Mon–Sat every 30min, Sun hourly; 40min).

By car There are car parks at North St and Grange Rd.

THE RISE AND FALL OF COWDRAY HOUSE

In its heyday, **Cowdray House** was one of the grandest homes in the country – an ostentatious display of wealth and power, with lavish interiors and a castle-like exterior that reflected its owners' status. Cowdray was built by the powerful **Sir William Fitzwilliam**, friend and favoured courtier of Henry VIII, who began work on it in 1529 on the site of an earlier house. When Fitzwilliam died without heir in 1542, the estate passed to his half-brother **Sir Anthony Browne**, who two years previously had been gifted Battle Abbey (see page 185) by King Henry VIII during the Dissolution of the Monasteries. King Henry VIII, the young Edward VI and Elizabeth I all visited Cowdray to hunt and feast during its golden years; the queen, according to a 1591 account of her stay, enjoyed a modest breakfast of "three oxen, and one hundred and fortie geese".

Despite their Catholic allegiances, Cowdray's owners all managed to keep on the right side of the royals throughout the turbulent sixteenth century, right up until a certain **Guy Fawkes** – butler at Cowdray under the second Viscount Montague – hatched his plot to blow up Parliament in 1605; the Viscount was unaccountably absent from parliament on the planned day of the explosion, and was sentenced to forty weeks in prison for his suspected involvement.

In 1793, disaster struck Cowdray: during renovation work, a careless carpenter left a smouldering piece of charcoal on some wood shavings and a fire broke out that engulfed the whole house, reducing it virtually to ruins. Later that year the eighth Viscount died while shooting rapids on the Rhine; his successor died childless, ending the family line. These events saw the fulfilment of the so-called **"curse of Cowdray"**, supposedly put on the family back in the sixteenth century when Sir Anthony Browne pulled down the church at Battle Abbey in the Dissolution, and the evicted monks swore his family line would perish "by fire and water".

THE SPORT OF KINGS: POLO AT COWDRAY PARK

Polo has been played on the lawns of **Cowdray Park**, just north of Midhurst, since 1910. It was introduced to the country much earlier – in 1834, by the 10th Hussars at Aldershot – but it's Cowdray that's credited as its spiritual home. During World War II polo had all but died out; that it didn't is due entirely to the late **third Viscount Cowdray**, whose passion for the sport turned Cowdray into one of the most famous polo clubs in the world and kick-started a polo renaissance around the country. In 1956, the **Cowdray Park Gold Cup** was inaugurated, and it remains the highlight of the Cowdray polo season today; the final is one of the most glamorous events in the sporting calendar, with world-class players in action on the field and celebrities looking on.

The **game** is fast and furious, played on horseback on a grass field 300yd long by 160yd wide, with two teams of four riders attempting to score goals against their opponents. Matches are divided into seven-minute periods of play called **chukkas**, and a match will generally be four to six chukkas long, with players changing ends after each goal. At half-time spectators take to the field for "treading in" – stomping back the loose divots on the field.

The season at Cowdray Park runs from the end of April to mid-September, with **matches** held every Saturday and Sunday and most weekdays at one of its two grounds – the Lawns and River grounds near Midhurst, and the Ambersham pitches between Midhurst and Petworth. To watch, all you need do is turn up on the day; **tickets** can be bought at the entrance gate (£5, more for the Gold Cup semi-finals and final). See ⓦ cowdraypolo.co.uk for details of fixtures, and to buy Gold Cup tickets in advance.

South Downs Centre Capron House, North St (Mon– Thurs 9am–5pm, Fri 9am–4.30pm; May–Oct also Sat & bank hols 9am–1pm; ☎ 01730 814810, ⓦ southdowns. gov.uk). Headquarters of the National Park Authority, the South Downs Centre contains a small exhibition about the national park and has plenty of leaflets and information on walks and public transport. There's also information on Midhurst (ⓦ visitmidhurst.com), including town maps and trails.

ACCOMMODATION

The Church House Church Hill, GU29 9NX ☎ 01730 812990, ⓦ churchhousemidhurst.com. Luxurious B&B with five gorgeous rooms in a great location by Market Square. It's worth splashing out on one of the suites (£165) if you can: two of them come with high oak-beamed ceilings and roll-top baths. **£140**

Park House Bepton, near Midhurst, GU29 0JB ☎ 01730 819000, ⓦ parkhousehotel.com. Small, luxurious country-house hotel with glorious views, elegant rooms (from standard rooms to suites, plus cottages in the grounds), a croquet lawn, grass tennis courts and a spa – a real retreat. Rates vary according to demand. **£200**

Spread Eagle Hotel South St, GU29 9NH ☎ 01730 816911, ⓦ hshotels.co.uk. This wisteria-covered former coaching inn, dating back in part to the fifteenth century, oozes antiquity, from the creaking corridors and stained-glass windows to the wonky-walled lounge. Standard rooms are comfortable, and rates include use of the hotel spa. **£179**

Two Rose Cottages 2 Rose Cottages, Chichester Rd, GU29 9PF ☎ 01730 813804, ⓦ tworosebandb.com. Friendly B&B in a Victorian cottage, with just two tasteful rooms, both en suite. A cosy sitting room, private front door, great breakfasts and plenty of local maps and books all round off a tip-top B&B experience. **£90**

EATING

MIDHURST

Cowdray Café Easebourne, 1 mile north of Midhurst, GU29 0AJ ☎ 01730 815152, ⓦ cowdrayfarmshop.co.uk. Attached to the Cowdray Farm Shop, this café is a popular spot for breakfast and lunch, with lots of local produce on the menu, from rarebit made with Sussex Charmer cheese to the Cowdray burger made from the Estate's organically reared beef (£8.50). Mon–Sat 8am–5pm, Sun & bank hols 9am–5pm.

Garton's Coffee House Market Square, GH29 9NJ ☎ 01730 817166, ⓦ gartons.net. Bright and airy coffee house situated in the Old Town Hall, with tables outside on the cobbles in the summer – the nicest place in Midhurst for an alfresco cuppa. Good sandwiches and salads range from £4 to £8. At the back you can still see the wooden-doored cells once used to house the town's criminals. Mon–Sat 8am–5pm, Sun 9.30am–5pm.

The Olive & Vine North Street, GU29 9DJ ☎ 01730 859532, ⓦ theoliveandvine.co.uk. Popular, contemporary restaurant-bar that covers all bases, from breakfasts through to evening meals and late-night cocktails. The dinner menu features burgers, salads, "Sharing Planks" (£30) and tasty, tapas-style "small plates" (around £6). Daily 9am–late.

AROUND MIDHURST

Some of the best food in the area can be found in the pubs in nearby villages, many of which have the added bonus of splendid views; booking ahead is recommended.

Duke of Cumberland Fernhurst, 5 miles north of Midhurst, just off the A286, GU27 3HQ ☎ 01428 652280, ⓦ dukeofcumberland.com. Fifteenth-century pub with bags of character and spectacular views. To see it in its full glory visit in summer and grab a table on the lovely deck or in the enormous sloping garden. Food is delicious but pricey: most mains cost £20 and upwards at dinner, although simpler lunch dishes (including sandwiches) are £9–16. Mon–Sat 11.30am–11.30pm, Sun noon–10.30pm; kitchen Mon & Sun noon–2pm, Tues–Sat noon–2pm & 7–9pm.

Lickfold Inn Highstead Lane, Lickfold, 6 miles northeast of Midhurst, GU28 9EY ☎ 01789 532535, ⓦ thelickfoldinn.co.uk. This foodie pub is a real gem. Downstairs, the bar offers log fires, local ales, comfy sofas and a long list of gourmet bar snacks (£2–14), while upstairs is a beautiful dining room where you can tuck into dishes such as halibut with yeast cauliflower and pickled sloes (£19–32). Wed–Sat 11am–11pm, Sun 11am–7pm; kitchen Wed–Fri noon–2.30pm & 6–9pm, Sat noon–2.30pm & 6–9.30pm, Sun 12.30–5.30pm.

Noah's Ark Inn The Green, Lurgashall, 7 miles northeast of Midhurst, GU28 9ET ☎ 01428 707346, ⓦ noahsarkinn.co.uk. Traditional village pub in a perfect setting looking out onto the pretty village green. Great food, from fish and chips and burgers to Sussex rib-eye (£15–24), plus kids' meals. Mon–Sat 11am–11.30pm, Sun noon–8pm (10pm in summer); kitchen Mon–Sat noon–2.30pm & 7–9.30pm, Sun noon–3.15pm.

SHOPPING

Cowdray Farm Shop Easebourne, 1 mile north of Midhurst, GU29 0AJ ☎ 01730 815152, ⓦ cowdray farmshop.co.uk. Award-winning farm shop selling Cowdray and other local produce, including meat and eggs from the estate. Mon–Sat 9am–6pm, Sun & bank hols 9am–5pm.

Cowdray Living Easebourne, 1 mile north of Midhurst, GU29 0AJ ☎ 01730 815152, ⓦ cowdray.co.uk. Finish off a visit to the Cowdray Farm Shop by popping into its sister shop across the courtyard, where you can buy a range of homeware and gifts, including slow-wax candles made on the Estate, and work from local artists and craftspeople. Mon–Sun 10am–5pm.

Harting Down Nature Reserve

Near South Harting • Open access • NT; parking £2 for non-members • ⓦ nationaltrust.org.uk/harting-down

Wonderful views, wildflowers, butterflies and skylarks abound at the National Trust-run **Harting Down Nature Reserve**, where there are plenty of options for walks including an easy four-mile circular route (see page 284) – walkers thin out the further you get from the hilltop car park. The highest point is steep-sided **Beacon Hill** (794ft), site of an Iron Age hillfort and home to the remains of a Napoleonic War telegraph station.

Uppark House

South Harting, Petersfield, GU31 5QR • **House** March–Oct daily 12.30–4pm; Servants' Quarters and dolls' house mid-Feb–Oct daily 11am–4pm, Nov to mid-Feb daily 11am–3pm • £12.50 (includes garden); NT • **Garden** Mid-Feb to Oct daily 10am–5pm; Nov to mid-Feb daily 10am–4pm; tours March–Oct Thurs 2pm • £9.95; NT • ☎ 01730 825857, ⓦ nationaltrust.org.uk/uppark

Handsome **Uppark House** sits, as it has done for centuries, perched high up on the Downs, with no hint that things might have been very different. For 1989, a fire caused by a workman's blowtorch started a blaze that virtually reduced it to ruin. The house was open at the time, and National Trust staff, volunteers and members of the family managed to carry most of the art and furniture collection to safety. The decision was made to restore the house as it would have been on the day before the fire broke out, and this kicked into action a £20-million restoration, involving hundreds of craftsmen, many of whom had to relearn skills that had been lost for decades. The house finally opened once more in 1995, and it's fascinating today to play detective and spot the (often seamless) joins between original and restored woodwork, curtains, carpets and wallpaper (with commendable foresight, strips were ripped from the walls as the fire blazed, so that colours and pattern could be matched later).

WALKS AROUND MIDHURST

There are some fabulous walks to be had in the countryside around Midhurst. The **South Downs Way** (see page 210) can be joined two miles south of town, accessed from the village of Cocking at the foot of the scarp (bus #60 from Midhurst; Mon–Sat every 30min, Sun hourly; 10min). From Cocking you can head east along the Way towards Upwaltham or west towards Harting Down (see page 283). The walks below are marked on OS *Explorer* **maps** OL33 and OL8.

Midhurst River Walk This easy three-mile circular route (waymarked Rother Walk) runs northwest from Midhurst's North Bridge Weir along the River Rother to Woolbeding, before returning via sweeping parkland to town.

Harting Down circular This four-mile route takes you east along the ridgetop South Downs Way, with panoramic views across the Weald, before cutting south around the lower slopes of Beacon Hill, and then heading back to your starting point through a cool, dark yew wood and up onto Harting Hill.

Serpent Trail Pick up the Serpent Trail, a 64-mile-long route which wends its way in a serpentine S-shape through beautiful heathland from Haslemere in Surrey past Black Down (see page 284), Petworth and Midhurst to Petersfield in Hampshire; the section from Midhurst to Petersfield is around 10 miles, and there's a handy bus for the return leg (bus #92: Mon–Sat every 1–2hr). You can download a trail map from ⓦ southdowns.gov.uk/enjoy/walking/serpent-trail.

Even before the fire, the house had seen its fair share of excitement. It was built in 1690, and bought some fifty years later by **Sir Matthew Fetherstonhaugh**, who lavished some of his huge fortune on furnishing the house with treasures acquired on the Continent. When he died, his playboy son **Sir Harry** took up the reins with some relish, installing the teenage Emma Hart (the future Lady Hamilton, Nelson's mistress) as his live-in lover in the house, where she would reportedly dance naked on the dining-room table. Harry certainly knew how to enjoy himself: at the ripe old age of 70 he scandalized Sussex society by marrying his 21-year-old dairymaid, Mary Ann Bullock.

The elegant Georgian **interior** is crammed with treasures from Sir Matthew's Grand Tour; highlights include the sumptuous gold and white Saloon, and an eighteenth-century doll's house with miniature oil paintings and tiny hallmarked silverware. The **servants' quarters** are presented as they would have been in the late nineteenth century when the mother of **H.G. Wells** was housekeeper here.

Uppark's beautiful **gardens** have lovely views over the Downs, and contain the elegant Georgian dairy where Mary Anne Bullock's singing first caught the roving Sir Harry's attention.

Black Down

Tennyson's Lane, GU27 3BJ • Open access • NT; parking free • ⓦ nationaltrust.org.uk/black-down

Black Down (917ft), up near the Surrey border, is the highest point in the national park – a wild and rich landscape of heathland, ancient woodland, bogs and wildflower meadows, crisscrossed by trails. **Tennyson** lived here for almost a quarter of a century before his death, and immortalized the beautiful view from his study in a poem: "You came, and looked and loved the view/Long-known and loved by me/Green Sussex fading into blue/With one gray glimpse of sea." To capture the view for yourself, park at the free car park on Tennyson Lane (southeast of the town of Haslemere) and follow the footpath for a mile to the **Temple of the Winds**, one of the finest viewpoints in Sussex, where the ground falls away before you and miles of patchwork fields and copses stretch into the distance, backed by the blue-green smudge of the South Downs; on a clear day you can indeed glimpse the sea, forty miles away. Black Down is also one of the best **star-gazing** destinations in the country: see ⓦ nationaltrust.org.uk/black-down/trails/summer-star-gazing-walk-at-black-down for a downloadable star-gazing walk.

Petworth

The honey-coloured, high stone walls of Petworth House loom over the handsome little town of **PETWORTH**, seven miles east of Midhurst. The town owes its existence to the great house and its estate: for centuries the Leconfield Estate employed virtually everyone in the town, and reminders of its importance can be seen in the brown-painted doors of the hundreds of estate cottages built in the mid-nineteenth century (and numbered according to when they first appeared in the rent records). Even today, it's **Petworth House** that brings in the tourists, and most visitors, justifiably, make a beeline straight for it; the rest of town, though, is a bit of a gem, with an extraordinary number of vibrant independent shops for its size, centred around a thriving **antiques trade**. East of the town, attractions include family-friendly **Fishers Farm Park** and the peaceful **Wey and Arun Canal**.

Market Square and around

The centre of town is **Market Square**, site of the town's marketplace since at least 1541. In the centre of the square is **Leconfield Hall**, built in 1794 as a courthouse; the old fire bells, which once served as the town's fire alarm, can be seen up on the pediment above the clock. The hall is one of the venues for July's **Petworth Festival** (ⓦpetworthfestival. org.uk), a two-week-long arts festival.

From Market Square, cobbled **Lombard Street** – once the town's busiest thoroughfare and still its prettiest – climbs north to Church Street and the **Church of St Mary's**; to the left of the church is the entrance to Petworth House, while to the right you'll see a fantastically elaborate iron **streetlamp**, designed by Charles Barry (of Houses of Parliament fame) and erected by the townspeople in 1851 as a token of thanks to Lord Leconfield for installing gas lighting in the town.

Petworth House

Petworth, GU28 9LR • **House** Mid-March to early Nov daily 11am–5pm; rest of year opening hours vary – check website • **Pleasure Ground** Daily: mid-March to Oct 10am–5pm; Nov–Feb 10am–4pm; early March 10am–4.30pm • House and Pleasure Ground mid-March to early Nov £14.40, rest of year £12; NT • Parking £4 • ☏ 01798 342207, ⓦ nationaltrust.org.uk/petworth

Petworth House, built in the late seventeenth century, is one of the Southeast's most impressive stately homes. The grounds alone are worth the visit: seven hundred acres of stunning parkland, ponds and woodland, roamed by the largest herd of fallow deer in the country and dotted with ancient oaks. The park – containing the thirty-acre woodland garden known as the **Pleasure Ground** – was landscaped by Capability Brown and is considered one of his finest achievements, but it was **Turner** who made the sweeping vistas famous, immortalizing the park in several of his paintings. Turner was a frequent visitor here, given virtual free rein of the house by the art-loving third Earl of Egremont; Mike Leigh's 2014 film *Mr Turner* was partly shot on location here.

Twenty of Turner's paintings are on view in the house, and form just part of Petworth's outstanding **art collection**, with works by Van Dyck, Titian, Gainsborough, Bosch, Reynolds and Blake. Other treasures include the **Molyneux globe**, dating from 1592 and believed to be the earliest terrestrial globe in existence, and the **Leconfield Chaucer** manuscript, one of the earliest surviving editions of the *Canterbury Tales*.

The opulent **decor** is equally jaw-dropping. Highlights are Louis Laguerre's murals around the **Grand Staircase**, which trace the myth of Prometheus and Pandora, and the dazzling **Carved Room**, where flowers, fruit, vines, musical instruments and birds have been carved in joyfully extravagant detail by master woodcarver Grinling Gibbons.

The **servants' quarters**, connected by a tunnel to the main house, contain an impressive series of kitchens bearing the latest in 1870s kitchen technology, and a copper *batterie de cuisine* of more than a thousand pieces – all polished by a team of strong-elbowed volunteers every winter.

8

Petworth Cottage Museum

346 High St, GU28 0AU • April–Oct Tues–Sat 2–4.30pm • £5 • ☎ 01798 342100, ⊚ petworthcottagemuseum.co.uk

For an alternative and intriguing view of the life of one of the great house's former employees, **Petworth Cottage Museum** is well worth a visit. Seamstress Mary Cummings lived in this gas-lit abode, which has been restored using her own possessions to show how it would have looked in 1910, with family photos on the wall, the washing-up by the sink and the kettle on the range.

ARRIVAL AND INFORMATION

By train and bus The closest stations are Haslemere (no bus connection) and Pulborough (bus #1: Mon–Sat hourly, Sun every 2hr; 15min). Bus #1 also connects Petworth with Midhurst (15min).

By car There's a large car park in the centre of town and another at Petworth House.

Website ⊚ discoverpetworth.com.

ACCOMMODATION AND EATING

E. Street Bar & Grill New Street, GU28 0AS ☎ 01798 345111 ⊛ theleconfield.co.uk. Classy restaurant serving up superb locally sourced food in a characterful seventeenth-century building. Dishes from the grill (ranging from spatchcock poussin to Wagyu blade steak; £14–36) sit alongside cheaper offerings from the "classic" menu (£11 and up). Mon–Sat noon–2.30pm & 6–9.30pm, Sun noon–3pm & 6–9pm.

★ **Horse Guards Inn** Upperton Rd, Tillington, GU28 9AF ☎ 01798 342332, ⊛ thehorseguardsinn.co.uk. Lovely little gastropub two miles west of Petworth, decked out with informal, shabby-chic panache; in summer you can grab a deckchair (or hay-bale) in the idyllic garden. Harveys and guest ales on tap, plus excellent seasonal food; mains (around £15) might include Selsey crab with sea vegetable salad in summer, or pheasant with hawthorn jelly in winter. The pub also has three serene, pretty B&B rooms. Daily noon–midnight; kitchen Mon–Thurs noon–2.30pm & 6.30–9pm, Fri noon–2.30pm & 6–9.30pm, Sat noon–3pm & 6–9.30pm, Sun noon–3.30pm & 6.30–9pm. **£110**

Hungry Guest Café Lombard St, GU28 0AG ☎ 01798 344564, ⊛ thehungryguest.com. This smart, modern café on cobbled Lombard Street serves up top-quality food, as you'd expect from the sister café of the excellent Hungry Guest Food Shop (see below). The breakfast menu offers freshly baked croissants from the bakery near Chichester, while the lunch menu features sourdough pizza (£10), sandwiches, burgers and more. Mon–Fri 8.30am–5.30pm, Sat 9am–5.30pm, Sun 9am–4pm.

★ **Old Railway Station** 2 miles south of Petworth on the A285, GU28 0JF ☎ 01798 342346, ⊛ old-station. co.uk. Petworth's former railway station (1892) has been converted into a smart, colonial-style B&B, with breakfast and cream teas served in the high-ceilinged old waiting room; in summer there are tables out on the platform. The largest rooms are upstairs in the station house, but for sheer character they can't compete with the rooms in the stylishly converted Pullman carriages on the platform. **£170**

Petworth Penthouse Park Rd, GU28 0EA ☎ 01798 215007, ⊛ penthousepetworth.com. If you're travelling in a small group, consider a stay at this luxurious three-bedroom self-catering penthouse, with a light-flooded, double-height open-plan living area and views over the rooftops to Petworth House. The space was once the studio of Victorian portrait photographer Walter Keevis (his dark room is now the kitchen) and, in a nice touch, some of his old photographs adorn the walls. Two-night minimum stay. Two people **£145**, six people **£345**

SHOPPING

Petworth has more than two dozen **antiques and arts** dealers within a mile of the centre – one of the greatest concentrations of any town in the Southeast. Check out ⊚ discoverpetworth.org/petworth-antiques for a comprehensive list or pick up the free town guide (with map) – most shops will have copies.

Hungry Guest Food Shop Middle St, GU29 0BE ☎ 01798 342803, ⊛ thehungryguest.com. This award-winning produce store sells its own bread, pastries and brownies (baked at its own wholesale artisan bakery), and sells local Wobblegate apple juice, a good selection of charcuterie and cheese from a dedicated cheese room – all you need for a picnic at Petworth Park. Mon–Sat 9am–6pm, Sun 10am–5pm.

Kevis House Gallery Lombard St, GU28 0AG ☎ 01798 215007, ⊛ kevishouse.com. Changing exhibitions of works on paper – prints, drawings and photography, including an annual wood-engraving exhibition. Tues–Sat 10am–5pm.

Wey and Arun Canal

Loxwood, RH14 0RH · April–Oct Sat, Sun & bank hols 3 cruises each afternoon (35min–2hr 30min); also open for occasional special mid-week events · £6 for 35min cruise, £12 for 2hr 30min · ☎ 01403 752404, ⓦ weyandarun.co.uk

"London's lost route to the sea", the 23-mile **Wey and Arun Canal** was built between 1813 and 1816 to provide an inland barge route between the capital and the south coast, carrying agricultural produce, coal and imported goods. The coming of the railways spelled an end to its brief period of usefulness, however, and in 1871 it was formally abandoned. The Wey and Arun Canal Trust, which began its quest to restore the canal in the 1970s and has today cleared more than half of it, runs **narrowboat trips** on the canal which take you through some of the restored locks.

Fishers Farm Park

Newpound Lane, Wisborough Green, RH14 0EG · Daily 10am–5pm · £9.75 low-, £12.75 mid- & £15.75 peak-season; under-2s free · ☎ 01403 700063, ⓦ fishersfarmpark.co.uk

If you've got younger kids, you really can't go wrong with the award-winning **Fishers Farm Park** – the farm park to end all farm parks. There are all the usual animals on show, ready for petting, bottle-feeding and riding, plus a ten-acre adventure play area featuring everything from swingboats, slides and sandpits to an assault course, treetop nets and a splash zone, with a few scare-free "rides" thrown in for good measure. It's not cheap, but it's friendly and well run, jam-packed with things to do, and once you're through the doors everything's included.

Arundel and around

Your first view of **ARUNDEL** if you're driving in from the east is a corker, with the turrets of its fairytale castle rising up out of the trees, and the huge bulk of the Gothic cathedral towering over the rooftops. The compact town's well-preserved appearance and picturesque setting by the banks of the River Arun draw the crowds on summer

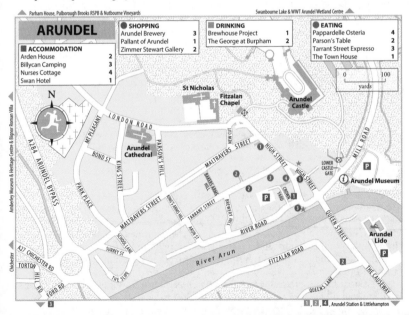

weekends, but at any other time a visit reveals one of West Sussex's least spoilt old towns. The main attractions are the **castle**, seat of the dukes of Norfolk, and the **WWT Arundel Wetland Centre** on the outskirts of town, but the rest of Arundel is pleasant to wander round, with some good independent shops, cafés and restaurants on the High Street and Tarrant Street. At the end of August, **Arundel Festival** (Ⓦarundelfestival. co.uk) features everything from open-air theatre to salsa bands.

Out of town, there are some lovely walks through the water meadows, as well as a handful of sights further afield, including **Bignor Roman Villa**, the **Amberley Museum** of industrial heritage and the graceful Elizabethan **Parham House**.

Arundel Castle

Mill Rd, BN18 9AB • April–Oct Tues–Sun & bank hols: keep 10am–4.30pm; Fitzalan Chapel & grounds 10am–5pm; castle rooms noon–5pm • Castle rooms, keep, grounds & chapel £20; keep, grounds & chapel £15; grounds & chapel £13 • ☏ 01903 882173, Ⓦ arundelcastle.org

Arundel's standout attraction is **Arundel Castle**, which, though pricey, has enough to keep you occupied for a whole day. Despite its romantic medieval appearance, most of what you see is little more than a century old: the original Norman castle was badly damaged in the Civil War in the seventeenth century, and was reconstructed from 1718 onwards, most extensively by the fifteenth duke at the end of the nineteenth century. Parts of the original structure still remain, notably the 100ft-high **motte** on which it stands, constructed in 1068 by **Roger de Montgomery**. The **keep**, built in 1190, is a steep climb up 131 stairs, but rewards with wonderful views over the town and out to sea. **Events** take place throughout the year, including re-created sieges and medieval tournaments – see the website for details.

Over in the main, remodelled part of the castle, the opulent **castle rooms** provide a dramatic contrast to the medieval keep, with cold stone walls replaced by extravagantly carved woodwork, fine tapestries, ornate sixteenth-century furniture and masterpieces by Gainsborough, Holbein, Van Dyck and Canaletto. Treasures peep out from every corner, easy to miss amid the general splendour: in the **dining room**, hidden away in a small cabinet, is the gold and enamel rosary carried by Mary, Queen of Scots at her execution. Other highlights include the palatial **Barons' Hall**, the Victorian **private chapel** and the stunning Regency **library**, carved out of Honduran mahogany.

In the castle grounds, the **Collector Earl's Garden** is a playfully theatrical take on a Jacobean garden, with exotic palms and ferns, and pavilions, obelisks and urns made from green oak rather than stone. Adjacent is the beautiful fourteenth-century **Fitzalan Chapel**, burial place of the dukes of Norfolk, who have owned the castle for over 850 years in a more-or-less unbroken line. Like the castle, the chapel was badly damaged in the Civil War, when encamped Roundheads stabled their horses among the tombs, but it was restored in the late nineteenth century. Carved stone tombs are dotted around the chapel, among them the rather gruesome twin effigies of the seventh duke – one as he looked when he died and, underneath, one of his emaciated corpse.

Arundel Cathedral

Corner of Parson's Hill & London Rd, BN18 9AY • Daily 9am–6pm or dusk • Free • ☏ 01903 882297, Ⓦ www.arundelcathedral.uk

The flamboyant **Arundel Cathedral** was constructed in the 1870s over the town's former Catholic church by the fifteenth duke of Norfolk; its spire was designed by John Hansom, inventor of the hansom cab. Inside are the enshrined remains of **St Philip Howard**, the canonized thirteenth earl, who was brought up Protestant but chose to return to the Catholic faith of his birth, thereby turning his back on a life of great favour at Elizabeth I's royal court; he was sentenced to death in 1585, aged 27, when he was caught fleeing overseas, and died of dysentery in the Tower of London ten years later, refusing till the very last to renounce his faith.

St Nicholas' church

London Rd, BN18 9AT • Daily 9am–5pm • Free • ☎ 01903 882262, ⊛ stnicholas-arundel.co.uk

What you see when you walk into the fourteenth-century **church of St Nicholas** is really only half a church: behind an iron grille and glass wall lies the Fitzalan Chapel, once the church's chancel but now part of Arundel Castle, and accessible only through the castle grounds. This unique state of affairs – which has resulted in a Church of England parish church and a Catholic chapel under one roof – came about in 1544 with the Dissolution, when Henry VIII sold off the chancel to the twelfth earl, and it became the private chapel and burial place of the earl's family. The screen has only been opened eight times in the last 35 years, most recently in 1995 for the funeral of Lavinia, Duchess of Norfolk. Elsewhere in the church, look out for the red consecration crosses on the walls, which date from the church's construction in 1380, and the beautiful carved stone **pulpit**, one of only six pre-Reformation pulpits in the country, believed to be the work of Henry Yevele, who also designed the nave in Canterbury Cathedral.

Arundel Lido

Queen St, BN18 9JG • May to mid-Sept daily noon–6/7pm, opens 10am Sat, Sun, bank hols & school hols • £8 • ☎ 01903 882404, ⊛ arundel-lido.com

Just south of the river lies **Arundel Lido**, which celebrates its sixtieth anniversary in 2020. It's a great spot for a dip on a hot day, with grassy lawns surrounding the heated pool, a separate paddling pool for kids and, best of all, a view of the castle as you swim along.

Mill Road

From the castle entrance, **Mill Road** curves north through an avenue of trees up to **Swanbourne Lake**, an old millpond encircled by trees, with **rowing boats** for hire (March–Oct Sat, Sun & school hols from 9/10am; £3.50/person for 30min) and a tearoom. Swanbourne Lake is the entrance to the thousand-acre **Arundel Park**, which is crisscrossed with footpaths that meet up with the South Downs Way three miles away near Houghton.

Arundel Museum

Mill Rd, BN18 9PA • Daily 10am–4pm • £3.50 • ☎ 01903 885866, ⊛ arundelmuseum.org

At the southern end of Mill Road by the river, the small and immaculately presented **Arundel Museum** tells the story of the town and the surrounding area through exhibits that range from 500,000-year-old Palaeolithic hand-axes to a model of Arundel Castle during the Civil War. There's also an informative display on the castle's owners over its almost 1000-year history, from the first Norman earls to the current dukes of Norfolk – well worth a read if you're planning to visit the castle.

WWT Arundel Wetland Centre

Mill Rd, BN18 9PB • Daily: April to mid-Oct 9.30am–5.30pm; mid-Oct to March 9.30am–4.30pm • £12.09, under-17s £6.50 • **Pond-dipping** May–Oct Sat, Sun & school hols • **Boat trips** Daily: spring–autumn 11am–4.30pm; winter 11am–3.30pm; 15–20min • ☎ 01903 883355, ⊛ wwt.org.uk/wetland-centres/arundel

The excellent **WWT Arundel Wetland Centre**, a mile out of town along Mill Road, is a great place to spend half a day, especially if you've got children in tow. The centre is home to endangered waterfowl from around the world, but a wander around the scenic 65-acre site, divided into different habitats, can also turn up sightings of native wildlife including water voles, kingfishers, sand martins, dragonflies and peregrines. Don't miss the tranquil, rustling **reedbed boardwalks** – where artist Chris Drury has created a camera obscura sculpture – or the free **boat trips**, probably your best chance of spotting water voles. There are a couple of imaginative play areas for kids, as well as popular **pond-dipping** sessions.

8

ARRIVAL AND INFORMATION

ARUNDEL AND AROUND

By train Arundel's station is half a mile south of the town centre over the river on the A27.

Destinations Brighton (hourly; 1hr 10min); Chichester (Mon–Sat 2 hourly, Sun hourly; 30–50min); London Victoria (every 30min; 1hr 20min).

By bus Buses arrive either on the High St or River Rd. Stagecoach bus #9 runs to Shoreham-by-Sea via Littlehampton (Mon–Sat hourly), and Compass bus #85

connects Arundel to Chichester (every 2hr; 45min).

By car There's free parking all along Mill Rd, though spaces fill up quickly on summer weekends; failing that try the large pay-and-display car park on Mill Rd.

Tourist information There's a visitor information point in Arundel Museum, open the same hours as the museum (ⓦ sussexbythesea.com).

ACCOMMODATION

SEE MAP PAGE 287

Arden House 4 Queens Lane, BN18 9JN ⓣ 01903 884184, ⓦ ardenhousearundel.com. Smart and very friendly B&B, in a great location just south of the river. The cheapest rooms share bathrooms (fluffy robes are provided to protect your modesty); en-suite rooms are just £10 more. There's bike storage, and muddy walking boots are welcomed. **£89**

Billycan Camping Manor Farm, Tortington, near Arundel, BN18 0BG ⓣ 07766 742533, ⓦ billycan camping.co.uk. You know you're onto a winner as soon as you arrive at this lovely campsite, a fifteen-minute walk from Arundel. The snug, vintage-style tents and yurts (available in various sizes) come decked out with bunting, pathways are lit by tealights at night, and campers are welcomed with a communal stew around the campfire on a Friday night. The two-night minimum stay includes a breakfast hamper stuffed with local goodies. Open May–Aug. Four-person scout tents **£122.50**, four-person bell tents **£122.50**, four-person yurt **£210**

Nurses Cottage Warningcamp, Arundel BN18 9QU ⓣ 01903 884718, ⓦ arundelnursescottage.com. One of the nicest places to stay in Arundel is this super-friendly B&B in the nearby hamlet of Warningcamp, a half-hour walk or five-minute drive from the town centre. A stay in one of the two beautiful B&B rooms gives you a perfect slice of rural tranquillity – there are gorgeous views out over the Arun valley and castle, and breakfast comes with homemade jams and eggs from the resident chickens. **£85**

Swan Hotel 27–29 High St, BN18 9AG ⓣ 01903 882314, ⓦ swanarundel.co.uk. The fifteen rooms above this pub have a bit of a seaside-chic vibe, with coir carpet or wooden boards underfoot, white tongue-and-groove panelling, shutters and seaside-themed photos and paintings. The cheapest rooms are on the small side, so consider paying extra for a superior double. Family rooms are also available. Prices fluctuate according to demand. **£120**

EATING

SEE MAP PAGE 287

★ **Pappardelle Osteria** 41 High St, BN18 9AG ⓣ 01903 882024, ⓦ pappardelle.co.uk. This friendly café-cum-wine-bar, with its long copper communal tables, has a sociable buzz about it, with people chatting over coffee or reading papers in the daytime. In the evening there are cocktails, over twenty different grappas, and more than thirty (mostly Italian) wines by the glass. Food is served all day, from breakfast through to pizza (£8.50 upwards), bruschetta, pasta and *cicchetti* (Italian-style canapés). Mon & Tues 9am–4pm, Wed–Sat 9am–11pm, Sun 10am–6pm.

Parson's Table 2 & 8 Castle Mews, Tarrant St BN18 9DG ⓣ 01903 883477, ⓦ theparsonstable.co.uk. Tucked away off Tarrant Street, this relaxed, informal restaurant has won itself plenty of fans (and a few awards) for its beautifully presented, imaginative food. Dishes feature plenty of local, seasonal ingredients, from South Coast mackerel to South Downs lamb (mains £16–26). Tues– Sat noon–2.30pm & 6– 9.30pm.

Tarrant Street Expresso 17 Tarrant St, BN18 9DG ⓣ 01903 885350. Stylish, pocket-sized coffee shop, with just a couple of tables inside and a few stools outside on the pavement in good weather. Coffee comes from Square Mile, milk from the nearby Goodwood Estate, and bread and pastries from the Hungry Guest Bakery (see page 286) in Petworth. Tues–Sat 7.30am–4pm, Sun 9am–2pm.

The Town House 65 High St, BN18 9AJ ⓣ 01903 883847, ⓦ www.thetownhouse.co.uk. The town's grandest place to dine is this Regency townhouse restaurant overlooking the castle walls, with starched linen tablecloths, a stunning ceiling – hand-carved and gilded in Florence in the late sixteenth century – and a menu that might feature lobster or local crab alongside Barbary duck or game (most mains £20–26). It's not at all stuffy, despite the grandeur, and is very popular, so book ahead. Wed–Thurs noon–2pm & 7–9.15pm, Fri 4–9.15pm, Sat noon–9.15pm.

DRINKING

SEE MAP PAGE 287

Brewhouse Project Lyminster Road, BN17 7QQ ⓣ 01903 889997, ⓦ brewhouseproject.co.uk. Set up

by two local businesses, Arundel Brewery and Edgcumbes Coffee, this unique place, housed in a stylish barn a mile east

of the town centre, is part brewery taproom (with a great selection of keg beers), part coffee house – the plan is to eventually bring both coffee roasting and brewing on site. A small menu of food is available, including wood-fired pizzas at weekends, and there's regular live music and other events – check the website for details. Tues & Wed 8am–5pm, Thurs 8am–8pm, Fri 8am–10pm, Sat 9am–10pm, Sun 10am–4pm.

The George at Burpham Burpham, BN18 9RR ☎ 01903 883131, ⓦ georgeatburpham.co.uk.   Seventeenth-

century pub in the gorgeous village of Burpham, three miles upstream of Arundel. There's a beamed, flagstone interior, picnic tables out front and plenty of Sussex ales behind the bar, as well as local champagne and spirits and a good-value house lager. The daily-changing, seasonal, local menu runs from sandwiches (£7.25) to burgers (£12.95) via fish, quiche and steaks. Mon–Fri 10.30am–3pm & 6–11pm, Sat 10.30am–11pm, Sun 10.30am–10pm; kitchen Mon–Fri noon–2.30pm & 6–9pm, Sat noon–3pm & 6–9.30pm, Sun noon–4pm; closed Sun & Mon eve in winter.

SHOPPING
SEE MAP PAGE 287

Arundel Brewery River Rd, BN18 9DF ☎ 01903 883577, ⓦ arundelbrewery.co.uk. Pick up some bottles of Arundel Brewery's own ales (also available from the cask from Thursday onwards) at the brewery shop on the quay. The shop also has a good wine selection (including English wines). Wed–Sat noon–5pm, Sun noon–4pm.

Pallant of Arundel 17 High St, BN18 9AD ☎ 01903 882288, ⓦ pallantofarundel.co.uk. Great little food shop, deli and wine merchant, with crusty bread from several

local bakeries, a well-stocked cheese counter, and plenty of tasty-looking homemade pork pies, Scotch eggs and the like, plus takeaway coffee. Mon–Sat 9am–6pm (5pm in Jan), Sun & bank hols 10am–5pm.

Zimmer Stewart Gallery 29 Tarrant St, BN18 9DG ☎ 01903 885867, ⓦ zimmerstewart.co.uk. This excellent small gallery features contemporary painting, prints and photos, as well as ceramics and sculpture. Exhibitions change every month or two. Tues–Sat 10am–5pm.

8 Amberley Museum and Heritage Centre

Amberley, on the B2139 between Arundel and Storrington, BN18 9LT • March–Oct Wed–Sun & bank hols 10am–4.30pm • £13.60 • ☎ 01798 831310, ⓦ amberleymuseum.co.uk • Amberley station is adjacent to the museum (regular trains from Littlehampton and the south coast)

Dedicated to the industrial heritage of the Southeast, the excellent **Amberley Museum and Heritage Centre** is an open-air museum spread around the 36-acre site of an old lime works and chalk pit. The museum contains dozens of workshops, re-created shops and listed buildings (many rescued from elsewhere in Sussex), housing everything from a brickyard drying shed to a re-created 1920s bus garage. Craftspeople are on hand to demonstrate traditional skills – woodturning, stained-glass making, letterpress printing, even broom making – and hop-on, hop-off vintage green-and-yellow Southdown buses trundle regularly round the site, with a narrow-gauge train running round the perimeter. There are a few larger exhibition halls, including a Railway Hall stuffed full of old engines and wagons, and a fun Telecommunications Exhibition, with a display of telephones from 1878 onwards – an exercise in nostalgia for anyone old enough to remember the old dial telephones and the first, brick-like mobiles.

ACCOMMODATION
AMBERLEY

Amberley Castle 4 miles north of Arundel, BN18 9LT ☎ 01798 831992, ⓦ amberleycastle.co.uk. For a real splurge, crunch up the sweeping gravel drive of this 800-year-old castle, complete with portcullis and sixty-foot curtain walls, and ensconce yourself in one of the nineteen

luxurious bedrooms. Many rooms come with four-posters, and a couple even have doorways leading directly to the battlements. Outside are acres of landscaped grounds, roamed by peacocks, and a grass-covered moat that serves as a croquet lawn. **£290**

Bignor Roman Villa

Bignor, RH20 1PH • March–Oct daily 10am–5pm; last entry 4pm • £6.50 • ☎ 01798 869259, ⓦ bignorromanvilla.co.uk

Six miles north of Arundel, in a beautiful spot at the bottom of the Downs scarp, the excavated third-century ruins of the **Bignor Roman Villa** aren't on the same scale as nearby first-century Fishbourne (see page 270), but they do contain some of the best Roman mosaics in the country. Bignor started life as a farmstead and was gradually expanded over the centuries, ending up by the fourth century as a seventy-room villa set in a square around a central courtyard. The western end of the north wing, and the bathhouse in the southeast corner, are all that remain today. The villa's location, for all that it seems like a sleepy backwater, was carefully chosen: **Stane Street**, one of the first paved roads in the country, passed just a few hundred yards away. Local materials were used to make the stunning **mosaics** (chalk for white, sandstone for yellow and orange, and Purbeck marble for blue and black), which increased in complexity and sophistication as the villa grew in size and wealth. Perhaps the finest mosaic is in the **winter dining room**, where the head of Venus stares out above a series of wonderful winged gladiators; adjacent to it you can see the original Roman hypocaust (underfloor heating system).

Pulborough Brooks RSPB nature reserve

Pulborough, RH20 2EL• Daily 9.30am–5pm • £6 • ☎ 01798 875851, ⓦ rspb.org.uk/pulboroughbrooks • Pulborough train station (services from Littlehampton and south coast), 2 miles away, then taxi; alternatively, Compass bus #100 from Steyning (Mon–Sat hourly; 25min) stops outside the reserve

Spread over the water meadows of the River Arun, the **Pulborough Brooks RSPB nature reserve** is one of the southeast's most important wetland habitats, supporting ducks, geese and swans in winter, wading birds and nightingales in the spring, and butterflies, dragonflies and nightjars in the summer, as well as a population of deer and shaggy Highland cattle year-round. Two short circular **nature trails** from the visitor centre – the 1.5-mile wooded heathland trail and the 2-mile wetland trail – meander through the different habitats of the site, the latter taking in four bird hides, where volunteers are often on hand to help identify species. Guided walks and hands-on family activities are held throughout the year, normally for an extra fee.

Parham House and Gardens

Storrington, near Pulborough, RH20 4HS • Mid-April to Oct Wed–Sun & bank hols: house 2–5pm; gardens noon–5pm • House & gardens £12, gardens only £9.50 • ☎ 01903 742021, ⓦ parhaminsussex.co.uk • Pulborough train station (services from Littlehampton and south coast), 4 miles away, then taxi; alternatively, Compass Bus #100 from Pulborough or Steyning (Mon–Sat hourly; 10–15min) stops outside the main gate

Built in 1577, **Parham House** has only ever been owned by three families: the Palmers, the Bisshopps and, most recently, the Pearsons, who took over in 1922 and rescued the beautiful but dilapidated Elizabethan house from decay – the Pearson family still lives there today. Inside, the highlights are the **Great Hall**, a magnificent Elizabethan room with tall leaded windows overlooking the grand sweep of the Downs (look out for the enormous narwhal horn hidden away in a corner), and the 160-foot **Long Gallery**, which runs the length of the house, with a flamboyant ceiling featuring vines, birds and butterflies designed by the famous theatre-set designer Oliver Messel in the 1960s.

Outside, the eighteenth-century **gardens** feature a four-acre walled garden containing an ornamental vegetable garden, herb garden and orchard, as well as exuberant mixed borders that supply the fresh flowers seen in every room in the house; a lavish two-storey Wendy House is built into the brickwork in the northwest corner, a gift from Clive Pearson to his three daughters in 1928. Beyond lie the pleasure grounds and deer park, where a three hundred-strong herd of dark fallow deer wander beneath ancient oaks.

Nutbourne Vineyards

Gay St, near Pulborough, RH20 2HH • May–Oct Tues–Fri 2–5pm, Sat & bank hols 11–5pm; Nov–Dec Sat 11am–3pm; at other times by appointment • Free • **Tours** Two days a month in summer – see website for details • 2–3hr • £15 • ☎ 01798 815196, ⓦ nutbournevineyards.com

The vines at family-run **Nutbourne Vineyards** were first planted way back in 1980, making this vineyard one of the pioneers of the now-thriving English wine industry. The vineyard is in an idyllic spot, with beautiful views across to the South Downs – you're free to wander around the vines before visiting the tasting room, uniquely sited in an old windmill tower. Scheduled **tours** of the vineyard, which include tutored tastings, also run in summer.

Steyning and around

The pretty little town of **Steyning**, fifteen miles east of Arundel, has plenty of appealingly rickety half-timbered buildings, a bustling main street and a ruined Norman castle in neighbouring **Bramber**, a one-street village that Steyning has all but swallowed up. Nearby are a couple of ancient hillforts at **Chanctonbury Ring** and **Cissbury Ring**; to the east is the popular beauty spot Devil's Dyke (see Chapter 6).

Steyning's oldest buildings can be found along **Church Street**, with Wealden and jettied timber-framed buildings rubbing shoulders with flint-walled cottages as the road slopes down to bulky **St Andrew's Church**, with its lofty double-height Norman nave and comparatively squat sixteenth-century tower. There are plenty of independent shops along the **High Street**, including the quirky **Cobblestone Walk** arcade at no. 74 (ⓦcobblestonewalk.co.uk); the town's excellent **farmers' market** takes place on the first Saturday of the month in the car park on the High Street.

Bramber Castle

Signposted from the A283, BN44 3XA • Open daylight hours • Free • ⓦ www.english-heritage.org.uk/visit/places/bramber-castle

Don't go to **Bramber Castle** expecting to clamber up the battlements: all that remains of this Norman stronghold is a section of fourteenth-century curtain wall and one tall finger of stone that once formed part of the eleventh-century gatehouse. Bramber was one of the six Rapes (districts) of Sussex established by William after the Conquest, and the castle was built here by **William de Braose** on a grassy knoll to defend the Adur gap through the South Downs. The tree-covered motte (mound) at the castle's centre, and the defensive ditch around the outer bailey, have both survived much better than the castle itself, which by 1558 was already being described as "the late castle of Bramber".

Sheltering on the hillside just below the ruins, the **Church of St Nicholas** was built at the same time as the castle and served as its chapel, making it one of the oldest Norman churches in Sussex, though in fact only the nave dates from this time.

ARRIVAL AND INFORMATION   **STEYNING AND AROUND**

By bus Bus #2 runs from Brighton via Shoreham (daily hourly; 1hr 15min); Compass bus #100 runs from Pulborough (Mon–Sat hourly; 30min).

By car The most central place to park is the pay-and-display car park on the High St (2hr max stay).

Website ⓦsteyningsouthdowns.co.uk.

EATING

Steyning Tea Rooms 32 High St, BN44 3YE ☏01903 810103, ⓦfacebook.com/steyningtearooms. This cosy, diminutive tearoom is a real treat, with cheery floral wallpaper, scrubbed wooden tables, bunting and mismatched furniture. Great cakes, and a pear-and-stilton rarebit that's to die for. No credit cards. Daily 10am–6pm.

Sussex Produce Company 88 High St, BN44 3RD ☏01903 815045, ⓦthesussexproducecompany.co.uk.

As you might expect from the name, there's plenty of Sussex produce on the menu at this award-winning café-cum-produce-store, which serves great breakfasts and wholesome, delicious lunches. The shop attached to the café is a great place to pick up picnic provisions: freshly baked bread, Sussex cheeses, and even Harveys ale on tap. Mon–Fri 8am–4pm, Sat 8.30am–4.30pm, Sun 9am–4pm.

Chanctonbury Ring

Three-mile walk from Steyning to Chanctonbury, or there's a car park nearer the Ring just off the A283

A SUSSEX SAFARI

Kent's Port Lympne Reserve may promise sightings of exotic giraffes and zebras on its African-style safari (see page 128), but Sussex's **Knepp Safaris**, based eight miles north of Steyning (☎01403 713230, ⓦkneppsafaris.co.uk), offers a very different – and altogether more local – experience. Here the animals you'll see are all native: herds of English longhorn cattle, red and fallow deer, Tamworth pigs, Exmoor ponies, turtle doves, bats, butterflies and beetles. The project is set on the Knepp Castle estate, where 3500 acres of Sussex countryside has been given over to one of the largest "**rewilding**" projects of its kind in lowland Europe; in the fifteen years or so that the project's been running it has seen the re-emergence of previously scarce species such as purple emperor butterflies, cuckoos and nightingales.

Knepp Safaris run various safaris (over 12s only) at different times of year from April through to October, all led by experts; these include dawn **walking safaris** (£35), half-day **vehicle safaris** (£40) and a raft of **specialist safaris** focusing on everything from bees to deer rutting to "reading trees". For the full experience, **stay overnight** and take advantage of the miles of footpaths, wild swimming pond, outdoor bathhouse and on-site wood-fired pizza ovens (pizza dough, sauces, cheese and toppings can be bought in the campsite shop). Shepherd's huts, treehouses and luxurious bell tents and yurts are all available (2 nights midweek in July/Aug from £170, 3 nights at the weekend from £240), as are regular tent pitches (£17/person).

The site of an Iron Age hillfort, and later two Roman-British temples, hilltop **Chanctonbury Ring** (783ft) gained its fame from the clump of beech trees planted in a circle in 1760 by **Charles Goring**, heir to the nearby Winton Estate. The hurricane of 1987 decimated the Ring, and although the trees have been replanted, it will take many years before the grove is fully regrown. Nothing, however, can detract from the magnificent views from the lofty hilltop lookout, stretching north across the patchwork of fields of the Weald and south towards Cissbury and the sea beyond.

Legend has it that if you run seven times anticlockwise around Chanctonbury Ring you'll conjure up the Devil, who'll offer you a bowl of soup that, if accepted, will cost you your soul. The Devil's the least of your worries if local **folklore** is to be believed: Sussex author Esther Meynell wrote in 1947 that the Ring was best avoided at midnight as "curious things are apt to happen", and over the years Chanctonbury's been the site of numerous alleged **UFO sightings**, mysterious lights and unexplained paranormal happenings, not to mention the odd black-magic ritual.

Cissbury Ring

Just above the village of Findon, 4 miles west of Steyning • Open access • Free • ⓦ nationaltrust.org.uk/cissbury-ring • There's a free car park (not NT) a 20min walk from the Ring, signposted off the A24; on foot, the Ring lies 2 miles off the South Downs Way, but is connected to it by footpaths

One of the biggest Iron Age hillforts in the south, **Cissbury Ring** would have been a magnificent site when it was built, with a 3ft-deep ditch backed by a raised bank topped with a 15ft-high timber palisade, stretching for over a mile around the hilltop. It's estimated it would have taken two hundred men over two years to complete, involving the excavation of a staggering 60,000 tonnes of chalk. Both ditch and bank can still clearly be seen today, and the half-hour stroll around the top of the earth ramparts will give you a good sense of the scale of this most massive of earthworks. The views from up here are beautiful, too, stretching across the Downs and over to the sea; wild ponies introduced by the National Trust to maintain the rare chalk grassland habitat only add to the charm.

At the westernmost end of the Ring, look out for bumps and hollows in the grass – the remains of **flint mines** dug by Neolithic man thousands of years before the hillfort was built. There are over two hundred mineshafts beneath the soil, some as deep as 40ft – quite a mind-boggling feat when you consider that the miners had only antlers for tools.

The coast: Bognor Regis to Shoreham-by-Sea

With the exception of the Manhood Peninsula (see page 274), the West Sussex coast is in the main one long ribbon of development, with only the odd pocket of undeveloped coastline here and there holding out against the sprawl. Heading west to east, you'll pass a trio of **seaside towns**, part of a wave of genteel resorts which grew up along the south coast in the eighteenth century, hoping to emulate the success of royally favoured Brighton. First stop is brash buckets-and-Butlins resort **Bognor Regis**, followed eight miles on by **Littlehampton** – the nicest of the bunch, with a great setting on the River Arun and two good beaches – and, another eight miles on, pleasant but unremarkable **Worthing**. The final worthwhile stop along this stretch of coast is the low-key port and town of **Shoreham-by-Sea** on the banks of the River Adur, just a few miles from Brighton. The **beaches** along this stretch are all pebbly, with sand at low tide; none get too crowded, and at their best – at the **nature reserves** at Shoreham-by-Sea, Littlehampton's West Beach and nearby Climping – they possess a wild, windswept beauty, with rare vegetated shingle that bursts into flower in summer.

GETTING AROUND   **BOGNOR TO SHOREHAM-BY-SEA**

By train Southern run trains along the coast from Chichester to Brighton via Worthing and Shoreham-by-Sea (every 30min); you'll need to change for Bognor Regis and Littlehampton.

By bus Stagecoach Coastliner bus #700 (every 10min) runs along the coast from Chichester to Brighton via Bognor Regis, Littlehampton, Worthing and Shoreham-by-Sea.

8 Bognor Regis

"Oh, bugger Bognor!", George V famously exclaimed of the little seaside town, and the words have stuck – perhaps a little unfairly. Despite its royal associations ("Regis" was added to its name after the king's visit in 1929), **Bognor Regis** is best known today for a slightly lower-brow connection – Billy Butlin of holiday-camp fame – and for its traditional, unpretentious seaside entertainments. Behind the Blue Flag pebble-and-sand beach you'll find tacky amusements aplenty, crazy golf, a miniature railway, a boating lake and fish-and-chip shops at every turn.

Butlin's

Upper Bognor Rd, PO21 1JJ • Funfair and indoor water park mid-Feb to Oct school hols & selected days: funfair 10am–8pm; water park noon–8pm • Day-tickets £17–28 depending on time of year, under-15s £10–15 • ☎ 0845 070 4754, ⓦ butlins.com

The flagship **Butlin's camp**, which opened here in 1960 and now boasts a couple of funky hotels alongside the more basic chalets, sits at the eastern end of the seafront; you can visit its funfair and indoor water park on a day-ticket – a good option for kids on a rainy day.

Littlehampton

The low-key seaside town of **LITTLEHAMPTON** ticks all the boxes for the perfect summer day-trip, with a lovely setting by the River Arun, good beaches, a stylish beach café and, as you'd expect of any self-respecting seaside town, plenty of fish and chips, crazy golf and traditional entertainment on tap. With Arundel just a few miles away up the river, Littlehampton is also worth considering as a good-value base for a longer stay.

The seafront

The seafront is an attractive affair, with lawns backing onto the promenade, and a pebble **beach** that at low tide reveals large swathes of sand. Along the prom runs **Britain's longest bench**, a funky ribbon of candy-coloured reclaimed slats that twists and loops its way for over 300m along the seafront, bending around bins and lampposts. The bench ends near the rippling, rusted steel shell that houses the **East**

THE INTERNATIONAL BOGNOR BIRDMAN

Brilliantly bonkers and quintessentially British, the **International Bognor Birdman competition** (⟁facebook.com/bognorbirdman) sees hundreds of daredevils strap themselves into human-powered flying machines and fling themselves off the end of Bognor pier in an attempt to fly 100m and gain the prized Birdman Trophy.

The event started back in 1971 in nearby Selsey, but moved to Bognor in 1978 and over the next decade started to gather interest internationally, with TV crews and competitors arriving from around the world. There's a (semi-) serious contingent who take part – the Condor Class is for standard hang-gliders, while the Leonardo da Vinci Class is for self-designed and -built flying machines – but what the competition's best known for is the fancy dress **"fun flyers"** taking the plunge for charity. Over the years flying doughnuts, vampires, pantomime horses, a Dr Who tardis and a chicken-and-mushroom pie have all tipped themselves over the edge. The date for the event varies year by year (and cancellations are not uncommon); check the website for the details.

Beach Café (see page 298); the award-winning design of the café was the work of design supremo Thomas Heatherwick, and when it opened back in 2006 it was to a fanfare of media attention – *Vogue* magazine even dubbed the town, rather overenthusiastically it has to be said, the "coolest British seaside resort".

Adjacent are Norfolk Gardens, from where the **Littlehampton Miniature Railway** (⟁littlehamptonminiaturerailway.com) trundles along in summertime to nearby **Mewsbrook Park**, where there's a large boating lake with pedalos and kayaks for rent. At the other, western, end of the seafront is **Harbour Park** (⟁harbourpark.com), a small-scale, run-of-the-mill amusement park that's been pulling in holidaymakers ever since Billy Butlin started operating the first rides here in 1932.

East Bank

Littlehampton prom comes to an abrupt halt at its western end as it meets the **River Arun** – one of the fastest-flowing rivers in the country – which rushes out to sea in a dead-straight channel. A riverside walkway leads up the regenerated **East Bank** of the river, past fish-and-chip shops, bobbing boats and kids waiting patiently with crabbing lines, before reaching the Harbour Office, where a passenger ferry crosses the river to West Beach (see below).

West Beach

Littlehampton Ferry (Easter–Sept weekends & school hols 10am–5pm; £2; ⟁littlehamptonferry.co.uk) crosses the River Arun by the Harbour Office; alternatively, cross using the pedestrian bridge 1km upstream of the river mouth, then follow Rope Walk down the western bank of the river; there's also a car park at West Beach, but it's a long detour inland to get to it

Over on the west bank of the River Arun, Littlehampton's wild and windswept **West Beach**, backed by sand dunes flecked with marram grass, feels a world away from the mini-golf and boating lakes of the town. Follow the beach westwards for 1.5 miles to reach **Climping Beach**, which together with West Beach is protected as a Site of Special Scientific Interest for its dunes, rare vegetated shingle and sand flats.

ARRIVAL AND INFORMATION   LITTLEHAMPTON

By train Trains running along the coast from Chichester or Brighton (every 30min) arrive at Littlehampton station, a few minutes' walk from the River Arun; from here it's a 10min walk down the East Bank of the river to the main beach.

By car There's plenty of pay-and-display parking along the seafront.

Website ⟁visitlittlehampton.co.uk.

ACCOMMODATION AND EATING

Bailiffscourt Hotel Climping St, Climping, BN17 5RW ☎01903 723511, ⟁hshotels.co.uk. With its flagstone floors, mullioned windows and weathered stonework, *Bailiffscourt Hotel* looks like it's been in this spot for centuries, but it was in fact only built in 1927. The 39 luxurious rooms vary hugely in size, price and decor – some are traditional, some full-blown medieval, others more contemporary. There's also an excellent spa, 30 acres of parkland roamed by peacocks and, best of all, wild and all-but-deserted Climping Beach right on your doorstep. **£275**

East Beach Café East Beach, BN17 5NZ ☎01903 731903, ⓦeastbeachcafe.co.uk. Right on the beach, this striking café (designed by Thomas Heatherwick) has won awards for its architecture, and the food's pretty good, too, featuring plenty of fish (mains £13–17), from fish and chips to salt-and-pepper chilli squid; there's a small breakfast menu, too. The cave-like interior, with its rippling ceiling, has wonderful floor-to-ceiling views out to sea, and there are also plenty of tables outside. It gets busy, so book ahead. Summer daily 10am–4pm & 6–9pm; winter Mon–Thurs & Sun 10am–4pm, Fri & Sat 10am–4pm & 6–9pm.

Regency Rooms 85 South Terrace, BN17 5LJ ☎01903 717707, ⓦregencyrooms.net. Stylish, friendly and brilliant value, this guesthouse opposite the beach is a little gem, with sleek bathrooms and rooms decked out with funky fabrics and furnishings. No breakfast, but the *East Beach Café* is only a short walk away. **£69**

Worthing

The seaside town of **Worthing** was, like nearby Brighton, a fishing village until the fashion for sea bathing took off in the eighteenth century. When the Prince Regent's younger sister, Amelia, was sent here to recover from tuberculosis in 1798 (Brighton being deemed too racy), Worthing's smart, respectable reputation was sealed. While Brighton has blossomed over the years into a brash, beautiful London-by-the-Sea, Worthing has struggled to throw off its rather boring reputation – "duller than a weekend in Worthing" was the phrase one newspaper used to describe tennis player Andy Murray in 2015.

That said, Worthing's low-key charms make a welcome breather from the frenetic pace of Brighton: the pebbly **beach**, backed by five miles of prom, never gets too busy, and the seafront boasts an elegant Art Deco pier and one of the oldest working **cinemas** in the country, the Dome (ⓦworthingdome.com), opened in 1911. The **Worthing Museum and Art Gallery**, set back 500m from the seafront on Chapel Road (Tues–Sat 10am–5pm; ⓦworthingmuseum.co.uk), is also well worth a look, especially for its excellent costume and archeological collections.

East of the pier, you can kick off your shoes and have a go at beach volleyball, beach tennis or sand soccer at the **Worthing Sand Courts** (£21/hr; ⓦworthingsandcourts. co.uk), while out on the waves you can try out **kitesurfing** or stand-up paddleboarding (see below) – Worthing has been described as the kitesurf capital of the UK, and the large bay in which the town sits is one of the best places in the country to learn.

INFORMATION AND ACTIVITIES

WORTHING

Tourist information There's a Visitor Information Point at Worthing Museum and Art Gallery, Chapel Rd, BN11 1HP (Tues–Sat 10am–5pm; ☎01903 221066, ⓦdiscoverworthing.uk).

Kitesurfing and stand-up paddleboarding Plenty of companies offer kitesurfing tuition in the area, including BN1 Kitesurfing (ⓦbn1kitesurfing.co.uk), Brighton Kitesurf and SUP Academy (ⓦbrightonkitesurfandsupacademy. com), the KiteSurf & SUP Company (ⓦthekitesurfandsup.co) and Lancing Kitesurf School (ⓦlancingkitesurfschool.com).

EATING

★**Crab Shack** 2 Marine Parade, BN11 3PN ☎01903 215070, ⓦcrabshackworthing.co.uk. Laidback seafood café in a top spot on the seafront, with tables outside. The regularly changing menu might feature crab sarnies, pil pil prawns, cockle popcorn or half a kilo of mussels (£14) – all exceptionally tasty. It's very popular, so book ahead. Tues–Thurs noon– 9pm, Fri & Sat noon–9.30pm, Sun noon–4pm.

Macaris Restaurant and Café 24–25 Marine Parade, next to the Dome, BN11 3PT ☎01903 532753, ⓦmacarisrestaurant.co.uk. A Worthing institution that's been serving up ice creams to holidaymakers since 1959. Mon–Fri 9am–5pm, Sat & Sun 9am–6pm.

Shoreham-by-Sea

The little town and port of **Shoreham-by-Sea** probably won't be top of anyone's list of Sussex must-sees, but you might well pass through to take in a comedy or music gig at the excellent Ropetackle Centre (ⓦropetacklecentre.co.uk), or to visit the award-winning **Farmers' market** or **Artisans' market** (every second and fourth Sat of the month respectively 9am–1pm). Once in town it's worth poking around a little further to find a couple of gems dating back to the twelfth century: the church of **St Mary de Haura**, set in a peaceful square along Church Street; and the diminutive, chequerboard **Marlipins Museum** of local history on the High Street (May–Oct Mon–Fri 10.30am–4.30pm, Sat 11am–3pm; £0.50; ☎01273 462994, ⊕sussexpast.co.uk).

It's a ten-minute wander from the centre to peaceful **Shoreham Beach**, a nature reserve with rare vegetated shingle habitat above the high tide mark and a good sweep of sand at low tide. En route, look out for the row of **houseboats** hauled up on the mudflats on the far side of the River Adur, converted into bohemian homes from an assortment of rusting ferries, gunboats, steamers and other retired vessels.

Just west of town, across the River Adur, the fabulous Art Deco **Brighton City Airport** – the oldest licensed airfield in the country – is the base for Brighton Scenic's sightseeing flights (see page 248).

EATING

SHOREHAM-BY-SEA

Ginger & Dobbs 31–32 East St, BN43 5ZD ☎01273 453359, ⊕facebook.com/GingerAndDobbs. This lovely little organic greengrocer-cum-café, in a tranquil spot opposite St Mary de Haura church, serves up local Pharmacie coffee, home-baked bread and cakes, salads and daily specials. Mon–Sat 9am–5pm, Sun 10am–4pm.

8

Surrey

BOXHILL VIEWPOINT

9 Surrey

Too often dismissed as little more than a well-heeled, stuffy swathe of suburbia, Surrey has much to recommend it, particularly for outdoors-lovers. Carpeted with woodlands, the county is bisected laterally by the chalk escarpment of the North Downs, which rise west of Guildford, peak around Box Hill near Dorking, and continue east into Kent. Within the Downs lie the Surrey Hills, an Area of Outstanding Natural Beauty, with a number of excellent year-round cycling paths and two gentle, long-distance walking paths: in the north, the North Downs Way, which starts at Farnham and follows ancient pilgrims' routes to finish in Dover; further south, the Greensand Way leads from Haslemere to Hamstreet, near Ashford. These, along with countless shorter footpaths and hedge-tangled bridleways, lead you within a hiking-boot's throw of ancient bluebell woods, gently undulating fields, butterfly-speckled chalk grasslands, and sleepy villages that have dozed here since medieval times.

Surrey's wealth dates largely from the sixteenth and seventeenth centuries, when farming and the local paper, gunpowder and iron industries were booming; later industrialization effectively passed the county by, and it remained largely rural until the coming of the railways. In the nineteenth century, before rampant road- and suburb-building changed Surrey's aspect forever, its vernacular architecture, bucolic beauty and pre-industrial ambience inspired many artists – among them architect Edwin Lutyens and his gardening partner Gertrude Jekyll, potter Mary Watts and her husband, painter G.F. Watts – to settle in these leafy surrounds. Fine examples of Arts and Crafts architecture include **Mary Watts'** astonishing **chapel** at Compton.

Other key attractions include the Surrey Hills, where grand estates, such as the Edwardian **Polesden Lacey**, and beauty spots, primarily **Box Hill** and Leith Hill, offer sweeping views over pristine countryside. These chalky slopes provide perfect conditions for viniculture, with Denbies, currently the largest vineyard in England, offering tours. The handsome market towns of **Guildford** and **Dorking** provide restaurants, hotels and train connections, but it's far nicer to stay out in the countryside, kicking back in peace and quiet just a handful of miles from the capital. In the pretty cluster of villages between Guildford and Dorking, Shere, Abinger and **Peaslake** offer sleepy, chocolate-box appeal and excellent local walks.

In the west, Surrey has a different flavour. Here protected areas of wild lowland heath dominate, with the eerie natural amphitheatre of the **Devil's Punch Bowl** near **Farnham** making a dramatic destination in the Greensand Hills. **North Surrey**, cut through by the roaring M25 orbital motorway, is far less rural, though beyond the collection of satellite towns and light industrial installations are a few attractions, chiefly **Wisley**, the Royal Horticultural Society's flagship garden.

Farnham and around

The attractive market town of **FARNHAM** lies tucked into Surrey's southwestern corner on its border with Hampshire. Notwithstanding its thousand-year history, its most striking buildings date from the eighteenth century, when hop farming boomed hereabouts. The Georgian architecture is at its best along **Castle Street**, which links

POLESDEN LACEY

Highlights

❶ **Devil's Punch Bowl** Swathed in myth, this dramatic natural amphitheatre has a wild, raw beauty unseen elsewhere in the county. See page 305

❷ **The Watts Chapel** The bucolic village of Compton is home to this extraordinary Arts and Crafts chapel, part of a fascinating complex devoted to the life and works of British artists George and Mary Watts. See page 306

❸ **Box Hill** Hikers, cyclists and Sunday strollers make a beeline for this popular beauty spot – as featured in Jane Austen's *Emma* – near Dorking. See page 309

❹ **Polesden Lacey** The immaculate, extensive estate, crisscrossed with walks, and the quirky Edwardian house give Polesden Lacey the edge over many other stately homes. See page 309

❺ **Hannah Peschar Sculpture Garden** Wander through another world in this magical, artistic spot. See page 310

the centre with the small, twelfth-century motte-and-shell **castle keep** – there are good views across to the Downs from here (Feb–Dec Mon–Fri 9am–5pm, Sat & Sun 10am–4pm; free; EH; ⓦwww.english-heritage.org.uk/visit/places/farnham-castle-keep). Meanwhile, the quirky **Museum of Farnham**, 38 West St (Tues–Sat 10am–5pm; free; ⓦfarnhammaltings.com/museum), offers a lively jog through local history, with a strong emphasis on crafts. The long-distance **North Downs Way** (150 miles) starts at Farnham, signposted from the railway station.

Devil's Punch Bowl

London Rd, Hindhead, GU26 6AB • Daily dawn–dusk • Free; NT • Parking £4 • ☎01428 681050, ⓦnationaltrust.org.uk/hindhead-commons-and-the-devils-punch-bowl • Haslemere station (on the line from Guildford) is 3 miles south

A large natural depression, created by subterranean springs eroding the clay soil from below, the **Devil's Punch Bowl**, some nine miles south of Farnham, offers a startling counterpoint to the softer countryside elsewhere in Surrey. Its wild heathland slopes carpeted with heather and gorse, surrounded by ancient woodlands, the Bowl is a daunting, occasionally eerie vision, offering long walks around the rim and down into the valley. No one quite knows how it got its name, though many folk tales describe it as the devil's handiwork – one story suggests the bowl was created when he flung clods of earth at the god Thor. The Punch Bowl segues seamlessly into neighbouring **Hindhead Commons**, particularly lovely in summer and early autumn when the heather is in flower; Sir Arthur Conan Doyle, who lived for ten years in the village of Hindhead, was inspired to write *Hound of the Baskervilles* here. Accessible on the Greensand Way, the Punch Bowl and commons are crisscrossed by bridleways and walking paths, including several NT trails that strike off from the café.

ARRIVAL AND INFORMATION | FARNHAM AND AROUND

By train Farnham station – on Station Hill, across the River Wey in the south of town – is a 10min walk from the centre. There are connections with London Waterloo (every 30min–1hr; 1hr) and Woking (every 30min–1hr; 23min).

Tourist information Pick up information at the town council offices on South St, midway between the station and the centre (Mon–Thurs 9am–5pm, Fri 9am–4.30pm; ☎01252 712667, ⓦfarnham.gov.uk).

ACCOMMODATION AND EATING

Dovecote B&B Pickhurst Rd, Chiddingfold, GU8 4TS ☎01428 682920, ⓦbedandbreakfastchiddingfold.co.uk. In a sixteenth-century house near Chiddingfold village green, this three-room B&B has a lush garden and a cosy, beamed guest lounge with a real fire. The best room, a large double, is en suite, while another double and twin share a bathroom, complete with clawfoot tub. **£110**

Farnham Maltings Bridge Square, Farnham, GU9 7QR ☎01252 745444, ⓦfarnhammaltings.com. Farnham's excellent community arts centre, which hosts live music, theatre and movies, and crafts workshops, also has a riverside café. Here you'll find books to browse, good coffee and cakes, breakfasts and simple homemade food, including sandwiches, wraps, soups and salad, from around

£5. Mon & Tues 9.30am–5pm, Wed–Fri 9.30am–8pm, Sat 10am–5pm; kitchen Mon & Tues 10am–2.30pm, Wed–Fri 10am–7.30pm, Sat 10.30am–2.30pm.

Swan Inn Petworth Rd, Chiddingfold, GU8 4TY ☎01428 684688, ⓦtheswaninnchiddingfold.com. One of a number of pubs with rooms in the village of Chiddingfold. Mains (£12–17) range from seafood spaghetti, via gammon, egg and chips to miso aubergine with couscous, with plenty of good veggie choices. You can also get lunchtime sandwiches from £6. The terraced garden is lovely, and they offer eleven bedrooms, which you can take with or without breakfast. Mon–Fri 7.30am–11pm, Sat 9am–11pm, Sun 9am–10.30pm; kitchen Mon–Thurs noon–3pm & 6–9pm, Fri & Sat noon–3pm & 6–9.30pm, Sun noon–8pm. **£90**

Guildford and around

GUILDFORD is an appealing county town, set on the River Wey and with lovely views across the surrounding countryside. To get a broad panorama, walk up to the medieval **Guildford Castle** (March & Oct Sat & Sun 11am–4pm; April–Sept daily 10am–5pm;

9

£3.50; ⓦguildford.gov.uk/castle), circled by flower-filled gardens, which has a viewing platform in the tower. Otherwise, the **river** itself is a nice place for a walk, as is the lively cobbled **high street**, lined with half-timbered townhouses and with an elaborate seventeenth-century bracket clock overhanging the Guildhall. At no. 155 – sharing a building with the tourist office – the **Guildford House Gallery** (May–Sept Mon–Sat 10am–4.45pm, Sun 11am–4pm; Oct–March Mon–Sat 10am–4.45pm; free; ⓦguildford. gov.uk/guildfordhouse) stages art and crafts exhibitions and has a courtyard **café**.

Watts Gallery Artists' Village

Down Lane, Compton, GU3 1DQ • **Watts Gallery, Watts Studios & grounds** Daily 10.30am–5pm • £11.50 • **Limnerslease tours** Usually Tues & Sat noon & 2pm, Wed–Fri & Sun 2pm; check website and book in advance; 1hr • £5 • **Chapel** Mon–Fri 9am–5pm, Sat & Sun 10am–5pm • Free • **Shop and visitor centre** Daily 10am–5pm • ☎ 01483 810235, ⓦ wattsgallery.org.uk • #46 bus (hourly Mon–Sat; 15min) from Guildford town centre

Hidden away in the leafy lanes of **Compton**, a pretty village on the North Downs Way just ten minutes' drive from Guildford, the fascinating **Watts Gallery Artists' Village** offers insight into not only a unique artistic partnership but also the important role Surrey played in the cultural life of the late nineteenth and early twentieth centuries. There is a great deal to see; reckon on at least three hours for a visit.

In 1891 husband and wife **George Frederic Watts** (1817–1904) and **Mary Seton Watts** (1849–1938) – he an esteemed painter, she a sculptor/decorative artist 32 years his junior – escaped the pollution and crowds of London to this peaceful Surrey Hills spot, setting up home in a solid, half-timbered pile designed for them by Arts and Crafts architect Sir Ernest George.

Here the ageing Watts, previously best known for his portraits, shifted his attention to landscape paintings and sculpture, while Mary began a furiously creative phase, making decorative panels for their home, designing the astonishing Compton chapel, teaching pottery classes and establishing the **Compton Pottery**, whose decorative terracotta pieces, hand-carved with distinctive Art Nouveau motifs, remained in production until the 1950s.

In 1903 the couple commissioned a simple museum to display George's art. He died just a year later, after which Mary lived and worked here until her death. Today the **Watts Gallery** still focuses on his paintings, its vibrant crimson and turquoise walls displaying his portraits, light-infused metaphysical landscapes and socially conscious think pieces. Around the corner in the **Sculpture Gallery**, life-size models of Watts' monumental works include *Physical Energy* (1878), a huge equestrian piece.

A ten-minute woodland walk away from the main complex, **Limnerslease**, the couple's home, is visitable only on **guided tours**. These are rich in personal snippets – not least that George, who modelled himself on Titian and liked to be called "signor", would keep his devoted (insomniac) wife awake with his pronouncements on the state of the world. None of the furnishings are original, but you can see Mary's lively ceiling panels, moulded in gesso (a mix of hemp, plaster and glue), packed with natural and spiritual imagery from around the world. In the east wing, the **Watts Studios** give glimpses into the pair's working methods, with George's canvases hung on easels next to paint-smeared palettes, illustrated explanations of Mary's gesso technique, and her detailed diaries, sketchbooks and beautifully decorated photograph albums.

The star of the show, though, is the **Watts Chapel** (1896–97), Mary's masterpiece, a three-minute walk from the museum. Within this little red-brick and terracotta building, reminiscent of a Byzantine church, every patch of wall and vaulted ceiling is covered in a riot of imagery – lustrous jewel colours and burnished bronze gesso reliefs, natural and floral motifs, Celtic knots, Art Nouveau styling and spiritual symbols combining to create a peaceful, profoundly spiritual whole.

The **tearoom** (daily 10am–5pm), in Mary's old pottery, serves cakes and light lunches on crockery based on Compton pottery, and has outdoor seating for sunny days, while the museum **shop** is a winner, packed with art books, cards, artsy gifts – and, of course, ceramics.

Winkworth Arboretum

Hascombe Rd, Godalming, GU8 4AD • Daily: Feb & March 10am–5pm; April–Oct 10am–6pm; Nov–Jan 10am–4pm • £10; NT • Parking free • ☎ 01483 208477, ⓦ nationaltrust.org.uk/winkworth-arboretum • Godalming station is 2 miles northwest

Surrey doesn't get much leafier than at **Winkworth Arboretum**, a dazzling hillside ensemble of trees seven miles south of Guildford. It is particularly spectacular in **autumn**, when the views down the steep wooded slopes into the valley below blaze with reds and oranges; but spring, with its haze of bluebells, cherry blossom and azaleas, is also stunning. The arboretum was the creation of Dr Wilfrid Fox, who in the 1930s and 1940s planted more than a thousand exotic and rare trees among the existing oak and hazel woods; exhibits in the old boathouse by the tranquil lake reveal intriguing historical snippets.

Shere and around

SHERE, its half-beamed and rough-plastered cottages clustered around the River Tillingbourne – more of a stream, really, dotted with ducks and with a tree-shaded green alongside – is among Surrey's prettiest villages. The likeable **Shere Museum**, on Gomshall Lane (Sat & Sun 2–5pm; free; ⓦ sheremuseum.co.uk), has two intriguing rooms packed with local curiosities, while walks and biking trails shoot off in all directions. Other appealing villages nearby include picturesque **Abinger Hammer** – once home to author E.M. Forster and complete with stream and village cricket pitch – and the quiet hamlet of **Peaslake**, whose surrounding woodlands and hills are perfect for rambles and mountain biking. There's **bike rental** at Pedal & Spoke (Mon–Fri by appointment; Sat 8.30am–4pm, Sun 9am–4pm; ☎ 01306 731639, ⓦ pedalandspoke.co.uk), and on fine weekends the village centre, with its one pub, fills up with super-keen cyclists.

ARRIVAL AND INFORMATION   GUILDFORD AND AROUND

By train Guildford station is a mile west of the centre, across the River Wey.

Destinations Godalming (every 10–20min; 8min); Gomshall (for Shere; hourly; 15min); Haslemere (every 10–25min; 15–25min); London Waterloo (every 5–20min; 35min–1hr 15min); Witley (every 30min–1hr; 20min).

Tourist office 155 High St (May–Sept Mon–Sat 9.30am–5pm, Sun 11am–4pm; Oct–April Mon–Sat 9.30am–5pm; ☎ 01483 444333, ⓦ guildford.gov.uk/visitguildford).

ACCOMMODATION

Angel Hotel 91 High St, Guildford, GU1 3DP ☎ 01483 564555, ⓦ angelpostinghouse.com. Ignore the chains and head for this timber-framed sixteenth-century inn in the centre of town. The standard rooms don't have the atmosphere of the public spaces – all creaking floorboards, rustic beams and maze-like corridors – but the history and location compensate. Breakfast costs extra, taken in *Bill's* downstairs. **£101**

★ **Hurtwood Hotel** Walking Bottom, Peaslake, GU5 9RR ☎ 01306 730514, ⓦ hurtwoodhotel.co.uk. This 1920s inn at the heart of Peaslake makes a great base for cycling and walking breaks, with stylish, comfy boutique rooms and a pub/Italian restaurant (ⓦ hurtwoodinn.com) – run by different people – downstairs. The front terrace is a sociable suntrap. **£100**

★ **Rookery Nook** The Square, Shere, GU5 9HG ☎ 07946 756344, ⓦ rookerynook.info. In the centre of Shere, this cute half-timbered fifteenth-century cottage offers friendly B&B accommodation in two clean, quiet rooms, one with North Downs views, with shared bath. Breakfasts are excellent. **£115**

EATING AND DRINKING

GUILDFORD AND AROUND

Café Mila 1 Angel Court, Godalming, GU7 1DT ☎ 01483 808569, ⓦ cafemila.co.uk. A light, airy, colourful café, walls lined with local art and tables filled with yoga bunnies (classes are held upstairs), offering tasty, homemade veggie food – avocado on toast, stuffed vegetables, falafel in pitta – plus fresh juices, coffee and fabulous cakes. Mains around £6. Mon (drinks and cakes only) 10am–2pm, Tues–Fri 8am–5pm, Sat 8.30am–5pm, Sun 9am–4pm.

Coffee Culture 2 Angel Gate, Guildford, GU1 4AE ☎ 01483 564200, ⓦ mycoffeeculture.co.uk. It's easy to while away time in this independent coffee shop – tucked

9

off the high street in a cobbled pedestrian lane – lingering over good coffee and freshly made cakes and sandwiches. Mon–Fri 8am–5pm, Sat 8am–6pm, Sun 9am–5pm.

★ **Onslow Arms** The Street, West Clandon, GU4 7TE ☎ 01483 222447, ⓦ onslowarmsclandon.co.uk. Friendly, unstuffy country pub with a cosy beamed dining room, a large patio garden (complete with a heated barn area) and great walking from the car park. The menu is a breath of fresh air, with a mix of the exotic (bang bang peanut chicken salad; Keralan roasted veg curry; tuna tartare) and comforting gastropub staples (bubble and squeak with ham and eggs; fish and chips; liver and bacon). Mains from £11 at lunch, £13 at dinner; three-course menu £29.95. Daily 11am–11pm; kitchen Mon–Thurs & Sun noon–9.30pm, Fri & Sat noon–10pm.

SHERE AND AROUND

The Abinger Hatch Abinger Lane, Abinger Common, RH5 6HZ ☎ 01306 730737, ⓦ theabingerhatch.com. This comfortable free house offers locally sourced food in a peaceful setting. Dog- and family-friendly, it's popular with walkers and cyclists, and on Sundays for its roasts, but worth visiting any time – whether you fancy bangers and mash, fish pie, jackfruit burger or pan-fried kale pancakes with grilled goat's cheese. Mains from £11.50. Mon–Sat 11.30am–11pm, Sun noon–11pm; kitchen Mon–Thurs noon–9pm, Fri & Sat noon–10pm, Sun noon–8pm.

Kinghams Gomshall Lane, Shere, GU5 9HE ☎ 01483 202168, ⓦ kinghams-restaurant.co.uk. In a seventeenth-century building surrounded by a gorgeous cottage garden, *Kinghams* offers upscale dining in cosy surroundings. Creative takes on classic British and French cuisine might include guinea fowl marinated in coriander and orange, served with sweet potato and coconut purée; risotto cake of piquillo and spinach; or fresh fish of the day. Mains from £16. Call ahead to book. Tues–Sat noon–3pm & 7–10pm, Sun noon–3pm.

The William Bray Shere Lane, Shere, GU5 9HS ☎ 01483 202275, ⓦ thebray.net. Large Edwardian pub where you can eat Modern British food in a smart dining room or buzzy bar, in a small garden or on the terrace. The menu (mains from £12) focuses on crowd-pleasing gastropub favourites, from sharing platters to sourdough pizza, pork belly to grilled sea bass, with a few creative daily specials for good measure. Mon–Sat 8am–11pm, Sun 8am–10pm; kitchen Mon–Sat 9am–3pm & 6–10pm, Sun 9am–6pm.

Dorking and around

Set at the mouth of a gap carved by the River Mole through the North Downs, the historic market town of **DORKING** has quite a crop of **antique stores** – the handsome sixteenth-century **West Street** is a good place to start – and is also surrounded by some of the Surrey Hills' biggest sights. **Box Hill**, on a chalk escarpment above the Mole north of Dorking, draws streams of walkers and cyclists at the weekend; you can also stroll around the nearby **Leith Hill**, in the grounds of **Polesden Lacey**, and through the vineyards at **Denbies**, which offers tours. Further south, the idiosyncratic **Hannah Peschar Sculpture Garden** is a glorious spot, hidden in the woods towards Sussex.

Denbies Wine Estate

London Rd, RH5 6AA • **Estate** Daily: April–Oct 9.30am–5.30pm; Nov–March 9.30am–5pm • Free • **Tours** Check website, but roughly March–Oct daily hourly 11am–4pm (not 1pm), sometimes with extra tours on Sat; Nov–Feb occasional tours • Indoor tours £11.50, £14.95 with sparkling wines, £16.95 with food; outdoor "train" tours (March–Oct only) £7.50, £12 with sparkling wine • ☎ 01306 876616, ⓦ denbies.co.uk • 15min walk north of Dorking train station

With 265 acres of vines, planted on the sunny south-facing slopes of a sheltered valley, **Denbies** is the largest privately owned vineyard in England. It's a commercial operation, centring on a busy restaurant and gift store where you can buy the wines; the estate is also home to the independent Surrey Hills Brewery (ⓦ surreyhills.co.uk), and a good farm shop, selling produce grown on site.

The chalky soil and the warm, dry microclimate in this area, remarkably similar to the Champagne region of France, are ideal for wine production – indeed, the Romans grew grapes just 300yd away – and nineteen varieties are now planted here. With many prestigious awards to its name, Denbies specializes in traditionally produced **sparkling wines** – champagne in all but name – including the delicious sparkling Greenfields, but they also offer superb whites (among them the Surrey Gold, a very drinkable blend of Müller-Thurgau, Ortega and Bacchus), the Noble Harvest dessert wine and the dry, light Chalk Ridge rosé.

Indoor **tours** lead you through the winery, explaining the process, with tastings at the end. Even nicer, though, especially on a sunny summer's day, is to ride the little "train" through the vineyards, which are part of a much larger estate, dipping in and out of beautiful dappled woodland and affording wonderful views over the slopes to Box Hill, Dorking and Leith Hill. You can also simply **walk** through the estate, following some seven miles of public footpaths.

Box Hill

Box Hill Rd, KT20 7LB • Daily dawn–dusk • Free; NT • Parking £4 • ☎ 01306 885502, ⓦ nationaltrust.org.uk/box-hill • Box Hill & Westhumble train station is 1.2 miles west; from Dorking take bus #465 (daily) to the foot of the hill

It's a stiff cycle ride up the zigzagging path to the top of **Box Hill**, a mile from the North Downs Way, where various walks and paths lead you through woodlands of rare wild box trees, yew, oak and beech, and across chalk grasslands, designated as a Site of Special Scientific Interest, scattered with wildflowers and fluttering with butterflies. A number of NT trails include an adventurous "natural play trail" for kids, the two-mile Stepping Stones walk along the River Mole, and some longer, more strenuous options. Brilliant views abound, most famously from the **Salomons Memorial** viewpoint near the café, where on a clear day you can see across the Weald to the South Downs.

Polesden Lacey

Near Great Bookham, RH5 6BD • **House** Daily: March–Oct 11am–5pm; Nov–Feb 11am–4pm; timed tours 11am–noon, self-guided tours from 12.30pm; last entry 1hr before closing • £13.60 (includes gardens), £9 during last hour of house opening; NT • Parking £5 • ☎ 01372 452048, ⓦ nationaltrust.org.uk/polesden-lacey • Box Hill & Westhumble station is 3 miles east

Four miles from Dorking, and minutes from the North Downs Way, the grand Edwardian estate of **Polesden Lacey** practically begs you to while away the day with a picnic. In summer, deckchairs and rugs are provided on the velvety lawn of the South Terrace, where you can enjoy uninterrupted views of the Surrey Hills. If you're feeling more active, take a wander around the gardens – which include a fragrant lavender garden, apple orchard and a stunning walled rose garden – and follow any of the four trails through the 1400-acre surrounding estate.

The **house** – remodelled in 1906 by the architects of the *Ritz* – is worth a look. It's largely set up to appear as it would have in the 1930s, when owned by wealthy socialite Margaret Greville (1863–1942). Guests here included Winston Churchill, the Queen Mother and three kings, including Edward VII and his lover Alice Keppel – Camilla Parker-Bowles' great-grandmother – and while filled with priceless artworks, it's the human details that linger. Make sure to take a quick shot in the billiards room, where nostalgic tunes crackle in the background.

Leith Hill

Near Coldharbour, Dorking • **Leith Hill Tower** Daily 10am–3pm • £3; NT • Parking £3.50 (donation) • ☎ 01306 712711, ⓦ nationaltrust. org.uk/leith-hill-tower-and-countryside • **Leith Hill Place** Leith Hill Lane, RH5 6LY (Sat Nav RH5 6LU) • March–Oct Fri–Sun 11am–5pm • £6; NT • Parking free • ☎ 01306 711685, ⓦ nationaltrust.org.uk/leith-hill-place • 5 miles west of Holmwood train station

Reaching the lofty heights of 967ft, **Leith Hill** is the highest point in the southeast, topped with a neo-Gothic eighteenth-century **tower**, a folly from the top of which you can peer through a telescope to see the sprawling mass of London in the north and the Channel to the south. Four designated trails wind through open heathlands and through the woods, particularly lovely in spring, when drifts of **bluebells** shimmer across the floor, and the **rhododendrons** burst into colour. Below the tower, you can also visit **Leith Hill Place**, childhood home of British composer Ralph Vaughan Williams. With a small

9

display dedicated to the composer and a forty-minute "soundscape tour" (an evocative musical sound installation) bringing the house to life, this is an informal, low-key visit, and the views are lovely. Tea can be taken on the lawn.

Hannah Peschar Sculpture Garden

Standon Lane, near Ockley, RH5 5QU • April–Oct Thurs–Sat 11am–6pm, Sun noon–5pm; last entry 1hr before closing • £12 • ☎ 01306 627269, ⓦ hannahpescharsculpture.com • Ockley station is 3 miles northeast

Tucked away off a hedgerow-tangled lane outside the hamlet of Ockley, a twenty-minute drive south of Dorking, the **Hannah Peschar Sculpture Garden** has a fairytale feel. Owned by an artist/landscape designer couple, the setting is a work of art in itself: a secret forest of lofty mature trees, giant ferns and towering broadleaf plants. A vision of impossibly green lushness, dappled with light, it's all amazingly peaceful, silent other than the burble of rushing streams and the rat-a-tat of distant woodpeckers. Follow winding, mossy paths and cross honeysuckle-tangled footbridges to discover modern sculptures hidden among the giant ferns, dangling from branches, or standing alone in glades. Some, made of weather-battered wood, or cool green and brown marble, look as if they have grown from the soil, while others, constructed from steel, cement and fibreglass, make a striking contrast with the organic world around them.

ARRIVAL AND INFORMATION

By train Dorking's main station, with services to London, is a mile north of the centre. The town's other two stations, Dorking Deepdene and Dorking West, only run a few local services.

Destinations Box Hill & Westhumble (every 5–30min; 2min); London Victoria (every 30min; 1hr); London Waterloo (every 30min; 50min); Ockley (hourly; 12min).

Website ⓦ visitdorking.com.

DORKING AND AROUND

ACCOMMODATION AND EATING

Denbies Vineyard Hotel Bradley Lane, Dorking, RH5 6AA ☎ 01306 876777, ⓦ denbies.co.uk. With a rather special setting on the Denbies estate, at the edge of the vineyards, this hotel offers seventeen luxurious en-suite rooms, a restaurant, a bar and a landscaped garden – there's even a wine dispenser machine. **£125**

Duke of Wellington Guildford Rd, East Horsley, KT24 6AA ☎ 01483 282312, ⓦ dukeofwellingtoneasthorsley. co.uk. This gastropub conversion of a sixteenth-century inn, near Polesden Lacey, is a local hit, with plump armchairs, an open fire and a nice outdoor space. The classy menu, focussing on quality ingredients, offers something for everyone – 14hr-braised beef and ale pie; spiced monkfish with chorizo; big, healthy salads. Mains from £14; Mon–Fri two/three-course menu £15.50/£18.50. Mon–Thurs & Sun 9.30am–11pm, Fri & Sat 9.30am–midnight; kitchen daily noon till late.

Running Horses Old London Rd, Mickleham, RH5 6DU ☎ 01372 372279, ⓦ therunninghorses.co.uk. Old coaching inn near Box Hill, with seven appealing B&B rooms and a little gatehouse sleeping two (£170); there's a shed for cyclists to store their bikes. You can get Brakspear ales in the bar (snack menu available) and seasonal food – chicken kiev, perhaps, or roasted duck breast – in the restaurant (mains £10–24). Mon–Fri 7.30–9.30am & 11am–11pm, Sat 8–10am & 11am–10.30pm, Sun 11am–10.30pm; kitchen Mon–Thurs 7.30–9.30am, noon–3pm &

6–9pm, Fri 7.30–9.30am, noon–3pm & 6–10pm, Sat 8–10am, noon–3pm & 6–10pm, Sun noon–8pm. **£120**

★ **Sorrel** 77 South St, Dorking, RH4 2JU ☎ 01306 889414, ⓦ sorrelrestaurant.co.uk. Dorking's best restaurant by a long shot, serving seasonal, wildly creative, Michelin-starred cuisine. The accomplished set menus (three courses lunch £45, dinner £70; five-/nine-course tasting menu £70/£95) roll out surprise upon divine surprise – "green, green, green" for example (you'll have to wait and see), or BBQ hen of the woods with seaweed and mushroom milk. Dishes are delicate but satisfying. Reservations are taken months in advance. Tues–Sat noon–2.15pm & 7–9pm.

★ **YHA Tanners Hatch** Off Ranmore Common Rd, nr Dorking, RH5 6BE ☎ 0345 371 9542, ⓦ yha.org.uk/ hostel/tanners-hatch. Deep in the woods (it's a 15min walk from the nearest car park) next to the Polesden Lacey estate, this charming seventeenth-century cottage, surrounded by an old English garden, has wonderful views. Inside is simple, rustic and snug, with low-beamed ceilings, creaky narrow stairs and a small lounge with a real fire. It's self-catering, and hostellers and campers alike can stoke up the BBQs and use the fire pits. The fifteen beds are spread across two dorms and a private double, with the toilet/ shower block outside; there are also two safari tents for glamping. No wi-fi. Camping/person **£5**, dorms **£13**, double **£29**, glamping **£60**

North Surrey

North Surrey, straggling out beyond the Greater London borders, lacks the rural atmosphere that defines the hills and heaths to the south. However, there are a few key attractions here, including the **Epsom Downs racecourse**, home of the Derby (ⓦepsomderby.co.uk) since 1780, and **RHS Garden Wisley**, a dream-come-true real-life catalogue for keen gardeners. The appealing village of **Ripley**, with its excellent eating options and luxury B&B, makes an obvious base.

RHS Garden Wisley

Four miles east of Woking, GU23 6QB • Mid-March to mid-Oct Mon–Fri 10am–6pm, Sat & Sun 9am–6pm (Glasshouse daily 10am–5.15pm); mid-Oct to mid-March Mon–Fri 10am–4.30pm, Sat & Sun 9am–4.30pm (Glasshouse daily 10am–3.45pm) • £14.50, £12.10 if you arrive car-free • Parking free • ☎ 01483 224234, ⓦ rhs.org.uk/gardens/wisley

Established in Victorian times to cultivate "difficult" plants, **RHS Garden Wisley**, given to the Royal Horticultural Society in 1903, is still today a working and demonstration garden, experimenting with new plants and cultivation techniques. Its sheer size – 240 acres – means it remains blessedly uncrowded even in summer (though the glasshouse can fill up); it is also, with its trails, woodlands and lakes, the kind of garden that even non-gardeners can enjoy.

Things are constantly evolving, but one perpetual crowd-pleaser is the vast, 40ft-high **Glasshouse**, with three climatic zones teeming with rare and exotic plants, all set around waterfalls and pools. It's particularly lovely during the **butterfly show**, when countless species of butterfly flutter around you. Elsewhere, don't miss the wildly colourful **mixed borders**, the summer **rose garden** and the historic **rock garden**. **Battleston Hill** comes into its own in late spring, when you might catch not only the bluebells but also the firework display of rhododendrons, along with exquisite wisteria, tumbling through the branches of a stand of silver birch; autumn sees the arrival of the unusual, purple-spotted toad lily. From the **orchard**, planted with hundreds of varieties of fruit trees, to the **pinetum**, with its mighty redwoods, Wisley's trees are as fascinating as its smaller plants. If you're here in autumn make for the **Seven Acres**, where the broad-leaved Wisley Bonfire and *Liquidambar* trees present a thrilling blaze of burned golds and fiery reds.

ACCOMMODATION AND EATING

NORTH SURREY

The Anchor High St, Ripley, GU23 6AE ☎ 01483 211866, ⓦ ripleyanchor.co.uk. This stylishly but simply restored historic pub serves terrific, intriguing food – roast guinea fowl with Jerusalem artichoke purée, perhaps, or bream with cauliflower, lime and curried mussel sauce. Mains from £16; two-/three-course lunch menu £21.95/£27.95. Tues–Sat noon–2.30pm & 6–9pm, Sun noon–4pm & 6–8pm.

★ **Broadway Barn** High St, Ripley, GU23 6AQ ☎ 01483 223200, ⓦ broadwaybarn.com. Luxury B&B in a historic building peacefully set back behind the high street. Each of the four rooms is different, balancing cosy comforts (home-baked biscuits; plump bedding; towelling robes), rustic cool and easy-going elegance to create a gorgeous retreat. The gourmet breakfast, an array of home-baked treats, is outstanding. **£125**

Inn at West End 42 Guildford Rd, West End, GU24 9PW ☎ 01276 858652 (pub) or ☎ 01276 485842 (rooms), ⓦ the-inn.co.uk. This light, good-looking food pub offers a wide-ranging menu (from crispy Chinese duck salad to grilled hake; pan-fried liver and bacon to roasted veg and butterbean pie), with a grapevine-draped courtyard for the warm weather. Mains from £13. They also have twelve contemporary B&B rooms. Mon–Fri 7am–11pm, Sat 8am–11pm, Sun 8am–10.30pm. **£125**

★ **Stovell's** 125 Windsor Rd, Chobham, GU24 8QS ☎ 01276 858000, ⓦ stovells.com. Special occasion, modern European food with hearty Mexican influence – from Guerrero-style octopus ceviche to Goosnargh duck with cherry, pistachio and wild nettles – dished up in a beautiful Tudor farmhouse. They distil their own gin, too. Two/three courses £24/£28 at lunch; five-course/Taste of Mexico menu at dinner £48/£75. Tues & Wed 6–10.30pm, Thurs–Sat noon–2.30pm & 6–10.30pm, Sun noon–2.30pm.

Swallow Barn Milford Green, Chobham, GU24 8AU ☎ 01276 856030, ⓦ swallow-barn.co.uk. Set in 4 acres of gardens, with an outdoor pool, the traditional *Swallow Barn* offers three double/twin B&B rooms in a quiet spot near Wisley. **£95**

Contexts

History

As the part of the country closest to mainland Europe, the southeast corner of England has played an important part in British history. It was here that Caesar landed his troops in the Roman invasion of Britain in 55 BC, and here too, more than a millennium later in 1066, that William of Normandy defeated King Harold in the last successful invasion of Britain. Over the years the coastline of Kent and Sussex has been at the frontline of potential invasion, facing off threats from Napoleon and Hitler among others, with the coast's iconic White Cliffs standing as a symbolic, and very real, bulwark against would-be invaders.

Prehistory

Southeast England has been inhabited, intermittently at least, for half a million years or more. For much of this period it was covered by snow during successive ice ages, but a land bridge to continental Europe allowed early man to come and go. The earliest hominid remains so far discovered in Britain – a shinbone and two teeth, alongside worked flint implements – were unearthed at **Boxgrove**, near Chichester in West Sussex, and date back between 524,000 and 478,000 years. "Boxgrove Man" was a nomadic hunter, over 5ft 10in tall, who roamed the shoreline, hunting large mammals using worked flint tools.

The last spell of intense cold began about 17,000 years ago, and it was the final thawing of this Ice Age around 7000 years ago that caused Britain to separate from the European mainland, with the warmer temperatures allowing natural woodland to cloak the land. The earliest farmers appeared about 4000 BC. These tribes were the first to make some impact on the environment, clearing forests, enclosing fields, constructing defensive ditches around their villages and digging mines to obtain flint used for tools and weapons. The **flint mines** in Sussex are among the oldest in England: they were begun around 4000 BC and continued until 2800 BC, with the resulting flint axes being used for barter and trade along the South Downs. At Cissbury Ring in West Sussex (see page 295) you can still see the bumps in the grass from the network of shafts, some 40ft deep.

The transition from the Neolithic to the **Bronze Age** began around 2000 BC with the importation from northern Europe of artefacts attributed to the **Beaker Culture** – named for the distinctive cups found at many burial sites. The 3500-year-old **Hove amber cup** – considered to be one of Britain's most important Bronze Age finds – is on show at Hove Museum in Brighton (see page 244). The spread of the Beaker Culture along European trade routes helped stimulate the development of a comparatively well-organized social structure with an established aristocracy. Large numbers of earthwork forts and round barrows, or burial mounds, were constructed in this period, with settlements across the Southeast, including just outside Eastbourne underneath

c.500,000 BC	4000 BC	2000 BC
Boxgrove Man roams the shore around present-day Chichester.	Farming and the mining of flint for trade begins.	The start of the Bronze Age; earthwork forts and villages are built.

THE PILTDOWN HOAX

The skull of "**Piltdown Man**" was discovered in a gravel pit in Piltdown in East Sussex in 1912 by **Charles Dawson**, a respected lawyer and amateur geologist, and sensationally hailed as the missing link between apes and humans, a paleontological find of immense significance. As the years went by, and more ancient hominid fossils were unearthed around the globe, it became increasingly clear that Piltdown Man was a bit of an anomaly that didn't quite fit with other discoveries. It took more than forty years, however, until 1953, to unearth the truth: what had been presented as a five-thousand-million-year-old skull had in fact been cleverly assembled from a medieval skull and an orang-utan jaw, and the Piltdown hoax passed into history as one of the greatest archeological hoaxes ever perpetrated.

Shinewater Park – thought to be one of the largest Bronze Age villages in Europe, though it remains unexcavated.

The Iron Age and the Romans

By 500 BC, the Southeast was inhabited by a number of different Celtic tribes, each with a sophisticated farming economy and social hierarchy. Familiar with Mediterranean artefacts through their far-flung trade routes, they gradually developed better methods of metalworking, ones that favoured **iron** rather than bronze, from which they forged not just weapons but also coins and ornamental works. Their principal contribution to the landscape was a network of **hillforts** and other defensive works, among them the hillforts of Mount Caburn near Lewes, Cissbury Ring (see page 295), Chanctonbury Ring (see page 294), the Trundle near Chichester and Oldbury near Ightham.

The Roman invasion of Britain began hesitantly, with small cross-Channel incursions in 55 and 54 BC led by **Julius Caesar**, who landed near Deal in Kent. Almost one hundred years later, the death of the king of southeast England, Cunobelin (Shakespeare's Cymbeline), presented **Emperor Claudius** with a golden opportunity and in August 43 AD a substantial Roman force landed, though the jury is still out on precisely where – possibly at Richborough (see page 107) in Kent, possibly further west beyond Chichester. The Roman army quickly fanned out, conquering the southern half of Britain and subsuming it into the Roman Empire.

Roman rule lasted nearly four centuries. Commerce flourished, cities such as Canterbury and Chichester prospered, and Roman civilization left its mark all over the Southeast: in coastal forts at Richborough and Pevensey (see page 184), a clifftop lighthouse at Dover (see page 114), arrow-straight roads, city walls still standing in Chichester, which also retains the original Roman cruciform street plan (see page 265), and wealthy **Roman villas** at Lullingstone in Kent (see page 153), and Bignor (see page 292) and Fishbourne (see page 270) in Sussex – the last of these the largest and best-preserved Roman dwelling in the country.

The Anglo-Saxons

From the late third century, Roman England was subject to **raids** by **Saxons**, leading to the eventual withdrawal of the Roman armies at the beginning of the fifth century.

500 BC	55 and 54 BC	43 AD	410
The Iron Age sees a network of hillforts established across the Downs.	Julius Caesar first arrives in Britain, landing on the Kentish coast.	The Romans invade under Emperor Claudius, and rule for nearly four centuries.	The Romans withdraw from Britain, leaving the Saxons and Jutes to settle the Southeast and establish the Anglo-Saxon kingdoms of Kent, Sussex and Wessex.

This gave the Saxons free rein to begin settling the country, which they did throughout the sixth and seventh centuries, with the **Jutes** from Jutland establishing themselves in eastern Kent. The southeast of England was divided into the **Anglo-Saxon kingdoms of Kent, Sussex and Wessex** – the last of these stretching west into Somerset and Dorset – with power and territory fluctuating and passing among them over the centuries that followed. The Anglo-Saxons all but eliminated Romano-British culture, with the old economy collapsing and urban centres emptying.

The early Anglo-Saxon period saw the countrywide revival of Christianity, which was driven mainly by **St Augustine** (see page 50), who was despatched by Pope Gregory I and landed on the Kent coast in 597, accompanied by forty monks. Ethelbert, the king of the Kingdom of Kent and the most powerful Anglo-Saxon overlord of the time, received the missionaries and gave Augustine permission to found a monastery at **Canterbury**, where the king himself was then baptized. The ruins of Augustine's abbey, including the remains of its seventh-century St Pancras church, can still be visited today (see page 49).

By the end of the ninth century the Kingdom of Wessex had established supremacy over the Southeast, with the formidable and exceptionally talented **Alfred the Great** recognized as overlord by several southern kingdoms. His successor, **Edward the Elder**, capitalized on his efforts to become the de facto overlord of all England. The relative calm continued under Edward's son, **Athelstan**, and **Edgar**, crowned King of England in 959.

After a brief period of Danish rule – most famously under the shrewd and gifted **Cnut**, whose failure to turn back the tide may have taken place at Bosham (see page 274) – the Saxons regained the initiative, installing **Edward the Confessor** on the throne in 1042. On Edward's death, **Harold** was confirmed as king, ignoring several rival claims including that of William, Duke of Normandy. William wasted no time: he assembled an army, set sail for England and famously routed the Saxons at the **Battle of Hastings** in 1066 (see page 186). On Christmas Day, **William the Conqueror** was crowned king in Westminster Abbey.

The Middle Ages

William I swiftly imposed a Norman aristocracy on his new subjects, reinforcing his rule with a series of strongholds. The strategically important kingdom of Sussex was divided into five **rapes** (administrative divisions), each with a newly built **castle** at its centre, controlled by one of William's most loyal supporters: Robert, Count of Eu, in Hastings (see page 177); Robert, Count of Mortain, in Pevensey (see page 184); William de Warrene in Lewes (see page 222); William de Braose in Bramber (see page 294); and Roger of Montgomery in Chichester and Arundel (see page 288). In Surrey castles sprang up at Guildford (see page 305) and Farnham (see page 302), and in Kent at Canterbury, Rochester, Leeds (see page 159) near Maidstone, one of the best-preserved Norman fortresses in the country (see page 66), and Dover (see page 114), although Kent itself retained some autonomy under Norman rule, possibly because of the resistance it put up against its invaders; the county motto, "Invicta", meaning undefeated, was adopted after the Conquest, and the "Man of Kent" term (see page 317) may also date from this time. The earliest Norman castles were motte-and-bailey earth-and-timber constructions, later replaced with more permanent stone castles.

597	**973**	**1066**
St Augustine lands on the Kent coast to spread Christianity around the country; he establishes a church and a monastery in Canterbury.	Edgar becomes the first king of England.	The Battle of Hastings sees the Norman William the Conqueror defeat King Harold, marking the end of Anglo-Saxon England.

Alongside the castles, mighty stone-built **cathedrals, abbeys and churches** were erected. William raised the great Benedictine Battle Abbey (see page 185) on the site of his famous victory and in Lewes, William de Warrene founded **St Pancras Priory** (see page 224), which was to become one of the largest and most powerful monasteries in England. The Saxon See at Selsey was moved to Chichester, where the mighty Chichester Cathedral (see page 265) was founded, and up in northern Kent, Rochester Cathedral was built on the site of an Anglo-Saxon place of worship. In Canterbury the Norman archbishop Lanfranc rebuilt the existing cathedral in 1070 following a huge fire, and the Normans established a Benedictine abbey on the site of the Saxon St Augustine's Abbey. A hundred years later the cathedral became an important pilgrimage site – second only to Rome – when the murder of Archbishop **Thomas Becket** ended up with Becket's canonization (see page 41).

In 1264, the countryside around Lewes in East Sussex saw one of just two major battles to have taken place in the Southeast (the other was at Battle in 1066). The **Battle of Lewes** was the bloody culmination of a clash between Henry III and a rebel army of barons under Simon de Montfort; the king was defeated and the resulting treaty, the **Mise of Lewes**, restricted his authority and forced him to assemble a governing council – often described as the first House of Commons. De Montfort's role as de facto ruler of England was short-lived; the following year Henry III's son Edward (later Edward I) routed the barons' army at the battle of Evesham in Worcestershire, killing De Montfort in the process.

The outbreak of the **Black Death** came in 1349. The plague claimed about a third of the country's population – and the scarcity of labour that followed gave the peasantry more economic clout than they had ever had before; for the first time dwellings such as the Clergy House in Alfriston (see page 214) were erected by wealthy yeoman farmers. Predictably, the landowners attempted to restrict the accompanying rise in wages, thereby provoking the widespread rioting that culminated in the abortive **Peasants' Revolt** of 1381, led by **Wat Tyler** of Kent. Another popular uprising, this time organized by Kentish man **Jack Cade**, took place in 1450, with Cade leading an army of five thousand to London, where he listed the grievances of the common people and demanded reform from the King; the rebellion was quickly crushed and the fleeing Cade was caught and killed while hiding in a garden in Lewes.

The Tudors and the Stuarts

The start of the **Tudor** period saw the country begin to assume the status of a major European power. Henry VIII – best remembered for his multiple wives, whose former homes can be found scattered all over the region, from Anne Boleyn's childhood home of Hever Castle (see page 157) to the various properties granted to Anne of Cleves in her divorce settlement – built coastal fortresses at Deal and Walmer (see page 111), designed to scare off the Spanish and the French, and around 1570 he founded the vast **Chatham Historic Dockyard** (see page 72), which quickly became the major base of the Royal Navy. This effectively spelled the end of the **Cinque Port federation** (see page 107), which had been established in 1278 and granted trading privileges to the south-coast ports of Dover, Hythe, Sandwich, Romney and Hastings in return for their

1170	1264	1450
Canterbury Cathedral becomes one of Christendom's greatest pilgrim shrines after Archbishop Thomas Becket is murdered within its walls.	The Battle of Lewes is fought between Henry III and Simon de Montfort's army of rebel barons.	Jack Cade marches an army from Kent to London, demanding reform for the common people.

KENTISH MEN AND MAIDS OF KENT

To call oneself a **Kentish Man (or Maid)**, or a **Maid (or Man) of Kent**, would seem at first to be simply a matter of semantics. However, these proudly held labels in fact refer to geographical areas: although the division is generally taken to be the River Medway, strictly speaking Kentish Maids and Men are born west of a line that cuts through a point just east of Gillingham, and Men and Maids of Kent in the more rural area to the east. Some believe that this east–west division may date back to the fifth century, when, following the departure of the Romans, **Saxons** moved into the west of the region, while the **Jutes**, who called themselves Kentings, or "Men of Kent", settled in the east. Others say that "Men of Kent" only became an accepted term after the **Norman invasion**, when people of East Kent resisted William the Conqueror with more force than those in the west, were granted certain privileges because of it, and were bestowed with the name as an unofficial form of honour.

providing maritime support in times of war – though their demise was only a matter of time anyway, with the shifting coastline leaving many of them stranded high and dry miles inland.

Henry VIII also presided over the establishment of the **Church of England** and the **Dissolution of the Monasteries**, which conveniently gave both king and nobles the chance to get their hands on valuable monastic property in the late 1530s, and reduced the monasteries at Battle, Lewes and elsewhere to ruin. In 1553 Henry's daughter Mary, a fervent Catholic, ascended the throne and returned England to the papacy. Her oppression of Protestants during the **Marian Persecutions** of 1555–57, when seventeen Protestants in the Sussex town of Lewes were condemned to be burned alive (along with 271 others around the country) is at the root of the Sussex town's riotous bonfire celebrations today (see page 225).

The country reverted to Protestantism with Elizabeth I, but tensions between Protestants and Catholics remained, and Protestants' worst fears were confirmed in 1605 when **Guy Fawkes** – butler at Cowdray House in West Sussex (see page 280) – and a group of Catholic conspirators were discovered preparing to blow up King and Parliament in the so-called **Gunpowder Plot**. During the ensuing hue and cry, many Catholics met an untimely end and Fawkes himself was hanged, drawn and quartered.

In the turbulent years of the **English Civil War** (1642–51), the Southeast, which remained almost entirely Parliamentarian, saw little serious fighting – though the castle at Arundel was reduced to rubble when it was held under siege first by Royalists and then by Parliamentarian troops. For the next eleven years England was a **Commonwealth** – at first a true republic, then, after 1653, a **Protectorate** with Cromwell as the Lord Protector and commander-in-chief. The turmoil of the Civil War unleashed a furious legal, theological and political debate, and spawned a host of leftist sects, the most notable of whom were the **Levellers**, who demanded wholesale constitutional reform and whose first manifesto was drafted at Guildford in Surrey, and the more radical Surrey-based **Diggers**, who proposed common ownership of all land. Cromwell died in 1658 to be succeeded by his son **Richard**, who ruled briefly and ineffectually, leaving the army unpaid while one of its more ambitious commanders, General Monk, conspired to restore the monarchy. Charles II, the exiled son of the

1509	**1555–57**	**1642–51**
Henry VIII comes to the throne and orders the Dissolution of the Monasteries.	The Marian Persecutions of Mary I sees hundreds of Protestants burned alive around the country, including at Lewes and Canterbury.	The Southeast escapes relatively unscathed from the English Civil War, though Arundel Castle is reduced to rubble.

previous king, entered London in triumph in May 1660. For the next 150 years the Southeast was to remain largely untroubled by conflict.

The Georgian era

The next serious threat to the region's peace came in the form of the most daunting of enemies, **Napoleon**. "All my thoughts are directed towards England. I want only for a favourable wind to plant the Imperial Eagle on the Tower of London," Napoleon threatened. Henry VIII's coastal fortresses were garrisoned once again; a thirty-mile canal – the Royal Military Canal (see page 128) – was dug between Hythe and Winchelsea in Kent, with a raised northern bank forming a parapet; and more than a hundred squat Martello towers (see page 125) were erected along the south coast, stretching from Suffolk all the way round to Sussex. In the event, by the time the fortifications were completed – the canal in 1809, the Martello towers by 1812 – the threat of invasion was long past, with Nelson's decisive victory over **Napoleon** at **Trafalgar** in 1805 helping to put paid to his plans for invasion. Final defeat for the French emperor came ten years later at the hands of the Duke of Wellington at **Waterloo**, signalling the end of the Napoleonic Wars (1803–15).

England's triumph over Napoleon was underpinned by its financial strength, which was itself born of the **Industrial Revolution**, the switch from an agricultural to a manufacturing economy that changed the face of the country in the space of a hundred years – though it only scratched the surface of life in the rural Southeast. By the time James Watt patented his **steam engine** in 1781, Sussex and Kent's industrial era had already been and gone, with the collapse both of the **Wealden iron industry** (see page 319) and of the **Wealden cloth industry** which had been centred around Cranbrook in Kent and had all but disappeared by 1700. Surrey's great **paper and gunpowder mills**, at their peak in the seventeenth century, fared a little better, clinging on until the late nineteenth and early twentieth centuries, and Kent did develop its own small but significant **coal-mining** industry, but overall the Southeast remained largely agricultural throughout the Industrial Revolution. Kent in particular relied heavily on **hop-growing**, which peaked in the late nineteenth century – and retained its rural landscape of small towns and villages.

While the landed gentry spent their money on splendid country estates, life for **agricultural labourers** was hard: low wages, high rents, soaring bread prices thanks to the Corn Laws, and the introduction of labour-displacing agricultural machinery all contributed to widespread discontent, and it was in Kent that the **Swing Riots** began in 1830, with peasants rising up to destroy the much-hated threshing machines, and unrest spreading throughout the whole of southern England and into East Anglia. It was really little wonder that **smuggling** (see page 214) was such an attractive proposition to the rural communities along the Sussex and Kent coasts: a desperately poor farm labourer could earn a week's salary in one lucrative night as a tubman, carrying contraband cargo. Smuggling reached its peak in the late eighteenth and early nineteenth centuries, and only really died out with the introduction of free-trade policies after 1840.

A series of judicious parliamentary acts made small improvements to the lot of the rural labourer: the **Reform Act** of 1832 established the principle (if not actually the

1685	1736	1783–1826
Protestant French Huguenots, fleeing religious persecution in their home country, flee to England, with significant numbers settling in Kent.	The first seawater baths open at Margate.	George IV frequents the small seaside town of Brighton, helping it become the south coast's most fashionable resort.

THE WEALDEN IRON INDUSTRY

Little evidence remains today of the great furnaces of the **Wealden iron industry** that once roared and blazed in the ancient forests of Kent, Sussex and Surrey. During the Tudor and early Stuart periods the Weald grew to become the most important iron-producing centre in Britain: wood from the forest was used not only for **shipbuilding** (Sussex oak was especially prized) but also to cheaply power the furnaces of the Weald's great **iron ore mines** – with the iron used not just to produce domestic firebacks and the like, but also the cannons and weaponry for the great Tudor and Stuart navies. By the mid-sixteenth century there were fifty **furnaces** and forges, and double that number 25 years later. **Ironmasters' houses** sprang up in the Weald, among them Gravetye Manor (see page 188) and Bateman's (see page 198).

The good times couldn't last forever; iron ore supplies started to dwindle, prices were undercut by foreign imports and production elsewhere in the country, and by 1717 the number of furnaces had dropped to fourteen. The ironworks at Hoathly near Lamberhurst in Kent lingered on until 1784, and those at Ashburnham in Sussex until 1796, but they simply couldn't compete with the great coke-fired factories of the North with its vast coalfields.

practice) of popular representation; the **Poor Law** of 1834 did something to alleviate the condition of the most destitute; and the repeal of the Corn Laws in 1846 cut the cost of bread. Significant sections of the middle classes were just as eager to see progressive reform as the working classes, as evidenced by the immense popularity of **Charles Dickens** (1812–70), whose novels – many set in and around his native town of Rochester (see page 70) – railed against poverty and injustice.

The general sense of inequity felt by the rural poor can't have been helped by the antics of their future monarch, **George IV** (see page 238), along the coast at **Brighton**, where he was living the high life with his mistress, helping turn the little fishing town into the most fashionable resort on the south coast. The town's transformation had begun in the second half of the eighteenth century when Dr Russell of Lewes began to recommend sea-bathing as an alternative to "taking the cure" at spa towns such as fashionable **Tunbridge Wells** (see page 136). Brighton was one of the earliest **seaside resorts** in the country, but it was not the first: that honour goes to Margate (see page 89) on the North Kent coast, where the first seawater baths opened in 1736. It was only in the Victorian era, however, that the phenomenon of the seaside town really took off.

The Victorian era

In 1837 **Victoria** came to the throne. Her long reign witnessed the zenith of British power: the British trading fleet was easily the mightiest in the world and it underpinned an empire upon which, in that famous phrase of the time, "the sun never set". Sussex-based author Rudyard Kipling (see page 190) became the poet of the English empire, coining such phrases as "the white man's burden"; wealthy landowners thought nothing of dispatching plant hunters to scour the globe searching for exotic specimens to populate their great Wealden gardens (see page 197); and Victorian explorers proudly displayed their hunting trophies in museums such as the Powell-

1796	**1803–15**	**1830**
The last furnace of the great Wealden iron industry closes, just as the Industrial Revolution is gathering steam elsewhere in the country.	Defences are erected along the south coast during the Napoleonic Wars, which end with the defeat of Napoleon at Waterloo.	Agricultural labourers rise up in the Swing Riots, which start in Kent and spread across the south.

Cotton Museum in Margate (see page 92). There were extraordinary intellectual achievements too – as typified by the publication of *On the Origin of Species* in 1859, written by Charles Darwin from his home in Kent (see page 155).

Perhaps the biggest change the Victorian era brought to the Southeast was the **arrival of the railway** between the 1830s and 1860s, which at one stroke opened up the region to Londoners, commuters and holidaymakers alike. The world's first scheduled steam passenger service, the **Canterbury & Whitstable Railway**, began puffing its way between cathedral town and coast in 1830, carrying day-trippers to the beach and back.

Newcomers built villas and country houses in the Weald, settlements grew up along the railway routes – the start of the **commuter belt** – and the **seaside town** boomed. All along the Sussex coast the resorts expanded rapidly: the population of Hastings grew from 3175 in 1801 to 17,621 in 1851, to a staggering 65,000 by the end of the century. The fishing industry in many towns dwindled as tourism became a major source of income, and piers and bandstands sprang up all along the coast. In Kent, Herne Bay, Margate, Broadstairs and Ramsgate all thrived, as the train replaced the slower, weather-dependent steamboats. Kent also saw another phenomenon on the rise, as thousands of **hoppers** from London's East End migrated down to the hop fields of Kent every autumn to pick up casual work during the harvest (see page 139).

The world wars

The outbreak of **World War I** in 1914 saw an ever-present threat of invasion hang over the southeast corner of the country. In Dover Castle you can visit a fire command post with a chart room – its broad table spread with maps, charts and tin mugs of tea – and an observation room, where binoculars and telescopes were used to keep a 24-hour watch on the harbour and the Straits.

The war dragged on for four miserable years, its key engagements fought in the trenches that zigzagged across northern France and west Belgium. Britain and her allies eventually prevailed, but the number of dead beggared belief. The Royal Sussex Regiment alone lost nearly seven thousand men. The number of men enlisting caused a severe shortage of agricultural labourers, and conscientious objectors moved to the countryside to work the land, thus exempting themselves from military service; among them were Duncan Grant and his lover David Garnett, who with Vanessa Bell set up house at Charleston, marking the beginning of Sussex's famous connection with the **Bloomsbury Group** (see page 219).

When **World War II** broke out in September 1939, the Southeast was once more at the frontline: the Nazis' **Operation Sea Lion** had gone so far as to identify Camber Sands, Winchelsea, Bexhill and Cuckmere Haven in Sussex as potential invasion points. Barbed wire was strung up along the coast, pillboxes and anti-tank obstacles put in place, the Martello towers, built in Napoleonic times, re-employed and the Home Guard mobilized. The Cuckmere Valley – where you can still see tank traps and crumbling pillboxes today (see page 212) – was lit up at night to look like the nearby port of Newhaven to confuse enemy planes, while the nearby Long Man of Wilmington hill figure was temporarily painted green so it could not be used for

1830–60	1859	1914–18	1939–45
The railway reaches Kent and Sussex; seaside resorts boom along the coast.	Charles Darwin publishes *On the Origin of Species*, much of which was written from his home in Kent.	World War I; the Bloomsbury Set arrives at Charleston Farmhouse.	World War II: the Southeast takes heavy bomb damage; Dunkirk rescue is planned from Dover Castle; Battle of Britain is fought in the Kent skies.

navigation. Idealized posters of the Sussex Downs ("Your Britain – Fight For It Now") were used in propaganda, and Dame Vera Lynn sang the iconic *(There'll be Bluebirds Over) The White Cliffs of Dover* (see page 118).

Kent in particular played a crucial role in the war. It was from here in 1940 that **Operation Dynamo** – the rescue of around three hundred thousand troops stranded at Dunkirk by a flotilla of large and little boats – was masterminded from secret underground tunnels beneath Dover Castle (see page 114). That same summer saw the **Battle of Britain** fought in the skies above Kent – a famous victory that put paid to Hitler's invasion plans and led charismatic prime minister **Winston Churchill**, who had his own home in Kent at Chartwell (see page 154), to dub it the nation's "finest hour".

As the war continued, both Kent and Sussex suffered heavily from **bombing raids**. In June 1942 a Luftwaffe raid on Canterbury left whole streets and hundreds of houses destroyed, though amazingly the cathedral came through unscathed. The ports of Ramsgate, Dover and Folkestone all took a battering too – citizens of Ramsgate took refuge in a network of underground tunnels as their homes were blown to bits above them (see page 99). In the summer of 1944, 1500 doodlebug bombs fell on Kent on their way to London, bestowing the unenviable nickname of "**doodlebug alley**" on the beleaguered county.

To the modern day

A very different **landscape** emerged after World War II, particularly in Sussex, where there had been widespread ploughing up of the Downs' chalkland turf for wartime grain production – a change from the traditional mixed "sheep and corn" farming that was practised before the war. The ploughing up of grassland continued in the postwar period, leading to an enormous loss of biodiversity that has only recently started to be reversed. Some estimate that during this period the percentage of chalk grassland on the eastern Downs fell from fifty percent to just three or four percent. As early as 1929 there had been calls for the South Downs to be protected as a national park, to guard against the urban sprawl fast swallowing up the countryside, but instead after World War II the government opted to give the Sussex Downs partial protection as an AONB (Area of Outstanding Natural Beauty), with the High Weald AONB following soon after. It was only in 2010 that the South Downs finally gained full **national park** status and protection.

Elsewhere in the region, the **transport** infrastructure improved dramatically, making the Southeast even busier, and cementing its status as affluent, prime commuting territory. Motorway building took off in the 1960s and 1970s; Gatwick Airport saw its first flights to the continent in 1949 and became Britain's second largest airport in 1988; and the Channel Tunnel opened in 1994. The Local Government Act of 1972 saw Sussex divided into the separate counties of **East** and **West Sussex** in 1974, spelling an end, on paper at least, to the ancient Saxon kingdom of Sussex.

Alongside the expansion there was also decline. By the 1960s, the **hop-farming industry** was on its last legs, as machines replaced hop-pickers and cheaper hops were imported from abroad. Kent's **coal mines** – discovered near Dover in 1890 but beset by difficulties from the beginning – were closed by the National Coal Board in the

1974	2010
Sussex is divided into the separate counties of East Sussex and West Sussex.	The South Downs National Park is created.

1980s; the county's miners were among the most vocal in the year-long **miners' strike** (1984–85).

Around the coast, the traditional **seaside towns** were suffering too. The rise of the package holiday (and later budget airlines) saw holidaymakers abandon the traditional train-served resorts in droves in the 1960s and 1970s. By the end of the twentieth century, seaside towns such as Margate had become sorry shadows of their former selves, with boarded-up shop fronts and derelict seafront attractions, and areas of huge social deprivation.

The new century, however, brought about a decided sea change at the seafront. In Margate the arrival of the **Turner Contemporary** gallery in 2011 brought a raft of young artists in its wake, with vintage shops, galleries and creative restaurants breathing new life into the Old Town. This artist-led gentrification process has been repeated around the coast at Folkestone, Hastings and elsewhere (see page 6); the Southeastern seaside, it seems, is in fashion once more.

2016	**2019**
The i360 – the world's tallest moving observation tower – opens on Brighton seafront. In the Brexit referendum, Kent and Sussex vote Leave (59 percent and 50.23 percent respectively), while Surrey sees 52.2 percent vote Remain.	In the general election, Kent and Surrey vote in Conservative MPs across the board. In Sussex, 13 of 16 constituencies elect Tory MPs, with Brighton and Hove's three seats bucking the trend.

Books

Many writers have lived or worked in Kent, Sussex and Surrey, using real-life historical incidents, people and locations to inspire them. The list below is necessarily selective – we've marked our very favourites with the ★ symbol.

FICTION AND POETRY

★ **Daisy Ashford** *The Young Visiters*. Written in 1890 by a 9-year-old from Lewes, this warm and witty tale of Victorian love was first published in 1919 – complete with wonderfully idiosyncratic spelling – and has never been out of print since.

★ **Jane Austen** *Emma*. Austen's slyly witty novel about a misguided matchmaker was written while the author was living in Surrey; the famous picnic scene, in which Emma attempts to enjoy a fashionable alfresco foray that all goes horribly wrong, is set on Box Hill.

★ **H.E. Bates** *The Pop Larkin Chronicles*. Made into a hugely popular TV series, *The Darling Buds of May*, Bates's stories of the ever-optimistic Larkin family, with their earthy, often transgressive ways, are splendid examples of storytelling, portraying Kent as a land, in many ways, unto itself – both deeply conservative and rumbustuously independent.

E.F. Benson *Mapp and Lucia*. Comic novel – one of a series – set between the wars, following snobbish rivals Emmeline Lucas and Elizabeth Mapp, each vying for social supremacy in the fictional town of Tilling (modelled very closely on Benson's hometown of Rye). Fans of the books can join town of *Mapp and Lucia*'s Tilling (see page 169).

A.S. Byatt *The Children's Book*. Set in 1895–1919, Byatt's complex, wordy novel – which gives more than a nod to the real lives of writer E. Nesbit and artist Eric Gill – tells the story of a tangled set of bohemian families tussling with their creative, and procreative, urges. While the characters can be too narcissistic to be likeable, the sense of time and place – Romney Marsh and around – is striking and original.

Nick Cave *The Death of Bunny Monroe*. Rock musician Cave's Brighton-based novel follows Bunny Munro – travelling salesman, sex addict and all-round loser – as he takes to the road with his son after the death of his wife. Funny, sad and downright filthy in equal measure, and as the title suggests, there's no happy ending.

Geoffrey Chaucer *The Canterbury Tales*. Chaucer's great work of poetry, written in the late fourteenth century, takes the form of a series of yarns recounted by a motley crew of pilgrims heading from Southwark to Canterbury (see page 48). Full of wit and deftly drawn characters, it changed English literature forever and remains an entertaining read today.

★ **Charles Dickens** *David Copperfield*; *Great Expectations*; *The Mystery of Edwin Drood*; *Nicholas Nickleby*; *Pickwick Papers*. Dickens frequently used North Kent locations in his books – including the opening pages of *Great Expectations*, which rank among the most atmospheric passages in English literature.

Edwin Drood is a complex and engaging mystery largely set in Rochester, where Dickens spent much of his childhood, while *David Copperfield*'s Miss Trotwood was inspired by a real person, in Broadstairs. Of course, Dickens hopped about all over southern England, with Surrey locations included in *Nicholas Nickleby* (Devil's Punchbowl) and *Pickwick Papers* (Dorking).

★ **T.S. Eliot** *Murder in the Cathedral*. Spare, visceral, overwrought and intellectual, Eliot's short play (see page 44) tells the story of the assassination of Thomas Becket in Canterbury Cathedral. A beautiful piece of writing, shedding light on the man whose violent death made the city one of the most important pilgrimage sites in the world.

E.M. Forster *A Room with a View*. The second part of Forster's Edwardian romance has his heroine, Lucy, return to life in Surrey after a tumultuous Grand Tour of Europe; inevitably, however, she's driven to reject the Home Counties' respectable civility for something rather more passionate.

Stella Gibbons *Cold Comfort Farm*. First published in 1932, this comic classic is a merciless parody of the rural melodramas popular at the time. The orphaned, no-nonsense Flora Poste descends on her crazy, gloomy relatives, the Starkadders, in deepest rural Sussex, and sets about tidying up their lives.

★ **Graham Greene** *Brighton Rock*. Melancholic thriller with heavy Catholic overtones, set in the criminal underworld of 1930s Brighton and featuring anti-hero Pinkie Brown, teenage sociopath and gangster, who is hunted down by middle-aged avenging angel Ida, representing the force of justice.

★ **Patrick Hamilton** *Hangover Square*. Hamilton's 1941 masterpiece, set in seedy 1930s London, Brighton and Maidenhead, tells the dark story of lonely, schizophrenic George Harvey Bone and his obsession with greedy, unscrupulous Netta, a failed actress, whose cruel rejection of him ultimately leads to tragedy.

★ **Russell Hoban** *Riddley Walker*. Cult sci-fi fantasy set in a loosely disguised, post-apocalyptic Kent – with towns including Ram Gut, Sam's Itch and Horny Boy – thousands of years after a nuclear holocaust. Told in a futuristic pidgin English, it's a compelling and hugely affecting read.

Peter James *Dead Simple*. The first title in a series of bestselling crime thrillers featuring Brighton-based detective superintendent Roy Grace, with the city and its surrounding area looming large on the covers and in the storylines.

Rudyard Kipling *The Collected Poems*. Collection of poems by Sussex-based poet and author Kipling, which includes the wonderful *Smuggler's Song*, as well as *Sussex*, his poem in praise of his adopted county (see page 190).

Marina Lewycka *Two Caravans*. Lewycka's follow-up to the wildly popular *A Short History of Tractors in Ukrainian* sees a young Ukrainian woman, Irina, working as a seasonal fruit-picker in a less-than-bucolic contemporary Kent, along with a ragged band of overseas workers dreaming of a better life. The wordplay, and humour, are as sharp as in the first novel, though the issues are dark.

W. Somerset Maugham *Of Human Bondage*; *Cakes and Ale*. As a youth Maugham lived in Whitstable with his aunt and taciturn uncle, a vicar. He writes about it, disguised as "Blackstable", near the cathedral town of "Tercanbury", in these two novels. The first, written in 1915, portrays the Kent coast as a lonely and rather bleak place, while the second, from 1930, is a little cheerier.

★ **Melanie McGrath** *Hopping*. The title is a little misleading – while the annual "hop", in which the main characters decamp from the East End to East Kent to work on the hop harvest, is key to this compelling family saga, the novel's scope reaches far beyond that, offering a detailed history of how London's East End changed through the course of the twentieth century.

★ **A.A. Milne** *Winnie the Pooh*; *The House at Pooh Corner*. Milne's much-loved children's classics, beautifully illustrated by E.H. Shepherd, were written from his home in Ashdown Forest, with many of the Forest's real-life locations appearing in the books (see page 194).

George Orwell *A Clergyman's Daughter*. Orwell's short novel tells the story of a young country woman who suffers a bout of amnesia and finds herself lost in London. The chapter in which she hooks up with a group of hop-pickers and travels to Kent draws on Orwell's own hopping seasons. Unsurprisingly, he reveals a bleaker side to the whole business than is usually described, conveying in detail the poor conditions and pay suffered by the transient workers.

Julian Rathbone *The Last English King*. Fictionalized account of the 1066 invasion seen through the eyes of Walt, the last surviving of King Harold's bodyguards. A lively, gripping story which vividly brings to life that most tumultuous, momentous year in English history.

★ **Vita Sackville-West** *The Edwardians*. This mischievous dig at the English upper classes, published in 1930 but set during the final years of the Edwardian era, is Sackville-West's most popular novel. On one level a coming-of-age tale about siblings Sebastian and Viola, who together create an amalgam of Vita herself, it's also an expression of the author's tortured ambivalence about her background – her passion for her childhood home (the vast Knole estate in Kent); her bitter disappointment at not being able to inherit; her shame at enjoying privilege based upon a feudal system. Above all, however, *The Edwardians* is a paean to Knole itself, as strong a character as any in the book and described in vivid and romantic detail.

★ **Graham Swift** *Last Orders*. Beautifully written, moving account of a group of ageing men on an expedition from London to Margate, where their recently deceased friend has asked them to scatter his ashes. Stop-offs include Rochester, Canterbury and a hopping farm, with the poignant climax taking place on the bleak, windy Harbour Arm at Margate.

Russell Thorndike *Doctor Syn* novels. Swashbuckling adventures of the wonderfully named vicar whose wife's betrayal turns him to revenge, piracy, murder and smuggling. The books, published between 1915 and 1945, take us from the sleepy Kentish village of Dymchurch in Romney Marsh, via the high seas and the American colonies and back again.

Sarah Waters *Tipping the Velvet*. Waters' debut, alive with the author's now-familiar storytelling genius, follows the fortunes of Nan, an oyster girl from Victorian Whitstable. After encountering a charismatic male impersonator, she sets off on a picaresque journey through the London lesbian demi-monde. The oysters' potential for erotic metaphor is, as you might expect, exploited with verve.

H.G. Wells *Kipps*; *The History of Mr Polly*; *Tono-Bungay*. Wells conveys a convincing sense of place – including Romney Marsh and Folkestone – in *Kipps*, his 1905 comic novel of an ordinary man, trapped in a stultifyingly lower-middle-class life, whose fortunes change with a huge inheritance. *Mr Polly* (1910), much of which is set around "Fishbourne" – based on Sandgate, near Folkestone – explores similar themes, but with a darker edge. The semi-autobiographical *Tono-Bungay* (1909) tells the tale of George, an apprentice chemist, whose uncle's medicine becomes a spectacular success despite having no medical benefits whatsoever. The first part of the book describes George's life as a servant's child at Bladesover House; Wells' own mother was housekeeper at Uppark House.

Virginia Woolf *Orlando*; *Between the Acts*. Nigel Nicolson, Vita Sackville-West's son, called *Orlando* the "longest and most charming love letter in literature". It's an astonishing gift to Sackville-West, with whom Woolf had an affair, and who in this book lives for three centuries, changes sexes, and muses on the nature of life, love, art and history. The book is populated with thinly disguised characters and real-life photos, and at the heart of it is Knole, the grand Kentish estate that Sackville-West was never able to inherit (see page 152). *Between the Acts* was Woolf's final novel, published in 1941, and follows the staging of a play at Pointz Hall, an Elizabethan manor house inspired by Firle Place and Glynde Place, near Woolf's home at Rodmell.

HISTORY, BIOGRAPHY AND TRAVELOGUE

★ **H.E. Bates** *Through the Woods*. This compelling, slim volume, beautifully illustrated with exquisite engravings, sees Bates weave a year's observations of his local Kentish woods into a musing on the particular quality and primeval allure of English woodlands as a whole. With the author's trademark deft touch, clear-eyed observations and determined lack of sentimentality, this is nature writing at its best: nostalgic, evocative, personal and profound.

Pieter and Rita Boogaart *A272: An Ode to a Road*. Now in its fourth edition, this eccentric homage to the A272, which runs from Poundford in East Sussex through West Sussex into Hampshire, has become a bit of a cult classic. Quirky, humorous and informative, it covers both the road itself and the surrounding countryside, with hundreds of photos.

Sophie Collins *A Sussex Miscellany*. Quirky dip-in-and-out-of collection of Sussex trivia – one of a series of beautifully produced and illustrated books published by Sussex-based Snake River Press (ⓦ snakeriverpress.co.uk). Other titles in the series include books on Sussex wildlife, writers and artists, food and drink, landscape, gardens (see page 197) and walks.

Richard Filmer *Hops and Hop Picking*. Written in 1982, this slim volume offers a deft historical account of the hopping industry in Britain, taking it from its Roman roots to its demise in the late twentieth century, with lots of clearly written technical detail and intriguing historic photos.

Tim Fort *Channel Shore*. Tim Fort's trip on two wheels along the southern coast takes him from the White Cliffs of Dover to Land's End in Cornwall, passing through the good, the bad and the ugly of Sussex and Kent's seaside towns en route. Packed with anecdotes, eccentricity and detail, it's a fun and informative read.

★ **Olivia Laing** *To the River*. This acclaimed account of the author's midsummer walk along the River Ouse from source to sea is beautifully observed, interweaving nature writing, history and folklore, with plenty on Virginia Woolf, who drowned herself in the river in 1941.

Terence Lawson and David Killingray (eds) *An Historical Atlas of Kent*. This intriguing, comprehensive history, sponsored by the Kent Archaeological Society, uses around 250 maps and short essays to illustrate everything from Anglo-Saxon churches to medieval almshouses, breweries to suburban sprawl.

Philip MacDougal *Chatham Dockyard: The Rise and Fall of a Military Industrial Complex*. A lengthy account, published in 2012, of the great royal dockyard, which founded in the late sixteenth century, built hundreds of warships for the Royal Navy before being wound down in the 1980s. It's a good read even if you're not wild about ships, putting the docks into a broader historical context.

★ **Judith Mackrell** *The Bloomsbury Ballerina*. Engrossing account of one of the fringe members of the Bloomsbury Group – Lydia Lopokova, the larger-than-life Russian ballet star who became the much-adored wife of sober

economist and Bloomsburyite John Maynard Keynes (who had previously identified as homosexual) – much to the disgust of Vanessa Bell, Virginia Woolf and Lytton Strachey, who snidely dismissed her as a "half-witted canary".

Frank McLynn *1066: The Year of the Three Battles*; **Marc Morris** *The Norman Conquest*; **Peter Rex** *1066: A New History of the Norman Conquest*. Three excellent books on the Norman Conquest of 1066. McLynn's book overturns some of the myths about the battle and takes a closer look at Harald Hardrada, whom Harold defeated at Stamford Bridge before his own defeat at the hands of William; Morris sleuths through the often contradictory evidence to produce a gripping, nuanced account of the epic battle and its aftermath; and Rex not only covers the background to the Norman invasion, but also continues the story to the final crushing of lingering English resistance in 1076.

Adam Nicolson *Sissinghurst: An Unfinished History*. Fascinating book by the grandson of Vita Sackville-West and Harold Nicolson about his struggles with the National Trust to revitalize the estate around Sissinghurst in Kent, with a broader, personal and lively history of both the estate and Kent itself thrown in.

Juliet Nicolson *A House Full of Daughters*. Just when you thought there couldn't be anything left to write about the Sackville-Wests, along comes this 2015 title. Nicolson, Vita's granddaughter, uses personal experience and historical record to explore seven generations of family history from the point of view of its fascinating women. Bold, emotionally honest and pulling no punches.

Richard Platt *Smuggling in the British Isles*. A good introduction to the smuggling trade that operated up and down the coastline of Britain in the eighteenth and early nineteenth centuries; Kent and Sussex's smuggling outfits – including the notorious Hawkhurst Gang – had the most fearsome reputation of the lot.

Vita Sackville-West *Pepita*. Sackville-West's biography of her grandmother, a half-Gypsy Spanish dancer, and her mother, the illegitimate, volatile Victoria, catapulted into the aristocracy to become mistress of the Knole estate, reads like a rollicking melodrama and is all the more compelling for being entirely true.

Isabella Tree *Wilding: The Return of nature to a British farm*. Award-winning and inspiring insider's account of the pioneering rewilding of the Knepp Castle estate in Sussex, a project that has been spectacularly successfully in renewing habitats and increasing wildlife numbers and diversity. The story of how the author and her husband's vision became a reality is beautifully written, interwoven with passionate ecological arguments and lyrical descriptions of nature.

ART

Quentin Bell and Virginia Nicholson *Charleston: a Bloomsbury House and Garden*. This fascinating account of the Bloomsbury Group's country home – written by Vanessa

Bell's son, Quentin, and his daughter – gives an insider's view of life in the bohemian household. With plenty of photographs of the farmhouse's inimitable decorative style, as well as snapshots from the family album, it's the perfect souvenir after a visit.

Desna Greenhow (ed) *The Diary of Mary Watts 1887–1904.* Watts was an accomplished potter, artist and designer who managed at once to be the perfect Victorian wife to famed painter George Frederic Watts and a major player in the Arts and Crafts movement. These diaries, kept meticulously and in great detail, chronicle the world of Surrey's turn-of-the-century artistic set, her own creative process and life with G.F. Watts – who liked to be called "Signor" – himself.

Anthony Penrose *The Home of the Surrealists: Lee Miller, Roland Penrose and Their Circle at Farley Farm House.* Written by the son of photographer Lee Miller and painter and biographer Roland Penrose, this illustrated book gives a first-hand account of life at Farley's House in Sussex (see page 189), which hosted some of the twentieth century's greatest artists, Picasso, Max Ernst and Miró among them.

★ **James Russell** *Ravilious in Pictures: Sussex and the Downs.* Twenty-two colour plates of Eric Ravilious's beautiful watercolours landscapes of Downs, painted in the 1930s before his death in World War II. Social historian James Russell's accompanying short essays provide the background on Ravilious's life (see page 206) and the quintessentially English scenes he painted.

GARDENS

Jane Brown *Sissinghurst: Portrait of a Garden.* Lavishly illustrated coffee-table book that brings the ebullience and abundance of Sackville-West's garden to life, as well as providing a good chunk of history about the estate itself.

★ **Lorraine Harrison** *20 Sussex Gardens.* A succinct, well-written tour of twenty of the best Sussex gardens, taking in various different historical periods and horticultural styles, from the excellent Snake River Press. A sister title, *Inspiring Sussex Gardeners*, focuses on the designers and plant hunters behind the gardens.

★ **Derek Jarman** *Derek Jarman's Garden.* A poignant diary, illustrated with arty photos, recording the last year of Jarman's life as he created his shingle garden in Dungeness. Bittersweet, poetic and full of simple joy, much like the garden itself. The preface is by Keith Collins, Jarman's friend and current inhabitant of Prospect Cottage (see page 131).

Stephen Lacey *Gardens of the National Trust.* Lavishly photographed volume on the National Trust's expansive national collection of gardens, which includes some of the finest gardens in Sussex, Kent and Surrey.

★ **Judith Tankard** *Gertrude Jekyll and the Country House Garden.* Using a wealth of luscious photos from *Country Life* magazine, for whom Jekyll was the gardening correspondent, this stunning coffee-table book celebrates the work of the influential Surrey-based garden designer, both with collaborators – including her great friend, the architect Edwin Lutyens – and on her own.

Various *Essays on the Life of a Working Amateur 1843–1932.* A highly readable compendium of personal essays about Gertrude Jekyll, written by members of her family and various experts, covering a broad range of Jekyll's work – including interior design – beyond her garden design.

FOOD AND DRINK

★ **Mandy Bruce** *The Oyster Seekers.* Charmingly illustrated tome, produced in association with *Wheelers Oyster Bar* in Whitstable (see page 85), which works as both an excellent recipe book and a lively, nostalgic history of the oyster industry and fishing on the east coast.

★ **Amanda Powley and Phil Taylor** *Terre à Terre: the Vegetarian Cookbook.* Innovative, exciting recipes – from Dunkin Doughnuts (parmesan and porcini-dust doughnuts served with chestnut soup) to No Cocky, Big Leeky (sausages and mash) – from Brighton's multi-award-winning vegetarian restaurant (see page 251), which is regularly voted among the best in the country.

WALKING AND CYCLING

AA *50 Walks in Kent; 50 Walks in Sussex & South Downs; 50 Walks in Surrey.* Easy-to-follow routes spanning anything from two to ten miles, with good, concise background on local history, wildlife and landscape. They also include useful details for dog-owners, include refreshment-break and public-toilet information, and suggest more detailed maps.

Deirdre Huston and Marina Bullivant *Cycling in Sussex.* Twenty bike rides, from 4km to 28km, on off-road trails or quiet roads, with routes divided into "family", "easy", "medium" and "hard". Huston's *Cycling Days Out: South East England* covers Sussex, Kent, Surrey and Hampshire, with half a dozen or so rides suggested for each county.

Pathfinder Walks Series of excellent practical walking guides with OS maps and route descriptions. Titles include *South Downs National Park and East Sussex; West Sussex and the South Downs; Kent;* and *Surrey.*

Helena Smith *The Rough Guide to Walks in London and the Southeast.* Handy, pocket-sized book covering walks for all abilities around the Southeast, all starting and finishing at train stations. Each walk suggests places to stop for lunch or a pint, and there's plenty of background information on everything from smugglers to stone circles.

Small print and index

A ROUGH GUIDE TO ROUGH GUIDES

Published in 1982, the first Rough Guide – to Greece – was a student scheme that became a publishing phenomenon. Mark Ellingham, a recent graduate in English from Bristol University, had been travelling in Greece the previous summer and couldn't find the right guidebook. With a small group of friends he wrote his own guide, combining a contemporary, journalistic style with a thoroughly practical approach to travellers' needs.

The immediate success of the book spawned a series that rapidly covered dozens of destinations. And, in addition to impecunious backpackers, Rough Guides soon acquired a much broader readership that relished the guides' wit and inquisitiveness as much as their enthusiastic, critical approach and value-for-money ethos. These days, Rough Guides include recommendations from budget to luxury and cover more than 120 destinations around the globe, from Amsterdam to Zanzibar, all regularly updated by our team of roaming writers.

Browse all our latest guides, read inspirational features and book your trip at **roughguides.com**.

Rough Guide credits

Editor: Helen Fanthorpe
Cartography: Carte
Managing editor: Rachel Lawrence
Picture editor: Tom Smyth

Cover photo research: Tom Smyth
Senior DTP coordinator: Dan May
Head of DTP and Pre-Press: Rebeka Davies
Layout: Ruth Bradley

Publishing information

Third edition 2020

Distribution

UK, Ireland and Europe
Apa Publications (UK) Ltd; sales@roughguides.com
United States and Canada
Ingram Publisher Services; ips@ingramcontent.com
Australia and New Zealand
Woodslane; info@woodslane.com.au
Southeast Asia
Apa Publications (SN) Pte; sales@roughguides.com
Worldwide
Apa Publications (UK) Ltd; sales@roughguides.com
Special Sales, Content Licensing and CoPublishing
Rough Guides can be purchased in bulk quantities
at discounted prices. We can create special editions,
personalised jackets and corporate imprints tailored to
your needs. sales@roughguides.com.
roughguides.com

Help us update

We've gone to a lot of effort to ensure that this edition
of **The Rough Guide to Kent, Sussex and Surrey** is
accurate and up-to-date. However, things change –
places get "discovered", opening hours are notoriously
fickle, restaurants and rooms raise prices or lower
standards. If you feel we've got it wrong or left something
out, we'd like to know, and if you can remember the
address, the price, the hours, the phone number, so
much the better.

Please send your comments with the subject line
"**Rough Guide Kent, Sussex and Surrey Update**" to
mail@uk.roughguides.com. We'll credit all contributions
and send a copy of the next edition (or any other Rough
Guide if you prefer) for the very best emails.

Acknowledgements

Sam Cook: Many thanks to Claire Saunders, Helen Fanthorpe and, above all, Greg Ward.

Claire Saunders: Thanks to Helen and the team at Rough Guides, my co-author Sam, my dad for Hastings tips, my mum
for Cuckmere trips, and – as ever – Ian, Tom and Mia.

Photo credits

(Key: T-top; C-centre; B-bottom; L-left; R-right)

Alamy 9B, 11C, 12T, 12C, 16B, 17T, 67, 117, 183, 221, 300/301
AWL Images 7
Chris Christoforou/Rough Guides 11TR, 13B, 14L, 14B,
15BR, 15BL, 17C, 7B, 18, 20, 55, 79, 105, 165, 200/201,
203, 312

Getty Images 13T, 162/163, 255
Peter Durant/arcblue.com 12B
Shutterstock 1, 2, 4, 9T, 10, 11B, 16T, 36/37, 39, 102/103,
134/135, 147, 232/233, 235, 260/261, 263, 291, 303
Visit Kent 11TL, 15T, 64/65, 137

Cover: Woodchurch windmill **Getty Images**

ABOUT THE AUTHORS

Sam Cook is a London-born and -based writer and editor. She researched and wrote the
Kent and Surrey chapters of this guide and has authored Rough Guides to London, Paris, New
Orleans and Chick Flicks, among others.

Claire Saunders grew up in Brighton, which wasn't anywhere near as cool then as it is now.
After almost ten years of working as an editor and then Managing Editor at Rough Guides, she
moved back down to Sussex, where she now lives in Lewes and works as a freelance writer
and editor. She researched and wrote the Sussex chapters for this book.

Index

Map symbols

The symbols below are used on maps throughout the book

County boundary	Point of interest	Observatory	Lighthouse
Chapter boundary	Museum	Airport	Hospital
Road	Castle	Minor airport/airfield	Swimming pool
Motorway	Stately/historic home	Rock formation	Statue
Pedestrianized/restricted access road	Abbey	Cliffs	Golf course
Steps	Gardens	Hill	Building
Railway & station	Ruins/archeological site	Bus/taxi stop	Church
Private/tourist railway & station	Viewpoint	Tourist office	South Downs National Park
Funicular railway	Zoo/wildlife park	Parking	Park/forest
Wall	Nature reserve	Post office	Cemetery
North Downs Way	Vineyard/wine estate	Internet access	Beach
South Downs Way	Arboretum/forest park	Public toilets	Marshland
Saxon Shore Way	Farm/farm park	Gate	Tidal flats
Greensand Way	Country park	Surf beach	Shingle
Other footpath/cycling route	Battle site	Windsurfing	

Listings key

Accommodation

Eating

Drinking/nightlife

Shopping